메가스터디 N제

영어영역 독해

332제

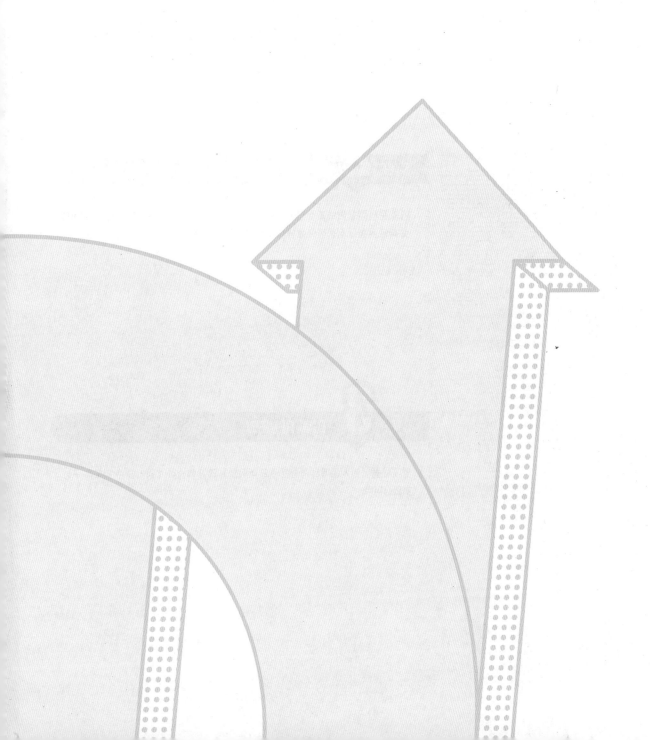

구성과 특징 STRUCTURE

⊘ 수능 영어 독해 28문항 19개 유형을 시험에 출제되는 순서로 구성한 교재로, 각 유형을 집중적으로 학습한 후 출제 예상 모의고사 문제들을 통해 실전 감각을 높일 수 있도록 하였습니다.

⊘ 수능 영어 독해에서 배점이 높고 출제되는 문항 수가 많은 유형은 더 비중 있게 수록하여 전 유형에 대한 균형 있는 학습이 될 수 있도록 구성하였습니다.

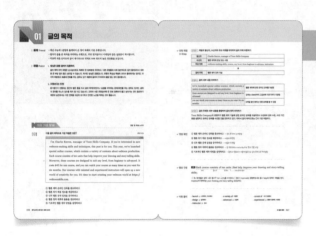

STEP 1 출제 Trend & 대표 기출 문제

출제 Trend와 해결 Point
수능 영어 독해의 유형별 출제 경향과 해결 전략들을 소개하여, 해당 유형을 보다 효율적으로 접근할 수 있도록 하였습니다.

대표 기출 문제 분석
3-Step으로 제시된 유형 해결 방법을 통해 최신 수능 기출 문제를 분석해 봄으로써, 유형별 해결 비법과 전략을 파악해 볼 수 있도록 하였습니다.

STEP 2 유형 연습 문제

기출 문제를 풀어보고 실전 감각을 익힌 후 최신 수능 경향을 반영한 엄선된 문항들로 해당 유형을 집중적으로 연습할 수 있도록 하였습니다.

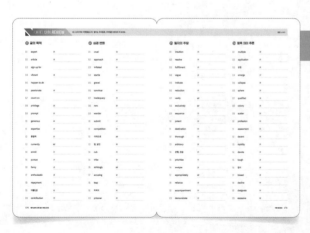

STEP 3 어휘 REVIEW

앞에서 풀어본 지문에서 학습한 주요 어휘들을 모아 복습하며 암기할 수 있도록 구성하였습니다.

STEP 4 적중 예상 문제 5회분

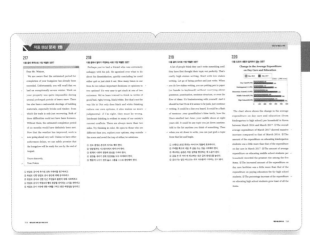

전 유형을 학습한 후 실전 감각을 익힐 수 있도록 12문항으로 구성한 모의고사 5회분을
제공합니다.

STEP 5 독해 실전 모의고사 2회분

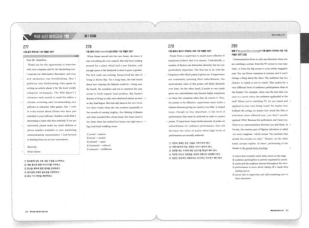

최종적으로 자신의 실력을 확인하고 실전에 대비할 수 있도록 28문항으로 구성된
Full 모의고사 2회분을 제공합니다.

친절하고 자세한 해설

모든 문제에 지문요약, 전문해석, 정답풀이, 구문풀이와 어휘풀이까지 친절하고 자세한
해설을 제공합니다.

미니 단어장

들고 다니면서 외울 수 있도록
전체 문항의 중요 어휘들만 모아
별책의 미니 단어장으로 구성하였습니다.

차례 CONTENTS

I 영어 독해 유형 연습

II 영어 독해 실전 연습

I 적중 예상 문제

II 독해 실전 모의고사

N I 영어 독해 유형 연습

N 01 글의 목적

│ 출제 Trend
- 매년 수능에 1문항씩 출제되어 온 영어 독해의 기본 유형입니다.
- 필자가 글을 쓴 목적을 파악하는 유형으로, 주로 편지글이나 이메일과 같은 실용문이 제시됩니다.
- 비교적 쉬운 난이도의 글이 제시되므로 대체로 90% 정도의 높은 정답률을 보입니다.

│ 해결 Point

1. 방심은 금물! 끝까지 집중하자.

글의 목적 파악 유형은 순서상으로도 독해의 맨 앞부분에 위치하고, 다른 유형들에 비해 일반적으로 쉽게 출제되어서 대부분 큰 부담 없이 풀고 넘어갈 수 있습니다. 하지만 방심은 금물입니다. 유형의 특성상 특별히 꼬아서 출제하지는 않지만, 마지막 부분에서 흐름에 변화를 주는 경우도 있기 때문에 끝까지 주의하여 글을 읽는 것이 중요합니다.

2. 요행보다는 안전!

듣기평가가 진행되는 중간의 짧은 틈을 타서 글의 목적(18번)이나 심경을 파악하는 문제(19번)를 푸는 경우도 있지만, 급하게 문제를 푸느라 실수를 하게 될 수도 있습니다. 오히려 쉬운 유형일수록 한 번에 정확하게 풀고 넘어가는 것이 중요하기 때문에 실전에서는 이런 전략을 과감히 포기하고 안전한 노선을 택하는 것이 좋습니다.

N 대표 기출 문제

정답 및 해설 p.003

001 다음 글의 목적으로 가장 적절한 것은?   2024 수능

I'm Charlie Reeves, manager of Toon Skills Company. If you're interested in new webtoon-making skills and techniques, this post is for you. This year, we've launched special online courses, which contain a variety of contents about webtoon production. Each course consists of ten units that help improve your drawing and story-telling skills. Moreover, these courses are designed to suit any level, from beginner to advanced. It costs $45 for one course, and you can watch your course as many times as you want for six months. Our courses with talented and experienced instructors will open up a new world of creativity for you. It's time to start creating your webtoon world at https://webtoonskills.com.

① 웹툰 제작 온라인 강좌를 홍보하려고
② 웹툰 작가 채용 정보를 제공하려고
③ 신작 웹툰 공개 일정을 공지하려고
④ 웹툰 창작 대회에 출품을 권유하려고
⑤ 기초적인 웹툰 제작 방법을 설명하려고

✔ 유형 해결
3-Step

STEP 1 메일의 발신자, 수신자와 주요 어휘를 파악하여 글의 주제 추론하기

발신자	Charlie Reeves, manager of Toon Skills Company
수신자	웹툰 제작에 관심 있는 사람
주요 어휘	webtoon-making skills, course, any level, from beginner to advance, instructors

↓

글의 주제	웹툰 제작 강좌 개설

STEP 2 글의 세부 내용 파악하기

we've launched special online courses, which contain a variety of contents about webtoon production	웹툰 제작에 관한 온라인 강좌를 개설함
these courses are designed to suit any level, from beginner to advanced	강좌는 초보반부터 고급반에 이르기까지 다양함
you can watch your course as many times as you want for six months	6개월 동안 원하는 만큼 강좌를 볼 수 있음

STEP 3 글의 주제와 세부 내용을 종합하여 글의 목적 파악하기

Toon Skills Company의 경영자가 웹툰 제작 기술에 관한 온라인 강좌를 개설하면서 수강료와 강좌 수준, 수강 기간 등을 설명하고 온라인 강좌를 수강할 것을 권유하고 있다. 따라서 글의 목적으로는 ①이 가장 적절하다.

✔ 정답 확인

① 웹툰 제작 온라인 강좌를 홍보하려고 → 글의 목적에 잘 부합함

② 웹툰 작가 채용 정보를 제공하려고 → 내용과 무관함

③ 신작 웹툰 공개 일정을 공지하려고 → 내용과 무관함

④ 웹툰 창작 대회에 출품을 권유하려고 → 글 후반부의 creativity라는 말로 만든 오답

⑤ 기초적인 웹툰 제작 방법을 설명하려고 → 홍보나 권유라는 내용이 없으므로 글의 목적으로 부적절함

✔ 중요 구문

4행 Each course consists of ten units [that help improve your drawing and story-telling skills].
주어 · 동사구 · 목적어 · 주격 관계대명사

: [ ]는 관계절로 앞에 나온 명사구 ten units를 수식하고, [ ]에서 improve는 원형부정사로 동사 help의 목적어 역할을 한다. improve의 목적어는 your drawing and story-telling skills이다.

✔ 어휘 풀이

• launch ⓥ 시작하다, 개시하다
• design ⓥ 설계하다
• instructor ⓝ 강사
• a variety of 다양한
• advanced ⓐ 고급의
• consist of ~로 구성되다
• experienced ⓐ 경험이 풍부한, 숙련된

002

다음 글의 목적으로 가장 적절한 것은?

To whom it may concern,

　My name is Michael Brown. I have been a bird-watcher since childhood. I have always enjoyed watching birds in my yard and identifying them by sight and sound. Yesterday, I happened to read an article about your club. I was surprised and excited to find out about a community of passionate bird-watchers who travel annually to go birding. I would love to join your club, but your website appears to be under construction. I could not find any information except for this contact email address. I would like to know how to sign up for the club. I look forward to your reply.

Sincerely,

Michael Brown

① 조류 관찰 클럽에 가입하는 방법을 문의하려고
② 조류 관찰 시 주의해야 할 사항을 전달하려고
③ 조류 관찰 협회의 새로운 규정을 확인하려고
④ 조류 관찰과 관련된 웹 사이트를 소개하려고
⑤ 조류 관찰 시 필요한 장비를 알아보려고

003

다음 글의 목적으로 가장 적절한 것은?

Dear Ms. Green,

　My name is Donna Williams, a science teacher at Rogan High School. I am planning a special workshop for our science teachers. We are interested in learning how to teach online science classes. I have been impressed with your ideas about using internet platforms for science classes. Since you are an expert in online education, I would like to ask you to deliver a special lecture at the workshop scheduled for next month. I am sure the lecture will help our teachers manage successful online science classes, and I hope we can learn from your insights. I am looking forward to hearing from you.

Sincerely,

Donna Williams

① 과학 교육 정책 협의회 참여를 독려하려고
② 과학 교사 워크숍의 특강을 부탁하려고
③ 과학 교사 채용 계획을 공지하려고
④ 과학 교육 프로그램 개발을 요청하려고
⑤ 과학 교육 워크숍 일정의 변경을 안내하려고

004

다음 글의 목적으로 가장 적절한 것은?

It is a real privilege and pleasure to be able to represent your interests in such a remarkable town for a further four years. I will do whatever is within my power to enhance the services that help make Middlewich such a wonderful place to live and bring up children. We will face serious challenges over the coming years, which I am sure we will overcome. I would like, however, to take this opportunity to encourage more of you to get involved. A town such as Middlewich is only as vibrant as its residents make it. Please come and support our many events over the coming year. You'll see how hard we try to do our best. Drop into the Victoria Buildings on Lewin Street for a chat with any of the officers. You will be certain of a friendly welcome.

① 선거 공약을 홍보하려고
② 투표에서의 패배를 인정하려고
③ 적극적인 투표 참여를 독려하려고
④ 당선된 이후 앞으로의 각오를 밝히려고
⑤ 현재의 위기를 극복하는 방안을 제안하려고

005

다음 글의 목적으로 가장 적절한 것은?

Dear Mr. Nelson,

Thank you for your application for employment at Brook Corporate. We have reviewed your résumé and application for an available job. As part of your application you granted permission to our human resources office to verify any information included on the application form. In checking your academic credentials, we contacted Lumbertown College to verify the M.B.A. degree you listed on the application; the college was unable to confirm that such a degree was granted. We need clarification of this matter before we can proceed with consideration of your application. If you need to contact the college to correct an error on their part, please do so. Your prompt response regarding this matter is greatly appreciated, as it will enable us to move forward with the evaluation of your application.

Sincerely,

Thomas Williams

*academic credentials: 학력

① 회사 면접시험 응시에 감사하려고
② 지원서에 누락된 학력 사항에 대해 문의하려고
③ 학력 사항의 허위 기재로 인한 불합격을 통보하려고
④ 지원서에 기재된 학력의 진위를 확증할 것을 요청하려고
⑤ 학력 사항 확인을 위해 개인정보의 열람 동의를 요청하려고

006

다음 글의 목적으로 가장 적절한 것은?

Dear Ms. Hart,

Have you "settled into" your new job by now, and do you still feel as enthusiastic about it as you did at the beginning? Of course, any job has its hard tasks, but we hope the job will be a good match for you. The reason why we are sending you this email is to ask when we can expect repayment of the $1,500 loan for your car. We were glad to help you with the purchase of your fancy SUV so that you'd have transportation to your new job and back home. You agreed to pay back all, or at least half, of the loan by June. If you cannot repay the total 1,500 dollars at once, we understand. As agreed upon, however, we do need to receive at least half that amount before July 1st. Please let us know how things are going.

Best Regards,

Jason Burton

① 차량 대출금 상환 계획을 문의하려고
② 금융거래 시 유의점에 대해 조언하려고
③ 새로 출시된 장기 저축 상품을 추천하려고
④ 자동차 보험료 절약 방법에 대해 조언하려고
⑤ 대출 신청 시 누락된 서류를 추가 요청하려고

007

다음 글의 목적으로 가장 적절한 것은?

Dear Westcott Residents,

Can you imagine what life would be like without the many wonderful offerings of the Westcott Community Center? It's a thought that very few of us want to even consider. We count on the center to provide music, theater, and civic events all through the year. Our children expect to be able to use the gym and the athletic fields. The entire operating budget for the center is paid by very modest membership fees, ticket sales, and the generous contributions of companies, organizations, and individuals like you. We are well aware that these are difficult times for everyone, but we believe that our town's culture is a necessity. I'm writing to ask you to join your neighbors and business associates in making a contribution to the Westcott Community Center. We will thank you for any amount you can give.

Sincerely,

Sue Stephens

① 지역 문화센터의 개관 소식을 알리려고
② 지역 문화센터를 위한 기부를 부탁하려고
③ 지역 문화센터의 운영 자금을 공개하려고
④ 지역 문화센터의 개방 시간 변경을 공지하려고
⑤ 지역 문화센터를 위한 자원봉사자를 모집하려고

008

다음 글의 목적으로 가장 적절한 것은?

Dear Sir,

Last month I bought a stationary bike for a Christmas present at your shop. I paid for it and, following my purchase, you sent a bike to my home and it arrived several days later. Thankfully it did arrive in time for Christmas Day. Upon using the bike, I immediately realized that there was something wrong with it. It is not the same one as the sample in the shop. It is another much more expensive model, but I do not want it. The stationary bike I bought doesn't have a computer monitor, but the one you sent me does. It is rather difficult for me to figure out and use. I called the customer service where you are the director and they said that there were not stationary bikes in stock like the one I bought. The one I chose was the oldest model, but it was the perfect choice for me. I only want you to understand that you destroyed my Christmas wishes.

Sincerely,

Fernando López Veloso

① 배송 지연에 대한 손해 배상을 요구하려고
② 고객 서비스 센터의 친절함에 대해 칭찬하려고
③ 배송 과정에서 제품에 생긴 흠집에 대해 지적하려고
④ 주문한 제품이 아닌 제품을 받은 것에 대해 불평하려고
⑤ 좋은 제품을 저렴하게 살 수 있게 해준 것에 감사하려고

009

다음 글의 목적으로 가장 적절한 것은?

Dear Ms. Thomas,

The position of executive drafting assistant sounds exciting. Thank you for considering me. However, the computer expertise this position requires for success demands more experience than I currently have. I want to do an excellent job; therefore, I am enrolling in a CAD course at Tulsa University (TU). In four months I will have the training to pursue a similar position with determination. Perhaps TU instructors can suggest names of recent students who are prepared now to accept the responsibilities of the job. Someone better trained than I am is waiting to discover Intercomp. Thank you again for thinking of me. It has been the incentive I needed to get the extra training I must have to continue in the drafting field. I intend to be prepared for the next executive drafting assistant opening.

Sincerely,

Cathy Jones

① 강좌 개설을 안내하려고
② 사원 모집에 지원하려고
③ 우수 학생을 추천하려고
④ 취업 제의를 거절하려고
⑤ 학생 추천을 의뢰하려고

출제 Trend • 등장인물의 심경이나 심경의 변화를 파악하는 유형으로 매년 수능에 1문항씩 출제됩니다.
• 문학 작품의 일부가 제시되는 경우가 많으며, 난이도는 낮은 편으로 대체로 90% 이상의 높은 정답률을 보입니다.

해결 Point **1. 심리 상태를 나타내는 형용사와 동사에 주목하자.**

심경 변화를 파악하는 문제는 처음과 마지막의 심경이 다르므로 처음 심경이 끝에 가서 어떻게 변하는지에 유의해서 글을 읽어야 합니다. 무엇보다 등장인물의 심리 상태를 나타내는 형용사와 동사에 주목하면서 글의 전체적인 분위기를 파악하도록 합니다.

2. 자주 등장하는 선택지 어휘들을 암기해 두자.

글을 해석하기가 어려워서라기보다는 선택지로 제시된 어휘를 몰라서 틀리는 경우가 있습니다. 다행히 심경 파악 문제의 선택지 어휘들은 매년 시험에 거의 반복하여 등장하기 때문에 교재에 수록된 문제의 선택지 어휘들만 모아서 외워도 실전에 도움이 될 것입니다.

N 대표 기출 문제

정답 및 해설 p.006

010 다음 글에 드러난 David의 심경 변화로 가장 적절한 것은?

2024 수능

David was starting a new job in Vancouver, and he was waiting for his bus. He kept looking back and forth between his watch and the direction the bus would come from. He thought, "My bus isn't here yet. I can't be late on my first day." David couldn't feel at ease. When he looked up again, he saw a different bus coming that was going right to his work. The bus stopped in front
⁵ of him and opened its door. He got on the bus thinking, "Phew! Luckily, this bus came just in time so I won't be late." He leaned back on an unoccupied seat in the bus and took a deep breath, finally able to relax.

① nervous → relieved
② lonely → hopeful
③ pleased → confused
④ indifferent → delighted
⑤ bored → thrilled

✔ 유형 해결
3-Step

(STEP 1) 인물 정보와 상황 및 초반 심경 파악하기

David was **starting a new job** in Vancouver, and he was **waiting for his bus.** / He **kept looking back and forth** between his watch and the direction the bus would come from. → 새 직장으로의 첫 출근을 위해
초조하게 버스를 기다림

→ David는 밴쿠버에서 새로운 일을 시작했고 버스를 기다리면서 시계와 버스가 올 방향을 계속 번갈아 쳐다보고 있었다.

(STEP 2) 전개되는 상황 파악하기

"My **bus isn't here yet.** I can't be late on my first day." / David **couldn't feel at ease.** / he saw a different bus coming that was going right to his work. → 첫 출근에 늦을까 봐 불안한 심경인데 다른 버스가 옴

→ 버스는 오지 않고 첫 출근에 늦을까 봐 불안감을 느끼고 있는데 직장으로 가는 다른 버스가 오고 있는 것을 보았다.

(STEP 3) 최종 상황 파악 및 변화된 심경 추론

"Phew! Luckily, this bus came just in time so I won't be late." / ~ and **took a deep breath, finally able to relax.** → 안도의 한숨을 쉬고 긴장이 풀림

→ 지각하지 않도록 버스가 시간에 맞춰 와 주어 다행이라고 생각하면서 안도의 한숨을 내쉬면서 긴장을 풀었다.

✔ 정답 확인

첫 출근길에 버스가 오지 않아서 지각할까 봐 초조해하다가 마침내 직장으로 가는 버스에 탈 수 있었고 지각하지 않겠다며 안심했다는 내용이므로, David의 심경 변화로 가장 적절한 것은 ① '초조한 → 안도하는'이다.

② 외로운 → 희망에 찬   ③ 기쁜 → 당황한
④ 무관심한 → 기쁜   ⑤ 지루한 → 신이 난

✔ 중요 구문

1행 He kept looking back and forth **between** his watch **and** the direction (which) [the bus would come
「between A and B(A와 B 사이에)」   선행사
from].

: 「keep -ing」는 '계속 ~하다'의 의미이며, 'A와 B 사이에'의 의미인 「between A and B」의 표현이 사용되고 있다. [ ]는 the direction을 수식하는 관계절이다.

✔ 어휘 풀이

• keep -ing 계속 ~하다   • back and forth 번갈아, 왔다 갔다   • direction *n* 방향
• feel at ease 마음을 놓다, 안도하다   • unoccupied *a* 빈, 비어 있는

011

2023 수능

다음 글에 드러난 Jamie의 심경 변화로 가장 적절한 것은?

Putting all of her energy into her last steps of the running race, Jamie crossed the finish line. To her disappointment, she had failed to beat her personal best time, again. Jamie had pushed herself for months to finally break her record, but it was all for nothing. Recognizing how she felt about her failure, Ken, her teammate, approached her and said, "Jamie, even though you didn't set a personal best time today, your performances have improved dramatically. Your running skills have progressed so much! You'll definitely break your personal best time in the next race!" After hearing his comments, she felt confident about herself. Jamie, now motivated to keep pushing for her goal, replied with a smile. "You're right! Next race, I'll beat my best time for surc!"

① indifferent → regretful
② pleased → bored
③ frustrated → encouraged
④ nervous → fearful
⑤ calm → excited

012

2022 수능

다음 글에 나타난 Evelyn의 심경 변화로 가장 적절한 것은?

It was Evelyn's first time to explore the Badlands of Alberta, famous across Canada for its numerous dinosaur fossils. As a young amateur bone-hunter, she was overflowing with anticipation. She had not travelled this far for the bones of common dinosaur species. Her life-long dream to find rare fossils of dinosaurs was about to come true. She began eagerly searching for them. After many hours of wandering throughout the deserted lands, however, she was unsuccessful. Now, the sun was beginning to set, and her goal was still far beyond her reach. Looking at the slowly darkening ground before her, she sighed to herself, "I can't believe I came all this way for nothing. What a waste of time!"

① confused → scared
② discouraged → confident
③ relaxed → annoyed
④ indifferent → depressed
⑤ hopeful → disappointed

013

다음 글에 드러난 Crystal의 심경 변화로 가장 적절한 것은?

The lights in the house went out. Joe carefully guided Crystal to the bedroom and told her to stay there. When they looked out a window that faced the neighbor's house, they found that their lights were still on. There was no doubt in their mind that their fuse box outside had been tampered with. Joe walked carefully through the dark house and went out. While Joe was gone, Crystal was so worried about him that she looked out the nearest window, but it was too dark outside to see anything. Then suddenly she heard a popping sound and saw a car driving into her driveway. Gravel crackled under tires and then an engine idled and she heard voices. Slowly she moved to the living room. Looking outside she saw a patrol car. Joe was talking to the officers who sat inside the car. He turned and was walking back to the house when suddenly the lights came back on. Crystal exhaled a sigh of relief while her eyes adjusted to the light. She hurried to join Joe and the officers outside.

*tamper: 손대다, 함부로 변경하다

① nervous → relieved
② pleased → disappointed
③ indifferent → regretful
④ anticipating → irritated
⑤ confident → embarrassed

014

다음 글에 드러난 John의 심경 변화로 가장 적절한 것은?

John had always struggled with mathematics, but he was determined to turn things around. He spent countless hours studying for his math exam, and when the results came back, he was thrilled to see that he had scored an A-. He felt a sense of pride and accomplishment that he had never felt before. But as he looked around the classroom, he realized that everyone else had scored higher than he did. He couldn't believe that even though he had worked so hard, he still couldn't measure up to his peers. As he left the classroom, he couldn't shake off the feeling of inadequacy. As he walked home, he tried to remind himself that his grade was still an improvement from before, but he couldn't help but feel like a failure. John knew he would have to work even harder if he wanted to improve his rank in the class. In fact, he couldn't shake off the feeling of dissatisfaction long after the exam had ended.

① satisfied → disappointed
② pleased → bored
③ frustrated → encouraged
④ nervous → relieved
⑤ confident → jealous

015

다음 글에 드러난 'I'의 심경 변화로 가장 적절한 것은?

The bus I was traveling in reached *Nogyin Erak*, a dangerous zone which is on the way to Rengging, a small village. This zone has always been famous among the hill tribes, not for its scenic beauty but for taking the lives of many. This moist and muddy, sliding zone has been a fear by travelers for many years. Boulders, pebbles, and mud would roll down at any moment without warning and bring an end to a traveler. With death lurking around, Siang river awaiting down below with her cruel smile was a nightmare scenario. Finally the driver and the passengers let out a big breath after crossing the danger zone. "Now we are safe," the driver said elated. "I didn't even look down! I was praying to God with my eyes closed," I said turning to the people around me with a sigh.

① bored → excited
② terrified → relieved
③ doubtful → satisfied
④ confident → worried
⑤ proud → embarrassed

016

다음 글에 드러난 Jenna의 심경 변화로 가장 적절한 것은?

Jenna and Johan Otter were celebrating Jenna's graduation from high school. They were on a father-daughter trip to Glacier National Park. Just before nine o'clock on a warm August morning, they were deciding how much farther to walk. The trail followed a ridge on a cliff. Jenna took the lead. She climbed rough steps for a while and stopped to admire the beautiful view. A golden eagle flew above them in blue skies with high clouds. Jenna was enjoying the time with her father while taking pictures of the wonderful scenery. Farther up the trail, a big boulder blocked their path. Jenna scooted around it. Behind the boulder was a mother grizzly bear with her two cubs. Jenna's sudden appearance startled the grizzly. When Johan saw the grizzly, he jumped in front of Jenna to protect her. She thought that soon the animal would leap and bite into his left thigh.

① pleasant → terrified
② indifferent → thrilled
③ envious → doubtful
④ irritated → shameful
⑤ bored → excited

017

다음 글에 드러난 Jerusha의 심경 변화로 가장 적절한 것은?

Mrs. Lippett allowed a moment of silence to fall, and then resumed in a slow, placid manner "Jerusha, as you know, the children are not kept after they are sixteen. Now you are sixteen and the orphanage cannot be responsible any longer for your support. Today the question of your future was brought up in the meeting and your record was discussed — thoroughly discussed." Mrs. Lippett brought accusing eyes to bear upon the prisoner in the dock, and Jerusha looked guilty because it seemed to be expected—not because she could remember any strikingly black pages in her record. "Fortunately for you, one of our trustees has offered to send you to college." "To college?" Jerusha's eyes grew big and her mind was numbed.

*dock: (법정의) 피고석

① nervous → surprised
② bored → excited
③ delighted → anxious
④ hopeful → discouraged
⑤ satisfied → resigned

018

다음 글에 드러난 'I'의 심경 변화로 가장 적절한 것은?

Bill was my student and he got great grades. He came early, stayed late, worked hard, and asked very good questions. He was one of my best students, and I was his writing mentor. He was supposed to submit an essay to enter a national competition. I taught him how to organize his writing for clarity. I was convinced that he would win a prize. Weeks later, when I heard that he won first prize, I was so proud of him and congratulated him on his achievement. However, our happiness didn't last long. It turned out that Bill didn't submit his own essay. He submitted an essay written by someone else as his own. He literally took the whole essay and put his name on and handed it in. He told me that he just wanted to make his parents and me happy. His words made me speechless.

① pleased → indifferent
② worried → determined
③ nervous → confident
④ suspicious → anticipating
⑤ delighted → disappointed

| 출제 Trend
- 거의 매년 수능에 1문항씩 출제되어 온 영어 독해의 기본 유형입니다.
- 사실(fact)을 기술하는 부분보다는 의견(opinion)을 제시하는 부분에 주목해야 하는 유형입니다.
- 선택지가 한글로 제시되어 글의 주제나 제목 유형보다 상대적으로 높은 정답률을 보입니다.

| 해결 Point

1. 핵심 문장을 찾는 연습을 한다.

일반적으로 필자의 주장 문제에는 필자의 주장을 한 문장으로 요약한 핵심 문장이 있습니다. 그 핵심 문장은 필자의 주장을 조금 돌려서 표현하는 경우가 많습니다. 간접적으로 주장을 표현한 문장을 보고, 선택지의 정답과 바로 연결해서 답을 내는 연습을 충분히 하는 것이 중요합니다.

2. 예시는 필자의 주장을 풀어 쓴 것이다.

필자의 주장을 찾는 문제는 지문에 주장을 나타내는 문장이 확실히 나와 있거나 여러 예시로 그 주장을 뒷받침하고 있는 경우가 많습니다. 따라서 주제문을 찾기 어려운 경우엔 제시되어 있는 예시들을 보고 필자의 주장을 추론할 수 있습니다.

대표 기출 문제

정답 및 해설 p.009

019 다음 글에서 필자가 주장하는 바로 가장 적절한 것은? 2024 수능

Values alone do not create and build culture. Living your values only some of the time does not contribute to the creation and maintenance of culture. Changing values into behaviors is only half the battle. Certainly, this is a step in the right direction, but those behaviors must then be shared and distributed widely throughout the organization, along with a clear and concise description of what is expected. It is not enough to simply talk about it. It is critical to have a visual representation of the specific behaviors that leaders and all people managers can use to coach their people. Just like a sports team has a playbook with specific plays designed to help them perform well and win, your company should have a playbook with the key shifts needed to transform your culture into action and turn your values into winning behaviors.

① 조직 문화 혁신을 위해서 모든 구성원이 공유할 핵심 가치를 정립해야 한다.
② 조직 구성원의 행동을 변화시키려면 지도자는 명확한 가치관을 가져야 한다.
③ 조직 내 문화가 공유되기 위해서 구성원의 자발적 행동이 뒷받침되어야 한다.
④ 조직의 핵심 가치 실현을 위해 구성원 간의 지속적인 의사소통이 필수적이다.
⑤ 조직의 문화 형성에는 가치를 반영한 행동의 공유를 위한 명시적 지침이 필요하다.

✔ 유형 해결
3-Step

STEP1 문제 제기 문장을 파악하여 필자의 입장이나 태도 파악하기

Changing values into behaviors is only half the battle.

→ 가치를 행동으로 옮기는 것은 전투의 절반이라고 했으므로, 가치를 행동으로 옮기는 것 이외의 다른 일이 필요함을 알 수 있고, 이것이 필자가 주장하고자 하는 내용임을 추론할 수 있다.

STEP2 주장이 드러나는 표현에 집중하여 주장하는 내용 파악하기

• those behaviors **must** then be shared and distributed widely throughout the organization, along with a clear and concise description ~
(그러한 행동은 명확하고 간결한 설명과 함께 조직 전체에 널리 공유되고 퍼뜨려져야 한다)

• It is **critical** to have a visual representation of the specific behaviors ~
(특정한 행동들의 시각적 표현을 갖는 것이 중요하다)

• your company **should** have a playbook ~
(여러분의 회사는 플레이 북을 가지고 있어야 한다)

→ 필자의 주장은 흔히 critical, must, should 등이 포함된 문장 안에 담겨 있다.

STEP3 근거를 종합해 필자의 주장 정리하기

스포츠팀이 플레이 북을 가지고 있는 것처럼, 조직(회사)도 가치를 반영한 행동이 공유될 수 있게 해주는, 시각적으로 명확하게 설명된 플레이 북을 가지고 있어야 한다고 했으므로 필자가 주장하는 바로 가장 적절한 것은 ⑤이다.

....

✔ 정답 확인

① 조직 문화 혁신을 위해서 모든 구성원이 공유할 핵심 가치를 정립해야 한다. → 조직 문화 혁신에 관한 내용은 없음

② 조직 구성원의 행동을 변화시키려면 지도자는 명확한 가치관을 가져야 한다. → 지도자의 가치관에 관한 글이 아님

③ 조직 내 문화가 공유되기 위해서 구성원의 자발적 행동이 뒷받침되어야 한다.
　　　→ 구성원의 자발적 행동에 관한 내용은 무관함

④ 조직의 핵심 가치 실현을 위해 구성원 간의 지속적인 의사소통이 필수적이다.
　　　→ 의사소통에 관한 내용은 언급되지 않음

⑤ 조직의 문화 형성에는 가치를 반영한 행동의 공유를 위한 명시적 지침이 필요하다.
　　　→ 필자가 주장한 내용을 종합해서 한 문장으로 표현한 내용이므로 정답!

....

✔ 중요 구문　　5행 It is critical [**to have** a visual representation of the specific behaviors {**that** leaders and all
　　　　　　　　　주어　　　　　진주어　　　　　　　　　　　　　　　　　　　　　　　　목적격 관계대명사
people managers can use to coach their people}].

: It은 가주어이고 to부정사구인 [ ]가 진주어이다. { }는 관계절로 선행사는 a visual representation of the specific behaviors이다. to coach their people은 to부정사의 부사적 용법으로 '목적'을 나타낸다.

....

✔ 어휘 풀이
　• contribute　v 기여하다　　　　• maintenance　n 유지　　　　• battle　n 전투
　• distribute　v 퍼뜨리다, 배포하다　• concise　a 간결한　　　　　• description　n 설명, 기술
　• critical　a 중요한, 결정적인　　　• visual　a 시각적인　　　　　• representation　n 표현, 묘사
　• specific　a 특정한, 구체적인　　• playbook　n 플레이 북(팀의 공수 작전을 그림과 함께 기록한 책), 작전집
　• shift　n 변화　　　　　　　　• transform　v 바꾸다

020

2023 수능

다음 글에서 필자가 주장하는 바로 가장 적절한 것은?

At every step in our journey through life we encounter junctions with many different pathways leading into the distance. Each choice involves uncertainty about which path will get you to your destination. Trusting our intuition to make the choice often ends up with us making a suboptimal choice. Turning the uncertainty into numbers has proved a potent way of analyzing the paths and finding the shortcut to your destination. The mathematical theory of probability hasn't eliminated risk, but it allows us to manage that risk more effectively. The strategy is to analyze all the possible scenarios that the future holds and then to see what proportion of them lead to success or failure. This gives you a much better map of the future on which to base your decisions about which path to choose.

*junction: 분기점 **suboptimal: 차선의

① 성공적인 삶을 위해 미래에 대한 구체적인 계획을 세워야 한다.
② 중요한 결정을 내릴 때에는 자신의 직관에 따라 판단해야 한다.
③ 더 나은 선택을 위해 성공 가능성을 확률적으로 분석해야 한다.
④ 빠른 목표 달성을 위해 지름길로 가고자 할 때 신중해야 한다.
⑤ 인생의 여정에서 선택에 따른 결과를 스스로 책임져야 한다.

021

2022 수능

다음 글에서 필자가 주장하는 바로 가장 적절한 것은?

One of the most common mistakes made by organizations when they first consider experimenting with social media is that they focus too much on social media tools and platforms and not enough on their business objectives. The reality of success in the social web for businesses is that creating a social media program begins not with insight into the latest social media tools and channels but with a thorough understanding of the organization's own goals and objectives. A social media program is not merely the fulfillment of a vague need to manage a "presence" on popular social networks because "everyone else is doing it." "Being in social media" serves no purpose in and of itself. In order to serve any purpose at all, a social media presence must either solve a problem for the organization and its customers or result in an improvement of some sort (preferably a measurable one). In all things, purpose drives success. The world of social media is no different.

① 기업 이미지에 부합하는 소셜 미디어를 직접 개발하여 운영해야 한다.
② 기업은 사회적 가치와 요구를 반영하여 사업 목표를 수립해야 한다.
③ 기업은 소셜 미디어를 활용할 때 사업 목표를 토대로 해야 한다.
④ 소셜 미디어로 제품을 홍보할 때는 구체적인 정보를 제공해야 한다.
⑤ 소비자의 의견을 수렴하기 위해 소셜 미디어를 적극 활용해야 한다.

022

다음 글에서 필자가 주장하는 바로 가장 적절한 것은?

Students and parents alike have been worried by the sense of namelessness that exists in many modern schools. Under the current system, some students are just faces in a classroom. The namelessness problem is usually not a teacher's fault. Many teachers have to work with over a hundred different students per day, as well as manage troublemakers, do paperwork, and, of course, try their best to teach! It can be difficult to remember a hundred names, never mind any more personal details. And it can be impossible to notice small changes in individual students that might indicate more serious problems. A reduction in class size could resolve these problems quickly. Teachers would have a much easier time getting to know their students, not just recognizing their faces. If a teacher knows a student's strengths and weaknesses, personality and interests, that can vastly improve the student's academic and personal experience. The teacher will be better able to help him or her, as well as communicate in more effective, meaningful ways.

① 내향적이거나 뛰어나지 않은 학생들을 위한 학급을 편성 운영해야 한다.
② 학생들 개개인이 모두 존중받을 수 있도록 학급 당 인원을 줄여야 한다.
③ 교사는 학생들 각자의 이름을 불러 존중받는 느낌을 만들어 주어야 한다.
④ 학생들의 개성을 발전시키기 위해 추가적인 교실 공간이 제공되어야 한다.
⑤ 학습 능률 향상과 교사의 업무 경감을 위해 전체 학급 수를 축소해야 한다.

023

다음 글에서 필자가 주장하는 바로 가장 적절한 것은?

Observation that replaces or at least postpones experimental manipulation contributes directly to animal welfare through a potential reduction in the number of animals that might have to be used in the experiments. Not only that, but someone who has acquired a good knowledge of their animals through having watched them carefully beforehand, is likely to be able to carry out the experiments in a much more animal-friendly way, for example, through understanding the animals' needs for shelter or social companions. Observation can thus contribute to a Reduction in the numbers of animals used as well as to a Refinement of experimental procedures. If, in addition, it leads to the Replacement of experiments altogether, it makes a major contribution to each one of what have come to be called the 'three Rs' of animal experimentation: Reduction, Refinement and Replacement. Observation should therefore be seen as one of the major alternatives to animal experimentation, a way of providing scientific data of a high standard while safeguarding animal welfare at the same time.

① 동물 실험의 세 가지 기준을 지켜야 한다.
② 동물 복지에 대한 사람들의 인식을 높여야 한다.
③ 동물 행동을 면밀히 관찰한 후에 실험을 진행해야 한다.
④ 동물 연구를 하는 데 있어 동물의 권리를 보장해야 한다.
⑤ 동물을 직접 실험하는 대신에 관찰을 통해 연구해야 한다.

024

다음 글에서 필자가 주장하는 바로 가장 적절한 것은?

Typically, presenters put their material into some kind of logical order, an order that makes sense — to them. You want to cover, say, the background, the opportunity, the strategic imperative, the competitive environment, the financial implications, the human resource implications, and so on. Boring. Begin your presentation with a pressing problem that your audience has and then tell them your proposed solution. Here's the important part: to decide where to go next, ask yourself, "If I were to stop right here, what is the first objection that would come from the audience?" Your response to that objection is what your next point should be. Make that point, and then repeat the question. This way you will progressively design a presentation sequenced in the way your audience wants to hear it, not in some arbitrary order that seems to make sense to you.

*imperative: 불가피한 것, 임무

① 발표 전에 청중의 관심사에 대한 조사가 선행되어야 한다.
② 발표자는 정보 제시 순서를 청중의 관점에서 결정해야 한다.
③ 발표에는 청중의 흥미를 끄는 다양한 자료가 포함되어야 한다.
④ 발표 중에 발표자와 청중이 상호작용할 기회가 주어져야 한다.
⑤ 청중은 발표자가 제시하는 정보를 선별적으로 받아들여야 한다.

025

다음 글에서 필자가 주장하는 바로 가장 적절한 것은?

Never make the mistake of thinking that the mere delivery of the criticism provides the explanation of what the receiver should do next. That's a bad practice! Take, for example, the employee who needs to prioritize his work better. Telling him that he needs to do a better job of setting priorities is helpful. But consider that if the employee knew how to prioritize his work appropriately, he would likely do it. Similarly, many managers receive criticism for not participating more in meetings. In all likelihood, if the managers knew how to participate more in meetings, they would. In each situation, it's necessary to explore further the specific actions that the receiver can perform in order to improve things. For instance, the boss could say, "What I mean by participating more in meetings is to go beyond coming prepared. What I'd like you to do is come up with one idea or introduce one good question to raise to the group. Also, if the meeting goes off track, I'd like you to take it upon yourself to get everyone back on point."

① 비판의 내용보다 전달 방식에 더 유의해야 한다.
② 비판을 할 때는 상대방과의 관계를 고려해야 한다.
③ 비판과 함께 구체적인 개선 방법도 제시해야 한다.
④ 사안에 따라 비판의 강도를 적절히 조절해야 한다.
⑤ 세세한 잘못의 지적보다는 개괄적인 비판을 해야 한다.

026

다음 글에서 필자가 주장하는 바로 가장 적절한 것은?

Why would you want to leave your prize stallion in the stable? While he stands there eating his hay, races are won and lost without him. He can't contribute to the winnings if he gets no chance to race. So often, we find organizations pushing away their star performers in spite of their zeal. The reason is that by overachieving, they make others look bad. The other people in the office do not have any awards or recognition. They just make the others jealous. However, instead of punishing those who are out of step with the rest, reward them for their drive. In the great production of life, there will always be headliners followed by back-up singers. If you silence the soloist, all you will be left with is background music. Shining stars need to be supported just as much as the slacker. Let the stallion out of the stable and give them room to run.

*stallion: 종마 **slacker: 태만한 사람

① 외적인 성과보다 내부 기여도로 직원을 평가해야 한다.
② 경기의 결과보다 경기를 준비하는 과정을 중시해야 한다.
③ 조직이 추구하는 목표를 구성원들에게 잘 이해시켜야 한다.
④ 재능 있는 사람들에게 능력을 발휘할 기회를 제공해야 한다.
⑤ 뛰어난 소수의 의견보다 평범한 다수의 의견에 주목해야 한다.

027

다음 글에서 필자가 주장하는 바로 가장 적절한 것은?

There is still too much reliance on producing exclusively print-based responses at school, yet in the world outside of school print rarely appears without the accompaniment of images. Indeed, print is itself a visual medium, and much more could be done to encourage pupils and students to think about, use, and package different print formats and different combinations of print and images, in presenting their work. In addition, of course, photographs, collected images, drawings, slide displays, audiotape and radio presentations, and simple video and film work all have exciting possibilities for the presentation of student ideas in every subject. Even a little encouragement by teachers for students to choose an appropriate media form in presenting their work would allow students to demonstrate any abilities they might possess in communicating via nonprint forms and to develop new skills.

① 수업 시간에는 학생들의 통신 매체 사용을 제한해야 한다.
② 학생들의 집중력을 해치는 과도한 매체 사용을 삼가야 한다.
③ 학생들의 매체 사용 능력 향상을 위한 교육이 실시되어야 한다.
④ 학생들이 다양한 매체를 활용하여 발표하도록 장려해야 한다.
⑤ 시청각 매체를 활용한 수업이 가능하도록 시설을 개선해야 한다.

04 함축 의미 추론

정답 및 해설 p.012

| 출제 Trend
- 2019학년도 6월 평가원 모의고사에서부터 출제되기 시작한 유형입니다.
- '지문의 전체적인 내용 이해'를 기반으로 '특정 부분의 의미까지 이해'하는 능력을 필요로 합니다.
- 지문이 쉽지 않고, 특정 어구의 사전적 의미가 아닌 문맥적 의미를 파악해야 하기 때문에 난이도가 높습니다.

| 해결 Point

1. 선택지를 먼저 읽을 필요는 없다.

함축 의미를 파악하는 문제는 밑줄 친 부분이 '문맥상' 어떤 의미인지를 묻기 때문에 선택지를 먼저 읽어서 얻을 수 있는 힌트가 없습니다. 함축된 의미는 지문의 전체적인 맥락을 이해해야 알 수 있는데, 선택지는 해당 표현의 의미만 서술하고 있기 때문입니다. 만약 선택지의 표현이 지문의 요지와 반대되는 개념을 담고 있는 경우라면 문제를 풀 때 헷갈리기만 하겠죠?

2. 함축된 의미는 이미 지문에서 풀어서 설명하고 있다.

보통은 지문에 밑줄 친 부분과 문맥상 유사한 의미로 사용된 표현들이 많이 나옵니다. 밑줄 친 부분을 대체할 수 있는 문장이나 어구를 찾아보세요. 또한 지문에 주어진 예시들도 함축된 의미로 표현할 수 있는 경우가 많습니다. 즉, 예시의 의미를 이해하면 함축된 의미를 유추할 수 있습니다.

대표 기출 문제

028 밑줄 친 a nonstick frying pan이 다음 글에서 의미하는 바로 가장 적절한 것은?　　　　2024 수능

How you focus your attention plays a critical role in how you deal with stress. Scattered attention harms your ability to let go of stress, because even though your attention is scattered, it is narrowly focused, for you are able to fixate only on the stressful parts of your experience. When your attentional spotlight is widened, you can more easily let go of stress. You can put in perspective many more aspects of any situation and not get locked into one part that ties you down to superficial and anxiety-provoking levels of attention. A narrow focus heightens the stress level of each experience, but a widened focus turns down the stress level because you're better able to put each situation into a broader perspective. One anxiety-provoking detail is less important than the bigger picture. It's like transforming yourself into a nonstick frying pan. You can still fry an egg, but the egg won't stick to the pan.

*provoke: 유발시키다

① never being confronted with any stressful experiences in daily life
② broadening one's perspective to identify the cause of stress
③ rarely confining one's attention to positive aspects of an experience
④ having a larger view of an experience beyond its stressful aspects
⑤ taking stress into account as the source of developing a wide view

✔ 유형 해결
3-Step

STEP 1 밑줄 친 말의 표면적 의미 해석하기

a nonstick frying pan(들러붙지 않는 프라이팬)

STEP 2 도입부에서 제기하는 문제 파악하기

문제 1 Scattered attention harms your ability to let go of stress ~
(분산된 주의는 스트레스를 해소하는 능력을 해친다)

문제 2 When your attentional spotlight is widened, you can more easily let go of stress.
(여러분의 주의의 초점이 넓어지면, 여러분은 스트레스를 더 쉽게 해소할 수 있다.)
→ 분산된 주의보다는 주의의 초점을 넓게 하는 것이 스트레스 해소에 도움이 됨

STEP 3 주제문을 토대로 밑줄 친 말의 의미 파악하기

주제문 ~ a widened focus turns down the stress level because you're better able to put each situation into a broader perspective. → 초점이 넓으면 상황을 더 넓은 시각으로 더 잘 볼 수 있기 때문에
스트레스 수준이 낮아진다는 것이 중심 내용임

밑줄 친 말 It's like transforming yourself into a nonstick frying pan.
→ 자신을 들러붙지 않는 프라이팬으로 만든다는 것은, 불안감을 유발하는 하나의 세부 사항에 얽매이지 않고 보다
넓은 관점에서 그것을 바라보면서 스트레스에서 벗어난다는 의미임

....

✔ 정답 확인
① 일상생활에서 스트레스가 많은 어떤 경험에도 결코 직면하지 않는 것
→ 스트레스를 주는 경험에 대처하는 방법에 관한 글이어서 부적절함

② 스트레스의 원인을 파악하기 위해 시각을 넓히는 것
→ 스트레스의 원인 파악이 아니라 발생한 스트레스에 어떻게 대처하느냐의 문제를 다루고 있어서 부적절함

③ 경험의 긍정적인 측면에 주의를 거의 제한하지 않는 것
→ 주의의 초점을 넓히면 어떠한 경험도 보다 균형 있는 시각으로 볼 수 있다고 설명하고 있으므로 부적절함

④ 스트레스를 주는 측면을 넘어 경험에 대한 더 넓은 시각을 갖는 것
→ 불안감을 주는 특별한 세부 사항을 넘어 보다 넓게 상황을 본다고 했으므로 정답!

⑤ 넓은 시각을 개발하는 원천으로 스트레스를 고려하는 것
→ 넓은 시각은 스트레스를 해소하기 위한 정치로 언급되고 있으므로 부적절함

....

✔ 중요 구문
4행 You can [put in perspective {many more aspects of any situation}] and [not get locked
　　　　　　can에 이어지는 동사1　　　　　　put의 목적어　　　　　　　　can에 이어지는 동사2
into one part {that ties you down to superficial and anxiety-provoking levels of attention}].
　　　　　　　주격 관계대명사

: [ ]로 표시된 두 부분은 병렬구조를 이루면서 can에 연결되고 있고, 첫 번째 { }는 put의 목적어 역할을 하는 명사구이다. 두 번째 { }는 one part를 수식하는 관계절이다.

....

✔ 어휘 풀이
• scatter *v* 분산시키다, 흩뜨리다　　• let go of ~을 해소하다, ~을 풀어주다　　• fixate on ~에 집착하다

• attentional spotlight 주의의 초점, 주의의 집중

• put ~ in perspective ~을 균형 있는 시각으로 보다　　　　• tie down to ~에 옭아매다

• superficial *a* 피상적인　　　• anxiety-provoking *a* 불안감을 유발하는

• the bigger picture 더 큰 전체적인 상황, 큰 그림　　　• transform *v* 변형시키다

• nonstick *a* 들러붙지 않는

029

2023 수능

밑줄 친 make oneself public to oneself가 다음 글에서 의미하는 바로 가장 적절한 것은?

Coming of age in the 18th and 19th centuries, the personal diary became a centerpiece in the construction of a modern subjectivity, at the heart of which is the application of reason and critique to the understanding of world and self, which allowed the creation of a new kind of knowledge. Diaries were central media through which enlightened and free subjects could be constructed. They provided a space where one could write daily about her whereabouts, feelings, and thoughts. Over time and with rereading, disparate entries, events, and happenstances could be rendered into insights and narratives about the self, and allowed for the formation of subjectivity. It is in that context that the idea of "the self [as] both made and explored with words" emerges. Diaries were personal and private; one would write for oneself, or, in Habermas's formulation, one would make oneself public to oneself. By making the self public in a private sphere, the self also became an object for self-inspection and self-critique.

*disparate: 이질적인 **render: 만들다

① use writing as a means of reflecting on oneself
② build one's identity by reading others' diaries
③ exchange feedback in the process of writing
④ create an alternate ego to present to others
⑤ develop topics for writing about selfhood

030

2022 수능

밑줄 친 whether to make ready for the morning commute or not이 다음 글에서 의미하는 바로 가장 적절한 것은?

Scientists have no special purchase on moral or ethical decisions; a climate scientist is no more qualified to comment on health care reform than a physicist is to judge the causes of bee colony collapse. The very features that create expertise in a specialized domain lead to ignorance in many others. In some cases lay people—farmers, fishermen, patients, native peoples—may have relevant experiences that scientists can learn from. Indeed, in recent years, scientists have begun to recognize this: the Arctic Climate Impact Assessment includes observations gathered from local native groups. So our trust needs to be limited, and focused. It needs to be very *particular*. Blind trust will get us into at least as much trouble as no trust at all. But without some degree of trust in our designated experts—the men and women who have devoted their lives to sorting out tough questions about the natural world we live in—we are paralyzed, in effect not knowing whether to make ready for the morning commute or not.

*lay: 전문가가 아닌 **paralyze: 마비시키다 ***commute: 통근

① questionable facts that have been popularized by non-experts
② readily applicable information offered by specialized experts
③ common knowledge that hardly influences crucial decisions
④ practical information produced by both specialists and lay people
⑤ biased knowledge that is widespread in the local community

031

밑줄 친 They are like blind people, searching for a wall.이 다음 글에서 의미하는 바로 가장 적절한 것은?

If I can hurt and overpower you, then I can do exactly what I want, when I want, even when you're around. I can torment you to appease my curiosity. I can take the attention away from you, and dominate you. I can steal your toy. Children hit first because aggression is innate, although more dominant in some individuals and less in others, and, second, because aggression facilitates desire. It's foolish to assume that such behaviour must be learned. A snake does not have to be taught to strike. It's in the nature of the beast. Two-year-olds, statistically speaking, are the most violent of people. They kick, hit and bite, and they steal the property of others. They do so to explore, to express outrage and frustration, and to gratify their impulsive desires. More importantly, they do so to discover the true limits of permissible behaviour. How else are they ever going to puzzle out what is acceptable? They are like blind people, searching for a wall. They have to push forward to see where the actual boundaries lie.

*appease: 달래다

① Children only act on adult guidance.
② Babies don't know that they are ignorant.
③ Children's curiosity often leads them to danger.
④ Parents should try to satisfy their babies' curiosity.
⑤ Infants explore and test the limits of acceptable behavior.

032

밑줄 친 "You can't move a string by pushing it, you have to pull it."이 다음 글에서 의미하는 바로 가장 적절한 것은?

Persuasion is not coercion, and it is also not an attempt to defeat your intellectual opponent with facts or moral superiority, nor is it a debate with a winner or a loser. Persuasion is leading a person along in stages, helping them to better understand their own thinking and how it could align with your message. You can't persuade another person to change their mind if that person doesn't want to do so, and as you will see, the techniques that work best focus on a person's motivations more than their conclusions. In many ways, persuasion is mostly encouraging people to realize change is possible. All persuasion is self-persuasion. People change or refuse based on their own desires, motivations, and internal counterarguing, and by focusing on these factors, an argument becomes more likely to change minds. As psychologist Joel Whalen once put it, "You can't move a string by pushing it, you have to pull it."

*coercion: 강제

① Let the other person do a great deal of the talking first.
② Use a direct and forceful approach in persuading others.
③ Admit your fallacy promptly when you realize you are wrong.
④ Coerce the other person to adopt a different belief immediately.
⑤ Motivate the other person to willingly embrace a new perspective.

033

밑줄 친 the brain is a decent scientist but an absolutely outstanding lawyer가 다음 글에서 의미하는 바로 가장 적절한 것은?

Scientists gather evidence, look for regularities, form theories explaining their observations, and test them. Attorneys begin with a conclusion they want to convince others of and then seek evidence that
5 supports it, while also attempting to discredit evidence that doesn't. The human mind is designed to be both a scientist and an attorney, both a conscious seeker of objective truth and an unconscious, impassioned advocate for what we want to believe. Together these
10 approaches vie to create our worldview. Believing in what you desire to be true and then seeking evidence to justify it doesn't seem to be the best approach to everyday decisions. For example, if you're at the races, it is rational to bet on the horse you believe is fastest,
15 but it doesn't make sense to believe a horse is fastest because you bet on it. Still, even though the latter approach doesn't make rational sense, it is the irrational choice that would probably make you happier. As it turns out, the brain is a decent scientist
20 but an absolutely outstanding lawyer.

*vie: 경쟁하다

① we generally see ourselves in an overly positive light
② the unconscious mind is a master at using limited information
③ our attorney-like unconscious mind completely dictates our decisions
④ the human mind which tends to seek happiness is not always rational
⑤ our rational conscious mind needs the help of attorneys to make decisions

034

밑줄 친 the "erosion of childhood"가 다음 글에서 의미하는 바로 가장 적절한 것은?

Educators are voicing worries about the overwhelming rapidity of information. In a 2012 report that surveyed four hundred British teachers, three-quarters reported a significant decline in their young students' attention spans. In the same year, a survey of more than two
5 thousand U.S. secondary school teachers showed that 87 percent of teachers believed that digital technologies are creating an "easily distracted generation with short attention spans," whereas 64 percent agreed that these technologies have more of a distracting effect than a
10 beneficial one on students academically. The diversity of different professions expressing the drawbacks of digital devices was well illustrated in an open letter written in September 2011 to the respected British newspaper the *Daily Telegraph* and signed by two
15 hundred teachers, psychiatrists, neuroscientists, and other experts expressing alarm over the "erosion of childhood".

*psychiatrist: 정신과 의사

① children's distrust of their parents and teachers
② problems caused by children's reduced playing time
③ the reality of children who are tired of studying too much
④ the decrease in students' attention due to the use of digital devices
⑤ the increased violence in children due to excessive use of video games

035

밑줄 친 to take a breather from interactions가 다음 글에서 의미하는 바로 가장 적절한 것은?

Sometimes it is wise to take a breather from interactions. People often signal when they are experiencing negative emotions, and pushing beyond that in such moments may result in things being said, or certain tones of voice being used, that irreversibly cause hardened dislike and conflict. People show their negative emotions through their body posture, their tone of voice, their withholding of thoughts, a frown or tightening around their eyes or mouth, and so on. Taking a step back is useful to reflect and digest what has been said. Perhaps the matter can be recast and even mutual gain outcomes suggested. Alternatives might come to mind later, and sometimes it is wise to bring others into the picture. At the very least, it is wise to give oneself more time to deal with conflict, if that is what it is going to be. It is useful to cool things down and then decide on one's options and next steps.

① to seek help from those who have experienced similar issues
② to take immediate steps to resolve the conflict with those involved
③ to have time to relax and think about the issue and the next move
④ to withdraw from relationships with those who started the conflict
⑤ to play an active role in building and maintaining relationships

036

밑줄 친 this trap이 다음 글에서 의미하는 바로 가장 적절한 것은?

Jessica Spungin found herself caught in this trap when she was promoted to the position of associate principal in McKinsey's London office. As an AP, a consultant is expected to take on more responsibilities of the partnership group, juggle multiple projects, serve as a team leader, and play an active role in office life. Spungin dove in to all these tasks headfirst. While she was handling two major client projects, she was asked to serve as a senior coach for six business analysts, get involved in internal training, and help out on a new project for a health care company. In her first round of feedback from the three project teams she oversaw, she was rated second from the bottom among her peers. Spungin realized that her desire to be indispensable sprang from a lack of confidence. "I never said no to a client who wanted me to be present at a meeting," she told us. "I did what I thought was expected—regardless of what I was good at, what was important, or what I could physically do."

① taking others' help for granted
② always sticking to one's opinion
③ blindly trying to please everyone
④ giving up the present for the future
⑤ influencing what others expect of her

글의 요지

│ 출제 Trend
- 매년 수능에 1문항씩 출제되어 온 영어 독해의 기본 유형입니다.
- 요지는 글쓴이의 주장(의견)이나 글의 핵심 내용(주제)을 하나의 문장으로 나타낸 것입니다.
- 선택지가 한글로 제시되어 글의 주제나 제목 유형보다 상대적으로 높은 정답률을 보입니다.

│ 해결 Point

1. 전체를 가리키는 단어를 살펴라!

every, always, all 같은 전체를 가리키는 단어들이 등장하는 문장은 보통 필자가 통념이라고 믿거나 지지하는 내용을 담고 있습니다. 반대로 '대부분의 경우는 이렇지만, 나는 그렇게 생각하지 않는다'와 같이 반전을 위해 그러한 단어들을 사용하는 경우도 있으니 뒤 문장의 연결어까지 추가적으로 확인하도록 합니다.

2. 필자의 견해를 드러내는 표현에 주목하자!

글의 요지 유형의 지문은 보통 무언가를 권하거나 강조하는 내용으로 이루어져 있습니다. 그렇기에 should, must, have to와 같이 특정 행동을 촉구하는 표현들에 주목할 필요가 있습니다. 혹은 더 직관적으로 I believe[suggest], In my opinion과 같은 표현을 쓸 수도 있으니 이러한 자신의 생각을 드러내는 표현을 통해 글의 요지를 찾도록 합니다.

대표 기출 문제

정답 및 해설 p.016

037 다음 글의 요지로 가장 적절한 것은? 2024 수능

Being able to prioritize your responses allows you to connect more deeply with individual customers, be it a one-off interaction around a particularly delightful or upsetting experience, or the development of a longer-term relationship with a significantly influential individual within your customer base. If you've ever posted a favorable comment — or any comment, for that matter — about a brand, product or service, think about what it would feel like if you were personally acknowledged by the brand manager, for example, as a result. In general, people post because they have something to say — and because they want to be recognized for having said it. In particular, when people post positive comments they are expressions of appreciation for the experience that led to the post. While a compliment to the person standing next to you is typically answered with a response like "Thank You," the sad fact is that most brand compliments go unanswered. These are lost opportunities to understand what drove the compliments and create a solid fan based on them.

*compliment: 칭찬

① 고객과의 관계 증진을 위해 고객의 브랜드 칭찬에 응답하는 것은 중요하다.
② 고객의 피드백을 면밀히 분석함으로써 브랜드의 성공 가능성을 높일 수 있다.
③ 신속한 고객 응대를 통해서 고객의 긍정적인 반응을 이끌어 낼 수 있다.
④ 브랜드 매니저에게는 고객의 부정적인 의견을 수용하는 태도가 요구된다.
⑤ 고객의 의견을 경청하는 것은 브랜드의 새로운 이미지 창출에 도움이 된다.

✔ 유형 해결
3-Step

(STEP 1) 특정 개념과 관련되어 반복되는 어휘나 어구를 통해 글 대강의 내용 추측하기

response(응답), customer(고객), comment(의견), post(게시하다), compliment(칭찬)
→ 고객이 칭찬의 의견을 게시하는 것에 관련된 글임을 추측할 수 있음

(STEP 2) 문장 간 내용의 유기적 연관성 파악하기

• Being able to prioritize your responses allows you to connect more deeply with individual customers, ~ → 응답에 우선순위를 정할 수 있는 것이 개별 고객들과 더 깊은 관계를 맺을 수 있게 함

• If you've ever posted a favorable comment about a brand, think about what it would feel like if you were personally acknowledged by the brand manager / people post because they have something to say → 이후 브랜드에 대해 의견을 게시한 후 브랜드 관리자로부터 개인적 인정을 받는 구체적 상황을 제시

• the sad fact is that most brand compliments go unanswered / These are lost opportunities to understand what drove the compliments and create a solid fan based on them. → 하지만 대부분 고객의 브랜드에 대한 의견 게시는 응답을 받지 못하며, 이는 결국 기업이 확고한 팬을 만들어 낼 수 있는 기회를 잃는 것임

(STEP 3) 결론 확인 및 요지 추론

고객은 브랜드에 대해 자신이 게시한 칭찬 글에 대해 인정을 받고자 하기 때문에, 기업이나 브랜드 관리자가 고객의 칭찬 글에 응답을 하면 확고한 팬으로서의 고객을 만들어 낼 수 있다고 말하고 있으므로 글의 요지로 가장 적절한 것은 ①이다.

⋯⋯⋯

✔ 정답 확인

① 고객과의 관계 증진을 위해 고객의 브랜드 칭찬에 응답하는 것은 중요하다.
→ 주요 어구 및 글의 흐름에 드러난 주요 내용을 포함하고 있으므로 정답!

② 고객의 피드백을 면밀히 분석함으로써 브랜드의 성공 가능성을 높일 수 있다.
→ 고객의 의견에 대한 분석보다는 '응답'이 중요하다고 말하고 있는 글이므로 오답

③ 신속한 고객 응대를 통해서 고객의 긍정적인 반응을 이끌어 낼 수 있다.
→ 고객 응대가 빠르거나 지연되었을 경우의 문제를 말하는 글은 아님

④ 브랜드 매니저에게는 고객의 부정적인 의견을 수용하는 태도가 요구된다.
→ 브랜드 매니저의 자격 요건이나 고객의 부정적 의견 수용에 대한 언급은 없음

⑤ 고객의 의견을 경청하는 것은 브랜드의 새로운 이미지 창출에 도움이 된다.
→ 단순한 경청을 넘어서 고객의 브랜드 칭찬에 '응답'하라는 요지의 글이므로 오답

⋯⋯⋯

✔ 중요 구문

1행 [Being able to prioritize your responses] [allows you to connect more deeply with
　　　　주어(동명사구)　　　　　　　　　　　동사구「allow + 목적어 + 목적격보어(to부정사)(~가 …할 수 있게 해주다)」
individual customers], [be it a one-off interaction around a particularly delightful or upsetting
　　　　　　　　　　　도치구문「whether it be ~ or …(~이든 …이든)」
experience, or the development of a longer-term relationship with a significantly influential

individual within your customer base].

: 첫 번째 [ ]는 동명사구로 문장의 주어 역할을 하고, 두 번째 [ ]가 술부이다. 세 번째 [ ]는 부사절인데 「whether it be ~ or …」의 의미(~이든 …이든)가 whether가 생략되면서 주어와 동사가 어순이 바뀌어 「be it ~ or …」로 표현된 형태이다.

⋯⋯⋯

✔ 어휘 풀이

• prioritize　*v* 우선순위를 정하다, 우선시하다　• one-off　*a* 일회성의　　　• interaction　*n* 상호 작용

• upsetting　*a* 속상하게 하는　　　　• acknowledge　*v* 인정하다　　• recognize　*v* 인정하다

• appreciation　*n* 감사　　　　　　　• solid　*a* 확고한, 탄탄한

038

다음 글의 요지로 가장 적절한 것은?

Urban delivery vehicles can be adapted to better suit the density of urban distribution, which often involves smaller vehicles such as vans, including bicycles. The latter have the potential to become a preferred 'last-mile' vehicle, particularly in high-density and congested areas. In locations where bicycle use is high, such as the Netherlands, delivery bicycles are also used to carry personal cargo (e.g. groceries). Due to their low acquisition and maintenance costs, cargo bicycles convey much potential in developed and developing countries alike, such as the *becak* (a three-wheeled bicycle) in Indonesia. Services using electrically assisted delivery tricycles have been successfully implemented in France and are gradually being adopted across Europe for services as varied as parcel and catering deliveries. Using bicycles as cargo vehicles is particularly encouraged when combined with policies that restrict motor vehicle access to specific areas of a city, such as downtown or commercial districts, or with the extension of dedicated bike lanes.

① 도시에서 자전거는 효율적인 배송 수단으로 사용될 수 있다.
② 자전거는 출퇴근 시간을 줄이기 위한 대안으로 선호되고 있다.
③ 자전거는 배송 수단으로의 경제적 장단점을 모두 가질 수 있다.
④ 수요자의 요구에 부합하는 다양한 용도의 자전거가 개발되고 있다.
⑤ 세계 각국에서는 전기 자전거 사용을 장려하는 정책을 추진하고 있다.

039

다음 글의 요지로 가장 적절한 것은?

Environmental hazards include biological, physical, and chemical ones, along with the human behaviors that promote or allow exposure. Some environmental contaminants are difficult to avoid (the breathing of polluted air, the drinking of chemically contaminated public drinking water, noise in open public spaces); in these circumstances, exposure is largely involuntary. Reduction or elimination of these factors may require societal action, such as public awareness and public health measures. In many countries, the fact that some environmental hazards are difficult to avoid at the individual level is felt to be more morally egregious than those hazards that can be avoided. Having no choice but to drink water contaminated with very high levels of arsenic, or being forced to passively breathe in tobacco smoke in restaurants, outrages people more than the personal choice of whether an individual smokes tobacco. These factors are important when one considers how change (risk reduction) happens.

*contaminate: 오염시키다 **egregious: 매우 나쁜

① 개인이 피하기 어려운 유해 환경 요인에 대해서는 사회적 대응이 필요하다.
② 환경오염으로 인한 피해자들에게 적절한 보상을 하는 것이 바람직하다.
③ 다수의 건강을 해치는 행위에 대해 도덕적 비난 이상의 조치가 요구된다.
④ 환경오염 문제를 해결하기 위해서는 사후 대응보다 예방이 중요하다.
⑤ 대기오염 문제는 인접 국가들과의 긴밀한 협력을 통해 해결할 수 있다.

040

다음 글의 요지로 가장 적절한 것은?

Given how ubiquitous and compelling networked devices are to most teens, we tacitly assume that these machines will help them learn what they need to know. But do they? In the early 2000s, economists Jacob Vigdor and Helen Ladd decided to test the idea systematically. Over five years, nearly one million American students in grades five to eight were assessed annually in math and reading and were asked to fill out detailed questionnaires about how they spent their time outside school. By tracking the students' academic progress against, for example, dates when their digital devices, such as computers and tablets, along with broadband Internet access became available to them, the researchers were able to assess the technology's impact. The news was not good. The economists say, "Students who gain access to a home computer while in grades five to eight tend to witness a persistent decline in reading and math test scores. The introduction of high-speed Internet service is similarly associated with significantly lower math and reading test scores."

*tacitly: 암묵적으로

① 디지털 학습은 대면 교육과 병행할 때만 학습 효과가 크다.
② 디지털 기기를 이용한 교육은 취약 계층에게 많은 도움이 된다.
③ 디지털 기기를 이용한 교육은 학습자의 흥미를 유발하기 어렵다.
④ 학교의 교육은 디지털 기기를 이용하여 학습 효과를 높일 수 있다.
⑤ 디지털 기기를 이용한 학습은 학력 저하를 초래하는 경향이 있다.

041

다음 글의 요지로 가장 적절한 것은?

There is no such thing as absolute freedom. All acts of genuine freedom are performed in contexts that limit in various ways and in varying degrees the choices that are practically available to the person doing the choosing. Among these limiting factors are such things as genetic makeups; familial, social, cultural, and institutional influences; prospects and restrictions of particular situations of choice; and present habits, dispositions, and beliefs of persons shaped to a significant extent by their past decisions in particular situations. Such causal factors play an important role. They not only limit the alternatives available to a person in a given situation. They also limit a person's ability or willingness to take all of the alternatives fully into account at any given time when making choices at that time. The person's freedom is therefore a freedom conditioned by causes, even though it is not entirely determined by them.

① 자유를 구성하는 요인들은 고정적이 아니라 가변적이다.
② 진정한 자유를 누리는 데 핵심 요소는 개인의 자발성이다.
③ 자유의 개념은 시대와 상황에 따라 서로 다르게 해석된다.
④ 자유는 인과 관계에 있는 여러 요인에 의해 제약을 받는다.
⑤ 자유의 제약을 철폐하려는 노력은 인간성 회복과 직결된다.

042

다음 글의 요지로 가장 적절한 것은?

In one sophisticated study, researchers studied brain activity in children who viewed nonviolent videos versus children who watched violent videos. The differences between the brain patterns of the two
5 groups were remarkable. Specifically, certain portions of the children's right brains were stimulated only when the children viewed violence on the screen. The study also found that viewing violence on television stimulated a network of brain regions involved in
10 regulating emotions, arousal, attention and memory coding. They concluded that children who watch media violence frequently are more likely to behave aggressively and that this phenomenon may be explained by the brain's ability to store violent scripts
15 in the child's long-term memory. Indeed, over the last fifteen years the amount of evidence tying heavy electronic media use to aggressive behavior in children has become overwhelming and irrefutable.

① 폭력성은 관찰이 아니라 직접적인 경험을 통해서 강화된다.
② 어린아이들은 본성에 의해서 공격적인 충동에 쉽게 굴복한다.
③ 미디어의 폭력성에 대한 연구는 범죄를 줄이는 데 도움을 준다.
④ 어린 시절 미디어 노출은 뇌손상을 유발하여 공격성을 증가시킨다.
⑤ 폭력적인 미디어 시청은 장기 기억으로 저장되어 공격성으로 이어진다.

043

다음 글의 요지로 가장 적절한 것은?

The activities of managers with regard to groups include coaching, motivating, training, evaluating, and providing feedback. However, group dynamics change the way managers approach these activities. For
5 example, a very small change in a procedure may easily be accomplished in some work groups but not so easily in others. If the change is easy to understand and is not burdensome, a simple memo to all department members may work very nicely in one department.
10 However, in another department, employees may resist change of any kind so that department supervisors may have to supplement an introductory memo with one-on-one direction. To ensure successful implementation, one employee may need reassurance,
15 another may have to be convinced of the need for a change, and yet a third may need additional instruction. It is clear that managers have to know their work groups well and to plan their management activities to meet the needs of diverse work groups.

① 집단의 특성에 따라 관리자의 행동 방식도 달라져야 한다.
② 관리자의 업무는 직원 감시보다는 동기 부여와 피드백이다.
③ 관리자의 성향에 따라 업무 중요도를 설정하는 방식이 다르다.
④ 변화에 저항하는 성향의 직원은 새로운 업무에 적합하지 않다.
⑤ 관리자의 미덕은 집단의 일원이라는 마음으로 일하는 자세이다.

044

다음 글의 요지로 가장 적절한 것은?

A well-functioning society requires a certain level of public health. Herd immunity produces benefits at the societal level because it improves public health and reduces the public costs of health-care as well as the economic losses associated with illnesses. Everybody benefits from herd immunity because living in a society with herd immunity means that less public resources need to be diverted to treat sick people; for example, in the US, the flu costs annually US$10.4 billion for hospitalizations and outpatient visits, and the total economic cost associated with annual influenza epidemics, including loss of earning caused by illness, has been estimated to be US$87.1 billion. Preserving or realizing herd immunity is therefore important for society, and there are strong economic reasons for a collective to realize herd immunity.

① 집단 면역 형성을 통해 특정 바이러스는 박멸될 수 있다.
② 백신은 변종을 생산하는 새로운 진화적 압력을 만들어낸다.
③ 집단 면역을 위한 비용은 국가에서 보조하는 것이 바람직하다.
④ 비용이 많이 드는 집단 면역을 목표로 삼는 것은 비효율적이다.
⑤ 집단 면역으로 인한 경제적인 이익은 모든 사회 구성원에게 돌아간다.

045

다음 글의 요지로 가장 적절한 것은?

If physical activity is effective, one important challenge facing scientists, health professionals, and governments is to help large segments of the population become more physically active. How this will be achieved is not likely to come through additional research in exercise physiology, although that discipline will undoubtedly provide answers to important questions such as how much activity is necessary to obtain the physiological benefits. As a science, exercise physiology does not concern itself with general issues associated with understanding and modifying behavior, influencing public opinion, motivating people, and changing people's attitudes. Nor is it a concern of the biomechanics, historians, or sociologists of sport and physical activity. Questions concerning human attitudes, moods, cognitions, and behavior fall directly under the mandate of psychology.

*biomechanics: 생체 역학 **mandate: 권한

① 운동에 대한 동기 부여는 개인적 경험에서부터 시작한다.
② 활동적인 신체 활동을 장려하는 것은 심리학이 할 일이다.
③ 개인에 맞지 않는 획일적인 운동량 권장은 바람직하지 않다.
④ 효율적인 운동 효과를 얻기 위해 전문가의 도움이 필요하다.
⑤ 운동의 필요성 증명을 위해서 운동 생리학의 추가 연구가 필요하다.

┃ 출제 Trend
- 매년 수능에 1문항씩 출제되어 온 영어 독해의 기본 유형입니다.
- 선택지가 영어로 제시되기 때문에 요지 및 주장 파악 유형보다 상대적으로 어려운 유형입니다.
- 특히 정치, 경제, 철학 등의 학문적 주제를 다루는 지문이 출제되면 다소 낮은 정답률을 보입니다.

┃ 해결 Point

1. 연구 결과는 중심 내용과 직결된다.

지문이 연구나 실험 등과 관련된 내용이라면 연구 결과는 글의 주제를 반영합니다. 연구 결과와 그에 따른 결론이 글의 핵심이므로 이 부분을 주의하여 읽어야 합니다.

2. 글 전체에서 반복되는 어구는 주제와 직결된다.

글의 중심 소재와 관련이 있는 핵심 어구는 글 전체를 통해 반복적으로 언급됩니다. 따라서 주제문이 드러나 있지 않은 경우에는 글 전체에서 반복되는 어구를 통해 글의 중심 소재를 파악하세요.

3. 연결어 확인은 필수! 특히 예시 앞부분에 주목하라.

대조의 연결어가 나온다면 대체로 뒷부분이 중심 내용일 것입니다. 인과의 연결어가 나온다면 원인보다는 결과가 중요할 것이고, 예시의 연결어가 나온다면 앞부분에 위치한 상위 개념이 중심 내용일 것입니다.

▶ 대표 기출 문제

정답 및 해설 p.019

046 다음 글의 주제로 가장 적절한 것은?

2024 수능

 Managers of natural resources typically face market incentives that provide financial rewards for exploitation. For example, owners of forest lands have a market incentive to cut down trees rather than manage the forest for carbon capture, wildlife habitat, flood protection, and other ecosystem services. These services provide the owner with no financial benefits, and thus are unlikely to influence management decisions. But the economic benefits provided by these services, based on their non-market values, may exceed the economic value of the timber. For example, a United Nations initiative has estimated that the economic benefits of ecosystem services provided by tropical forests, including climate regulation, water purification, and erosion prevention, are over three times greater per hectare than the market benefits. Thus cutting down the trees is economically inefficient, and markets are not sending the correct "signal" to favor ecosystem services over extractive uses.

*exploitation: 이용 **timber: 목재

① necessity of calculating the market values of ecosystem services
② significance of weighing forest resources' non-market values
③ impact of using forest resources to maximize financial benefits
④ merits of balancing forests' market and non-market values
⑤ ways of increasing the efficiency of managing natural resources

✓ **유형 해결**
3-Step

STEP1 **특정 개념과 관련되어 반복되는 어구 파악하기**

forest(숲), market incentive(시장 인센티브), non-market value(비시장적 가치)
→ 비시장적인 관점에서 보는 삼림의 가치에 관한 글임을 알 수 있음

STEP2 **글의 흐름 따라가기**

천연자원의 관리자는 이용에 대한 재정적 보상을 주는 시장 인센티브를 마주함 → 그 예로, 삼림 지대 소유자는 나무를 베어 이득을 얻는 시장 인센티브를 갖고 있음 → 생태계 도움은 소유자에게 재정적 이익을 주지 않기 때문에 소유자의 관리 결정에 영향을 미치지 않음 → 그러나 삼림 지대가 주는 생태계 도움의 비시장적 가치는 경제적 가치를 초과할 수 있음 → 따라서 나무를 베는 것은 경제적으로 비효율적임

STEP3 **글의 주제 파악하기**

천연자원의 관리자는 시장 인센티브를 마주하게 되는데, 삼림 지대가 주는 생태계 도움의 비시장적 가치는 목재의 경제적 가치를 초과할 수도 있다는 점에 주목해야 함을 다루고 있으므로, **산림 자원의 비시장적 가치를 따져 보는 것의 의의**에 관해 쓴 글임을 알 수 있다.

✓ **정답 확인**

① 생태계 도움의 시장 가치 산정의 필요성 → 생태계 도움을 시장 가치로 산정한다는 내용은 언급되지 않음

② 산림 자원의 비시장적 가치를 따져 보는 것의 의의 → 글의 주제를 잘 표현하고 있으므로 정답!

③ 재정적 이익을 극대화하기 위한 산림 자원 이용의 영향 → 산림 자원 이용이 초래하는 영향까지는 다루고 있지 않음

④ 숲의 시장 가치와 비시장 가치의 균형을 맞추는 장점 → 시장 가치와 비시장 가치의 균형에 대한 언급은 없음

⑤ 천연자원 관리의 효율성을 높이는 방법 → 천연자원 관리의 효율성에 대한 언급은 없음

✓ **중요 구문**

6행 For example, a United Nations initiative has estimated [that the economic benefits of ecosystem services {provided by tropical forests}, {including climate regulation, water purification, and erosion prevention}, are over **three times greater** per hectare **than** the market benefits].

목적절을 이끄는 접속사 ← / 주어 / 동사 / that절 주어 / 과거분사구 / 현재분사구 / that절 동사 / 비교 구문

: [ ]는 has estimated의 목적어 역할을 하는 명사절이다. 이 명사절의 주어는 the economic benefits of ecosystem services, 동사는 are이다. 두 개의 { }는 각각 명사절(that절)의 주어를 수식한다.

✓ **어휘 풀이**

- typically *ad* 일반적으로
- habitat *n* 서식지
- estimate *v* 추정하다
- extractive *a* 채취의, 채광의
- market incentive 시장 인센티브
- exceed *v* 초과하다
- purification *n* 정화
- carbon capture 탄소 포집
- initiative *n* 계획
- erosion *n* 침식

047

다음 글의 주제로 가장 적절한 것은?

An important advantage of disclosure, as opposed to more aggressive forms of regulation, is its flexibility and respect for the operation of free markets. Regulatory mandates are blunt swords; they tend to
5 neglect diversity and may have serious unintended adverse effects. For example, energy efficiency requirements for appliances may produce goods that work less well or that have characteristics that consumers do not want. Information provision, by
10 contrast, respects freedom of choice. If automobile manufacturers are required to measure and publicize the safety characteristics of cars, potential car purchasers can trade safety concerns against other attributes, such as price and styling. If restaurant
15 customers are informed of the calories in their meals, those who want to lose weight can make use of the information, leaving those who are unconcerned about calories unaffected. Disclosure does not interfere with, and should even promote, the autonomy (and quality)
20 of individual decision-making.

*mandate: 명령 **adverse: 거스르는 ***autonomy: 자율성

① steps to make public information accessible to customers
② benefits of publicizing information to ensure free choices
③ strategies for companies to increase profits in a free market
④ necessities of identifying and analyzing current industry trends
⑤ effects of diversified markets on reasonable customer choices

048

다음 글의 주제로 가장 적절한 것은?

Scientists *use* paradigms rather than believing them. The use of a paradigm in research typically addresses related problems by employing shared concepts, symbolic expressions, experimental and mathematical
5 tools and procedures, and even some of the same theoretical statements. Scientists need only understand *how* to use these various elements in ways that others would accept. These elements of shared practice thus need not presuppose any comparable unity in scientists'
10 beliefs about what they are doing when they use them. Indeed, one role of a paradigm is to enable scientists to work successfully without having to provide a detailed account of what they are doing or what they believe about it. Thomas Kuhn noted that scientists "can agree
15 in their *identification* of a paradigm without agreeing on, or even attempting to produce, a full *interpretation* or *rationalization* of it. Lack of a standard interpretation or of an agreed reduction to rules will not prevent a paradigm from guiding research."

① difficulty in drawing novel theories from existing paradigms
② significant influence of personal beliefs in scientific fields
③ key factors that promote the rise of innovative paradigms
④ roles of a paradigm in grouping like-minded researchers
⑤ functional aspects of a paradigm in scientific research

049

다음 글의 주제로 가장 적절한 것은?

Influencing people to exercise as a means to improve their health — and subsequently, reduce the cost of medical care — has been a primary focus of the health insurance industry. This is the case in countries such as the United States that has a largely private healthcare system as well as in countries such as Canada that has a largely public healthcare system. In both types of healthcare systems, there are policies designed to encourage people to become fit and stay fit. In the United States, many private health insurance companies offer discounts on insurance premiums or reimburse people for gym memberships. In Canada, the government encourages citizens to be active through public physical activity campaigns and tax credits. For example, the government reimburses parents for enrolling their children in an organized physical activity such as youth soccer. Increased profits and reduced spending are used both by the private and public systems to justify encouraging people to pursue fitness, demonstrating how politics is almost always part of the equation in encouraging a physically active culture.

*reimburse: 환급하다   **tax credit: 세액 공제

① the role of private health insurance
② ways to improve access to healthcare
③ reasons why you need to get health insurance
④ ways healthcare systems encourage members' fitness
⑤ effects of health insurance on medical service utilization

050

다음 글의 주제로 가장 적절한 것은?

BMI is easy to use, requiring only a scale and measurement of height. BMI is the primary classification system used to drive discussions between doctor and patient about health. BMI does not measure health or behaviors; however, healthy behaviors are correlated with improved health across BMI categories. Matheson et al. studied the association between mortality and lifestyle habits (specifically, not smoking, eating at least five servings of fruits and vegetables daily, physical activity, and moderate alcohol intake) and found increasing health benefits with increased healthy behaviors for people of all sizes, including those classified as "normal" weight under BMI. When health is evaluated by BMI, slender people (and their doctors) may assume they are healthy and have no need to engage in health promoting behaviors. Health improvements in people pursuing weight loss may be due to changes in behavior but are assumed to be caused by the weight loss. The almost inevitable weight regain is perceived as "failure," resulting in abandonment of the health-promoting behaviors.

*BMI: 체질량 지수

① emergence of a new measurement replacing the flawed BMI
② why sometimes healthy behaviors lead to sudden weight gain
③ limits of health-promoting behaviors in weight management
④ BMI as a reliable indicator of body fatness for ordinary people
⑤ wrong assumption of equaling weight loss to improved health

051

다음 글의 주제로 가장 적절한 것은?

Popper introduced the concept of situational logic which explains human behaviour as various attempts to achieve goals or aims within limited means. Marro too, has paid particular attention to the analysis and structure of social episodes in understanding human action. The theologian Fletcher caused a great stir with his book *Situation Ethics* in which he argued that goodness and badness are not inherent, essential, unchangeable human qualities, but are rather descriptions of actions in different situations. Thus, for situation ethicists, what is good or bad, right or wrong is dependent on specific situational factors. Lawyers too are concerned with different aspects of situational behavioural determinants — not only how the circumstances in which crimes are tried and examined affect the testimony but also how situational factors contributed to the crime being committed.

① invalidity of situational logic in understanding human action
② effects of social situations on various forms of behaviour
③ importance of ethics in developing positive social behavior
④ similar behavioural determinants in different situations
⑤ influences of personality and the situation in determining behaviour

052

다음 글의 주제로 가장 적절한 것은?

As a child, curiosity comes naturally. Even though the pursuit of new knowledge is work, it doesn't feel like work. The world is a child's laboratory, and everything is mysterious. As our minds begin to consolidate our imaginary and real experiences into one cohesive view of the world, our neural networks form patterns of understanding that help us predict what will happen next, mostly so that we can learn to spot opportunity and danger. We see everything unfamiliar within the framework of what we already know, and we discard information that isn't relevant. While this may allow us to process and assimilate new information more efficiently, it also creates conceptual boxes that we have to work hard to push out of if we want to reclaim that sense of wonder. We must build disciplines that help us develop our innate curiosity and allow us to embrace mystery.

① process of forming conceptual boxes for knowledge
② importance of experiences in predicting what will happen
③ necessity of overcoming patterns for developing curiosity
④ effects of curiosity on integrating experiences into knowledge
⑤ roles of neural networks in interpreting new experiences

053

다음 글의 주제로 가장 적절한 것은?

Compare the oral word in a conversation, the written word on a flyer or in a newspaper, and the word transmitted by electronic means. In the first case, the word is usually ephemeral and irreversibly lost after the encounter. Nevertheless, it may have a deep impact once we feel that the speaker is honest and authentic. Conversely, mimicry or tone may tell us that the speaker is unsure or may even be lying. In the second case, we can assume that the word was not spontaneously chosen but well-reflected, probably being the result of a long process of deliberation. In the case of an electronic message, we tend to give more weight to speed than to accuracy. Moreover, if messages come from unknown persons, we can assume in many cases that they did not pass the filter of professional journalistic criteria such as providing a correct, balanced account and checking the credibility of sources. Thus we may read electronic information from an unknown sender with more suspicion than the same information in a well-established newspaper.

*ephemeral: 일시적인

① the similarities in meaning of the spoken and written word
② the importance of body language in delivering true intentions
③ the problem caused by wrong or fake online information
④ the impact of words varying with the type of communication
⑤ the reliability and credibility of information from unknown sources

054

다음 글의 주제로 가장 적절한 것은?

It is especially important for social workers to recognize that there is an essentially "political" aspect to their identification and endorsement of core social work values. Social work emerged in the context of Western capitalism, and the profession's values, particularly those focused on individual worth and dignity, self-determination, and distributive justice, have been influenced by Western political views. In important respects, therefore, all social work values reflect a particular political ideology that ultimately influences the nature of its practice. For example, social workers in a capitalist society who support and attempt to promote their clients' right to self-determination may be embracing a form of individualism that runs counter to values found in other political contexts, such as a socialist society that places greater emphasis on collectivism. Similarly, the rights to privacy and to give informed consent that are now so prominent in Western society may seem quite foreign in cultures that have fundamentally different views of the boundaries between people and those in authority positions.

① effects of political ideology on social work values
② roles of capitalism in the development of social work
③ contribution of social work to the promotion of human rights
④ reasons why political views should be excluded from social work
⑤ factors affecting the relationship between social workers and clients

| 출제 Trend
- 매년 수능에 1문항씩 출제되어 온 영어 독해의 기본 유형입니다.
- 영어로 된 선택지가 글의 주제 유형보다는 함축적으로 제시되며 특히 어려운 소재의 지문일 경우 낮은 정답률을 보입니다.

| 해결 Point

1. '더 큰 방향'의 주제 찾기

글의 제목 유형은 글의 주제 유형을 풀 때의 접근 방식과 거의 같지만, 선택지의 성격이 좀 다릅니다. 제목은 글의 주제를 훨씬 더 포괄적, 함축적, 상징적, 비유적으로 나타내므로, 글 전체의 방향을 좀 더 넓게 보는 연습을 하면서 구체적인 내용을 통해 필자가 말하고자 하는 큰 틀을 찾는 방식으로 접근하는 것이 좋습니다.

2. '선택지에서 지문으로' 공부하기

글의 중심 내용은 쉽게 찾는데 제목과 연결하는 것이 어렵다면 '선택지에서 지문으로' 공부하는 방법을 추천합니다. 각 선택지에 제시된 제목들을 보고 '이게 제목인 글은 어떤 내용을 담고 있을까?' 생각해 보는 것입니다. 이런 방식으로 정답과 헷갈렸던 선택지를 떠올려 보면 중심 내용이 실제 지문과 확실히 차이가 있음을 알 수 있습니다.

대표 기출 문제

정답 및 해설 p.023

055 다음 글의 제목으로 가장 적절한 것은?   2024 수능

The concept of overtourism rests on a particular assumption about people and places common in tourism studies and the social sciences in general. Both are seen as clearly defined and demarcated. People are framed as bounded social actors either playing the role of hosts or guests. Places, in a similar way, are treated as stable containers with clear boundaries. Hence, places can be full of tourists and thus suffer from overtourism. But what does it mean for a place to be full of people? Indeed, there are examples of particular attractions that have limited capacity and where there is actually no room for more visitors. This is not least the case with some man-made constructions such as the Eiffel Tower. However, with places such as cities, regions or even whole countries being promoted as destinations and described as victims of overtourism, things become more complex. What is excessive or out of proportion is highly relative and might be more related to other aspects than physical capacity, such as natural degradation and economic leakages (not to mention politics and local power dynamics).

*demarcate: 경계를 정하다

① The Solutions to Overtourism: From Complex to Simple
② What Makes Popular Destinations Attractive to Visitors?
③ Are Tourist Attractions Winners or Losers of Overtourism?
④ The Severity of Overtourism: Much Worse than Imagined
⑤ Overtourism: Not Simply a Matter of People and Places

STEP 1 글의 전반부에서 글의 소재 파악하기

overtourism rests on a particular assumption about people and places / Both are seen as clearly defined and demarcated

(도입부에서 과잉 관광이 사람과 장소에 대한 특정한 가정에 기반한다고 하면서 사람과 장소에 대한 정의와 설명이 제시됨)

STEP 2 글의 내용 따라가기

관광 명소와 같은 장소가 사람으로 가득 차는 것이 과잉 관광이라고 하면서 에펠탑을 사례로 든 다음, However가 나오면서 필자가 언급하고 싶은 측면에 대한 설명이 이어지는데, 장소의 물리적 수용력이 아닌 다른 측면이 있다고 하면서 상황이 더 복잡해진다는 언급이 제시된다.

STEP 3 적절한 글의 제목 찾기

과잉 관광의 기본 요소는 사람과 장소나 그것보다 더 복잡한 요인들이 있다고 하면서 물리적인 수용력 문제가 아니라 자연의 질적 저하, 경제적 유출, 정치적 역학 관계 등을 언급하고 있으므로, **과잉 관광의 문제가 단순히 사람과 장소만의 문제가 아님**을 말하고 있다.

....

✓ 정답 확인

① 과잉 관광의 해결책: 복잡한 것에서 단순한 것으로 → 과잉 관광의 해법에 관한 글이 아님

② 무엇이 인기 있는 목적지를 방문객에게 매력적으로 만드는가? → 목적지를 매력적으로 만드는 요인과 무관함

③ 관광 명소는 과잉 관광의 승자인가 아니면 패자인가? → 관광 명소인 에펠탑을 가지고 그럴듯해 보이게 하는 오답

④ 과잉 관광의 심각성: 상상했던 것보다 훨씬 더 나쁘다 → 과잉 관광의 심각함에 대한 설명이 나오지 않음

⑤ 과잉 관광: 단순히 사람과 장소의 문제가 아니다 → 글의 내용을 가장 잘 표현하는 제목이므로 정답!

....

✓ 중요 구문

10행 [**What** is excessive or out of proportion] [**is** highly relative] and [**might be** more related **to** other aspects than physical capacity, {**such as** natural degradation and economic leakages (**not to mention** politics and local power dynamics)}].

주어 / 동사1 / 동사2 / to의 목적어 / ~와 같은 / ~은 말할 것도 없이

: 선행사를 포함한 관계대명사 What이 이끄는 절인 첫 번째 [ ]가 문장의 주어 역할을 하고 있다. 두 번째와 세 번째 [ ]는 and로 연결된 술부이다. { }는 other aspects than physical capacity의 사례를 보여준다.

....

✓ 어휘 풀이

- concept *n* 개념
- frame *v* 표현하다
- container *n* 용기, 그릇
- capacity *n* 수용력, 용량
- construction *n* 건축물
- excessive *a* 과도한
- aspect *n* 측면
- not to mention ~은 말할 것도 없이

- overtourism *n* 과잉 관광
- bounded *a* 한정된
- boundary *n* 경계
- not least 특히
- destination *n* 목적지
- out of proportion 균형이 안 맞는
- degradation *n* (질적) 저하
- dynamics *n* 역학

- assumption *n* 가정, 추정
- stable *a* 안정적인
- attraction *n* (관광) 명소
- man-made *a* 인공의
- victim *n* 피해자
- relative *a* 상대적인
- leakage *n* 유출

056

2023 수능

다음 글의 제목으로 가장 적절한 것은?

Different parts of the brain's visual system get information on a need-to-know basis. Cells that help your hand muscles reach out to an object need to know the size and location of the object, but they don't need to know about color. They need to know a little about shape, but not in great detail. Cells that help you recognize people's faces need to be extremely sensitive to details of shape, but they can pay less attention to location. It is natural to assume that anyone who sees an object sees everything about it — the shape, color, location, and movement. However, one part of your brain sees its shape, another sees color, another detects location, and another perceives movement. Consequently, after localized brain damage, it is possible to see certain aspects of an object and not others. Centuries ago, people found it difficult to imagine how someone could see an object without seeing what color it is. Even today, you might find it surprising to learn about people who see an object without seeing where it is, or see it without seeing whether it is moving.

① Visual Systems Never Betray Our Trust!
② Secret Missions of Color-Sensitive Brain Cells
③ Blind Spots: What Is Still Unknown About the Brain
④ Why Brain Cells Exemplify Nature's Recovery Process
⑤ Separate and Independent: Brain Cells' Visual Perceptions

057

2022 수능

다음 글의 제목으로 가장 적절한 것은?

Mending and restoring objects often require even more creativity than original production. The preindustrial blacksmith made things to order for people in his immediate community; customizing the product, modifying or transforming it according to the user, was routine. Customers would bring things back if something went wrong; repair was thus an extension of fabrication. With industrialization and eventually with mass production, making things became the province of machine tenders with limited knowledge. But repair continued to require a larger grasp of design and materials, an understanding of the whole and a comprehension of the designer's intentions. "Manufacturers all work by machinery or by vast subdivision of labour and not, so to speak, by hand," an 1896 *Manual of Mending and Repairing* explained. "But all repairing *must* be done by hand. We can make every detail of a watch or of a gun by machinery, but the machine cannot mend it when broken, much less a clock or a pistol!"

① Still Left to the Modern Blacksmith: The Art of Repair
② A Historical Survey of How Repairing Skills Evolved
③ How to Be a Creative Repairperson: Tips and Ideas
④ A Process of Repair: Create, Modify, Transform!
⑤ Can Industrialization Mend Our Broken Past?

058

다음 글의 제목으로 가장 적절한 것은?

Archaeologists have to do more to make aspects of archaeological research applicable to the modern world and to better communicate this to the public, if the field is to survive and flourish. One archaeologist has noted: "On the face of it, the study of archaeology, however fascinating, seems a luxury we can ill afford in a world beset by economic uncertainties and widespread poverty and famine." He goes on to say: "But to regard archaeology in such a way would be to treat the entire cultural heritage of humanity as irrelevant and unnecessary to the quality of our lives; in reality it is integral." However, many archaeologists would contend that the results of archaeological research do not significantly affect contemporary society and the major problems facing the world today. While I concur that this view of the current situation is probably an accurate one, I am convinced archaeologists can alter it, as the field of archaeology is in a better position than ever before to make itself pertinent to key modern issues such as the sustainability of our planet.

*beset: 괴롭히다 **pertinent: 관련 있는

① How to Achieve Sustainability in Archaeology
② Can Archaeology Be Influential in Modern Society?
③ Archaeologists' Efforts to Obtain Academic Successes
④ The Future of Archaeology Depends on Communication
⑤ Archaeology as an Academically Unjustifiable Discipline

059

다음 글의 제목으로 가장 적절한 것은?

Coaches play a critical role in forming the culture of their team. The attitudes and behaviors displayed by coaches around concussions influence the willingness of their athletes to report them. Athletes may feel more pressure to continue playing with a concussion if their coach has ridiculed them or given negative feedback for reporting injuries in the past. Coaches control playing time, and if the coach feels an athlete is weak or unwilling to sacrifice for the team, they may be less likely to play that athlete. Some coaches make statements about concussions not being as serious as a broken leg, or not believing that an athlete has symptoms. Even if the coach doesn't explicitly tell their athletes not to report, the culture of safety (or lack of it) that they create, and their overall attitudes toward injured players, can give the perception, real or not, that the coach would not support the athlete in reporting a concussion. In contrast, athletes who feel the coach supports them in reporting their concussion symptoms are more likely to follow the right protocols if they suspect they have a concussion.

*concussion: 뇌진탕 **protocol: 의료 치료 계획

① The Surprising Influence of Peer Coaching
② The Power of Coaching: Emotional Intelligence
③ How to Develop High-Performance Work Teams
④ Benefits of Coaching & Feedback in the Workplace
⑤ The Coach as the Leader: Setting the Team Culture

060

다음 글의 제목으로 가장 적절한 것은?

Human beings are selfish by nature. I'm willing to bet we instinctively spend over 90 percent of our time thinking about ourselves and 10 percent of our time thinking about other people. The secret to developing 5 supreme confidence lies in our own ability to reverse those numbers by spending 90 percent of our time thinking of others and 10 percent of our time thinking of ourselves. This way of thinking completely goes against the grain because as human beings our greatest 10 desire is to continuously experience the feeling of self-importance. We live for recognition. However, living only for ourselves does absolutely nothing to create the confidence. It is only when we take our eyes off ourselves and place them firmly on other people that 15 our confidence soars. If we can somehow lose the "what about me?" attitude and replace it with a servant mentality, we will begin to feel a power from within that we have never quite experienced before.

① Know Your Limitations, You'll Lead Better
② Self-confidence: A Basis for Our Creative Growth
③ Build Your Confidence by Thinking of Others First
④ In Defense of Selfishness: Don't Sacrifice Yourself
⑤ Stop Comparing Yourself to Others and Focus on You

061

다음 글의 제목으로 가장 적절한 것은?

Suppose you are about to buy a car, but you are torn between a van and a subcompact. You know that each has advantages and disadvantages: The van would be convenient; you can sleep in it, and it has plenty of power, but it gets poor mileage and it's hard to park. 5 The subcompact is a lot less roomy, and you wonder about its safety. But it is less expensive to buy and operate. Before you decide, you will probably get as much information as you can. Chances are you will talk with friends who own a van or a subcompact. 10 You'll probably visit automobile dealers to test-drive the vehicles to see how each one feels. Now, let's assume you decide to buy the subcompact. What happens next? You will begin to think more and more about the number of miles to the gallon as though 15 it were the most important thing in the world. Simultaneously, you will almost certainly downplay the fact that you can't sleep in your subcompact. Similarly, you will barely remember that your new car can put you at considerable risk of harm in a collision. 20

① Post-purchase Rationalization
② Finding the Right Car for You
③ Tips to Be a Smarter Consumer
④ Types of Stupid Consumer Behaviors
⑤ Benefits of Buying a Subcompact Car

062

다음 글의 제목으로 가장 적절한 것은?

Physicist John Archibald Wheeler noted, "Even to observe so minuscule an object as an electron, a physicist must shatter the glass. He must reach in. He must install his chosen measuring equipment. Moreover, the measurement changes the state of the electron. The universe will never afterward be the same." In other words, the act of studying an event can change it. Social scientists often encounter this phenomenon. Anthropologists know that when they study a tribe, the behavior of the members may be altered by the fact they are being observed by an outsider. Subjects in a psychology experiment may alter their behavior if they know what experimental hypotheses are being tested. This is why psychologists use blind and double-blind controls. Lack of such controls is often found in tests of paranormal powers and is one of the classic ways that thinking goes wrong in the pseudosciences. Science tries to minimize and acknowledge the effects of the observation on the behavior of the observed; pseudoscience does not.

*pseudoscience: 사이비 과학

① The Observer Changes the Observed
② Pseudoscience: A Product of Blind Faith
③ Why Process Is More Important than Result
④ Observation: A Passage to the Essence of Things
⑤ How to Exclude External Influences in Experiments

063

다음 글의 제목으로 가장 적절한 것은?

Man has been able to transcend the limitations of his genetic endowments and natural environments because of his cultures. The study of adaptation deals not only with man's relationships to his habitats but also, and more important, with his ability to come to terms with and exploit changing habitats. His capacity for culture — unmatched anywhere else in nature — has made this possible. But while man's capacity for culture contains his greatest potential for adapting to changing habitats and although he is able to adapt himself to different habitats without having to await genetic modifications in his constitution, to assume that man's cultural adaptations have replaced his biological adaptations would be a serious misconception. The adaptive process in man is as much biological as it is cultural. Man's biological evolution has not ceased, although students of evolution agree that it has probably slowed down drastically.

① Evidence of Cultural Adaptation in Nonhuman Beings
② Replacement of Biological Adaptation by a Cultural One
③ Genetic Modification: Destined to Cease Sooner or Later
④ Culture: An Outcome of Adaptation to a Specific Habitat
⑤ Human Adaptive Process: Biological as Well as Cultural

| 출제 Trend
- 주어진 도표를 보고 도표의 내용과 일치하지 않는 문장을 고르는 유형으로 매년 수능에 1문항씩 출제됩니다.
- 다양한 통계 자료가 제시되며 지문과 도표를 하나하나 비교해 가며 문제를 풀어야 합니다.
- 비교적 쉬운 유형에 속해서 대부분 높은 정답률을 보입니다.

| 해결 Point
1. 비교급과 배수 표현에 주목하라.

동등비교, 우등비교, 열등비교 혹은 최상급이 나오면 도표에 나타난 변화를 올바르게 묘사하고 있는지 확인하고 두 대상을 비교할 경우, 비교 대상끼리 몇 배의 차이가 나는지 꼭 확인하도록 합니다.

2. 증감 여부에 주목하라.

단순히 증가하거나 감소한다면 파악하기 쉽겠지만, continuously, steadily 같은 표현이 나온다면 큰 변동 없이 꾸준하게 증가하거나 감소하는지 확인해야 합니다. 또, gap이나 difference가 증가하거나 감소하는지 물어보는 문제도 많습니다. 실수할 수 있으니 도표 자체의 증감 여부를 묻는 건지 혹은 증가폭[감소폭]에 대한 증감 여부를 묻는 건지 꼭 확인하세요.

대표 기출 문제

정답 및 해설 p.026

064 다음 도표의 내용과 일치하지 <u>않는</u> 것은?

2024 수능

Percentages of Respondents Who Sometimes or Often Actively Avoided News in Five Countries in 2017, 2019, and 2022

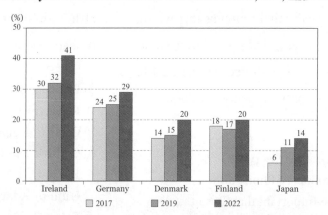

The above graph shows the percentages of the respondents in five countries who sometimes or often actively avoided news in 2017, 2019, and 2022. ① For each of the three years, Ireland showed the highest percentage of the respondents who sometimes or often actively avoided news, among the countries in the graph. ② In Germany, the percentage of the respondents who sometimes or often actively avoided news was less than 30% in each of the three years. ③ In Denmark, the percentage of the respondents who sometimes or often actively avoided news in 2019 was higher than that in 2017 but lower than that in 2022. ④ In Finland, the percentage of the respondents who sometimes or often actively avoided news in 2019 was lower than that in 2017, which was also true for Japan. ⑤ In Japan, the percentage of the respondents who sometimes or often actively avoided news did not exceed 15% in each of the three years.

✔ **유형 해결**
3-Step

STEP 1 도표 제목 및 세부 사항 파악하기

• 제목 또는 첫 문장을 통해 무엇에 대한 도표인지 파악하기

the percentages of the respondents in five countries who sometimes or often actively avoided news in 2017, 2019, and 2022
(2017년과 2019년, 2022년에 다섯 개 나라에서 때때로 또는 자주 적극적으로 뉴스를 회피한 응답자 비율)

• 비교 범위 및 비교 항목 파악하기
비교 범위 2017년, 2019년, 2022년
비교 항목 5개국(Ireland, Germany, Denmark, Finland, Japan)

STEP 2 선택지 문장과 도표를 일대일로 대조하여 내용 일치 여부 파악하기

① 세 해 각각에 대해, 도표에 있는 나라들 중에서 아일랜드는 때때로 또는 자주 적극적으로 뉴스를 회피한 응답자의 가장 높은 비율을 보여주었다. → 일치

② 독일의 경우, 세 해 각각에서 때때로 또는 자주 적극적으로 뉴스를 회피한 응답자 비율은 30%보다 낮았다. → 일치

③ 덴마크의 경우, 2019년에 때때로 또는 자주 적극적으로 뉴스를 회피한 응답자 비율이 2017년의 비율보다 더 높았으나 2022년의 그것보다는 더 낮았다. → 일치

④ 핀란드의 경우, 2019년에 때때로 또는 자주 적극적으로 뉴스를 회피한 응답자 비율이 2017년의 그것보다 더 낮았으며, 이는 일본도 마찬가지였다. → 일치하지 않음

⑤ 일본의 경우, 세 해 각각에서 때때로 또는 자주 적극적으로 뉴스를 회피한 응답자 비율이 15%를 초과하지 않았다. → 일치

STEP 3 정답 재확인하기

④ In Finland, the percentage of the respondents who sometimes or often actively avoided news in 2019 was lower than that in 2017, which was also true for Japan.
→ 핀란드의 경우, 2019년에 때때로 또는 자주 적극적으로 뉴스를 회피한 응답자 비율이 2017년보다 더 낮았지만, 일본은 2019년의 비율(11%)이 2017년의 비율(6%)보다 더 높았다.

✔ **중요 구문**
5행 In Denmark, the percentage of the respondents [who sometimes or often actively avoided news] in 2019 was higher than **that** in 2017 but lower than **that** in 2022.
핵심 주어 ─ 주격 관계대명사 ─ 동사 ─ 대명사 ─ 대명사

: [ ]는 the respondents를 수식하는 관계절이며, the percentage가 핵심 주어이므로 단수 동사인 was가 쓰였다. than 다음에 있는 that은 둘 다 the percentage of the respondents who sometimes or often actively avoided news를 대신한다.

✔ **어휘 풀이**
• respondent *n* 응답자
• actively *ad* 적극적으로
• avoid *v* 회피하다
• exceed *v* 초과하다

065

다음 도표의 내용과 일치하지 <u>않는</u> 것은?

**Americans' Preferred Type of Place to Live
(surveyed in 2020)**

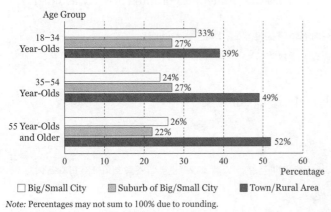

Note: Percentages may not sum to 100% due to rounding.

The above graph shows the percentages of Americans' preferred type of place to live by age group, based on a 2020 survey. ① In each of the three age groups, Town/ Rural Area was the most preferred type of place to live. ② In the 18–34 year-olds group, the percentage of those who preferred Big/Small City was higher than that of those who preferred Suburb of Big/Small City. ③ In the 35–54 year-olds group, the percentage of those who preferred Suburb of Big/Small City exceeded that of those who preferred Big/Small City. ④ In the 55 year-olds and older group, the percentage of those who chose Big/Small City among the three preferred types of place to live was the lowest. ⑤ Each percentage of the three preferred types of place to live was higher than 20% across the three age groups.

066

다음 도표의 내용과 일치하지 <u>않는</u> 것은?

**Share of the Global Middle Class by Region
in 2015 and in 2025**

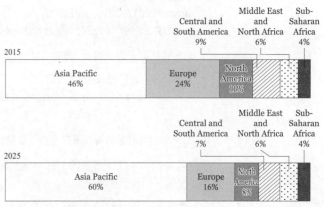

Note: Percentages may not sum to 100% due to rounding.

The above graphs show the percentage share of the global middle class by region in 2015 and its projected share in 2025. ① It is projected that the share of the global middle class in Asia Pacific will increase from 46 percent in 2015 to 60 percent in 2025. ② The projected share of Asia Pacific in 2025, the largest among the six regions, is more than three times that of Europe in the same year. ③ The shares of Europe and North America are both projected to decrease, from 24 percent in 2015 to 16 percent in 2025 for Europe, and from 11 percent in 2015 to 8 percent in 2025 for North America. ④ Central and South America is not expected to change from 2015 to 2025 in its share of the global middle class. ⑤ In 2025, the share of the Middle East and North Africa will be larger than that of sub-Saharan Africa, as it was in 2015.

067

다음 도표의 내용과 일치하지 <u>않는</u> 것은?

Distribution of global time spent on mobile phone apps from 2020 to 2022

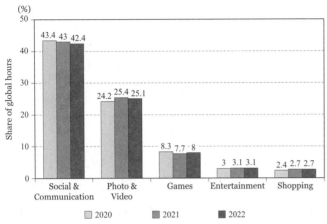

The graph above shows distribution of global time spent on mobile phone apps from 2020 to 2022, by category. ① During the period, Social & Communication apps always accounted for more than 42 percent of the time users worldwide spent on mobile phone apps. ② Photo & Video apps had the next highest percentage, accounting for more than 25 percent of mobile phone users' time in each of the three years. ③ Time spent on Games apps slightly fluctuated in the period from 2020 to 2022, with mobile phone users spending 8 percent of their time on Games in 2022. ④ From 2020 to 2022, the time people spent using Social & Communication apps was more than five times the time they spent on Games apps. ⑤ During the same period, the least used app was Shopping, with mobile users spending 2.7 percent of their time on Shopping apps in both 2021 and 2022.

068

다음 도표의 내용과 일치하지 <u>않는</u> 것은?

Acid Level in Mouth from Consumption of Sugar/Honey

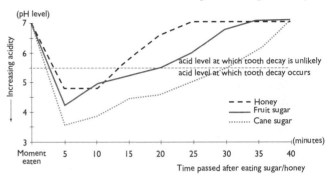

When the pH level in the mouth is kept above 5.5, acidity is such that teeth are unlikely to be in danger of decay. ① Among fruit sugar, cane sugar and honey, cane sugar lowers pH levels for the longest period, thus producing the greatest risk of tooth decay. ② Approximately five minutes after consuming cane sugar, pH levels drop to as low as pH 3.5. ③ They then begin to rise slowly, but do not rise above pH 5.5 until at least 30 minutes have passed. ④ By contrast, fruit sugar, which causes the mouth's pH level to fall to just above pH 4, poses a danger for a shorter period: tooth decay is unlikely 20 minutes after consumption. ⑤ Though acidity falls to about pH 4.75 within five minutes of consumption of honey, it returns to above pH 5.5 within ten minutes.

069

다음 도표의 내용과 일치하지 <u>않는</u> 것은?

Percentage distribution of School-age Children in the U.S.
by race / ethnicity: 2000 and 2013

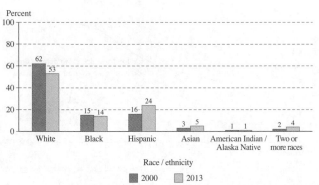

The above graph shows the racial/ethnic distribution of the school-age population in the United States in 2000 and in 2013. ① The percentage of school-age children who were White decreased from 62 percent to 53 percent during this time period. ② Also, the percentage of children who were Black decreased from 15 to 14 percent. ③ In contrast, the percentage of school-age children from other racial/ethnic groups increased during this time period: Hispanics increased from 16 to 24 percent, Asians from 3 to 5 percent, and children of Two or more races from 2 to 4 percent. ④ The percentages of children who were Hispanics in 2000 and 2013 were second to none respectively. ⑤ The percentages of school-age American Indians/Alaska Natives remained at 1 percent in both time periods.

070

다음 도표의 내용과 일치하지 <u>않는</u> 것은?

Regional Distribution of Catholics, 1910 and 2010

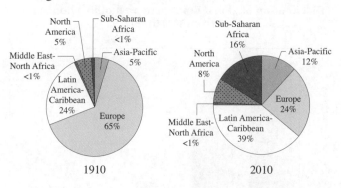

The graphs above show the regional distribution of Catholics in the world in 1910 and in 2010, which is shown by the percentage of all Catholics that lived in each region. ① In 1910, almost two-thirds of the world Catholics lived in Europe, and about a quarter in Latin America-Caribbean. ② In the same year, North America and Asia-Pacific had the same percentage of Catholics, both accounting for 5% of the world Catholics. ③ In 2010, more Catholics lived in Latin America-Caribbean than any other region in the world, accounting for over three-fifths of the world Catholics. ④ Over the 100-year-period, Europe saw a dramatic decline in the percentage of the world Catholics, and less than a fourth lived there in 2010. ⑤ Both the percentages of the world Catholics in Asia-Pacific and in North America went up from 1910 to 2010, especially the former being more than doubled.

071

다음 도표의 내용과 일치하지 <u>않는</u> 것은?

Waste Disposal in Four Cities

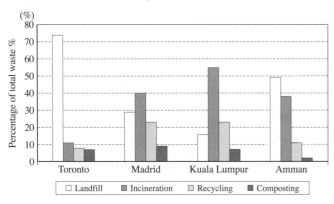

The above graph shows four cities and their percentages for four different types of waste disposal: landfill, incineration, recycling and composting. ① Toronto and Amman used landfill as a method of waste disposal the most with almost three-quarters and just under a half of waste in those cities respectively being disposed of in landfills. ② Incineration was the most popular method of waste disposal in Madrid and Kuala Lumpur, at approximately 40% and about 55% respectively. ③ No city disposed of more than 25% of its waste by recycling and in the case of Toronto, it was about 8%. ④ Madrid and Kuala Lumpur had almost equal percentages of waste that were landfilled. ⑤ The least popular method of waste disposal was by composting, which accounted for less than 10% in all four cities.

072

다음 도표의 내용과 일치하지 <u>않는</u> 것은?

Share of Online Transactions Based on Devices in 2018, by Region

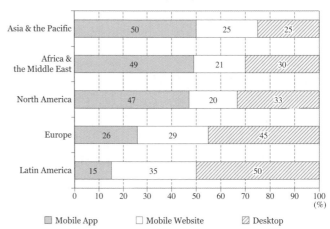

The graph above shows the share of online transactions based on three devices (via mobile app, mobile website and desktop) in 2018 by region. ① When it comes to the transactions via mobile app, Asia and the Pacific showed the most utilization, but Latin America showed the least. ② On the category of mobile website for online transactions, Latin America relied the most heavily on it, whereas North America relied the least on it. ③ The share of online transactions using a desktop in Latin America was exactly twice as large as that in Asia and the Pacific. ④ In Europe, the combined share of mobile app and mobile website transactions exceeded the share of online transactions using a desktop. ⑤ The gap between the share of mobile app and that of desktop was the largest in Latin America, but the smallest in Africa and the Middle East.

09 내용 불일치

ㅣ출제 Trend
- 지문에서 특정 정보를 파악해 한글 선택지에서 내용과 일치하지 않는 것을 고르는 문제로 매년 수능에 1문항 씩 출제됩니다.
- 특정 사물이나 인물, 동식물 등을 설명하는 글이 지문으로 등장하는 경우가 많습니다.
- 선택지가 지문에 언급되는 순서이므로 선택지와 지문을 하나하나 대조하면서 글을 읽어 나가면 됩니다.

ㅣ해결 Point

1. 선택지와 지문을 동시에 읽자.

선택지 순서대로 지문 내용이 전개되므로, 지문을 읽으면서 선택지를 하나하나 확인해 나가는 방법이 문제 풀이에 효율적입니다.

2. 정답은 주로 후반부에 나온다.

내용 불일치 유형은 정답이 후반부에 나오는 경우가 많습니다. 그래서 ③, ④, ⑤번 선택지를 먼저 확인한 뒤에 ①, ②번 선택지를 확인하는 식으로 문제를 푸는 것도 시간을 절약하는 한 방법입니다. 내용 불일치 유형의 문제에서 정답이 ①, ②번일 확률이 낮긴 하지만 언제나 예외가 있을 수 있다는 점을 유념하세요.

대표 기출 문제

정답 및 해설 p.029

073

Charles H. Townes에 관한 다음 글의 내용과 일치하지 <u>않는</u> 것은?   2024 수능

　　Charles H. Townes, one of the most influential American physicists, was born in South Carolina. In his childhood, he grew up on a farm, studying the stars in the sky. He earned his doctoral degree from the California Institute of Technology in 1939, and then he took a job at Bell Labs in New York City. After World War II, he became an associate professor of physics at
5　Columbia University. In 1958, Townes and his co-researcher proposed the concept of the laser. Laser technology won quick acceptance in industry and research. He received the Nobel Prize in Physics in 1964. He was also involved in Project Apollo, the moon landing project. His contribution is priceless because the Internet and all digital media would be unimaginable without the laser.

① 어린 시절에 농장에서 성장하였다.
② 박사 학위를 받기 전에 Bell Labs에서 일했다.
③ 1958년에 레이저의 개념을 제안하였다.
④ 1964년에 노벨 물리학상을 수상하였다.
⑤ 달 착륙 프로젝트에 관여하였다.

✔ 유형 해결
3-Step

STEP 1 지문 첫 부분에서 글의 소재 파악하기

Charles H. Townes, one of the most influential American physicists, was born in South Carolina.
(Charles H. Townes라는 사람은 가장 영향력 있는 미국의 물리학자이고 South Carolina에서 태어남)
→ Charles H. Townes라는 한 인물에 관한 글임을 파악할 수 있음

STEP 2 지문과 선택지를 일대일로 대조하여 일치 여부 파악하기

① 어린 시절에 농장에서 성장하였다. → 일치
  → 2행: In his childhood, he grew up on a farm, studying the stars in the sky.에서 알 수 있음

② 박사 학위를 받기 전에 Bell Labs에서 일했다. → 불일치
  → 2행: He earned his doctoral degree from the California Institute of Technology in 1939, and
    then he took a job at Bell Labs in New York City.에서 해당 진술이 틀렸음을 알 수 있음

③ 1958년에 레이저의 개념을 제안하였다. → 일치
  → 5행: In 1958, Townes and his co-researcher proposed the concept of the laser.에서 알 수 있음

④ 1964년에 노벨 물리학상을 수상하였다. → 일치
  → 6행: He received the Nobel Prize in Physics in 1964.에서 알 수 있음

⑤ 달 착륙 프로젝트에 관여하였다. → 일치
  → 7행: He was also involved in Project Apollo, the moon landing project.에서 알 수 있음

STEP 3 정답 확인하기

글의 초반부 He earned his doctoral degree from the California Institute of Technology in 1939, and
then he took a job at Bell Labs in New York City. 부분에서 California Institute of Technology에서 박사
학위를 받았고 그 후 뉴욕시에 있는 Bell Labs에서 일자리를 얻었다고 했으므로, ②는 글의 내용과 일치하지 않는다.

✔ 중요 구문
1행 Charles H. Townes, [one of the most influential American physicists], was born in South
        주어 └──── 동격 ────┘   동사
Carolina.

: Charles H. Townes가 주어이고, was born이 동사이다. [ ]는 문장의 주어를 부연 설명하는 동격구이다.

✔ 어휘 풀이
• influential a 영향력 있는
• concept n 개념
• contribution n 공헌, 기여

• doctoral degree 박사 학위
• acceptance n 인정
• priceless a 대단히 귀중한

• associate professor 부교수
• be involved in ~에 관여하다
• unimaginable a 상상할 수 없는

074

2023 수능

Niklas Luhmann에 관한 다음 글의 내용과 일치하지 <u>않는</u> 것은?

Niklas Luhmann, a renowned sociologist of the twentieth century, was born in Lüneburg, Germany in 1927. After World War II, he studied law at the University of Freiburg until 1949. Early in his career,
5 he worked for the State of Lower Saxony, where he was in charge of educational reform. In 1960 — 1961, Luhmann had the chance to study sociology at Harvard University, where he was influenced by Talcott Parsons, one of the most famous social system
10 theorists. Later, Luhmann developed his own social system theory. In 1968, he became a professor of sociology at the University of Bielefeld. He researched a variety of subjects, including mass media and law. Although his books are known to be difficult to
15 translate, they have in fact been widely translated into other languages.

① 제2차 세계 대전 이후에 법을 공부했다.
② State of Lower Saxony에서 교육 개혁을 담당했다.
③ Harvard University에 있을 때 Talcott Parsons의 영향을 받았다.
④ 다양한 주제에 관해 연구했다.
⑤ 그의 책은 번역하기가 쉽다고 알려져 있다.

075

2022 수능

Donato Bramante에 관한 다음 글의 내용과 일치하지 <u>않는</u> 것은?

Donato Bramante, born in Fermignano, Italy, began to paint early in his life. His father encouraged him to study painting. Later, he worked as an assistant of Piero della Francesca in Urbino. Around 1480, he built
5 several churches in a new style in Milan. He had a close relationship with Leonardo da Vinci, and they worked together in that city. Architecture became his main interest, but he did not give up painting. Bramante moved to Rome in 1499 and participated
10 in Pope Julius II's plan for the renewal of Rome. He planned the new Basilica of St. Peter in Rome — one of the most ambitious building projects in the history of humankind. Bramante died on April 11, 1514 and was buried in Rome. His buildings influenced other
15 architects for centuries.

① Piero della Francesca의 조수로 일했다.
② Milan에서 새로운 양식의 교회들을 건축했다.
③ 건축에 주된 관심을 갖게 되면서 그림 그리기를 포기했다.
④ Pope Julius II의 Rome 재개발 계획에 참여했다.
⑤ 그의 건축물들은 다른 건축가들에게 영향을 끼쳤다.

076

Robert Baden-Powell에 관한 다음 글의 내용과 일치하지 <u>않는</u> 것은?

Robert Baden-Powell was a British Army officer, writer, and the founder of the Scout Movement. He was born in London in 1857 and joined the British Army in 1876. He served in India, Africa, and the Mediterranean, and was awarded the Victoria Cross for his bravery in the Battle of Rorke's Drift during the Zulu War of 1879. In 1908, Baden-Powell published a book called *Scouting for Boys*, which described a new educational program for young men. The book was based on Baden-Powell's experiences in the Army and was designed to teach boys skills such as camping, tracking, and first aid. The book was a huge success, and within a few years Scout troops were being formed all over the world. In 1910, Baden-Powell retired from the Army to devote himself full-time to the Scout Movement. He wrote many books about Scouting, including *Scouting for Girls*, which was co-written with his sister Agnes. Baden-Powell died in 1941 at the age of 83 and was buried in Nyeri, Kenya.

① 영국 육군 장교이자 작가였다.
② 인도와 아프리카 지역에서 근무했다.
③ 군 경험을 바탕으로 책을 출판했다.
④ 저술 작업에 전념하기 위해 전역했다.
⑤ 80대에 사망 후 케냐에 묻혔다.

077

Bertha Suttner에 관한 다음 글의 내용과 일치하지 <u>않는</u> 것은?

Bertha Suttner was born in 1843 in Prague, and grew up in a military family and witnessed the devastating effects of war firsthand. She became interested in the peace movement at a young age. In 1876, she published an anti-war novel *Lay Down Your Arms!* that was widely read and influential in spreading the message of peace. Soon, her name came to be closely associated with the ideals of peace and a strong stance against war. At male-dominated peace congresses, she stood out as a liberal and forceful leader. She became a close friend of Alfred Nobel's in the 1870s, and they corresponded for years on the subject of peace. She was the first woman to be awarded the Nobel Peace Prize, which she received in 1905 for her efforts to promote peace and international understanding.

① 군인 가정에서 자라며 전쟁의 참혹함을 목격했다.
② 젊은 나이에 평화 운동에 관심을 갖게 되었다.
③ 반전 소설을 출판했지만 주목받지 못했다.
④ Alfred Nobel과 평화를 주제로 편지를 주고받았다.
⑤ 여성으로는 최초로 노벨 평화상을 수상했다.

078

John Logie Baird에 관한 다음 글의 내용과 일치하지 <u>않는</u> 것은?

John Logie Baird was the first person to show that it was possible to transmit visual images, and so his name will always be part of television's history. Baird's first jobs as an engineer were so miserable that when he was 26 he decided to abandon that profession and become an inventor. His early ideas were completely unsuccessful and by the time he was 35, he had lost all his money. But in 1923, he started work on a machine to transmit pictures, as well as sound, by radio. Soon he was able to send crude images by wireless transmitter to a receiver a few feet away. In January 1926 he gave a television demonstration to the public at the Royal Institution in London. This was the very first demonstration of television. In 1929 the BBC made the first television broadcast, using Baird's equipment. But he failed to make use of the cathode-ray tubes on which modern televisions depend and thus, by 1933, his invention had lost out to this rival system.

*cathode-ray tube: 브라운관

① 시각적 이미지의 전송이 가능하다는 것을 최초로 보여주었다.
② 엔지니어를 그만두고 발명가가 되기로 결심했다.
③ 초기의 아이디어가 실패하여 35세가 될 무렵 모든 돈을 잃었다.
④ 1926년 1월에 대중들에게 처음으로 텔레비전을 시연했다.
⑤ 브라운관을 도입하여 텔레비전이 발달하는 데 공헌했다.

079

Walter Gropius에 관한 다음 글의 내용과 일치하지 <u>않는</u> 것은?

Walter Gropius was the son of an architect. From early on in his career he designed buildings that used only modern materials. In 1914 he built some factories constructed only from glass and steel. He also borrowed ideas from modern art, sometimes making his buildings look like abstract paintings. In 1919 he founded the 'Bauhaus' in Germany, a school of design. Gropius himself created the new building for the school. Students there were taught how to use smooth surfaces, bright colors and three-dimensional design in their buildings. In 1933 the Bauhaus was closed down by the Nazis. Gropius, who had left the Bauhaus five years before that, moved to England in 1934 because of the growing power of the Nazi government. After designing more striking modern buildings in Britain he finally settled in America.

① 유리와 강철만으로 구성된 공장을 건설했다.
② 종종 추상화처럼 보이는 건물을 만들기도 했다.
③ 독일에 디자인 학교인 Bauhaus를 설립했다.
④ Bauhaus가 폐교한 지 5년 후에 영국으로 떠났다.
⑤ 영국에서 건축가로 활동한 후에 미국으로 건너갔다.

080

guacharo에 관한 다음 글의 내용과 일치하지 <u>않는</u> 것은?

  In South America, in the mountain caves along the coast lives a bird called the guacharo or oilbird. For centuries the fat of the young guacharos has been boiled to obtain a clear, yellow, odorless oil. People use
5 it to cook and for lighting for their homes. The guacharo spends most of its life in darkness. It has large, blue eyes, short legs, weak feet, and a strong, hooked bill. When it spreads its wings, they stretch out to 36 inches. The color of the guacharo is reddish-
10 brown, spotted with black and white. Around its mouth are long, stiff bristles. As it flies around in the dark cave, the guacharo gives off clicking sounds, echoes coming back to the bird. This helps it avoid bumping into anything that is in the way. It lays two to
15 four white eggs in the saucer-shaped nest. Both parents take turns sitting on the eggs until they hatch. At night it leaves the cave to get food. It is the only fruit-eating bird in the world that flies at night.

*bristle: 뻣뻣한 털

① 남미의 동굴에 서식하는 야행성 조류이다.
② 지방을 끓여 만든 기름은 조명을 위해 사용된다.
③ 입 주변에 길고 뻣뻣한 털이 나 있다.
④ 반사되는 소리를 이용해서 동굴에서 먹이를 찾는다.
⑤ 암컷과 수컷이 번갈아 가며 알을 품는다.

081

Antonio Gramsci에 관한 다음 글의 내용과 일치하지 <u>않는</u> 것은?

  Antonio Gramsci was born in Sardinia, Italy, in 1891. He was a cofounder of the Italian Communist Party. While serving as the party's leader, he was sentenced to 20 years imprisonment in 1928 by Benito Mussolini, Italy's prime minister and dictator at the time. Gramsci
5 wrote prolifically while in prison. Although he had an exceptional memory, without the help of his relative, Tania, who was a frequent visitor, his ideas would not have come to light. This intellectual work did not emerge until several years after World War II, when it
10 was published posthumously in what are known as the *Prison Notebooks*. By the 1950s, his prison writings attracted interest not only in Western Europe but also in the Soviet bloc. Due to the poor diet, illness, and bad health he suffered in prison, Gramsci died of a stroke
15 at the age of only 46 in the prison.

*posthumously: 사후에

① 이탈리아 공산당의 공동 창설자였다.
② 공산당의 지도자로 활동하다가 20년 형을 선고받았다.
③ 감옥에서 친척의 도움을 받았다.
④ 제2차 세계 대전이 일어난 해에 〈Prison Notebooks〉를 출판했다.
⑤ 수감 생활로 인한 건강상의 문제로 46세에 사망했다.

│ 출제 Trend
- 안내문을 읽고 일치하는 정보와 일치하지 않는 정보를 선택지에서 고르는 문제로 매년 수능에 일치 1문항, 불일치 1문항이 출제됩니다.
- 다양한 내용의 안내문이 제시되며, 지문의 내용과 선택지의 진술을 비교해 가며 문제를 풀어야 합니다.
- 비교적 쉬운 유형에 속해서 대부분 높은 정답률을 보입니다.

│ 해결 Point
1. 숫자 정보의 내용을 명확하게 파악하자.
안내문의 내용 일치를 묻는 문제는 일정, 비용, 나이, 상금액 등 다양한 숫자 정보가 등장하므로 이 정보를 정확히 파악하여 선택지의 진술과 비교하도록 합시다.

2. 자주 등장하는 어휘의 뜻을 정확히 외워 두자.
안내문에는 제출, 등록, 예약, 자격 등과 관련하여 자주 쓰이는 어휘가 있는데, 이 어휘의 뜻을 알지 못하면 선택지 진술이 일치하는지를 판단하는 것 자체가 불가능합니다. 이 유형의 문제를 다룰 때마다 반복하여 등장하는 주요 어휘들을 모아서 외우면 실전에 큰 도움이 됩니다.

대표 기출 문제
정답 및 해설 p.032

082 Turtle Island Boat Tour에 관한 다음 안내문의 내용과 일치하지 <u>않는</u> 것은?　　2024 수능

Turtle Island Boat Tour

The fantastic Turtle Island Boat Tour invites you to the beautiful sea world.

Dates: From June 1 to August 31, 2024

Tour Times

Weekdays	1 p.m. — 5 p.m.
Weekends	9 a.m. — 1 p.m.
	1 p.m. — 5 p.m.

※ Each tour lasts four hours.

Tickets & Booking
- $50 per person for each tour
  (Only those aged 17 and over can participate.)
- Bookings must be completed no later than 2 days before the day of the tour.
- No refunds after the departure time
- Each tour group size is limited to 10 participants.

Activities
- Snorkeling with a professional diver
- Feeding tropical fish

※ Feel free to explore our website, www.snorkelingti.com.

① 주말에는 하루에 두 번 운영된다.

② 17세 이상만 참가할 수 있다.

③ 당일 예약이 가능하다.

④ 출발 시간 이후에는 환불이 불가능하다.

⑤ 전문 다이버와 함께 하는 스노클링 활동이 있다.

✔ 유형 해결
3-Step

STEP 1 안내문 전체의 중심 소재와 내용 파악하기

• Boat Tour(보트 투어), Tour Times(투어 시간), aged 17 and over(참가 연령), no later than 2 days before the day of the tour(예약 가능일)

• No refunds after the departure time(환불 방침), Snorkeling with a professional diver(활동)

STEP 2 안내문과 선택지 내용 비교하기

• 안내문: Bookings must be completed no later than 2 days before the day of the tour.
　　　　(예약은 늦어도 투어 당일 이틀 전에 완료되어야 합니다.)

• 선택지: 당일 예약이 가능하다.

STEP 3 안내문과 일치하지 않는 진술 고르기

예약은 늦어도 투어 당일 이틀 전에 완료되어야 한다고 했으므로 당일 예약은 불가함을 알 수 있다. 따라서 안내문의 내용과 일치하지 않는 것은 ③이다.

✔ 정답 확인
① 주말에는 하루에 두 번 운영된다. → 'Weekends 9 a.m. — 1 p.m., 1 p.m. — 5 p.m.)'로 보아 일치함

② 17세 이상만 참가할 수 있다. → 'Only those aged 17 and over can participate.'로 보아 일치함

④ 출발 시간 이후에는 환불이 불가능하다. → 'No refunds after the departure time'으로 보아 일치함

⑤ 전문 다이버와 함께 하는 스노클링 활동이 있다. → 'Snorkeling with a professional diver'로 보아 일치함

✔ 중요 구문
12행 Bookings must be completed [no later than 2 days before the day of the tour].
　　　　　　　　 수동태　　　　　　　　 늦어도

: 주어 Bookings는 complete가 나타내는 동작의 주체가 아니라 대상이므로 수동태가 사용되었다. [ ]는 시간을 나타내는 부사구이며 no later than은 '늦어도'라는 뜻을 나타낸다.

✔ 어휘 풀이
• fantastic _a_ 환상적인
• booking _n_ 예약
• refund _n_ 환불
• feed _v_ 먹이를 주다

083

2023 수능

2022 Valestown Recycles Poster Contest에 관한 다음 안내문의 내용과 일치하는 것은?

2022 Valestown Recycles Poster Contest

Join this year's Valestown Recycles Poster Contest and show off your artistic talent!

Guidelines

- Participation is only for high school students in Valestown.

- Participants should use the theme of "Recycling for the Future."

Submission Format

- File type: PDF only

- Maximum file size: 40MB

Judging Criteria

- Use of theme   - Creativity   - Artistic skill

Details

- Submissions are limited to one poster per person.

- Submissions should be uploaded to the website by 6 p.m., December 19.

- Winners will be announced on the website on December 28.

For more information, please visit www.vtco.org.

① Valestown의 모든 학생들이 참여할 수 있다.
② 참가자는 포스터의 주제 선정에 제약을 받지 않는다.
③ 출품할 파일 양식은 자유롭게 선택 가능하다.
④ 심사 기준에 창의성이 포함된다.
⑤ 1인당 출품할 수 있는 포스터의 수에는 제한이 없다.

084

2022 수능

Cornhill No Paper Cup Challenge에 관한 다음 안내문의 내용과 일치하지 <u>않는</u> 것은?

Cornhill No Paper Cup Challenge

Cornhill High School invites you to join the "No Paper Cup Challenge." This encourages you to reduce your use of paper cups. Let's save the earth together!

How to Participate

1) After being chosen, record a video showing you are using a tumbler.

2) Choose the next participant by saying his or her name in the video.

3) Upload the video to our school website within 24 hours.

※ The student council president will start the challenge on December 1st, 2021.

Additional Information

• The challenge will last for two weeks.

• All participants will receive T-shirts.

If you have questions about the challenge, contact us at cornhillsc@chs.edu.

① 참가자는 텀블러를 사용하는 자신의 동영상을 찍는다.
② 참가자가 동영상을 업로드할 곳은 학교 웹사이트이다.
③ 학생회장이 시작할 것이다.
④ 두 달 동안 진행될 예정이다.
⑤ 참가자 전원이 티셔츠를 받을 것이다.

085

Big Bookend Book Review Competition에 관한 다음 안내문의 내용과 일치하는 것은?

Big Bookend Book Review Competition

Submissions are now being accepted!

- You must be attending a middle or high school in Leeds to enter.

- Book reviews can be of any book of your choice and should be no more than 500 words long.

- The age categories are 12-14, 15-16 and 17-18. There will be one prize for each age category.

• The winners will be announced on May 16th and prizes will be awarded at the Big Bookend Book Review Party on the evening of June 5th.

• The winner's book reviews will be published on the Big Bookend's website.

• To enter, just complete the entry form available on the Big Bookend's website at www.theleedsbigbookend.com and send it, along with your review, to info@bigbookend. co.uk by May 2nd.

---

① Leeds에 있는 학교에 다니지 않아도 참가할 수 있다.
② 서평은 적어도 500단어를 넘어야 한다.
③ 연령 부문별로 각각 세 개의 상이 있을 것이다.
④ 수상자는 6월 5일에 발표된다.
⑤ 참가 신청서는 서평과 함께 보내면 된다.

086

Queen Mary Wasafiri New Writing Prize 2023에 관한 다음 안내문의 내용과 일치하지 <u>않는</u> 것은?

Queen Mary Wasafiri New Writing Prize 2023

Deadline

30 May 2023, 5 p.m.

Who may enter

The competition is open to anyone who has not published a book.

Short description

• The competition is organized by Wasafiri, a quarterly British literary magazine.

• There are prizes in three categories: Fiction, Poetry and Life Writing.

• The word limit is 3,000 maximum.

• Entries must not have been previously published in any form.

Entry fees

A single entry costs £10, two entries are £16.

Prizes

The winner of each category will receive £1,000 and his/her work be published in *Wasafiri* magazine.

For further information, visit the official competition website.

---

① 책을 출간하지 않은 사람은 누구나 참가할 수 있다.
② 3가지 부문을 심사하여 상을 준다.
③ 단어 수에 별도의 제한이 없다.
④ 출품작이 하나이면 참가비는 10파운드이다.
⑤ 수상작은 *Wasafiri* 잡지에 실릴 예정이다.

087

Hands Craft Store Gift Voucher에 관한 다음 안내문의 내용과 일치하는 것은?

Hands Craft Store Gift Voucher

Shopping for someone else but not sure

what to give them?

Give them the gift of choice

with a Hands Craft Store Gift Voucher!

- You can choose a $10, $25, $50, or $100 voucher.
- You can buy a minimum of one gift voucher and a maximum of five gift vouchers in a single purchase.
- Gift vouchers are delivered by email.
- Gift vouchers contain a code to redeem them at a website of our store.
- Or the recipient can bring the email voucher in store to redeem it.
- Our gift vouchers have no additional processing fees.
- Once purchase of the voucher is confirmed, it cannot be cancelled and the payment you made is not refundable.

① 금액이 다른 3종류의 상품권이 판매되고 있다.
② 한 번에 최대 4장의 상품권을 구입할 수 있다.
③ 구입한 상품권은 우편으로 배달된다.
④ 상품권은 온라인상에서만 사용할 수 있다.
⑤ 구매한 상품권은 취소나 환불이 불가능하다.

088

Manhattan Camera Club 사진 전시회에 관한 다음 안내문의 내용과 일치하지 <u>않는</u> 것은?

Manhattan Camera Club PHOTO EXHIBITION
at
Manhattan Community Center
November 15th–19th 2018
11 a.m. to 9 p.m.

WEDNESDAY 15TH NOVEMBER

- Inaugural ceremony conducted by Robert Tyler, the President of the Royal Photographic Society will be held at 7 p.m.
- The ceremony will be followed by a commentary on work in the Exhibition.

SUNDAY 19TH NOVEMBER

- Barnet Saidman, chief photographer of a leading New York newspaper will give a public lecture on his work.
- Free Cheese & Wine Event will be held after the lecture.

You are cordially invited to visit the Exhibition and to attend the functions announced above.

ADMISSION IS FREE

For further information, call us at 419-1199.

① 5일 동안 지역 문화회관에서 개최된다.
② 첫날 오후 7시에 개막식이 열린다.
③ 개막식 전에 작품 해설 행사가 있다.
④ 마지막 날에 사진작가의 강연이 있다.
⑤ 강의 후에는 치즈와 와인을 무료로 즐길 수 있다.

089

T-shirt Design Competition에 관한 다음 글의 내용과 일치하는 것은?

T-shirt Design Competition

BrandNew Studios invites high school students to create a design for a promotional T-shirt to be sold at the Contemporary Art Gallery.

The winner will receive a pair of good-quality headphones valued at $200 and the design will be printed onto T-shirts and promoted widely at the gallery.

All entrants also benefit from having their designs seen by the judging panel mainly composed of local designers from creative business. The top 5 designs will also be exhibited at the gallery as posters from August 12th to 17th 2019.

Deadline: at 5 p.m. on August 5th 2019

Stylistic Guidelines

- Design must display the BrandNew Studio Logo
- Two colour design on a colored T-shirt (not white)
- Artwork on the front side only

Submit your entry to tshirtcompetition@umbrella.org.

① 고등학교 졸업생들이 출품할 수 있다.
② 참가자 전원에게 상금과 상품이 수여된다.
③ 최고상 수상자 1인의 작품만 미술관에 전시된다.
④ 반드시 **BrandNew** 스튜디오 로고를 포함해야 한다.
⑤ 흰색 티셔츠에 다양한 색으로 디자인한 작품을 제출한다.

090

Peach Grove One-stop Health Education Event에 관한 다음 안내문의 내용과 일치하지 <u>않는</u> 것은?

Peach Grove One-stop Health Education Event

This is a fulfilling and informative event arranged for Peach Grove residents. Health screenings can find diseases and conditions early when they are easier to treat. Events include lectures and health tests:

Lectures

- Promoting Good Health Habits for Children and Teens
- Making Nutritious Lunches for a Healthy Diet

Health Tests

- Eye Exams & Hearing Screenings (free)
- Dental Screenings ($5 per person; free for senior citizen, 65 or older)
- Blood tests for diabetes and cholesterol ($10 per person)

Licensed medical doctors will be on hand to answer any questions.

- Sponsored by Peach Grove Hospital
- Saturday, September 7, from 9 a.m. to 1:30 p.m.
- Located at Peach Grove Hospital's Health Education Center

For more information, visit our website at www.peachhospital.com.

① Peach Grove 주민을 위한 행사이다.
② 어린이와 청소년의 건강을 위한 강연이 있다.
③ 65세 이상의 노인은 치과 검사가 5달러이다.
④ Peach Grove 병원에서 후원하는 행사이다.
⑤ 9월 7일 9시부터 4시간 30분 동안 실시한다.

| 출제 Trend
- 밑줄 친 다섯 개의 어법 사항 중 쓰임이 올바르지 않은 것을 고르는 밑줄 어법 유형과 두 가지 어법 요소 중 알맞은 표현을 고르는 네모 어법 유형이 있습니다.
- 2014 수능 이후로 밑줄 어법 유형만 1문항씩 출제되고 있습니다.

| 해결 Point

1. 기본적인 문법 사항들을 숙지한다.

수능에 출제되는 문법 사항이 비교적 정해져 있으므로 자주 출제되는 문법 사항(수의 일치, 동사와 준동사, 관계사와 접속사, 병렬구조, 동명사와 부정사, 형용사와 부사 등)은 그 개념을 완벽하게 정리해 두도록 합니다.

2. 어떤 어법 요소를 묻는지 파악한다.

밑줄 친 부분에 어떤 문법 요소가 쓰였는지를 먼저 파악하고 수능에 자주 출제되는 관련 문법 사항들을 떠올려 보세요. 예를 들어, 동사에 밑줄이 있다면 '주어와의 수 일치, 본동사와 준동사의 구분을 묻겠구나!'라고 생각하고 그 부분에 초점을 맞춰 문장을 분석해 볼 수 있습니다.

대표 기출 문제

정답 및 해설 p.035

091 다음 글의 밑줄 친 부분 중, 어법상 틀린 것은?   2024 수능

A number of studies provide substantial evidence of an innate human disposition to respond differentially to social stimuli. From birth, infants will orient preferentially towards the human face and voice, ① seeming to know that such stimuli are particularly meaningful for them. Moreover, they register this connection actively, imitating a variety of facial gestures that are presented to them — tongue protrusions, lip tightenings, mouth openings. They will even try to match gestures ② which they have some difficulty, experimenting with their own faces until they succeed. When they ③ do succeed, they show pleasure by a brightening of their eyes; when they fail, they show distress. In other words, they not only have an innate capacity for matching their own kinaesthetically experienced bodily movements with ④ those of others that are visually perceived; they have an innate drive to do so. That is, they seem to have an innate drive to imitate others whom they judge ⑤ to be 'like me'.

*innate: 타고난 **disposition: 성향 ***kinaesthetically: 운동감각적으로

✔ 유형 해결
3-Step

(STEP 1) 대략적인 글의 흐름 파악

• 인간은 사회적 자극에 차별적으로 반응하는 성향을 가지고 태어난다(an innate human disposition to respond differentially to social stimuli)는 내용의 글

(STEP 2) 각 항목의 어법성 판단

• 문맥과 어법을 동시에 고려하여 밑줄 친 부분의 어법성을 판단한다.

• 앞부분에서 정답으로 판단한 것이 나왔다고 해서 끝까지 읽지 않고 다음 문항으로 넘어가지 않도록 특히 유의한다.

②의 which는 바로 앞의 선행사 gestures를 받고 있어서 올바른 형태의 관계대명사처럼 보이지만 뒤에 이어지는 문장이 필요한 문장 성분을 다 갖춘 완전한 문장이어서 문제가 있다.
→ 선행사와 관계절이 연결되려면 부사적인 역할을 할 수 있는 '전치사+관계대명사'의 구조가 필요함

(STEP 3) 정답으로 판단한 항목의 재확인

② 관계대명사 which 뒤에는 주어, 동사, 목적어의 문장 성분을 모두 갖춘 완전한 절이 이어지고 있으므로 앞의 선행사 gestures가 이 절과 연결되려면 부사적인 역할을 해야 한다. they have some difficulty with gestures로 생각해 볼 수 있으므로 **which는 with which와 같은 표현으로 바꿔야 한다.**

....

✔ 정답 확인

① 문장의 주어인 infants의 상태를 부가적으로 설명하는 분사구문으로, 아기들이 알고 있는 것 같다는 문맥의 능동의 의미이므로 현재분사 seeming은 어법상 적절하다. → 분사구문의 태

③ 일반동사 succeed를 강조하려고 쓰인 조동사 do는 어법상 적절하다. → 동사의 강조

④ bodily movements를 대신하여 사용되었으므로, 복수형 대명사인 those는 어법상 적절하다. → 지시대명사의 수 일치

⑤ judge의 목적격보어 역할을 하고 있으므로 to be는 어법상 적절하다. 「judge+목적어+목적격보어(to부정사)」(~을 …라고 판단하다)의 구문인데 목적어가 whom으로 바뀌어 앞부분에 위치하고 있어 동사 다음에 목적격보어가 바로 연결된 구조이다. → 목적격보어의 형태

....

✔ 중요 구문

4행 Moreover, they register this connection actively, [imitating a variety of facial gestures
            주어   동사   분사구문
{that are presented to them} — tongue protrusions, lip tightenings, mouth openings].
    주격 관계대명사

: [ ]는 주절에 이어지는 부수적 상황을 나타내는 분사구문으로 의미상의 주어는 주절의 주어와 동일한 they이다. { }는 a variety of facial gestures를 수식하는 관계절이고, 대시(—) 이하는 a variety of facial gestures that are presented to them의 구체적인 예를 열거하는 부분이다.

....

✔ 어휘 풀이

• substantial *a* 상당한	• differentially *ad* 차별적으로	• stimulus *n* 자극(*pl.* stimuli)
• infant *n* 아기, 유아	• orient *v* 향하다	• preferentially *ad* 우선적으로
• register *v* 마음속에 새기다, 명심하다	• protrusion *n* 내밀기	• tighten *v* (입을) 다물다
• distress *n* 괴로움	• perceive *v* 지각하다, 인지하다	• drive *n* 욕구, 추진력

092

2023 수능

다음 글의 밑줄 친 부분 중, 어법상 **틀린** 것은?

Trends constantly suggest new opportunities for individuals to restage themselves, representing occasions for change. To understand how trends can ultimately give individuals power and freedom, one must first discuss fashion's importance as a basis for change. The most common explanation offered by my informants as to why fashion is so appealing is ①that it constitutes a kind of theatrical costumery. Clothes are part of how people present ②them to the world, and fashion locates them in the present, relative to what is happening in society and to fashion's own history. As a form of expression, fashion contains a host of ambiguities, enabling individuals to recreate the meanings ③associated with specific pieces of clothing. Fashion is among the simplest and cheapest methods of self-expression: clothes can be ④inexpensively purchased while making it easy to convey notions of wealth, intellectual stature, relaxation or environmental consciousness, even if none of these is true. Fashion can also strengthen agency in various ways, ⑤opening up space for action.

*stature: 능력

093

2022 수능

다음 글의 밑줄 친 부분 중, 어법상 **틀린** 것은?

Like whole individuals, cells have a life span. During their life cycle (cell cycle), cell size, shape, and metabolic activities can change dramatically. A cell is "born" as a twin when its mother cell divides, ①producing two daughter cells. Each daughter cell is smaller than the mother cell, and except for unusual cases, each grows until it becomes as large as the mother cell ②was. During this time, the cell absorbs water, sugars, amino acids, and other nutrients and assembles them into new, living protoplasm. After the cell has grown to the proper size, its metabolism shifts as it either prepares to divide or matures and ③differentiates into a specialized cell. Both growth and development require a complex and dynamic set of interactions involving all cell parts. ④What cell metabolism and structure should be complex would not be surprising, but actually, they are rather simple and logical. Even the most complex cell has only a small number of parts, each ⑤responsible for a distinct, well-defined aspect of cell life.

*metabolic: 물질대사의 **protoplasm: 원형질

094

다음 글의 밑줄 친 부분 중, 어법상 틀린 것은?

Automatic thinking helps us ① <u>understand</u> new situations by relating them to our prior experiences. When we meet someone ② <u>new</u>, we don't start from scratch to figure out what he or she is like; we categorize the person as "an engineering student" or "like my cousin Helen." The same goes for places, objects, and situations. When we walk into a fast-food restaurant ③ <u>where</u> we've never been to, we know, without thinking, not to wait at a table for a waiter and a menu. We know that we have to go to the counter to order ④ <u>because</u> our mental "script" automatically tells us that this is what we do in fast-food restaurants, and we assume that this one is no different. More formally, people use schemas, which are mental structures that ⑤ <u>organize</u> our knowledge about the social world. These mental structures influence the information we notice, think about, and remember. The term schema is very general; it encompasses our knowledge about many things — other people, ourselves, social roles, and specific events.

*schema: 스키마, 인지 틀

095

다음 글의 밑줄 친 부분 중, 어법상 틀린 것은?

With the acceleration of technical progress after the Second World War, it became evident that there was a real challenge to ensure that legislation ① <u>related</u> to technical products or issues would remain up to date. A nice solution was found in Europe in the 1980s ② <u>when</u> some EU Directives were streamlined to contain only "Essential Requirements", while leaving to standardization committees the task to produce the necessary supporting standards, called "harmonised standards". Therefore, since these Essential Requirements were very "stable", there was no need to continuously amend the legislation, while the standards could be more ③ <u>rapidly</u> improved and adapted to technical innovation. Experience has shown the great benefit of such a procedure, ④ <u>which</u> could/should usefully be expanded to cover new fields, whenever applicable! The fact that all stakeholders can have an input in the drafting of such standards ⑤ <u>to enhance</u> both the practicability of these standards and the acceptability of these directives and regulations.

*directive: 지침, 지시

096

다음 글의 밑줄 친 부분 중, 어법상 틀린 것은?

Research shows many benefits of help-seeking. Not only ①does asking for help make it likely that we will get what we need (more likely than we think), but we also tend to be judged less harshly than we might imagine — we may even strengthen our relationships by soliciting help. Yet, this is an area ②in which research findings never seem to fit into the "real world." Although there is great value in help-seeking, few ③seem to appreciate its potential value. Take, for example, a typical employee performance appraisal. Almost every performance appraisal measures ④what employees offer help to their co-workers. In contrast, performance appraisals rarely measure the employees' ability to ask for help when needed. Yet, ⑤being willing and able to access the expertise of one's co-workers would seem to be a critical driver of collaboration in organizations.

097

다음 글의 밑줄 친 부분 중, 어법상 틀린 것은?

When children are young, parents can begin developing their kindness by teaching them to speak well of others. Speech and behavior go together. ①Train a child to speak well of others, and over time he or she will treat those people better. Disciplining a child to talk differently will make him or her ②think differently. This technique works beautifully. If a parent insists that a child ③stop talking negatively about a friend, for instance, over time he or she will either forget about the friend's bad habits or actually learn to like him or her. When children are prohibited from complaining, they become happier. The way a child talks about someone ④causing him or her to think about that person the same way. Children think on ⑤what they say. If they complain, negative thoughts not only precede the complaints, they follow them. Then, a child forms a very negative pattern of thinking. When this happens, he or she not only complains more but begins to act unhappy.

098

다음 글의 밑줄 친 부분 중, 어법상 틀린 것은?

In 1790, the U.S. Census recorded 697,624 slaves; by the time of the Civil War, that number ① had grown to nearly 4 million. The increasing reliance on slave labor in the southern states in the nineteenth century ② was due largely to the invention of the cotton gin in 1793. This device automated the process of separating the seeds from the cotton fibers. While the device eliminated the need for humans to perform that task, ③ they vastly increased the overall need for human labor in cultivation and processing. U.S. production of cotton increased from 2 million pounds in 1790 to 1 billion pounds in 1860, ④ dominating the world market by mid-century. The national economy (not just the southern economy) was quite dependent on cotton by this time, which helps to explain both the aversion of southerners to ⑤ giving up their slaves and the reluctance of northerners to tamper with the system.

*cotton gin: 조면기(면화에서 솜과 씨를 분리하는 기계)

099

다음 글의 밑줄 친 부분 중, 어법상 틀린 것은?

We must distinguish *rules of thumb*, which are useful guides but ① do not, even when accepted, provide reasons for action in themselves, from *mandatory rules*. Mandatory rules, when accepted, furnish reasons for action simply by virtue of their existence *qua* rules, and thus generate normative pressure even in those cases ② which the justifications (rationales) underlying the rules indicate the contrary result. This is not to say that it is necessarily *wrong*, all things considered, ③ to violate a mandatory rule. What we have a reason to do is different from ④ what, all things considered, we *should* do. Even when a mandatory rule supplies a reason for conforming to the indications of the rule, other features of the situation may provide reasons for acting in some other way. To exceed the speed limit in order to rush a critically injured person to hospital is still to *break* the speed limit, but other reasons for action may justify breaking ⑤ it.

*qua: ~로서, ~의 자격으로

| 출제 Trend
- 글의 흐름을 고려하여 밑줄 친 다섯 개의 낱말 중 글의 흐름에 적절하지 않은 것을 고르는 밑줄 어휘 유형과 두 낱말 중 하나를 고르는 네모 어휘 유형이 있습니다.
- 2019 수능부터 1지문 2문항에도 밑줄 어휘 유형이 출제되고 있어서 그 중요성이 더 커졌다고 볼 수 있습니다.

| 해결 Point

1. 문맥을 정확히 파악하자!

어휘 문제에서 밑줄로 제시되는 어휘 자체는 어렵지 않습니다. 그런데 많은 학생들이 어휘 문제를 풀 때 지문 전체를 읽지 않고 밑줄이나 네모 어휘가 있는 구, 절 또는 문장만 읽습니다. 하지만 주어진 어휘의 단순한 의미를 파악할 것이 아니라, 지문의 전체적인 맥락을 이해하고 그에 따라 어휘의 적절성을 판단하는 것이 중요합니다.

2. 밑줄 친 어휘의 반의어를 떠올려 보자!

밑줄 어휘 유형은 주로는 해당 어휘의 반의어를 제시하고 글의 흐름에서 벗어나는지를 판단하게 하는 방식으로 출제됩니다. 따라서 먼저 밑줄 친 어휘를 훑어보고 각 어휘의 반의어를 떠올려 보는 것이 도움이 됩니다.

3. 어휘의 의미를 정확히 알아두자!

유사한 철자의 어휘, 반의어, 파생어 등 혼동하기 쉬운 어휘들은 따로 외우고 정리해 두어야 합니다. 특히 어휘를 외울 때 반의어를 활용하여 문제를 출제할 수 있는 동사, 형용사 그리고 부사를 눈여겨보도록 합니다.

대표 기출 문제

정답 및 해설 p.039

100 다음 글의 밑줄 친 부분 중, 문맥상 낱말의 쓰임이 적절하지 <u>않은</u> 것은?

2024 수능

Bazaar economies feature an apparently flexible price-setting mechanism that sits atop more enduring ties of shared culture. Both the buyer and seller are aware of each other's ①<u>restrictions</u>. In Delhi's bazaars, buyers and sellers can ②<u>assess</u> to a large extent the financial constraints that other actors have in their everyday life. Each actor belonging to a specific economic class understands what the other sees as a necessity and a luxury. In the case of electronic products like video games, they are not a ③<u>necessity</u> at the same level as other household purchases such as food items. So, the seller in Delhi's bazaars is careful not to directly ask for very ④<u>low</u> prices for video games because at no point will the buyer see possession of them as an absolute necessity. Access to this type of knowledge establishes a price consensus by relating to each other's preferences and limitations of belonging to a ⑤<u>similar</u> cultural and economic universe.

*constraint: 압박 **consensus: 일치

STEP 1 글의 도입부에서 핵심 소재 및 요지 파악하기

상점가 경제의 유연한 가격 설정 메커니즘(Bazaar economies feature an apparently flexible price-setting mechanism)에 관한 글이다.

STEP 2 전후 맥락을 고려하여 각 선택지의 적절성 여부 판단하기

① **restrictions**: 다음 문장에 다른 행위자(구매자와 판매자) 서로의 재정적 압박에 관한 내용이 기술되고 있다. 따라서 구매자와 판매자 둘 다 서로의 '제약(restrictions)'을 알고 있다고 할 수 있다.

② **assess**: 다음 문장에 특정 경제 계층에 속하는 행위자의 필수품과 사치품을 이해한다는 내용이 기술되고 있다. 따라서 구매자와 판매자는 대체로 다른 행위자들이 그들의 일상생활에서 가지는 재정적인 압박을 '평가할(assess)' 수 있다고 할 수 있다.

③ **necessity**: 비디오 게임과 식품을 비교하며 전자를 사치품으로 규정하고 있다. 따라서 식품과 같은 다른 가정 구매품은 '필수품(necessity)'이라고 할 수 있다.

④ **low**: 앞에서 비디오 게임은 필수품이 아니라고 했고, 뒤에서는 구매자가 비디오 게임 소유를 절대적 필수 사항으로 볼 이유가 전혀 없다고 확언하고 있다. 따라서 판매자가 비디오 게임에 대해 곧바로 매우 '낮은(low)' 가격을 요구하지 않도록 주의한다는 문맥은 어색하다.

⑤ **similar**: 앞에서 판매자와 구매자가 특정 경제 계층에 속한다고 언급했으므로, 둘 다 서로의 '비슷한(similar)' 문화적, 경제적 세계를 고려하여 선호와 한계를 토대로 가격 일치에 도달할 것임을 추론할 수 있다.

STEP 3 정답으로 판단한 항목의 재확인

④ 델리의 상점가에서의 거래는 구매자와 판매자가 서로가 가진 제약을 알고 있으므로, 필수품으로 여겨지지 않는 비디오 게임의 경우에 판매자는 구매자가 구매 의사가 생기도록 너무 '높은' 가격을 제시하지 않도록 주의해야 한다는 문맥이 되도록 low(낮은)를 high(높은)와 같은 어휘로 바꿔야 한다.

✔ 중요 구문

4행 Each actor [**belonging** to a specific economic class] understands [**what** the other sees **as a**
　　　　주어 ←──┘ 현재분사구　　　　　　　　　　동사　　　　목적어(의문사절)　　　전치사(~로)
necessity and a luxury].

: 첫 번째 [ ]는 문장의 주어인 Each actor를 수식하는 분사구이고, 두 번째 [ ]는 understand의 목적어 역할을 하는 명사절이다.

✔ 어휘 풀이

- **bazaar** *n* 상점가, 시장 거리
- **flexible** *a* 유연한
- **restriction** *n* 제약
- **necessity** *n* 필수품, 필수 사항
- **establish** *v* 정립하다, 확립하다

- **feature** *v* 특징으로 하다
- **mechanism** *n* 메커니즘(사물의 작용 원리)
- **assess** *v* 평가하다
- **luxury** *n* 사치품
- **limitation** *n* 한계, 제한

- **apparently** *ad* 겉보기에
- **atop** *p* 위에, 맨 꼭대기에
- **financial** *a* 재정적인
- **absolute** *a* 절대적인

101

다음 글의 밑줄 친 부분 중, 문맥상 낱말의 쓰임이 적절하지 <u>않은</u> 것은?

Everywhere we turn we hear about almighty "cyberspace"! The hype promises that we will leave our boring lives, put on goggles and body suits, and enter some metallic, three-dimensional, multimedia otherworld. When the Industrial Revolution arrived with its great innovation, the motor, we didn't leave our world to go to some ① <u>remote</u> motorspace! On the contrary, we brought the motors into our lives, as automobiles, refrigerators, drill presses, and pencil sharpeners. This ② <u>absorption</u> has been so complete that we refer to all these tools with names that declare their usage, not their "motorness." These innovations led to a major socioeconomic movement precisely because they entered and ③ <u>affected</u> profoundly our everyday lives. People have not changed fundamentally in thousands of years. Technology changes constantly. It's the one that must ④ <u>adapt</u> to us. That's exactly what will happen with information technology and its devices under human-centric computing. The longer we continue to believe that computers will take us to a magical new world, the longer we will ⑤ <u>maintain</u> their natural fusion with our lives, the hallmark of every major movement that aspires to be called a socioeconomic revolution.

*hype: 과대광고 **hallmark: 특징

102

다음 글의 밑줄 친 부분 중, 문맥상 낱말의 쓰임이 적절하지 <u>않은</u> 것은?

It has been suggested that "organic" methods, defined as those in which only natural products can be used as inputs, would be less damaging to the biosphere. Large-scale adoption of "organic" farming methods, however, would ① <u>reduce</u> yields and increase production costs for many major crops. Inorganic nitrogen supplies are ② <u>essential</u> for maintaining moderate to high levels of productivity for many of the non-leguminous crop species, because organic supplies of nitrogenous materials often are either limited or more expensive than inorganic nitrogen fertilizers. In addition, there are ③ <u>benefits</u> to the extensive use of either manure or legumes as "green manure" crops. In many cases, weed control can be very difficult or require much hand labor if chemicals cannot be used, and ④ <u>fewer</u> people are willing to do this work as societies become wealthier. Some methods used in "organic" farming, however, such as the sensible use of crop rotations and specific combinations of cropping and livestock enterprises, can make important ⑤ <u>contributions</u> to the sustainability of rural ecosystems.

*nitrogen fertilizer: 질소 비료 **manure: 거름 ***legume: 콩과(科) 식물

103

다음 글의 밑줄 친 부분 중, 문맥상 낱말의 쓰임이 적절하지 <u>않은</u> 것은?

The brilliance of the market is that it rewards workers for producing things that others value. Soon after its beginnings, the market was ① <u>extended</u> to reward innovators for producing ideas that others value. In 1449, the world's first patent was issued to John Utyman, a Venetian glassmaker, for his process of creating colored glass. Utyman was granted a twenty-year monopoly on the technique in England, in exchange for which he was required to teach his technique to apprentices, ② <u>preventing</u> that the knowledge would spread. From there, patents took hold. With these patent laws in place, an inventor had a greater chance of making a fortune from a new invention. With greater ③ <u>profits</u> to be made, more of the educated class turned their efforts to innovation. The inventors of the first several steam engines, the incandescent light bulb, the mechanical loom, the cotton gin, and the automobile were all motivated, at least in part, by the ④ <u>availability</u> of patents. And the rewarding of inventors by the patent system ⑤ <u>accelerated</u> the creation of new ideas.

*incandescent: 백열의, 백열광을 내는   **loom: 베틀, 직조기
***cotton gin: 조면기

104

(A), (B), (C)의 각 네모 안에서 문맥에 맞는 낱말로 가장 적절한 것은?

According to Kuhn, a scientific discipline has reached a certain degree of maturity when a paradigm has been established and becomes dominant. The phase of normal science that then begins is characterized by unconditional confidence that all problems can be solved within the existing paradigm for the time being. Therefore, in normal science, according to Kuhn, scientists do not seek falsifications of the fundamental laws, but work within a(n) (A) accepted / disputed framework provided by the paradigm. This framework is also reflected in school and university curricula. It significantly shapes the background knowledge and approach of scientists. Pupils and students grow up naturally with the prevailing paradigm and accept the established scientific principles. The (B) adaptation / adoption of the paradigm is thus part of scientific socialization and shapes the common worldview. Due to its openness and complexity, a paradigm is never fully conscious to scientists. As a rule, it contains numerous (C) implicit / explicit assumptions and metaphysical interpretations that are not reflected in the textbooks, but nevertheless influence the scientific enterprise like unwritten laws.

*falsification: 반증

	(A)	(B)	(C)
①	accepted	adoption	implicit
②	accepted	adoption	explicit
③	accepted	adaptation	explicit
④	disputed	adoption	implicit
⑤	disputed	adaptation	explicit

105

다음 글의 밑줄 친 부분 중, 문맥상 낱말의 쓰임이 적절하지 <u>않은</u> 것은?

In large part, the changing nature of mobility is linked closely with the changing nature of ① <u>transportation</u> systems. Throughout the early stages of human history, the means of human mobility was limited to walking. This meant that mobility was constrained by the limitations of human endurance. With the ② <u>advent</u> of domestication and certain technological developments (e.g., harnesses), the use of animal power became a means of increasing the mobility of individuals. Thus, the scope of activity was ③ <u>shrunk</u> because horses and other animals have greater physical endurance than do humans. By the beginning of the 20th century, the mobility of individuals was ④ <u>transformed</u> once again by the invention of the automobile (the "horseless carriage"). In addition to these developments, railroads, shipping lines, and airplanes have expanded the ⑤ <u>geographic</u> scope of personal mobility, potentially allowing individuals to become global citizens.

106

다음 글의 밑줄 친 부분 중, 문맥상 낱말의 쓰임이 적절하지 <u>않은</u> 것은?

Resistance is the tug-of-war partner of persuasion. Just as it takes two opposing teams for a tug-of-war competition, resistance and persuasion are opposing yet integral parts of a persuasive interaction. Knowing about an upcoming persuasion attempt ① <u>motivates</u> us to resist whatever the message is; this is called *reactance* (or the boomerang effect). Reactance refers to the feeling that people have when their freedom is threatened so that they want to ② <u>abandon</u> that freedom. If your parents really hate someone you are dating and try to break it off, how might you react? You might become even more attached to this person as a way of ③ <u>avoiding</u> letting your parents restrict your freedom. In these cases, persuasion ④ <u>backfires</u>. Reactance explains why banning television violence or using warning labels on particular television shows or movies can ⑤ <u>increase</u> people's interest in watching these programs.

*reactance: 반발

107

(A), (B), (C)의 각 네모 안에서 문맥에 맞는 낱말로 가장 적절한 것은?

Economies of scale are present in virtually all sectors of the media, from magazine publishing to radio broadcasting to music publishing. Consequently, horizontal expansion is a(n) (A) advantageous / disadvantageous strategy for most media firms. In newspaper publishing, for example, the marginal costs involved in selling one additional copy of the same edition of a newspaper are relatively low, so product-specific economies of scale will arise as circulations expand. Marginal costs are positive since (unlike broadcasting) the product is delivered in a(n) (B) tangible / intangible form, involving some printing and distribution costs. But editorial overheads tend to be the largest single component of expenditure for print media publishers and these do not necessarily change as consumption of the product expands or contracts. The editorial overheads associated with publishing any given newspaper title tend to be (C) changed / fixed, regardless of actual circulation volume, and so economies of scale can be gained as larger levels of readership are translated into more revenue.

*economies of scale: 규모의 경제(생산 요소의 투입량을 증가시켜 이익이 증가되는 현상)
**overheads: 간접비

	(A)		(B)		(C)
①	advantageous	………	tangible	………	changed
②	advantageous	………	intangible	………	changed
③	advantageous	………	tangible	………	fixed
④	disadvantageous	………	intangible	………	fixed
⑤	disadvantageous	………	tangible	………	changed

108

(A), (B), (C)의 각 네모 안에서 문맥에 맞는 낱말로 가장 적절한 것은?

Envy is an emotion which occurs when a person lacks another's quality, skill, achievement, or possession and either desires it or wishes that the other lacked it. It is easy to understand why this emotion is such a prevalent, pan-cultural emotion. People who are superior on valued attributes reap greater power and attention as well as higher self-esteem. (A) Excellence / Inferiority leads to less power and attention as well as lower self-esteem. It would be bizarre for other people's consequential advantages to have no emotional effect on us. Furthermore, from an evolutionary perspective, as evolutionary psychologists Sarah Hill and David Buss argue, it would hardly be adaptive to be inclined to feel that another person's advantage is a fully (B) satisfactory / unsatisfactory outcome. In this sense, a capacity to feel envy, although it has an unpleasant edge to it, serves a necessary adaptive function. If we, as evolving beings, had (C) failed / managed to develop an emotion designed to help us keep up with the Joneses, perhaps we would have withered away on the evolutionary vine.

*bizarre: 기이한 **Joneses: 사회적 지위가 비슷비슷한 사람들

	(A)		(B)		(C)
①	Excellence	………	satisfactory	………	managed
②	Excellence	………	unsatisfactory	………	failed
③	Inferiority	………	satisfactory	………	failed
④	Inferiority	………	unsatisfactory	………	failed
⑤	Inferiority	………	satisfactory	………	managed

01 글의 목적

01 expert _n_ _____

02 article _n_ _____

03 sign up for _____

04 vibrant _a_ _____

05 happen to _do_ _____

06 passionate _a_ _____

07 count on _____

08 privilege _n_ _____

09 prompt _a_ _____

10 generous _a_ _____

11 expertise _n_ _____

12 통찰력 _n_ _____

13 currently _ad_ _____

14 enroll _v_ _____

15 pursue _v_ _____

16 fancy _a_ _____

17 enthusiastic _a_ _____

18 repayment _n_ _____

19 대출(금) _n_ _____

20 contribution _n_ _____

02 심경 변화

01 cruel _a_ _____

02 approach _v_ _____

03 irritated _a_ _____

04 startle _v_ _____

05 gravel _n_ _____

06 convince _v_ _____

07 inadequacy _n_ _____

08 rare _a_ _____

09 wander _v_ _____

10 submit _v_ _____

11 competition _n_ _____

12 극적으로 _ad_ _____

13 말, 발언 _n_ _____

14 cub _n_ _____

15 tribe _n_ _____

16 strikingly _ad_ _____

17 accusing _a_ _____

18 leap _v_ _____

19 허벅지 _n_ _____

20 prisoner _n_ _____

03 필자의 주장

01	intuition	n	
02	resolve	v	
03	fulfillment	n	
04	vague	a	
05	indicate	v	
06	reduction	n	
07	vastly	ad	
08	exclusively	ad	
09	sequence	v	
10	potent	a	
11	destination	n	
12	thorough	a	
13	arbitrary	a	
14	관행, 관습	n	
15	prioritize	v	
16	analyze	v	
17	appropriately	ad	
18	reliance	n	
19	accompaniment	n	
20	demonstrate	v	

04 함축 의미 추론

01	multiple	a	
02	application	n	
03	강점	n	
04	emerge	v	
05	collapse	n	
06	sphere	n	
07	qualified	a	
08	colony	n	
09	scatter	v	
10	profession	n	
11	assessment	n	
12	decent	a	
13	rapidity	n	
14	devote	v	
15	tough	a	
16	침식	n	
17	biased	a	
18	decline	n	
19	designate	v	
20	excessive	a	

05 글의 요지

01	elimination	n	
02	congested	a	
03	acquisition	n	
04	maintenance	n	
05	implement	v	
06	district	n	
07	반박할 수 없는	a	
08	extension	n	
09	hazard	n	
10	promote	v	
11	exposure	n	
12	contaminant	n	
13	전염병	n	
14	distribution	n	
15	outrage	v	
16	overwhelming	a	
17	modify	v	
18	disposition	n	
19	entirely	ad	
20	absolute	a	

06 글의 주제

01	as opposed to		
02	equation	n	
03	mortality	n	
04	blunt	a	
05	appliance	n	
06	interfere	v	
07	typically	ad	
08	relevant	a	
09	subsequently	ad	
10	primary	a	
11	account	n	
12	moderate	a	
13	aggressive	a	
14	flexibility	n	
15	inevitable	a	
16	consolidate	v	
17	discard	v	
18	conceptual	a	
19	타고난, 선천적인	a	
20	interpretation	n	

⑰ 글의 제목

01	poverty	n
02	extension	n
03	integral	a
04	이해, 파악	n
05	detect	v
06	betray	v
07	separate	a
08	fascinating	a
09	archaeology	n
10	현상	n
11	famine	n
12	contend	v
13	flourish	v
14	concur	v
15	anthropologist	n
16	heritage	n
17	alter	v
18	hypothesis	n
19	paranormal	a
20	contemporary	a

⑱ 도표

01	ethnic	a
02	survey	n
03	slightly	ad
04	dispose of	
05	exceed	v
06	점유율	n
07	project	v
08	fluctuate	v
09	approximately	ad
10	racial	a
11	distribution	n
12	based on	
13	respectively	ad
14	dramatic	a
15	decline	n
16	suburb	n
17	landfill	n
18	decay	n
19	account for	
20	when it comes to	

09 내용 불일치

01	influence	*v*
02	a variety of	
03	translate	*v*
04	widely	*ad*
05	ambitious	*a*
06	bury	*v*
07	stroke	*n*
08	describe	*v*
09	dictator	*n*
10	forceful	*a*
11	correspond	*v*
12	reform	*n*
13	이론	*n*
14	settle	*v*
15	주제	*n*
16	give off	
17	prolifically	*ad*
18	exceptional	*a*
19	stiff	*a*
20	retire	*v*

10 안내문

01	nutritious	*a*
02	질환, (몸의) 이상	*n*
03	show off	
04	submission	*n*
05	complete	*v*
06	competition	*n*
07	resident	*n*
08	description	*n*
09	quarterly	*a*
10	literary	*a*
11	previously	*ad*
12	recipient	*n*
13	confirm	*v*
14	lecture	*n*
15	conduct	*v*
16	cordially	*ad*
17	function	*n*
18	fulfilling	*a*
19	informative	*a*
20	refundable	*a*

⑪ 어법

01	a host of	
02	ambiguity	*n*
03	notion	*n*
04	mature	*v*
05	differentiate	*v*
06	logical	*a*
07	distinct	*a*
08	figure out	
09	evident	*a*
10	legislation	*n*
11	stable	*a*
12	amend	*v*
13	adapt	*v*
14	discipline	*v*
15	prohibit	*v*
16	complain	*v*
17	precede	*v*
18	cultivation	*n*
19	aversion	*n*
20	harshly	*ad*
21	solicit	*v*
22	잠재적인	*a*
23	appraisal	*n*
24	critical	*a*

⑫ 어휘

01	regardless of	
02	revenue	*n*
03	be inclined to *do*	
04	wither	*v*
05	contract	*v*
06	advent	*n*
07	absorption	*n*
08	prevailing	*a*
09	integral	*a*
10	fundamentally	*ad*
11	aspire	*v*
12	sensible	*a*
13	assumption	*n*
14	patent	*n*
15	issue	*v*
16	monopoly	*n*
17	significantly	*ad*
18	as a rule	
19	profoundly	*ad*
20	constrain	*v*
21	endurance	*n*
22	관점	*n*
23	yield	*n*
24	grant	*v*

| 출제 Trend
- 단일 유형으로는 가장 큰 비중을 차지하여 4문항이 출제되며 3점짜리 고난이도 문항이 보통 2개가 포함됩니다.
- 수능에서 가장 많은 문제가 출제되면서 또한 가장 낮은 정답률을 보이는 유형입니다.
- 빈칸에 들어갈 말로는 핵심어(구)나 주제문이 주로 제시됩니다.

| 해결 Point

1. 글의 주제를 파악해야 하는 유형이다.

지문 속 각 문장들은 논리적으로 연결되어 있으므로 각 문장 사이의 논리 관계를 파악하면서 읽어야 합니다. 이때 대명사나 지시어, 대용 표현이 정확하게 무엇을 나타내는지 파악할 수 있어야 합니다. 또한 지문 속 주제를 나타내는 핵심어구와, 주제와 대립되는 개념을 내포하는 어구를 구분할 수 있어야 합니다.

2. 주제문을 정리한 후 선택지를 보자.

빈칸에 들어갈 내용은 대개 주제와 관련이 있으므로, 글의 주제와 지문 속 내용을 근거로 빈칸에 들어갈 내용을 추론해야 합니다. 이때 빈칸의 앞 문장이 주제를 뒷받침하는 문장인지, 주제와 상반되는 문장인지 꼭 확인합니다. 참고로, 지문에 나온 단어가 직접적으로 사용된 선택지보다는 글의 핵심어를 유사한 의미의 다른 표현으로 바꿔 사용한 선택지가 답일 가능성이 높습니다.

N 대표 기출 문제

정답 및 해설 p.044

109 다음 빈칸에 들어갈 말로 가장 적절한 것은?

2024 수능

Over the last decade the attention given to how children learn to read has foregrounded the nature of *textuality*, and of the different, interrelated ways in which readers of all ages make texts mean. 'Reading' now applies to a greater number of representational forms than at any time in the past: pictures, maps, screens, design graphics and photographs are all regarded as text. In addition to the innovations made possible in picture books by new printing processes, design features also predominate in other kinds, such as books of poetry and information texts. Thus, reading becomes a more complicated kind of interpretation than it was when children's attention was focused on the printed text, with sketches or pictures as an adjunct. Children now learn from a picture book that words and illustrations complement and enhance each other. Reading is not simply _____. Even in the easiest texts, what a sentence 'says' is often not what it means.

*adjunct: 부속물

① knowledge acquisition
② word recognition
③ imaginative play
④ subjective interpretation
⑤ image mapping

✔ 유형 해결 3-Step

STEP 1 글 전체의 중심 소재와 중심 생각 파악하기

Reading(읽기), reader(독자), textuality(텍스트성)

STEP 2 빈칸의 앞과 뒤에 이어지는 문장에서 단서 찾기

- 빈칸 앞의 문장:

Children learn from a picture book that **words and illustrations complement and enhance each other.** (어린이들은 그림책을 통해 글과 삽화가 서로 보완하여 향상한다는 것을 배운다.)

→ 글 또는 삽화만으로는 읽기가 완성되지 않음을 추론할 수 있음

- 빈칸 문장:

Reading is not simply _____. (읽기는 단순히 _____가 아니다.)

- 빈칸 뒤의 문장:

Even in the easiest texts, what a sentence 'says' is often not what it means.

(가장 쉬운 텍스트에서도, 문장이 '말하는' 것은 흔히 그것이 의미하는 것이 아니다.)

→ 읽기 과정은 단순히 문장을 읽는 것만으로는 부족함을 추론할 수 있음

STEP 3 찾은 단서를 종합하여 빈칸에 들어갈 말 고르기

빈칸 전후의 내용을 종합할 때, 텍스트는 단순히 글자만을 의미하는 것이 아니며, 정보를 제공하는 모든 것이 텍스트이므로, 읽기는 단순히 쓰인 글자를 인식하는 것을 넘어서는 활동임을 알 수 있다. 따라서 빈칸에 들어갈 말로 가장 적절한 것은 ② '단어 인식'이다.

✔ 정답 확인

① 지식 습득 → 본문에 언급되어 있지 않음

② 단어 인식 → 읽기가 단순한 글자 인식을 넘어서는 활동이라는 의미이므로 정답! 빈칸이 있는 문장에 부정어 not이 있음에 유의!

③ 창의적인 놀이 → 어린이와 읽기가 중심 소재로서 언급되고 있지만 창의적 놀이와는 무관함

④ 주관적인 해석 → 본문에 언급되어 있지 않음

⑤ 이미지 맵핑 → 본문의 단어 pictures, maps, graphics 등을 가지고 만든 오답

✔ 중요 구문

1행 Over the last decade the attention [**given** to how children learn to read] has foregrounded the nature [of *textuality*], and [of the different, interrelated ways {**in which** readers of all ages make texts mean}].

「make + 목적어 + 목적격보어(동사원형)」

: 첫 번째 [ ]는 형용사구로 문장의 주어인 the attention을 수식한다. { }는 관계절로 선행사 the different, interrelated ways를 수식한다. make는 사역동사로 '~하게 하다'의 의미이며, 목적어 texts 뒤에 동사원형 mean이 쓰였다.

✔ 어휘 풀이

- foreground *v* 전면으로 불러오다
- textuality *n* 텍스트성
- interrelated *a* 상호 연관된
- representational *a* (있는 그대로) 표현의, 나타내는
- feature *n* 특징, 특색
- predominate *v* 두드러지다, 지배적이다
- complicated *a* 복잡한
- illustration *n* 삽화
- complement *v* 보완하다
- enhance *v* 향상시키다
- recognition *n* 인식

110

다음 빈칸에 들어갈 말로 가장 적절한 것은?

There is something deeply paradoxical about the professional status of sports journalism, especially in the medium of print. In discharging their usual responsibilities of description and commentary,
5 reporters' accounts of sports events are eagerly consulted by sports fans, while in their broader journalistic role of covering sport in its many forms, sports journalists are among the most visible of all contemporary writers. The ruminations of the elite
10 class of 'celebrity' sports journalists are much sought after by the major newspapers, their lucrative contracts being the envy of colleagues in other 'disciplines' of journalism. Yet sports journalists do not have a standing in their profession that corresponds to the
15 size of their readerships or of their pay packets, with the old saying (now reaching the status of cliché) that sport is the 'toy department of the news media' still readily to hand as a dismissal of the worth of what sports journalists do. This reluctance to take sports
20 journalism seriously produces the paradoxical outcome that sports newspaper writers are much read but little _____ .

*discharge: 이행하다 **rumination: 생각 ***lucrative: 돈을 많이 버는

① paid
② admired
③ censored
④ challenged
⑤ discussed

111

다음 빈칸에 들어갈 말로 가장 적절한 것은?

Humour involves not just practical disengagement but cognitive disengagement. As long as something is funny, we are for the moment not concerned with whether it is real or fictional, true or false. This is why
5 we give considerable leeway to people telling funny stories. If they are getting extra laughs by exaggerating the silliness of a situation or even by making up a few details, we are happy to grant them comic licence, a kind of poetic licence. Indeed, someone listening to a
10 funny story who tries to correct the teller — 'No, he didn't spill the spaghetti on the keyboard and the monitor, just on the keyboard' — will probably be told by the other listeners to stop interrupting. The creator of humour is putting ideas into people's heads
15 for the pleasure those ideas will bring, not to provide _____ information.

*cognitive: 인식의 **leeway: 여지

① accurate
② detailed
③ useful
④ additional
⑤ alternative

112

다음 빈칸에 들어갈 말로 가장 적절한 것은?

The economist Fabian Waldinger examined the impact of the purge of Jewish professors at German universities before World War II and found something striking. Waldinger's research strategy was based on the fact that different university departments suffered very different rates of dismissal. For example, in Göttingen, which the influential mathematician Hilbert loved, 60 per cent of the mathematicians were forced to leave, but the chemistry department lost nobody. Using such random variations across Germany, Waldinger was able to show how serious the impact was of losing, say, 10 per cent of the scientists in a department. Then he compared it to the impact of bombing raids on university departments during the war. He found the damage from losing Jewish or dissident scientists was far greater and longer lasting than the damage to offices or laboratory facilities. Insisting on a racially pure scientific establishment inflicted permanent harm both to research output and to the productivity of young Ph.D. students who lost some of their best mentors. Stripped of their _____, German universities could not bounce back.

*purge: 숙청, 제거 **dissident: 반체제적인

① funding　　　　② diversity
③ authority　　　④ credibility
⑤ reputation

113

다음 빈칸에 들어갈 말로 가장 적절한 것은?

As parents we all have different standards of acceptable behaviour that we demand from our children. As long as your toddler is aware of your rules and boundaries and you stick to them, he will feel secure and reassured by your _____. You may occasionally get comments, such as, "Jane is having sweets, can I have some please?" If you decide that your answer is *no*, then don't back down. If you do, your toddler will remember that and be determined to persevere with asking you repeatedly next time, until you give in again. If you feel pressure to let your child do something he wouldn't normally do in a social situation, because others are, then it is better to say *yes* as soon as you are asked, rather than as a result of continued pressure. For example, in the case of asking for sweets, let him know it is a special treat: "Okay, Mummy will let you have the sweets as we are on a special outing, but usually we have sweets 'after' lunch, don't we?" That small reminder will reinforce your usual rules and mean that you're making the decision rather than being pressured by your toddler.

① honesty　　　　② patience
③ diligence　　　④ accuracy
⑤ consistency

114

다음 빈칸에 들어갈 말로 가장 적절한 것은?

_____ is perhaps most visible — as well as dramatic and spectacular — in large animals, but far more of it occurs in plants, where the most biomass is concentrated. Plants get their nutrients from the soil and the air in the form of chemicals — all bodies are built of carbons linked together, later to be disassembled and released as carbon dioxide — but nevertheless they are still "living off" other life. The carbon dioxide that plants take up to build their bodies is made available through the agency of bacteria and fungi and is sucked up massively from the enormous pool of past and present life. The carbon building blocks that make a daisy or a tree come from millions of sources: a decaying elephant in Africa a week ago, an extinct plant of the Carboniferous age, an Arctic poppy returning to the earth a month ago. Even if those molecules were released into the air the previous day, they came from plants and animals that lived millions of years ago.

*Carboniferous age: 석탄기

① Destroying   ② Evolving
③ Diversifying   ④ Recycling
⑤ Harmonizing

115

다음 빈칸에 들어갈 말로 가장 적절한 것은?

The adequacy criterion is important in psychiatric diagnosis. For example, a diagnosis of major depression requires that 'the person's symptoms are a cause of great distress or difficulty in functioning at home, work, or other important areas.' We all have fears, some sensible and some irrational. A fear is only classified as abnormal — that is, a phobia — if 'the avoidance, anxiety, or distress about the feared situation(s) interferes significantly with one or more of the following areas in a person's life: normal daily routine, occupational (or academic) functioning, social activities, or personal relationships. Introducing these sorts of elements to diagnosis is very helpful because it defines where the cut-off points should be between unusual and abnormal, and because it ensures we take into account the _____ of the person as well as social norms.

① welfare   ② morality
③ genetics   ④ confidence
⑤ background

116

다음 빈칸에 들어갈 말로 가장 적절한 것은?

It is useful to consider praise in terms of _____. When we *encourage* a boy, our focus is on the future — we try to convince him that he will overcome any current difficulty to be successful thereafter. We therefore generate faith, hope and confidence and give him heart. When we clearly *enjoy* his company and his achievements, we indicate our happiness and pleasure with who he is, in the present. When we *endorse* his actions, his view of the world, his approaches to learning and his feelings, we are accepting those bits of him that have been fashioned by his past. If boys are comfortable with their past behaviour and experiences, even if these were difficult, they are better able to look optimistically at the future. It is not helpful for parents or significant others to make a boy feel either ashamed of or guilty about his past or to wipe it out in any attempt to refocus and start again.

① time zones
② an indirect warning
③ behavior correction
④ personality differences
⑤ the pursuit of goals

117

다음 빈칸에 들어갈 말로 가장 적절한 것은?

Nelson Mandela's sage observation that "there can be no keener revelation of a society's soul than the way in which it treats its children," invites concern about our own society's soul as big business ruthlessly squeezes childhood into practices designed to _____. From the self-interested perspective of corporations, children are little more than opportunities to exploit — opportunities such as markets for fast food or standardized tests, for example. And as corporations become dominant forces in children's and parents' lives, that morally myopic perspective and the practices it inspires define more and more of what we, as a society, think and do about childhood. Our societal aspirations to manifest the values of childhood — caring for, nurturing, protecting, and supporting children — end up getting pushed aside by strategies devised to maximize the economic value of children.

*myopic: 근시안적인

① yield profits
② teach morals
③ share information
④ overcome poverty
⑤ improve knowledge

정답 및 해설 p.048

118 다음 빈칸에 들어갈 말로 가장 적절한 것은?   2024 수능

Everyone who drives, walks, or swipes a transit card in a city views herself as a transportation expert from the moment she walks out the front door. And how she views the street _____. That's why we find so many well-intentioned and civic-minded citizens arguing past one another. At neighborhood meetings in school auditoriums, and in back

5 rooms at libraries and churches, local residents across the nation gather for often-contentious discussions about transportation proposals that would change a city's streets. And like all politics, all transportation is local and intensely personal. A transit project that could speed travel for tens of thousands of people can be stopped by objections to the loss of a few parking spaces or by the simple fear that the project won't work. It's not a challenge of the data or the

10 traffic engineering or the planning. Public debates about streets are typically rooted in emotional assumptions about how a change will affect a person's commute, ability to park, belief about what is safe and what isn't, or the bottom line of a local business.

*swipe: 판독기에 통과시키나 **contentious: 논쟁적인 ***commute: 통근

① relies heavily on how others see her city's streets
② updates itself with each new public transit policy
③ arises independently of the streets she travels on
④ tracks pretty closely with how she gets around
⑤ ties firmly in with how her city operates

✓ **유형 해결**
3-Step

STEP 1 **글 전체의 중심 소재와 내용 파악하기**

• transportation(교통), local(지역적인), personal(개인적인)
• emotional assumption(감정적 추정), commute(통근), park(주차하다), the bottom line(순익)

STEP 2 **빈칸 문장과 빈칸 이후의 문장 파악하기**

• 빈칸 문장:
  - (as a transportation expert) how she views the street _____ .
  - (거리에서 교통을 이용하는 사람 각각은 모두 교통 전문가로서) 그 사람들이 거리를 바라보는 방식은 _____ 다.)

• 빈칸 이후의 문장:
  - all transportation is **local and intensely personal**
    (모든 교통은 지역적이고 지극히 개인적이다)
  - Public debates about streets are typically rooted in **emotional assumptions** about how a change will affect **a person's commute, ability to park, belief about what is safe and what isn't,** or **the bottom line of a local business.**
    (개인의 통근, 주차 능력, 안전한 것과 안전하지 않은 것에 대한 믿음, 또는 지역 사업체의 순익에 어떤 영향을 미칠지에 대한 감정적인 추정에 뿌리를 두고 있다.)

STEP 3 **찾은 단서를 종합하여 빈칸에 들어갈 말 고르기**

빈칸 문장과 빈칸 이후의 문장들의 내용을 종합할 때, 도시에서 각 교통 사용자가 거리를 바라보는 방식은 지역적이고 개인적이어서 자신의 통근, 주차 능력, 안전성, 또는 지역 사업체의 순익과 같은 각자의 이해관계와 직결된다는 내용이므로, 빈칸에는 ④ '그 사람이 돌아다니는 방식과 매우 긴밀하게 맞아떨어진다'가 적절하다.

✓ **정답 확인**

① 다른 사람들이 그 사람의 도시 거리를 어떻게 보느냐에 크게 의존한다
  → 한 도시의 교통 사용자에 관해서만 언급했을 뿐, 외부인의 견해나 태도는 언급되지 않음

② 각각의 새로운 대중교통 정책에 맞춰 자체를 업데이트한다 → 자신의 편의와 안전을 토대로 새로운 대중교통 정책을 제안한다는 내용은 있지만, 정책 변화에 따른 개인의 대응에 관한 내용은 언급되지 않음

③ 그 사람이 이동하는 거리와 관계없이 발생한다 → 각 교통 사용자는 개인의 통근, 주차 능력 등에 뿌리를 두고 대중 토론에 참가한다고 했으므로 글의 내용에 위배됨

⑤ 그 사람의 도시가 운영되는 방식과 확고하게 연계되어 있다
  → 도시의 교통 운영 방식에 따라 개인의 교통 사용이 좌우된다는 내용은 언급되지 않음

✓ **중요 구문**

7행 A transit project [**that** could speed travel for tens of thousands of people] can be stopped
　　　　　　 └─┘ 주격 관계대명사　　　　　　　　　　　　　　　　　　　　　 동사(수동태)
[by objections to the loss of a few parking spaces] or [by the simple fear {**that** the project
전치사구1　　　　　　　　　　　　　　　　　　　　　 전치사구2　　　　└─ 동격 ─┘
won't work}].

: 첫 번째 [ ]는 문장의 주어인 A transit project를 수식하는 관계절이다. or로 연결된 두 번째와 세 번째 [ ]는 '~에 의해'라는 뜻을 나타내는 두 개의 전치사구이고, { }는 the simple fear의 구체적인 내용을 설명하는 동격의 명사절이다.

✓ **어휘 풀이**

• transit card 교통 카드
• auditorium n 강당
• objection n 반대
• bottom line 순익
• transportation n 교통, 운송
• resident n 주민
• engineering n 공학
• track with ~와 맞아떨어지다
• well-intentioned a 선의의
• intensely ad 지극히, 몹시
• assumption n 추정, 가정

119

다음 빈칸에 들어갈 말로 가장 적절한 것은?

We understand that the segregation of our consciousness into present, past, and future is both a fiction and an oddly self-referential framework; your present was part of your mother's future, and your children's past will be in part your present. Nothing is generally wrong with structuring our consciousness of time in this conventional manner, and it often works well enough. In the case of climate change, however, the sharp division of time into past, present, and future has been desperately misleading and has, most importantly, hidden from view the extent of the responsibility of those of us alive now. The narrowing of our consciousness of time smooths the way to divorcing ourselves from responsibility for developments in the past and the future with which our lives are in fact deeply intertwined. In the climate case, it is not that _____. It is that the realities are obscured from view by the partitioning of time, and so questions of responsibility toward the past and future do not arise naturally.

*segregation: 분리 **intertwine: 뒤얽히게 하다 ***obscure: 흐릿하게 하다

① all our efforts prove to be effective and are thus encouraged
② sufficient scientific evidence has been provided to us
③ future concerns are more urgent than present needs
④ our ancestors maintained a different frame of time
⑤ we face the facts but then deny our responsibility

120

다음 빈칸에 들어갈 말로 가장 적절한 것은?

Precision and determinacy are a necessary requirement for all meaningful scientific debate, and progress in the sciences is, to a large extent, the ongoing process of achieving ever greater precision. But historical representation puts a premium on a proliferation of representations, hence not on the refinement of one representation but on the production of an ever more varied set of representations. Historical insight is not a matter of a continuous "narrowing down" of previous options, not of an approximation of the truth, but, on the contrary, is an "explosion" of possible points of view. It therefore aims at the unmasking of previous illusions of determinacy and precision by the production of new and alternative representations, rather than at achieving truth by a careful analysis of what was right and wrong in those previous representations. And from this perspective, the development of historical insight may indeed be regarded by the outsider as a process of creating ever more confusion, a continuous questioning of _____, rather than, as in the sciences, an ever greater approximation to the truth.

*proliferation: 증식

① criteria for evaluating historical representations
② certainty and precision seemingly achieved already
③ possibilities of alternative interpretations of an event
④ coexistence of multiple viewpoints in historical writing
⑤ correctness and reliability of historical evidence collected

121

다음 빈칸에 들어갈 말로 가장 적절한 것은?

In general, _____ can be extremely helpful to the creative process. For instance, an argument people used in the sixteenth and seventeenth centuries to prove that Earth does not move was to say that a rock dropped from a tower lands at its base. If Earth were moving, they argued, it would fall elsewhere. Galileo, a man who habitually thought in terms of analogies, saw Earth in his mind as a kind of sailing ship in space. As he explained to doubters of Earth's movement, a rock dropped from the mast of a moving ship still lands at its base. These analogies can be tight and logical, such as Isaac Newton's comparison of the falling apple from a tree in his garden to the moon falling in space. Or they can be loose and somewhat irrational, such as jazz artist John Coltrane's thinking of his own compositions as cathedrals of sound he was constructing. In any event, thinking in terms of analogies and metaphors can expand your ideas.

*analogy: 비유 **mast: 돛대

① convincing doubters of their irrational arguments
② explaining uncontroversial ideas with common language
③ developing loose analogies and metaphors into tight logic
④ taking greater advantage of the associative powers of the mind
⑤ citing great figures of the scientific world as well as great artists

122

다음 빈칸에 들어갈 말로 가장 적절한 것은?

A practical example of falsely assuming that _____ can be found with the advent of antibiotics, which began with the production of penicillin in the late 1940s. When penicillin was first used therapeutically in humans, it was observed that the administration of penicillin in patients infected with some contagious diseases caused by bacteria was uniformly efficacious in killing off the bacteria. One might be tempted to conclude a general principle — that penicillin kills the bacteria. In fact, this became an accepted practical truth, and penicillin was listed by the medical community as the definitive treatment for those diseases. However, given the selective pressure of widespread penicillin use, some strains of the bacteria acquired resistance to penicillin through evolutionary processes. Thus, whereas essentially 100% of the bacteria was observed to be sensitive to penicillin yesterday, such is not the case today, a clear example of the fallibility of induction in being able to predict tomorrow.

*therapeutically: 치료 목적으로 **efficacious: 효능이 있는
***fallibility: 틀리기 쉬움

① there is no cure-all solution
② the future will resemble the past
③ evolution can happen in an instant
④ a discovery can be made by accident
⑤ today will be different from yesterday

123

다음 빈칸에 들어갈 말로 가장 적절한 것은?

Consider the relationship between facial expressions and felt emotions. We often assume that we feel an emotion and then the appropriate expression plays across our face. In fact there's evidence showing that the relationship can run the other way, too. Pulling a smiling face has been shown to lead some people to feel happier and to be biased toward retrieving more positive events from their memory. One pertinent study involved participants holding a pen between their teeth — which forced them to imitate a smiling expression — while watching cartoons. Those with their face in this smiling position rated the cartoons as funnier than other participants who posed with the pen held between their lips (which prevents smiling). There's even evidence that the cosmetic use of Botox can interfere with people's experience of emotions, presumably because they're unable to stretch their faces into the appropriate facial expressions, resulting in _____.

① the development of body language
② a confusion among diverse emotions
③ a temporary paralysis of the whole body
④ a lack of feedback from the face to the brain
⑤ the wrong transmission of signals from the brain

124

다음 빈칸에 들어갈 말로 가장 적절한 것은?

It is wrong to imagine ourselves and others as _____. Science is now showing us more clearly than ever that whatever genetic limitations we may have, the specific boundaries of these limitations are unknown to us. Therefore, it makes no sense to pretend that we know these prison walls and then navigate our lives accordingly. Genetic inheritance is a huge factor in intellectual potential, of course. Sure, people really are born with brains that will never produce Nobel Prize-winning achievements no matter how hard they work or how many opportunities they have. But how exactly do we know who falls into which category? All we can do is measure current ability. We cannot determine intelligence that might have been or intelligence that could be. Therefore, we must never let the lie of known genetic limits to our intelligence hold us back either as individuals, as groups, or as a species.

① top consumers in the food chain
② prisoners fenced in by our genes
③ poor collaborators with other species
④ specimens of inefficiency in food use
⑤ creatures with an infinite power of evolution

125

다음 빈칸에 들어갈 말로 가장 적절한 것은?

People can create a new sense of identity by behaving like the person that they want to be. The same principle can also help bring people together by getting them _____ . In one study, for example, one group of students was asked to behave as if they had recently been paralyzed in a road accident and were now confined to a wheelchair. The students spent twenty minutes working their way around a prespecified route in a wheelchair and so had to navigate several lifts, ramps, and doors. Another group of students walked behind the wheelchairs and witnessed everything that happened. Both groups were then asked about their attitudes about issues related to the disabled, including, for example, whether public funds should be spent on a new rehabilitation center. A remarkable difference emerged between the groups, with those who had spent time in a wheelchair showing far greater empathy for the disabled.

① to have equal opportunities
② to organize volunteer work days
③ to see how the world looks to others
④ to plan some great outdoor activities
⑤ to take cultural differences into account

126

다음 빈칸에 들어갈 말로 가장 적절한 것은?

It should be obvious that circulation and advertisements, whether they are print or digital, account for a majority of the revenue sources for commercial magazines. As a medium dependent both on subscription payments from the audience and on advertising revenues, a magazine must recognize the interdependence of its two major revenue sources. When faced with higher costs entailed in both production and promotion, a publisher feels tempted to hike its subscription prices to make up for higher costs. Higher subscription prices in turn reduce circulation and therefore lower advertising revenue, offsetting the gains from higher prices. The same kind of scenario plays out with a publisher which, in an attempt to resolve the same kind of issue of higher production and promotion costs, looks for a solution in raising advertising prices. Because many members of the audience may value advertisements, especially those with pricing and other specific information, as well as noncommercial content, a reduction in advertising resulting from higher prices for advertisements reduces circulation, again _____ .

① prompting the publisher to seek another solution
② inducing a delicately balanced profit-cost analysis
③ necessitating cutting production costs wherever possible
④ creating tension between the audience and the publisher
⑤ canceling out the gains from more expensive advertising

127

다음 빈칸에 들어갈 말로 가장 적절한 것은?

Very much at the forefront of our ancestors' minds was, 'whatever you do today, don't get eaten'. First and foremost was not ending up on the menu of local lions and tigers. But second was remaining within the tribe. Early tribes were not particularly forgiving of members who did not contribute, who were greedy or lazy—for the survival of the tribe, they couldn't afford to be. These members were ejected from the group, which, for a toothless, clawless, and hairless mammal, meant certain death. The result of this is that those of our ancestors who survived were the ones who were vigilant. They were cautious and looked out for lions and tigers. Also, they were cautious in the tribe, vigilant for cues they were _____. Those who tended to be relaxed, easy-going, a little carefree and not bothered about what others thought of them, tended not to stick around long enough to successfully pass on their genes.

① being hunted down
② not trying to stay fit
③ not pulling their weight
④ hiding food from others
⑤ running after their mates

128

다음 빈칸에 들어갈 말로 가장 적절한 것은?

Consider now a very different model, called the "prisoners' dilemma." It has its origins in research by mathematicians, but it is a cornerstone of much contemporary work in economics. Assume that two competing firms must decide whether to have a big advertising budget. Advertising would allow one firm to steal some of the other's customers. But when they both advertise, the effects on customer demand cancel out. The firms end up having spent money needlessly. We might expect that neither firm would choose to spend much on advertising, but the model shows that _____. When the firms make their choices independently and they care only about their own profits, each one has an incentive to advertise, regardless of what the other firm does. When the other firm does not advertise, you can steal customers from it if you do advertise; when the other firm does advertise, you have to advertise to prevent a loss of customers. So the two firms end up in a bad equilibrium in which both have to waste resources. This market is not at all efficient.

① this logic is off base
② advertising is the best strategy
③ competition brings gains in efficiency
④ cooperation increases the overall benefits
⑤ rational decisions bring a good equilibrium

129

다음 빈칸에 들어갈 말로 가장 적절한 것은?

In the classic model of the Sumerian economy, the temple functioned as an administrative authority governing commodity production, collection, and redistribution. The discovery of administrative tablets from the temple complexes at Uruk suggests that token use and consequently writing evolved as a tool of centralized economic governance. Given the lack of archaeological evidence from Uruk-period domestic sites, it is not clear whether individuals also used the system for _____. For that matter, it is not clear how widespread literacy was at its beginnings. The use of identifiable symbols and pictograms on the early tablets is consistent with administrators needing a lexicon that was mutually intelligible by literate and nonliterate parties. As cuneiform script became more abstract, literacy must have become increasingly important to ensure one understood what he or she had agreed to.

*archaeological: 고고학적인 **lexicon: 어휘 목록
***cuneiform script: 쐐기 문자

① religious events
② personal agreements
③ communal responsibilities
④ historical records
⑤ power shifts

130

다음 빈칸에 들어갈 말로 가장 적절한 것은?

The most important reason for asking a questions when a friend has a problem is because *people can't fully think and feel at the same time* — it involves two different areas of the brain. If I give you a math problem when you're upset you're going to do one of two things: solve the problem because anger took a back-seat, or not be able to solve the problem because your feelings got in the way of thinking it through. One of the two will dominate. The best way to de-escalate hurt feelings is to make that transition from feelings (emotional logic) to thought (rational logic). So, if you ask a question, especially one that requires some self-analysis, you're helping your friend move past reacting, and on to *thinking* about what's going on — *Why did that actually hurt?* You're still asking about his or her feelings, true, but you're _____. You're helping your friend find some emotional distance from the problem in order to resolve the problem; and you're de-escalating the tension at the same time.

① putting it on an objective level
② adding fuel to his or her anger
③ trying to cover up your own mistake
④ sympathizing with his or her feelings
⑤ realizing the difference between emotions and thought

131

다음 빈칸에 들어갈 말로 가장 적절한 것은?

In a study that tested the frustration-aggression theory, participants were waiting in long lines at various stores, banks, restaurants, ticket windows, and airport passenger check-in stands, when a confederate, somebody who is secretly working for the researcher, crowded in front of them in line. The participants didn't even realize they were in a study. By the flip of a coin, the confederate crowded in front of the 2nd person in line or in front of the 12th person in line. According to the frustration-aggression theory, events are more frustrating if you _____. The confederate then recorded the participant's reaction. The results showed that participants 2nd in line responded more aggressively to the confederate who crowded in front of them than did participants 12th in line, which is consistent with the frustration-aggression theory. Indeed, it must be very frustrating if you can "almost taste it," but someone gets in your way.

① are close to the goal
② are unwilling to yield
③ are particularly in a hurry
④ expect a long waiting time
⑤ have nothing to do with them

132

다음 빈칸에 들어갈 말로 가장 적절한 것은?

In the post-World War II years after 1945, unparalleled economic growth fueled a building boom and a massive migration from the central cities to the new suburban areas. The suburbs were far more dependent on the automobile, signaling the shift from primary dependence on public transportation to private cars. Soon this led to the construction of better highways and freeways and the decline and even loss of public transportation. With all of these changes came a _____ of leisure. As more people owned their own homes, with more space inside and lovely yards outside, their recreation and leisure time was increasingly centered around the home or, at most, the neighborhood. One major activity of this home-based leisure was watching television. No longer did one have to ride the trolly to the theater to watch a movie; similar entertainment was available for free and more conveniently from television.

*unparalleled: 유례없는

① downfall　　　　② uniformity
③ restoration　　　④ privatization
⑤ customization

133

다음 빈칸에 들어갈 말로 가장 적절한 것은?

How do you know that men have walked on the moon? You haven't personally been to the moon, nor were you present in Apollo 11 to witness the first manned lunar landing with your own eyes. When we ask you, then, to tell us what you remember about the moon landing, and you tell us that you know that the Lunar Module, *Eagle*, landed on the moon as part of the Apollo 11 mission on 20 July 1969, and that Neil Armstrong, as he took the first human steps on the moon, famously marked the occasion with the memorable description: "One small step for man; one giant leap for mankind," you are remembering information that other people amassed and recorded. Perhaps you have a relative who remembers watching the moon landing on television. Perhaps you have seen the video footage. Perhaps you have read about the event in history books, or you've seen the news articles from the time. Your knowledge of the moon landing is personal, in that you personally know it, but it is also _____. That is, the reason you know about the moon landing is that other people — the vast majority of whom you have not met — have documented it and stored it in our cultural memory.

*Lunar Module: 달 착륙선

① shared with other people
② developed through action
③ open to personal interpretation
④ dangerous when it is superficial
⑤ superior to any worldly pleasures

134

다음 빈칸에 들어갈 말로 가장 적절한 것은?

Tribal peoples usually distinguish between gifts and capital. "One man's gift," they say, "must not be another man's capital." Wendy James, a British social anthropologist, tells us that among the Uduk in northeast Africa, "any wealth transferred from one subclan to another, whether animals, grain or money, is in the nature of a gift, and should be consumed, and not invested for growth. If such transferred wealth is added to the subclan's capital — cattle in this case — and kept for growth and investment, the subclan is regarded as being _____."
If a pair of goats received as a gift from another subclan is kept to breed or to buy cattle, "there will be general complaint that the so-and-sos are getting rich at someone else's expense, behaving without regard for morality by hoarding and investing gifts, and therefore being in a state of severe debt. It will be expected that they will soon suffer storm damage."

*subclan: (부족 내의) 소(小)부족, 하위 부족   **hoard: 축적하다

① in the position to use the gift at their own free will
② in accordance with the donors' intentions embedded in the gift
③ in a moral obligation to invest the gift for growth and get richer
④ in opposition to the donors who want their gift to be capital
⑤ in an immoral relation of debt to the donors of the original gift

135

다음 빈칸에 들어갈 말로 가장 적절한 것은?

Choices about art objects that go on and off display in art museums are shaped by, and in turn give shape to, the canon of art history. Art history is so influential in this respect that Donald Preziosi even calls it 'museography' — the writing-down of what the museum shows. Decisions about what goes on show and what stays in storage are affected by the taking into consideration of a few concerns. When a curator is confronted with many objects of the same type, and must choose one to put on display, it may seem likely that her or his decision would be guided by aesthetics. Yet even this kind of curatorial decision-making is different in art museums, museums of everyday objects, and museums of science and technology, natural history, anthropology or local history, to name only a few genres of museums. A bronze sculpture that would be rejected as second-rate and unworthy of showing by an art curator, might be displayed by a science curator who wishes to highlight those exceptional qualities of the alloy that the art curator is unconcerned about. Thus, what is worthy of display and what is not, depends greatly upon the _____ of the display.

*canon: 정전(正典) **alloy: 합금

① cost   ② space
③ context   ④ span
⑤ popularity

136

다음 빈칸에 들어갈 말로 가장 적절한 것은?

A key message that modern science provides us with is that _____. For any strategy or trait to evolve, it simply has to out-compete other ones. There is an old joke which goes: 'You don't have to run faster than the wolf. You just have to run faster than your friend.' Okay — so it does nothing for friendship, but it does demonstrate that some of the things that evolution has bestowed on animals to give them an advantage in one area can compromise their abilities in another. This trade-off can be seen in the peacock's tail, which is great for attracting mates but a handicap when trying to escape from predators. Also consider how giraffes have to struggle to get their necks down to drink water. Any alien visiting this planet would regard them as rather bizarre animals — how could such an animal have evolved? Then we discover that the long neck is actually an adaptation that allows giraffes to eat leaves from the higher branches of trees. So an advantage in one area can actually produce serious disadvantages in another.

*bestow: 부여하다 **bizarre: 이상한

① nothing is designed without effort and pain
② the process of competition is not always fair
③ evolved design can bring unintended consequences
④ the process is more important than the final result
⑤ there is always a big element of chance in evolution

137

다음 빈칸에 들어갈 말로 가장 적절한 것은?

When we look at ourselves from the evolutionary point of view, we see that not only are we very recent arrivals on Earth, but that our emergence as a new species on the planet was originally an event of no particular importance to the entire scheme of things. Earth was filled with life long before we appeared. Putting the point metaphorically, we are relative newcomers, entering a home that has been the residence of others for hundreds of millions of years, a home that must now be shared by all of us together. The comparative brevity of human life on Earth may be vividly depicted by imagining the geological time scale in _____ terms. Suppose we start with algae, which have been around for at least 600 million years. If the time that algae have been here were represented by the length of a football field (300 feet), then the period during which sharks have been swimming in the world's oceans and spiders have been spinning their webs would occupy three quarters of the length of the field; reptiles would show up at about the center of the field; mammals would cover the last third of the field; hominids the last two feet; and the species Homo sapiens the last six inches.

*brevity: 짧음, 간결

① causal　　　　　② spatial
③ abstract　　　　④ competitive
⑤ comprehensive

138

다음 빈칸에 들어갈 말로 가장 적절한 것은?

We buy something at the overpriced convenience store on the corner because it's easier than getting in the car and driving to the store where prices are lower. We put our dishes in the sink instead of the dishwasher because one less step is required. We let our teenager text through dinner because it's easier than inviting an argument by trying to enforce the no-phones rule. We accept the first, minimally credible information we find online about a subject because it's the easiest way to get our questions answered. And so on. From an evolutionary perspective, this bias for ease is useful. For most of human history it's been crucial to our survival and progress. Just imagine if humans had a bias for doing things the hardest possible way. What if our ancestors had been wired to ask, "What's the hardest way to obtain food? To provide shelter for our family? To maintain good relationships within our tribe?" They wouldn't have made it! Our survival as a species grows out of our innate preference for _____.

① choosing peace rather than war
② taking the path of least resistance
③ seeking companionship over solitude
④ learning about the world around ourselves
⑤ striving for success despite hard challenges

139

다음 빈칸에 들어갈 말로 가장 적절한 것은?

A human being has many different roles over the course of a lifetime. Where do these roles come from? Often they are part of the social system. If you lived in a small peasant farming village where most people historically used to live, then many roles would not be available to you. The limited opportunities in that village's social system mean that you could not be a basketball coach, for example, or a software consultant, or a movie star because the only other people you ever meet are peasant farmers. Most roles are ways of relating to other people within a cultural system. If you lived alone in the forest, it would be silly to describe yourself as a police officer, a bartender, a schoolteacher, or vice president of telemarketing. A person's social identity thus shows the interplay of the individual and the larger cultural system: Society creates and defines the roles, and individual people seek them out, adopt them, and sometimes impose their own style on them. Without society, _____.

① the self would not exist in full
② there would not be conflicts at all
③ no technology would ever be developed
④ individual roles would take on more importance
⑤ living in harmony with nature would be impossible

140

다음 빈칸에 들어갈 말로 가장 적절한 것은?

When psychologists first showed that animals appeared to construct cognitive "maps" of the mazes in which they ran, skeptics argued that perhaps the animals laid down a record of their sequence of responses as they ran through a maze. These "behaviorists" called each component in this sequence a "fractional anticipatory goal response", which was about as far as they would concede that any animals, including us, have a mental life. On this account, my mind doesn't contain a representation of the spatial relations between my chair and Nassau Street. All it contains is a sequence of "fractional" responses: turn left, proceed forwards for ten feet, go through the sitting room door, turn left, go out the front door, and so on. It was easy to show to the contrary that rats do construct internal maps. They learned a dog-legged route to a box containing food. When the experimenter blocked this route, they were able to choose a direct path to the food box. They couldn't have made this switch if _____. Studies of foraging animals also refute the skeptics: chimpanzees and birds can recover food from various caches in an order that differs from the one in which they were shown the caches.

*dog-legged: 급커브의 **cache: 은닉처

① they didn't know how to use tools
② all they had was a record of responses
③ the temptation of the prey were not intense
④ their sense of direction were not very sensitive
⑤ the structure of the maze were not known to them

141

2020 수능

다음 빈칸에 들어갈 말로 가장 적절한 것은?

The future of our high-tech goods may lie not in the limitations of our minds, but in _____. In previous eras, such as the Iron Age and the Bronze Age, the discovery of new elements brought forth seemingly unending numbers of new inventions. Now the combinations may truly be unending. We are now witnessing a fundamental shift in our resource demands. At no point in human history have we used *more* elements, in *more* combinations, and in increasingly refined amounts. Our ingenuity will soon outpace our material supplies. This situation comes at a defining moment when the world is struggling to reduce its reliance on fossil fuels. Fortunately, rare metals are key ingredients in green technologies such as electric cars, wind turbines, and solar panels. They help to convert free natural resources like the sun and wind into the power that fuels our lives. But without increasing today's limited supplies, we have no chance of developing the alternative green technologies we need to slow climate change.

*ingenuity: 창의력

① our ability to secure the ingredients to produce them
② our effort to make them as eco-friendly as possible
③ the wider distribution of innovative technologies
④ governmental policies not to limit resource supplies
⑤ the constant update and improvement of their functions

142

다음 빈칸에 들어갈 말로 가장 적절한 것은?

In my experience, when a freeloader, a person not as committed as others, comes into a team and can't be rejected because of bureaucratic policy, the other hard-working members of the team immediately and drastically reduce their work level and channel their attention and commitment to other parts of their lives. Why? This is because it's human nature for team members to want to maximize their efforts. Especially as time becomes limited, each of us wants to apply our attention to that which will produce the greatest result. Whether we say it aloud or not, everyone knows that freeloaders leverage our efforts downward, not upward. Thus, the uncomfortable truth is that _____. Smart team leaders and savvy team members appreciate this principle and address motivation issues early, directly, and regularly. To do less may seem easier for team members, but in the long run it could cause the demise of the team.

*leverage: 영향을 주다

① teams will have to tolerate their least committed members
② bosses won't be able to assess each member's performance
③ teams will perform to the level of their least-invested coworker
④ bosses will assign more work to the other hard-working members
⑤ team leaders will let some team members do less work than usual

무관한 문장

| **출제** Trend
- 글의 흐름상 중심 내용과 무관한 문장을 고르는 유형으로 매년 수능에 1문항씩 출제됩니다.
- 짧은 시간 안에 문맥을 정확히 파악하는 능력이 필요한 유형입니다.
- 주제와 관련이 있어 보이지만 실제로는 글의 통일성을 해치는 문장이 삽입되어 제시되는 경향이 있습니다.

| **해결** Point

1. 핵심은 글의 주제를 파악하는 것이다.

문장 하나하나에 지나치게 집중해서 앞뒤 문장과의 관계만을 따지다 보면, 정답을 정확히 찾기 힘들 수 있습니다. 무관한 문장도 글의 핵심어를 포함하여 글의 주제와 연관이 있는 것처럼 보이도록 함정을 만들기 때문입니다. 그러므로 시야를 넓혀서 일단 글의 주제와 요지를 먼저 파악한 다음, 각 문장의 내용을 그와 비교하여 답을 찾아야 합니다.

2. 연결어를 눈여겨보자!

무관한 문장은 글의 전체적인 흐름에서 벗어나는 문장을 의미합니다. 그리고 연결어는 글의 흐름을 분명히 나타내기 위해 사용됩니다. 즉, 글에 쓰인 연결어들을 잘 살펴보면 글의 흐름을 보다 명확히 파악할 수 있고 문맥에 어긋나는 문장도 더 쉽게 찾아낼 수 있습니다.

대표 기출 문제

정답 및 해설 p.059

143

다음 글에서 전체 흐름과 관계 <u>없는</u> 문장은?

2024 수능

Speaking fast is a high-risk proposition. It's nearly impossible to maintain the ideal conditions to be persuasive, well-spoken, and effective when the mouth is traveling well over the speed limit. ① Although we'd like to think that our minds are sharp enough to always make good decisions with the greatest efficiency, they just aren't. ② In reality, the brain arrives at an intersection of four or five possible things to say and sits idling for a couple of seconds, considering the options. ③ Making a good decision helps you speak faster because it provides you with more time to come up with your responses. ④ When the brain stops sending navigational instructions back to the mouth and the mouth is moving too fast to pause, that's when you get a verbal fender bender, otherwise known as filler. ⑤ *Um, ah, you know*, and *like* are what your mouth does when it has nowhere to go.

(STEP 1) **글의 도입부에 주목하면서 글의 요지를 추론하기**

첫 문장과 두 번째 문장에서 글의 요지를 추론한다. 즉, 빨리 말하는 것은 의사를 효과적으로 표현하는 방법이 아니라는 (Speaking fast is a high-risk proposition) 것이 요지임을 파악할 수 있다.

(STEP 2) **글의 요지와의 연관성에 주목하면서 글의 흐름에서 벗어난 문장 찾기**

문장① → 정신이 항상 최고의 효율로 좋은 결정을 내릴 수 있다고 생각하지만 그렇지 않다는 내용이므로 빨리 말하는 것의 단점과 관련이 있음.

문장② → 뇌는 말할 가능성이 있는 여러 가지의 것들이 있을 때 머뭇거린다는 내용이므로 글의 요지와 관련이 있음.

문장③ → 좋은 결정을 내리면 응답을 생각해 낼 시간이 더 많아지기 때문에 더 빨리 말할 수 있다는 내용이므로 빨리 말하는 것의 단점과는 무관함.

문장④ → 입이 너무 빨리 움직여 멈출 수 없을 때, 가벼운 언어적 장애를 겪는다는 내용이므로 글의 요지와 관련이 있음.

문장⑤ → '음, 아, 알다시피, 그러니까'라는 말은 빨리 말하는 것이 초래하는 언어적 위험 부담에 대한 것으로 ④의 내용을 보완하므로 글의 요지와 관련이 있음.

(STEP 3) **글의 흐름을 살피면서 무관한 문장을 제외하고 나머지 문장 간의 흐름이 자연스러운지 확인하기**

'좋은 결정을 내리는 것은 응답을 생각해 낼 시간이 더 많아지기 때문에 여러분이 더 빨리 말하는 데 도움이 된다'라는 ③의 내용은 빨리 말하는 것의 단점을 언급하고 있는 다른 문장의 내용과는 관계가 없다. 문장③을 빼고 다시 읽어 보면 글의 요지와 일치하는 자연스러운 흐름의 글이 된다.

✓ 중요 구문　　[4행] In reality, the brain **arrives** at an intersection of four or five possible things [to say] and
　　　　　　　　　　　　주어　　　동사1
sits idling for a couple of seconds, [**considering** the options].
동사2　　　　　　　　　　　　　　　　　　분사구문

: 주어는 the brain이고 동사는 arrives와 sits로 두 개의 동사가 병렬구조를 이루고 있다. 첫 번째 [ ]는 앞에 나온 명사구 four or five possible things를 수식하는 to부정사이고, 두 번째 [ ]는 앞 절의 주어 the brain을 의미상의 주어로 하는 분사구문이다.

✓ 어휘 풀이　　• proposition　*n* 일, 문제　　• persuasive　*a* 설득력이 있는　　• efficiency　*n* 효율성
　　　　　　　　• intersection　*n* 교차점　　• idle　*v* 빈둥거리다　　• come up with　~을 생각해 내다
　　　　　　　　• navigational　*a* 항해의　　• instruction　*n* 지시　　• fender bender　가벼운 접촉 사고
　　　　　　　　• filler　*n* (중요하지는 않고, 시간·공간 등을) 채우기 위한 것

144

다음 글에서 전체 흐름과 관계 <u>없는</u> 문장은?

Actors, singers, politicians and countless others recognise the power of the human voice as a means of communication beyond the simple decoding of the words that are used. Learning to control your voice and use it for different purposes is, therefore, one of the most important skills to develop as an early career teacher. ① The more confidently you give instructions, the higher the chance of a positive class response. ② There are times when being able to project your voice loudly will be very useful when working in school, and knowing that you can cut through a noisy classroom, dinner hall or playground is a great skill to have. ③ In order to address serious noise issues in school, students, parents and teachers should search for a solution together. ④ However, I would always advise that you use your loudest voice incredibly sparingly and avoid shouting as much as possible. ⑤ A quiet, authoritative and measured tone has so much more impact than slightly panicked shouting.

145

다음 글에서 전체 흐름과 관계 <u>없는</u> 문장은?

Since their introduction, information systems have substantially changed the way business is conducted. ① This is particularly true for business in the shape and form of cooperation between firms that involves an integration of value chains across multiple units. ② The resulting networks do not only cover the business units of a single firm but typically also include multiple units from different firms. ③ As a consequence, firms do not only need to consider their internal organization in order to ensure sustainable business performance; they also need to take into account the entire ecosystem of units surrounding them. ④ Many major companies are fundamentally changing their business models by focusing on profitable units and cutting off less profitable ones. ⑤ In order to allow these different units to cooperate successfully, the existence of a common platform is crucial.

146

다음 글에서 전체 흐름과 관계 없는 문장은?

Applying context comes naturally to humans. ① It's one way our brains handle so much data without having to consciously figure things out constantly. ② Our brain does the work in the background without any noticeable effort, nearly as effortlessly as breathing. ③ A strong chess player knows in a glance that a certain type of move is good in a certain type of position and you know you will enjoy a pastry that looks a particular way. ④ Whether you play chess in person or online, you are able to improve a number of your social skills in the process, including communication, sportsmanship, and collaboration. ⑤ Of course, these background intuition processes are sometimes wrong, leaving you with a lost position or a second-rate snack, and as a result your conscious mind will probably assert itself a little more next time you are in that situation and second-guess your intuition.

147

다음 글에서 전체 흐름과 관계 없는 문장은?

The more abundant goods become and the more removed they are from basic physical and social needs, the more open we are to appeals which are psychologically grounded. Although the goods on display in shops and supermarkets do not usually relate to our urgent needs, we nonetheless desire them. ① Advertising's central function is to create desires that previously did not exist. ② The experience of the advanced nations shows that advertising is greatly responsible for raising the living standards of the people. ③ Thus advertising arouses our interests and emotions in favour of goods and more goods, and thereby actually creates the desires it seeks to satisfy. ④ Our desires are aroused and shaped by the demands of the system of production, not by the needs of society or of the individual. ⑤ It is thus the advertiser's task to try to persuade rather than inform.

148

다음 글에서 전체 흐름과 관계 없는 문장은?

For the vast majority of children between the ages of thirteen and twenty, male or female, peer approval is enormously important. ① The reason for this does not lie as much in the desire for friendships in themselves as it does in the desire to be an accepted member of a group. ② Caught in an awkward transition period between childhood and adulthood, teenagers are psychologically insecure as individuals — much more so than during the so-called latency period that extends roughly from age six to age twelve. ③ Membership in a specific group of peers brings with it a precious feeling of being worthy as a person, having social power, and belonging somewhere in the world outside the family. ④ Although the major physical developmental milestones of adolescence happen to everyone, some adolescents exhibit physical signs of maturity sooner than their peers, and others exhibit them later. ⑤ In fact, being popular is such a major issue for teenagers in general that it's often a sign of emotional problems if an individual teenager is not a fiercely involved member of a particular group of peers.

*latency period: 잠재연령기(정신분석 이론에서 6세에서 12세 사이의 발달 단계)

149

다음 글에서 전체 흐름과 관계 없는 문장은?

The marvellous telephone and television network that enmeshed the whole world, making all human beings neighbours, cannot be extended into space. *It will never be possible to converse with anyone on another planet.* Do not misunderstand this statement. ① Even with today's radio equipment, the problem of sending speech to the other planets is almost trivial. ② But the messages will take minutes — sometimes hours — on their journey, because radio and light waves travel at the same limited speed of 186,000 miles a second. ③ Twenty years from now you will be able to listen to a friend on Mars, but the words you hear will have left his mouth at least three minutes earlier, and your reply will take a corresponding time to reach him. ④ Any spacecraft that could be built with today's technology would take six to nine months to reach Mars. ⑤ In such circumstances, an exchange of verbal messages is possible — but not a conversation.

*enmesh: 하나로 묶다, 얽어 넣다

150

다음 글에서 전체 흐름과 관계 <u>없는</u> 문장은?

If you are sincere, focused, and willing to give back something extra as you search for a mentor, you'll find that most people are kind enough to be willing to help you reach your goals. ① If you fear taking the first step toward seeking a mentor, remember that mentoring is a two-way street. ② In asking for help, you must be willing to give back to your mentor at every opportunity, both in the appreciation you express and in the information, contacts, or assistance you can provide as you grow in your career. ③ Don't forget that in a two-way mentor relationship, your own achievements can help validate your mentor's success, and you can provide your mentor with valuable insights into a different age group. ④ The mentor may be older or younger than the person being mentored, but he or she must have a certain area of expertise. ⑤ So please don't be stopped by thinking, "she's far too busy and important to talk to me."

151

다음 글에서 전체 흐름과 관계 <u>없는</u> 문장은?

Musical gifts are multiple and not always found together in the same person. There is often a wide discrepancy between musical interest and musical talent. ① Many of those to whom music is immensely important struggle for years to express themselves as composers or executants in vain. ② Others who are auditorily gifted, as shown by musical aptitude tests, are not necessarily very interested in music. ③ This discrepancy between interest and talent is more often encountered in music than in other subjects. ④ Music is believed to be a powerful instrument of education which could alter the characters of those who studied it, inclining them toward inner order and harmony. ⑤ For example, those who are not mathematically gifted seldom long to be mathematicians; but musical enthusiasts often confess that their lack of musical talent is their greatest disappointment.

*executant: 연주자

출제 Trend
- 주어진 글 다음에 올 (A), (B), (C) 세 개의 글을 논리적인 순서로 배열하는 유형으로 매년 수능에 2문항씩 출제됩니다.
- 글의 선후 관계를 논리적으로 판단하는 사고 능력이 필요한 유형으로, 정답률이 낮은 편입니다.

해결 Point

1. 연결어가 힌트이다.

연결어에 문제 해결의 힌트가 숨어 있는데, 특히 지금까지의 흐름과 반대되는 내용이 올 것을 예고하는 However, Nevertheless 같은 연결어는 아주 중요한 힌트입니다. 따라서 (A), (B), (C) 각 글의 첫 문장과 마지막 문장에 연결어가 있는지 확인하고, 이러한 연결어를 바탕으로 앞뒤에 올 내용을 짐작합니다.

2. 정관사와 지시어에 주목하자.

영어에서는 한 번 언급한 대상에 정관사 the를 붙이므로 the가 붙은 명사가 있다면, 앞에 그 명사가 처음 등장하는 글이 와야 한다는 뜻입니다. 비슷한 맥락으로, 이미 앞에서 설명하거나 언급한 대상은 that 또는 this와 같은 지시어로 받아 서술하는 경우가 많습니다. 이렇듯 인칭대명사나 지시대명사 같은 지칭 표현은 글의 순서를 정하는 데 중요한 단서가 됩니다.

대표 기출 문제

정답 및 해설 p.062

152 주어진 글 다음에 이어질 글의 순서로 가장 적절한 것은?

2024 수능

Norms emerge in groups as a result of people conforming to the behavior of others. Thus, the start of a norm occurs when one person acts in a particular manner in a particular situation because she thinks she ought to.

(A) Thus, she may prescribe the behavior to them by uttering the norm statement in a prescriptive manner. Alternately, she may communicate that conformity is desired in other ways, such as by gesturing. In addition, she may threaten to sanction them for not behaving as she wishes. This will cause some to conform to her wishes and act as she acts.

(B) But some others will not need to have the behavior prescribed to them. They will observe the regularity of behavior and decide on their own that they ought to conform. They may do so for either rational or moral reasons.

(C) Others may then conform to this behavior for a number of reasons. The person who performed the initial action may think that others ought to behave as she behaves in situations of this sort.

*sanction: 제재를 가하다

① (A) — (C) — (B) ② (B) — (A) — (C) ③ (B) — (C) — (A)
④ (C) — (A) — (B) ⑤ (C) — (B) — (A)

STEP 1 주어진 글을 통해 글의 소재, 주제, 전개 방향 등 예측하기

Norms emerge in groups as a result of people conforming to the behavior of others. / the start of a norm occurs when one person acts in a particular manner in a particular situation
(규범은 다른 사람들의 행동에 순응하는 결과로 집단 내에 생겨남, 한 사람이 특정 상황에서, 특정 방식으로 행동할 때 규범이 발생함)
→ 핵심 소재: 집단과 규범
→ 전개 방향 예측: 규범이 생기는 원인으로 특정한 방식의 행동에 순응하는 것에 대해 말하고 있으므로 '순응과 규범의 발생과의 관계'를 다룬 글임을 예측할 수 있음

STEP 2 단서를 통해 이어질 단락 찾기 → 연결어, 반복 어구 파악 / 지시어, 대명사 등이 가리키는 것 파악

• **(A)**: Thus가 있으므로 어떤 내용 다음에 이어지는 결과임을 알 수 있고, she와 them이 누구인지 파악해야 한다. (A)에서는 어떤 사람이 다른 사람에게 규범 진술, 몸짓, 또는 제재를 가하겠다고 겁을 주면서 자신이 원하는 대로 행동하기, 즉 '순응을 요구하는 것'에 대해 말하고 있다.

• **(B)**: But으로 시작하고 있으므로 앞의 내용과 반대되는 내용이 전개된다. some others는 (C)에 나온 Others 다음에 이어질 것을 추론할 수 있다. (B)에서는 행동이 지시되게 할 필요가 없는 사람, 즉 행동의 순응 여부를 '스스로 결정하는 사람'에 대해 언급했다.

• **(C)**: this behavior가 어떤 행동을 가리키는지 파악해야 하고, 최초의 순응하는 행동을 하는 사람을 she로 지칭했다. she가 자신이 행동하는 것처럼 다른 사람이(others) 행동해야 한다고 생각한다는 내용이 어디에 이어질지 파악해야 한다.

STEP 3 세 단락의 내용을 요약하여 자연스러운 글의 순서 구성하기 → 파악한 단서 활용하여 전후 관계 찾기

• **(A)**: she는 (C)에 나온 최초의 행동을 하는 사람을 가리키고, them도 (C)에서 언급한 others를 가리킨다. 접속사 Thus로 보아 (A)는 (C)에 대한 결과이며, she가 여러 가지 방법으로 순응에 대한 요망을 전달하는(communicate that conformity is desired in other ways) 것을 언급했다. → (A)는 (C) 다음에 온다.

• **(B)**: (A)에서 다른 사람들이 she가 요망하는 대로 행동하는 것과는 달리 순응할지 여부를 스스로 결정하는 것(decide on their own that they ought to conform)에 대해 말하고 있다. → (B)는 (A) 다음에 온다.

• **(C)**: this behavior는 주어진 글의 acts in a particular manner를 가리키며, 최초의 순응을 하는 사람(The person who performed the initial action)은 주어진 글 다음에 와야 한다. → 적절한 글의 순서는 (C) - (A) - (B)이다.

✔ 중요 구문

~해야 한다 ←┐
11행 [The person {**who** performed the initial action}] may think [**that** others ought to behave
　　　　　주어　↑──┘ 주격 관계대명사　　　　　　　　　동사　목적절을 이끄는 접속사
{**as** she behaves in situations of this sort}].
접속사(~처럼)

: 첫 번째 [ ]가 주어이고 그 안의 { }는 The person을 수식하는 관계절이다. 두 번째 [ ]는 think의 목적어로 쓰인 명사절이다.

✔ 어휘 풀이

• **norm** _n_ 규범
• **prescribe** _v_ 지시하다, 규정하다
• **alternately** _ad_ 다른 방식으로, 번갈아, 교대로
• **threaten** _v_ 겁을 주다, 위협하다
• **moral** _a_ 도덕적인

• **emerge** _v_ 생겨나다, 나타나다
• **utter** _v_ 말하다, 소리를 내다
• **regularity** _n_ 규칙성
• **initial** _a_ 최초의, 초기의

• **conform to** ~에 순응하다, ~을 따르다
• **statement** _n_ 진술, 성명
• **conformity** _n_ 순응, 따름, 일치
• **rational** _a_ 이성적인, 합리적인

153

2023 수능

주어진 글 다음에 이어질 글의 순서로 가장 적절한 것은?

> A fascinating species of water flea exhibits a kind of flexibility that evolutionary biologists call *adaptive plasticity*.

(A) That's a clever trick, because producing spines and a helmet is costly, in terms of energy, and conserving energy is essential for an organism's ability to survive and reproduce. The water flea only expends the energy needed to produce spines and a helmet when it needs to.

(B) If the baby water flea is developing into an adult in water that includes the chemical signatures of creatures that prey on water fleas, it develops a helmet and spines to defend itself against predators. If the water around it doesn't include the chemical signatures of predators, the water flea doesn't develop these protective devices.

(C) So it may well be that this plasticity is an adaptation: a trait that came to exist in a species because it contributed to reproductive fitness. There are many cases, across many species, of adaptive plasticity. Plasticity is conducive to fitness if there is sufficient variation in the environment.

*spine: 가시 돌기 **conducive: 도움되는

① (A) — (C) — (B) ② (B) — (A) — (C)
③ (B) — (C) — (A) ④ (C) — (A) — (B)
⑤ (C) — (B) — (A)

154

2022 수능

주어진 글 다음에 이어질 글의 순서로 가장 적절한 것은?

> According to the market response model, it is increasing prices that drive providers to search for new sources, innovators to substitute, consumers to conserve, and alternatives to emerge.

(A) Many examples of such "green taxes" exist. Facing landfill costs, labor expenses, and related costs in the provision of garbage disposal, for example, some cities have required households to dispose of all waste in special trash bags, purchased by consumers themselves, and often costing a dollar or more each.

(B) Taxing certain goods or services, and so increasing prices, should result in either decreased use of these resources or creative innovation of new sources or options. The money raised through the tax can be used directly by the government either to supply services or to search for alternatives.

(C) The results have been greatly increased recycling and more careful attention by consumers to packaging and waste. By internalizing the costs of trash to consumers, there has been an observed decrease in the flow of garbage from households.

① (A) — (C) — (B) ② (B) — (A) — (C)
③ (B) — (C) — (A) ④ (C) — (A) — (B)
⑤ (C) — (B) — (A)

155

주어진 글 다음에 이어질 글의 순서로 가장 적절한 것은?

One of the most profound transitions in the history of life was the evolution of multicellular eukaryotes.

(A) This gave way to a key trait of more advanced multicellular organisms: division of labour. Over time, cells became structurally and functionally distinct. For example, some cells may have specialized in harvesting energy, whereas others developed a role related to the motility of the organism.

(B) Perhaps a group of individual cells of a particular species came together to form a colony, or a single cell divided and the resulting two cells did not separate. In the simplest of multicellular organisms, all cells are structurally and functionally autonomous (independent).

(C) Clear evidence of multicellularity, in the form of species of algae, appears in the fossil record starting about 1.2 billion years ago. The actual events that led to the development of multicellularity are a mystery but it is easy to envision how it may have occurred.

*eukaryote: 진핵생물 **motility: 운동성

① (A) — (C) — (B)　　② (B) — (A) — (C)
③ (B) — (C) — (A)　　④ (C) — (A) — (B)
⑤ (C) — (B) — (A)

156

주어진 글 다음에 이어질 글의 순서로 가장 적절한 것은?

Direct rebound effects relate to individual energy services, such as heating, lighting and refrigeration and are confined to the energy required to provide that service.

(A) But any increase in energy service consumption will reduce the 'energy savings' achieved by the energy-efficiency improvement. In some circumstances it could offset those savings altogether.

(B) Similarly, consumers may choose to heat their homes for longer periods and/or to a higher temperature following the installation of attic insulation, because the operating cost per square meter has fallen. The extent to which this occurs may be expected to vary widely from one energy service to another, from one circumstance to another and from one time period to another.

(C) Since improved energy efficiency will reduce the marginal cost of supplying the relevant service it could lead to an increase in the consumption of that service. For example, consumers may choose to drive further and/or more often following the purchase of a fuel-efficient car because the operating cost per kilometer has fallen.

① (A) — (C) — (B)　　② (B) — (A) — (C)
③ (B) — (C) — (A)　　④ (C) — (A) — (B)
⑤ (C) — (B) — (A)

157

주어진 글 다음에 이어질 글의 순서로 가장 적절한 것은?

> The more we investigate what our ancestors ate, the more we find out about what is healthy for us.

(A) Potassium is found in fruits and vegetables too often lacking in the American diet. By going back to nature, we're able to solve many problems that have been created over thousands of years. We've been doing some things wrong for so many years we have forgotten the correct course to follow.

(B) Salt was not readily available during the Stone Age. Excess salt in our diet may raise blood pressure, while ingesting higher dietary levels of potassium will lower blood pressure. Guess what?

(C) For example, we now realize that sooner or later around 90 percent of Americans will develop high blood pressure. Causes of high blood pressure include excessive weight, a lack of physical activity, kidney disease, and excess intake of salt from processed foods or overuse at mealtime.

*potassium: 칼륨

① (A) — (C) — (B) ② (B) — (A) — (C)
③ (B) — (C) — (A) ④ (C) — (A) — (B)
⑤ (C) — (B) — (A)

158

주어진 글 다음에 이어질 글의 순서로 가장 적절한 것은?

> We humans have long held that a person's eyes are the "windows to the soul," and we tend to give meaning to how a person maintains — or avoids — eye contact during conversation. It is here that the "reading" can get a little tricky.

(A) On the contrary, deceivers may actually be consciously forcing themselves to maintain eye contact to convince you that they are truthful and interested. Or they may even be trying in some way to manipulate you with their steady, unwavering gaze.

(B) Some people aren't inclined to make heavy eye contact, and tend to look away frequently. This doesn't necessarily support conventional wisdom, which says that such people are usually deceitful.

(C) They may simply be shy. On the other hand, just because someone looks unceasingly into your eyes when he or she speaks doesn't mean this person is necessarily a model of integrity.

① (A) — (C) — (B) ② (B) — (A) — (C)
③ (B) — (C) — (A) ④ (C) — (A) — (B)
⑤ (C) — (B) — (A)

159

주어진 글 다음에 이어질 글의 순서로 가장 적절한 것은?

> In most cases similarity trumps dissimilarity when it comes to attraction. People generally associate with similar others, and they are repulsed by those who are dissimilar to them.

(A) Instead, he will respond more positively to those who accept his guidance. Similarly, individuals who are forming a group may realize that the members' skills and abilities must complement each other if the group is to be successful. These cases suggest that people are attracted to those who possess characteristics that complement their own personal characteristics.

(B) If, however, people's qualities complement each other — they are dissimilar but they fit well together — then this unique form of dissimilarity may encourage people to associate with one another. If, for example, Claude enjoys leading groups, he will not be attracted to other individuals who also strive to take control of the group.

(C) In one-on-one relations, people are sometimes attracted to individuals who have very desirable personal qualities, but when evaluating groups people base their preferences on the degree of similarity between the group and themselves.

① (A) — (C) — (B)   ② (B) — (A) — (C)
③ (B) — (C) — (A)   ④ (C) — (A) — (B)
⑤ (C) — (B) — (A)

160

주어진 글 다음에 이어질 글의 순서로 가장 적절한 것은?

> Our genus Homo has been evolving for a couple million years. Brain evolution happens over many thousands or millions of years, but we've lived in civilized society for less than 1 percent of that time.

(A) Among humans and many other animals, voice seems to play a role in meeting one of those demands — choosing a mate. One way we can understand the importance of voice is to examine which aspect of it is most highly valued by one sex when evaluating the other sex.

(B) For example, women may disagree on whether they prefer dark-skinned men with beards, or clean-shaven blonds, or men of any appearance sitting in the driver's seat of a sports car — but when asked to rate men they can hear but not see, women miraculously tend to agree: men with deeper voices are more attractive.

(C) That means that though we may pack our heads full of 21st century knowledge, the organ inside our skull is still a Stone-Age brain. We think of ourselves as a civilized species, but our brains are designed to meet the challenges of an earlier era.

① (A) — (C) — (B)   ② (B) — (A) — (C)
③ (B) — (C) — (A)   ④ (C) — (A) — (B)
⑤ (C) — (B) — (A)

161

주어진 글 다음에 이어질 글의 순서로 가장 적절한 것은?

> The brain is often thought of as an input/output system, processing information from the outside to generate an appropriate behavioral response, and most brain-scanning studies examine which areas become active, or 'light up', during a particular action or perception.

(A) This 'baseline' activity is continuously running in the background, changing very little regardless of what we are doing. This is the brain's 'default mode', a network of brain regions that comes online when the brain is awake but resting.

(B) However, what's particularly intriguing is its metabolic activity. The brain is a hungry organ that consumes about 20 percent of the body's energy, despite accounting for just 2 percent of its mass.

(C) Yet its metabolic activity changes very little when it is actively engaged in performing a task. In other words, the brain remains active when we are doing nothing at all, and has an intrinsic pattern of activity that uses up most of its energy.

① (A) — (C) — (B) ② (B) — (A) — (C)
③ (B) — (C) — (A) ④ (C) — (A) — (B)
⑤ (C) — (B) — (A)

162

주어진 글 다음에 이어질 글의 순서로 가장 적절한 것은?

> In some studies, a mother straps her months-old infant into a car seat and interacts with her baby normally for a moment or two. Then she looks away, but after a few minutes she turns back toward the infant with an expressionless face.

(A) This is disconcerting for the baby, who attempts to engage her, usually first by smiling. When this fails and the mother maintains her stony expression as instructed, the baby escalates his attempts to bring her to life, crying imploringly.

(B) This is emotion-focused coping as the baby realizes that, without help from the mother, all he can do is soothe himself. The baby appears to give up looking for help or solutions on the outside, but he escapes on the inside in an attempt to save himself.

(C) When he smiles and then cries, the baby is using problem-focused coping as he tries to compel his mother to change her indifferent behavior toward him. When this is not successful, the baby switches strategies, looking away and withdrawing into himself, sucking on fingers or arms or toes.

*disconcerting: 당황하게 하는 **imploringly: 애원하듯이

① (A) — (B) — (C) ② (A) — (C) — (B)
③ (B) — (C) — (A) ④ (C) — (A) — (B)
⑤ (C) — (B) — (A)

163

주어진 글 다음에 이어질 글의 순서로 가장 적절한 것은?

Politics was instrumental in the history of port and continued to play an important role throughout the wine's development. In 1678, Britain declared war on France and blocked all its ports, creating an immediate wine shortage.

(A) Wine was shipped down the Douro River for export to England. However, these wines did not travel well, so brandy was added to stop the fermentation process and act as a stabilizer for shipment back to England. This created a sweet, fruity, and strong wine and was the birth of port.

(B) As Portugal and England had a close trading partnership since the fourteenth century, the British logically looked to Portugal to provide the wine they could no longer get from France.

(C) But they soon realized that Portuguese wines were not of the same quality as the French, and they would need to oversee its production to ensure the quality to which they had become accustomed. The Douro Valley, it was found, had the ideal climate to produce grapes of a more intense flavor and deep color, so desired in a quality wine.

*port: 포트와인(단맛이 나는 포르투갈산 적포도주)

① (A) ― (C) ― (B) 　② (B) ― (A) ― (C)
③ (B) ― (C) ― (A) 　④ (C) ― (A) ― (B)
⑤ (C) ― (B) ― (A)

164

주어진 글 다음에 이어질 글의 순서로 가장 적절한 것은?

Most economists view themselves as scientists seeking the truth about the way people behave. They make speculations about economic behavior, and then, ideally, they assess the validity of those predictions based on human experience.

(A) For example, the following is a positive statement: If rent controls are imposed, vacancy rates will fall. This statement is testable. A positive statement does not have to be a true statement, but it does have to be a testable statement.

(B) This objective, value-free approach, based on the scientific method, is called positive analysis. In positive analysis, we want to know the impact of variable *A* on variable *B*. We want to be able to test a hypothesis.

(C) Their work emphasizes how people *do* behave, rather than how people *should* behave. In the role of scientist, an economist tries to observe patterns of behavior objectively, without reference to the appropriateness or inappropriateness of that behavior.

*positive: 실증적인(경험상으로 판단할 수 있는)

① (A) ― (C) ― (B) 　② (B) ― (A) ― (C)
③ (B) ― (C) ― (A) 　④ (C) ― (A) ― (B)
⑤ (C) ― (B) ― (A)

165

2020 수능

주어진 글 다음에 이어질 글의 순서로 가장 적절한 것은?

> Movies may be said to support the dominant culture and to serve as a means for its reproduction over time.

(A) The bad guys are usually punished; the romantic couple almost always find each other despite the obstacles and difficulties they encounter on the path to true love; and the way we wish the world to be is how, in the movies, it more often than not winds up being. No doubt it is this utopian aspect of movies that accounts for why we enjoy them so much.

(B) The simple answer to this question is that movies do more than present two-hour civics lessons or editorials on responsible behavior. They also tell stories that, in the end, we find satisfying.

(C) But one may ask why audiences would find such movies enjoyable if all they do is give cultural directives and prescriptions for proper living. Most of us would likely grow tired of such didactic movies and would probably come to see them as propaganda, similar to the cultural artwork that was common in the Soviet Union and other autocratic societies.

*didactic: 교훈적인 **autocratic: 독재적인

① (A) ― (C) ― (B)　　② (B) ― (A) ― (C)
③ (B) ― (C) ― (A)　　④ (C) ― (A) ― (B)
⑤ (C) ― (B) ― (A)

166

주어진 글 다음에 이어질 글의 순서로 가장 적절한 것은?

> Suppose you're sitting in some public place and notice someone looking at you. If you return the gaze and the other person smiles, you'll probably feel good about the exchange. But if the other person continues to stare without any hint of a smile, you'll probably feel uncomfortable.

(A) As a result, if, say, a submissive monkey wants to check out a dominant one, it will bare its teeth as a peace signal. In monkey talk, bared teeth means "Pardon my stare. True, I'm looking, but I don't plan to attack, so please don't attack me first."

(B) In trading the currency of smiles, we are sharing a feeling experienced by many of our primate cousins. In the societies of nonhuman primates, a direct stare is an aggressive signal. It often precedes an attack — and, therefore, can cause one.

(C) In chimpanzees, the smile can also go the other way — a dominant individual may smile at a submissive one, saying, analogously, "Don't worry, I'm not going to attack you." So when you pass a stranger in the corridor and that person flashes a brief smile, you're experiencing an exchange with roots deep in our primate heritage.

① (A) ― (C) ― (B)　　② (B) ― (A) ― (C)
③ (B) ― (C) ― (A)　　④ (C) ― (A) ― (B)
⑤ (C) ― (B) ― (A)

167

주어진 글 다음에 이어질 글의 순서로 가장 적절한 것은?

Descartes made a very significant contribution to the understanding of behavior when he formulated the concept of the reflex. The basic idea that behavior can reflect a triggering stimulus remains an important building block of behavior theory.

(A) He thought that nerves were hollow tubes, and neural transmission involved the movement of gases called animal spirits. The animal spirits, released by the pineal gland, were assumed to flow through the neural tubes and enter the muscles, causing them to swell and create movement.

(B) However, Descartes was mistaken in his beliefs about the details of reflex action. He believed that sensory messages going from sense organs to the brain and motor messages going from the brain to the muscles traveled along the same nerves.

(C) In addition, Descartes considered all reflexive movements to be innate and to be fixed by the anatomy of the nervous system. Over the course of several hundred years since Descartes passed away, all of these ideas about reflexes have been proven wrong.

*pineal gland: 송과선(솔방울 모양의 내분비 기관)

① (A) — (C) — (B) ② (B) — (A) — (C)
③ (B) — (C) — (A) ④ (C) — (A) — (B)
⑤ (C) — (B) — (A)

168

주어진 글 다음에 이어질 글의 순서로 가장 적절한 것은?

Social loafing refers to a decline in motivation and effort found when people combine their efforts to produce a group product. People tend to generate less output or to contribute less effort when working on a task collectively where contributions are combined than when working individually.

(A) This is also similar to the *sucker effect*, whereby people withhold their contributions to a group to avoid being the victim of the social loafing or free riding efforts of other group members.

(B) However, the *free rider effect* and the *sucker effect* are narrower terms that refer to specific causes of social loafing. Social loafing is a broader construct that refers to any reduction in motivation and effort that occurs when contributions are pooled compared with when they are not pooled.

(C) The consequence is that people are less productive when working as part of a group than when working individually. Social loafing is similar to the *free rider effect*, whereby people contribute less to a collective effort when they perceive their contributions are dispensable.

*social loafing: 사회적 태만 **sucker effect: 편승 효과

① (A) — (C) — (B) ② (B) — (A) — (C)
③ (B) — (C) — (A) ④ (C) — (A) — (B)
⑤ (C) — (B) — (A)

│ 출제 Trend
- 지문에서 주어진 문장이 들어갈 위치를 찾는 유형으로 매년 수능에 2문항씩 출제됩니다.
- 글을 논리정연하게 완성할 수 있는 사고 능력이 필요한 유형으로, 정답률이 낮은 편입니다.

│ 해결 Point

1. 지문의 논리적 전개 구조를 파악한다.

특정한 주장에 대한 예시 또는 근거를 제시하는 등 영어 지문에는 이야기를 전개하는 다양한 구조들이 존재하므로 출제된 지문이 어떤 구조에 해당하는지를 파악하는 것이 우선입니다. 그리고 주장을 뒷받침하는 데에 있어서 어떤 논리적 비약이나 공백은 없는지 파악하고, 있다면 그 부분에 주어진 문장이 위치해야 합니다.

2. 제시어 힌트를 사용한다.

문장에 쓰인 연결어와 지시어가 힌트가 될 수 있습니다. 예를 들어, this와 같은 지시대명사가 등장했는데 그것이 가리키는 대상이 앞에 나오지 않았다면, 그 부분 앞이 주어진 문장의 위치가 됩니다. 또, 연결어는 글의 논리적인 구조를 명시적으로 드러내기 때문에 주어진 문장의 위치를 파악하는 데 도움을 줍니다. 예를 들어, therefore라는 연결어 다음에는 어떤 원인에 대한 결과가 제시되어야 하는데, 그것이 빠져 있으면 그곳에 주어진 문장이 들어가야 합니다.

대표 기출 문제

정답 및 해설 p.068

169 글의 흐름으로 보아, 주어진 문장이 들어가기에 가장 적절한 곳은?   2024 수능

> Yes, some contests are seen as world class, such as identification of the Higgs particle or the development of high temperature superconductors.

Science is sometimes described as a winner-take-all contest, meaning that there are no rewards for being second or third. This is an extreme view of the nature of scientific contests. (①) Even those who describe scientific contests in such a way note that it is a somewhat inaccurate description, given that replication and verification have social value and are common in science. (②) It is also inaccurate to the extent that it suggests that only a handful of contests exist. (③) But many other contests have multiple parts, and the number of such contests may be increasing. (④) By way of example, for many years it was thought that there would be "one" cure for cancer, but it is now realized that cancer takes multiple forms and that multiple approaches are needed to provide a cure. (⑤) There won't be one winner — there will be many.

*replication: 반복   **verification: 입증

STEP 1 주어진 문장의 의미와 중심 소재 파악하기

Yes, some contests are seen as world class, such as identification of the Higgs particle or the development of high temperature superconductors.

(물론, 힉스 입자의 확인 또는 고온 초전도체 개발과 같은 몇몇 대회는 세계적인 수준으로 여겨진다.)

→ 힉스 입자의 확인 또는 고온 초전도체 개발과 같은 대회에 관한 내용으로, 이 글이 과학 대회에 관한 글임을 대략적으로 파악한다.

STEP 2 연결사나 대명사를 살펴 글의 흐름에 논리적 비약이 일어나는 곳 찾기

앞 부분: 과학은 때때로 승자독식 대회로 묘사되는데, 이는 2등이나 3등인 것에 대한 보상이 없다는 뜻이다. 이는 과학 대회의 본질에 대한 극단적인 견해이다.

① 과학 대회를 그렇게(in such a way) 설명하는 사람들조차도 그것이 다소 부정확한 설명이라고 말하는데, 반복과 입증이 사회적 가치를 지니고 있으며 과학에서는 일반적이라는 것을 감안할 때 그렇다. → 앞의 내용을 지칭함

② 또한(also) 그것은(It) 단지 소수의 대회만 존재한다는 것을 보여 줄 경우에 부정확하다. → 앞의 내용에 부가적인 설명이 제시됨

③ 하지만 다른 많은 대회에는(many other contests) 다양한 부분이 있고, 그런 대회의 수는 증가하고 있을 것이다.
→ 앞 문장과 자연스럽게 이어지지 않음. some contests가 포함된 주어진 문장이 ③의 위치에 들어가면, many other contests가 포함된 이 문장과 자연스럽게 연결됨

④ 예를 들어(By way of example), 여러 해 동안 암에 대해 '하나'의 치료법만 있다고 생각되었지만, 암은 여러 가지 형태를 띠고 치료를 제공하기 위해 다양한 접근 방식이 필요하다고 이제 인식된다. → 앞 문장의 내용에 대한 구체적인 예가 제시됨

⑤ 승자는 한 명이 아니라 여러 명이 있을 것이다. → ④와 같은 맥락의 문장임

STEP 3 단절이 있는 곳에 주어진 문장을 넣고 글의 흐름 확인하기

힉스 입자의 확인 또는 고온 초전도체 개발과 같은 몇몇 대회(some contests)는 세계적인 수준으로 여겨진다는 주어진 문장의 내용은 ③ 앞의 소수의 대회만 존재한다는 내용의 예이며, ③ 뒤에 이어지는 문장의 many other contests의 내용과 But으로 연결되므로 ③에 들어가는 것이 가장 적절하다.

✔ 중요 구문

4행 Even those [who describe scientific contests in such a way] note [that it is a somewhat inaccurate description, {given that replication and verification have social value and are common in science}].

주어 / 관계절 / 동사 / 접속사 / note의 목적절
~을 고려하면 / 주어 / 동사1 / 동사2

: 문장의 주어는 those이고, 동사는 note이다. 첫 번째 [ ]는 those를 수식하는 관계절이고, that절인 두 번째 [ ]는 note의 목적어이다. given that ~은 분사구로 '~을 고려하면'의 의미이고, { } 안에서 동사인 have와 are는 병렬구조를 이룬다.

✔ 어휘 풀이
- identification *n* 확인
- inaccurate *a* 부정확한
- superconductor *n* 초전도체
- a handful of 소수의
- winner-take-all *a* 승자독식의
- multiple *a* 다양한

170

2023 수능

글의 흐름으로 보아, 주어진 문장이 들어가기에 가장 적절한 곳은?

> There's a reason for that: traditionally, park designers attempted to create such a feeling by planting tall trees at park boundaries, building stone walls, and constructing other means of partition.

Parks take the shape demanded by the cultural concerns of their time. Once parks are in place, they are no inert stage — their purposes and meanings are made and remade by planners and by park users. Moments of park creation are particularly telling, however, for they reveal and actualize ideas about nature and its relationship to urban society. (①) Indeed, what distinguishes a park from the broader category of public space is the representation of nature that parks are meant to embody. (②) Public spaces include parks, concrete plazas, sidewalks, even indoor atriums. (③) Parks typically have trees, grass, and other plants as their central features. (④) When entering a city park, people often imagine a sharp separation from streets, cars, and buildings. (⑤) What's behind this idea is not only landscape architects' desire to design aesthetically suggestive park spaces, but a much longer history of Western thought that envisions cities and nature as antithetical spaces and oppositional forces.

*aesthetically: 미적으로 **antithetical: 대조적인

171

2022 수능

글의 흐름으로 보아, 주어진 문장이 들어가기에 가장 적절한 곳은?

> As long as the irrealism of the silent black and white film predominated, one could not take filmic fantasies for representations of reality.

Cinema is valuable not for its ability to make visible the hidden outlines of our reality, but for its ability to reveal what reality itself veils — the dimension of fantasy. (①) This is why, to a person, the first great theorists of film decried the introduction of sound and other technical innovations (such as color) that pushed film in the direction of realism. (②) Since cinema was an entirely fantasmatic art, these innovations were completely unnecessary. (③) And what's worse, they could do nothing but turn filmmakers and audiences away from the fantasmatic dimension of cinema, potentially transforming film into a mere delivery device for representations of reality. (④) But sound and color threatened to create just such an illusion, thereby destroying the very essence of film art. (⑤) As Rudolf Arnheim puts it, "The creative power of the artist can only come into play where reality and the medium of representation do not coincide."

*decry: 공공연히 비난하다 **fantasmatic: 환상의

172

글의 흐름으로 보아, 주어진 문장이 들어가기에 가장 적절한 곳은?

> Unfortunately, the Precautionary Principle works better in theory than in practice.

All versions of the Precautionary Principle hold this axiom in common: A technology must be shown to do no harm before it is embraced. It must be proven to be safe before it is disseminated. If it cannot be proven safe, it should be prohibited, restricted, modified, junked, or ignored. In other words, the first response to a new idea should be inaction until its safety is established. When an innovation appears, we should pause. Only after a new technology has been confirmed okay by the certainty of science should we try to live with it. (①) On the surface, this approach seems reasonable and prudent. (②) Harm must be anticipated and preempted. (③) Better safe than sorry. (④) "The precautionary principle is very, very good for one thing — stopping technological progress," says philosopher and consultant Max More. (⑤) Cass R. Sunstein, who devoted a book to debunking the principle, says, "We must challenge the Precautionary Principle not because it leads us in a bad direction, but because it leads in no direction at all."

*axiom: 공리 **disseminate: 전파하다 ***debunk: (실체를) 폭로하다

173

글의 흐름으로 보아, 주어진 문장이 들어가기에 가장 적절한 곳은?

> However, they have little understanding of the causal relationships between inanimate objects.

Causal understanding is unique to humans — the weight of a falling rock clearly 'forces' the log to splinter. How did this ability to have causal beliefs evolve, for animals do not have such beliefs? There are of course cognitive similarities between human and mammalian and especially primate cognition. (①) Primates remember their local environment, take novel detours, follow object movement, recognise similarities and have some insight into problem solving. (②) They also recognise individuals, predict their behaviour, and form alliances. (③) They do not view the world in terms of underlying 'forces' that are fundamental to human thinking and do not understand the world in intentional or causal terms. (④) Non-human primates do not understand the causal relation between their acts and the outcomes they experience. (⑤) Apes, for example, cannot select an appropriate tool for a simple physical manipulation without extensive teaching.

*inanimate: 생명이 없는 **detour: 우회로

174

글의 흐름으로 보아, 주어진 문장이 들어가기에 가장 적절한 곳은?

> Psychological factors, such as preconceived ideas based on appearance or on previous experiences with a similar food, also affect a person's perception of taste.

Not everyone perceives the taste of apple pie the same way. There is considerable genetic variation among individuals in sensitivity to basic tastes. (①) Tasting abilities may also vary within the individual, depending on a number of outside influences. (②) One such factor affecting taste is the temperature of a food or beverage: Taste buds operate best at temperatures of around 30°C. (③) As the temperature of foods or beverages goes below 20°C or above 30°C, it becomes harder to distinguish their tastes accurately. (④) For instance, cherry-flavored foods are expected to be red, but if they are colored yellow, they become difficult to identify as cherry. (⑤) Also, unpleasant experiences associated with a food may influence the perceived taste of that food in the future.

175

글의 흐름으로 보아, 주어진 문장이 들어가기에 가장 적절한 곳은?

> While celebrities are most often cast to sound like themselves, there is a growing market for voice-over artists who can imitate celebrities when the celebrities themselves are too busy or the pay is too small.

A more recent problem for voice-over artists is the use of celebrity voices. Businessmen feel that known celebrity names will bring in an audience, especially to films. (①) Fans may go to see a celebrity's work, even when they can't see the celebrity himself. (②) And a celebrity can give a film publicity by making rounds of the television talk show circuit and talking about the film. (③) Jeff Bridges was chosen for the voice of Big Z in *Surf's Up*, not only for his celebrity name, but also because of this gravelly voice and, because as a surfer himself, he was a close match for the character. (④) Of course, the more celebrity voices are used, the less work there is for professional voice actors. (⑤) So the use of celebrities can, occasionally, actually bring in work, as well as take it away.

*gravelly: (목소리가) 걸걸한

176

글의 흐름으로 보아, 주어진 문장이 들어가기에 가장 적절한 곳은?

A leader might make claims that initially sound absurd and that people generally know are not true.

One very surprising aspect of persuasive communication is that we tend to perceive messages as more true when we have heard them repeatedly. This is known as the validity effect and researchers have shown that it operates separately from actual evidence for a claim. (①) In other words, we perceive a statement that we have heard repeatedly as more true than a statement we have heard less often or not at all — even when no evidence supporting the statement has been offered. (②) When we shop at the supermarket and believe that one brand of soft drink is superior to another, we don't realize that our belief stems from hearing repeated commercials touting that particular brand. (③) The validity effect even plays a role in political propaganda. (④) However, as the leader makes the same claims repeatedly over time, people often increasingly believe that the statements are true. (⑤) Although saying something is true does not make it true, it can make it seem true in people's minds.

*tout: 광고하다, 홍보하다 **propaganda: (정치와 관련된 허위·과장된) 선전

177

글의 흐름으로 보아, 주어진 문장이 들어가기에 가장 적절한 곳은?

In contrast, a mate who provided abundant resources, who protected us and our children, and who devoted time, energy, and effort to our family would be a great asset.

Nowhere do people have an equal desire for all members of the opposite sex. Everywhere some potential mates are preferred, others shunned. (①) Imagine living as our ancestors did long ago. (②) They struggled to keep warm by the fire, hunted meat for our kin, gathered nuts, berries, and herbs, and avoided dangerous animals and hostile humans. (③) If we were to select a mate who failed to deliver the resources promised, who was lazy, who lacked hunting skills, or who heaped physical abuse on us, our survival would be tenuous, our reproduction at risk. (④) As a result of the powerful survival and reproductive advantages reaped by those of our ancestors who chose mates wisely, many specific desires evolved. (⑤) As descendants of those winners in the evolutionary lottery, modern humans have inherited a specific set of mate preferences.

178

글의 흐름으로 보아, 주어진 문장이 들어가기에 가장 적절한 곳은?

> The Victorian government also pursued a "retreat and resettlement" strategy by creating a voluntary buyback program allowing the government to purchase land with an unacceptably high risk of fire.

The severity of the risks posed by more extreme storms, bigger wildfires, and higher sea levels requires that "no more" must truly mean "no more" for some locales: people will have to move out of harm's way. Australia's "no more" moment came when some four hundred bushfires ignited in the state of Victoria on a single Saturday in 2009. (①) The so-called Black Saturday fires destroyed thousands of homes, killed almost two hundred people, and burned over a million acres. (②) In the aftermath of the fires' destruction, Australia fast-tracked new building regulations for bushfire-prone areas. (③) Standards now require a risk assessment for all properties, including those outside wildfires areas, and builders in high-risk areas must obtain a special permit for new construction. (④) But then Australia took it a step further. (⑤) In that moment, Australia prepared proactively for increasing wildfire risk by reconsidering not just "how", but also "where to build".

*ignite: 불이 붙다

179

글의 흐름으로 보아, 주어진 문장이 들어가기에 가장 적절한 곳은?

> However, there is growing evidence that the mind and body are interwoven so deeply that it is impossible to make that separation any longer.

The philosopher Descartes held the notion of duality or separateness of the body and mind. Conventional medicine, which treats only the body with painkilling drugs, perpetuates that concept. (①) They often only treat the symptoms, not the cause. (②) Even pain which originates in the mind clearly affects the body. (③) A kind of pain that demonstrates this blending of mind and body is "phantom limb pain." (④) Phantom limb pain is experienced by people who have had an amputation, but still feel often excruciating sensations in the missing limb. (⑤) It was once supposed that the damaged nerve endings in the stump were the cause of this pain, but this theory is not consistent with the evidence.

*amputation: 절단 **stump: (절단하고) 남은 부분

180

글의 흐름으로 보아, 주어진 문장이 들어가기에 가장 적절한 곳은?

> This is a short-term fix and doesn't work in the long term because the micro-ecosystems of healthy soils are ignored.

Today's Food Industry generates more tons of food per hectare than ever before. But these increased yields come at the expense of quality. Continuous growing of the same crops in the same soils removes the nutrients. (①) In turn, these depleted soils lead to crops with fewer nutrients. (②) Industrial farming tries to correct the soil depletion by fertilizing with micro-nutrients. (③) The USDA (United States Department of Agriculture) studied 43 crops that it consistently tracked since the 1950s. (④) On average, the Vitamin C content in today's crops was down 20 percent; iron was down 15 percent; riboflavin was down 38 percent and calcium was down 16 percent. (⑤) As a specific example, an apple from 1940 contained three times as much iron as one of today's apples.

*riboflavin: 리보플라빈(비타민 B2)

181

글의 흐름으로 보아, 주어진 문장이 들어가기에 가장 적절한 곳은?

> Instead, both TV watching and violent behavior could be caused by a third variable, such as having neglectful parents who do not pay much attention to their kids.

If a researcher finds that there is a correlation between two variables, it means that there are three possible causal relationships between these variables. (①) For example, researchers have found a correlation between the amount of violent television children watch and how aggressive they are. (②) One explanation for this correlation is that watching TV violence causes kids to become more violent themselves. (③) It is equally probable, however, that the reverse is true: that kids who are violent to begin with are more likely to watch violent TV. (④) Or there might be no causal relationship between these two variables. (⑤) When using the correlational method, it is wrong to jump to the conclusion that one variable is causing the other to occur because a correlation does not prove causation.

182

글의 흐름으로 보아, 주어진 문장이 들어가기에 가장 적절한 곳은?

> If, for example, you were contrasting the driving habits of your old boyfriend with those of your new boyfriend, the part of your paper about your old boyfriend would be written in the past tense, and the part about your new boyfriend would be written in the present tense.

Every time you use a verb in a sentence, you are using a specific tense. The most important thing to remember about tense is that you must be consistent. (①) You cannot randomly shift from one tense to another. (②) For example, if you were telling a story about what happened to you on your vacation last summer, you would stay in the past tense. (③) If, on the other hand, you were explaining the difference between your German Shepherd and your Irish Setter, you would stay in the present tense. (④) There will be times, of course, when you have to move to a different tense. (⑤) You should not move to a different tense, however, unless you have a good reason, so proofread your papers carefully and make sure your writing contains no unnecessary shifts in tense.

*Irish Setter: 아이리시 세터(적갈색의 새 사냥개)

183

글의 흐름으로 보아, 주어진 문장이 들어가기에 가장 적절한 곳은?

> In fact, some believe that online surveys soon will replace other, more traditional survey methods.

The main disadvantage of online surveys concerns the representativeness of the respondents. This disadvantage is relevant to social work surveys of people who are poor or elderly. (①) People who use the Internet and who are most apt to respond to online surveys are likely to be younger, more affluent, and more highly educated than the rest of your target population. (②) However, this problem may be waning as more and more people gain access to the Internet. (③) Depending on the type of respondents being targeted, evidence is emerging to suggest that online survey response rates may be comparable to mail surveys, especially when the online survey is accompanied by a postcard reminder encouraging respondents to participate. (④) This "mixed method" of combining online surveys and postal surveys has largely been developed by Don Dillman. (⑤) Nevertheless, the poor and the elderly remain likely to be underrepresented in online social work surveys in the foreseeable future.

184

글의 흐름으로 보아, 주어진 문장이 들어가기에 가장 적절한 곳은?

> Some highly processed foods may be more easily or quickly consumable, potentially overriding the body's satiety mechanisms.

The caloric value of a food does not tell us how satiating a food is and how it might meet our nutritional needs in a way that may reduce hunger cravings and increase the gap between meals. (①) While the question of satiety is independent of the energy-balance equation, it has practical significance in terms of the quantity of food we eat. (②) If calorie values do not determine how full we feel after a meal or drink, then selecting lower calorie foods is not necessarily the best strategy to weight loss. (③) We also need other strategies for selecting foods, which may at times contradict a narrow focus on calories and the accompanying "eat less" messages. (④) On the other hand, some whole foods — such as nuts or full-fat milk — may be relatively energy dense yet may have a number of beneficial nutritional qualities that ultimately promote satiety and limit excessive food consumption. (⑤) Being told to eat more good-quality foods may turn out to be a more effective public health message than to eat less calories.

185

글의 흐름으로 보아, 주어진 문장이 들어가기에 가장 적절한 곳은?

> Some industry readers may disagree with this statement and point out that there are companies that indeed "go beyond compliance."

We must recognize that since we do not live in a utopian society, economics overshadows many decisions. For industry, sustainability and growth are tied to profitability. (①) To sustain businesses and to maintain or grow profit margins, among other things companies must meet their environmental obligations in a cost-effective manner. (②) Few companies, if any, will spend more to protect the environment than is necessary beyond their legal requirements. (③) But even these businesses are in fact relying on economic forces that enhance their profitability. (④) Companies that allocate more funds toward exceeding environmental performance reap financial benefits from such areas as public opinion and investor confidence that provide them competitive advantages. (⑤) These impacts ultimately result in positive effects on profit margins.

요약문 완성

| 출제 Trend
- 주어진 글의 내용을 요약한 문장에 두 개의 빈칸이 주어지고 각 빈칸에 들어갈 말을 고르는 유형으로, 매년 수능에 1문항씩 출제됩니다.
- 빈칸에는 글의 내용과 연관된 핵심어 또는 이를 달리 표현한 유의어나 파생어가 들어가는 경우가 많습니다.

| 해결 Point

1. 어휘력을 기르자.

요약문 완성 유형은 지문의 길이는 길지만 사실 난이도는 그렇게 높지 않습니다. 선택지로 반대의 뜻을 가진 단어가 함께 제시되거나 지문을 모두 이해했는지를 확인하기 위해 지문에 나온 단어의 유의어가 제시되는 경우가 있으므로, 어휘를 최대한 폭넓게 접해 보는 것이 요약문 완성 유형을 푸는 데 도움이 됩니다.

2. 요약문부터 읽자.

요약문은 해당 지문의 핵심과도 같으므로 요약문을 먼저 읽고 지문이 어떤 내용일지 짐작해 보면 답을 조금 더 빨리 찾을 수 있습니다. 그리고 정답으로 고른 선택지를 요약문의 빈칸에 넣어 제시된 지문의 내용을 모두 포괄하는지 확인합니다. 참고로, 요약문에 부정어가 사용된 경우라면 빈칸에 핵심어의 반의어가 들어가야 한다는 것에 유의하세요.

N 대표 기출 문제

정답 및 해설 p.075

186 다음 글의 내용을 한 문장으로 요약하고자 한다. 빈칸 (A), (B)에 들어갈 말로 가장 적절한 것은? 2024 수능

Even those with average talent can produce notable work in the various sciences, so long as they do not try to embrace all of them at once. Instead, they should concentrate attention on one subject after another (that is, in different periods of time), although later work will weaken earlier attainments in the other spheres. This amounts to saying that the brain adapts to
5 universal science in *time* but not in *space*. In fact, even those with great abilities proceed in this way. Thus, when we are astonished by someone with publications in different scientific fields, realize that each topic was explored during a specific period of time. Knowledge gained earlier certainly will not have disappeared from the mind of the author, but it will have become simplified by condensing into formulas or greatly abbreviated symbols. Thus, sufficient space
10 remains for the perception and learning of new images on the cerebral blackboard.

*condense: 응축하다 **cerebral: 대뇌의

↓

Exploring one scientific subject after another _____(A)_____ remarkable work across the sciences, as the previously gained knowledge is retained in simplified forms within the brain, which _____(B)_____ room for new learning.

	(A)	(B)		(A)	(B)		(A)	(B)
①	enables	leaves	②	challenges	spares	③	delays	creates
④	requires	removes	⑤	invites	diminishes			

✔ **유형 해결**
3-Step

(STEP 1) **글의 전반부에서 중심 소재 파악하기**

~ **can produce notable work in the various sciences**, so long as they do not try to embrace all of them at once / they should concentrate attention on one subject after another (that is, in different periods of time)

(다양한 과학을 한 번에 수용하려고 하지 말고, 한 번에 하나씩 차례로 탐구하면 주목할 만한 작업을 만들어 낼 수 있다)

(STEP 2) **글의 전개를 통해 주제 및 그와 관련된 구체적인 내용 파악하기**

과학을 탐구하는 방식이 글의 소재임을 파악하고, 요지와 관련된 세부적인 내용을 찾는다.

• This amounts to saying that **the brain adapts to universal science in *time* but not in *space***.
  (뇌는 보편적인 과학에 '공간'이 아니라 '시간' 속에서 적응한다.)

• **Knowledge gained earlier** certainly will not have disappeared from the mind of the author, but it will **have become simplified by condensing** into formulas or greatly abbreviated symbols.
  (더 이전에 얻은 지식은 저자의 마음에서 사라지지 않고, 공식이나 축약된 기호로 응축되어 단순화된다.)

• Thus, **sufficient space remains for the perception and learning of new images** on the cerebral blackboard.
  (그래서 대뇌에 새로운 이미지를 인식하고 학습할 수 있는 충분한 공간이 남아 있다.)

(STEP 3) **글의 요약문을 확인하고 적절한 선택지 고르기**

과학 분야들을 차례로 탐구하는 것은 과학 전반에서 주목할 만한 작업을 '가능하게 하는' 접근 방식이고, 그것이 가능한 이유는 이전에 습득된 지식이 뇌 속에서 단순화된 형태로 유지되어 뇌에는 새로운 것을 받아들일 공간이 충분히 '남아 있기' 때문이므로, 요약문의 빈칸 (A), (B)에 각각 들어갈 말로 가장 적절한 것은 ① '가능하게 하다 – 남겨두다'이다.

✔ **중요 구문**

1행 Even those [with average talent] can produce notable work in the various sciences, /
　　　　　주어(= people)　　　　　　　동사　　　　목적어
so long as they do not try to embrace all of them at once.
= if　　　　　　　　　　　　　　　　= the various sciences

: 주절과 부사절로 이루어진 문장이다. 주절의 주어는 Even those with average talent이고 동사는 can produce이며, 목적어는 notable work이다. so long as는 조건의 부사절을 이끄는 접속사이다.

✔ **어휘 풀이**
• notable *a* 주목할 만한
• attainment *n* 성취
• universal *a* 보편적인
• simplify *v* 단순화하다
• symbol *n* 기호, 상징
• remarkable *a* 놀랄 만한, 주목할 만한

• embrace *v* 수용하다
• sphere *n* 영역
• proceed *v* 나아가다, 진행하다
• formula *n* 공식
• sufficient *a* 충분한
• spare *v* 할애하다, 내주다

• at once 한 번에
• amount to ~인 셈이다, ~과 같은 뜻이다
• astonish *v* 놀라게 하다
• abbreviated *a* 축약된
• perception *n* 인식
• diminish *v* 감소하다

187

다음 글의 내용을 한 문장으로 요약하고자 한다. 빈칸 (A), (B)에 들어갈 말로 가장 적절한 것은?

"Craftsmanship" may suggest a way of life that declined with the arrival of industrial society — but this is misleading. Craftsmanship names an enduring, basic human impulse, the desire to do a job well for its own sake. Craftsmanship cuts a far wider swath than skilled manual labor; it serves the computer programmer, the doctor, and the artist; parenting improves when it is practiced as a skilled craft, as does citizenship. In all these domains, craftsmanship focuses on objective standards, on the thing in itself. Social and economic conditions, however, often stand in the way of the craftsman's discipline and commitment: schools may fail to provide the tools to do good work, and workplaces may not truly value the aspiration for quality. And though craftsmanship can reward an individual with a sense of pride in work, this reward is not simple. The craftsman often faces conflicting objective standards of excellence; the desire to do something well for its own sake can be weakened by competitive pressure, by frustration, or by obsession.

*swath: 구획

↓

Craftsmanship, a human desire that has ___(A)___ over time in diverse contexts, often encounters factors that ___(B)___ its full development.

	(A)		(B)
①	persisted	········	limit
②	persisted	········	cultivate
③	evolved	········	accelerate
④	diminished	········	shape
⑤	diminished	········	restrict

188

다음 글의 내용을 한 문장으로 요약하고자 한다. 빈칸 (A), (B)에 들어갈 말로 가장 적절한 것은?

Philip Kitcher and Wesley Salmon have suggested that there are two possible alternatives among philosophical theories of explanation. One is the view that scientific explanation consists in the *unification* of broad bodies of phenomena under a minimal number of generalizations. According to this view, the (or perhaps, a) goal of science is to construct an economical framework of laws or generalizations that are capable of subsuming all observable phenomena. Scientific explanations organize and systematize our knowledge of the empirical world; the more economical the systematization, the deeper our understanding of what is explained. The other view is the *causal/mechanical* approach. According to it, a scientific explanation of a phenomenon consists of uncovering the mechanisms that produced the phenomenon of interest. This view sees the explanation of individual events as primary, with the explanation of generalizations flowing from them. That is, the explanation of scientific generalizations comes from the causal mechanisms that produce the regularities.

*subsume: 포섭(포함)하다   **empirical: 경험적인

↓

Scientific explanations can be made either by seeking the ___(A)___ number of principles covering all observations or by finding general ___(B)___ drawn from individual phenomena.

	(A)		(B)		(A)		(B)
①	least	·····	patterns	②	fixed	·······	features
③	limited	·····	functions	④	fixed	·······	rules
⑤	least	·····	assumptions				

189

다음 글의 내용을 한 문장으로 요약하고자 한다. 빈칸 (A), (B)에 들어갈 말로 가장 적절한 것은?

The Diderot effect was first described in 1769, in the French philosopher Denis Diderot's essay "*Regrets on Paining with My Old Dressing Gown.*" In the paper, he tells how the gift of a beautiful scarlet dressing gown leads to unexpected results, eventually plunging him into debt. Initially pleased with the gift, Diderot came to rue his new garment. Compared to his elegant new dressing gown, the rest of his possessions began to seem tawdry and he became dissatisfied that they did not live up to the elegance and style of his new possession. He replaced his old straw chair, for example, with an armchair covered in Moroccan leather, his old desk was replaced with an expensive new writing table; his formerly beloved prints were replaced with more costly prints, and so on. "I was absolute master of my old dressing gown," Diderot writes, "but I have become a slave to my new one ... Beware of the contamination of sudden wealth. The poor man may take his ease without thinking of appearances, but the rich man is always under a strain."

*rue: 안쓰럽게 생각하다 **tawdry: 저급한

↓

> Obtaining a higher quality item than the quality of the item in our present possession creates feelings of ____(A)____ for old possessions leading to the subsequent ____(B)____ of nicer items.

	(A)		(B)
①	affection	········	purchase
②	affection	········	rejection
③	inadequacy	········	exclusion
④	discontentment	········	avoidance
⑤	discontentment	········	acquisition

190

다음 글의 내용을 한 문장으로 요약하고자 한다. 빈칸 (A), (B)에 들어갈 말로 가장 적절한 것은?

Exposure can add to the complexity of the therapeutic relationship since anxiety disorder patients need to feel particularly safe within any therapeutic environment. A trusting and safe relationship forms the emotional platform upon which patients allow themselves to risk exposure to the triggers of their anxiety, and the resultant discomfort and uncertainty that it can bring. Anxiety creates a sense of danger, and that danger is best tolerated within the context of a positive relationship with the therapist. It is a challenge for any therapist to maintain a sense of safety within the therapeutic relationship while deliberately encouraging the patient to undertake feeling of being in danger; as therapists, our instincts push us to reassure and comfort patients whenever they are uncomfortable. Anxiety disorder therapy requires that we must frequently resist these instincts.

↓

> During anxiety disorder therapy, to help the patient ____(A)____ his or her problem, the therapist has to create a therapeutic environment in which the patient feels both safe and ____(B)____ .

	(A)		(B)
①	conceal	········	positive
②	classify	········	comfortable
③	reveal	········	uneasy
④	internalize	········	inferior
⑤	eliminate	········	lonely

191

다음 글의 내용을 한 문장으로 요약하고자 한다. 빈칸 (A), (B)에 들어갈 말로 가장 적절한 것은?

The need to belong is one of the strongest core motivations, and it affects people's thoughts, feelings, and behaviors frequently. It is therefore not surprising that when people have been excluded from a social
5 group, they will engage in behaviors that help them to create liking and allow them to reenter the group. Recent research conducted by Lakin and Chartrand has shown that mimicking the nonverbal behaviors of group members may be one such strategy. When
10 participants were excluded from a computerized ball-tossing game and then interacted with a confederate in a different context, they mimicked the behaviors of the confederate more than when they had not been excluded during the ball-toss game. In other words,
15 participants who were trying to create liking and affiliation were able to pursue this goal through mimicking another person. The findings from Lakin and Chartrand suggest that people can pursue a goal to develop rapport or liking by mimicking the behaviors
20 of others automatically.

*confederate: 실험 보조자 **affiliation: 연대, 소속 ***rapport: 친밀한 관계

↓

A recent social ____(A)____ which a person experienced is likely to lead the person to increase his or her behavioral ____(B)____ .

	(A)		(B)
①	acceptance	········	flexibility
②	alienation	········	imitation
③	interaction	········	deviance
④	acceptance	········	imitation
⑤	alienation	········	deviance

192

다음 글의 내용을 한 문장으로 요약하고자 한다. 빈칸 (A), (B)에 들어갈 말로 가장 적절한 것은?

New technologies, the elevator and the proliferation of materials like steel allowed the construction of ever-escalating high-rise buildings that now are a ubiquitous part of our society. However, technologies
5 not directly linked to the building industry also significantly influenced building design. The steam engine and then the automobile erased geographic distances that were once insurmountable. Materials and technologies can now be shipped all over the globe
10 and the idea of building locally became a thing of the past. Building materials were no longer confined to the local stone, brick, wood or earth that was available and a region's architectural character changed significantly because it was no longer limited by regional limits. As
15 materials changed so did form, and building designs were exported around the world regardless of culture and climate. Since technology could now take care of all our comfort needs, regionalism was deemed by many to be irrelevant. Buildings could now look the
20 same regardless of whether they were located in Anchorage, Alaska or Hilo, Hawaii.

↓

Technological advances in ____(A)____ had a significant impact on architecture, ____(B)____ regional distinctions in building materials and designs.

	(A)		(B)
①	communication	········	minimizing
②	communication	········	highlighting
③	manufacturing	········	reflecting
④	transportation	········	promoting
⑤	transportation	········	diminishing

193

다음 글의 내용을 한 문장으로 요약하고자 한다. 빈칸 (A), (B)에 들어갈 말로 가장 적절한 것은?

Spices come from plants — flowers, roots, seeds, shrubs, and fruits. Spices emit unique smells and have specific tastes due to chemicals called "secondary compounds." These compounds usually function in plants as defense
5 mechanisms to prevent macroorganisms(herbivores, or plant-eating animals) and microorganisms(pathogens) from attacking them. The use of spice plants among humans goes back thousands of years. Explorers such as Marco Polo and Christopher Columbus took great
10 risks to search for lands with abundant spices. It is difficult to find in a modern book of recipes a single dish that does not contain spices. Why are humans so concerned with spices and their addition to the foods eaten? According to the antimicrobial hypothesis,
15 spices kill or inhibit the growth of microorganisms and prevent the production of toxins in the foods we eat and so help humans to solve a critical problem of survival. Of the thirty spices for which we have solid data, all killed many of the species of food-borne
20 bacteria on which they were tested. Can you guess which spices are most powerful in killing bacteria? They are onion, garlic, allspice, and oregano.

*antimicrobial: 항균성의

↓

The use of spices in foods is one potential   (A)   that humans have used to   (B)   the dangers carried in the foods we eat.

    (A)   (B)
① tradition ········ combat
② tradition ········ minimize
③ risk ········ hide
④ solution ········ hide
⑤ solution ········ combat

194

다음 글의 내용을 한 문장으로 요약하고자 한다. 빈칸 (A), (B)에 들어갈 말로 가장 적절한 것은?

For centuries, doctors considered diseases exclusively as something stemming from outside the body attacking it — a contagious germ, a draft of cold air, poisonous vapors, and so on. Treatment depended on
5 finding drugs of some sort that could counteract the harmful effects of these environmental agents of disease. Then, in the early twentieth century, the biochemist Frederick Gowland Hopkins, studying the effects of scurvy, had the idea to reverse this
10 perspective. What caused the problem in this particular disease, he speculated, was not what was attacking from the outside, but what was missing from within the body itself — in this case what came to be known as vitamin C. Thinking outside the box helped him solve
15 the problem. This led to his groundbreaking work on vitamins and completely altered our concept of health.

*scurvy: 괴혈병

↓

Frederick Gowland Hopkins broke new ground for disease treatment by focusing on what was   (A)   from the body, not   (B)   agents of diseases.

    (A)   (B)
① absent ········ temporary
② absent ········ external
③ developed ········ temporary
④ recovered ········ external
⑤ recovered ········ internal

18 장문(1지문 2문항)

| 출제 Trend
- 보통 한두 개의 단락으로 이루어진 긴 지문에 2문항이 출제됩니다.
- 2019 수능부터 첫 번째 문제로 글의 제목 유형이, 두 번째 문제로 밑줄 어휘 유형이 출제되고 있습니다.

| 해결 Point **지문이 길어도 문제 풀이 요령은 같다!**

하나의 지문에 글의 제목, 밑줄 어휘 유형이 출제되며, 지문이 길다는 점만 빼면 앞에서 풀던 유형과 접근법은 동일합니다. 제목 파악 문제는 글의 앞부분에서 중심 소재와 글의 방향을 잡은 다음, 글의 요지를 담고 있는 중심 문장을 찾아야 합니다. 밑줄 어휘 문제는 중심 문장을 파악하며 밑줄 친 어휘가 글의 전체적인 논리 전개와 일치하는지를 판단해야 하는데, 반의어가 있는 어휘들을 유심히 보고 혹시 반의어가 오는 게 맞지 않을까 의심하면서 읽으면 정답을 찾을 수 있습니다.

대표 기출 문제

정답 및 해설 p.078

195~196 다음 글을 읽고, 물음에 답하시오. 2024 수능

One way to avoid contributing to overhyping a story would be to say nothing. However, that is not a realistic option for scientists who feel a strong sense of responsibility to inform the public and policymakers and/or to offer suggestions. Speaking with members of the media has (a)advantages in getting a message out and perhaps receiving favorable recognition, but it runs the risk of misinterpretations, the need for repeated
5 clarifications, and entanglement in never-ending controversy. Hence, the decision of whether to speak with the media tends to be highly individualized. Decades ago, it was (b)unusual for Earth scientists to have results that were of interest to the media, and consequently few media contacts were expected or encouraged. In the 1970s, the few scientists who spoke frequently with the media were often (c)criticized by their fellow scientists for having done so. The situation now is quite different, as many scientists feel a responsibility to speak out
10 because of the importance of global warming and related issues, and many reporters share these feelings. In addition, many scientists are finding that they (d)enjoy the media attention and the public recognition that comes with it. At the same time, other scientists continue to resist speaking with reporters, thereby preserving more time for their science and (e)running the risk of being misquoted and the other unpleasantries associated with media coverage.

*overhype: 과대광고하다 **entanglement: 얽힘

195 윗글의 제목으로 가장 적절한 것은?

① The Troubling Relationship Between Scientists and the Media
② A Scientist's Choice: To Be Exposed to the Media or Not?
③ Scientists! Be Cautious When Talking to the Media
④ The Dilemma over Scientific Truth and Media Attention
⑤ Who Are Responsible for Climate Issues, Scientists or the Media?

196 밑줄 친 (a)~(e) 중에서 문맥상 낱말의 쓰임이 적절하지 <u>않은</u> 것은?

① (a)   ② (b)   ③ (c)   ④ (d)   ⑤ (e)

✓ **유형 해결**
3-Step

(STEP 1) **글의 전반적인 흐름 파악하기**

과학자들이 언론과 대화하는 것은 대중에게 정보를 전달하고 정책에 영향을 미치기 위한 중요한 수단이 될 수 있지만, 오해와 논란의 위험도 있어서 과학자들은 언론과 대화할지 여부를 신중하게 결정하는 경향이 있다고 하며, 현재 일부 과학자들의 언론과의 소통이 활발해지고 있으나 다른 과학자들은 언론 보도의 편향성이나 과학적 오해의 가능성을 우려하여 언론과의 소통을 피하기도 한다는 내용의 글이다.

(STEP 2) **글의 요지를 파악하여 제목 선택하기**

언론과 소통하는 것을 활발히 하는 과학자들도 있지만, 다양한 이유로 그것을 피하는 과학자들도 있다는 내용이므로 ② '과학자의 선택: 언론에 노출될 것인가, 말 것인가?'가 글의 제목으로 가장 적절하다.

(STEP 3) **글의 주제나 요지의 큰 맥락을 고려하여 어휘의 적절성 판단하기**

일부 언론과 접하는 과학자들이 많아지고 있지만, 다른 과학자들은 기자들과의 대화를 거부하며 과학을 위해 더 많은 시간을 유지해 언론 보도와 관련하여 잘못 인용되거나 불쾌한 일을 '피한다'는 맥락이 되어야 하므로, (e)의 running은 avoiding과 같은 어휘로 바꿔야 한다.

✓ **정답 확인**

195

① 과학자와 언론 간의 골치 아픈 관계 → 관계 자체가 좋거나 나쁘다는 것에 대해 말하는 글은 아님

③ 과학자여! 언론에 말할 때 조심하시오 → 연구 시간을 확보하고 부정적 상황을 피하기 위해 일부 과학자들이 언론 노출을 기피한다고는 했지만, 조심하라는 내용의 글은 아니므로 오답

④ 과학적 진실과 언론의 주목에 대한 딜레마 → 언론 노출에 대한 입장을 달리하는 과학자들에 대한 글이므로 오답

⑤ 누가 기후 문제에 책임이 있는가, 과학자인가, 언론인가? → 지구 온난화는 언급만 되었을 뿐 글의 요지가 아님

196

(a) advantages → 언론 구성원들과의 긍정적 상호 관계를 말하는 부분으로 '이점'이 있다는 내용은 적절함

(b) unusual → 언론 노출에 대해 비난을 받는 상황이 이후에 언급되고 있으므로, 과학자가 연구 결과를 발표하는 것이 '드물다'는 내용은 적절함

(c) criticized → 뒤에 이어지는 내용에서 오늘날에는 상황이 다르다고 하며 언론 공개에 대해 책임감을 느낀다고 했으므로 그와 반대로 과거에는 '비난받았다'는 내용은 적절함

(d) enjoy → 앞서 언론 공개에 대한 책임감을 느낀다는 내용에, '게다가(In addition)'라고 하며 같은 맥락의 말을 첨언하고 있으므로 언론의 주목과 대중의 인정을 '즐긴다'는 문맥은 적절함

✓ **중요 구문** **3행** [{Speaking with members of the media} {has advantages in getting a message out and perhaps receiving favorable recognition}], but [it runs the risk of {misinterpretations}, {the need for repeated clarifications}, and {entanglement in never-ending controversy}].

: 두 개의 절 [ ]가 but으로 연결된 구조로, 첫 번째 [ ] 안에 두 개의 { }는 각각 주어와 술부이다. 두 번째 [ ] 안의 세 개의 { }는 and로 연결되어 전치사 of에 이어지는 명사(구)이다.

✓ **어휘 풀이**
- policymaker *n* 정책 입안자
- recognition *n* 인식, 인정
- run the risk 위험이 있다
- misinterpretation *n* 오해
- clarification *n* 해명
- controversy *n* 논란
- come with ~이 딸려 있다
- thereby *ad* 그렇게 함으로써
- preserve *v* 유지하다, 지키다
- misquote *v* (말이나 글을) 잘못 인용하다
- unpleasantry *n* 불쾌한 상황, 불쾌한 사건
- coverage *n* (언론의) 보도

197~198 다음 글을 읽고, 물음에 답하시오.　2023 수능

There is evidence that even very simple algorithms can outperform expert judgement on simple prediction problems. For example, algorithms have proved more (a) accurate than humans in predicting whether a
5 prisoner released on parole will go on to commit another crime, or in predicting whether a potential candidate will perform well in a job in future. In over 100 studies across many different domains, half of all cases show simple formulas make (b) better significant
10 predictions than human experts, and the remainder (except a very small handful), show a tie between the two. When there are a lot of different factors involved and a situation is very uncertain, simple formulas can win out by focusing on the most important factors and
15 being consistent, while human judgement is too easily influenced by particularly salient and perhaps (c) irrelevant considerations. A similar idea is supported by further evidence that 'checklists' can improve the quality of expert decisions in a range of
20 domains by ensuring that important steps or considerations aren't missed when people are feeling (d) relaxed. For example, treating patients in intensive care can require hundreds of small actions per day, and one small error could cost a life. Using checklists
25 to ensure that no crucial steps are missed has proved to be remarkably (e) effective in a range of medical contexts, from preventing live infections to reducing pneumonia.

*parole: 가석방　**salient: 두드러진　***pneumonia: 폐렴

197

윗글의 제목으로 가장 적절한 것은?

① The Power of Simple Formulas in Decision Making
② Always Prioritise: Tips for Managing Big Data
③ Algorithms' Mistakes: The Myth of Simplicity
④ Be Prepared! Make a Checklist Just in Case
⑤ How Human Judgement Beats Algorithms

198

밑줄 친 (a)~(e) 중에서 문맥상 낱말의 쓰임이 적절하지 않은 것은?

① (a)　　② (b)　　③ (c)
④ (d)　　⑤ (e)

199~200 다음 글을 읽고, 물음에 답하시오.

Consider the case of a client of mine who is a professional musician. As some people do, my client tends toward (a)negative thinking and has a habit of mentally beating himself up. Despite his success at his work he continually struggles with self-doubt. We worked together to loosen up his creativity and generate ideas for a new album. Even as the ideas tumbled forth onto the page and into the strings of his guitar, I frequently heard him saying such things as, "this song probably won't work out anyway," and, "people probably won't like this particular song much." This is defensive pessimism at work: by (b)predicting failure you won't be surprised when it comes, and you will be delighted on the off chance that you are successful. Where courage is concerned, defensive pessimism is a dead end. It typically (c)energizes people and holds them back from the enthusiastic and automatic responding we often associate with bravery.

Just imagine a mountain rescue worker who is afraid that he will not find the lost climbers. This is exactly the (d)opposite of the outlook that is required for rescue work. Emergency personnel need to have robust mindsets that cling feverishly to even a (e)slim chance of success. It is this optimism that helps them persevere and gives them the energy they need to face danger.

199

윗글의 제목으로 가장 적절한 것은?

① Optimism and Self-Confidence
② The Positive Power of Negative Thinking
③ Optimism: What Rescue Workers Need Most
④ Why Pessimists Fail When Optimists Succeed
⑤ Defensive Pessimism: A Mental Preparation Strategy

200

밑줄 친 (a)~(e) 중에서 문맥상 낱말의 쓰임이 적절하지 <u>않은</u> 것은?

① (a)   ② (b)   ③ (c)
④ (d)   ⑤ (e)

201~202 다음 글을 읽고, 물음에 답하시오.

Negotiations occur because people who are giving something up — either because they made it or already own it — will always feel that loss more (a)heavily than the buyer will feel the gain. In one study, participants approached people on the street who had recently purchased lottery tickets. They offered these people the chance to sell their tickets for eight times as much money as they paid! Of course, this sale would have allowed the lottery ticket buyers to buy two to eight times as many tickets as they'd already bought, obviously (b)increasing their chances of winning the lottery. Seems like an easy deal, doesn't it? Remember, the human mind is not rational. Even though lottery ticket buyers had no reason at all to believe they held the winning tickets, they still, on the whole, refused to sell their tickets for an astronomically higher price. This was a clear example of loss aversion: they knew that if they'd given the winning ticket away, the emotional price would be much (c)higher than their potential emotional relief they'd gain from increasing their odds of actually winning the lottery. For no reason at all, these people ascribed extra value to the ticket they already held and (d)dismissed the potential value in the eight tickets they could gain. This is a perfect example of the human brain working (e)rationally. Keep in mind that the lady at the flea market may not be trying to rip you off; in fact, she, like you, will always ascribe a higher value to what she's selling than what she's buying.

201

윗글의 제목으로 가장 적절한 것은?

① The Lottery: Is It Ever Worth Playing?
② When Do Gains Look Larger than Losses?
③ A Reason Why People Buy Lottery Tickets
④ Psychological Mechanisms of Loss Aversion
⑤ Negotiation: The Only Way for Both Parties to Win

202

밑줄 친 (a)~(e) 중에서 문맥상 낱말의 쓰임이 적절하지 <u>않은</u> 것은?

① (a) ② (b) ③ (c)
④ (d) ⑤ (e)

203~204 다음 글을 읽고, 물음에 답하시오.

Impression management (presentation of self) refers to people's efforts to present themselves to others in ways that are most favorable to their own interests or image. For example, suppose that a professor has
5 returned graded exams to your class. Will you discuss the exam and your grade with others in the class? If you are like most people, you probably play your student role (a)differently depending on whom you are talking to and what grade you received on the exam.
10 Your "presentation" may vary depending on the grade earned by the other person (your "audience"). In one study, students who all received high grades ("Ace-Ace encounters") (b)willingly talked with one another about their grades and sometimes engaged in a little
15 bragging about how they had "aced" the test. However, encounters between students who had received high grades and those who had received low or failing grades ("Ace-Bomber encounters") were uncomfortable. The Aces felt as if they had to (c)exaggerate their own
20 grade. Consequently, they tended to attribute their success to "luck" and were quick to offer the Bombers words of encouragement. On the other hand, the Bombers believed that they had to (d)praise the Aces and hide their own feelings of frustration and
25 disappointment. Students who received low or failing grades ("Bomber-Bomber encounters") were more (e)comfortable when they talked with one another because they could share their negative emotions. They often indulged in self-pity and relied on face-saving
30 excuses (such as an illness or an unfair exam) for their poor performances.

*bomber: (폭탄 맞은 것처럼) 성적이 엉망인 학생

203

윗글의 제목으로 가장 적절한 것은?

① First Impressions Often Turn Out to Be Wrong
② Aces Can Be a Good Audience, but Bombers Cannot
③ Discuss the Exam Even When You Performed Poorly
④ Presentation Skills: Getting More and More Important
⑤ The Social Situation: The Key Determinant of Interaction

204

밑줄 친 (a)~(e) 중에서 문맥상 낱말의 쓰임이 적절하지 않은 것은?

① (a)   ② (b)   ③ (c)
④ (d)   ⑤ (e)

| 출제 Trend · 하나의 지문을 4개의 단락으로 나누어 순서를 섞어 제시합니다. 첫 번째는 단락의 순서를 배열하는 문제, 두 번째는 지칭 대상을 파악하는 문제, 세 번째는 내용 일치 여부를 묻는 문제가 주로 출제됩니다.

| 해결 Point

1. 어려운 문제는 건너뛰고 복합 장문 먼저 풀어라!

복합 장문은 대부분 가벼운 스토리텔링으로 지문이 출제되어 내용이 쉽기 때문에 큰 어려움 없이 풀 수 있습니다. 그런데 마지막에 위치해 있어 시간에 쫓겨 실수를 할 수 있으므로 빈칸 추론 등의 어려운 유형을 풀기 전에 이 유형을 먼저 풀어 점수를 확보하는 것도 좋은 전략입니다.

2. 문제 풀이 요령은 같다!

글의 순서를 정할 때는 곳곳에 등장하는 연결어, 정관사, 지시어 등을 놓치지 말고 단서로 삼아 확실한 순서부터 정해 갑니다. 지칭 대상을 파악할 때는 가장 먼저 나오는 (a)의 지칭 대상을 파악하고 나머지가 (a)의 지칭 대상과 동일한 대상인지 아닌지를 판단하면서 글을 읽도록 합니다. 내용 불일치 문제는 선택지를 먼저 읽으면 지문에서 확인해야 할 내용이 무엇인지 알 수 있어 문제 풀이 시간을 절약할 수 있습니다.

▶ 대표 기출 문제

정답 및 해설 p.082

205~207 다음 글을 읽고, 물음에 답하시오.

2024 수능

(A)

Emma and Clara stood side by side on the beach road, with their eyes fixed on the boundless ocean. The breathtaking scene that surrounded them was beyond description. Just after sunrise, they finished their preparations for the bicycle ride along the beach road. Emma turned to Clara with a question, "Do you think this will be your favorite ride ever?" Clara's face lit up with a bright smile as she nodded. "Definitely! (a) I can't wait to ride while watching those beautiful waves!"

(B)

When they reached their destination, Emma and Clara stopped their bikes. Emma approached Clara, saying "Bicycle riding is unlike swimming, isn't it?" Clara answered with a smile, "Quite similar, actually. Just like swimming, riding makes me feel truly alive." She added, "It shows (b) me what it means to live while facing life's tough challenges." Emma nodded in agreement and suggested, "Your first beach bike ride was a great success. How about coming back next summer?" Clara replied with delight, "With (c) you, absolutely!"

(C)

Clara used to be a talented swimmer, but she had to give up her dream of becoming an Olympic medalist in swimming because of shoulder injuries. Yet she responded to the hardship in a constructive way. After years of hard training, she made an incredible recovery and found a new passion for bike riding. Emma saw how the painful past made her maturer and how it made (d) her stronger in the end. One hour later, Clara, riding ahead of Emma, turned back and shouted, "Look at the white cliff!"

(D)

Emma and Clara jumped on their bikes and started to pedal toward the white cliff where the beach road ended. Speeding up and enjoying the wide blue sea, Emma couldn't hide her excitement and exclaimed, "Clara, the view is amazing!" Clara's silence, however, seemed to say that she was lost in her thoughts. Emma understood the meaning of her silence. Watching Clara riding beside her, Emma thought about Clara's past tragedy, which (e) she now seemed to have overcome.

205 주어진 글 (A)에 이어질 내용을 순서에 맞게 배열한 것으로 가장 적절한 것은?

① (B) — (D) — (C)　　　　② (C) — (B) — (D)　　　　③ (C) — (D) — (B)

④ (D) — (B) — (C)　　　　⑤ (D) — (C) — (B)

206 밑줄 친 (a)~(e) 중에서 가리키는 대상이 나머지 넷과 다른 것은?

① (a)　　　　② (b)　　　　③ (c)　　　　④ (d)　　　　⑤ (e)

207 윗글에 관한 내용으로 적절하지 않은 것은?

① Emma와 Clara는 자전거 탈 준비를 일출 직후에 마쳤다.
② Clara는 자전거 타기와 수영이 꽤 비슷하다고 말했다.
③ Clara는 올림픽 수영 경기에서 메달을 땄다.
④ Emma와 Clara는 자전거를 타고 하얀 절벽 쪽으로 갔다.
⑤ Emma는 Clara의 침묵의 의미를 이해했다.

✔ **유형 해결**
3-Step

STEP 1 (A) 문단을 읽고 등장인물 및 이야기의 상황 파악하기

• **등장인물**　Emma와 Clara
• **상황**　두 사람이 해변 도로를 따라 자전거를 타려 준비하고 있음

STEP 2 사건의 전개, 시간의 흐름, 연결어나 대명사에 유의하면서 이야기의 연결성 파악하기

(D) Emma와 Clara가 하얀 절벽을 향해 페달을 밟기 시작했고, 자전거를 타며 Emma는 Clara의 과거 비극에 대해 생각함 → (A)에는 두 사람이 해변 도로에서 자전거를 타고 싶어 했음

(C) Clara는 재능 있는 수영 선수였지만 꿈을 포기해야만 했음 → (D)에서 언급한 Clara의 과거 비극

(B) Emma와 Clara는 목적지에 도착해서 내년 여름에도 이곳에 오자고 약속함 → 이야기의 마무리

STEP 3 이야기의 흐름을 바탕으로 문제 해결

205 주어진 글 (A) 다음에 '(D)-(C)-(B)'의 순서로 이야기가 전개됨을 알 수 있다.

206 (a), (b), (d), (e)는 Clara를 가리키지만, (c)는 Clara가 Emma에게 하는 말이므로 Emma를 가리킨다.

207 (C)에서 Clara는 어깨 부상으로 올림픽 수영 메달리스트의 꿈을 포기해야만 했다(She had to give up her dream of becoming an Olympic medalist in swimming because of shoulder injuries)고 했으므로, ③은 글의 내용으로 적절하지 않다.
① Emma와 Clara는 자전거 탈 준비를 일출 직후에 마쳤다. → (A)의 내용으로 일치함
② Clara는 자전거 타기와 수영이 꽤 비슷하다고 말했다. → (B)의 내용으로 일치함
④ Emma와 Clara는 자전거를 타고 하얀 절벽 쪽으로 갔다. → (D)의 내용으로 일치함
⑤ Emma는 Clara의 침묵의 의미를 이해했다. → (D)의 내용으로 일치함

(A)

"Hailey, be careful!" Camila yelled uneasily, watching her sister carrying a huge cake to the table. "Don't worry, Camila," Hailey responded, smiling. Camila relaxed only when Hailey had safely placed the cake on the party table. "Dad will be here shortly. What gift did (a) you buy for his birthday?" Camila asked out of interest. "Dad will be surprised to find out what it is!" Hailey answered with a wink.

(B)

"Dad, these glasses can help correct your red-green color blindness," said Hailey. He slowly put them on, and stared at the birthday presents on the table. Seeing vivid red and green colors for the first time ever, he started to cry. "Incredible! Look at those wonderful colors!" He shouted in amazement. Hailey told him in tears, "Dad, I'm glad you can now finally enjoy the true beauty of rainbows and roses. Red represents love and green represents health. You deserve both." Camila nodded, seeing how happy (b) her gift of the glasses had made their dad.

(C)

"Happy birthday! You're fifty today, Dad. We love you!" Camila said before (c) her sister handed him a small parcel. When he opened it, he discovered a pair of glasses inside. "Hailey, Dad doesn't have eyesight problems," Camila said, puzzled. "Actually Camila, I recently found out he has long been suffering from color blindness. He's kept it a secret so as not to worry us," Hailey explained.

(D)

"I bet (d) you bought a wallet or a watch for him," Camila said. In reply, Hailey answered, "No. I bought something much more personal. By the way, there's something (e) you should know about Dad..." They were suddenly interrupted by the doorbell ringing. It was their dad and they were overjoyed to see him. "My lovely ladies, thank you for inviting me to your place for my birthday." He walked in joyfully, hugging his daughters. They all walked into the dining room, where he was greeted with a rainbow-colored birthday cake and fifty red roses.

208

주어진 글 (A)에 이어질 내용을 순서에 맞게 배열한 것으로 가장 적절한 것은?

① (B) ― (D) ― (C)　　　② (C) ― (B) ― (D)
③ (C) ― (D) ― (B)　　　④ (D) ― (B) ― (C)
⑤ (D) ― (C) ― (B)

209

밑줄 친 (a)~(e) 중에서 가리키는 대상이 나머지 넷과 다른 것은?

① (a)　　　② (b)　　　③ (c)
④ (d)　　　⑤ (e)

210

윗글에 관한 내용으로 적절하지 않은 것은?

① Hailey는 생일 케이크를 테이블로 무사히 옮겨 놓았다.
② 아버지는 생일 선물로 받은 안경을 직접 써 보았다.
③ Hailey는 아버지가 색맹이라는 사실을 최근에 알게 되었다.
④ Hailey와 Camila는 아버지의 집을 방문하였다.
⑤ 아버지는 자신의 나이와 똑같은 수의 장미를 받았다.

211~213 다음 글을 읽고, 물음에 답하시오.

(A)

One sunny afternoon in June, my sister Jenny and I were walking home from school when we noticed a loud chirping coming from an empty trash can on the curb. We walked over to it and peered inside. A sad little
5 sparrow was sitting at the bottom of the trash can, chirping her heart out. Her right wing stuck out from her body at a strange angle. Jenny said it was probably broken. She reached in and cupped the bird in her hands, cooing to her so (a)she wouldn't be scared. The
10 sparrow chirped all the way to our house. *coo: '구구' 소리를 내다

(B)

Once the splint was on, we fed the bird water and bits of bread. At first she wouldn't eat, but then after a while, (b)she wouldn't stop. The little bird earned the name Peep. We kept her in an empty cage. After a
15 while, Peep's wing got better, and we removed the splint. Mom told us it was probably time to let her go. The next morning when we opened the cage door, she flew about fifty feet into the air before coming back. From then on, Peep flew further each morning, but
20 (c)she always came back. *splint: 부목

(C)

Mom took one look at the little bird and said, "No way! I'm not having another animal in the house." But once she got a closer look at those big, sad eyes and heard that pathetic chirping, (d)her heart melted. We
25 were counting on that. Mom said her right wing was definitely broken, so she designed a splint out of a Popsicle stick and carefully taped it to her wing.

(D)

Two weeks later, on a Sunday morning, when Jenny let Peep out of her cage, she just kept flying. We left her cage outside with the door open, but she never 30 came home all that day. At night, we faced the truth that Peep would never come back. Mom said (e)she probably found some other sparrows and decided it was time to be with her own kind. My eyes filled with tears, and so did Jenny's. 35

211

주어진 글 (A)에 이어질 내용을 순서에 맞게 배열한 것으로 가장 적절한 것은?

① (B) — (D) — (C)   ② (C) — (B) — (D)
③ (C) — (D) — (B)   ④ (D) — (B) — (C)
⑤ (D) — (C) — (B)

212

밑줄 친 (a)~(e) 중에서 가리키는 대상이 나머지 넷과 <u>다른</u> 것은?

① (a)   ② (b)   ③ (c)
④ (d)   ⑤ (e)

213

윗글에 관한 내용으로 적절하지 <u>않은</u> 것은?

① Jenny는 쓰레기통 안에서 참새 한 마리를 발견했다.
② 새는 처음에 먹이를 먹으려고 하지 않았다.
③ 엄마는 처음에는 참새를 데려온 것을 못마땅해했다.
④ 엄마는 다친 참새를 치료해 주었다.
⑤ Peep은 부상에서 회복한 후 곧바로 친구들에게 날아갔다.

214~216 다음 글을 읽고, 물음에 답하시오.

(A)

The first time I met George Kissell, one of the Cardinals' minor-league coaches, I had just gotten to the ballpark in Sarasota. On the morning of my first day, I was in that "B" game, I guess you'd call it. I don't know what it was, really. But when that game was over, at about 3:30 in the afternoon, I went back to the hotel and then (a) that coach said, "Report back at five o'clock for the night game."

(B)

I leaned around the light pole and looked at the scoreboard and read him the stuff he asked me about. I was thinking, "This guy can't even see the scoreboard." (b) He said to me, "Don't ever be on the bench not knowing the count and how many outs there are. You always have to be involved in the game. If you're gonna sit there, learn something!" I'd only been here a day, and I was thinking, "Are you kidding me? I don't even want to be here." But now I know he was right. George was always right!

(C)

We got to the ballpark and the game started. There were rain delays, and I wasn't even playing, and I basically hadn't slept for two days. There was a huge light pole in the middle of the dugout, and I was kind of sitting behind it. (c) This guy walked right in front of me and said, "What's the count and how many outs are there?" I figured I better find out the answers (d) he wanted.

(D)

I hadn't slept in almost two days, coming in from Sacramento, so I went up to my room and I overslept. I woke up at a quarter to five, and I just jumped in a cab. I got to the ballpark where we had played the day game, and I just gathered up my baseball stuff and ran to the bus. It was leaving right at five for the ballpark where we played night games. And Ray Hathaway, the manager, came up to me when I was getting on the bus. And the only thing (e) he said to me was, "Don't ever be late." That was it.

214

주어진 글 (A)에 이어질 내용을 순서에 맞게 배열한 것으로 가장 적절한 것은?

① (B) — (D) — (C)   ② (C) — (B) — (D)
③ (C) — (D) — (B)   ④ (D) — (B) — (C)
⑤ (D) — (C) — (B)

215

밑줄 친 (a)~(e) 중에서 가리키는 대상이 나머지 넷과 <u>다른</u> 것은?

① (a)   ② (b)   ③ (c)
④ (d)   ⑤ (e)

216

윗글의 'I'에 관한 내용으로 적절하지 <u>않은</u> 것은?

① Sarasota에 있는 야구장에서 George를 처음 만났다.
② 첫 경기가 끝나고 호텔로 돌아갔다.
③ 볼카운트를 물어보는 George를 무시했다.
④ 우천으로 지연된 경기에서 대기석에 앉아 있었다.
⑤ 늦잠을 자서 집합 장소에 택시를 타고 이동했다.

⑬ 빈칸 추론

01	fashion	v		21	in terms of		
02	induction	n		22	entail	v	
03	dismissal	n		23	striking	a	
04	comparative	a		24	eject	v	
05	considerable	a		25	definitive	a	
06	criterion	n		26	nurture	v	
07	discipline	n		27	paralysis	n	
08	reinforce	v		28	revenue	n	
09	abnormal	a		29	infinite	a	
10	spectacular	a		30	accordingly	ad	
11	persevere	v		31	consistent with		
12	endorse	v		32	ramp	n	
13	extinct	a		33	governance	n	
14	live off			34	migration	n	
15	concentrate	v		35	circulation	n	
16	sensible	a		36	induce	v	
17	manifest	v		37	delicately	ad	
18	distress	n		38	우울증	n	
19	disengagement	n		39	strain	n	
20	adequacy	n		40	contagious	a	

41	bureaucratic	*a*		61	exceptional	*a*
42	budget	*n*		62	confront	*v*
43	end up -ing			63	greedy	*a*
44	equilibrium	*n*		64	fractional	*a*
45	domestic	*a*		65	ingredient	*n*
46	desperately	*ad*		66	commodity	*n*
47	목격하다	*v*		67	abstract	*a*
48	compromise	*v*		68	depict	*v*
49	crowd	*v*		69	고독	*n*
50	impose	*v*		70	enforce	*v*
51	massive	*a*		71	forage	*v*
52	signal	*v*		72	refute	*v*
53	confined to			73	peasant	*n*
54	cancel out			74	shift	*n*
55	relative	*n*		75	channel	*v*
56	superficial	*a*		76	address	*v*
57	mutually	*ad*		77	reptile	*n*
58	embed	*v*		78	bring forth	
59	obligation	*n*		79	element	*n*
60	fuel	*v*		80	confederate	*n*

⑭ 무관한 문장

01	profitable	a	
02	assert	v	
03	abundant	a	
04	awkward	a	
05	지속 가능한	a	
06	trivial	a	
07	validate	v	
08	measured	a	
09	approval	n	
10	discrepancy	n	
11	aptitude	n	
12	verbal	a	
13	in a glance		
14	sparingly	ad	
15	come up with		
16	adolescence	n	
17	marvellous	a	
18	직관	n	
19	panicked	a	
20	in vain		

⑮ 글의 순서 파악

01	manipulate	v	
02	landfill	n	
03	reproductive	a	
04	complement	v	
05	두개골, 두뇌	n	
06	precede	v	
07	trigger	v	
08	conserve	v	
09	desirable	a	
10	복도	n	
11	profound	a	
12	integrity	n	
13	readily	ad	
14	deceitful	a	
15	strive	v	
16	account for		
17	offset	v	
18	envision	v	
19	appropriateness	n	
20	intriguing	a	

21	unceasingly	ad	
22	다락방	n	
23	prescription	n	
24	excessive	a	
25	intrinsic	a	
26	withdraw	v	
27	distinct	a	
28	영장류의 동물	n	
29	compel	v	
30	anatomy	n	
31	assess	v	
32	시대, 시기	n	
33	validity	n	
34	hollow	a	
35	aggressive	a	
36	ship	v	
37	stimulus	n	
38	intense	a	
39	decline	n	
40	아기, 유아	n	

⑯ 문장 삽입

01	embody	v	
02	precautionary	a	
03	celebrity	n	
04	stem from		
05	contradict	v	
06	a handful of		
07	circuit	n	
08	be apt to *do*		
09	statement	n	
10	차원	n	
11	imitate	v	
12	inert	a	
13	affluent	a	
14	principle	n	
15	splinter	v	
16	neglectful	a	
17	absurd	a	
18	hostile	a	
19	유전의	a	
20	anticipate	v	

21	compliance	n	
22	depletion	n	
23	extensive	a	
24	fix	n	
25	prudent	a	
26	포만감	n	
27	reveal	v	
28	allocate	v	
29	pose	v	
30	variable	n	
31	coincide	v	
32	yield	n	
33	severity	n	
34	novel	a	
35	후손	n	
36	override	v	
37	illusion	n	
38	retreat	n	
39	reap	v	
40	come into play		

01	manual	a	
02	scarlet	a	
03	herbivore	n	
04	astonish	v	
05	for one's own sake		
06	proliferation	n	
07	impulse	n	
08	undertake	v	
09	inhibit	v	
10	garment	n	
11	집착	n	
12	strain	n	
13	abbreviated	a	
14	alienation	n	
15	think outside the box		
16	conflicting	a	
17	live up to		
18	sphere	n	
19	attainment	n	
20	speculate	v	

18 장문 (1지문 2문항)

01	feverishly	ad
02	commit	v
03	결정 요인	n
04	brag about	
05	odds	n
06	coverage	n
07	live	a
08	cling to	
09	aversion	n
10	mindset	n
11	clarification	n
12	dismiss	v
13	indulge in	
14	struggle	v
15	풀어주다, 석방하다	v
16	robust	a
17	ascribe A to B	
18	refer to	
19	slim	a
20	controversy	n

19 복합 장문 (1지문 3문항)

01	peer	v
02	비극	n
03	interrupt	v
04	be involved in	
05	curb	n
06	greet	v
07	definitely	ad
08	hardship	n
09	chirp	v
10	deserve	v
11	stick out from	
12	pathetic	a
13	꾸러미, 소포	n
14	sparrow	n
15	pole	n
16	report back	
17	destination	n
18	vivid	a
19	count on	
20	lean	v

영어 독해 실전 연습

217

다음 글의 목적으로 가장 적절한 것은?

Dear Mr. Watson,

We are aware that the estimated period for completion of your bungalow has already been exceeded. Unfortunately, you will recall that we had an exceptionally severe winter. Work on your property was quite impossible during several prolonged periods of heavy snow. There has also been a nationwide shortage of building materials, especially bricks and timber, from which the trade is only just recovering. Both of these difficulties could not have been foreseen. Without them, the estimated completion period of six months would have definitely been met. Now that the weather has improved, work is now going ahead very well. Unless we have other unforeseen delays, we can safely promise that the bungalow will be ready for you by the end of August.

Yours sincerely,

Tom Peters

① 방갈로 공사에 추가된 건축 자재비를 청구하려고
② 폭설로 인한 방갈로 공사 중단에 대해 공지하려고
③ 방갈로 공사로 인한 인근 주민들의 불편에 대해 사과하려고
④ 방갈로 공사가 예정보다 빨리 완공될 것이라는 소식을 전하려고
⑤ 방갈로 공사 지연에 대한 이해를 구하고 완공 예정일을 알리려고

218

다음 글에서 필자가 주장하는 바로 가장 적절한 것은?

Perhaps you've had a friend who was extremely unhappy with his job. He agonized over what to do about his dissatisfaction, quickly concluding he could either quit or just stick it out. How many times in our lives do we reduce important decisions or opinions to two options? It's very easy to get stuck at one of two extremes. We've been trained to think in terms of good/bad, right/wrong, black/white. But that's not the way life is! Not only does black and white thinking reduce our own options, it also makes us more judgmental: if I'm right, they must be wrong. Intolerant thinking is evident in many of our society's current conflicts. There are always more than two sides. Try thinking in color. Be open to those who are different than you, explore your options, step outside the norm and avoid the trap of either/or solutions.

① 진로 결정은 본인의 의지로 해야 한다.
② 양분법적인 사고방식에서 벗어나야 한다.
③ 현재의 사회적 쟁점에 관심을 가져야 한다.
④ 결정을 내리기 전에 장단점을 모두 따져봐야 한다.
⑤ 행동에 나서기 전에 옳고 그름을 스스로 판단해야 한다.

219

다음 글의 요지로 가장 적절한 것은?

A lot of people think they can't write something until they have first thought their topic out perfectly. That's really high stakes writing. Start with low stakes writing. Let go of being perfect and just write. When you do low stakes writing, you are putting pen to paper (or hands to keyboard) without worrying about grammar, punctuation, sentence structure, or even the flow of ideas. It's brainstorming with yourself. And it should be fun! Even if it seems to be junk, just continue writing. It could be a line you heard. It could be a flash of memory: your grandfather's false teeth; how the lilacs smelled last June; your saddle shoes at eight years old. It could be any topic you jot down anytime. Add to the list anytime you think of something. Then when you sit down to write, you can just grab a topic from that list and begin.

① 브레인스토밍 회의는 아이디어 창출에 효과적이다.
② 주제를 확고히 세운 후 글을 쓰는 것을 시작해야 한다.
③ 메모하는 습관은 작문 실력을 향상하는 데 도움이 된다.
④ 글을 쓴 후 여러 번 퇴고하는 것은 글의 완성도를 높인다.
⑤ 글쓰기는 일단 떠오르는 대로 자유롭게 시작하는 것이 좋다.

220

다음 도표의 내용과 일치하지 <u>않는</u> 것은?

**Change in the Average Expenditure
on Day Care and Education**

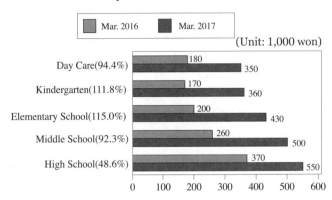

The chart above shows the change in the average expenditure on day care and education (from kindergarten to high school) per household in Korea between March 2016 and March 2017. ① The overall average expenditure of March 2017 showed massive increase compared to that of March 2016. ② The amount of the expenditure on educating kindergarten students was a little more than that of the expenditure on day care in March 2017. ③ The amount of average expenditure on educating middle school students per household recorded the greatest rise among the five items. ④ The increased amount of the expenditure on day care facilities was a little more than that of the expenditure on paying education fee for high school students. ⑤ The percentage increase of the expenditure on educating high school students grew least of all the items.

221

Jeremy Bentham에 관한 다음 글의 내용과 일치하지 <u>않는</u> 것은?

Jeremy Bentham was born in London in 1748. He was a gifted child, reading history and other "serious" books at age 3, playing the violin at age 5, and studying Latin and French when he was only 6. At 12, he
5 entered Queens College, in Oxford, where he studied law. In his late teens, Bentham decided to concentrate on his writings. With funding provided by his father, he wrote a series of books on philosophy, economics, and politics. He would often write for 8 to 12 hours a
10 day, a practice that continued through his life, leaving scholars material to compile for years to come. Most of his writings were not published until well over a century after his death. His most famous contribution to economics was the idea of utility and how it was a
15 driving force in economic and social behavior.

① 여섯 살 때 두 개의 외국어를 공부했다.
② Queens College에 입학하여 법을 공부했다.
③ 부친의 재정적 뒷받침을 받아 저술 활동을 했다.
④ 대부분의 저작물이 사망하기 전에 출판되었다.
⑤ 유용성이라는 개념으로 경제학에 기여했다.

222

다음 빈칸에 들어갈 말로 가장 적절한 것은?

Consider a scientist who feels stupid for not having read a journal article that is being discussed heatedly among his colleagues. A mindless hindsight makes him feel this way. He sees himself as having had the choice
5 of either reading or not reading the important article, and having stupidly made the wrong choice. This is, however, an example of faulty comparisons. Had he been less fixated on the outcome of the choice, he might have realized that the choice had not been
10 between reading the article and doing nothing, but rather between reading the article and working in the lab, taking a much-needed rest, or reading to his daughter. This example shows that awareness of _____ makes it less likely that we
15 will feel guilty in retrospect. On occasion, after learning the consequences of a choice, we may wish we had chosen differently, but we still tend not to be quite as hard on ourselves when we know why we made a certain choice and what we did instead.

① the freedom of choosing
② avoiding making decisions
③ the options that are being ignored
④ the negative effects of our choices
⑤ the process of making real choices

223

다음 빈칸에 들어갈 말로 가장 적절한 것은?

It is a common observation that people with great talents are often indifferent students. No one, for example, could have predicted Einstein's great achievements on the basis of his mediocre record in school. The reason for mediocrity is obviously not the absence of ability. It may result, instead, from self-absorption and the inability to pay attention to the ordinary tasks at hand. The only sure way an individual can interrupt daydreaming like preoccupation and self-absorption is to form a deep attachment to a great teacher or other person who understands and has the ability to communicate with the gifted individual. Whether gifted individuals find what they need in one-to-one relationships depends on _____. Fortunately, when this happens, we learn more about how to develop leaders and how talented people of different generations influence each other.

*mediocre: 보통의, 평범한

① how early their extraordinary qualities are found
② whether their parents can afford a special education for them
③ the availability of teachers who know how to cultivate their talents
④ their willingness not to be distracted from the tasks at hand
⑤ the level of difficulty of the schoolwork they are given

224

다음 글에서 전체 흐름과 관계 <u>없는</u> 문장은?

Anyone who follows sweatshops or international labor standards is by now familiar with the importance of transparency and monitoring of supply chains. ① Large multinational corporations rarely own their own factories these days. ② Instead, they produce their goods via a tangled web of contractors and subcontractors. ③ This way of doing business allows companies to get the lowest price possible for each component of their product, and shift production swiftly without having to shut down an old factory or build a new one. ④ The relationship between the contractors and subcontractors is one of the keys to the successful construction of a new factory. ⑤ Unfortunately, it also makes it extremely difficult for labor watchers to monitor which companies are using child labor or cheating their workers out of overtime.

*sweatshop: (저임금으로 노동자를 장시간 혹사시키는) 착취 공장

225

글의 흐름으로 보아, 주어진 문장이 들어가기에 가장 적절한 곳은?

> This stimulates job creation in the higher productivity industrial and service sectors of the economy, and eventually draws labor out of agriculture.

Rice research contributes to poverty alleviation through several pathways, and these contributions benefit both producers and consumers. (①) The direct pathway leads to higher productivity and higher profits for farmers. (②) The indirect pathway arises from the lower prices for consumers that are the inevitable result of higher farm productivity for any given level of demand. (③) In the short run, lower prices for consumers reduce poverty because many poor people are net buyers of rice, and lower prices increase their effective incomes. (④) In the long run, lower prices for consumers reduce the cost to employers of hiring workers. (⑤) This structural transformation of the economy is essential for long-term poverty alleviation.

226

다음 글의 내용을 한 문장으로 요약하고자 한다. 빈칸 (A), (B)에 들어갈 말로 가장 적절한 것은?

Science typically progresses not by rejecting previous theories outright but by extending them: new theories do not necessarily contradict older ones; rather, they reconceive the older ones as limited to certain conditions. The new theories extend the older ones to different domains so that more conditions can be explained. For example, Galileo's theory about falling objects (that they all fall at the same speed) works in a vacuum, but Newton's laws work in vacuums and extend to non-vacuums. It became clear in the twentieth century that Newtonian mechanics could not adequately describe objects that are moving very fast (approaching the speed of light) or massive (like black holes). Newtonian physics generated significant errors in these cases, so broader theories were needed that extended to these conditions, which is exactly what Einstein's special theory of relativity did for high speeds and his general theory of relativity did for gravity.

↓

> When a scientific theory is found to be ___(A)___ to a new situation, a new theory is developed and it ___(B)___ the existing theory.

	(A)		(B)
①	effective	········	replaces
②	effective	········	integrates
③	similar	········	complements
④	inapplicable	········	replaces
⑤	inapplicable	········	integrates

227~228 다음 글을 읽고, 물음에 답하시오.

James Steyer wrote a thought-provoking book entitled *The Other Parent: The Inside Story of the Media's Effect on Our Children.* Unfortunately, the media serve as another parent by being a force that shapes children's minds and reality, (a) influences behavior, sets expectations, defines self-image, and dictates interests, choices, and values. In actuality, this other parent is composed of a few large media corporations that include such giants as Time Warner, News Corporation, Disney, Viacom, Vivendi, and Sony. Sadly, these corporations are not concerned about children's well-being. Rather, they are in the business to (b) maximize profits. It's all about money — short-term profit.

One way that these media conglomerates maximize profits is through cross-promotions between branded properties and products — movies, TV shows, videos, merchandise, theme parks, books, magazines, music, and on and on. This means that no one dares (c) admit the decency and merit of what someone produces within their mega-structured corporate family. The conglomerates also censure their own network news programs and magazine articles to protect and promote their own interests. A common practice is to minimize or kill stories that might (d) offend advertisers. It is interesting to see the attitude that the CEOs of media corporations take when it comes to their own children. Ironically, many will not (e) allow their own children to see or hear the works that they produce and market for other people's kids. Media literacy education needs to be offered in every school, from grade school on up, to help our children healthfully deal with the other parent's influence for good and bad.

*conglomerate: 거대 복합 기업

227

윗글의 제목으로 가장 적절한 것은?

① Fall into the Sea of Media
② Beware of *the Other Parent*
③ Bad Reading Habits Die Hard
④ Be a Role Model to Your Kids
⑤ The Effect of Using Media on Education

228

밑줄 친 (a)~(e) 중에서 문맥상 낱말의 쓰임이 적절하지 <u>않은</u> 것은?

① (a) 　　② (b) 　　③ (c)

④ (d) 　　⑤ (e)

229

다음 글에 드러난 'I'의 심경 변화로 가장 적절한 것은?

I sat one evening in my laboratory. The sun had just set and the moon was rising from the sea. There was not enough light for my work. I left the room and locked the door. Then I went to the seashore. I was alone. There was nobody to help or comfort me. Several hours passed. I remained there gazing at the sea. It seemed almost motionless. The winds made no noise and all nature seemed to be resting under the quiet eye of the moon. A few fishing boats were on the water. Suddenly I heard the sound of a voice carried on the wind. It was warm and soft. I turned my head and saw some children walking along with their mother. Then I realized that I also had my children waiting for me in the house. It gave me the courage to carry on. I put all other thoughts out of my mind and hurried to my house.

① angry → calm
② lonely → refreshed
③ joyful → sorrowful
④ concerned → envious
⑤ excited → embarrassed

230

다음 글에서 필자가 주장하는 바로 가장 적절한 것은?

There are times when it is necessary to correct someone's grammar, pronunciation, or misuse of a word. If your employees or children use words in ways that will adversely affect the impression they make on others, you have an incentive, and often even a responsibility, to help them improve their impression by correcting them tactfully. But you almost never need to do so in public if your action will result in embarrassment. When you are in conversation with someone whom you have no reason to correct, why feel compelled to correct him at all if he misspeaks? Why not just let it pass? To the extent it makes you seem smarter to point out his error, it will make him feel dumber. Sometimes you need to be critical as a friend, lover, employee, coworker or parent. But how often does that criticism need to be expressed in public? The worst kind of embarrassment can't exist in private. It needs witnesses.

① 상대방의 사생활을 침해해서는 안 된다.
② 서로 발전할 수 있도록 건전한 비판을 해야 한다.
③ 타인에 대한 비판은 공개적으로 하지 말아야 한다.
④ 상대방의 사소한 실수는 지적하지 않는 것이 좋다.
⑤ 말하는 방식이 아니라 말하는 내용을 지적해야 한다.

231

다음 글의 요지로 가장 적절한 것은?

With complacency, no matter what people say, if you look at what they do it is clear that they are mostly content with the status quo. They pay insufficient attention to wonderful new opportunities and frightening new hazards. They continue with what has been the norm in the past. As an outsider, you may correctly see that internal complacency is dangerous, that past successes have created sluggishness or arrogance, but complacent insiders — even very smart people — just don't have that perspective. They may admit there are difficult challenges, but the challenges are over there in that other person's department. They think they know what to do and they do it. In a world that moves slowly and in which you have a strong position, this attitude certainly is a problem, but no more so than a dozen other problems. In a fast-moving and changing world, a sleepy or steadfast contentment with the status quo can create disaster — literally, disaster.

*status quo: 현재의 상황

① 현실에 안주하는 것은 매우 위험한 상황을 초래할 수 있다.
② 문제를 해결하려면 그 문제에 대한 철저한 분석이 필요하다.
③ 조직 내부의 시각이 아닌 외부의 시각으로 문제를 바라봐야 한다.
④ 초기에 큰 성과를 거둔 사람은 과거의 기준에 집착하는 경향이 있다.
⑤ 새로운 사업 분야에 뛰어들기 전에 현재의 사업 기반을 다져야 한다.

232

밑줄 친 the Australian salute has become a dwindling gesture가 다음 글에서 의미하는 바로 가장 적절한 것은?

Australian scientist George Bornemissza researched dung beetles native to thirty-two different countries to find the most suitable dung beetle species to handle the cowpat problem in Australia. Cowpats were indeed a serious problem in Australia because they were ideal breeding grounds for the very pesky bush fly. After the larvae turn into flies, they terrorize human since bush flies are attracted to bodily fluids such as sweat, nasal mucus, saliva, blood and tears. As a result, people have to wave their hands in front of the face at regular intervals in order to prevent the flies from landing on their body, or entering their nose or mouth. The term "the Australian salute," meaning such gesturing, was coined to explain these actions. Eventually Bornemissza found beetles that were able to recycle cow dung so he introduced fifty-five dung beetle species into Australia, solving the problem in one stroke. Now the Australian salute has become a dwindling gesture.

*cowpat: 소똥 **bush fly: 덤불파리 ***nasal mucus: 콧물

① Native dung beetles have rapidly disappeared in Australia.
② The Australian salute is used to show respect for Australia.
③ Bornemissza's action has reduced the number of bush flies.
④ Bush flies are the immediate cause of the Australian salute.
⑤ Annoying bush flies have increased due to the cowpat problem.

233

Ashokashtami에 관한 다음 글의 내용과 일치하지 <u>않는</u> 것은?

Ashokashtami is a festival for the Hindu deity Shiva held annually across eastern India, and central India. It is based on a story from the ancient Hindu texts, the Puranas, concerning the attempts of Lord Rama to kill
5 the demon Ravana. His efforts were being thwarted as Ravana had the favor and protection of the Goddess Kali. He was advised that the way to defeat Ravana was to worship and please Kali and thus change her allegiance away from the demon. Rama subsequently
10 engaged in seven days of elaborate rituals that led to Kali withdrawing her support of Ravana, whom Rama subsequently killed easily. Rama celebrated his victory by taking Shiva and Durga, the two Gods who helped him defeat Ravana, on a ride in his chariot. The
15 modern Ashokashtami festival operates as a dramatic reenactment of the chariot ride of Rama, Shiva, and Durga. Then Rama reunited with his wife, Sita, who was held captive by Ravana.

*thwart: 좌절시키다 **chariot: 전차

① 해마다 인도 동부와 중부 지방에서 열리는 축제이다.
② 신화에서 Ravana는 처음에 Kali 여신의 총애와 보호를 받았다.
③ 신화에서 Rama는 결국 Ravana를 죽였다.
④ 현대에는 Rama가 승리를 축하하며 전차를 탄 것을 재현한다.
⑤ 신화에서 Rama는 아내인 Sita와 재회하지 못했다.

234

Smoky Mountains National Park에 관한 다음 안내문의 내용과 일치하는 것은?

Smoky Mountains National Park

LOCATION: 107 Park Headquarters Road
Gatlinburg, North Carolina

OPEN: All year. Hours of operation vary from
season to season.
March − May: 9 am − 6 pm
June − October: 8 am − 7 pm
November − February: 8 am − 6 pm
The visitor center is open daily.

PHONE: Recorded information: (865) 436−1232

WEBSITE: http://www.nps.gov/grsm

COST: Fee for camping is 5 dollars a night.

Smoky Mountains National Park is a great place to bring the family and enjoy the view. Pack a basket, pick a spot and enjoy a meal or a snack near a rushing stream with a breathtaking view. The park is home to miles and miles of clear mountain streams, great for both trout fishing and swimming on a hot summer day. Much of the park can be enjoyed from your vehicle.

NOTE: Most trails in Smoky Mountains National Park are steep and rugged.

① 개방시간은 1년 내내 같은 시간이다.
② 캠핑을 위한 별도의 입장료는 없다.
③ 시냇물에서 수영과 낚시를 할 수 있다.
④ 산림 보존을 위해 자동차 출입은 통제된다.
⑤ 산길은 가파른 구간이 거의 없다.

235

다음 빈칸에 들어갈 말로 가장 적절한 것은?

A critical rule of life is _____. During a crisis at work it is often critical and/or desirable to seek assistance from those outside of your organization. In many cases you may need the assistance of an organization in your community. Having relationships with these entities prior to an incident will make it easier to work with them and for them to be responsive. If you have to figure out who you need to call and then you need to explain everything about yourself and your organization to them, it is going to take a lot longer to obtain assistance and the longer it takes the more damage that is being caused to your organization. Not only is building external relationships important, but also building internal relationships is just as critical. If you have a working relationship with the help desk manager, legal affairs department and public relations, asking for their assistance during an incident is going to be a lot easier and smoother.

① do not accept illegal gifts from anyone
② put public interests before private interests
③ do not expose the flaws of your organization
④ make an evacuation plan in case of a natural disaster
⑤ do not wait until you need a favor to build a friendship

236

다음 글에서 전체 흐름과 관계 <u>없는</u> 문장은?

In a 2015 article, a research team at the University of Southern California (USC) revealed that they might have discovered a treatment for human hair loss through experiments on laboratory animals. ① As strange as it sounds, they found that pulling hairs out could actually stimulate new hair growth. ② The USC scientists based the claims on their investigation of a microbiological phenomenon known as "quorum sensing." ③ Men with balding fathers have been shown to be more likely to bald themselves, so it can't just be the genes people inherit from their mothers that determine the risk of balding. ④ This phenomenon is not a new discovery, and four decades ago, it was seen by a group of Harvard scientists in colonies of bacteria. ⑤ It was observed that when bacteria are under attack, they send signals to one another in order to maintain healthy population densities.

*quorum: 정족수(필요한 구성원의 수)

237

글의 흐름으로 보아, 주어진 문장이 들어가기에 가장 적절한 곳은?

> Ecocentrics, on the other hand, believe in a greater degree of equality between humans and nature, and even the subordination of man to nature.

Religion and spiritual values are not the only factors which affect our attitudes to the environment. Philosophical and political values can also have a strong influence. (①) O'Riordan divides environmentalists into two broad groups: technocentrics and ecocentrics. (②) Technocentrics have more faith in science and technology. (③) They believe in man's dominance over nature, and furthermore are more optimistic that future scientific and technological developments will enable us to overcome environmental problems and constraints. (④) As such, they believe we are just one part of a global ecosystem, which must be respected. (⑤) Important issues shaping the extent to which someone is technocentric or ecocentric include their faith in the ability of science and technology to resolve environmental problems, and belief or skepticism regarding science and technology as driving forces in economic development.

238~240 다음 글을 읽고, 물음에 답하시오.

(A)

About 15 years ago, a little girl was sitting in a rusty wheelchair outside the central hospital of Maputo, the capital of Mozambique. She had no legs and was perhaps ten years old. When I passed, I stopped and exchanged a few words with her. I still do not know why. Her name was Sofia. Today, many years later, (a)she is one of my dearest friends.

(B)

After I heard about her story, I spoke to the doctor who took care of Sofia when she arrived at the hospital. The doctor said, "I will now tell you something that no doctor ever should. Nevertheless, I will do it so you will fully comprehend the remarkable strength of this young girl." And (b)she continued, "Since she was so seriously damaged, we were hoping that Sofia would die along with her sister. Her legs were torn apart, and her chest blown to pieces."

(C)

What happened to Sofia was that she and her sister were running along a small road close to their village. Sofia knew very well that she and her sister should keep to the road. There was something she called "earth crocodiles" buried in the ground by the side of the road. With her right foot, Sofia accidentally stepped by the side of the road. (c)She put her foot on a landmine. However, the major part of the explosion that followed was directed at her sister Maria. She died instantly, and Sofia was brought to the hospital.

(D)

Yet Sofia survived in spite of these serious damages. Even though (d)she was deeply frustrated with her sister's death, she had greater strength than the entire military industrial complex which tried to take her life. Within her body and mind, Sofia carried with her the strong will to resist of the poor people of the world. And she overcame. Today, Sofia has two children. She is a very good seamstress, she studies and she wants to become a teacher. But more than this, she has become a symbol all around the world for the resistance against the usage of landmines. For many young people, (e)she has become a heroine.

238

주어진 글 (A)에 이어질 내용을 순서에 맞게 배열한 것으로 가장 적절한 것은?

① (B) ― (D) ― (C) ② (C) ― (B) ― (D)
③ (C) ― (D) ― (B) ④ (D) ― (B) ― (C)
⑤ (D) ― (C) ― (B)

239

밑줄 친 (a)~(e) 중에서 가리키는 대상이 나머지 넷과 다른 것은?

① (a) ② (b) ③ (c)
④ (d) ⑤ (e)

240

윗글에 관한 내용으로 적절하지 않은 것은?

① 필자는 15년 전에 병원에서 Sofia를 만났다.
② Sofia는 지뢰 파편으로 다리와 가슴 부위를 심하게 다쳤다.
③ 지뢰를 밟은 Maria는 죽고 Sofia는 병원으로 이송되었다.
④ Sofia는 현재 재봉사이나 교사가 되기 위해 공부하고 있다.
⑤ Sofia는 지뢰 사용을 반대하는 상징적 인물이 되었다.

241

밑줄 친 a similar absence가 다음 글에서 의미하는 바로 가장 적절한 것은?

A reporter for *TechCrunch* recently observed, "Uber, the world's largest taxi company, owns no vehicles. Alibaba, the most valuable retailer, has no inventory. And Airbnb, the world's largest accommodation provider, owns no real estate. Something interesting is happening." Indeed, digital media exhibits a similar absence. Netflix, the world's largest video hub, allows me to watch a movie without owning it. Spotify, the largest music streaming company, lets me listen to whatever music I want without owning any of it. Amazon's Kindle Unlimited enables me to read any book in its 800,000-volume library without owning books, and PlayStation Now lets me play games without purchasing them. Every year I own less of the entertainment products I consume because I am able to consume whatever I desire by using these rental stores. Why would anyone own anything these days? You can quickly and easily rent whatever you want to watch or listen to. Instant renting gives you most of the benefits of owning and few of its disadvantages. You have no responsibility to clean, to repair, to store, to sort, to insure, to upgrade, to maintain.

① we can access entertainment products without possessing them
② small start-up companies can be key competitors to large corporations
③ there should be more investment in innovative ideas for new companies
④ lack of knowledge can be a problem in the knowledge-based economy
⑤ we need to find a balance between our online social life and our offline one

242

다음 글의 주제로 가장 적절한 것은?

The increasingly urbanized global society depends on the capacity of ecosystems of all kinds worldwide to support urban life with essential ecosystem services, even though people may not perceive this support or believe it valuable. For example, shrimp farmed in ponds in Thailand for export to cities in industrial countries are fed with fish meal derived from the harvests of fish in marine ecosystems worldwide. Or consider evolving changes in the variability of rainfall patterns that will likely trigger changes in the frequency, magnitude, and duration of droughts, fires, storms and floods, affecting food production, trade, migration, and possibly sociopolitical stability. And it has been suggested that the wildfires in Russia in 2010 — fueled by record temperatures and a summer drought — burned away much of Russia's wheat harvest and halted exports, contributing to the rising food prices that are seen as one of the triggers of the Arab Spring.

① the importance of global commerce and trade
② harmful effects of economic and political intervention
③ the influence of technological innovation on food supply
④ societies interconnected globally through Earth's ecosystems
⑤ international organizations working for environmental policy

243

다음 글의 제목으로 가장 적절한 것은?

The widespread belief that environmental regulation has an adverse effect on the economy can be traced back to the 1970s when a significant slowing down of growth was attributed to the advent of environmental
5 regulation. In China, on the other hand, rapid economic growth has brought about serious environmental degradation, with widespread air and water pollution, causing premature deaths, illness and health problems. Policy makers believe their dilemma is the choice
10 between environmental degradation and economic growth as they believe environmental regulation hurts growth but sustains the environment and saves lives. This is the commonly held view, but there are those who believe that growth and environmental quality are
15 not necessarily mutually exclusive and that the choice between environmental and economic goals is not necessarily governed by a trade-off of some sort.

① What Are the Main Causes of Environmental Pollution?
② China's Strenuous Efforts to Clean Up the Environment
③ Can Environmental Protection and Economic Growth Coexist?
④ A Dark Side of Industrial Development and Economic Growth
⑤ How Are People's Misconceptions about the Environment Formed?

244

다음 도표의 내용과 일치하지 <u>않는</u> 것은?

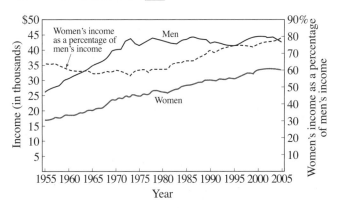

The graph above shows the average income for full-time, year-round workers by gender from 1955 to 2005 in 2005 dollars. ① The average income for male workers dramatically rose until the 1970s, but since then it has leveled off and actually fell in some years. 5 ② The average income for female workers shows a steady increase throughout the same time period. ③ At the start of the time period, the average income for female workers was less than half of the average income for male workers, but the figure rose to almost 10 four-fifths by the end of the time period. ④ The biggest gap between the average income for male and female workers was recorded in the early 1970s and female workers earned about 60% of what male workers earned. ⑤ In 2005, a gap of about 20% still persisted 15 between male and female workers' wages, even though society had moved closer to gender equity in pay.

245

다음 글의 밑줄 친 부분 중, 어법상 틀린 것은?

While some educators believe students who use English as a second language should be educated in their native language as well, critics insist such an approach ① doesn't work. The critics believe the best path to academic achievement for language-minority students in most cases ② are to learn English and learn it quickly. Too many bilingual programs, they say, place LEP(Limited English Proficient) students into slower learning tracks ③ where they rarely learn sufficient English and from which they may never emerge. These critics basically support an immersion model of bilingual education but ④ oppose the transitional and maintenance models. But supporters of transitional and maintenance models argue that students can best keep up academically with their English-speaking peers if they are taught at least partly in their native languages while ⑤ learning English.

246

다음 글의 밑줄 친 부분 중, 문맥상 낱말의 쓰임이 적절하지 않은 것은?

We are often remarkably ① resilient in responding to painful setbacks, largely because of what Gilbert and Wilson call the "psychological immune system," which enables us to get beyond stressful experiences and traumas. Just as our biological immune system protects us from toxins and disease, our psychological immune system protects us from psychological ② distress. We have a great capacity to find the silver lining, the humor, the potential for insight and growth, in the face of painful setbacks and traumatic experiences; and these "immune-related" processes ③ forbid us to return to satisfying lives in the face of negative experiences. But sometimes we overestimate our psychological immune system. So, when estimating the effects of traumatic events like breakups or failures at work, we ④ fail to consider how effectively they will take hold or how quickly they will exert their effects. As a consequence, we ⑤ inaccurately predict our future happiness.

247

다음 빈칸에 들어갈 말로 가장 적절한 것은?

Language is often used to claim a group identity. Interestingly, groups sometimes purposefully change words to accentuate their distinction from other groups. Typically, teenagers use words that will not be understood by their parents to mark the difference. This use of language is very common. Yet it has a perverse effect. It is that some dialects or accents might lead people to classify their speakers into categories based solely on the language or the accent. It is here that _____ meet language. Kinzler and DeJesus have interviewed children aged 5 or 6 about the northern and southern accents in the U.S. They did not really find noticeable differences. The children are simply too young to categorize people according to accents. They repeated the experimental procedure with children aged around 10. Then, the children have attributed the label of 'nice' to the southern accents and of 'smart' to the northern accent. Here, we can see that language properties (accent) were associated with concepts ('nice' vs. 'smart') that led the children to judge the temperament of the speaker.

*perverse: (일이) 기대를 벗어난, 심술궂은

① errors
② stereotypes
③ competencies
④ characteristics
⑤ interpretations

248

주어진 글 다음에 이어질 글의 순서로 가장 적절한 것은?

> The neutral colors are white, black, and gray. They make tints and shades but do not affect the hue of any color.

(A) The darks are still darks; the lights are still lights. Colors at the highest level of intensity are sometimes described as saturated. Any addition of a neutral color will diminish a hue's intensity. In other words, pink is lighter in value than a pure red but not nearly as intense.

(B) For example, no matter how much black, white, or gray is mixed into blue, it could not change it into purple. Neutral colors do, however, change the value of any hue with which they are mixed.

(C) Value means the relative lightness or darkness of a color. It is not the same as color intensity, which refers to the vividness of a particular hue. For example, when you bring up the color setting on your television, you increase the intensity of the colors. The relative values between the colors remain the same.

*saturated: 채도가 높은

① (A) — (C) — (B)
② (B) — (A) — (C)
③ (B) — (C) — (A)
④ (C) — (A) — (B)
⑤ (C) — (B) — (A)

249

글의 흐름으로 보아, 주어진 문장이 들어가기에 가장 적절한 곳은?

> Member contributions and discussions in online communities reveal the consumer needs, values, norms and behaviors.

Increasing number of people gathering in cyberspace has created the phenomenon called social media. Over a billion people now participate in various forms of social media, since the new social world is online. (①) People join online communities for the reasons of social enhancement, entertainment and enjoyment, as well as forming and retaining relationships. (②) Online communities have the potential to be a rich information source not only for consumers but also for marketers. (③) Marketers can therefore learn how consumers use the product, what they like or dislike about the product. (④) In addition, what the product means for the community and the various consumer groups can be learned. (⑤) Thus, marketers can better understand the processes underlying the purchasing behavior, by analyzing the online consumer-generated content.

250

다음 글의 내용을 한 문장으로 요약하고자 한다. 빈칸 (A), (B)에 들어갈 말로 가장 적절한 것은?

Is a judge likely to be affected by whether she is sitting, on a three-judge panel, with either conservative or liberal colleagues? It is tempting to suggest that this won't matter at all. Maybe judges simply follow the law as they see it. But this suggestion turns out to be wrong. If accompanied by two other judges appointed by a Republican president, a Republican-appointed judge is especially likely to vote according to conservative stereotypes — to invalidate environmental regulations, to strike down affirmative action programs or campaign finance laws, and to reject claims of discrimination made by women and handicapped people. The same pattern holds for Democrat-appointed judges, who are far more likely to vote according to liberal stereotypes if accompanied by two other Democratic appointees.

↓

> In court, a judge's ideological inclinations are _____(A)_____ by sitting with other judges who belong to the _____(B)_____ political party.

	(A)		(B)
①	disregarded	········	identical
②	neutralized	········	different
③	diminished	········	neutral
④	magnified	········	identical
⑤	maintained	········	different

251~252 다음 글을 읽고, 물음에 답하시오.

All too often, a great deal of energy is placed on establishing teaching-related goals, but far less attention is given to how progress toward them can be monitored. Once goal setting is completed, the pace
5 of the school year overwhelms us, and we don't give (a)sufficient attention to what progress is being made and what modifications should be made in our strategies. Opportunities for student and teacher learning are lost when goals are set in the fall and ignored until spring.
10 The best way to (b)construct this trap is to schedule periodic times throughout the school year when individuals will touch base and share their progress. Scheduled in the fall when the goals are developed, these (c)interactions could be formal, one-on-one
15 meetings between a teacher and an administrator, or they could be small-group conversations among teachers at faculty meetings or through e-mail exchanges. At my school, we sometimes designate faculty meetings for updates on goal progress.
20 Teachers are also placed into discussion groups based on the similarity of their goals, and these groups meet a few times during the year. The small settings and common focus (d)allow teachers to share their progress and learn from what others are doing to
25 address similar issues. At least one face-to-face meeting between teachers and administrators that is focused on teaching-related goals must take place each year. After all, if administrators don't take the time to talk to teachers about goals, what is the message we
30 give about their (e)importance?

251

윗글의 제목으로 가장 적절한 것은?

① The Role of Administrators in Education Reform
② Set Goals for Students, not for Teachers or Administrators
③ The Necessity of Monitoring Goal-related Progress at Schools
④ Increasing Student Academic Performance: The Number One Goal
⑤ Teacher Collaboration Can Lead to Student Learning Improvement

252

밑줄 친 (a)~(e) 중에서 문맥상 낱말의 쓰임이 적절하지 <u>않은</u> 것은?

① (a)　　　　② (b)　　　　③ (c)
④ (d)　　　　⑤ (e)

253

다음 글에 드러난 Hannah의 심경 변화로 가장 적절한 것은?

During her last week at the hospital, Hannah was starting to eat solid foods again. One afternoon, her close friends came to see her. They wheeled her to the second-floor lounge, where an outside terrace overlooked the park and the lake. From the terrace, they all watched Hannah's husband, Kenneth, on the street. He waved to them, leaning against a new-model red Jetta. Tied around the car was a ridiculous large gold bow. Everyone applauded. Hannah smiled looking at her nice new car. Kenneth joined them on the terrace. He brought a bottle of champagne and paper cups. Everyone toasted to Hannah's remarkable recovery. The celebration didn't last long. Her friends and Kenneth had to return to work. For a few minutes, Hannah was stuck on the terrace with her nurse. Hannah sat in her wheelchair and gazed out at the choppy gray water. The sky was turning dark. Then Hannah started to cry. She cried out at the sudden realization that she had been left alone again.

① bored → sad
② pleased → lonely
③ gloomy → touched
④ excited → nervous
⑤ relieved → regretful

254

다음 글의 주제로 가장 적절한 것은?

Although the lifespan of annual plant species is relatively fixed and short, that of many other plant species is relatively flexible. Even many biennial species, which normally die at the end of the second growing season after flowering and leaving seeds, will live for years (without flowering) if they do not receive the environmental cues that signal the normal progression through the seasons. The timing of progression through the life cycle in many other species is highly flexible, depending on the conditions under which a plant grows and develops. Reproduction is typically delayed when resources are limiting, and occurs sooner in plants that grow in high-light, nutrient-rich sites. Overall development, at both the organ (e.g., leaf) and whole plant level, is generally accelerated under resource-rich conditions.

① various ways of plant reproduction
② worldwide reduction of plant habitats
③ the importance of diversity in plant species
④ the ability of plants to adjust their life cycles
⑤ the absence of flexibility in the growing season

255

다음 글의 제목으로 가장 적절한 것은?

When you think about innovative people that never seem to run out of ideas, what is the first thing that comes to your mind? What immediately comes to my mind is that they have a reputation for listening to their people. Romano's Macaroni Grill is one of the nation's best-run food service chains according to *Restaurants and Institutions* magazine. Almost 80 percent of its restaurants' menu items have come from suggestions made by unit managers. What's good for effective companies is good for individuals. When you consistently listen to others, you never suffer for ideas. If you give people opportunities to share their thoughts, and you listen with an open mind, you gain fresh insights into problems and make good decisions. And even if you hear ideas that won't work, just listening to them can often spark other innovative thoughts in you and others.

① How Communication Drives Innovation
② Seek First to Listen, Then to Be Understood
③ Listening Builds Up Your Innovative Muscle
④ Main Principle of Leadership: Listen to Others
⑤ Some Key Characteristics of Innovative Organizations

256

Joseph-Marie Jacquard에 관한 다음 글의 내용과 일치하지 않는 것은?

Joseph-Marie Jacquard was born on July 7, 1752, in Lyon, France. Since both his parents were employed in the weaving industry, it was just a simple matter of time before Jacquard, as a young man, would become involved in that industry. Starting at the age of 10, Jacquard worked in the monotonous environment of the late eighteenth century textile industry. In 1790, Jacquard came up with the creative notion of an automated loom. However, his efforts to develop an automated loom were interrupted by the French Revolution. During the civil conflict that gripped France, Jacquard fought on the side of the revolutionaries and participated in the defense of his home city of Lyon. Following the revolution, Jacquard resumed his efforts to develop a device that would help automate the textile industry in France. In 1801, he introduced his punch-card system for programming the pattern of a carpet as it is being made on a loom. The Napoleonic government of France quickly recognized the value of Jacquard's device. He was awarded a medal and lifetime pension.

*loom: 직조기, 베틀 **punch-card: 천공 카드

① 양친 모두 직물업에 종사했다.
② 10살부터 직물업에 종사했다.
③ 자동화된 직조기에 대한 아이디어를 생각해냈다.
④ 프랑스 혁명에서 반혁명군 편에서 싸웠다.
⑤ 나폴레옹 정부로부터 자신이 만든 장치를 인정받았다.

257

다음 글의 밑줄 친 부분 중, 어법상 틀린 것은?

"Stop and smell the roses." This is a phrase you often hear but, maybe, are not quite sure that you understand. It does not mean to stop and actually smell roses each time you see them ① although that practice couldn't
5 hurt. What it means to me is that in spite of all the trials and adversity the world may seem to throw at you, ② it also provides beauty and serenity. But it is up to you to notice it. You will find it is out there, but so many people just pass it by, all the while ③ complaining
10 about how awful the world is with all the crime, violence, and poverty. I am not saying that crime, violence, and poverty do not exist, but so ④ are love, support, and abundance. In many instances, the negativity out there seems impossible to avoid, and in
15 many instances, ⑤ that may be true. What must be done in that instance is for us to seek out an example demonstrating love and support of our fellow man.

258

(A), (B), (C)의 각 네모 안에서 문맥에 맞는 낱말로 가장 적절한 것은?

The agricultural system has adapted so that it now relies on pesticides. This has occurred because farmers, extension services, agricultural policies, and agricultural research systems depend on and support the use of pesticides. This makes the parties involved
5 (A) resistant / vulnerable to change, making it difficult for new technologies to gain a foothold. For example, the slow adoption of disease-resistant wheat cultivars in Belgium was not a result of poor technical characteristics but of resistance at all levels of the food
10 chain, from farmers to input suppliers to policymakers. Dominant wheat systems were organized around a system that favored the use of chemical inputs, and the incumbents made it difficult for new entrants and new technology, such as disease-resistant wheat cultivars,
15 to (B) disrupt / maintain the food-growing practices in place. Private stakeholders could focus on changing three crop protection practices: an internal bias in supply companies in favor of agrochemicals rather than seed sales; a bias toward agrochemical applications
20 among supplier salespeople; and a (C) high / low priority attached to breeding for disease and pest resistance in seed companies.

*extension service: (미국의) 농사 조사 기관 **cultivar: (재배) 품종
***incumbent: 현존 업자, 현직자

	(A)	(B)	(C)
①	resistant	disrupt	high
②	resistant	maintain	high
③	resistant	disrupt	low
④	vulnerable	maintain	low
⑤	vulnerable	disrupt	high

259

다음 빈칸에 들어갈 말로 가장 적절한 것은?

Journalism is, and always has been, an exciting and controversial industry and one which for centuries has been subject to intense scrutiny of its purposes, practices and standards. Journalism serves many different, and sometimes conflicting, functions and interests. The role of news providers is to unearth facts of public interest and to mediate them for their audience in a neutral way. Thus, the public can make informed judgments and opinions of others' actions, which may in turn benefit society as a whole. Yet it must not be forgotten that the vast bulk of this diverse and dynamic industry _____. News is a commodity that makes profits for shareholders and delivers customers to advertisers. If journalism does not sell its products, there will not be enough money to fund the next reporting cycle. So journalism has to be attractive to its audiences, to maximize circulations and guarantee a return on its costs.

① relies on a strong business imperative
② gets low productivity from its workers
③ is being threatened by digital technology
④ strives for the realization of social justice
⑤ greatly promotes social conflict and division

260

다음 빈칸에 들어갈 말로 가장 적절한 것은?

Any large-scale human cooperation — whether a modern state, a medieval church, an ancient city or an archaic tribe — is rooted in common myths that _____. Churches are rooted in common religious myths. Two Catholics who have never met can nevertheless go together on a crusade or pool funds to build a Catholic church because they both believe that God was incarnated in human flesh and allowed Himself to be crucified to redeem our sins. States are rooted in common national myths. Two Serbs who have never met might risk their lives to save one another because both believe in the existence of the Serbian nation, the Serbian homeland and the Serbian flag. Judicial systems are rooted in common legal myths. Two lawyers who have never met can nevertheless combine efforts to defend a complete stranger because they both believe in the existence of laws, justice, and human rights.

① mistakenly cause us to fear failure
② exist only in people's collective imagination
③ make religious fundamentalists more extreme
④ control people's behavior based on collectivism
⑤ help us to realize the importance of companionship

261

주어진 글 다음에 이어질 글의 순서로 가장 적절한 것은?

Masters runners have confidence in their own judgment. The views of others, including their coach, teammates, and friends, matter less than they used to.

(A) A second opinion has saved many masters runners, including me. A well-known orthopedic surgeon told me in my late 40s that I had arthritis and should only run two miles (3.2 km) a week henceforth. I sought a second opinion from another doctor.

(B) Masters runners are also more discerning about advice from health specialists and about whether a diagnosis feels right. If a specialist says something that doesn't feel right, they are more likely to seek a second opinion.

(C) He said my bones were those of a 30-year-old and I could continue to run 30 to 40 miles (48 — 64 km) a week. The second diagnosis felt right. That was about eight years ago and I've continued running since then.

*orthopedic surgeon: 정형외과 의사 **arthritis: 관절염

① (A) — (C) — (B)　　　　② (B) — (A) — (C)
③ (B) — (C) — (A)　　　　④ (C) — (A) — (B)
⑤ (C) — (B) — (A)

262

글의 흐름으로 보아, 주어진 문장이 들어가기에 가장 적절한 곳은?

But theorists such as Newcomb have stressed the tentative nature of attitudes and pointed out that an individual will evaluate the new situation afresh and form an attitude about it on the spot.

Psychologists from many schools have preferred to think of attitudes as permanent, an 'enduring' aspect of character, 'an integral part of personality.' (①) Thus, attitudes are anchored and consistent. (②) Attitudes become predictable because the individual forms them as he interacts with the same things and people in his environment; he makes a mental organization — what Eysenck refers to as being 'programmed' and others prefer to call habit. (③) For such theorists, the individual is an impulsive, spontaneous creature; self theorists and sociologists belong to this school of thought. (④) Eminent social psychologist Allport is among those pointing out that there is no inner consistency in personality. (⑤) Since we are bundles of tendencies in a situation, it is only the environments in which we move that elicit characteristic behaviour in given situations.

Our brains are greedy energy-hungry organs. Despite comprising just 2 per cent of our body weight, they use up to 25 per cent of its energy. Clearly, anything that the brain can do to use less power will be of (a)advantage, as it would stop the person running out of energy and starving. Over time, our ancestors' brains evolved shortcuts to thinking that would save energy. As nothing seems to give our brains the glucose-munchies like conscious, rational, and deliberative thinking, we needed an 'energy saving' mode of thought. Equally, in situations of possible (b)threat, if our hunter-gatherer ancestors had taken the time to consciously, rationally weigh up the chances that the movement they saw in the corner of their eye was a lion, they may not have survived for very long. To underscore the point: it typically takes up to half a second or more for our brains to digest incoming sensory information and present a meaningful experience to our conscious mind. This may seem fast, but its implications for avoiding predators could be (c)fatal. Even today, our consciousness is constantly half a second behind reality, meaning that most activities — from sport to walking and even talking — are largely taken care of by our non-conscious minds, although the brain creates the bizarre illusion that our consciousness is in complete (d)autonomy! Therefore, for millions of years Mother Nature has sculpted our brains with a (e)preference for fast shortcut thinking.

*glucose-munchies: 포도당 간식거리   **bizarre: 기이한

263

윗글의 제목으로 가장 적절한 것은?

① Why Do Our Brains Need So Much Energy?
② Evolution: The History of Struggling to Secure Energy
③ Survival Strategy: Find It Outside, Not Inside the Brain
④ Unconscious Thinking to Save Energy: Our Survival Tool
⑤ Expand Your Conscious Thinking Against Potential Threats

264

밑줄 친 (a)~(e) 중에서 문맥상 낱말의 쓰임이 적절하지 <u>않은</u> 것은?

① (a)   ② (b)   ③ (c)
④ (d)   ⑤ (e)

265

다음 글의 목적으로 가장 적절한 것은?

To Whom It May Concern:

I've known John Brown for several years. While John was in high school, he helped me coach a community soccer team of 9- and 10-year-old boys. With patience and an ability to explain and demonstrate strategy clearly, he drew out the very best from these boys, who, in turn, looked up to him. I know John to be dependable, responsible, honest and courteous. He is by far the most popular server in the restaurant where he currently works. While dining there, I've often overheard customers asking to be seated in his section. John will be an assct to any organization. I can confidently recommend him for any position in your company. Please do not hesitate to call me if you would like to discuss what I've mentioned above further.

Sincerely,

Fred Miller (303) 444—1313

① 새로운 축구 코치 영입을 요청하려고
② 유소년 축구 클럽 코치를 추천하려고
③ 식당 직원 처우의 개선을 촉구하려고
④ 채용과 관련하여 지인을 추천하려고
⑤ 직원 채용 관련 정보를 문의하려고

266

다음 글에서 필자가 주장하는 바로 가장 적절한 것은?

A physician sets limits on his expertise with a difficult-to-diagnose case. "If the tests show that the problem is X, I can help you with medication. But if the X-rays indicate Y, I'm going to have to send you to a specialist for more testing." You don't respect the doctor any less for setting the boundaries. If anything, you're glad that he's honest about the limits of his expertise rather than experimenting. You may have similar limits, either because of a lack of expertise or simply because you prefer not to answer. Say so. "In this meeting, I'd rather not go into issues of costs. I'm here to respond to technical questions about how the system works." And if a question about cost surfaces later, stick to your limits: "As I mentioned earlier, I am not prepared to discuss costs." People will respect your boundaries if you yourself do.

① 자신의 약점보다는 강점을 찾아내도록 노력하라.
② 현재의 위치에 안주하지 말고 늘 새로움을 추구하라.
③ 자신이 처리할 일에 한계를 설정하고 그것을 준수하라.
④ 합리적인 근거를 들어 상대방을 설득하도록 노력하라.
⑤ 어려운 문제에 대해서는 전문가의 도움을 기꺼이 구하라.

267

다음 글의 요지로 가장 적절한 것은?

Are there advantages to demanding perfection? You might think that this will motivate you to find the best solution — but does it really lead to the best solution? Rejecting all alternatives because they are not perfect does not guarantee any solution whatsoever. Or you might think that demanding perfection will reduce any chances of regret. Again, perfectionism actually leads to the opposite — if you demand perfection, then you will look back on any decisions that you make that do not lead to the best possible outcome as a reason for regret. Your regrets will be magnified by your demand for perfection. In contrast to this, if you allow yourself some room for error, then you will accept that some decisions can possibly lead to a negative outcome, and you will consider this as something that comes with the territory.

① 완벽을 요구하지 않음으로써 후회를 줄일 수 있다.
② 완벽함을 추구해야 최선의 해결책을 찾을 수 있다.
③ 사람에 따라 완벽에 대해 갖고 있는 기준이 다르다.
④ 세상에 완벽함이란 존재하지 않으며 실현할 수 없다.
⑤ 어느 한 가지만 잘하고 다른 것에는 평범한 사람이 많다.

268

다음 도표의 내용과 일치하지 <u>않는</u> 것은?

Household Packaging Recycling Rates

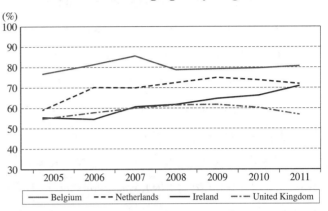

The graph above shows the household recycling rate for packaging of four selected European countries between 2005 and 2011. ① Belgium had the highest household recycling rate during this period and recycled about 80% of its packaging in 2011. ② In 2011, the Netherlands and Ireland had nearly the same recycling rate. ③ Between 2005 and 2006, the Netherlands, having the second highest recycling rate after Belgium, experienced a drastic 10% increase in its recycling rate. ④ From 2006 to 2011, the household recycling rate for packaging in Ireland steadily increased. ⑤ In 2006 the recycling rate in the United Kingdom was the lowest among these four European countries.

269

Charles Lyell에 관한 다음 글의 내용과 일치하지 <u>않는</u> 것은?

Born at Kinnordy, Scotland to a botanist father who possessed considerable literary tastes, Charles Lyell graduated from Oxford in 1821 and joined the bar in 1825. He soon realized that his ambitions were more
5 towards science, so, in 1827, he finally chose geology over the law. The first volume of his legendary book *Principles of Geology* was published in 1830. The third and last volume was published three years later. His other work, *Antiquity of Man*, was published in 1863,
10 and discussed the proofs of the long existence of human beings on the earth. Lyell's geological approach tends to be an assessment of evolutionism in the wider sense. He was one of the earliest men to embrace Darwin's theory of natural selection in biology. In
15 1866, Charles Lyell was made a foreign member of the Royal Swedish Academy of Sciences. Lyell died on February 22, 1875. He was 77 years old. He was buried in Westminster Abbey.

*bar: 변호사

① 아버지는 상당한 문학적 취향을 가진 식물학자였다.
② Oxford 대학을 졸업하고 처음에는 법조계에 들어갔다.
③ 1830년에 〈Principles of Geology〉의 첫 권을 출간했다.
④ Darwin의 자연 선택설을 반대한 사람들 중 한 명이었다.
⑤ 스웨덴 왕립 과학원의 외국인 구성원이 되었다.

270

다음 글의 밑줄 친 부분 중, 어법상 틀린 것은?

"Education is not the filling of a pail but the lighting of a pail," as the poet William Yeats wrote. Lighting that fire, creating thinking, informed, inspired and self-actualized individuals and citizens, ① is the
5 purpose of liberal education. That ideal was embraced by democratic societies in the previous century not only to help individuals reach their potentials, but also ② to help democracy survive and thrive. Democracy needs informed and thinking citizens as much as it
10 needs considerate and thoughtful citizens. Education is not, in other words, only about ③ what we provide for our children; it is also about what our children are likely to provide to the world. How we educate youth, how we cultivate their minds, how we guide their social
15 and moral development — these are key parts not only of who and what they become as individuals, but also of how we, as a society, ④ creating our future and collective destiny. It may be cliché, but it is also profoundly true that youth are our future and that upon
20 our children ⑤ rests the fate of tomorrow's world.

271

(A), (B), (C)의 각 네모 안에서 문맥에 맞는 낱말로 가장 적절한 것은?

Getting people to agree with you is an art — the art of persuasion. It turns out that the majority has an enormous advantage. They don't really need to try to persuade us. The simple fact that they are the majority
5 is almost always enough for people to agree with them or to follow them. The majority has the ability to (A) bend / comprehend reality. In fact, their power is so immediate and compelling that we follow them even when our own senses tell us they are wrong. Minority
10 views, on the other hand, have an uphill battle to persuade us. We don't agree readily. In fact, we find many reasons to resist agreement. It has to be done over time, through a systematic method of persuasion. However, this (B) deliberate / random process of
15 persuasion is what ultimately ensures that our support for a minority view is truly genuine. When we do agree with a minority view, it is usually based on a real change in attitude. It means that we now follow or agree with that view because we have been (C) conditioned /
20 convinced.

	(A)		(B)		(C)
①	bend	········	deliberate	········	conditioned
②	comprehend	········	random	········	convinced
③	bend	········	deliberate	········	convinced
④	comprehend	········	deliberate	········	conditioned
⑤	bend	········	random	········	convinced

272

다음 빈칸에 들어갈 말로 가장 적절한 것은?

The most important self-regulatory skill that top performers use during their work is controlling their thoughts of _____. Elite runners, for example, focus intensely on themselves; among other
5 things, they count their breaths and simultaneously count their strides in order to maintain certain ratios. In contrast, ordinary endurance runners in a race tend to think about anything other than what they're doing; it's painful, and they want to take their minds off it.
10 Most of us don't exert ourselves in such a significant physical manner, but the same principle applies to purely mental work. The best performers monitor themselves closely. They are in effect able to step outside themselves, monitor what is happening in their
15 own minds, and ask how it's going. Researchers call this metacognition — knowledge about your own knowledge, thinking about your own thinking. Top performers do this much more systematically than others do; it's an established part of their routine.

① self-defense
② self-expression
③ self-confidence
④ self-observation
⑤ self-contentment

273

주어진 글 다음에 이어질 글의 순서로 가장 적절한 것은?

> People from a sequential culture would argue that proceeding in a straight line is reasonable because it is orderly, efficient, and involves a minimum of effort.

(A) Even though each customer is not served in order, the whole process is more efficient because it involves far less unwrapping and rewrapping of the various types of meat.

(B) Trompenaars and Hampden-Turner cite the example of the butcher shop in Italy (a sequential culture). In the shop, the butcher unwraps and slices an order of salami for one customer and then yells out, "Anyone want salami before I rewrap it?"

(C) However, this type of straight-line thinking may not always be the best way of doing something, because it is blind to certain efficiencies of shared activities and interconnections. Sometimes juggling a number of different tasks at the same time may in fact be the most time efficient.

① (A) — (C) — (B)
② (B) — (A) — (C)
③ (B) — (C) — (A)
④ (C) — (A) — (B)
⑤ (C) — (B) — (A)

274~276 다음 글을 읽고, 물음에 답하시오.

(A)

I was a single parent of four small children, working at a minimum-wage job. Money was always tight, but we had a roof over our heads, food on the table, clothes on our backs and, if not a lot, always enough. My kids told me that in those days they didn't know we were poor. They just thought Mom was cheap. (a) I've always been glad about that. It was Christmastime, and although there wasn't money for a lot of gifts, we planned to celebrate with church and family, parties and friends, drive downtown to see the Christmas lights and have special dinners.

(B)

Back in the car driving home, everyone was in high Christmas spirits, laughing and teasing each other with hints and clues about what they had bought. My younger daughter, Ginger, who was eight years old, was unusually quiet. (b) I noted she had only one small, flat bag with her after her shopping spree. I could see enough through the plastic bag to tell that she had bought candy bars — fifty-cent candy bars! I was so angry. I wanted to yell at her, but I didn't say anything until we got home. I called her into my bedroom and closed the door, ready to be angry again when (c) I asked her what she had done with the money.

(C)

But the big excitement for the kids was the fun of Christmas shopping at the mall. They talked and planned for weeks ahead of time, asking each other and their grandparents what they wanted for Christmas. I dreaded it. (d) I had saved $120 for

presents to be shared by all five of us. The big day
30 arrived and we started out early. I gave each of the four
kids a twenty-dollar bill and reminded them to look for
gifts that cost about four dollars each. Then everyone
scattered. We had two hours to shop; then we would
meet back at the "Santa's workshop" display.

(D)

35 This is what she told me: "I was looking around,
thinking of what to buy, and I stopped to read the little
cards on one of the Salvation Army's 'Giving Trees.'
One of the cards was for a little girl, four years old, and
all she wanted for Christmas was a doll with clothes
40 and a hairbrush. So (e)I took the card off the tree and
bought the doll and the hairbrush for her and took
them to the Salvation Army booth. I only had enough
money left to buy candy bars for us," Ginger continued.
"But we have so much and she doesn't have anything."
45 I never felt so rich as I did that day.

274

주어진 글 (A)에 이어질 내용을 순서에 맞게 배열한 것으로 가장 적절한 것은?

① (B) — (C) — (D)　　　② (C) — (B) — (D)
③ (C) — (D) — (B)　　　④ (D) — (B) — (C)
⑤ (D) — (C) — (B)

275

밑줄 친 (a)~(e) 중에서 가리키는 대상이 나머지 넷과 다른 것은?

① (a)　　　② (b)　　　③ (c)
④ (d)　　　⑤ (e)

276

윗글의 필자에 관한 내용으로 적절하지 <u>않은</u> 것은?

① 배우자가 없이 네 자녀를 키우는 어머니였다.
② 집으로 오는 길에 Ginger가 산 선물을 보고 화가 났다.
③ 집에 도착한 후에 Ginger를 자기 방으로 불렀다.
④ 자녀에게 선물 살 돈을 20달러씩 나누어 주었다.
⑤ 인형과 머리빗을 사서 구세군에게 선물로 주었다.

277

다음 글의 목적으로 가장 적절한 것은?

Dear Mr. Hamilton,

Thank you for the opportunity to interview with your company and for the fascinating tour. I enjoyed our informative discussion, and your new animation was breathtaking. May I publicize your forthcoming video game by writing an article about it for the local weekly computer newspaper, *The Web-Byter?* I volunteer each month to send the editor a column reviewing and recommending new software or computer video games. Also, I want to write stories about clients who have just switched to your software. Readers would find it interesting to learn why they switched. If you are interested, please make my email address or phone number available to your marketing communications representative. I look forward to hearing from you at your convenience.

Sincerely,

Brian Adams

① 홍보물에 실린 오류 내용 수정을 요구하려고
② 제품 홍보에 관한 아이디어를 구하려고
③ 홍보물 배부에 관한 절차를 안내하려고
④ 홍보업체 교체의 필요성을 주장하려고
⑤ 홍보 기사 작성을 제안하려고

278

다음 글에 드러난 Susan의 심경 변화로 가장 적절한 것은?

When Susan moved into her new home, she knew it was everything she ever wanted. She had been looking around for a place which had a new kitchen, and enough space in the backyard to start to grow a garden. The first week was exciting. Susan loved the idea of living in Byron Bay. For a long time, she had heard about how relaxing the lifestyle could be—living near the beach, the sunshine and not to mention the easy access to fresh organic local produce. But Susan's dreams of living in calm were shattered almost as soon as they had begun. She had only been in her new home two short weeks when she was awoken repeatedly to the sounds of roaring laughter, the clinking of glasses and what sounded like a brass band. Her heart sank in her chest when she realized her house was right near a big, loud hotel wedding venue.

① proud → jealous
② bored → excited
③ pleased → upset
④ frustrated → relieved
⑤ annoyed → indifferent

279

다음 글에서 필자가 주장하는 바로 가장 적절한 것은?

Praise from a supervisor is much more effective if employees believe that it is sincere. Undoubtedly, a number of factors can determine sincerity, but two are particularly important. The first has to do with the frequency with which praise is given out. If supervisors are constantly praising their subordinates, the motivational value of this praise will likely diminish over time. On the other hand, if praise is very rarely given out, subordinates may become highly suspicious on those few occasions when they do receive it. Thus, for praise to be effective, supervisors must strike a balance between giving too much or too little. A related issue, though no less important, is the level of performance that must be achieved in order to receive praise. If supervisors heap lavish amounts of praise on subordinates for ordinary performance, this will decrease the value of praise when high levels of performance are actually achieved.

① 칭찬과 질책은 같은 비율로 이루어져야 한다.
② 아랫사람에게 하는 칭찬은 아끼지 말아야 한다.
③ 칭찬할 때는 무엇에 관한 것인지를 확실히 해야 한다.
④ 적당한 빈도로 칭찬받을 성과에 대해서만 칭찬해야 한다.
⑤ 칭찬은 일상적인 대화보다는 공식적인 자리에서 해야 한다.

280

밑줄 친 the purest form of acting이 다음 글에서 의미하는 바로 가장 적절한 것은? [3점]

Communication flows in only one direction when you are watching a screen: from the TV screen to your easy chair, or from the big screen to your sticky megaplex seat. You can throw tomatoes at screens and it won't change a thing about the show. The audience has two choices: to watch or not to watch. This makes for a very different level of audience participation than at the theater. For example, when was the last time you were at a movie where the audience applauded at the end? When you're watching TV, do you stand and applaud in your own living room? No matter how brilliant the acting, no matter how much the film or television show affected you, you don't usually applaud. Why? Because the performers can't hear you. There is no communication between you and them. In Yoruba, the western part of Nigeria, television is called 'ero asoro maghese,' which means "the machine that speaks but accepts no reply." Theater, on the other hand, accepts replies. In short, performing in the theater is the purest form of acting.

① actors don't actually watch other actors on the stage
② audience participation is actively requested by actors
③ actors and the audience interact throughout the show
④ performance is more about taking off a mask than putting one on
⑤ actors like to improvise and add something new to their characters

281

다음 글의 요지로 가장 적절한 것은?

We have seen that for many people living close to nature and being self-sufficient are important components of an ideally simple rural lifestyle. But as David Owen argues in *Green Metropolis*, there are
5 times when the truth is counterintuitive. Living in the countryside usually means a detached house, which takes a lot more energy to heat than a city apartment that is typically more compact and surrounded on all sides but one by other apartments. It also usually
10 involves a lot more driving compared to life in big cities where there is extensive public transport and where walking is often preferable to driving. If part of being self-sufficient in the countryside is heating the house with wood you've cut, this is probably worse for
15 the environment than heating with gas. Even when the wood is properly dried and burned in an efficient modern stove of the type approved by the US Environmental Protection Agency, burning wood still gives off far more fine-particle pollution than does
20 heating with oil or gas furnaces.

*furnace: 난로, 보일러

① 일상 생활에서 환경 보호를 실천하는 것이 중요하다.
② 도시에서 친환경적으로 생활하는 것은 많은 비용이 든다.
③ 도시나 시골 생활의 환경 파괴의 정도를 계측하기는 어렵다.
④ 시골에서의 생활 방식이 도시 생활보다 환경에 악영향을 끼친다.
⑤ 도시 생활은 시골 생활보다 비용 효율적이지만 환경에는 해롭다.

282

다음 글의 주제로 가장 적절한 것은? [3점]

Advocates of genetically modified (GM) foods argue that, contrary to popular belief, GM foods cause less environmental damage than their unmodified counterparts. For some crops, it is not cost-effective to
5 remove weeds by physical means such as tilling, so farmers will often spray large quantities of different herbicides to destroy weeds, a time-consuming and expensive process that requires care so that the herbicide doesn't harm the crop plant or the environment. Crop
10 plants genetically-engineered to be resistant to one very powerful herbicide could help prevent environmental damage by reducing the amount of herbicides needed. For example, Monsanto has created a strain of soybeans genetically modified to be not affected by their
15 herbicide product Roundup. A farmer grows these soybeans which then only require one application of weed-killer instead of multiple applications, reducing production cost and limiting the dangers of agricultural waste run-off.

① the best weed-killer for crops
② the disadvantages of herbicides on crops
③ the long-term health effects of pesticides
④ the environmental benefit of genetically modified plants
⑤ potential health hazards of genetically engineered foods

283

다음 글의 제목으로 가장 적절한 것은?

Real life is seldom as dramatic as the cinematic world and minorities in situations such as a jury room rarely win the day. Nevertheless, they do occasionally convert the majority. The success of minorities is dependent on the behavioral style of the individuals involved. If the minority is consistent and flexible, and their arguments are relevant, then they may eventually win over the opinions of the majority. The first of these factors, the consistency with which the group defends and advocates its position, is the most crucial. This consistency must be maintained between the minority group and over time. If the minority members agree among themselves and continue to do so, they may persuade the majority to question its own assumptions and seriously consider those of the minority. To be successful, those people in the minority must not appear to be rigid and dogmatic but flexible in their approach and willing to discuss the reasons why they disagree with the majority.

① Attitude Is Not Everything!
② Democracy as a System of Majority Rule
③ How Can the Minority Influence the Majority?
④ Real Life Differs from the Life on the Big Screen
⑤ The Impact of Political Reform on Minority Rights

284

다음 도표의 내용과 일치하지 않는 것은?

% of U.S. workers employed in jobs that are the most exposed to AI in 2022

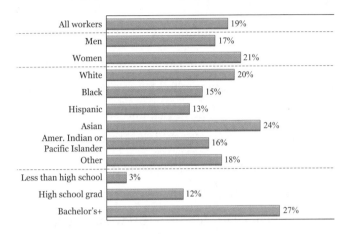

The above graph shows the percentages of U.S. workers who were exposed to Artificial Intelligence (AI) in their jobs in 2022. ① In 2022, almost one in five U.S. workers (19%) were in jobs exposed to AI. ② Women were exposed to AI in their jobs at a four-percentage-point higher rate than men. ③ While white workers had a five-percentage-point higher exposure rate than black workers, American Indian or Pacific Islander workers had a three-percentage-point higher exposure rate than Hispanic workers. ④ Nearly a quarter of Asian workers were exposed to AI in their jobs, representing the highest AI exposure level among all the racial groups. ⑤ Workers with a bachelor's degree or higher had about three times the AI exposure level in their professions compared to those with only a high school diploma and nine times more than those without a high school diploma.

285

Richard Arkwright에 관한 다음 글의 내용과 일치하지 <u>않는</u> 것은?

Richard Arkwright was the youngest of 13 children. He had no schooling and did not learn to read and write until he was middle-aged. At the age of ten he was sent to work in a barber's shop. While working
5 there he discovered a method for dyeing hair that did not fade, and he became a rich and successful barber and wigmaker. However, Arkwright's real claim to fame is his invention of the 'spinning frame', a machine for spinning cotton. He made it with the help of a
10 skilled watchmaker, John Kay. Arkwright went on to invent and improve other machines used in textile manufacture. Many workers found their jobs were taken over by the new machines. They became very angry and tried to destroy the machines and even
15 threatened Arkwright. But he was a determined man and his factories helped his home county of Lancashire become the centre of the world's cotton industry.

*spinning frame: 정방기(실을 뽑는 기계)

① 중년이 되어서야 비로소 읽고 쓰기를 배웠다.
② 10살에 이발소에서 일을 시작하여 성공적인 이발사가 되었다.
③ John Kay의 정방기 발명을 도왔다.
④ 직물 제조공장 노동자들에게 위협을 받기도 했다.
⑤ Lancashire를 세계 면화 산업의 중심지로 만드는 데 기여했다.

286

2024 Spring Job Fair에 관한 다음 안내문의 내용과 일치하지 <u>않는</u> 것은?

2024 Spring Job Fair

Saturday April 6, 2024
2:00 p.m. — 6:00 p.m.
Bayshore Community Center

Last year's Job Fair was the largest ever held in
5 this area with more than 80 employers and over 1,000 job seekers. This year, we're moving to an even larger location with plenty of space for all attendees.

Enhanced Services to Employers
10
• 5m×5m booth with tables
• Free Wi-fi
• Open areas and interview spaces
• Employer-only lounge and refreshments

The cost to register is $50, which will help offset
15 the enhanced event and the services provided for this year's event.

Register Now! (click here)

The Job Fair is a collaborative event supported by Grey County, Georgian College and the Four
20 County Labour Market Planning Board.

For more information, please email Peter Kalina at P_Kalina@jobfair.org or call 541-2345-4321.

① 전년보다 더 큰 행사장에서 개최된다.
② 테이블이 있는 부스가 설치된다.
③ 별도의 인터뷰 공간이 마련된다.
④ 등록 비용은 50달러이다.
⑤ 지역 대학에서 단독 후원하는 행사이다.

287

Lake George Bike Rentals에 관한 다음 안내문의 내용과 일치하는 것은?

Lake George Bike Rentals

Whether you have come for a nice relaxing vacation or want to actively discover all Lake George has to offer, there is no better way to experience the area than on a bike. You can rent a bike at a low price at one of our rental shops.

Rental Shop Operating Hours

– 9:00 am — 6:00 pm (March — October)

– All bikes must be returned by 5:45 pm.

Rental Rates

– Standard bikes: $5 by the hour; $20 by the day

– Bikes with attached trailer: $10 by the hour; $30 by the day

– Helmet rental fee is included in the bike rental fee.

Safety Checklist

– Bikers must only ride on paved bicycle paths.

– All bikers are required to wear a helmet.

– Only the person renting the bike is allowed to ride it.

– Only one child per trailer

Reservations are not needed.

First-come, first-served.

---

① 3월부터 10월까지 하루 10시간 영업을 한다.
② 트레일러가 부착된 자전거의 대여료는 시간당 30달러이다.
③ 헬멧 대여 비용은 자전거 대여료와 별도로 지불해야 한다.
④ 포장된 자전거 도로에서만 자전거를 타야 한다.
⑤ 자전거 대여를 위해서 예약이 필수적이다.

288

다음 글의 밑줄 친 부분 중, 어법상 틀린 것은? [3점]

The second law of thermodynamics states that each time useful energy is converted from one state to another, there always is a lesser amount of useful energy available in the second state ① than there was in the first state. For example, in the case of an incandescent light bulb, electrical energy is converted to 'useful' light energy as well as some useless heat, ② which you can detect by touching a light bulb that has been turned on for a few minutes. For incandescent light, approximately 5 percent of the electrical energy becomes light and 95 percent becomes heat: a 5 percent energy efficiency. Similarly, the fossil fuel energy used to do the work of moving an automobile ③ generating a substantial amount of useless heat that must be dissipated through the 'cooling system,' or it will ruin the motor. Therefore, in ④ any transformation of energy, in terms of energy quality (useful energy) there is an apparent loss of available energy. This phenomenon ⑤ is referred to as the principle of energy degradation, and it is universally applicable.

*thermodynamics: 열역학

289

다음 글의 밑줄 친 부분 중, 문맥상 낱말의 쓰임이 적절하지 <u>않은</u> 것은?

Evolution-oriented researchers have a plausible explanation for the dramatic increase in the ① <u>prevalence</u> of obesity. They point out that over the course of history, most animals and humans have lived in environments in which there was fierce competition for limited, unreliable food resources and ② <u>starvation</u> was a very real threat. As a result, warm-blooded, foraging animals evolved a propensity to ③ <u>consume</u> more food than immediately necessary when the opportunity presented itself, because food might not be available later. Excess calories were stored in the body to prepare for food shortages, and having extra fat on the body was actually considered to be an ④ <u>unappealing</u> quality. This approach to eating remains adaptive for most species of animals that continue to struggle with the ebb and flow of ⑤ <u>unpredictable</u> food supplies.

*propensity: 경향, 기질

290 ~ 293 다음 빈칸에 들어갈 말로 가장 적절한 것을 고르시오.

290

Teachers with a growth mind-set encourage students to work hard, or to make an effort, in order to grow academically. That encouragement is well founded in terms of the critical role of effort in success. When it comes to grading, however, the vocabulary needs to shift a bit. It's not possible to observe effort accurately, and we can't (or ought not try to) grade what we can't observe. So there is a vocabulary shift from *effort* to *process*. We can observe that a student willingly revises his work to improve its quality. We can observe that a student seeks help when she is stuck on some aspect of her work. We can observe that a student develops a time line for completing a complex task and adheres to it. Those sorts of "habits of mind and work" are indicators of the sorts of "intelligent processes" that are associated with successful people. Good grading practice requires that we use _____ indicators.

① visible
② mutual
③ technical
④ academic
⑤ qualitative

291

As Napoleon said, victory _____.
Most people tend to underestimate the time it takes to
achieve something of value, but to be successful, you
have to be willing to pay your dues. James Watt spent
5 twenty years laboring to perfect his steam engine.
William Harvey labored night and day for eight years
to prove how blood circulated in the human body. And
it took another twenty-five years for the medical
profession to acknowledge he was right. Cutting
10 corners is really a sign of impatience and poor self-
discipline. But if you are willing to follow through, you
can achieve a breakthrough. That's why Albert Gray
says, "The common denominator of success lies in
forming the habit of doing things that failures don't
15 like to do." Self-discipline is a quality that is won
through practice. Psychologist Joseph Mancusi noted,
"Truly successful people have learned to do what does
not come naturally. Real success lies in experiencing
fear or aversion and acting in spite of it."

*denominator: 분모

① belongs to the most persevering
② comes when you desire it eagerly
③ requires strength, wisdom, and skills
④ is the child of opportunity and chance
⑤ lies in the process, not in the attainment

292

Even in an ambiguous statement, each word has a
clear and distinct meaning (as in the various meanings
of "work"). We just don't know which meaning to
accept as the intended one. For example, in the sample
5 sentence, "The auditor's work is done," the speaker
could mean that the entire audit has been completed
or the auditor is done for the day and is going home.
Here both "work" and "done" must be clarified. Had the
speaker said, "The auditor's review of the accounting
10 records is complete for today," the potential confusion
would be eliminated. Ambiguity in meaning, called
semantic ambiguity, can be avoided by substituting an
unambiguous word or phrase for the ambiguous one.
Or, the semantic ambiguity can be explained away by
15 providing clarifying information that makes only one
interpretation possible. For example, we could avoid
the ambiguity by saying, "The auditor's work is done.
He does not need to come back until next year." Thus,
_____. [3점]

*auditor: 회계 감사관 **semantic: 어의의, 의미론의

① the additional context avoids ambiguity
② a metaphor is used to clarify the ambiguity
③ ambiguous words slow down comprehension
④ an ambiguous statement cannot be stated clearly
⑤ simplifying words often fails to eliminate ambiguity

293

A prime illustration of how dangerous emotionally based reform can be to the health of a society, particularly when those reforms attack the traditions and institutions supporting society, can be found in the French Revolution. In attempting to create a completely new order, the French revolutionaries through force and terror sought to destroy all social and political institutions. Undermining the traditional family, the right to property, and religious authority, the Revolution tried to refashion society by destroying its past and its social traditions, and by attacking the inherited foundations of French civilization — its art, moral ideas, science, and reason. The result was a mass murder and a complete breakdown of authority, culminating in the dictatorship of Napoleon Bonaparte. Unlike the more limited American Revolution, the French Revolution _____. [3점]

① was led by rational and credible leaders
② marked a destructive break from the past
③ brought a balance between liberty and order
④ allowed greater independence and democracy
⑤ led to the surprising survival of an old authority

294

다음 글에서 전체 흐름과 관계 없는 문장은?

In the Islamic world, the tribes and peoples had their own long history of stargazing. ① This was, at first, partly for navigating the deserts where they lived, which had few landmarks on the ground, but countless ones overhead in the cloudless, starry skies. ② But later it was for judging the right time and direction to face for Islamic prayer times. ③ The Islamic scholars translated ancient Greek writings, and adapted their ideas and instruments to produce calendars and star-charts of their own. ④ The political conflicts between the Muslim and non-Muslim groups affected the interactions of a specific civilization or society with another group. ⑤ Scholars like Abd Allah Muhammad Ibn Jabir Sinan al-Battani wrote and rewrote many important works on astrology, and started to draw out the differences between astrology, used for fortune-telling, and astronomy as a pure and accurate study of 'the heavens' for its own sake.

295 ~ 296 주어진 글 다음에 이어질 글의 순서로 가장 적절한 것을 고르시오.

295

A term connected to approaches that focus on the audience is *reception*. Studies of reception focus on how the text, cultural object, or experience is received by particular audiences.

(A) These kinds of approaches recognize that different audiences read or receive the same esthetic experience in different ways. Alongside the question of what these things may have meant to the original audiences, we can explore what they mean to those who "read" them today.

(B) Rather than focusing on the relationship between the author and the text, reception studies look at the relationship between the text and the audience. The reception approach is also applied to non-textual esthetic creation and cultural experience.

(C) Just as we can consider what happens when someone reads a text, we can ask what happens when someone gazes at a painting or watches a movie, or even when someone hears a piece of music. Religious texts, images, architecture and ritual can all be "read" in this way.

① (A) — (C) — (B)   ② (B) — (A) — (C)
③ (B) — (C) — (A)   ④ (C) — (A) — (B)
⑤ (C) — (B) — (A)

296

Although it is misleading simply to assume, without argumentation, that findings on laboratory animals are extrapolable to humans, many defenders of animal experimentation appear to do just that. When they do defend the practice, they typically do so by citing examples of experimental success.

(A) Basically they simply stated, on grounds of their authority, that animal experimentation was crucial for a variety of biomedical discoveries. The evidence they provided was merely historical: the presence of some animal experiments before a particular biomedical discovery was said to show that those experiments were the cause of that discovery.

(B) Consider, for example, the now classic 1974 article titled "Ben Franklin and Open Heart Surgery." This article presumably showed just how pervasive and how important animal experimentation was in the development of new medical treatments. What evidence did the authors offer in support of this claim?

(C) However, more care must be taken before we claim that the former caused the latter. Although examples may establish a correlation, there is a large gulf between a correlation and a cause. And this is especially so for animal experimentation. [3점]

*extrapolable: 확대 적용[일반화]할 수 있는

① (A) — (C) — (B)   ② (B) — (A) — (C)
③ (B) — (C) — (A)   ④ (C) — (A) — (B)
⑤ (C) — (B) — (A)

297~298 글의 흐름으로 보아, 주어진 문장이 들어가기에 가장 적절한 곳을 고르시오.

297

> They take plenty of effort and care, but are accompanied by far less guilt, drama, and intensity than that which attends the catching and slaughtering of animals.

Meat is good to use for a solemn ceremony because it is rich and expensive; it used to be eaten comparatively rarely and usually only on special occasions. (①) Until recent times, meat has had exceptionally poor storage qualities, which meant that it had to be eaten quickly. (②) For thousands of years it was placed before the family as a result of male enterprise and triumph. (③) And men, with their knives, have insisted on carving it up, and even cooking it before the expectant and admiring crowd. (④) Vegetables, on the other hand, were most often the result of the steady, cooperative, and often mainly female work required for collecting and tending them in the fields. (⑤) A joint of meat served for dinner also restricts the number of guests invited; vegetarian meals permit far more elastic arrangements because they are easily shared and extended.

298

> Their solutions are usually obtained by some degree of learning, observing others, and a lot of trial-and-error experimentation.

Many primates innovate when challenged by the environment outside of just food acquisition. (①) Orangutans take large leaves and hold them over their heads when it rains; chimpanzees eat certain bad-tasting leaves covered with tiny bristles when they have intestinal worms, and the leaves help clean out their systems. (②) Many other animals rise to ecological challenges via taking items in the world around them and using them for novel purposes. (③) While such behavior must include some curiosity, nearly all of these innovations are driven by functional goals: hunger, thirst, illness, comfort, and so on. (④) The process of evolution has honed many species' responses to the challenges of the world into amazing and innovative capacities. (⑤) But remember, it takes a young chimpanzee many months, if not years, to learn how to effectively use a rock to crack open nuts, whereas the same skill can be taught to a young human in a day. [3점]

*bristle: 강모(뻣뻣한 털) **intestinal: 장에 있는 ***hone: 연마하다

299

다음 글의 내용을 한 문장으로 요약하고자 한다. 빈칸 (A), (B)에 들어갈 말로 가장 적절한 것은?

Suppose that one night you and your spouse are preparing dinner. Suppose, too, that midway through the preparations, your spouse discovers that you forgot to buy the dinner's most important ingredient. Suppose then that your spouse grabs the car keys, curls a lip, glares at you, and hisses, "I'm going to the store." Nearly everyone with an intact brain would understand two things about the words just uttered. First, your spouse is heading to Safeway. Second, your spouse is pissed. Your left hemisphere figured out the first part — that is, it deciphered the sounds and syntax of your spouse's words and arrived at their literal meaning. But your right hemisphere understood the second aspect of this exchange — that the ordinarily neutral words "I'm going to the store" weren't neutral at all. The glare of the eyes and the hiss of the voice signal that your spouse is angry.

*hiss: (화난 어조로) 낮게 말하다   **pissed: 화가 난

↓

> The brain's left hemisphere pays more attention to the ___(A)___, whereas the right hemisphere thinks a lot about the ___(B)___.

	(A)		(B)
①	content	········	translation
②	process	········	result
③	empathy	········	logic
④	content	········	context
⑤	process	········	efficiency

▶ 300번 ~ 304번 뒤에 계속...

300~301 다음 글을 읽고, 물음에 답하시오.

If scientific articles are written to be read, then it is important for you as a writer to have a realistic impression of the sort of person who is likely to be a reader and how they go about reading. In reality, potential readers are not likely to be motivated much (a)<u>differently</u> than you are. That means that they are probably busy, lazy, impatient, grumpy and preoccupied with other things just as you are. They have other things than reading scientific articles on their daily agenda and they will be happy to convince themselves that they don't need to read many of the articles in the journals that cross their desk or computer screen. They certainly will not be reading articles just in case they contain some (b)<u>unforeseen</u> but useful material hidden in some obscure paragraph. So, your first task is to attract their attention and then try to hold that attention until the last full stop. That should be your goal but, even with a well-written article, it is (c)<u>unlikely</u> that you will often achieve it. From the beginning, readers are selective until they get a feeling for the article and what it has to offer them. Then, if it really (d)<u>interests</u> them, they will come back and scrutinise the whole article carefully and with scientific interest. The challenge is to make sure that, even if they spend just a few moments perusing your article, they will pick up the essentials of what it has to say. This means that they must find the most important parts clearly presented and in the places where they expect to find them. If they are forced to find your most interesting data buried in a heterogeneous mass of information in the Results or your most brilliant inspiration among a series of problematical comments in the Discussion, you will have (e)<u>much</u> chance of having your work acknowledged or appreciated.

*grumpy: 기분이 언짢은 **peruse: 정독하다

300

윗글의 제목으로 가장 적절한 것은?

① A Tip on Making Scientific Articles Be Read
② Credibility: A Key Element of Scientific Articles
③ Why Scientific Articles Require a Lot of Verification
④ Writing as an Important Part of Scientific Research
⑤ Differences Between Scientific Articles and General Writings

301

밑줄 친 (a)~(e) 중에서 문맥상 낱말의 쓰임이 적절하지 <u>않은</u> 것은?

① (a)   ② (b)   ③ (c)
④ (d)   ⑤ (e)

302~304 다음 글을 읽고, 물음에 답하시오.

(A)

Many years ago, in the Smokey Mountains of Tennessee, some domesticated hogs escaped from a farmer's pen. Over a period of several generations of hogs, these pigs became wilder and wilder until they were a menace to anyone who crossed their path. A number of skilled hunters tried to locate and kill (a)<u>them</u>, but the hogs proved to be too elusive. One day an older man leading a small donkey pulling a cart came into the village closest to the habitat of these wild hogs.

*hog: (육용) 돼지

(B)

The village people coaxed him into telling them how he had accomplished such a feat. "The first thing I'd done was find the spot where the hogs came to eat. Then I put a little grain right in the middle of the
15 clearing. The hogs was scared at first but curiosity finally got to (b)them and the old boar started sniffing around. After he took the first bite the others joined in and I knew right then and there I had them." *boar: 수퇘지

(C)

The cart was loaded with lumber and grain. The local
20 citizens were curious about what he was going to do. He told (c)them he had come "to catch the wild hogs." They laughed in disbelief that the old man could accomplish what the local hunters were unable to do. Two months later the old man returned to the village
25 and told the citizens that the hogs were trapped in a pen near the top of the mountain.

(D)

"Next day I put some more grain out and laid one plank a few feet away. That plank kind of spooked them for a while, but that free lunch was a powerful
30 appeal. It wasn't long before (d)they were back eating. All I had to do was add a couple of boards each day until I had everything I needed for my trap. Then I dug a hole and put up my first corner post. Every time I did something they'd stay away a spell. But they always
35 came back to eat. Finally, the pen was built and the trapdoor was set. Next time (e)they came to eat they walked right into the pen and I sprung the trap."

302

주어진 글 (A)에 이어질 내용을 순서에 맞게 배열한 것으로 가장 적절한 것은?

① (B) — (D) — (C) ② (C) — (B) — (D)
③ (C) — (D) — (B) ④ (D) — (B) — (C)
⑤ (D) — (C) — (B)

303

밑줄 친 (a)~(e) 중에서 가리키는 대상이 나머지 넷과 다른 것은?

① (a) ② (b) ③ (c)
④ (d) ⑤ (e)

304

윗글에 관한 내용으로 적절하지 않은 것은?

① 우리를 탈출한 돼지들이 사람들에게 위협이 되었다.
② 노인은 돼지들을 잡기 위해 공터 한가운데 곡물을 놓아두었다.
③ 노인의 짐마차에는 목재와 곡물이 실려 있었다.
④ 지역 주민들은 처음에 노인이 돼지들을 잡을 수 있을 거라고 믿지 않았다.
⑤ 노인이 울타리를 세우자 돼지들은 다시는 먹이를 먹으러 오지 않았다.

305

다음 글의 목적으로 가장 적절한 것은?

Dear Mr. Browning,

My present appointment carries an annual salary of £28,500; this was reviewed in March last year. During my five years with the company, I feel I have carried out my duties conscientiously and have recently acquired additional responsibilities. I feel that my qualifications and the nature of my work justify a higher salary and I have already been offered a similar position with another company at a salary of £30,000 per annum. My present duties are interesting and I thoroughly enjoy my work. Although I have no wish to leave the company, I cannot afford to turn down this offer unless some improvement in my salary can be arranged. I hope a salary increase will be possible, and look forward to hearing from you soon.

Yours sincerely,
Roger Moore

① 보직 변경을 신청하려고
② 급여 인상을 요구하려고
③ 이직 제안을 거절하려고
④ 업무 평가 결과를 보고하려고
⑤ 업무 개선 방안을 제안하려고

306

다음 글에 드러난 'I'의 심경 변화로 가장 적절한 것은?

Last Saturday I wanted to visit my grandmother, who lives on the other side of London. I had not seen her for ages, and I was looking forward to eating a piece of her delicious cake. I got onto the train, and found an empty seat next to an elderly man. I sat there and looked out the window. I imagined the joyful reunion with Grandmother, and I said to myself, "I miss you, Grandma!" Then I felt that the elderly man was watching me. I took out my book, and he kept watching me. Finally, the train pulled into Kings Cross Station, and I began walking towards my grandmother's house. After a few moments, I had a strange feeling that someone was following me. I turned round. The elderly man was running towards me. I tried to run, but couldn't even move a step.

① grateful → worried
② horrified → relieved
③ anticipating → scared
④ delighted → sorrowful
⑤ disappointed → excited

307

다음 글에서 필자가 주장하는 바로 가장 적절한 것은?

Time is our most precious commodity, and it is definitely a finite resource. Therefore, we just can't do it all. Too often, we fill our schedules with minutiae and seem too busy to accomplish our goals. We play
5 this trick on ourselves; it's what Steven Pressfield calls in *The War of Art*, "the resistance." Subconsciously, we know if we keep ourselves busy and over-scheduled, we won't have to face the great work we know that we should be doing. We have to do what Stephen Covey
10 described as putting the big rocks (your priorities) in your jar of life first. The less important things can fill the extra time, just don't allow them to steal time from your priorities. Realize that any time you say yes to something, you are saying no to something else. Learn
15 to say yes to the significant, and no to projects and activities that diminish the time and energy you need to fulfill your major purpose.

*minutia: 사소한 점

① 지나간 일보다 앞으로 할 일에 집중해야 한다.
② 어떤 일이든 사소하게 여기지 말고 완수해야 한다.
③ 일을 시작할 때 계획을 세우는 습관을 가져야 한다.
④ 중요한 일을 할 시간을 다른 일에 뺏겨서는 안 된다.
⑤ 때로는 자기 충전을 위한 휴식의 시간을 가져야 한다.

308

밑줄 친 politics is more meteorology than astronomy가 다음 글에서 의미하는 바로 가장 적절한 것은? [3점]

Debates rage about the possibilities and limits of prediction in politics. On one side are those who argue that reliable excellence (though not infallibility) is possible. Philip Tetlock's "superforecasters" are quintessential foxes, ordinary people who predict 5
extraordinarily well by cultivating open, curious, and self-critical habits of enquiry. Bruce Bueno de Mesquita's "predictioneers" claim similar success by a different route (in their case, a 90 percent rate of prediction accuracy), by applying refined models built 10
from the rigorous logic of "expected utility" to decisions that produce political outcomes. On the other side are skeptics who doubt the possibility, even in principle, of reliable political prediction. The obstacles are not merely technical ones that might be 15
overcome with enough data or computing power, but are inherent in the complex nature of political systems: dynamic, non-linear, chaotic, and highly sensitive to tiny changes in initial conditions. A solar eclipse can be calculated centuries in advance to the minute, but 20
the weather cannot be predicted more than a few days ahead, and then only imperfectly. Earthquakes cannot be predicted at all. The skeptics argue that politics is more meteorology than astronomy.

*infallibility: 절대 확실함 **quintessential: 전형적인
***meteorology: 기상학

① There are many factors that influence political outcomes.
② The views of political experts are unlikely to be predicted.
③ Political outcomes are determined by intentional activities.
④ Predicting politics is highly complex, uncertain, and difficult.
⑤ Unlike other domains, predictive accuracy is high for politics.

309

다음 글의 요지로 가장 적절한 것은?

Children's biological strengths and weaknesses influence their developing self-esteem, but so too do their interactions with family and the social environment. Self-esteem is a social process in that how people come to see themselves is heavily influenced by how others see and treat them. Though self-esteem refers to self-judgment, this judgment is easily influenced by the way children are treated by others and whether or not they have a positive experience of themselves while interacting with others. Therefore, parents play a vital role in helping children to develop positive self-esteem since parents are the "others" that children interact with most frequently. There are no people in the world more important to young children than their parents. Parents exert this influence over children's self-esteem by paying attention to how they communicate, express love and attention, encourage children to take on challenges, foster independence, and encourage socialization.

① 사회성은 자존감의 발달에 필수적인 요소이다.
② 부모의 자존감은 아이들의 자존감에 영향을 미친다.
③ 부모는 아이들의 자존감 형성에 중요한 역할을 한다.
④ 자존감의 발달은 타고난 성격에 많은 영향을 받는다.
⑤ 자존감이 높은 사람은 다른 사람의 영향을 덜 받는다.

310

다음 글의 주제로 가장 적절한 것은? [3점]

Suppose you stop at a roadside restaurant for a piece of pie. The server comes over to take your order, but you are having a hard time deciding which pie you want. While you are hesitating, she impatiently taps her pen against her notepad, rolls her eyes toward the ceiling, scowls at you, and finally snaps, "Hey, I haven't got all day, you know!" Like most people, you would probably think that she is a nasty or unpleasant person. But suppose, while you are deciding whether to complain about her to the manager, a regular customer tells you that your "crabby" server is a single parent whose car broke down on her way to work and she has no idea where she will find the money to have it repaired; and that the short-order cook keeps screaming at her because she is not picking up the orders fast enough to please him. Given all that information, you might conclude that she is not necessarily a nasty person, just an ordinary human living under enormous stress.

*crabby: 신경질적인

① learning how to complain effectively
② drawing a line between public and private lives
③ explaining someone's behavior in terms of personality
④ developing empathy skills to maintain social relationships
⑤ understanding stemming from a consideration of the situation

311

다음 글의 제목으로 가장 적절한 것은?

For any organism to survive, its constituent parts must be diverse enough to carry on a wide variety of very different tasks. Where there is a loss of diversity, weakness necessarily results. In plant species such as rice, for example, the most rugged and strong plants are hybrids that result from the interbreeding of different varieties. Unfortunately, many people have not understood this simple truth. Hitler and the Nazis, for example, thought that they could engineer a super race of human beings by breeding human beings that are genetically uniform and pure. Little did they realize that such uniformity, far from leading to a super-race, actually leads to inbreeding and loss of diversity in the human gene pool. Had such misinformed people known that diversity should be cultivated rather than destroyed, they might have conceivably encouraged racial, religious, and ideological diversity, instead of stamping it out.

*constituent: 구성하는

① The Importance of Purity
② Only the Fittest Can Survive
③ Diversity: A Source of Strength
④ Negative Effects of Racial Hatred
⑤ Potential Dangers of Interbreeding

312

다음 도표의 내용과 일치하지 <u>않는</u> 것은?

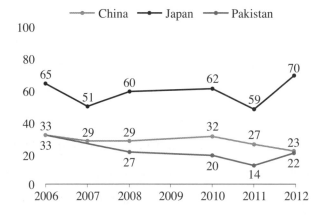

% Favorable toward India

The graph above shows the percent of people in three Asian nations having a favorable view of India in the time period between 2006 and 2012. ① Among these three Asian nations, Japan had the highest percentage of people with a favorable opinion of India throughout the given time period. ② Increasing 11%p from 2011, in 2012 70% of Japanese people had a favorable opinion of India. ③ In contrast, in 2012, only 23% of Chinese people saw India in a favorable light, down 10%p from 2006. ④ And in 2011 only 14% of Pakistanis were favorably disposed toward India. ⑤ In 2012, the Pakistani appraisal of India was up 8%p from the previous year, but down 2%p from the percentage in 2006.

313

berberis에 관한 다음 글의 내용과 일치하지 않는 것은?

There are over 500 species of berberis growing in every country on the planet, in all climates, apart from Antarctica and Australia. All varieties of berberis are edible. Italians call the shrub the holy thorn, since they
5 believe this is the plant that was used to make Christ's crown of thorns. Some varieties, for example Berberis darwinii, are indeed hellishly prickly and require thick gauntlets should you need to prune it. While you're pruning, you might notice that the inner part of the
10 woody stems is a bright orange colour. A similarly coloured dye can be made from the plant. Berberis shrubs are tough and frost-hardy, happy to grow in all sorts of soil and weather conditions. Berberis flowers appear either singly or in dangling racemes of yellow
15 or orange blossoms, and the ripe berries vary in colour from red to dark purple and can be either rounded or distinctly oval-shaped.

*raceme: (식물) 총상(總狀) 꽃차례

① 모든 품종이 식용이다.
② 이탈리아인들은 신성한 가시라고 부른다.
③ 줄기의 내부는 밝은 오렌지색이다.
④ 자랄 수 있는 토양과 날씨 조건이 제한적이다.
⑤ 다 익은 열매는 둥글거나 타원형일 수 있다.

314

After-School Martial Arts Program에 관한 다음 안내문의 내용과 일치하지 않는 것은?

After-School Martial Arts Program

Daily martial arts classes provide your child with a character building education.

Our After-School Martial Arts Program is the answer to your child's after-school needs:
• Free transportation provided from local schools.
• We are open for most of the holidays.

Program Includes:
Martial Arts Lessons every day / Snack Time / Homework Time

Friday Fun Days include activities like soccer, basketball, obstacle courses & games, rock climbing, and swimming, etc.

Sign up by February 15th, 2024 for our year-round program and save $100!

Christmas Holidays: We will be open and offer a Christmas camp for those who need it.

Call us now! 410-555-1234

① 학교에서부터 무료 교통편이 제공된다.
② 간식 시간과 숙제 시간이 포함되어 있다.
③ 금요일에는 축구나 농구 등의 활동도 한다.
④ 2024년 2월 15일까지는 100달러에 등록할 수 있다.
⑤ 크리스마스 휴일 기간에는 캠프를 제공한다.

315

Marine Technology Research Program에 관한 다음 안내문의 내용과 일치하는 것은?

> ### Marine Technology Research Program
>
> **Program Entrance Requirements**
> - College level student interested in marine technology applications
>
> **Program Fee**
> - $1,500 which includes food, accommodations and local travel as part of the program
>
> **Registration Deadline**
> - May 19, 2024
>
> **Cancellation / Refund Policy**
> - Minimum of 10 students required for program to be operated
> - Full refund of program fees paid if minimum enrollment is not met
> - Registered students will be notified on May 31, 2024 if the minimum enrollment number has not been met, so it is recommended not to purchase airline tickets in advance of being notified.

① 해양 기술 응용에 관심 있는 고등학생을 대상으로 한다.
② 프로그램 비용에는 현지 여행비가 포함되지 않는다.
③ 최대 수용 인원은 10명이다.
④ 최소 등록 인원이 충족되지 않으면 전액 환불된다.
⑤ 2024년 5월 31일에 프로그램이 시작된다.

316

다음 글의 밑줄 친 부분 중, 어법상 틀린 것은?

For the past half-century, social justice has been an active area of study for social psychologists. Do most people care about justice? Cynics say no and point out people's inhumanity to each other ① as proof. But Melvin Lerner proposed a theory called *belief in a just world*, ② stating that all people want to imagine that they live in a just world. Experiments show people's desire ③ maintains the illusion of fairness often leads them to do cruel acts. If someone receives bad outcomes, others look at the person and believe ④ that he or she did something to deserve the bad outcomes. This belief shields observers from feeling ⑤ vulnerable to unjust outcomes because they know that they themselves are not bad people, but the process also results in victim blaming.

*victim blaming: 피해자 책임 전가(피해자에게 책임의 일부를 전가시키는 것)

317

(A), (B), (C)의 각 네모 안에서 문맥에 맞는 낱말로 가장 적절한 것은? [3점]

Not all problems require extensive critical thinking. Sometimes assumptions about the cause of a problem are easily made and are evident to everyone in the organization. For example, if the owners of a local souvenir shop see their customers' cars across the street in the parking lot of a recently opened discount souvenir store, the problem is (A) clear / unclear . Little questioning is needed to challenge the assumption that the customers are buying the competitor's product because of cost. The assumption might be made that research is needed to determine how much to (B) lower / raise prices. However, if the shop's owners, who take pride in their product, instead conducted research on what benefits visitors desire when buying souvenirs they might find that visitors are also interested in products being locally made. This could then provide the owners with an idea for countering the competitive threat by (C) concealing / promoting the locally made products in their shop.

	(A)		(B)		(C)
①	clear	....	lower	....	concealing
②	clear	....	raise	....	concealing
③	clear	....	lower	....	promoting
④	unclear	....	lower	....	concealing
⑤	unclear	....	raise	....	promoting

318 ~ 321 다음 빈칸에 들어갈 말로 가장 적절한 것을 고르시오.

318

Specific, definite, concrete, particular details — these are the life of fiction. Details (as every good liar knows) are the stuff of _____. Mary is sure that Ed forgot to go pay the gas bill last Tuesday, but Ed says, "I know I went, because this old guy in a knit vest was in front of me in the line, and went on and on about his twin granddaughters" — and it is hard to refute a knit vest and twins even if the furnace doesn't work. John Gardner in *The Art of Fiction* speaks of details as "proofs," as indicators for truthfulness, rather like the steps that together demonstrate a geometric theorem or evidence in a court case. The novelist, he says, "gives us such detail about the streets, stores, weather, politics, and concerns of Cleveland (or wherever the setting is) and such detail about the looks, gestures, and experiences of his characters that we cannot help believing that the story he tells us must be true."

① persuasiveness
② preciseness
③ wholeness
④ sympathy
⑤ vividness

319

When the first animal, Dolly the sheep, was cloned, it hit the headlines and gave rise to a heated moralistic debate. Today there is a big furor about human cloning and stem cells. Meanwhile, animal cloning has largely been accepted and the cloning of yet another species scarcely qualifies as front-page news anymore. When "test tube babies" first appeared, they were the subjects of intense ethical debate by self-appointed leaders in human morality. Louise Brown, the world's first test tube baby, was born on July 25, 1978, in England. Since then there have been more than a million others, and today the procedure is covered by most health insurance plans. The "morality" of this topic is rarely even discussed anymore. The fact that _____ at much the same rate as fashions in women's clothing brings their deep significance into question. [3점]

*furor: 열광

① the debates in biotechnology get heated
② the problems of biotechnology are settled
③ most fundamental ethical issues fade away
④ the cost of test tube babies is covered by insurance
⑤ the moral decline in scientific research has increased

320

The role of scientific models can be compared to that of the scaffolds and cranes built around large buildings as they are being built. There is no way to construct the building without these scaffolds and cranes, but once the building is completed, they need to be removed. Thus, in his classic book *The Character of Physical Law*, Richard Feynman argued that theory should always try to separate itself from the models upon which it was built. "It always turns out that the greatest discoveries take attention away from the model and the model never does any good," he wrote. "Maxwell's discovery of electro-dynamics was first made with a lot of imaginary wheels in space. But when you get rid of all the wheels and things in space, the thing is okay." Models help us gain mastery of concepts, but should not be confused with the concepts themselves. As the greatest philosopher Chuang-tzu says, "_____." [3점]

*scaffold: (건축 공사장의) 비계, 임시 가설물

① A shortcut isn't always quicker
② Any tool is a weapon if you hold it right
③ You look back to understand the present
④ The trees don't allow one to see the forest
⑤ The purpose of a rabbit trap is to catch a rabbit

321

Cooking has always been a part of human culture as long as we've flourished on this planet. With both the aspect of survival and pleasure, food and cooking has always been something that we humans were attracted to. Through cooking we learned how to use tools, and some even argue that it is our ability to cook that separated us from the rest of the animals. A few thousand years later, we have a much different view on food and cooking. Though it still continues to be an essential part of our daily lives, thanks to industrialization, much fewer people cook today than they used to. In our highly organized and sophisticated culture, many food preparations are done inside factories where most of us do not know what happens. Here, every ingredient is perfectly controlled and measured, bringing us the same taste that we love every time. Cheap and tasty — but not necessarily healthy — food has become an essential part of human culture, _____.

① allowing people to enjoy more leisure time
② causing ecological destruction in the process
③ encouraging people to prefer meat to vegetables
④ excluding more and more people from the kitchen
⑤ making more and more people look for tastier foods

322

다음 글에서 전체 흐름과 관계 없는 문장은?

Depending solely on honey bees for pollination is dangerous, as honey bees alone are ineffective in terms of biodiversity. A number of pollinators — not just one — are necessary, because that will insure more substitutes in pollination. ① That is, even if one group of pollinators were to disappear or be badly affected by conditions, other groups could make up for their decreased pollination. ② Biodiversity is extremely important now, as honey bees are being subjected to a myriad of problems that are threatening their population. ③ Possibly because many honey bees are regularly transported instead of being kept stationary, they are exposed to a number of diseases and pests that negatively affect honey bee numbers. ④ Commercialized honey bees are easy to work with and produce measurable economic products, honey and beeswax, as well as pollination services. ⑤ Worse still, now honey bees are disappearing in great numbers in what has been termed Colony Collapse Disorder, whose cause is unknown.

323 ~ 324 주어진 글 다음에 이어질 글의 순서로 가장 적절한 것을 고르시오.

323

> Isolation has several interesting aspects to it. One truly fascinating aspect is the isolation from predators, including that noteworthy predator, man himself.

(A) It is not necessary to do this in the Galapagos, and the picture-taking opportunities are unbelievable — to the point that you will shoot 2-3 times more than your usual daily quota.

(B) So, the animals in the Galapagos have not learned or adapted themselves to flee or shy away when approached. One can get to within arm's length distance of many of the Galapagos animals, and amazingly they will not dash or fly off.

(C) This experience is a constant source of pleasure and amazement, and it's one that is very difficult for many of us to get used to. We are very accustomed to slowly approaching an animal, camera in hand, using very powerful telephoto lenses to cut down the distance.

① (A) — (C) — (B) ② (B) — (A) — (C)
③ (B) — (C) — (A) ④ (C) — (A) — (B)
⑤ (C) — (B) — (A)

324

> Smokejumpers are often dropped into fires that are too remote for ground based firefighting resources to reach. In most scenarios, when people parachute recreationally they choose wide open meadows so they have little trouble finding safe spots to land.

(A) While coming down, sometimes their gear gets tangled in trees, so smokejumpers must be adept at climbing and descending trees in order to free anything, all the while remaining calm and ready for action.

(B) Once on the ground, smokejumpers are self-sufficient for between 48 and 72 hours, and they fight any fires that ignite or are already under way, typically with just the use of simple, yet highly effective hand tools.

(C) Smokejumpers, however, must often come down on rough terrain that is thick with vegetation in order to access the fires they need to fight, making the task much more complex. To accomplish it, they have spotters on every team who are skilled at assessing the current conditions and determining the best jump spot. [3점]

*smokejumper: 삼림 소방대원 **parachute: 낙하산으로 강하하다

① (A) — (C) — (B) ② (B) — (A) — (C)
③ (B) — (C) — (A) ④ (C) — (A) — (B)
⑤ (C) — (B) — (A)

325 ~ 326 글의 흐름으로 보아, 주어진 문장이 들어가기에 가장 적절한 곳을 고르시오.

325

> But these blessings, allied with the region's summer monsoon climate, are also a curse.

If Bangladesh were to count her blessings, they would number three: the Brahmaputra, the Meghna and the mighty Ganges. (①) These great rivers are practically Bangladesh's only natural resources. (②) In a predominantly rural country in which agriculture and freshwater fishing are the keys to the economy, the rivers are the people's lifeblood. (③) Although almost two meters of rain fall on Bangladesh each year, more than two-thirds arrive in just four months. (④) For much of the year, the vast delta formed by the three rivers is parched, but in many summers their banks burst, causing massive floods. (⑤) Lacking proper sanitation and water storage facilities, Bangladesh is also prone to epidemics of water-borne disease.

*monsoon: (동남아시아 지역의) 우기   **delta: (하구의) 삼각주

326

> Social Security does not follow this savings-and-investment model.

The Social Security program in the United States is not based on principles of insurance. Private insurance and pension programs invest the current payments of customers in buildings, farms, or other real assets. (①) Alternatively, they buy stocks and bonds that finance the development of real assets. (②) These real assets generate income that allows the pension fund (or insurance company) to fulfill its future obligations to its customers. (③) Instead, it taxes current workers and uses the revenues to finance benefits for existing retirees. (④) There is no buildup of productive assets that the federal government can use to fund the future benefits promised today's workers. (⑤) When current workers retire, their promised Social Security benefits will have to come from taxes levied on future generations.

327

다음 글의 내용을 한 문장으로 요약하고자 한다. 빈칸 (A), (B)에 들어갈 말로 가장 적절한 것은?

Susan Perry, a primatologist at UCLA who has observed capuchin monkeys in Costa Rica for many years, has reported that these primates periodically test the patience of their favorite social partners by subjecting them to all kinds of physically intrusive and annoying behaviors. For example, a young capuchin monkey may walk up to his favorite social partner, stick a finger up his nose, and wait for a reaction. If their relationship is good, nothing will happen, but if the partner has lost some of the initial enthusiasm about the partnership, the annoying monkey will get smacked. Perry noticed that two capuchin monkeys who have a strong social bond sometimes simultaneously insert their fingers up each other's nose and sit in this pose for up to several minutes with happy expressions on their faces, sometimes swaying. Capuchin monkeys also torture their favorite coalition partners by pulling hairs from their face, biting their ears, or sucking their fingers or toes.

*smack: 세게 때리다

↓

Some expressions of affection among capuchin monkeys are ___(A)___ for their close friends, but their friend's acceptance of that behavior provides reliable evidence of their ___(B)___ to continue the relationship.

	(A)		(B)
①	irritating	………	reluctance
②	irritating	………	willingness
③	protective	………	inability
④	protective	………	willingness
⑤	supportive	………	reluctance

▶ 328번 ~ 332번 뒤에 계속...

328~329 다음 글을 읽고, 물음에 답하시오.

How do children mediate and negotiate the experiences of poverty and exclusion? Without sufficient money to go into town with friends or take part in activities, children find themselves caught by

5 their circumstances. Poverty and disadvantage place considerable (a)constraints on children's capacity for autonomous action and their ability to negotiate and resolve their social dilemmas.

Previous research has shown that children are very

10 (b)protective of their parents and this can take many forms, including self-denial of need and the moderation of demands. For some children, this can mean (c)self-exclusion from activities — by not pursuing opportunities or failing to draw attention

15 to activities perceived by them as too costly — in a bid to alleviate pressures within the home. These children are active social agents and they employ a range of strategies to try to mediate or mitigate their circumstances. One way in which children can

20 gain some measure of control over their circumstances is to (d)ban alternative ways of gaining access to economic resources that can be used to enable them to participate more fully with their peers. Taking on part-time employment is one example,

25 providing an opportunity for a measure of freedom and independence. Income from the paid employment can (e)release children, to some degree, from the economic constraints of their family environment and render them economic agents in their own right.

328

윗글의 제목으로 가장 적절한 것은?

① The Miserable Reality of Child Labor
② The Importance of a Self-Motivated Lifestyle
③ Poverty: A Constraint on Children's Activities
④ The Danger of Excessive Neglect in Parenting
⑤ Childhood: The Foundation That Determines Our Whole Life

329

밑줄 친 (a)~(e) 중에서 문맥상 낱말의 쓰임이 적절하지 않은 것은? [3점]

① (a)   ② (b)   ③ (c)
④ (d)   ⑤ (e)

330~332 다음 글을 읽고, 물음에 답하시오.

(A)

When I started my teaching career at age twenty-five, Peter Miller, a colleague who was eight years older, "took me under his wing." (a)He took the time to point out the things I was doing wrong and explained what some of my students didn't like about me. I always 5 appreciated his criticism and worked hard to improve in these areas. Sometimes I wondered if I'd ever become the teacher or the person that I wanted to be. But at least I always had someone to show me where I was going wrong. 10

(e) he helped me see some things that had never gotten 40 my attention before: what I was doing *right* both as a teacher and as a person.

(B)

As I began the sixth year of my career, our faculty was joined by Tim Hansel, who had transferred from another school. Since we were teaching the same two subjects and became team teachers in one of them, we 15 had daily contact. Tim was so effective and so well liked. (b) He seemed to have a special talent for bringing out the best in other people. With his students, instead of emphasizing their mistakes, he emphasized either what they did right or what they 20 *could* do.

(C)

What became of these two friendships? Sadly, the first one ended after many years. I say *sadly* because this is a person I'd greatly admired. Most of his criticism of me was valid, and I learned a great deal 25 from him. But one of the main reasons it ended was that the criticism was so constant. It was never balanced with any form of praise, and eventually it wore me down. The other friendship continues to flourish, even after thirty years. (c) He still reminds me 30 about what's good in the world and what's good in me.

(D)

But it didn't stop there. Tim always had something good to say to me, too. He pointed out all the things I was doing well. He said that (d) he admired me for my dedication and that it was obvious that my hard work 35 was paying off. He reminded me often how much my students liked me and how much they were learning because of my teaching. As we began to spend time together outside of school, he found other things to compliment me about. The effect of all this was that

330

주어진 글 (A)에 이어질 내용을 순서에 맞게 배열한 것으로 가장 적절한 것은?

① (B) ― (C) ― (D)　　② (B) ― (D) ― (C)
③ (C) ― (B) ― (D)　　④ (C) ― (D) ― (B)
⑤ (D) ― (B) ― (C)

331

밑줄 친 (a)~(e) 중에서 가리키는 대상이 나머지 넷과 다른 것은?

① (a)　　② (b)　　③ (c)
④ (d)　　⑤ (e)

332

윗글에 관한 내용으로 적절하지 않은 것은?

① Peter는 필자보다 나이가 여덟 살 많았다.
② 필자는 Tim과 동일한 과목을 가르쳤다.
③ Peter는 필자를 아무런 근거도 없이 비판했다.
④ 필자는 아직도 Tim과 친분을 유지하고 있다.
⑤ Tim은 주로 필자의 좋은 점에 대해 말해 주었다.

❶ 적중 예상 문제

01	facility	*n*	
02	in retrospect		
03	transparency	*n*	
04	outright	*ad*	
05	massive	*a*	
06	via	*p*	
07	compile	*v*	
08	vacuum	*n*	
09	prolonged	*a*	
10	net	*a*	
11	faulty	*a*	
12	덫	*n*	
13	at hand		
14	agonize	*v*	
15	censure	*v*	
16	punctuation	*n*	
17	decency	*n*	
18	adequately	*ad*	
19	비범한, 보통이 아닌	*a*	
20	dictate	*v*	

❷ 적중 예상 문제

01	coin	*v*	
02	발음	*n*	
03	elaborate	*a*	
04	sorrowful	*a*	
05	evacuation	*n*	
06	contentment	*n*	
07	laboratory	*n*	
08	rusty	*a*	
09	concerning	*p*	
10	trout	*n*	
11	adversely	*ad*	
12	phenomenon	*n*	
13	entity	*n*	
14	rugged	*a*	
15	density	*n*	
16	hazard	*n*	
17	saliva	*n*	
18	explosion	*n*	
19	desirable	*a*	
20	군체	*n*	

❸ 적중 예상 문제

01	gender	n	
02	keep up with		
03	real estate		
04	exert	v	
05	고정관념	n	
06	variability	n	
07	immersion	n	
08	designate	v	
09	resilient	a	
10	inventory	n	
11	retain	v	
12	halt	v	
13	discrimination	n	
14	temperament	n	
15	보수적인	a	
16	retailer	n	
17	norm	n	
18	distinction	n	
19	inclination	n	
20	hue	n	

❹ 적중 예상 문제

01	adjust	v	
02	run out of		
03	pesticide	n	
04	applaud	v	
05	단조로운	a	
06	deliberative	a	
07	serenity	n	
08	fatal	a	
09	gaze	v	
10	stakeholder	n	
11	pension	n	
12	absence	n	
13	comprise	v	
14	imperative	n	
15	중세의	a	
16	implication	n	
17	strive for		
18	elicit	v	
19	reputation	n	
20	impulsive	a	

5 적중 예상 문제

01	look up to	
02	persuasion	*n*
03	courteous	*a*
04	turn out	
05	tease	*v*
06	steadily	*ad*
07	deliberate	*a*
08	simultaneously	*ad*
09	확대하다	*v*
10	dread	*v*
11	sequential	*a*
12	asset	*n*
13	thrive	*v*
14	ratio	*n*
15	profoundly	*ad*
16	flat	*a*
17	be blind to	
18	literary	*a*
19	인색한	*a*
20	botanist	*n*

1 독해 실전 모의고사

01	triumph	*n*
02	intact	*a*
03	구문	*n*
04	give off	
05	exchange	*n*
06	lumber	*n*
07	obscure	*a*
08	hemisphere	*n*
09	gulf	*n*
10	statement	*n*
11	brilliant	*a*
12	목록, 의제	*n*
13	figure out	
14	question	*v*
15	distinct	*a*
16	have to do with	
17	domesticated	*a*
18	농산물	*n*
19	feat	*n*
20	correlation	*n*
21	unforeseen	*a*

22	sniff	v	
23	breathtaking	a	
24	ambiguous	a	
25	glare	v	
26	slaughter	v	
27	decipher	v	
28	plausible	a	
29	lavish	a	
30	menace	n	
31	contrary to		
32	venue	n	
33	convert	v	
34	fade	v	
35	박람회	n	
36	빈도	n	
37	metaphor	n	
38	textile	n	
39	prevalence	n	
40	not to mention		
41	diminish	v	
42	rigid	a	

43	adhere to		
44	herbicide	n	
45	the ebb and flow		
46	기아, 굶주림	n	
47	apparent	a	
48	foraging	a	
49	advocate	v	
50	dogmatic	a	

② 독해 실전 모의고사

01	competitive	a	
02	mediate	v	
03	숙박	n	
04	descend	v	
05	conscientiously	ad	
06	pollinator	n	
07	피해자, 희생자	n	
08	sophisticated	a	
09	sway	v	
10	carry out		

11	separate	v		31	make up for		
12	constraint	n		32	finite	a	
13	turn down			33	감추다, 숨기다	v	
14	moderation	n		34	appraisal	n	
15	conceivably	ad		35	neglect	n	
16	vulnerable	a		36	take on		
17	be subjected to			37	torture	v	
18	admire	v		38	ignite	v	
19	edible	a		39	rage	v	
20	mighty	a		40	compliment	v	
21	thorn	n		41	substitute	n	
22	curse	n		42	vital	a	
23	commodity	n		43	목초지	n	
24	재회	n		44	pay off		
25	flourish	v		45	nasty	a	
26	sign up for			46	chaotic	a	
27	epidemic	n		47	retiree	n	
28	to some degree			48	intrusive	a	
29	qualification	n		49	revenue	n	
30	sanitation	n		50	alleviate	v	

메가스터디 N제

메가스터디 N제

메가스터디 N제

영어영역 독해

수능 완벽 대비 예상 문제집

정답 및 해설

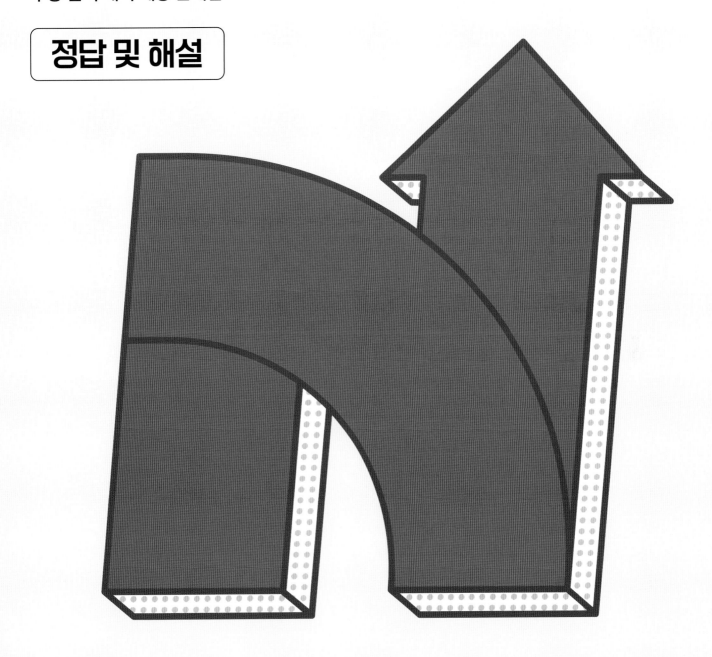

332제

메가스터디 N제

영어영역 독해

332제

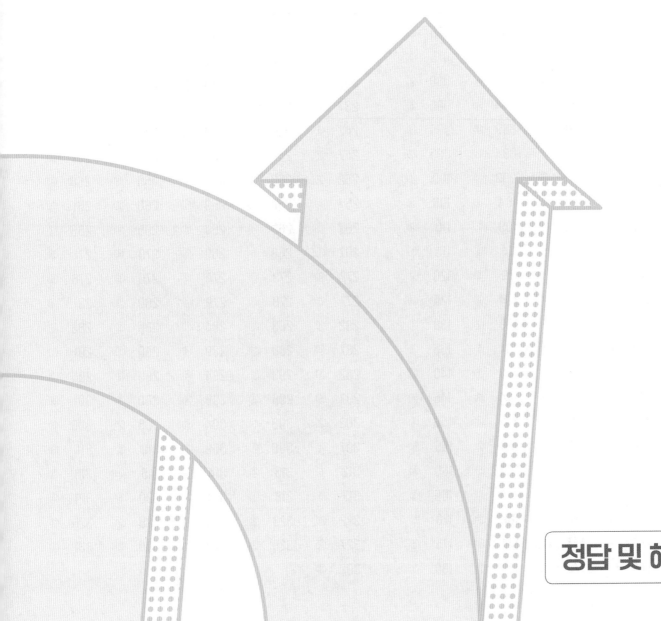

정답 및 해설

I 영어 독해 유형 연습

001 ①	002 ①	003 ②	004 ④	005 ④
006 ①	007 ②	008 ④	009 ④	010 ①
011 ③	012 ⑤	013 ①	014 ①	015 ②
016 ①	017 ①	018 ⑤	019 ⑤	020 ③
021 ①	022 ②	023 ⑤	024 ②	025 ③
026 ④	027 ④	028 ④	029 ①	030 ⑤
031 ⑤	032 ⑤	033 ④	034 ④	035 ③
036 ③	037 ①	038 ①	039 ①	040 ⑤
041 ④	042 ⑤	043 ①	044 ④	045 ②
046 ②	047 ②	048 ⑤	049 ④	050 ⑤
051 ②	052 ③	053 ④	054 ①	055 ⑤
056 ⑤	057 ①	058 ②	059 ⑤	060 ③
061 ①	062 ①	063 ⑤	064 ④	065 ④
066 ④	067 ②	068 ⑤	069 ④	070 ③
071 ④	072 ⑤	073 ②	074 ⑤	075 ③
076 ④	077 ③	078 ⑤	079 ④	080 ④
081 ④	082 ③	083 ④	084 ④	085 ⑤
086 ③	087 ⑤	088 ③	089 ④	090 ③
091 ②	092 ②	093 ④	094 ③	095 ⑤
096 ④	097 ④	098 ④	099 ②	100 ④
101 ⑤	102 ③	103 ②	104 ①	105 ③
106 ②	107 ③	108 ③	109 ②	110 ②
111 ①	112 ②	113 ⑤	114 ④	115 ①
116 ①	117 ①	118 ④	119 ⑤	120 ②
121 ④	122 ②	123 ④	124 ②	125 ③
126 ⑤	127 ③	128 ①	129 ③	130 ①
131 ①	132 ④	133 ①	134 ⑤	135 ③
136 ③	137 ②	138 ③	139 ①	140 ②
141 ①	142 ③	143 ③	144 ③	145 ④
146 ④	147 ②	148 ④	149 ④	150 ④
151 ④	152 ④	153 ②	154 ②	155 ⑤
156 ⑤	157 ②	158 ⑤	159 ⑤	160 ④
161 ③	162 ②	163 ③	164 ⑤	165 ④
166 ②	167 ②	168 ④	169 ③	170 ⑤
171 ④	172 ④	173 ③	174 ④	175 ⑤
176 ④	177 ④	178 ⑤	179 ②	180 ③
181 ⑤	182 ⑤	183 ③	184 ④	185 ③
186 ①	187 ①	188 ①	189 ⑤	190 ③
191 ②	192 ⑤	193 ③	194 ②	195 ②
196 ⑤	197 ①	198 ①	199 ⑤	200 ③
201 ④	202 ⑤	203 ③	204 ③	205 ⑤
206 ③	207 ③	208 ⑤	209 ⑤	210 ④
211 ②	212 ④	213 ⑤	214 ⑤	215 ⑤
216 ③				

II 영어 독해 실전 연습

217 ⑤	218 ②	219 ⑤	220 ④	221 ④
222 ⑤	223 ③	224 ④	225 ⑤	226 ⑤
227 ②	228 ③	229 ②	230 ③	231 ①
232 ③	233 ⑤	234 ③	235 ⑤	236 ③
237 ④	238 ②	239 ②	240 ③	241 ①
242 ④	243 ③	244 ③	245 ②	246 ④
247 ②	248 ③	249 ③	250 ④	251 ③
252 ②	253 ③	254 ④	255 ③	256 ④
257 ④	258 ③	259 ①	260 ②	261 ②
262 ③	263 ④	264 ④	265 ④	266 ③
267 ①	268 ⑤	269 ④	270 ④	271 ③
272 ④	273 ⑤	274 ②	275 ⑤	276 ⑤
277 ⑤	278 ③	279 ④	280 ③	281 ④
282 ③	283 ③	284 ⑤	285 ③	286 ⑤
287 ④	288 ③	289 ④	290 ①	291 ①
292 ①	293 ②	294 ④	295 ③	296 ②
297 ⑤	298 ⑤	299 ④	300 ①	301 ⑤
302 ②	303 ③	304 ⑤	305 ②	306 ③
307 ④	308 ④	309 ③	310 ⑤	311 ③
312 ⑤	313 ④	314 ④	315 ④	316 ③
317 ③	318 ①	319 ③	320 ③	321 ④
322 ④	323 ③	324 ③	325 ③	326 ③
327 ②	328 ③	329 ④	330 ②	331 ①
332 ③				

영어 독해 유형 연습

01 글의 목적
본문 pp.006~011

001 ①	002 ①	003 ②	004 ④	005 ④
006 ①	007 ②	008 ④	009 ④	

001 답 ①

📖 웹툰 제작 온라인 강좌 홍보

전문해석

저는 Toon Skills Company의 경영자인 Charlie Reeves입니다. 새로운 웹툰 제작 기술과 기법에 관심이 있으시다면, 이 게시물은 여러분을 위한 것입니다. 올해, 저희는 웹툰 제작에 관한 다양한 콘텐츠가 담겨 있는 특별 온라인 강좌를 시작했습니다. 각 강좌는 그림 그리기와 스토리텔링 기술을 향상하는 데 도움을 주는 10개의 단원으로 구성되어 있습니다. 게다가, 이 강좌들은 초급에서 고급까지 어떤 수준에도 맞게 설계되었습니다. 한 강좌당 45달러의 비용이 들며, 여러분은 6개월 동안 여러분의 강좌를 원하는 만큼 여러 번 보실 수 있습니다. 재능 있고 경험이 풍부한 강사들과 함께하는 저희 강좌는 여러분에게 창의력의 새로운 세계를 열어줄 것입니다. 이제 https://webtoonskills.com에서 여러분의 웹툰 세계를 창조하는 것을 시작할 때입니다.

002 답 ①

📖 조류 관찰 클럽 가입 방법 문의

전문해석

관계자분께,

제 이름은 Michael Brown입니다. 저는 어린 시절부터 조류 관찰자였습니다. 저는 항상 저의 뜰에서 새들을 관찰하고 모습과 소리로 그것들을 식별하는 것을 즐겼습니다. 어제 저는 우연히 귀하의 클럽에 관한 기사를 읽었습니다. 저는 조류 관찰을 하기 위해 매년 여행하는 열정적인 조류 관찰자들의 공동체에 대해 알게 되어 놀랐고 신이 났습니다. 저는 귀하의 클럽에 가입하고 싶지만, 귀하의 웹사이트가 공사 중인 것 같습니다. 저는 이 이메일 주소 외에 다른 정보를 찾을 수가 없었습니다. 저는 **클럽에 가입하는 방법을 알고 싶습니다.** 귀하의 답장을 기다리겠습니다.

Michael Brown 드림

정답풀이

글의 마지막 부분에서 글을 쓴 이유를 명확히 알 수 있다. 조류 관찰 클럽에 대한 기사를 읽고 클럽에 가입하는 방법을 알고 싶다고 했으므로, 글의 목적으로는 ①이 가장 적절하다.

구문풀이

6행 I was surprised and excited to find out about [a community of passionate bird-watchers {who travel annually to go birding}].

: [ ]로 표시한 명사구가 전치사 about의 목적어이며, { }는 passionate bird-watchers를 수식하는 관계절이다.

어휘풀이
- childhood *n* 어린 시절
- happen to *do* 우연히 ~하다
- identify *v* 식별하다
- article *n* 기사, 글

- passionate *a* 열정적인
- under construction 공사 중인
- annually *ad* 매년
- sign up for ~에 가입하다

003 답 ②

📖 과학 교사들을 위한 워크숍의 특강 요청

전문해석

Green 씨께,

제 이름은 Donna Williams이며, Rogan 고등학교의 과학 교사입니다. 저는 우리 학교의 과학 교사들을 위한 특별 워크숍을 계획하고 있습니다. 저희는 온라인 과학 수업을 가르치는 방법을 배우는 데 관심을 가지고 있습니다. 저는 과학 수업에 인터넷 플랫폼을 사용하는 데 대한 귀하의 아이디어에 감명을 받았습니다. 귀하가 온라인 교육의 전문가이시기에, **저는 다음 달에 예정된 워크숍에서 귀하가 특강을 해주시기를 부탁드리고자 합니다.** 저희 교사들이 성공적인 온라인 과학 수업을 해내는 데 강의가 도움이 되리라고 확신하며 귀하의 통찰력으로부터 저희가 배울 수 있기를 희망합니다. 귀하의 답변을 기다리고 있겠습니다.

Donna Williams 드림

정답풀이

특별 워크숍을 계획하고 있다고 했고 중반부 I would like to ask you to deliver a special lecture ~ next month.에서 다음 달에 특강을 해 달라고 요청하고 있으므로 글의 목적으로는 ②가 가장 적절하다.

구문풀이

11행 I am sure [the lecture will help our teachers manage successful online science classes], / and I hope [we can learn from your insights].

: 두 개의 절이 and로 연결된 구조이며, 첫 번째 [ ]는 명사절로 the lecture 앞에 접속사 that이 생략되었다. 이 절에는 「help+목적어+목적격보어」 구조가 쓰여 '~가 …하는 것을 돕다'의 의미를 나타내고 help의 목적격보어로 동사원형 manage가 사용되었다. 두 번째 [ ]는 hope의 목적어 역할을 하는 명사절로 앞에 목적절을 이끄는 접속사 that이 생략되었다.

어휘풀이
- workshop *n* 워크숍, 연수회
- expert *n* 전문가
- deliver a special lecture 특강을 하다
- manage *v* 해내다, 성공하다
- impressed *a* 감명을 받은
- scheduled *a* 예정된
- insight *n* 통찰력

004 답 ④

📖 당선된 후 밝히는 앞으로의 포부

전문해석

이렇게 놀라운 마을에서 앞으로 4년 더 여러분의 이익을 대변할 수 있게 되어 정말 영광스럽고 기쁘게 생각합니다. 저는 Middlewich가 생활하고 자녀들을 양육하기에 정말 좋은 곳이 되도록 도움을 주는 서비스들을 향상시키기 위해 제 힘이 닿는 한 무엇이든 할 것입니다. 우리는 앞으로 몇 년간 심각한 문제들에 직면할 것이지만, 저는 우리가 극복할 수 있으리라고 확신합니다. 그러나 저는 더 많은 분들이 동참하도록 장려하기 위해 이 기회를 잡고 싶습니다. Middlewich와 같은 마을은 거주민들이 노력하는 만큼 활기를 띱니다. 다가오는 해 동안 우리의 많은 행사에 오셔서 후원해 주시길 바랍니다. 여러분은 저희가 최선을 다하기 위해 얼마나 열심히 노력하는지 보게 될 것입니다. 직원들과 이야기를 나누고 싶으시면 Lewin 가에 있는 Victoria 건물에 들르세요. 여러분은 친절한 환대를 받을 것입니다.

정답풀이

당선된 이후에, 앞으로 열심히 노력하겠으니 주민 여러분의 적극적인 참여를 바란다는 당선 소감을 밝히는 글이므로 글의 목적으로는 ④가 가장 적절하다.

구문풀이

1행 It is a real privilege and pleasure [to be able to represent your interests {in such a remarkable town} {for a further four years}].

: 「가주어 It – 진주어 to부정사구」 구문으로 [ ]로 표시한 to부정사구가 문장의 진주어에 해당한다. 이때, to부정사구에 쓰인 두 개의 { }는 부사구로, 각각 장소와 시간을 나타낸다.

3행 I will do [whatever is within my power] [to enhance the services {that help make Middlewich such a wonderful place (to live and bring up children)}].

: 첫 번째 [ ]는 do의 목적어 역할을 하며, whatever는 복합관계대명사로 '~하는 것[일]은 무엇이든'으로 해석된다. 두 번째 [ ]는 부사적 용법으로 쓰인 to부정사구로 목적(~하기 위해)의 의미를 나타낸다. { }는 the services를 수식하는 관계절인데 여기에는 동사 help 다음에 목적어로 make라는 원형부정사가 쓰였다. 또한, '~를 …하게 만들다'의 의미를 나타내는 「make+목적어+목적격보어」 구문이 쓰였는데, 목적격보어로 「such a+형용사+명사(그렇게[정말] ~한)」의 표현이 쓰였다. 그리고 이는 형용사적 용법으로 쓰인 to부정사구 ( )의 수식을 받고 있다.

어휘풀이

- privilege *n* 특권, 영광
- enhance *v* 향상시키다
- vibrant *a* 활기찬
- represent *v* 대변하다, 대표하다
- get involved 관련되다, 관여하다
- resident *n* 거주민

005 답 ④

📖 입사 지원서에 기재된 학력의 진위 여부 확인 요청

전문해석

Nelson 씨께,

Brook Corporate에 입사 지원해 주셔서 감사합니다. 저희는 귀하의 이력서와 입사 지원서를 검토했습니다. 지원서의 일부로, 귀하는 지원서에 포함된 모든 정보를 확인할 수 있도록 우리 인사부에 권한을 부여했습니다. 귀하의 학력을 확인하는 과정에서 귀하가 지원서에 기재한 경영학석사 학위를 확인하기 위해 Lumbertown College에 연락했으나 (해당) 대학에서 해당 학위가 수여되었는지 확인할 수 없었습니다. **지원서 검토를 진행하기 전에 저희는 이 문제에 대한 명확한 설명이 필요합니다.** 대학 측의 오류를 수정하기 위해 해당 대학에 연락해야 하는 경우 그렇게 하시기 바랍니다. 이 문제에 대해 신속하게 답변해 주시면 대단히 감사하겠습니다. 그렇게 해주셔야 저희가 귀하의 지원서 평가를 진행할 수 있겠습니다.

Thomas Williams 드림

정답풀이

회사 인사부에서 입사서류를 제출한 지원자에게 학력을 확인하는 과정에서 지원서에 기재한 경영학석사 학위를 확인할 수 없다는 대학 측의 입장을 전하며 학력의 진위를 확인해달라고 하고 있다. 따라서 글의 목적으로는 ④가 가장 적절하다.

구문풀이

16행 Your prompt response regarding this matter is greatly appreciated, / **as** it will enable us to move forward with the evaluation of your application.

: 주절과 부사절로 이루어진 문장으로, as는 이유의 부사절을 이끄는 접속사로 쓰였다. 이 부사절에는 '…에게 ~이 가능하게 하다'라는 의미의 「enable+목적어+to부정사」 구문이 쓰였다.

어휘풀이

- application *n* 지원서
- résumé *n* 이력서
- permission *n* 허락, 허가
- human resources office 인사 부서, 인력 자원 부서
- verify *v* 확인하다, 검증하다
- confirm *v* 확인하다, 확정하다
- proceed *v* 진행하다, 계속하다
- employment *n* 고용, 취업
- grant *v* 부여하다, 허락하다
- M.B.A. degree 경영학 석사 학위
- clarification *n* 명확화, 설명
- prompt *a* 즉각적인, 신속한

006 답 ①

📖 차량 관련 대출금 상환 계획 요청

전문해석

Hart 씨께,

귀하는 지금쯤 새 직장에 '정착하셨나요', 그리고 아직도 처음에 그랬던 것처럼 그 일을 굉장히 좋아하시나요? 물론, 어떤 직장이든 고된 업무는 있지만, 우리는 그 직장이 귀하에게 잘 맞기를 바랍니다. **제가 이 이메일을 드리는 이유는 귀하의 차에 대한 1,500달러 대출금의 상환을 언제쯤 예상할 수 있을지 문의드리기 위해서입니다.** 저희는 귀하가 새로운 직장으로 가고 집으로 돌아올 수 있도록 귀하의 멋진 SUV 구입을 도울 수 있어서 기뻤습니다. 귀하는 대출금의 전부 또는 적어도 절반을 6월까지 지불하기로 동의하셨습니다. 만약 귀하가 총액 1,500달러를 한 번에 상환할 수 없더라도, 저희는 이해합니다. 하지만 합의한대로, 저희는 7월 1일 전에 최소한 그 금액의 절반을 수령해야 합니다. **진행 상황을 알려 주십시오.**

Jason Burton 드림

정답풀이

이메일 수신자의 새 직장의 적응과 관련한 안부를 물으면서 시작하는 이메일로, 이메일을 쓴 궁극적인 이유는 자동차 구매를 위해 대출한 금액의 전액 혹은 부분 상환 계획을 요청하기 위한 것이다. 따라서 글의 목적으로는 ①이 가장 적절하다.

구문풀이

6행 [The reason {why we are sending you this email}] **is** [to ask {when we can expect repayment of the $1,500 loan for your car}].

: 첫 번째 [ ]가 주어, is가 동사이다. 핵심 주어인 The reason은 { }로 표시한 관계절의 수식을 받는다. 두 번째 [ ]는 문장의 보어로 쓰인 to부정사구이며, 그 안의 { }로 표시한 when절은 ask의 목적어인 의문사절이다.

어휘풀이

- settle into ~에 정착하다
- repayment *n* 상환
- fancy *a* 고급의, 엄청난
- enthusiastic *a* 열광적인
- loan *n* 대출(금)
- transportation *n* 운송, 이동 수단

007 답 ②

📖 지역 문화센터에 대한 기부 요청

전문해석

Westcott 거주자 여러분께,

Westcott 지역 문화센터에서 제공하는 많은 멋진 것들이 없다면 생활이 어떠할지 여러분은 상상하실 수 있습니까? 그것은 우리 중 극히 일부가 고려라도 해보길 바라는 생각입니다. (그것은 우리 대부분이 심지어 생각도 하기 싫은 것입니다.) 우리들은 일년 내내 음악, 연극, 그리고 시민 활동을 제공하는 센터에 의존하고 있습니다. 우리 아이들은 체육관과 경기장을 사용할 수 있기를 기대하고 있습니다. 센터의 전체 운영 예산은 매우 저렴한 회비, 입장권 판매, 그리고 회사, 단체, 그리고 여러분과 같은 개인들의 후한 기부금에 의해 지불됩니다. 모두에게 지금이 힘든 시기라는 것

을 잘 알고 있지만, 우리는 우리 시의 문화가 꼭 필요한 것이라고 믿습니다. **저는 여러분이 Westcott 지역 문화센터에 기부하는 여러분의 이웃과 사업 동료들과 함께 참여해 주시길 요청하기 위해 이 글을 쓰고 있습니다.** 여러분이 어떤 액수를 기부하시더라도 우리는 여러분에게 감사드릴 겁니다.

Sue Stephens 드림

정답풀이

지역 문화센터가 시의 문화를 위해 꼭 필요한 곳임을 강조하면서 센터의 운영 자금을 위해 기부를 해달라고 요청하고 있으므로, 글의 목적으로는 ②가 가장 적절하다.

구문풀이

`2행` Can you imagine [what life would be like without the many wonderful offerings of the Westcott Community Center]?

: [ ]는 동사 imagine의 목적어 역할을 하는 명사절(의문사절)이며, without은 if it were not for ~(~이 없다면)의 의미로 주절의 would be와 호응하여 현재 사실의 반대를 가정하는 가정법 과거를 나타내고 있다.

어휘풀이

- offering *n* 제공(하는 것)
- civic *a* 시민의
- budget *n* 예산
- contribution *n* 기부(금)
- count on ~에 의존하다
- athletic field 경기장
- generous *a* 후한
- business associate 사업 동료

008 답 ④

📖📖 **주문한 제품이 아닌 다른 제품이 배송된 것에 대한 불만 표시**

전문해석

담당자님께,

지난 달에 저는 당신의 가게에서 크리스마스 선물로 실내 운동용 고정식 자전거를 샀습니다. 저는 돈을 지불했고, 구매 후에 당신은 자전거를 저희 집으로 보냈고 그것은 며칠 후에 도착했습니다. 고맙게도 그것은 크리스마스 날에 맞춰 도착했습니다. 자전거를 사용하자마자 저는 자전거에 문제가 있다는 것을 곧바로 깨달았습니다. **그것은 가게의 견본과 같은 것이 아니었습니다.** 그것은 다른 훨씬 더 비싼 모델이지만 저는 그것을 원하지 않습니다. 제가 산 실내 운동용 고정식 자전거에는 컴퓨터 모니터가 없지만, 당신이 보내준 것에는 컴퓨터 모니터가 있습니다. 알아내서 사용하는 것이 저에게는 꽤 어렵습니다. 저는 당신이 책임자로 있는 고객 서비스 부서에 전화를 걸었고 그들은 제가 산 것과 같은 실내 운동용 고정식 자전거는 재고가 없다고 말했습니다. 제가 고른 모델은 가장 오래된 모델이지만 제게는 완벽한 선택이었습니다. **저는 당신이 제 크리스마스 소망을 망쳤다는 것만 알아줬으면 합니다.**

Fernando López Veloso 드림

정답풀이

필자가 주문한 실내 운동용 고정식 자전거의 재고가 없어 다른 모델을 배송받고 이에 대해 불만 사항을 전달하는 글이므로, 글의 목적으로는 ④가 가장 적절하다.

구문풀이

`13행` I called the customer service [where you are the director] / and they said [that there were not stationary bikes in stock like the one {I bought}].

: 두 개의 절이 접속사 and로 연결된 구조이다. 첫 번째 [ ]는 the customer service를 수식하는 관계부사절이고, 두 번째 [ ]는 동사 said의 목적어 역할을 한다. { }는 the one을 수식하는 관계절로 목적격 관계대명사가 생략되었다.

어휘풀이

- stationary bike 실내 운동용 고정식 자전거

- immediately *ad* 즉시
- director *n* (부서의) 책임자
- destroy *v* 망치다
- figure out 이해하다, 알아내다
- in stock 재고로

009 답 ④

📖📖 **취업 제의에 대한 거절**

전문해석

Thomas 씨께,

부 설계 관리자 직위는 흥미롭게 들립니다. 저를 고려해 주셔서 감사합니다. **하지만 성공적인 업무 수행을 위해서 이 직위가 요구하는 컴퓨터 전문성은 제가 현재 갖고 있는 경험보다 더 많은 것을 요구합니다.** 저는 탁월하게 업무를 수행하기를 원합니다. 그래서 저는 Tulsa 대학교(TU)의 CAD(컴퓨터 이용 설계) 강좌에 등록할 것입니다. 네 달 후에 저는 이와 비슷한 직위를 단호하게 해 나갈 수 있는 훈련을 받게 될 것입니다. 아마 TU의 강사들이 현재 그 일의 책임을 받아들일 준비가 되어 있는 최근 학생들의 명단을 제안해 줄 수 있을 것입니다. 저보다 더 잘 훈련된 누군가가 Intercomp를 찾기 위해 기다리고 있습니다. 저를 고려해 주신 것에 대해 다시 한 번 감사드립니다. 그것은 설계 분야에서 계속 일하기 위해 제가 갖추어야만 하는 추가적인 훈련을 받기 위해서 제게 필요했던 자극이 되었습니다. 저는 다음 번 부 설계 관리자 채용에 준비할 생각입니다.

Cathy Jones 드림

정답풀이

취업 제의를 받고 현재 그러한 업무를 담당할 수 있는 역량이 되지 않아 그 제의를 받아들일 수 없다는 내용의 글이므로, 글의 목적으로는 ④가 가장 적절하다.

구문풀이

`4행` However, [the computer expertise {this position requires for success}] demands [**more** experience **than** I currently have].

: 첫 번째 [ ]가 주어, demands가 동사이며, 핵심 주어인 the computer expertise는 목적격 관계대명사가 생략된 관계절 { }의 수식을 받고 있다. 두 번째 [ ]는 목적어로, 여기서 「more ~ than ....은 '…보다 더 많은 ~'이라는 뜻이다.

어휘풀이

- executive *a* 관리자의, 간부의
- assistant *n* 부(副) ~; 조수
- currently *ad* 현재
- CAD 컴퓨터 이용 설계(= computer-aided design)
- pursue *v* 해 나가다
- with determination 결연하게, 단호하게
- instructor *n* 강사
- incentive *n* 자극
- drafting *n* 설계
- expertise *n* 전문성
- enroll *v* 등록하다
- responsibility *n* 책임

---

02 심경 변화

본문 pp.012~017

010 답 ①

📖 새 직장의 첫 출근일에 버스를 기다리는 David

전문해석

David는 밴쿠버에서 새로운 일을 시작하게 되었고, 그는 자신이 탈 버스를 기다리고 있었다. 그는 계속 자신의 시계와 버스가 올 방향을 번갈아 보고 있었다. 그는 "내가 탈 버스가 아직 오지 않아. 내가 첫날 지각할 수는 없어."라고 생각했다. David는 **마음을 놓을 수가 없었다.** 그가 다시 고개를 들어 보았을 때, 그는 바로 자신의 직장으로 가는 다른 버스가 오고 있는 것을 보았다. 그 버스는 그의 앞에 섰고 문을 열었다. 그는 버스에 오르며, "후유! 다행히도 내가 지각하지 않도록 이 버스가 딱 맞춰 왔네."라고 생각했다. 그는 버스의 빈 좌석에 등을 기대며 **깊은 한숨을 내쉬었고, 마침내 긴장을 풀 수 있었다.**

011 답 ③

📖 달리기에서 최고 기록을 깨는 데 실패했지만 용기를 얻은 Jamie

전문해석

Jamie는 자신의 모든 에너지를 달리기 경주의 마지막 발걸음에 쏟으면서 결승선을 통과했다. 실망스럽게도, 그녀는 자신의 개인 최고 기록을 깨는 데 또 실패했다. **Jamie는 기어코 자신의 기록을 깨기 위해 몇 달 동안 자신을 몰아붙였지만, 그것은 모두 수포가 되었다.** 그녀가 자신의 실패에 대해 어떻게 느끼는지 알아차리자, 그녀의 팀 동료 Ken은 그녀에게 다가와 말했다. "Jamie, 비록 오늘 네가 개인 최고 기록을 세우지 않았지만 너의 경기력은 극적으로 향상되었어. 너의 달리기 기량이 무척 발전했어! 다음 경주에서 너는 분명히 너의 개인 최고 기록을 깰 거야!" 그의 말을 들은 후, 그녀는 자신에 대해 자신감을 느꼈다. **이제 자신의 목표를 계속 밀고 나갈 의욕이 생긴 Jamie가 미소를 지으며 대답했다.** "네 말이 맞아! 다음 경주에서 나는 틀림없이 내 최고 기록을 깰 거야!"

정답풀이

Jamie는 달리기 경주에서 자신의 개인 최고 기록을 깨는 데 실패한 후 그간 자신의 노력이 결실을 보지 못한 것에 낙담하고 있었는데, 팀 동료인 Ken이 경기력 향상을 이야기하며 격려해 주자 새로운 의욕을 갖게 되었다. 따라서 Jamie의 심경 변화로 가장 적절한 것은 ③ '좌절한 → 용기를 얻은'이다.

① 무관심한 → 후회하는 ② 기쁜 → 지루한
④ 초조한 → 무서워하는 ⑤ 차분한 → 신이 난

구문풀이

6행 [Recognizing {how she felt about her failure}], Ken, her teammate, approached her and said, ["Jamie, {even though you didn't set a personal best time today}, your performances have improved dramatically].

: 첫 번째 [ ]는 동시상황을 나타내는 분사구문이고, 그 안의 { }는 Recognizing의 목적어 역할을 하는 명사절(의문사절)이다. 두 번째 [ ]는 said의 목적어이며, 그 안의 { }는 '~이지만'이라는 뜻을 나타내는 양보의 부사절이다.

어휘풀이

- all for nothing 수포가 된
- approach v 다가가다, 접근하다
- dramatically ad 극적으로
- definitely ad 분명히
- motivate v 의욕을 갖게 하다
- failure n 실패
- performance n (운동선수의) 경기력
- progress v 진전을 보이다
- comment n 말, 발언

012 답 ⑤

📖 아무것도 얻지 못한 첫 공룡 화석 탐험

전문해석

캐나다 전역에서 수많은 공룡 화석으로 유명한 Alberta 주의 Badlands를 탐험한 것은 Evelyn에게는 처음이었다. **젊은 아마추어 뼈 발굴자로서, 그녀는 기대감이 넘쳐났다.** 그녀는 평범한 공룡 종의 뼈를 얻기 위해 이렇게 멀리까지 여행한 적이 없었다. 희귀한 공룡 화석을 찾겠다는 그녀의 평생의 꿈이 막 이루어지려고 했다. 그녀는 그것들을 열심히 찾기 시작했다. 몇 시간 동안 황량한 땅을 헤매고 다녔지만, 그녀는 성공하지 못했다. 이제 해가 지기 시작했고, 그녀의 목표는 여전히 그녀의 힘이 미치지 않는 곳에 있었다. 자신 앞에 서서히 어두워지는 땅을 바라보며 그녀는 혼자 **한숨을 쉬며, "이렇게나 멀리 와서 아무것도 얻지 못하다니 믿을 수가 없어. 시간 낭비였어!"라고 말했다.**

정답풀이

처음에는 기대에 차서 탐험을 시작했으나 화석 발굴에 성공하지 못해 한숨을 쉬는 상황을 통해, Evelyn의 심경 변화로 적절한 것은 ⑤ '기대에 찬 → 실망스러운'임을 추론할 수 있다.

① 혼란스러운 → 무서워하는 ② 낙담한 → 자신에 찬
③ 느긋한 → 짜증이 난 ④ 무관심한 → 낙심한

구문풀이

11행 [Looking at the slowly darkening ground before her], **she** sighed to herself, "I can't believe [I came all this way for nothing]. [What a waste of time]!"

: 첫 번째 [ ]는 문장의 주어인 she를 의미상의 주어로 하는 분사구문이며, 두 번째 [ ]는 목적절을 이끄는 접속사 that이 생략된 절로 believe의 목적어 역할을 한다. 세 번째 [ ]는 감탄문으로 time 뒤에 it was가 생략된 것으로 볼 수 있다.

어휘풀이

- explore v 탐험하다
- fossil n 화석
- overflow v 넘쳐나다
- rare a 희귀한
- wander v 헤매다
- sigh v 한숨을 쉬다
- numerous a 수많은
- bone-hunter n 뼈 발굴자
- anticipation n 기대감
- eagerly ad 열심히
- deserted a 황량한

013 답 ①

📖 갑작스런 정전과 복구

전문해석

집에 전등이 나갔다. Joe는 조심스럽게 Crystal을 침실로 데려가 그녀에게 그곳에 있으라고 말했다. 그들이 이웃집과 마주한 창문을 내다보았을 때, 그 집 전등은 여전히 켜져 있는 것을 발견했다. 그들의 마음속에는 외부에 있는 그들의 두꺼비집을 (누군가가) 손댔음이 의심의 여지가 없었다. Joe는 조심스럽게 깜깜한 집 안을 지나 밖으로 걸어 나갔다. Joe가 나가 있는 동안, Crystal은 그가 너무 걱정스러워 가장 가까운 창문 밖을 내다보았지만, 밖은 너무 어두워 아무것도 볼 수 없었다. 그때 갑자기 그녀는 펑 소리를 들었고 차 한 대가 그녀의 차도로 들어오는 것을 보았다. 자갈들이 타이어 밑에서 탁탁 소리를 냈고, 이내 엔진이 잦아들었으며, 그녀는 목소리를 들었다. 천천히 그녀는 거실로 이동했다. 밖을 내다보자 그녀는 순찰차를 보게 되었다. Joe가 차 안에 앉아 있는 경찰관들에게 이야기하고 있었다. 그는 뒤돌아서 다시 집으로 걸어오고 있었는데, **그때 갑자기 불이 다시 들어왔다. Crystal은 자기 눈이 불빛에 맞춰지는 동안 안도의 숨을 내쉬었다.** 그녀는 Joe와 경찰관들과 함께하기 위해 서둘러 나갔다.

정답풀이

Crystal은 전등이 나가자 Joe가 밖에 나간 후 집에 홀로 남겨져 어둠 속에서 걱정하고 있었는데, 경찰차가 들어오고 Joe와 경찰관이 이야기를 나누는 것

을 본 후 집에 다시 불이 들어와서 안도의 숨을 내쉬었다. 따라서 Crystal의 심경 변화로 가장 적절한 것은 ① '불안한 → 안심한'이다.

② 기쁜 → 실망한 　　　　　③ 무관심한 → 후회하는
④ 기대에 찬 → 짜증이 난 　　⑤ 자신만만한 → 당혹스러운

구문풀이

3행 [When they looked out a window {that faced the neighbor's house}], they found [that their lights were still on].

: 첫 번째 [ ]는 시간의 부사절이고, 그 안의 { }는 a window를 수식하는 관계절이다. 두 번째 [ ]는 found의 목적어 역할을 하는 명사절이다.

어휘풀이

- fuse box 두꺼비집, 퓨즈 함
- popping *a* 펑 하는
- driveway *n* 차도(차고에서 외부 도로까지의 길)
- gravel *n* 자갈
- crackle *v* 탁탁 소리를 내다
- idle *v* 잦아들다, 천천히 돌다
- patrol car 순찰차
- officer *n* 경찰관
- exhale *v* 숨을 내쉬다
- sigh *n* 한숨
- relief *n* 안도, 안심
- adjust *v* 맞추다, 조절하다
- irritated *a* 짜증이 난

014 답 ①

📖 수학 점수를 잘 받았지만 친구들은 더 잘 받은 것을 알게 된 John

전문해석

John은 늘 수학에서 고생했지만, 상황을 바꾸기로 결심했다. 그는 수학 시험공부를 하면서 많은 시간을 보냈고, 결과가 나왔을 때 A-를 받은 것을 확인하고 짜릿함을 느꼈다. **그는 이전에 느껴보지 못한 자부심과 성취감을 느꼈다.** 그러나 교실을 둘러보았을 때, 그는 다른 모든 사람들이 그가 받은 것보다 높은 점수를 받은 것을 알았다. 그는 아주 열심히 공부했지만, 여전히 친구들에게 미치지 못했다는 것을 믿을 수 없었다. 교실을 떠날 때, 그는 열등감을 떨쳐낼 수 없었다. 집으로 걸어가면서 그는 자신의 점수가 그래도 이전보다 나아진 것임을 상기시키려 노력했지만, 실패자처럼 느끼지 않을 수 없었다. John은 반에서 자신의 등수를 올리길 원한다면 훨씬 더 열심히 공부해야 한다는 것을 알았다. 사실은, 그는 **시험이 끝나고 오랜 시간이 지난 후에도 불만족감을 떨쳐낼 수 없었다.**

정답풀이

수학 시험에서 A-를 받아 자부심과 성취감을 느낀 John은 주변의 친구들이 더 좋은 점수를 받은 것을 알고 열등감과 불만족감을 느꼈다고 했으므로, John의 심경 변화로 가장 적절한 것은 ① '만족스러운 → 실망한'이다.

② 기쁜 → 지루한 　　　　　③ 좌절한 → 자신감이 생긴
④ 초조한 → 안도하는 　　　⑤ 자신 있는 → 질투하는

구문풀이

2행 He spent countless hours studying for his math exam, / and when the results came back, he was thrilled [to see {that he had scored an A-}].

: [ ]는 to부정사의 부사적 용법으로 '감정의 원인'을 나타낸다. { }는 see의 목적어 역할을 하는 명사절이다.

12행 As he walked home, he tried to remind himself [that his grade was still an improvement from before], / but he couldn't help but feel like a failure.

: 명사절인 [ ]는 remind의 직접목적어이다. 「cannot help but+동사원형」은 '~하지 않을 수 없다, ~할 수밖에 없다'라는 의미이다.

어휘풀이

- struggle *v* 애쓰다, 열심히 노력하다
- determine *v* 결심하다

- countless *a* 무수한, 많은
- accomplishment *n* 성취감
- measure up to ~에 능력이 미치다
- peer *n* 친구, 또래, 동료
- shake off 떨쳐내다
- inadequacy *n* 열등감
- remind *v* 상기시키다
- improvement *n* 향상
- cannot help but *do* ~하지 않을 수 없다
- failure *n* 실패, 실패자
- dissatisfaction *n* 불만

015 답 ②

📖 위험 지역인 Nogyin Erak을 건너가면서 느낀 경험담

전문해석

내가 타고 가고 있는 버스가 Rengging이라는 작은 마을로 가는 길에 있는 위험 지역인 'Nogyin Erak'에 도착했다. 이 지역은 경치가 아름다운 것이 아니라 많은 사람들의 목숨을 앗아가는 것으로 산악 부족들 사이에서 늘 유명했다. **이 습하고 진흙 투성이인, 미끄러운 지역은 여러 해 동안 여행자들 사이에 두려움의 대상이었다.** 바위, 자갈, 진흙은 경고도 없이 언제라도 굴러 내려와 여행자의 목숨을 빼앗아 가곤 했다. 도처에 죽음이 도사리고 있는 상태에서, 아래에서 Siang 강이 잔인한 미소를 지으며 기다리고 있는 것은 악몽과 같은 시나리오였다. 마침내 운전자와 승객들은 위험 지역을 건너간 후에 숨을 크게 내쉬었다. "이제 우리는 안전해요."라고 운전사가 의기양양하게 말했다. "나는 심지어 내려다보지도 않았어요! 나는 눈을 감고 신께 기도하고 있었어요."하고 나는 한숨을 쉬며 내 주위 사람들을 향해 말했다.

정답풀이

많은 여행객들이 목숨을 잃는 위험 지역인 Nogyin Erak을 버스를 타고 건너는 상황으로, 'I'는 두려움에 눈을 뜨지 못하고 있다가 무사히 건넌 후에 안도의 한숨을 쉬고 있다. 따라서 글에 드러난 'I'의 심경 변화로 가장 적절한 것은 ② '겁에 질린 → 안심한'이다.

① 지루해 하는 → 신이 난 　　　③ 의심스러운 → 만족한
④ 자신만만한 → 걱정스러운 　　⑤ 자랑스러워 하는 → 당혹스러운

구문풀이

3행 This zone has always been famous among the hill tribes, [**not** {for its scenic beauty} **but** {for taking the lives of many}].

: 문맥상 과거부터 현재까지 계속된 상황을 나타내므로 현재완료로 표현했고, { }의 이유를 나타내는 두 개의 전치사구가 'A가 아니라 B인'의 뜻을 나타내는 상관접속사 「not A but B」로 연결되어 있다.

어휘풀이

- tribe *n* 부족, 집단
- scenic *a* 경치가 좋은
- moist *a* 습한
- muddy *a* 진흙투성이의
- boulder *n* 바위
- pebble *n* 자갈, 조약돌
- lurk *v* 도사리다, 숨어 있다
- await *v* 기다리다
- cruel *a* 잔인한
- elated *a* 의기양양한

016 답 ①

📖 국립공원 여행 중 곰의 습격을 받을 위기에 처한 부녀

전문해석

Jenna와 Johan Otter는 Jenna의 고등학교 졸업을 축하하고 있었다. 그들은 Glacier 국립공원으로 부녀 여행 중이었다. 어느 따뜻한 8월 아침 9시 직전, 그들은 얼마나 더 걸어야 할지 결정하고 있었다. 그 오솔길은 절벽 위의 산등성이를 따라나 있었다. Jenna가 앞장섰다. 그녀는 한동안 험한 계단을 올랐고, 아름다운 경치를 감상하기 위해 멈춰 섰다. 그들 위로 검독수리가 높은 구름이 있는 푸른 하늘을 날았다. Jenna는 멋진 풍경을 사진 찍으며 아버지와 함께 즐거운 시간을 보내고 있었다. 오솔길 더 위쪽에서, 커다란 바위가 그들의 길을 막고 있었다. Jenna는 그것 주

위를 뛰어다녔다. 그 바위 뒤에 어미 회색곰이 두 마리의 새끼를 데리고 있었다. Jenna의 갑작스러운 등장이 회색곰을 깜짝 놀라게 했다. Johan은 회색곰을 보았을 때, Jenna를 보호하기 위해 그녀 앞으로 뛰어들었다. 그녀는 곧 그 동물이 뛰어올라 그의 왼쪽 허벅지를 덥석 물 거라고 생각했다.

정답풀이

고등학교 졸업 축하를 위해 부녀가 함께 여행을 하며 아름다운 경치를 보고 사진을 찍으며 즐거운 시간을 보내고 있던 중, 거대한 바위 뒤에 있던 회색곰이 나타나 아버지의 허벅지를 물 상황이므로 Jenna의 심경 변화로 가장 적절한 것은 ① '즐거운 → 겁에 질린'이다.

② 무관심한 → 흥분한   ③ 부러운 → 의심하는
④ 짜증이 난 → 부끄러운   ⑤ 지루한 → 신이 난

구문풀이

12행 [Behind the boulder] was [a mother grizzly bear {with her two cubs}].

: 첫 번째 [ ]로 표시한 장소를 나타내는 부사구가 문장의 맨 앞에 오면서 주어와 동사가 도치된 구조이다. 전치사구인 { }는 문장의 주어인 a mother grizzly bear를 수식한다.

어휘풀이

- trail *n* 오솔길
- cliff *n* 절벽
- golden eagle 검독수리
- scoot *v* 뛰다, 질주하다
- cub *n* (곰·사자·여우 등의) 새끼
- leap *v* 뛰어오르다
- thigh *n* 허벅지
- ridge *n* 산등성이
- take the lead 앞장서다
- boulder *n* 바위
- grizzly bear 회색곰
- startle *v* 깜짝 놀라게 하다
- bite into ~을 덥석 물다

017 답 ①

📖 Jerusha가 이사진에게 받은 제안

전문해석

Lippett 여사는 잠시 침묵이 드리울 시간을 두고 나서 느리고 조용하게 다시 말을 이었다. "Jerusha, 너도 알다시피 아이들은 16살이 되면 더 이상 머물지 못해. 이제 너는 16살이 되었기 때문에 고아원은 더 이상 널 지원할 책임을 질 수가 없구나. 오늘 회의에서 너의 장래에 관한 이야기가 나왔고, 너의 기록이 논의되었단다. 아주 자세히 말이지." Lippett 여사는 피고석에 앉아 있는 죄수에게 던지는 듯한 책망의 눈초리를 던졌다. 그리고 Jerusha는 그녀의 기록에 어떠한 명백한 잘못을 기억할 수 있어서가 아니라, 단지 그렇게 보이도록 기대되었기 때문에 죄를 지은 듯 보였다. "너에게는 다행히도, 우리 이사진들 중 한 분이 너를 대학에 보내주신다고 하는구나." "대학에요?" Jerusha의 눈이 커졌고 정신이 멍해졌다.

정답풀이

고아원 회의에서 자신에 대한 논의가 있었다는 이야기에 Jerusha는 죄지은 사람처럼 긴장하고 있었고, 이사진들 중 한 명이 자신을 대학에 보내준다는 갑작스런 말에 눈이 커지고 정신이 멍해졌다고 했으므로 Jerusha의 심경 변화로 가장 적절한 것은 ① '긴장한 → 놀란'이다. 마지막 부분의 Fortunately for you라는 표현으로 보아 부정적인 심경, 즉 anxious, discouraged, resigned는 정답에서 제외된다.

② 지루한 → 신이 난   ③ 기쁜 → 걱정하는
④ 희망에 찬 → 낙담한   ⑤ 만족한 → 체념한

구문풀이

8행 Mrs. Lippett **brought** accusing eyes **to bear upon** the prisoner in the dock, / and Jerusha **looked** guilty [because it seemed to be expected — {not because she could remember any

---

strikingly black pages in her record}].

: 두 개의 절이 and로 연결된 구조이며, 첫 번째 절에는 「bring A to bear upon B」 구문이 쓰여 'A를 B에 쏟아붓다'의 의미를 나타낸다. 두 번째 절에서 동사 look은 2형식 동사로 형용사를 보어로 취해 '~해 보이다'의 의미를 나타낸다. [ ]는 이유를 나타내는 부사절로, 대시(—) 이하의 { }에서 이 부사절에 대한 부연 설명이 제시되고 있다.

어휘풀이

- resume *v* 다시 시작하다, 계속하다
- in a(n) ~ manner ~인 식으로, ~한 태도로
- placid *a* 차분한, 조용한
- bring up (문제를) 꺼내다, 제기하다
- bring A to bear upon B A를 B에 쏟아붓다
- accusing *a* 비난하는 (듯한), 고발하는 (듯한)
- prisoner *n* 죄수
- strikingly *ad* 두드러지게, 눈에 띄게
- trustee *n* 보관인, 평의원, 이사
- resigned *a* 체념한
- orphanage *n* 고아원
- thoroughly *ad* 철저하게
- guilty *a* 유죄의
- black page 좋지 못한 기록
- numb *v* 멍하게 만들다

018 답 ⑤

📖 표절로 선생님을 실망시킨 Bill

전문해석

Bill은 내 학생이었고 우수한 점수를 받았다. 그는 일찍 왔고, 늦게까지 남았고, 열심히 공부했고, 아주 좋은 질문을 했다. 그는 나의 최고의 학생들 중 한 명이었으며, 나는 그의 글쓰기 멘토였다. 그는 전국 대회에 참가할 에세이를 제출할 예정이었다. 나는 그에게 명료하게 그의 글을 구성하는 법을 가르쳤다. 그가 상을 탈 것임을 확신했다. 몇 주 후에 나는 그가 일등상을 탔다는 것을 들었을 때, **그가 매우 자랑스러웠고 그의 성취에 대해 그에게 축하를 보냈다.** 하지만, 우리의 행복은 오래 가지 않았다. Bill이 자기 자신의 에세이를 제출하지 않은 것이 드러났다. 그는 다른 사람이 쓴 에세이를 자기 자신의 것으로 제출했다. 그는 문자 그대로 전체 에세이를 가져다가 자신의 이름을 쓰고 그것을 제출했다. 그는 내게 그저 자신의 부모님과 나를 행복하게 만들고 싶었다고 말했다. **그의 말은 내 말문을 막히게 했다.**

정답풀이

제자인 Bill이 전국 대회에서 일등상을 받았을 때 그의 글쓰기 멘토인 'I'는 자랑스러워했으나, 나중에 Bill의 에세이가 표절로 밝혀지자 실망했을 것이므로 'I'의 심경 변화로 가장 적절한 것은 ⑤ '기쁜 → 실망한'이다.

① 즐거운 → 무관심한   ② 걱정스러운 → 단호한
③ 초조한 → 자신만만한   ④ 의혹을 갖는 → 기대하는

구문풀이

10행 It turned out [**that** Bill didn't submit his own essay].

: It은 가주어이고 [ ]로 표시된 that절이 진주어이다.

11행 He submitted an essay [**written** by someone else] **as** his own.

: [ ]는 an essay를 수식하는 과거분사구이며, as는 '~로(서)'의 의미로 쓰인 전치사이다.

어휘풀이

- submit *v* 제출하다
- clarity *n* 명료성, 명확성
- achievement *n* 성취
- speechless *a* (충격 등으로) 말이 안 나오는
- competition *n* 대회, 시합, 경쟁
- convince *v* 확신시키다, 납득시키다
- literally *ad* 문자 그대로

019　답 ⑤

📖 **조직 문화 형성을 위한 명시적 지침의 필요성**

전문해석

가치만으로는 문화를 창조하고 구축하지 않는다. 일부 시간에만 가치에 따라 생활하는 것은 문화의 창조와 유지에 기여하지 않는다. 가치를 행동으로 바꾸는 것은 전투의 절반에 불과하다. 물론, 이것은 올바른 방향으로 내딛는 한 걸음이지만, 그러한 행동은 그다음에 기대되는 것에 대한 명확하고 간결한 설명과 함께 조직 전체에 널리 공유되고 퍼뜨려져야 한다. 단순히 그것에 관해 이야기하는 것만으로는 충분하지 않다. 리더와 모든 인력 관리자가 자신의 팀을 지도하기 위해서 사용할 수 있는 특정한 행동들의 시각적 표현을 갖는 것이 중요하다. 스포츠팀이 좋은 성과를 내고 승리하는 데 도움이 되도록 고안된 특정 플레이를 담고 있는 플레이 북을 가지고 있는 것과 마찬가지로, 여러분의 회사는 여러분의 문화를 행동으로 바꾸고 여러분의 가치를 승리하는 행동으로 바꾸는 데 필요한 핵심적인 변화를 담은 플레이 북을 가지고 있어야 한다.

020　답 ③

📖 **어떤 선택의 성공 가능성을 확률적으로 분석해야 할 필요성**

전문해석

평생을 두고 우리 여정의 모든 단계에서 우리는 먼 곳으로 이어지는 많은 다른 길들이 있는 분기점을 만난다. 각각의 선택은 어떤 길이 여러분의 목적지로 데려다줄지에 대한 불확실성을 포함한다. 선택을 하기 위해 우리의 직관을 믿는 것은 흔히 우리가 차선의 선택을 하는 것으로 결국 끝난다. 불확실성을 숫자로 바꾸는 것은 여러분의 목적지로 가는 길을 분석하고 지름길을 찾는 강력한 방법으로 입증되었다. 확률에 대한 수학적 이론은 위험을 제거하지는 않았지만, 우리가 그 위험을 더 효과적으로 관리할 수 있게 해준다. 미래가 가지고 있는 모든 가능한 시나리오를 분석한 다음, 그것들이 성공이나 실패로 이어질 비율이 얼마나 되는지를 살펴보는 것이 전략이다. 이것은 여러분이 어떤 길을 선택할 것인지에 관한 결정을 내릴 때 그 근거로 삼을 수 있는 미래에 대한 훨씬 더 나은 지도를 여러분에게 제공한다.

정답풀이

글의 중반부에 필자의 주장이 명확히 드러난다. 우리의 선택은 불확실성을 포함하는데, 이 불확실성을 확률적으로 분석하는 것이 불확실성에 대한 위험을 더 효과적으로 관리할 수 있게 해준다는 내용이므로, 필자가 주장하는 바로 가장 적절한 것은 ③이다.

구문풀이

1행 [At every step in our journey through life] we encounter junctions with many different pathways [leading into the distance].

: 첫 번째 [ ]는 부사구이고, we가 문장의 주어, encounter가 동사이다. 두 번째 [ ]는 many different pathways를 수식하는 현재분사구이다.

어휘풀이
- journey *n* 여정
- pathway *n* 길, 방향
- destination *n* 목적지
- encounter *v* 만나다
- uncertainty *n* 불확실성
- intuition *n* 직관

- end up with 결국 ~하게 되다
- analyze *v* 분석하다
- probability *n* 확률
- strategy *n* 전략
- proportion *n* 비율
- potent *a* 강력한, 강한
- mathematical *a* 수학의, 수학적인
- eliminate *v* 제거하다, 없애다
- scenario *n* 시나리오, 각본

021　답 ③

📖 **소셜 미디어 프로그램을 만들 때, 조직 자체의 목표에 대한 이해의 필요성**

전문해석

소셜 미디어로 실험을 하는 것을 처음 고려할 때 조직이 가장 흔히 저지르는 실수들 중 하나는 소셜 미디어 도구와 플랫폼에 지나치게 집중하고 자신들의 사업 목표에는 충분히 집중하지 않는다는 것이다. 기업을 위한 소셜 웹에서의 성공의 실제는 소셜 미디어 프로그램을 만들어내는 것이 최신 소셜 미디어 도구와 채널에 대한 통찰이 아니라 조직 자체의 목적과 목표에 대한 철저한 이해와 함께 시작된다는 것이다. 소셜 미디어 프로그램은 단지 '다른 모든 사람들이 그것을 하고 있기' 때문에 인기 있는 소셜 네트워크에서 '존재'를 관리할 막연한 필요를 실행시키는 것이 아니다. '소셜 미디어에 있다는 것'은 그 자체로 아무런 쓸모가 없다. 조금이라도 쓸모가 있으려면 소셜 미디어 존재는 조직과 고객의 문제를 해결하거나 어떤 종류의 개선(가급적이면 측정 가능한 것)을 가져와야 한다. 모든 일에서, 목적은 성공을 이끈다. 소셜 미디어의 세계도 다르지 않다.

정답풀이

조직이 소셜 미디어 프로그램을 만들어낼 때 소셜 미디어 도구나 플랫폼에 집중하는 것은 아무 쓸모가 없으며, 조직 자체의 목적과 목표에 대한 철저한 이해를 기반으로 해야만 문제를 해결하고 개선을 이룰 수 있다는 내용이므로, 필자가 주장하는 바로 가장 적절한 것은 ③이다.

구문풀이

1행 [One {of the most common mistakes (made by organizations when they first consider experimenting with social media)}] is [**that** they focus {too much on social media tools and platforms} and {not enough on their business objectives}].

: 주어에 「One of the 최상급+복수명사」 구문이 쓰인 문장으로 '가장 ~한 것들 중 하나'의 뜻을 나타낸다. 이때, 핵심 주어는 One이므로 단수동사 is가 쓰였으며, ( )는 the most common mistakes를 수식하는 과거분사구이다. 두 번째 [ ]는 접속사 that이 이끄는 보어절이며, 이 명사절에는 동사구 「focus on ....」의 표현이 쓰여 접속사 and를 앞뒤로 대구를 이루고 있다.

어휘풀이
- organization *n* 조직
- insight *n* 통찰력
- fulfillment *n* 이행, 충족
- in and of itself 그것 자체로는
- preferably *ad* 될 수 있으면, 되도록이면
- measurable *a* 측정 가능한
- objective *n* 목표
- thorough *a* 철저한
- vague *a* 막연한

022　답 ②

📖 **학교에 만연한 학생의 무명감 문제 극복**

전문해석

학생들과 부모들은 똑같이 많은 현대 학교에 존재하는 무명감으로 걱정해 왔다. 현재의 체제하에서 어떤 학생들은 단지 교실 속의 얼굴들일 뿐이다. 무명의 문제는 보통 교사의 잘못이 아니다. 많은 교사들은 말썽쟁이들을 관리하고, 서류작업을 하고, 물론 최선을 다해 가르치는 것뿐만 아니라 하루에 백 명도 넘는 여러 다른 학생들과

함께 일해야 한다! 어떤 더 개인적인 세부 사항은 고사하고, 백 개의 이름을 기억하기는 어려울 수 있다. 그리고 더 심각한 문제를 내비칠지도 모르는 개별 학생들의 작은 변화를 알아차리는 것은 불가능할 수 있다. **학급 규모의 축소가 이러한 문제들을 빠르게 해결해 줄 수 있을 것이다.** 교사들은 단지 자신의 학생들의 얼굴을 알아보는 것뿐만 아니라 학생들을 알게 되는 데에 훨씬 더 수월한 시간을 보낼 것이다. 교사가 학생의 강점과 약점, 성격과 관심사를 안다면, 그것이 그 학생의 학문적, 개인적 경험을 대단히 향상시켜줄 수 있다. 교사는 좀 더 효과적이고 유의미한 방식으로 소통할 뿐만 아니라 학생을 더 잘 도울 수 있을 것이다.

정답풀이
현재 학교에서는 일부 학생들이 이름 없는 존재가 된다는 문제가 있는데, 학급의 규모를 축소하여 교사가 학생을 깊이 있게 이해하게 되면 문제를 극복할 수 있을 것이라는 내용이므로, 필자가 주장하는 바로 가장 적절한 것은 ②이다.

구문풀이
10행 And **it** can be impossible [to notice small changes in individual students {that might indicate more serious problems}].

: it은 가주어이고, [ ]로 표시된 to부정사구가 문장의 진주어에 해당한다. { }는 small changes를 수식하는 주격 관계대명사절이다.

어휘풀이
- namelessness *n* 무명
- never mind ~은 고사하고
- reduction *n* 축소, 감소
- recognize *v* 알아보다, 인식하다
- academic *a* 학업의, 학문의
- current *a* 지금의, 현재의
- indicate *v* 나타내다, 내비치다
- resolve *v* 해결하다
- vastly *ad* 대단히

023 답 ⑤

📖📖 동물 실험을 대체하는 동물 관찰의 이점

전문해석
(동물 실험을) 대체하거나 적어도 실험 조작을 연기하는 관찰은 실험에서 사용되어야 할 수도 있는 동물 수의 잠재적 감소를 통해서 동물 복지에 직접적으로 기여한다. 그뿐만 아니라 사전에 동물들을 주의 깊게 관찰함으로써 동물에 대한 깊은 지식을 얻은 사람은, 예를 들어 은신처나 친구에 대한 동물의 필요를 이해함으로써 훨씬 더 동물 친화적인 방식으로 실험을 실행할 수 있을 것이다. 관찰은 따라서 실험 절차의 '개선'뿐만 아니라 사용되는 동물 수의 '감소'에도 기여할 수 있다. 게다가, 만일 그것이 완전히 실험의 '대체'로 이어진다면 동물 실험의 '3R'이라고 불리는 것, 즉 '감소, 개선, 대체'의 각각에 크게 기여한다. 그러므로 관찰은 동물 실험에 대한 주된 대안 중 하나로, 동시에 동물 복지를 지키면서 높은 수준의 과학적 데이터를 제공하는 방식으로 여겨져야 한다.

정답풀이
동물을 대상으로 직접 실험을 하는 대신에 주의 깊게 관찰함으로써 동물을 연구하는 것이 실험 절차의 개선, 사용되는 동물 수의 감소로 인한 동물 복지에의 기여 등 여러 장점이 있음을 설명하고 있는 글이다. 따라서 필자가 주장하는 바로 가장 적절한 것은 ⑤이다.

구문풀이
1행 Observation [that replaces or at least postpones experimental manipulation] contributes directly to animal welfare through a potential reduction in the number of animals [that might have to be used in the experiments].

: 첫 번째 [ ]는 문장의 주어인 Observation을 수식하는 관계절이고, 주어에 이어지는 술어 동사는 contributes이다. 두 번째 [ ]는 animals를 수식하는 관계절이다.

10행 Observation can thus **contribute** [**to** a Reduction in the numbers of animals used] **as well as** [**to** a Refinement of experimental procedures].

: 두 개의 [ ]는 contribute에 이어지는 전치사구로 「A as well as B(B뿐만 아니라 A도)」에 의해 병렬구조로 연결되어 있다. used는 앞의 명사 animals를 수식하는 과거분사로 그 앞에 which are가 생략된 것으로 볼 수 있다.

어휘풀이
- observation *n* 관찰
- postpone *v* 연기하다, 미루다
- manipulation *n* 조작
- welfare *n* 복지
- reduction *n* 감소
- shelter *n* 은신처
- refinement *n* 개선, 개량
- alternative *n* 대안
- replace *v* 대체하다
- experimental *a* 실험의
- contribute to ~에 기여하다
- potential *a* 잠재적인
- carry out ~을 실행하다
- companion *n* 친구
- procedure *n* 절차, 과정
- safeguard *v* 보호하다, 지키다

024 답 ②

📖📖 발표 자료의 제시 순서를 청중의 관점에서 정하기

전문해석
일반적으로, 발표자들은 자신의 자료를 일종의 논리적 순서로 배열하는데, 자신들에게 합당한 순서이다. 예컨대 여러분은 배경, 기회, 전략적 임무, 경쟁 환경, 재정적 영향, 인적 자원 등에 대한 영향 등을 다루고자 한다. 지루하다. **여러분의 발표를 여러분의 청중이 가지고 있는 시급한 문제와 더불어 시작하고, 그다음에 그들에게 여러분이 제안하는 해결책을 말하라.** 여기가 중요한 부분인데, 다음에는 어디로 가야 할지 정하기 위해 자신에게 물어라. "내가 여기서 멈추게 된다면 청중에게서 나올 첫 번째 반대는 무엇인가?" 그 반대에 대한 여러분의 반응이 여러분의 다음 지점이다. 그 지점으로 나아가고, 그다음에 그 질문을 반복하라. **이런 식으로 여러분은 여러분에게 합당해 보이는 어떤 임의적인 순서가 아니라, 청중이 듣고자 하는 방식으로 배열된 발표를 점진적으로 설계할 것이다.**

정답풀이
발표자는 발표를 할 때 본인에게 합당한 순서가 아니라 청중의 관점에서 청중이 가지고 있는 문제와 더불어 시작하고 해결책을 제안하며, 발표가 진행되는 동안에도 계속 청중이 듣기를 원하는 것이 무엇인지를 고려해서 순서를 정해가야 한다는 내용이다. 따라서 필자가 주장하는 바로 가장 적절한 것은 ②이다.

구문풀이
6행 [Begin your presentation with a pressing problem {**that** your audience has}] / and then [tell them your proposed solution].

: [ ]로 표시된 두 개의 명령문이 and로 연결되어 있다. a pressing problem은 { }로 표시한 목적격 관계대명사절의 수식을 받고 있으며, 두 번째 명령문에는 「tell A B(A에게 B를 말하다)」 구문이 쓰였다.

14행 This way you will progressively design a presentation [sequenced in the way {your audience wants to hear it}], not in some arbitrary order [**that** seems to make sense to you].

: 첫 번째 [ ]는 a presentation을 수식하는 과거분사구이고, 그 안의 { }는 the way를 수식하는 관계부사절이다. 두 번째 [ ]의 that은 주격 관계대명사로, 이 관계절은 앞의 명사구 some arbitrary order를 수식한다.

어휘풀이
- typically *ad* 일반적으로, 보통
- make sense 합당하다, 이치에 맞다
- competitive *a* 경쟁의
- implications *n* (예상되는) 영향, 결과
- logical *a* 논리적인
- strategic *a* 전략적인
- financial *a* 재정적인
- pressing *a* 시급한, 절박한

- objection *n* 반대, 이의
- sequence *v* 배열하다
- progressively *ad* 점진적으로
- arbitrary *a* 임의적인

025 답 ③

📖 개선 방법을 구체적으로 제시하는 비판의 필요성

전문해석

비판을 단순히 전달하는 것으로 비판을 받는 사람이 다음에 무엇을 해야 하는지에 대한 설명을 제공한다고 생각하는 실수를 범하지 마라. 그건 나쁜 관행이다! 업무의 우선순위를 더 잘 정할 필요가 있는 직원을 예로 들어보자. 그에게 우선순위를 정하는 일을 더 잘할 필요가 있다고 말하는 것은 도움이 된다. 그러나 그 직원이 업무 우선순위를 적절하게 정하는 방법을 안다면 그가 그렇게 할 가능성이 높을 것이라는 점을 고려하라. 마찬가지로, 많은 관리자들은 회의에서 더 많이 참여하지 않는 것에 대해 비판을 받는다. 십중팔구, 관리자들이 회의에서 더 많이 참여하는 방법을 알고 있다면 그들은 그렇게 할 것이다. **각 상황에서, 비판을 받는 사람이 일을 개선하기 위해 수행할 수 있는 구체적인 조치를 더 깊이 탐구하는 것이 필요하다.** 예를 들어, 상사는 "회의에서 더 많이 참여한다는 것은 준비하는 것을 넘어서는 것입니다. 저는 여러분이 한 가지 아이디어를 내거나 집단에 제기할 좋은 질문을 하나 소개해주었으면 합니다. 또한, 회의가 경로를 벗어나면, 모든 사람이 논의 사항으로 돌아오게 하는 일을 당신이 직접 해주었으면 합니다."라고 말할 수 있다.

정답풀이

비판을 할 때는 단순하게 비판만 전달하지 말고 구체적으로 어떻게 개선을 해야 하는지에 관한 내용도 함께 전달해야 한다는 내용이므로, 필자의 주장으로 가장 적절한 것은 ③이다.

구문풀이

1행 Never make the mistake of thinking [that the mere delivery of the criticism provides the explanation of {what the receiver should do next}].

: [ ]로 표시한 that절은 thinking의 목적어 역할을 하는 명사절로, the mere delivery of the criticism이 이 명사절의 주어, provides가 동사이다. { }는 of의 목적어 역할을 하는 명사절이다.

어휘풀이

- delivery *n* 전달
- explanation *n* 설명
- prioritize *v* 우선순위를 정하다
- appropriately *ad* 적절히
- in all likelihood 십중팔구
- specific *a* 구체적인, 명확한
- go off track 경로를 벗어나다
- criticism *n* 비판
- practice *n* 관행, 관습
- priority *n* 우선순위
- participate *v* 참여하다
- explore *v* 탐구하다
- come up with ~을 생각해 내다

026 답 ④

📖 뛰어난 자질을 가진 사람들에게 기회를 줄 필요성

전문해석

여러분은 왜 상을 받을 만한 여러분의 종마를 마구간에 남겨두려고 하는가? 그것이 건초를 먹으며 거기 서 있는 동안에, 경기는 그것 없이 이기기도 하고 지기도 한다. 그것이 경기를 할 기회를 가지지 못하면 그것은 승리에 기여할 수 없다. 너무나 자주, 우리는 자신들의 스타급 직원들을 그들의 열정에도 불구하고 밀어내는 회사들을 본다. 이유는 기대 이상의 성과를 냄으로써 그들이 다른 사람들을 형편없게 보이게 한다는 것이다. 사무실의 다른 사람들은 어떤 상이나 인정도 받지 못한다. 그들은 단지 다른 사람들에게 질투심이 일게 한다. 하지만, 나머지 사람들과 보조를 맞추지 않

는 사람들을 벌하는 대신에, 그들의 동기에 대해 그들에게 보상을 하라. 삶이라는 훌륭한 작품에는 뒤를 받쳐주는 가수들이 따라다니는 스타들이 항상 있을 것이다. 독주자를 침묵하게 하면 여러분에게 남는 전부는 배경 음악일 것이다. 빛나는 스타들도 태만한 사람들만큼 지원을 받을 필요가 있다. **종마를 마구간 밖에 나오게 해 그것들에게 달릴 수 있는 여지를 제공하라.**

정답풀이

뛰어난 자질을 가진 사람들을 견제하고 그들의 능력을 억제하기보다는 재능을 마음껏 발휘하도록 기회를 줘야 한다는 내용이므로, 필자의 주장으로 가장 적절한 것은 ④이다.

구문풀이

13행 If you silence the soloist, / all [you will be left with] is background music.

: if절과 주절로 이루어진 문장으로, 주절에서 주어는 all, 동사는 is가 된다. [ ]는 all을 수식하는 관계절로, 목적격 관계대명사 that이 생략되어 있다.

어휘풀이

- prize *a* 상을 받을 만한, 귀중한
- hay *n* 건초, 여물
- zeal *n* 열의
- overachieve *v* 기대 이상의 성과를 내다
- recognition *n* 인정, 인식
- out of step 보조를 맞추지 않고, 조화되지 않고
- drive *n* 동기, 추진력
- headliner *n* 스타, 인기 배우
- stable *n* 마구간, 외양간
- contribute to ~에 기여하다
- punish *v* 처벌하다
- production *n* (영화 등의) 상연, 작품

027 답 ④

📖 학생들이 다양한 매체를 활용해 발표하도록 장려하기

전문해석

학교에서는 여전히 오로지 인쇄물을 기반으로 하는 결과물을 만들어 내는 것에 지나치게 의존하고 있지만, 학교 밖의 세상에서는 인쇄물이 이미지 자료의 수반 없이 등장하는 경우가 거의 없다. 진정, 인쇄물은 그 자체가 시각적인 매체이고, **학생들이 자신들의 학습 결과를 발표할 때 다양한 인쇄 형식과, 인쇄물과 이미지 자료의 다양한 조합에 대해 생각하고, 사용하고, 제시하도록 장려하기 위해 더 많은 것이 행해질 수 있을 것이다.** 게다가, 물론 사진, 수집된 이미지 자료, 도안, 슬라이드 상영, 오디오테이프, 라디오 상영, 그리고 간단한 비디오와 영화 작품은 모두, 모든 과목에서 학생 아이디어 발표를 위한 흥미로운 가능성을 가지고 있다. **학생들이 자신들의 학습 결과를 발표하는 데에 적절한 미디어 형태를 선택하도록 교사들이 조금만 장려하면** 학생들이 비인쇄물 형태를 매개로 한 의사소통에서 소유하고 있을지도 모르는 능력을 드러내 보이고 새로운 역량을 개발할 수 있을 것이다.

정답풀이

아직도 학생들의 발표가 단순히 인쇄물을 이용하는 수준에 머물러 있다는 점을 지적하면서 학생들이 다양한 형식과 매체를 이용해 학습 결과를 발표할 수 있도록 교사들이 권장해야 한다는 취지를 담고 있는 글이다. 따라서 필자가 주장하는 바로 가장 적절한 것은 ④이다.

구문풀이

4행 Indeed, print is itself a visual medium, / and much more could be done [**to encourage** pupils and students to think about, use, and package different print formats and different combinations of print and images, in presenting their work].

: 두 개의 절이 접속사 and로 연결된 구조이다. 두 번째 절에서 주어는 much more, 동사는 could be done이다. [ ]는 목적을 나타내는 부사적 용법의 to부정사구이며, 여

기에는 '~가 …하도록 장려하다'라는 의미의 「encourage+목적어+목적격보어(to부정사)」 구문이 사용되었다. think (about), use, package는 병렬구조를 이룬다.

13행 Even a little encouragement by teachers [for students **to choose** an appropriate media form in presenting their work] would **allow** students to demonstrate any abilities [they might possess in communicating via nonprint forms] and to develop new skills.

: Even a little encouragement by teachers가 주어, would allow가 동사이다. 첫 번째 [ ]는 주어를 수식하는 형용사적 용법의 to부정사구로 for students가 의미상의 주어이다. 문장의 동사에는 '~가 …하게 해주다'라는 의미의 「allow+목적어+목적격보어(to부정사)」 구문이 쓰였으며, to demonstrate와 to develop은 병렬구조를 이룬다. 두 번째 [ ]는 any abilities를 수식하는 관계절로 목적격 관계대명사 that 또는 which가 생략되었다.

어휘풀이
- reliance *n* 의존, 의지
- accompaniment *n* 수반, 동반
- package *v* 제시하다
- combination *n* 조합, 결합
- demonstrate *v* 드러내 보이다, 보여주다
- via *p* ~을 매개로 하여
- exclusively *ad* 오로지, 독점적으로
- pupil *n* 학생
- format *n* 형식, 형태

---

04 함축 의미 추론

본문 pp.024~029

028 ④	029 ①	030 ②	031 ⑤	032 ⑤
033 ④	034 ④	035 ③	036 ③	

---

028 답 ④

📖 주의의 초점을 넓혀 보다 넓은 시각을 통해 스트레스 상황에 대처하기

전문해석
여러분의 주의를 집중하는 방식은 여러분이 스트레스에 대처하는 방식에 중요한 역할을 한다. 분산된 주의는 스트레스를 해소하는 능력을 해치는데, 왜냐하면 여러분의 주의가 분산되더라도, 여러분은 여러분의 경험 중 스트레스가 많은 부분에만 집착할 수 있어서 그것이 좁게 집중되기 때문이다. 여러분의 주의의 초점이 넓어지면, 여러분은 스트레스를 더 쉽게 해소할 수 있다. 여러분은 어떤 상황이라도 그것의 더 많은 측면을 균형 있는 시각으로 볼 수 있으며, 피상적이고 불안을 유발하는 주의력 수준으로 여러분을 옭아매는 한 부분에 갇히지 않을 수 있다. **초점이 좁으면 각 경험의 스트레스 수준이 높아지는데, 초점이 넓으면 여러분은 각 상황을 더 넓은 시각으로 더 잘 볼 수 있기 때문에 스트레스 수준이 낮아진다.** 불안감을 유발하는 하나의 세부 사항은 더 큰 전체적인 상황보다 덜 중요하다. 그것은 여러분 자신을 들러붙지 않는 프라이팬으로 변형시키는 것과 같다. 여러분은 여전히 달걀을 부칠 수 있지만, 그 달걀이 팬에 들러붙지 않을 것이다.

---

029 답 ①

📖 현대적 주체성 구성을 가져온 개인 일기

전문해석
18세기와 19세기에 발달하면서, 개인 일기는 현대적인 주체성을 구성하는 데 중심

적인 존재가 되었는데, 그것의 중심에는 세계와 자아의 이해에 대한 이성과 비평의 적용이 있어서, 이것이 새로운 종류의 지식이 생겨나게 해 주었다. **일기는 계몽되고 자유로운 주체가 구성되도록 하는 중심 매체였다.** 그것은 사람들이 날마다 자신의 행방, 감정, 생각에 대해 적을 수 있는 공간을 제공했다. 시간이 흐르면서, 그리고 재차 읽어봄으로써, 이질적인 기입 내용, 사건, 우연한 일이 자아에 관한 통찰과 이야기로 만들어질 수 있었고, 주체성의 형성을 가능하게 했다. '말로 만들어지기도 하고 탐구되기도 하는 (대로의) 자아' 개념이 나타나는 곳은 바로 그런 맥락이다. 일기는 개인적이고 사적이었는데, 사람들이 자신을 위해 쓰거나, 혹은 Habermas의 간결한 표현으로 하자면, 사람들이 자신을 자신에게 알려지게 하곤 했다. **사적 영역에서 자아를 알려지게 함으로써, 자아는 자기 점검과 자기비판의 대상이 되기도 했다.**

정답풀이
개인 일기는 주체가 구성되도록 하는 중심 매체로서 자아에 관한 통찰과 이야기가 형성되어 결국 자기 점검과 자기비판이 가능하도록 했다는 내용이다. 결국 개인 일기가 자기 성찰의 계기를 준다는 것이 핵심 내용이므로, 밑줄 친 부분이 의미하는 바로 가장 적절한 것은 ① '글을 자신을 되돌아보는 수단으로 사용하다'이다.
② 다른 사람들의 일기를 읽음으로써 자신의 정체성을 확립하다
③ 글 쓰는 과정에서 의견을 교환하다
④ 다른 사람들에게 보이기 위한 대체 자아를 만들어 내다
⑤ 자아에 관한 글쓰기 주제를 개발하다

구문풀이
1행 [Coming of age in the 18th and 19th centuries], the personal diary became a centerpiece in the construction of a modern subjectivity, [at the heart of which is the application of reason and critique to the understanding of world and self], [which allowed the creation of a new kind of knowledge].

: 첫 번째 [ ]는 '~하면서'라는 의미를 나타내는 분사구문이며, the personal diary가 문장의 주어, became이 동사이다. 두 번째 [ ]는 the construction of a modern subjectivity를 부가적으로 설명하는 관계절이고, 세 번째 [ ]는 the application ~ self를 부가적으로 설명하는 관계절이다.

어휘풀이
- come of age 발달하다; 성년이 되다
- construction *n* 구성, 구축
- application *n* 적용
- critique *n* 비평, 비판
- whereabouts *n* 소재, 행방
- happenstance *n* 우연(한 일)
- context *n* 맥락, 문맥
- formulation *n* 간결한 표현
- self-inspection *n* 자기 점검
- alternate *a* 대신의
- centerpiece *n* 중심적인 존재
- subjectivity *n* 주체성, 주관성
- reason *n* 이성, 사고력
- enlightened *a* 계몽된
- entry *n* 기입 (내용)
- insight *n* 통찰(력)
- emerge *v* 나타나다, 등장하다
- sphere *n* 영역, 분야
- identity *n* 정체성
- ego *n* 자아

---

030 답 ②

📖 전문화된 전문가들이 가진 특정 지식에 대한 신뢰성 필요

전문해석
과학자들은 도덕적 또는 윤리적 결정에 대한 특별한 강점이 없는데, 기후 과학자가 의료 개혁에 관한 견해를 밝힐 자격이 없는 것은 물리학자가 꿀벌 군체의 붕괴 원인을 판단할 자격이 없는 것과 같다. 전문화된 영역에서의 전문 지식을 만들어내는 바로 그 특징이 많은 다른 영역에서의 무지로 이어진다. 어떤 경우에는, 전문가가 아닌 사람들, 즉 농부, 어부, 환자, 토착민이, 과학자들이 배울 수 있는 관련 경험을 가지고 있을 수도 있다. 실제로, 최근 과학자들은 이 점을 인식하기 시작했는데, 북극 기

후 영향 평가는 지역 토착 집단에게서 수집된 관찰을 포함한다. 그러므로 우리의 신뢰는 한정되고 초점이 맞춰질 필요가 있다. 그것은 매우 '특정할' 필요가 있다. 맹목적 신뢰는 최소한 신뢰가 전혀 없는 것만큼이나 우리를 문제에 봉착하게 할 것이다. 하지만 우리의 지정된 전문가들, 즉 우리가 사는 자연 세계에 관한 어려운 질문들을 처리하는 데 평생을 바친 남녀에 대한 어느 정도의 신뢰가 없으면, 우리는 마비되고, 사실상 아침 통근을 위해 준비해야 할지 말아야 할지를 알지 못할 것이다.

정답풀이
과학자들의 전문 지식에 대한 신뢰는 한정되고 초점이 맞춰져야 하며, 과학자들의 전문 분야에 대해서도 일반인들의 생활 속 경험으로부터 배워야 할 경우가 있으므로 자연 세계에 관한 어려운 문제들을 해결하는 데 평생을 바친 전문가들의 전문성에 대한 어느 정도의 신뢰가 없다면 아침에 통근 준비를 해야 할지의 여부도 알 수 없을 것이라는 내용이다. 따라서 밑줄 친 부분이 의미하는 바로 가장 적절한 것은 ② '전문화된 전문가들에 의해 제공된 쉽게 적용할 수 있는 정보'이다.
① 비전문가들에 의해 보급된 의심스러운 사실
③ 중대한 결정에 거의 영향을 주지 않는 일반 지식
④ 전문가와 전문가가 아닌 사람들 모두에 의해 생산된 실용적인 정보
⑤ 지역 공동체에 널리 퍼져 있는 편향된 지식

구문풀이
1행 Scientists have no special purchase on moral or ethical decisions; a climate scientist **is no more** qualified to comment on health care reform **than** a physicist **is** to judge the causes of bee colony collapse.

: 「A is no more B than C is D」 구문이 쓰여 'A가 B가 아닌 것은 C가 D가 아닌 것과 같다'라는 의미를 나타내고 있다.

15행 But without some degree of trust in our designated experts — [the men and women {who have devoted their lives to sorting out tough questions about the natural world (we live in)}] — / we are paralyzed, in effect [not knowing {**whether to make** ready for the morning commute or not}].

: 첫 번째 [ ]는 our designated experts를 부연 설명하는 동격구이고, 그 안의 { }는 the men and women을 수식하는 관계절이다. 그 안의 ( )는 목적격 관계대명사가 생략된 형태로 the natural world를 수식하는 관계절이다. 두 번째 [ ]는 동시상황을 나타내는 분사구문이고, 그 안의 { }는 knowing의 목적어 역할을 하는 「whether+to부정사구」로 whether we should make ~의 명사절이 변형된 형태로 이해할 수 있다.

어휘풀이
- purchase *n* 강점
- qualified *a* 자격이 있는
- colony *n* (개미·벌 등의) 집단, 군체
- expertise *n* 전문 지식
- relevant *a* 관련이 있는
- designate *v* ~을 지정하다
- sort out (문제 등을) 해결하다
- in effect 실제로, 사실상
- popularize *v* ~을 보급하다, ~을 널리 알리다
- applicable *a* 적용[응용]할 수 있는
- ethical *a* 윤리적인
- physicist *n* 물리학자
- collapse *n* 붕괴, 와해
- ignorance *n* 무지
- assessment *n* 평가
- devote *v* ~을 바치다
- tough *a* 어려운, 힘든
- biased *a* 편향된

031 답 ⑤

📖 아이들이 보이는 폭력성의 이유

전문해석
내가 여러분을 해치고 제압할 수 있다면, 여러분이 주변에 있을 때조차도, 나는 내가 원하는 것을 내가 원하는 때에 바로 할 수 있다. 나는 여러분을 괴롭혀 내 호기심을 달랠 수 있다. 나는 여러분의 관심을 빼앗아 여러분을 지배할 수 있다. 나는 여러분의 장난감을 훔칠 수 있다. **공격성은 첫 번째로 어떤 사람에게는 더 지배적이고 어떤 사람에게는 덜 지배적이기는 하지만 선천적으로 타고난 것이어서, 그리고 두 번째로 공격성이 욕망을 촉진하기 때문에, 아이들은 공격한다.** 그러한 행동은 학습되는 것이 틀림없다고 가정하는 것은 어리석은 일이다. 뱀은 공격하는 법을 배울 필요가 없다. 그것은 짐승의 본성 안에 있다. 통계적으로 말하자면, 두 살짜리 아이들이 사람들 중에서 가장 폭력적이다. 그들은 발로 차고, 때리고, 깨물고, 다른 사람의 소유물을 훔친다. 그들은 탐구하고, 분노와 좌절을 표현하고, 충동적인 욕구를 충족시키기 위해 그렇게 한다. 더 중요한 것은, 허용할 수 있는 행동의 진정한 한계를 발견하기 위해 그렇게 한다는 것이다. 그러지 않고서야 아이들이 무엇이 허용되는지 어떻게 알아낼 수 있을까? 그들은 벽을 찾고 있는 눈먼 사람과 같다. 그들은 실제 경계가 어디에 있는지 확인하기 위해 앞으로 나아가야 한다.

정답풀이
아이들의 공격적 행동이 탐구, 감정 표현, 욕구 충족 등의 목적으로 나타날 수 있으며, 이것은 그들이 허용 가능한 행동의 한계를 발견하기 위해 그렇게 하는 것이라는 내용의 글이다. 밑줄 친 부분 다음에 나오는 마지막 문장에서 '실제 경계가 어디에 있는지 확인하기 위해 앞으로 나아가야 한다'라고 말하고 있으므로, 밑줄 친 부분이 의미하는 바로 가장 적절한 것은 ⑤ '유아는 허용 가능한 행동의 한계를 탐색하고 시험한다.'이다.
① 아이들은 어른들의 지도에 따라서만 행동한다.
② 아기들은 자신들이 무지하다는 것을 모른다.
③ 아이들의 호기심은 종종 그들을 위험에 빠뜨린다.
④ 부모들은 아기들의 호기심을 만족시키기 위해 노력해야 한다.

구문풀이
1행 If I can hurt and overpower you, / then I can **do** exactly [what I want], [when I want], [even when you're around].

: 조건절과 주절로 이루어진 문장이다. 첫 번째 [ ]는 do의 목적어이고, 두 번째와 세 번째 [ ]는 주절에 포함된 부사절이다.

5행 Children hit first [**because** aggression is innate, {although more dominant in some individuals and less in others}], and, [second, **because** aggression facilitates desire].

: and로 연결된 두 개의 [ ]는 주절에 이어지는 부사절이다. { }는 첫 번째 because절에 포함된 부사절이다.

어휘풀이
- overpower *v* 제압하다
- dominate *v* 지배하다
- innate *a* 선천적인, 타고난
- assume *v* 가정하다
- statistically speaking 통계적으로 말하자면
- property *n* 재산, 소유물
- gratify *v* 충족시키다
- desire *n* 욕구, 욕망
- puzzle out 알아내다
- torment *v* 괴롭히다
- aggression *n* 공격성
- facilitate *v* 촉진하다
- beast *n* 짐승
- outrage *n* 분노
- impulsive *a* 충동적인
- permissible *a* 허용되는
- boundary *n* 경계

032 답 ⑤

📖 설득의 기술

전문해석
설득은 강제가 아니며, 또한 사실이나 도덕적 우월함으로 지적인 상대방을 이기려는 시도도 아니며, 승자나 패자가 있는 논쟁도 아니다. 설득은 한 사람을 단계적으로 이

끌어, 그들이 자기 자신의 생각을 더 잘 이해하고 당신의 메시지와 어떻게 조정할 수 있는지를 돕는다. **당신은 다른 사람이 마음을 바꾸기를 원하지 않으면 설득할 수 없으며, 알다시피, 가장 잘 작동하는 기술은 결론보다 한 사람의 동기에 더 중점을 두는 것이다.** 여러모로 볼 때 대체로 설득은 사람들이 변화하는 것이 가능하다는 것을 깨닫도록 격려하는 것이다. 모든 설득은 자기 설득이다. 사람들은 자신의 욕망, 동기, 내적인 반론 등을 토대로 마음을 바꾸기도 하고 바꾸지 않기도 하는데, 그래서 이러한 요인들에 집중함으로써 토론으로 마음을 바꿀 가능성은 더 높아진다. 심리학자 Joel Whalen이 언젠가 말한 것처럼, "끈을 밀어서는 움직일 수 없고 잡아당겨야 한다."

정답풀이

설득은 강제로 상대방과 견해를 싸워서 이기는 것이 아니라 자기 설득이라서 상대방의 내부에서 변화가 일어나야 성공하는 것이라는 내용의 글이다. 끈을 민다는 것은 상대방을 강제로 이기려는 것이고, 잡아당긴다는 것은 상대방이 자발적으로 마음을 바꾸도록 유도한다는 것이다. 따라서 밑줄 친 부분이 의미하는 바로 가장 적절한 것은 ⑤ '상대방이 기꺼이 새로운 관점을 받아들이도록 동기를 부여하라.'이다.

① 상대방이 먼저 말을 많이 하게 하라.
② 상대방을 설득할 때 직접적이고 강력한 접근법을 사용하라.
③ 당신이 틀렸다는 것을 깨달았을 때 즉시 당신의 오류를 인정하라.
④ 상대방이 즉시 다른 신념을 채택하도록 강요하라.

구문풀이

1행 Persuasion is not coercion, and it is also not an attempt to defeat your intellectual opponent with facts or moral superiority, [**nor** is it {a debate with a winner or a loser}].

: [ ]는 도치 구문으로 부정어 nor를 강조하기 위해 '부사어+동사+주어'의 어순으로 도치가 되었다. { }는 동사 is의 보어이다.

13행 People change or refuse [**based** on their own desires, motivations, and internal counterarguing], and {by focusing on these factors}, an argument becomes more likely to change minds.

: [ ]는 동시상황을 나타내는 분사구로 based 앞에는 being이 생략되었다. based on 의 목적어로 their own desires, motivations, internal counterarguing이 병렬 구조로 연결되어 있다. { }는 부사구로 「by -ing」는 '~함으로써'라는 의미를 나타낸다. 「be[become] likely+to부정사」는 '~할 가능성이 있다, ~할 것 같다'의 의미이다.

어휘풀이

- persuasion *n* 설득
- defeat *v* 패배시키다
- opponent *n* 상대방, 반대자
- debate *n* 논쟁
- persuade *v* 설득하다
- counterargue *v* 항변하다, 상대방의 주장을 반박하다
- argument *n* 토론, 논의
- fallacy *n* 오류
- embrace *v* 받아들이다, 수용하다
- attempt *n* 시도
- intellectual *a* 지적인
- superiority *n* 우월성
- align with ~에 맞추어 조정하다
- desire *n* 욕망
- string *n* 끈, 줄
- promptly *ad* 신속하게
- perspective *n* 관점

033 답 ④

📖📖 언제나 합리적이지는 않은 인간의 사고방식

전문해석

과학자들은 증거를 수집하고, 규칙성을 찾고, 그들의 관찰을 설명하는 이론을 만들고, 그것들을 검증한다. 변호사들은 다른 사람들을 설득하기를 원하는 결론으로 시작한 후 그것을 뒷받침하는 증거를 찾는데, 또한 그렇지 않은 증거를 믿지 않으려고 한다. 인간의 마음은 과학자와 변호사 모두가 되도록 설계되었으며, 객관적인 진실

의 의식적인 추구이면서 우리가 믿고 싶어 하는 것의 무의식적이고 열렬한 옹호자이다. 이 접근법들은 함께 우리의 세계관을 만들기 위해서 경쟁한다. 당신이 진실이기를 바라는 것을 믿고 그것을 정당화하는 증거를 찾는 것은 매일의 결정에 최선의 접근법으로 보이지 않는다. 예를 들어, 만일 당신이 경마 대회에 있다면 당신이 가장 빠르다고 믿는 말에 내기를 거는 것은 합리적이지만, 당신이 어떤 말에 내기를 했기 때문에 그 말이 가장 빠르다고 믿는 것은 말이 되지 않는다. 그러나 **비록 후자의 접근법이 합리적이지는 않지만, 아마도 우리를 더 행복하게 만드는 것은 바로 그 비합리적인 선택이다.** 그것이 밝혀진 것처럼, 뇌는 괜찮은 과학자이지만 절대적으로 뛰어난 변호사이다.

정답풀이

변호사처럼 결론을 먼저 내리고 증거를 찾는 것은 합리적인 것이 아닌데도, 인간의 뇌는 행복을 위해서 이런 비합리적인 사고를 한다는 내용의 글이다. 따라서 밑줄 친 부분이 의미하는 바로 가장 적절한 것은 ④ '행복을 추구하는 인간의 마음이 언제나 합리적인 것은 아니다'이다.

① 우리는 일반적으로 우리 자신을 지나치게 긍정적인 관점에서 본다
② 무의식적인 마음은 제한된 정보를 사용하는 데 대가이다
③ 우리의 변호사와 같은 무의식적인 마음은 우리의 결정을 완전히 좌우한다
⑤ 우리의 이성적인 의식은 결정을 내리기 위해 변호사의 도움을 필요로 한다

구문풀이

10행 [**Believing in** {what you desire to be true} and then **seeking** evidence {to justify it}] doesn't seem [to be the best approach to everyday decisions].

: 첫 번째 [ ]는 문장의 주어로 동명사구인 Believing in ~과 seeking ~이 등위접속사 and로 연결된 구조이다. 문맥상 두 동명사구를 하나의 개념으로 보아 단수 취급(doesn't seem)했다. 첫 번째 { }는 전치사 in의 목적어이며, what은 관계대명사로 the thing that ~으로 바꿔 쓸 수 있다. 두 번째 { }는 앞의 명사 evidence를 수식하는 형용사적 용법의 to부정사구이며, 두 번째 [ ]는 2형식 동사 seem의 보어이다.

어휘풀이

- regularity *n* 규칙성
- attorney *n* 변호사
- convince ~ of … ~에게 …를 납득시키다
- discredit *v* 신용하지 않다
- impassioned *a* 열정적인
- approach *n* 접근법
- justify *v* 정당화하다
- irrational *a* 비합리적인, 비이성적인
- outstanding *a* 뛰어난
- dictate *v* ~을 좌우하다, ~에 영향을 끼치다
- theory *n* 이론
- conclusion *n* 결론
- conscious *a* 의식적인
- advocate *n* 옹호자
- desire *v* 바라다
- rational *a* 합리적인, 이성적인
- decent *a* 괜찮은

034 답 ④

📖📖 디지털 기술의 발달로 인한 학생들의 주의력 감소

전문해석

교육자들은 정보의 압도적인 신속성에 대해 우려를 나타내고 있다. 400명의 영국 교사들을 대상으로 한 2012년 보고서에서, 4분의 3이 자신들의 **어린 학생들의 주의 지속 시간이 현저히 떨어졌다**고 보고했다. 같은 해, 2,000명 이상의 미국 중등학교 교사들을 대상으로 한 설문조사는 교사들의 87퍼센트가 디지털 기술이 '**짧은 주의 지속 시간을 가진 쉽게 산만해지는 세대**'를 만들고 있다고 믿는데, 64퍼센트는 이러한 기술들이 학생들에게 학업적으로 유익한 효과보다는 **산만한 효과를 준다**는 데 동의했다. 디지털 기기의 결점을 표현하는 여러 직업의 다양성이 2011년 9월에 저명한 영국 신문인 〈Daily Telegraph〉에 기고되어 '어린 시절의 침식'에 대한 경종을 표명한 200명의 교사, 정신과 의사, 신경과학자 및 기타 전문가들이 서명한 공개 서한에 잘 설명되었다.

디지털 기술의 발달이 아이들을 짧은 주의 지속 시간을 가진 쉽게 산만해지는 세대로 만들고 학업적으로도 산만한 효과를 준다고 하며, 이를 '어린 시절의 침식'이라고 표현하고 있다. 따라서 밑줄 친 부분이 의미하는 바로 가장 적절한 것은 ④ '디지털 기기의 이용으로 인한 학생들의 주의력 감소'이다.
① 부모와 교사에 대한 아이들의 불신
② 아이들의 줄어든 놀이 시간에 의해 야기되는 문제
③ 너무 많은 학업에 지친 아이들의 현실
⑤ 과도한 비디오 게임 이용으로 인한 아이들의 증가된 폭력성

구문풀이

5행 In the same year, a survey of more than two thousand U.S. secondary school teachers showed [that {87 percent of teachers believed (that digital technologies are creating an "easily distracted generation with short attention spans,")} {whereas 64 percent agreed (that these technologies have more of a distracting effect than a beneficial one on students academically)}].

: that절인 [ ]는 문장의 동사 showed의 목적절로, 이 절에서는 첫 번째 { }가 주절, 두 번째 { }가 부사절이다. ( )로 표시한 두 개의 that절은 각각 앞의 동사 believed와 agreed의 목적절이다. whereas는 '그런데, 반면에'라는 의미의 접속사이며, agreed의 목적절에는 'B라기보다는 A'의 의미인 「more A than B」 구문이 쓰였다. 대명사인 one은 앞에 나온 명사 effect를 대신한다.

어휘풀이

- voice *v* (말로) 나타내다
- rapidity *n* 신속, 빠르기
- attention span 주의 지속 시간
- beneficial *a* 유익한
- diversity *n* 다양성
- illustrate *v* 설명하다, 예증하다
- erosion *n* 침식
- excessive *a* 지나친, 과도한
- overwhelming *a* 압도적인
- decline *n* 감소
- distracted *a* 산만해진
- academically *ad* 학업적으로
- profession *n* 직업
- neuroscientist *n* 신경과학자
- violence *n* 폭력, 폭행

035 답 ③

📖 갈등 상황에서 잠시 생각해볼 시간 갖기

전문해석

때때로 상호작용에서 한숨을 돌리는 것이 현명하다. 사람들은 흔히 그들이 부정적인 감정을 경험하고 있을 때 신호를 보내는데, 그런 순간에 그것을 넘어 몰아세우는 것은 반감과 갈등이 돌이킬 수 없이 굳어지도록 하는 말을 내뱉는 것, 즉 어떤 말투를 사용하는 결과를 가져올 수도 있다. 사람들은 몸의 자세, 말투, 생각의 보류, 찡그림 또는 눈이나 입 주변이 팽팽해지는 것 등을 통해 자신의 부정적인 감정을 드러낸다. **한걸음 물러서는 것이 상대방이 한 말의 뜻을 숙고하고 음미하는 데 유용하다.** 아마도 그 문제가 재구성되고 심지어 상호 이득의 결과물이 제안될 수도 있다. 후에 대안이 마음속에 떠오를 수도 있으며, 때로는 다른 사람들을 그 상황 속으로 데려오는 것이 현명하다. 적어도 갈등이 피할 수 없는 것이라면 그 갈등을 처리할 더 많은 시간을 스스로에게 주는 것이 현명하다. 상황을 진정시키고 그런 다음 자신의 선택 사항과 다음 행보를 결정하는 것이 유용하다.

정답풀이

부정적인 감정에 휩싸여 있을 때는 한걸음 물러서는 것이 상대방의 말을 숙고하고 되짚어보는 시간을 갖게 해주고 그렇게 함으로써 대안을 생각해내거나 다른 사람들의 중재를 받거나 최소한 자신의 행동 방침을 세울 시간을 얻을 수 있다고 말하고 있다. 따라서 밑줄 친 부분이 의미하는 바로 가장 적절한 것은 ③ '여유를 갖고 문제와 그 다음 행동에 대해 생각하는 것'이다.

① 비슷한 문제를 경험한 사람들로부터 도움을 구하는 것
② 관련된 사람들과 갈등을 해결하는 즉각적인 조치를 취하는 것
④ 갈등을 시작한 사람들과의 관계로부터 물러서는 것
⑤ 관계를 형성하고 유지하는 데 있어서 능동적인 역할을 하는 것

구문풀이

2행 [People often signal {when they are experiencing negative emotions}], and [pushing beyond that in such moments may result in {**things** being said}, {or **certain tones of voice** being used}, {that irreversibly cause hardened dislike and conflict}].

: [ ]로 표시한 두 개의 등위절이 and로 연결된 구조이며, 각 절의 밑줄 친 부분이 주어와 동사이다. 첫 번째 [ ]에는 부사절(when절)이 포함되어 있다. 두 번째 [ ]에서 첫 번째 { }는 전치사 in의 목적어로 쓰인 동명사구이며, 두 번째 { }는 첫 번째 { }와 동격을 이루는 어구이다. 이때, things와 certain tones of voice가 각각 동명사의 의미상 주어로 쓰였다. 세 번째 { }는 things를 수식하는 관계절이다.

어휘풀이

- breather *n* 숨을 돌림, 잠시의 휴식
- harden *v* 굳어지다, 단단하게 하다
- posture *n* 자세
- frown *n* 찡그림
- digest *v* (뜻을) 음미하다
- mutual *a* 상호간의, 서로의
- at the very least 적어도
- withdraw from ~로부터 물러나다
- irreversibly *ad* 돌이킬 수 없이
- conflict *n* 갈등
- withhold *v* 보류하다
- reflect *v* 숙고하다
- recast *v* 재구성하다
- alternative *n* 대안
- resolve *v* 해결하다

036 답 ③

📖 모든 사람의 기대에 맞추려는 노력의 무용함

전문해석

Jessica Spungin은 Mckinsey 런던 지사에서 부파트너 자리로 승진했을 때 자기 자신이 이 덫에 걸린 것을 발견했다. 부파트너로서, 컨설턴트는 파트너십 그룹의 더 많은 책임을 맡고, 다수의 프로젝트를 잘 처리하고, 팀 리더로서 일하고, 회사 생활에서 적극적인 역할을 할 거라는 기대를 받는다. Spungin은 이 모든 업무에 무모하게 뛰어났다. 그녀는 두 개의 중요한 고객 프로젝트를 처리하는 동안, 여섯 명의 비즈니스 애널리스트에게 선임 코치 역할을 하고, 내부 교육에 관여하고, 건강관리 회사를 위한 새로운 프로젝트를 도울 것을 요청받았다. 그녀가 감독하는 세 개의 프로젝트 팀에서 받은 첫 번째 피드백에서, 그녀는 동료 가운데 꼴찌에서 두 번째라는 평가를 받았다. Spungin은 없어서는 안 될 존재가 되려는 자신의 바람이 자신감의 결여에서 비롯되었음을 깨달았다. "나는 내가 회의에 참석하기를 바라는 고객에게 거절한 적이 없었다."라고 그녀가 우리에게 말했다. "**나는 내가 잘하는 것, 중요한 것 또는 내가 육체적으로 할 수 있는 것과 상관없이, (남들이) 나에게 기대하고 있다고 생각되는 일을 했다.**"

정답풀이

마지막 문장에서 알 수 있듯이 Spungin은 회사에서 모든 사람들의 기대에 부응하기 위해서 무작정 열심히 했지만, 이것이 좋은 결과를 가져오지 않았다고 한다. 따라서 밑줄 친 '이 덫(this trap)'이 의미하는 바로 가장 적절한 것은 ③ '모든 사람을 기쁘게 하기 위해 무작정 노력함'이다.

① 다른 사람의 도움을 당연하게 여김
② 언제나 자신의 의견을 고수함
④ 미래를 위해서 현재를 포기함
⑤ 다른 사람들이 그녀에게 기대하는 것에 영향을 미침

구문풀이

17행 I did [what {I thought} was expected] — **regardless of** [what

I was good at], [what was important], **or** [what I could physically do].

: 첫 번째 [ ]는 did의 목적어인 관계절이고, 그 안의 { }는 삽입절이다. 전치사구 regardless of 다음에는 [ ]로 표시한 세 개의 목적어(what절)가 「A, B, or C」의 형태로 이어진다.

어휘풀이

- promote *v* 승진시키다
- associate principal 부파트너
- consultant *n* 컨설턴트
- take on 떠맡다, (책임을) 지다
- juggle *v* 잘 처리하다
- multiple *a* 다수의
- headfirst *ad* 무모하게, 몹시 서둘러서
- analyst *n* 애널리스트, 분석가
- internal *a* 내부의
- oversee *v* 감독하다
- indispensable *a* 없어서는 안 될, 필수인
- spring from ~에서부터 비롯되다[야기되다]
- confidence *n* 자신감
- stick to ~을 고수하다
- blindly *ad* 맹목적으로, 무작정

05	**글의 요지**			본문 pp.030~035
037 ①	**038** ①	**039** ①	**040** ⑤	**041** ④
042 ⑤	**043** ①	**044** ⑤	**045** ②	

---

037 답 ①

📖📖 고객의 브랜드 칭찬에 응답하는 것의 필요성

전문해석

여러분의 응답에 우선순위를 정할 수 있는 것은, 그것이 특별히 즐겁거나 속상하게 하는 경험에 대한 일회성 상호 작용이든, 고객 기반 내에서 상당히 영향력이 있는 개인과의 장기적 관계의 발전이든 간에, 여러분이 개별 고객들과 더 깊은 관계를 맺을 수 있게 한다. 만약 여러분이 어떤 브랜드, 제품 또는 서비스에 관해 호의적인 의견이나 혹은 그 문제에 대해서 어떠한 의견이라도 게시해 본 적이 있다면, 그 결과로, 예를 들어, 그 브랜드의 관리자로부터 개인적으로 인정을 받는다면 기분이 어떨지 생각해 보라. 일반적으로, 사람들은 할 말이 있기 때문에, 그리고 그것을 말한 것에 대해 인정받고 싶어 하기 때문에 글을 올린다. 특히, 사람들이 긍정적인 의견을 게시할 때 그것은 그 게시물을 작성하도록 한 경험에 대한 감사의 표현이다. 여러분 옆에 서 있는 사람에 대한 칭찬은 보통 '고맙습니다'와 같은 응답을 받지만, 슬픈 사실은 대부분의 브랜드 칭찬은 응답을 받지 못한다는 것이다. 이것은 무엇이 칭찬을 이끌어 냈는지 이해해 그것들을 바탕으로 하여 확고한 팬을 만들어 낼 수 있는 기회를 잃은 것이다.

---

038 답 ①

📖📖 도심 및 혼잡한 지역에서 자전거 기반 배송 서비스의 잠재적 가치

전문해석

도시 배송 수단은 흔히 자전거를 포함해 밴과 같은 더 작은 차량을 수반하는 도시 분포의 밀도에 더 잘 맞게 조정될 수 있다. 후자(자전거)는 특히 고밀도 및 혼잡 지역에서 선호되는 '최종 단계의' 수송 수단이 될 가능성이 있다. 네덜란드와 같이 자전거 사용이 높은 지역에서, 배달 자전거는 또한 개인 화물(예를 들어, 식료품)을 운반하는 데 사용된다. 낮은 매입 및 유지 비용 때문에, 화물 자전거는 인도네시아의 '베

짝'(3륜 자전거)과 같이 선진국 및 개발도상국에서 똑같이 많은 잠재력을 전한다. 전기 보조 배달 세발자전거를 사용하는 서비스는 프랑스에서 성공적으로 실행되어 왔고 소포 및 음식 공급 배달처럼 다양한 서비스를 위해 유럽 전역에서 점차 채택되고 있다. 시내 또는 상업 지구와 같은 도시의 특정 지역에 대한 자동차 접근을 제한하는 정책 또는 자전거 전용 도로의 확장과 함께 결합될 때 자전거를 화물 수송 수단으로 사용하는 것이 특히 장려된다.

정답풀이

도심 및 혼잡한 지역에서의 배송 수단으로서의 자전거와 그 서비스의 잠재적 가치에 대해 말하고 있는 글이므로 글의 요지로 가장 적절한 것은 ①이다.

구문풀이

12행 Services [using electrically assisted delivery tricycles] [have been successfully implemented in France] and [are gradually being adopted across Europe for services {**as** varied **as** parcel and catering deliveries}].

: 첫 번째 [ ]는 바로 앞의 주어 Services를 수식하는 분사구이고, 두 번째와 세 번째 [ ]는 and로 연결되어 주어에 이어지는 술부이다. { }는 바로 앞의 services를 수식하는 형용사구로, 「as ~ as ...(…만큼 ~한)」의 표현이 사용되었다.

16행 [Using bicycles as cargo vehicles] is particularly encouraged [when combined {with policies (that restrict motor vehicle access to specific areas of a city, such as downtown or commercial districts)}, or {with the extension of dedicated bike lanes}].

: 첫 번째 [ ]는 주어 역할을 하는 동명사구이다. 두 번째 [ ]는 부사절로, when과 combined 사이에 it(= using bicycles as cargo vehicles) is 정도가 생략되었다. 두 개의 { }는 or로 연결되어 combined에 이어지는 전치사구이며, ( )는 policies를 수식하는 관계절이다.

어휘풀이

- vehicle *n* 수송 수단
- adapt *v* 조정하다
- suit *v* 맞추다, 적합하게 하다
- density *n* 밀도
- distribution *n* 분포
- the latter 후자
- last-mile *a* 최종 단계의
- congested *a* 혼잡한
- cargo *n* 화물
- acquisition *n* 취득, 매입
- maintenance *n* 유지
- convey *v* 운반하다, 전하다
- implement *v* 실행하다
- catering *n* 음식 공급
- restrict *v* 제한하다
- commercial *a* 상업의
- district *n* 지구, 지역
- extension *n* 확장
- dedicated *a* 전용의

---

039 답 ①

📖📖 개인 수준에서 피할 수 없는 환경 위험 요인에 대한 사회적 대응의 필요성

전문해석

환경 위험 요인들에는 노출을 조장하거나 허용하는 인간의 행동과 함께 생물학적, 물리적, 화학적 위험 요인이 포함된다. (오염된 공기의 호흡, 화학적으로 오염된 공공 식수의 음용, 개방된 공공장소에서의 소음처럼) 일부 환경 오염물질들은 피하기가 어렵고, 이런 상황에서 노출은 대개 자기도 모르게 이루어진다. 이러한 요인들의 감소 또는 제거에는 대중의 인식 및 공중 보건 조치와 같은 사회적 조치가 필요할 수도 있다. 많은 국가에서, 일부 환경적 위험 요인들이 개인적 수준에서 피하기 어렵다는 사실은 피할 수 있는 그 위험 요인들보다 도덕적으로 더 매우 나쁜 것으로 느껴진다. 어쩔 수 없이 매우 높은 수준의 비소로 오염된 물을 마실 수밖에 없는 것이나, 식당에서 담배 연기를 수동적으로 들이마시도록 강요당하는 것은 개인이 담배를 피울지 말지에 대한 개인적인 선택보다 더 사람들을 화나게 한다. 이러한 요인들은 변화(위험 감소)가 어떻게 일어나는지를 고려할 때 중요하다.

정답풀이

개인적 수준에서 피할 수 없는 환경 위험 요인을 줄이거나 제거하려면 사회적 대응과 조치가 필요하다는 내용이므로 글의 요지로 가장 적절한 것은 ①이다.

구문풀이

13행 [Having no choice but to drink water contaminated with very high levels of arsenic], or [being forced to passively breathe in tobacco smoke in restaurants], outrages people more than the personal choice of [**whether** an individual smokes tobacco].

: 동명사구인 첫 번째와 두 번째 [ ]는 or로 연결되어 「A or B」의 형태로 문장의 주어 역할을 하며, 이 주어는 단수동사 outrages에 연결되어 있다. 첫 번째 [ ]에는 「have no choice but to+동사원형」 구문이 쓰여 '어쩔 수 없이 ~하다, ~하는 수밖에 없다'의 의미를 나타내고, 세 번째 [ ]는 of의 목적어 역할을 하는 명사절(~인지 아닌지)이다.

어휘풀이

- hazard *n* 위험 (요인)
- exposure *n* 노출, 접함
- involuntary *a* 자기도 모르게 하는
- elimination *n* 제거
- measures *n* 조치
- passively *ad* 수동적으로
- promote *v* 조장하다, 촉진하다
- contaminant *n* 오염물질
- reduction *n* 감소
- societal *a* 사회의
- arsenic 〈화학〉 비소
- outrage *v* 격분하게 만들다

040 답 ⑤

📖 디지털 기기를 이용한 학습이 초래한 학력 저하

전문해석

대부분의 10대에게 네트워크로 연결된 기기들이 얼마나 보편적이고 매력적인지를 고려해 볼 때, 우리는 이 기계들이 그들이 알아야 하는 것을 배우는 데 도움을 줄 거라고 암묵적으로 가정한다. 그러나 그것들이 그런가? 2000년대 초, 경제학자 Jacob Vigdor와 Helen Ladd는 그 생각을 체계적으로 시험해 보기로 했다. 5년에 걸쳐, 거의 백만 명의 5학년에서 8학년의 미국 학생들이 매년 수학과 읽기 시험에서 평가를 받았고, 학교 밖에서 어떻게 시간을 보냈는지에 대한 상세한 설문지를 작성하도록 요구받았다. 예를 들어, 광대역 인터넷 접속과 함께 컴퓨터와 태블릿과 같은 그들의 디지털 기기를 그들이 이용할 수 있게 된 날짜에 학생들의 학업 진행을 추적함으로써, 연구자들은 그 기술의 영향을 평가할 수 있었다. 그 결과를 전하는 소식은 좋지 않았다. 그 경제학자들은 "5학년에서 8학년 동안에 **가정용 컴퓨터에 접근하는 학생들은 읽기와 수학 시험 점수의 지속적인 하락을 목격하는 경향이 있다.** 유사하게 초고속 인터넷 서비스의 도입은 현저히 낮은 수학과 읽기 시험 점수와 관련이 있다."고 말한다.

정답풀이

컴퓨터나 태블릿 등의 디지털 기기를 이용한 학습이 예상과 달리 학생들의 학력 저하를 가져왔다는 내용의 글이다. 따라서 글의 요지로 가장 적절한 것은 ⑤이다.

구문풀이

10행 By tracking the students' academic progress against, for example, dates [when their digital devices, such as computers and tablets, along with broadband Internet access became available to them], / the researchers were able to assess the technology's impact.

: 부사구(~함으로써)와 절로 이루어진 문장으로, 문장의 주어는 the researchers, 동사는 were이다. [ ]는 관계부사절로 앞에 나온 dates를 수식하며 이 관계절의 주어는 their digital devices, 동사는 became이다.

어휘풀이

- ubiquitous *a* 만연한, 어디에나 존재하는
- compelling *a* 흥미를 돋우는
- assess *v* 평가하다, 판단하다

- fill out 작성하다
- academic *a* 학문적인, 학교의
- available *a* 이용할 수 있는
- persistent *a* 지속적인, 끊임없는
- introduction *n* 도입, 소개
- significantly *ad* 현저히, 상당히
- questionnaire *n* 설문지
- broadband *n* 광대역 인터넷
- impact *n* 영향, 효과
- decline *n* 하락, 감소
- be associated with ~와 관련되다

041 답 ④

📖 인과 관계에 있는 여러 요인에 의해 제약을 받는 개인의 자유

전문해석

절대적인 자유와 같은 것은 없다. 진정한 자유의 모든 행위는 선택을 하는 사람에게 실질적으로 이용 가능한 선택을 다양한 방식으로 그리고 다양한 정도로 제한하는 상황에서 수행된다. 이러한 제한하는 요소들 중에는 유전적 구성, 가족적·사회적·문화적·제도적 영향, 특정한 선택 상황의 전망과 제한, 그리고 특정한 상황에서 과거의 결정에 의해 상당한 정도로 형성되는 사람들의 현재 습관과 성향과 믿음 등이 있다. 그러한 인과적 요소들은 중요한 역할을 한다. 그것들은 단지 어떤 특정한 상황에서 한 개인에게 이용 가능한 대안들을 제한하는 것만이 아니다. 그것들은 또한 어떤 특정한 때이든 그 시점에서 선택을 할 때 대안들을 모두 완전히 고려하려는 개인의 능력이나 자발성을 제한하기도 한다. 따라서 **개인의 자유는 비록 그것이 이유들에 의해 전적으로 결정되지는 않지만, 그것들에 의해 조건화되는 자유이다.**

정답풀이

절대적인 자유는 없으며 자유의 행위를 다양한 방식과 다양한 정도로 제한하는 상황에서 자유가 수행되는데, 이용 가능한 선택 사항을 제한하는 요소들은 모두 특정한 원인에 의해 야기된 요인들이라는 내용이므로, 글의 요지로 가장 적절한 것은 ④이다.

구문풀이

1행 All acts of genuine freedom are performed in contexts [that limit in various ways and in varying degrees the choices {that are practically available to the person doing the choosing}].

: All acts of genuine freedom이 주어, are performed가 동사이다. [ ]는 contexts를 수식하는 관계절이고 { }는 the choices를 수식하는 관계절이다.

어휘풀이

- absolute *a* 절대적인
- context *n* 맥락, 상황
- genetic *a* 유전적인
- institutional *a* 제도의
- prospect *n* 전망, 가능성
- disposition *n* 성향, 기질
- alternative *n* 대안
- take ~ into account ~을 고려하다
- entirely *ad* 전적으로, 완전히
- genuine *a* 진정한
- practically *ad* 실질적으로
- makeup *n* 구성, 기질
- influence *n* 영향
- restriction *n* 제한
- to a significant extent 상당한 정도로
- willingness *n* 자발성
- condition *v* 조건화하다

042 답 ⑤

📖 폭력적인 미디어 시청으로 야기되는 아이들의 공격성

전문해석

한 정교한 연구에서, 연구자들은 비폭력적인 비디오를 보는 아이들과 폭력적인 비디오를 보는 아이들의 뇌 활동을 대비해서 연구했다. 두 집단의 뇌 패턴 간의 차이는 놀라웠다. 구체적으로 말해서, 아이들이 화면에서 폭력을 볼 때만 아이들의 오른쪽 뇌의 특정 부분이 자극을 받았다. 이 연구는 또한 텔레비전에서 폭력을 보는 것은 감정, 흥분, 주의 그리고 기억의 코드화를 통제하는 데 관여하는 뇌의 부분들의 네트워

크를 자극한다는 것을 발견했다. 그들은 미디어 폭력을 자주 시청하는 아이들이 폭력적으로 행동하는 경향이 더 많으며, 이 현상은 아이의 장기 기억에 폭력적인 대본을 저장하는 뇌의 능력으로 설명될 수 있다고 결론 내렸다. 정말로, 지난 15년 동안 심각한 전자매체 사용과 아이들의 공격적인 행동을 연결시키는 증거의 양은 압도적이고 반박할 수 없게 되었다.

정답풀이

폭력적인 장면을 자주 본 아이들이 폭력적으로 행동하기 쉬운 것은 그것을 장기 기억에 저장하는 뇌의 능력 때문으로, 전자매체의 이용 빈도와 아이들의 공격적인 행동 간에 연관성이 높다고 말하고 있다. 따라서 글의 요지로 가장 적절한 것은 ⑤이다.

구문풀이

15행 Indeed, over the last fifteen years / the amount of evidence [**tying** heavy electronic media use **to** aggressive behavior in children] has become overwhelming and irrefutable.

: 부사구와 절로 이루어진 문장이며, 밑줄 친 부분이 각각 주어, 동사, 보어가 된다. [ ]는 evidence를 수식하는 현재분사구이며, 「tie A to B」는 'A와 B를 연결시키다'의 의미이다.

어휘풀이

- sophisticated *a* 정교한
- versus *p* ~와 대비하여, ~대
- specifically *ad* 구체적으로 말하면
- stimulate *v* 자극하다
- regulate *v* 통제하다
- frequently *ad* 자주
- phenomenon *n* 현상
- electronic *a* 전자의
- irrefutable *a* 반박할 수 없는
- nonviolent *a* 비폭력의
- remarkable *a* 놀라운
- portion *n* 부분
- region *n* 부분, 부위
- arousal *n* 흥분
- aggressively *ad* 공격적으로
- script *n* 대본
- overwhelming *a* 압도적인, 굉장한

043 답 ①

📖📖 집단의 특성에 맞춰야 하는 관리자의 행동 방식

전문해석

집단과 관련된 관리자의 활동에는 코칭, 동기 부여, 교육, 평가 및 피드백 제공이 포함된다. 그러나 **집단의 역학은 관리자가 이러한 활동에 접근하는 방식을 변화시킨다.** 예를 들어, 절차의 아주 작은 변화가 일부 작업 집단에서는 쉽게 이행될 수 있지만 다른 작업 집단에서는 그리 쉽지 않을 수 있다. 변화가 이해하기 쉽고 부담스럽지 않다면, 모든 부서 구성원들에게 보내는 간단한 메모가 한 부서에서 매우 잘 작동할 수 있다. 그러나 다른 부서에서는 직원들이 어떤 종류의 변화도 거부할 수 있기 때문에 부서장들은 일대일로 보내는 소개 메모를 추가해야만 할 수도 있다. 성공적인 실행을 보장하기 위해 한 직원은 안심시키기가 필요할 수 있고, 다른 직원은 변화의 필요성을 확신해야 할 수 있으며, 덧붙여 세 번째 직원은 추가 지침을 필요로 할 수도 있다. 관리자들이 다양한 작업 집단의 요구를 충족하기 위해 자신의 작업 집단을 잘 알고 자신들의 관리 활동을 계획해야 한다는 것은 분명하다.

정답풀이

집단에는 다양한 유형의 직원이 있고 그들에게 성공적으로 영향을 미칠 수 있는 방법이 모두 다르기 때문에, 관리자는 이것을 고려해 관리 활동에 접근하는 방식을 달리해야 한다는 내용이다. 따라서 글의 요지로 가장 적절한 것은 ①이다.

구문풀이

17행 It is clear [**that** managers have to know their work groups well and to plan their management activities {to meet the needs of diverse work groups}].

: It은 가주어이고 [ ]로 표시된 that절(명사절)이 진주어이다. 그 안의 { }는 목적을 나타내는 부사적 용법으로 쓰인 to부정사구로 '~하기 위해'라고 해석한다. to know와 to plan은 병렬구조를 이룬다.

어휘풀이

- with regard to ~와 관련하여
- dynamics *n* 역학
- accomplish *v* 실행하다
- supervisor *n* 감독관
- introductory *a* 소개의
- reassurance *n* 안심시키기
- instruction *n* 지시
- evaluate *v* 평가하다
- procedure *n* 절차
- burdensome *a* 부담스러운
- supplement *v* 보충[추가]하다
- implementation *n* 실행, 이행
- be convinced of ~을 확신하다

044 답 ⑤

📖📖 집단 면역의 경제적 이익

전문해석

잘 작동하는 사회는 일정 수준의 공중 보건이 필요하다. 집단 면역은 공공 건강을 개선하고 질병과 관련된 경제적 손실뿐만 아니라 공공 의료 비용을 감소시키기 때문에 사회적 수준에서 이익을 창출한다. **집단 면역이 있는 사회에 사는 것은 아픈 사람들을 치료하기 위해 더 적은 공공 자원이 전용될 필요가 있다는 것을 의미하기 때문에, 모든 사람들이 집단 면역으로부터 이익을 얻는다.** 예를 들어, 미국에서는 독감 비용이 입원 및 외래 환자 방문에 매년 104억 달러가 들고, 질병으로 인한 수입 손실을 포함하여 연간 인플루엔자 전염병과 관련된 총 경제적 비용은 871억 달러로 추산된다. 따라서 집단 면역을 보존하거나 실현하는 것은 사회를 위해 중요하며, 공동체가 집단 면역을 실현하는 데는 강력한 경제적 이유가 있다.

정답풀이

집단 면역이 형성되면 공공 의료 비용이 줄어들기 때문에 모든 사람이 그로 인한 이익을 얻는다는 내용의 글이므로, 글의 요지로 가장 적절한 것은 ⑤이다.

구문풀이

5행 Everybody benefits from herd immunity / **because** {living in a society with herd immunity} means [that less public resources need to be diverted to treat sick people]; ~.

: 주절과 이유 부사절로 이루어진 문장으로, Everybody가 주절의 주어, benefits가 동사이며 benefits from은 '~로부터 이익을 얻다'의 의미이다. { }로 표시된 동명사구가 부사절의 주어 역할을 하며, [ ]는 부사절의 동사 means의 목적절이다.

어휘풀이

- well-functioning *a* 잘 작동하는
- illness *n* 병, 아픔
- hospitalization *n* 입원
- epidemic *n* 전염병
- herd immunity 집단 면역
- divert *v* (돈 등을) 전용[유용]하다
- outpatient *n* 외래 환자
- estimate *v* 추산하다

045 답 ②

📖📖 신체 활동 장려를 위한 심리학의 역할

전문해석

신체 활동이 효과가 있다면, 과학자, 건강 전문가, 그리고 정부가 직면하는 하나의 중요한 과제는 인구의 많은 부분이 신체적으로 더 활동적으로 되도록 돕는 것이다. 이것이 성취될 방법은, 운동 생리학이 생리학적 이로움을 얻는 데 얼마나 많은 활동이 필요한지와 같은 중요한 질문에 대한 답을 의심의 여지 없이 제공하겠지만, 그 학문 분야에서의 추가적인 연구에서 나올 것 같지는 않다. 학문으로서, 운동 생리학은 행동을 이해하여 바꾸고, 대중의 의견에 영향을 미치고, 사람들에게 동기를 부여하고, 사람들의 태도를 바꾸는 것과 관련된 일반적인 문제에 관심을 기울이지 않는다. 그것은 또한 생체 역학자, 사학자, 혹은 스포츠 및 신체 활동 사회학자의 관심사도 아니다. **인간의 태도, 기분, 인식, 그리고 행동과 관련된 질문은 심리학의 권한 하에 직접적으로 들어간다.**

많은 사람이 활발한 신체 활동을 하도록 장려하는 과제를 수행할 수 있는 분야는 운동 생리학이나 생체 역학, 역사학, 사회학이 아니라 인간의 태도, 기분, 인식, 그리고 행동과 관련된 질문에 대한 답을 연구하는 심리학 분야라는 내용이다. 따라서 글의 요지로 가장 적절한 것은 ②이다.

구문풀이

9행 As a science, exercise physiology does not concern itself with general issues [associated with {understanding and modifying behavior}, {influencing public opinion}, {motivating people}, and {changing people's attitudes}].

: As는 '~로서'라는 의미의 전치사로 쓰였다. [ ]는 general issues를 수식하는 과거분사구이고, 그 안에 and로 연결된 네 개의 { }는 모두 with의 목적어로 쓰인 동명사구이다.

어휘풀이

- professional *n* 전문가
- exercise physiology 운동 생리학
- undoubtedly *ad* 의심할 여지없이
- modify *v* 바꾸다, 변경하다
- segment *n* 부분, 조각
- discipline *n* 학문 분야
- physiological *a* 생리학적인
- cognition *n* 인식

06 글의 주제

본문 pp.036~041

046 ②	047 ②	048 ⑤	049 ④	050 ⑤
051 ②	052 ③	053 ④	054 ①	

046 답 ②

📖 삼림 지대의 비시장적 가치를 따져 보는 것의 의의

전문해석
천연자원의 관리자는 일반적으로 이용에 대한 재정적 보상을 제공하는 시장 인센티브를 마주한다. 예를 들어, 삼림 지대의 소유자는 탄소 포집, 야생 동물 서식지, 홍수 방어 및 다른 생태계 도움을 위해 숲을 관리하기보다는 나무를 베어 내는 시장 인센티브를 가지고 있다. 이러한 (생태계) 도움은 소유자에게 어떠한 재정적 이익도 제공하지 않으므로, 관리 결정에 영향을 미칠 것 같지 않다. 그러나 이러한 도움이 제공하는 경제적 이익은, 그것의 비시장적 가치에 근거하여, 목재의 경제적 가치를 초과할 수도 있다. 예를 들어, 유엔의 한 계획은 기후 조절, 수질 정화 및 침식 방지를 포함하여 열대 우림이 제공하는 생태계 도움의 경제적 이익이 시장 이익보다 헥타르당 3배 이상 더 크다고 추정했다. 따라서 나무를 베는 것은 경제적으로 비효율적인데, 시장은 채취하는 사용보다 생태계 도움을 선호하게 하는 올바른 '신호'를 보내지 않고 있다.

047 답 ②

📖 개인 의사 결정의 자율성과 질을 촉진하는 정보 공개

공개의 중요한 이점은 더 공격적인 형태의 규제와는 반대로 자유 시장의 작용에 대한 유연성과 존중이다. 규제하는 명령은 무딘 칼인데, 그것들은 다양성을 무시하는 경향이 있고 의도하지 않은 심각한 역효과를 발생시킬 수도 있다. 예를 들어, 가전제품에 대한 에너지 효율 요건은 덜 잘 작동하거나 소비자가 원하지 않는 특성을 가진 제품을 만들어 낼 수도 있다. 반대로 정보 제공은 선택의 자유를 존중한다. 자동차 제조사가 자동차의 안전 특성을 측정하고 공개해야 한다면, 잠재적 자동차 구매자들은 가격과 스타일 같은 다른 속성과 안전에 대한 우려를 맞바꿀 수 있다. 식당 손님들에게 그들의 식사에 들어 있는 칼로리를 알려주면, 살을 빼고 싶은 사람들은 그 정보를 이용할 수 있고, 칼로리에 신경 쓰지 않는 사람들은 영향을 받지 않은 채로 있게 된다. **공개는 개인 의사 결정의 자율성(과 질)을 방해하지 않으며 심지어 촉진할 것이다.**

정답풀이
어떤 제품의 정보를 공개하는 것은 자유 시장에서 개인이 스스로 자유롭게 의사 결정을 내릴 수 있는 자율성을 촉진한다는 내용이므로, 글의 주제로 가장 적절한 것은 ② '자유로운 선택을 보장하기 위해 정보를 공개하는 것의 이점'이다.
① 공공의 정보를 고객이 이용할 수 있도록 하는 절차
③ 기업들이 자유 시장에서 이윤을 높이는 전략들
④ 현재의 산업 동향을 파악하고 분석할 필요성
⑤ 다양화된 시장이 합리적인 고객 선택에 미치는 영향

구문풀이

6행 For example, energy efficiency requirements for appliances may produce goods [that work less well] or [that have characteristics {that consumers do not want}].

: energy ~ appliances가 주어, may produce가 동사이므로, 두 개의 [ ]는 문장의 목적어인 goods를 수식하는 관계절이고 { }는 characteristics를 수식하는 관계절이다.

14행 If restaurant customers are informed of the calories in their meals, / those [who want to lose weight] can make use of the information, [leaving those {who are unconcerned about calories} unaffected].

: If절과 주절로 이루어진 문장으로, 첫 번째 [ ]는 주절의 주어 those(= people)를 수식하는 관계절이다. 두 번째 [ ]는 주절에 이어지는 분사구문이며 { }는 바로 앞의 those를 수식하는 관계절이다.

어휘풀이

- disclosure *n* (정보 등의) 공개
- aggressive *a* 공격적인
- flexibility *n* 유연성
- regulatory *a* 규제하는
- diversity *n* 다양성
- efficiency *n* 효율(성)
- appliance *n* 가전제품
- publicize *v* 알리다
- make use of ~을 이용하다
- interfere *v* 방해하다
- as opposed to ~와는 대조적으로
- regulation *n* 규제
- operation *n* 작용
- blunt *a* 무딘
- unintended *a* 의도하지 않은
- requirement *n* 요건
- manufacturer *n* 제조사
- attribute *n* 특성, 속성
- unaffected *a* 영향을 받지 않는
- reasonable *a* 합리적인

048 답 ⑤

📖 과학자에게 있어서의 패러다임

전문해석
과학자들은 패러다임을 믿기보다는 '사용한다'. 연구에서 패러다임의 사용은 일반적으로 공유된 개념, 상징적 표현, 실험 및 수학적 도구와 절차, 그리고 심지어 동일한

이론적 진술의 일부를 사용함으로써 관련된 문제들을 다룬다. 과학자들은 다른 사람들이 받아들일 방식으로 이러한 다양한 요소들을 사용하는 '방법'을 이해하기만 하면 된다. 따라서 이러한 공유된 실행의 요소들은 과학자들이 그것들을 사용할 때 그들이 하고 있는 것에 관한 그들의 믿음에서 그 어떤 비슷한 통일성을 전제로 할 필요는 없다. 실제로, 패러다임의 한 가지 역할은 과학자들이 그들이 무엇을 하고 있는지 또는 그들이 그것에 관해 무엇을 믿고 있는지에 대한 상세한 설명을 제공할 필요 없이 성공적으로 일할 수 있게 하는 것이다. Thomas Kuhn이 언급하기를, 과학자들은 "패러다임에 대한 완전한 '해석'이나 '이론적 설명'에 동의하거나, 심지어 그런 것을 만들어 내려고 시도조차 하지 않고도, 그것(패러다임)을 '식별'하는 데 있어서 일치를 보일 수 있다. 표준적인 해석이나 규칙으로 축약되어 합의된 것이 없다고 해도 패러다임이 연구를 안내하는 것을 막지는 못할 것이다."

정답풀이

과학자들에게 있어 패러다임의 의미에 대해 언급하고 과학적 연구에서 패러다임이 어떻게 사용되며 어떤 역할을 하는지 설명하고 있으므로, 글의 주제로 가장 적절한 것은 ⑤ '과학 연구에서 패러다임의 기능적 측면'이다.
① 기존의 패러다임으로부터 새로운 이론을 도출하는 데 있어서의 어려움
② 과학 분야에서 개인 신념의 상당한 영향력
③ 혁신적 패러다임의 출현을 고취하는 핵심 요인
④ 생각이 비슷한 연구원들을 분류하는 데 있어서 패러다임의 역할

구문풀이

11행 Indeed, one role of a paradigm is [to **enable** scientists **to work** successfully {without having to provide a detailed account of (what they are doing) or (what they believe about it)}].

: to부정사구인 [ ]는 명사적 용법으로 쓰여 문장의 동사 is의 보어 역할을 하며 여기에는 '~가 …할 수 있게 하다'라는 의미의 「enable+목적어+to부정사」 구문이 쓰였다. 또한, 이 to부정사구는 { }로 표시된 전치사구를 포함하고 있으며, 이 전치사구 내의 두 ( )는 등위접속사 or로 연결된 간접의문문으로 of의 목적어 역할을 하고 있다.

어휘풀이

- paradigm *n* 패러다임
- address *v* 다루다
- mathematical *a* 수학적인
- theoretical *a* 이론적인
- comparable *a* 비슷한
- account *n* 설명
- interpretation *n* 해석
- reduction *n* 축약, 축소
- functional *a* 기능적인
- typically *ad* 일반적으로
- employ *v* 사용하다
- procedure *n* 절차
- presuppose *v* 전제로 하다
- unity *n* 통일성
- identification *n* 식별, 확인
- rationalization *n* 이론적 설명
- draw *v* 도출해 내다

049 답 ④

📖 민간/공공 의료 시스템의 국민 건강 증진 방법

전문해석

사람들이 건강을 개선하고 그 뒤에 의료 비용을 절감하기 위한 수단으로 운동을 하도록 유도하는 것은 건강보험 업계의 주요 관심사였다. 이는 주로 공공 의료 시스템을 갖춘 캐나다와 같은 국가들에서뿐만 아니라 주로 민간 의료 시스템을 갖춘 미국과 같은 국가들의 경우도 마찬가지이다. 두 유형의 의료 시스템 모두에서, 사람들이 건강해지고 건강을 유지하도록 장려하기 위해 고안된 정책이 있다. 미국에서는 많은 민간 의료 보험 회사에서 보험료 할인을 제공하거나 헬스장 멤버십 비용을 환급해 준다. 캐나다에서는 정부가 공공 신체 활동 캠페인과 세액 공제를 통해 시민들의 활동을 장려하고 있다. 예를 들면, 정부가 자녀를 유소년 축구와 같은 조직적인 신체 활동에 등록하는 부모에게 환급해 주는 것이다. 민간 및 공공 시스템 모두에서 수익 증가와 지출 감소를 통해 사람들의 체력 증진을 장려하는 것을 정당화하며, 이는 정

치가 신체적으로 활동적인 문화를 장려하는 데 있어 거의 항상 방정식 일부가 된다는 것을 보여준다.

정답풀이

미국과 캐나다에서의 구체적인 예를 들면서 민간이나 공공 의료 시스템이 수익 증가와 지출 감소를 위해 가입자의 건강 증진에 관심을 두고 있다는 것을 설명하는 글이므로, 글의 주제로 가장 적절한 것은 ④ '의료 시스템이 구성원들의 건강을 증진시키는 방법'이다.
① 민간 의료보험의 역할
② 의료 서비스 접근성을 개선하는 방법
③ 의료보험에 가입해야 하는 이유
⑤ 의료보험이 의료 서비스 이용에 미치는 영향

구문풀이

1행 [Influencing people to exercise as a means to {improve their health} — and subsequently, {reduce the cost of medical care}] — has been a primary focus of the health insurance industry.

: 동명사구인 [ ]가 문장의 주어이며, has been이 동사이다. as a means to는 '~하기 위한 수단으로'로 해석하며 여기에 두 개의 { }가 and로 연결되어 이어진다.

17행 Increased profits and reduced spending are used both by the private and public systems [to justify encouraging people to pursue fitness], [demonstrating how politics is almost always part of the equation in encouraging a physically active culture].

: Increased ~ spending이 주어, are used가 동사이다. 첫 번째 [ ]는 목적을 나타내는 to부정사구이며, 두 번째 [ ]는 분사구로써, 앞에 나온 주절의 내용을 부연 설명한다.

어휘풀이

- subsequently *ad* 그 뒤에, 나중에
- primary *a* 주요한
- fit *a* 건강한
- enroll *v* 등록하다
- fitness *n* 체력, 건강
- equation *n* 방정식
- reduce *v* 절감하다
- policy *n* 정책
- insurance premium 보험료
- pursue *v* 추구하다, 계속하다
- demonstrate *v* 보여주다
- utilization *n* 이용, 활용

050 답 ⑤

📖 BMI로 인한 체중과 건강에 대한 잘못된 가정

전문해석

BMI(체질량 지수)는 사용하기 쉬우며, 오직 저울과 신장 측정만이 필요하다. BMI는 의사와 환자 사이의 건강에 관한 논의를 이끄는 데 사용되는 주요 분류 체계이다. BMI는 건강 또는 행동을 측정하지 않지만, 건강에 좋은 행동은 BMI 범주 전체에 걸쳐 건강 개선과 상호 관련된다. Matheson 등은 사망률과 생활 습관(구체적으로, 비흡연, 일일 최소 다섯 번의 과일과 채소 먹기, 신체 활동, 그리고 과하지 않은 음주) 간의 연관성을 연구했고, BMI 하에 '정상적인' 체중으로 분류된 사람들을 포함하여 모든 체구의 사람들에게 건강에 좋은 행동의 증가에 따라 건강상의 이점의 증가를 발견했다. 건강이 BMI로 측정될 때, 호리호리한 사람들(그리고 그들의 의사들)은 그들이 건강해서 건강 증진 행동을 할 필요가 없다고 가정할 수도 있다. 체중 감량을 추구하는 사람들에게 있어서 건강 개선은 행동 변화로 인해서인데도 체중 감량으로 인해서라고 추정된다. 거의 필연적인 체중 재증가는 '실패'로 인식되어 건강 증진 행동의 포기라는 결과를 가져온다.

정답풀이

사람들은 BMI를 신뢰하여 체중이 줄면 건강이 좋아지는 것으로 가정하지만 실은 그런 효과를 가져오는 것은 건강 증진 행동이라는 내용의 글이다. 호리호리한 사람들, 즉 정상 체중인 사람들은 건강 증진 행동을 할 필요가 없다는

가정은 잘못되었다는 것이 핵심 내용이므로, 글의 주제로 가장 적절한 것은 ⑤ '체중 감량을 건강 개선과 동일시하는 잘못된 가정'이다.
① 결함이 있는 BMI를 대체하는 새로운 측정 수단의 출현
② 때때로 건강에 좋은 행동이 갑작스러운 체중 증가로 이어지는 이유
③ 체중 관리에서 건강 증진 행동의 한계
④ 일반인들에게 믿을 수 있는 체지방 지표로서의 BMI

구문풀이

7행 Matheson et al. [studied the association between mortality and lifestyle habits (specifically, not smoking, eating at least five servings of fruits and vegetables daily, physical activity, and moderate alcohol intake)] and [found increasing health benefits with increased healthy behaviors for people of all sizes, {including those classified as "normal" weight under BMI}].

: and로 연결된 두 개의 동사구 [ ]는 주어 Matheson et al.에 이어지는 문장의 두 술부이다. the association ~ habits와 increasing ~ all sizes는 각각 앞의 동사 studied와 found의 목적어이다. ( )로 묶인 부분은 lifestyle habits를 구체적으로 설명한다. { }는 '~을 포함하여'라는 의미를 나타내는 전치사구이다.

어휘풀이

- measurement *n* 측정
- primary *a* 주요한
- drive *v* 이끌다, 몰다
- be correlated with ~와 상호 관련되다
- association *n* 연관성
- specifically *ad* 구체적으로
- intake *n* 섭취
- slender *a* 호리호리한, 가냘픈
- inevitable *a* 필연적인
- abandonment *n* 포기
- indicator *n* 지표
- height *n* 신장, 키
- classification *n* 분류
- mortality *n* 사망률
- moderate *a* 과하지 않은, 적당한
- evaluate *v* 평가하다
- pursue *v* 해 나가다, 추구하다
- perceive *v* 인식하다, 여기다
- emergence *n* 출현, 발생
- assumption *n* 가정, 가설

051 답 ②

📖 사회적 상황이 인간 행동에 미치는 영향

전문해석

Popper는 인간 행동을 제한된 수단 내에서 목표와 목적을 성취하려는 다양한 시도로 설명하는 상황적 논리라는 개념을 도입하였다. Marro 역시 인간 행동의 이해에서 사회적 사건들의 분석과 구조에 각별한 관심을 기울여 왔다. 신학자 Fletcher는 선과 악은 내재적이고, 본질적이며, 변하지 않는 인간 특성이 아니라 오히려 상이한 상황에서의 행동에 대한 기술이라는 것을 주장한 자신의 저서 〈Situation Ethics〉로 커다란 논란을 일으켰다. 이와 같이 상황 윤리학자들에게는 **좋거나 나쁜 것, 옳거나 그른 것은 특정한 상황 요인에 의존한다.** 변호사들 역시 상황적 행동 결정 요인의 여러 다른 측면들에 관심이 많은데, (예컨대) 범죄가 심리되고 조사되는 상황이 증언에 어떻게 영향을 미치는지에 대해서 뿐만 아니라 상황 요인이 어떻게 범죄가 일어나는 데 원인을 제공하는지에도 관심이 많다.

정답풀이

글에 언급된 Popper의 상황적 논리, Marro의 인간 행동 이해, Fletcher의 상황 윤리 이론, 변호사의 상황적 행동 결정 요인에 대한 관심은 모두 인간의 행동 유형이 사회적 상황에 따라 결정된다는 입장을 담고 있으므로, 글의 주제로 가장 적절한 것은 ② '사회적 상황이 다양한 형태의 행동에 미치는 영향'이다.
① 인간 행동 이해에서 상황 논리의 무효성
③ 긍정적 사회 행동 발달에서 윤리의 중요성
④ 상이한 상황에서의 유사한 행동 결정 요인

⑤ 행동을 결정하는 데 있어 성격과 상황의 영향력

구문풀이

6행 The theologian Fletcher caused a great stir / with his book *Situation Ethics* [**in which** he argued that goodness and badness {are **not** inherent, essential, unchangeable human qualities, **but** are rather descriptions of actions in different situations}].

: The theologian Fletcher가 주어, caused가 동사이며, with 이하가 부사구이다. [ ]는 *Situation Ethics*를 수식하는 관계절이고 in which는 관계부사 where로 바꿔 쓸 수 있다. 이 관계절 안에는 「not A but B(A가 아니라 B)」 구문이 사용되었다.

어휘풀이

- analysis *n* 분석
- theologian *n* 신학자
- inherent *a* 내재적인
- description *n* 기술, 묘사
- determinant *n* 결정 요인
- try *v* (범죄를) 심리하다
- invalidity *n* 무효(성)
- episode *n* 사건
- cause a stir 논란을 일으키다
- quality *n* 특성, 자질
- factor *n* 요인
- circumstance *n* 상황
- testimony *n* 증언

052 답 ③

📖 호기심을 되찾기 위해 개념의 틀에서 벗어나야 할 필요성

전문해석

어렸을 때 호기심은 자연스럽게 나온다. 비록 새로운 지식의 추구가 일이라고 할지라도, 그것은 일처럼 느껴지지 않는다. 세상은 아이의 실험실이고 모든 것이 신비스럽다. 우리의 정신이 우리의 상상의 경험과 실제 경험을 세상에 대한 하나의 결합된 관점으로 통합하기 시작하면서, 우리의 신경망은 주로 우리가 기회와 위험을 알아채는 것을 배울 수 있도록 하기 위해 다음에 무슨 일이 일어날지를 예측하는 데 도움을 주는 이해의 패턴을 형성한다. 우리는 낯선 모든 것을 우리가 이미 알고 있는 것의 틀 안에서 보며, 적절하지 않은 정보는 버린다. 이것은 우리가 새로운 정보를 더 효율적으로 처리하고 완전히 이해하게 해 줄 수 있지만, 이것은 또한 우리가 그 경이로움의 느낌을 되찾기를 원한다면 (거기서) 밀고 나오기 위해 열심히 노력해야 하는 개념적인 상자를 만들어 낸다. 우리는 우리의 타고난 호기심을 개발하도록 도와주고 우리가 신비를 받아들이도록 허용해주는 훈련법을 만들어야만 한다.

정답풀이

어렸을 때는 타고난 호기심으로 인해 세상의 모든 것이 신비스럽게 보이지만 성장하면서 세상 일을 예측하는 데 도움을 주는 이해의 패턴을 형성하게 되는데, 이것이 새로운 정보를 효율적으로 처리하는 데는 도움이 되지만 어린 시절의 호기심과 경이로움을 되찾기 위해서는 그러한 패턴에서 벗어날 필요가 있다는 내용이다. 따라서 글의 주제로 가장 적절한 것은 ③ '호기심을 개발하기 위해 패턴을 극복할 필요성'이다.
① 지식을 위한 개념적 상자를 형성하는 과정
② 일어날 일을 예측하는 데 있어서 경험의 중요성
④ 호기심이 경험을 지식으로 통합하는 데 미치는 영향
⑤ 새로운 경험을 해석하는 데 있어서 신경망의 역할

구문풀이

11행 **While** this may allow us to process and assimilate new information more efficiently, / it also creates conceptual boxes [**that** we have to work hard to push out of / if we want to reclaim that sense of wonder].

: 접속사 While(~이지만, ~인 반면에)이 부사절을 이끌고 있으며, 이 절에는 '~가 … 하게 하다'라는 의미의 「allow+목적어+목적격보어(to부정사)」 구문이 쓰였다. [ ]로 표시된 that절은 conceptual boxes를 수식하는 관계절로 that은 목적격 관계대명사로 쓰였다.

- **curiosity** *n* 호기심
- **consolidate** *v* 통합하다
- **neural network** 신경망
- **framework** *n* 틀, 구조, 뼈대
- **relevant** *a* 적절한
- **assimilate** *v* 완전히 이해하다, 동화시키다
- **conceptual** *a* 개념적인
- **innate** *a* 타고난, 선천적인
- **integrate** *v* 통합하다
- **pursuit** *n* 추구
- **cohesive** *a* 결합된
- **predict** *v* 예측하다
- **discard** *v* 버리다
- **discipline** *n* 훈련법; 규율
- **embrace** *v* 받아들이다, 포용하다
- **interpret** *v* 해석[설명]하다

053 답 ④

📖 의사소통 형태에 따라 달라지는 말의 영향력

전문해석
대화할 때의 구어, 전단지나 신문에 쓰인 문어, 그리고 전자 수단에 의해 전송되는 말을 비교해 보라. 첫 번째 경우에, 그 말은 대개 일시적이고 접한 후에 되돌릴 수 없게 사라진다. 그럼에도 불구하고, 일단 화자가 정직하고 진실하다고 우리가 느끼면 그것은 깊은 영향을 미칠 수도 있다. 반대로, 흉내 또는 어조는 화자가 확신하지 못하거나 심지어 거짓말을 하고 있을지도 모른다고 우리에게 알려준다. 두 번째의 경우에, 우리는 그 단어가 즉흥적으로 선택된 것이 아니라 매우 숙고한 것이었다고 추정할 수 있는데, 아마도 오랜 숙고의 과정을 거친 결과일 것이다. 전자 메시지의 경우에, 우리는 정확도보다는 속도에 더 많은 비중을 두는 경향이 있다. 게다가, 만약 메시지가 알지 못하는 사람들로부터 온다면, 우리는 많은 경우에 그것들이 정확하고 균형 잡힌 기사를 제공하고 출처의 신뢰성을 확인하는 것과 같은 전문적인 저널리즘 기준의 필터를 통과하지 않았다고 추정할 수 있다. 따라서 우리는 잘 확립된 신문에 실린 동일한 정보보다 알지 못하는 발신처로부터 온 전자 정보를 더 많은 의심을 품으며 읽을지도 모른다.

정답풀이
입으로 하는 말, 문자로 전달되는 말, 전자적 수단에 의해 전달되는 말의 세 가지 경우를 예로 들어서 메시지가 전달되는 유형에 따라서 그 메시지의 영향력이 어떻게 달라지는지에 대해 설명하는 글이다. 따라서 글의 주제로 가장 적절한 것은 ④ '의사소통의 유형에 따라 달라지는 말의 영향'이다.
① 구어와 문어의 의미상의 유사성
② 진정한 의도를 전달하는 데 있어서 몸짓 언어의 중요성
③ 잘못된 혹은 가짜 온라인 정보에 의해 발생되는 문제
⑤ 출처를 알 수 없는 정보의 신뢰성과 신빙성

구문풀이
5행 Nevertheless, it may have a deep impact / **once** we feel [that the speaker is honest and authentic].

: 주절과 접속사 once가 이끄는 부사절로 이루어진 문장이다. once는 '일단 ~하면'으로 해석한다. [ ]는 feel의 목적절이다.

13행 Moreover, **if** messages come from unknown persons, / we can assume in many cases [that they did not pass the filter of professional journalistic criteria {**such as** providing a correct, balanced account and checking the credibility of sources}].

: 조건절과 주절로 이루어진 문장으로, [ ]는 주절의 동사 can assume의 목적절이다. '~와 같은'이라는 의미의 such as가 이끄는 구는 바로 앞의 명사구 professional journalistic criteria를 수식한다.

어휘풀이
- **oral** *a* 구두의, 구술의
- **transmit** *v* 전송하다, 전달하다
- **flyer** *n* 전단지
- **irreversibly** *ad* 되돌릴 수 없게

- **encounter** *n* 만남, 조우
- **conversely** *ad* 반대로
- **spontaneously** *ad* 즉흥적으로
- **accuracy** *n* 정확도, 정확
- **credibility** *n* 신뢰성
- **similarity** *n* 유사성
- **authentic** *a* 진실한, 진짜인
- **mimicry** *n* 흉내
- **deliberation** *n* 숙고, 신중함
- **criteria** *n* 기준(criterion의 복수형)
- **suspicion** *n* 의심

054 답 ①

📖 정치적인 이념의 영향을 받는 사회 복지의 가치관

전문해석
사회 복지사들이 핵심적인 사회 복지의 가치를 확인하고 승인하는 데는 본질적으로 '정치적' 측면이 있다는 것을 인식하는 것은 특히 중요하다. 사회 복지는 서구 자본주의의 배경에서 생겨났고, 그 직업의 가치관들, 특히 개인의 가치와 존엄성, 자기 결정, 그리고 분배 정의에 초점을 맞춘 가치관들은 서양의 정치적 견해에 의해 영향을 받았다. 그러므로 중요한 측면에서, 모든 사회 복지의 가치관들은 실행의 본질에 궁극적으로 영향을 미치는 특정한 정치적 이념을 반영한다. 예를 들어, 그들의 고객(사회 복지의 수혜자들)의 자기결정권을 지지하고 촉진하려고 시도하는 자본주의 사회의 사회 복지사들은 집단주의를 더 강조하는 사회주의 사회와 같은 다른 정치적 배경에서 발견되는 가치관들과 반대되는 개인주의의 형태를 포용할 수도 있다. 마찬가지로, 서구 사회에서 현재 너무나 중요한 사생활 권리와 정보에 입각한 동의를 제공할 권리는 일반인들과 권력자들 사이의 경계에 대해 근본적으로 다른 관점을 가진 문화에서는 상당히 이질적으로 보일 수 있다.

정답풀이
사회 복지의 가치관들은 기본적으로 그것이 실행되는 사회의 정치적 이념에 의해 영향을 받는다는 것이 중심 내용이므로, 글의 주제로 가장 적절한 것은
① '정치적 이념이 사회 복지의 가치관에 미치는 영향'이다.
② 사회 복지 발달에 있어서 자본주의의 역할
③ 인권 촉진에 대한 사회 복지의 기여
④ 정치적 관점이 사회 복지에서 배제되어야 하는 이유
⑤ 사회 복지사들과 고객들 사이의 관계에 영향을 미치는 요소

구문풀이
11행 For example, social workers in a capitalist society [**who** support and attempt to promote their clients' right to self-determination] may be embracing a form of individualism [**that** runs counter to values found in other political contexts, such as a socialist society {that places greater emphasis on collectivism}].

: social workers in a capitalist society가 주어, may be embracing이 동사, a form of individualism이 목적어이다. 주어는 주격 관계대명사 who절, 목적어는 주격 관계대명사 that절의 수식을 각각 받고 있다. { }는 선행사 a socialist society를 수식하는 관계절이다.

어휘풀이
- **social worker** 사회 복지사
- **identification** *n* 확인
- **core** *a* 핵심적인
- **capitalism** *n* 자본주의
- **dignity** *n* 존엄성
- **distributive** *a* 분배의
- **ideology** *n* 이데올로기, 이념
- **embrace** *v* 포용하다
- **run counter to** ~와 반대되다, ~을 거스르다
- **collectivism** *n* 집단주의
- **informed consent** 정보에 입각한 동의
- **political** *a* 정치적인
- **endorsement** *n* 승인, 지지
- **emerge** *v* 나오다, 생겨나다
- **profession** *n* (전문적인) 직업, 직종
- **self-determination** *n* 자기 결정
- **justice** *n* 정의, 공정
- **ultimately** *ad* 궁극적으로

- **prominent** *a* 중요한, 저명한
- **boundary** *n* 경계, 한계
- **fundamentally** *ad* 근본적으로
- **authority** *n* 지휘권, 권위

07 글의 제목 본문 pp.042~047

055 ⑤	056 ⑤	057 ①	058 ②	059 ⑤
060 ③	061 ①	062 ①	063 ⑤	

055 답 ⑤

과잉 관광을 유발하는 요인들

전문해석

과잉 관광의 개념은 관광학과 사회 과학 전반에서 일반적인 사람과 장소에 관한 특정 가정에 기초한다. 둘 다 명확하게 정의되고 경계가 정해진 것으로 간주된다. 사람들은 주인이나 손님의 역할을 하는 한정된 사회적 행위자로 표현된다. 비슷한 방식으로, 장소는 명확한 경계가 있는 안정적인 용기로 취급된다. 그러므로 장소는 관광객으로 가득 찰 수 있고, 따라서 과잉 관광으로 고통받을 수 있다. 하지만 어떤 장소가 사람으로 가득 차 있다는 것은 무엇을 의미하는가? 정말로, 제한된 수용력을 가지고 있고 더 많은 방문객을 수용할 공간이 실제로 없는 특정 명소의 사례들이 있다. 이것은 특히 에펠탑과 같은 일부 인공 건축물에 해당하는 경우이다. 하지만 목적지로 홍보되고 과잉 관광의 피해자로 묘사되고 있는 도시, 지역 또는 심지어 국가 전체와 같은 장소들에서는 상황이 더 복잡해진다. **과도하거나 균형이 안 맞는 것은 매우 상대적이며 자연적 (질적) 저하와 경제적 유출(정치와 지역의 권력 역학은 말할 것도 없이)과 같은, 물리적 수용력이 아닌 다른 측면과 더 관련이 있을 수도 있다.**

056 답 ⑤

뇌세포의 시각 정보 처리 방식

전문해석

뇌 시각 체계의 여러 다른 부분은 알아야 할 필요가 있는 것을 토대로 정보를 얻는다. 여러분의 손 근육이 어떤 물체에 닿도록 돕는 세포들은 그 물체의 크기와 위치를 알아야 하지만, 색깔에 대해서는 알 필요가 없다. 그것들은 모양에 대해서는 약간 알아야 하지만, 매우 세부적으로는 아니다. 여러분이 사람의 얼굴을 알아보도록 돕는 세포는 모양의 세부 사항에 극도로 민감해야 할 필요가 있지만, 위치에는 신경을 덜 쓸 수 있다. 어떤 물체를 보는 사람은 누구든 모양, 색깔, 위치, 움직임 등 그것에 관한 모든 것을 보고 있다고 추정하는 것은 당연하다. **하지만 여러분 뇌의 한 부분은 그것의 모양을 보고, 다른 한 부분은 색깔을 보며, 또 다른 한 부분은 위치를 감지하고, 또 다른 한 부분은 움직임을 인식한다.** 따라서 국부적 뇌 손상 후에 물체의 어떤 측면은 볼 수 있으면서도 다른 측면은 볼 수 없는 것이 가능하다. 수 세기 전에, 사람들은 어떻게 누군가가 어떤 물체의 색깔이 무엇인지는 보지 못하면서도 그것을 볼 수 있는지를 상상하기가 어려웠다. 심지어 오늘날에도, 여러분은 물체가 어디에 있는지 보지 못하면서도 그것을 보거나, 또는 그것이 움직이고 있는지를 보지 못하면서도 그것을 보는 사람들에 대해 알게 되면 놀라워할 수 있을 것이다.

정답풀이

뇌의 시각 체계는 알아야 할 필요가 있는 사항만 선별하여 정보를 처리하므로 뇌세포마다 인지하는 물체의 측면이 다르다는 내용의 글이다. 결국 뇌세포의 시각 정보 처리는 모양, 색깔, 위치, 움직임 별로 따로따로 진행된다는 것이

핵심 내용이므로, 글의 제목으로 가장 적절한 것은 ⑤ '분리되고 독립적인: 뇌세포의 시각 인식'이다.

① 시각 체계는 결코 우리의 신뢰를 저버리지 않는다!
② 색에 예민한 뇌세포의 비밀 임무
③ 맹점: 뇌에 관해 아직 알려지지 않은 것
④ 뇌세포가 자연의 회복 과정에 관한 좋은 예가 되는 이유

구문풀이

18행 Even today, you might find it surprising [to learn about people {who see an object without seeing (where it is), or see it without seeing (whether it is moving)}].

: it은 가목적어이고, [ ]가 진목적어로 쓰인 to부정사구이다. { }는 people을 수식하는 관계절이고, 그 안에 두 개의 ( )는 각각 seeing의 목적어 역할을 하는 명사절이다.

어휘풀이

- **on a need-to-know basis** 꼭 필요한 때 꼭 필요한 것만 알려주는 방식으로
- **location** *n* 위치
- **sensitive** *a* 민감한
- **perceive** *v* 인식하다
- **localized** *a* 국부적인
- **betray** *v* 배반하다
- **recovery** *n* 회복
- **extremely** *ad* 극도로
- **detect** *v* 감지하다
- **consequently** *ad* 따라서
- **aspect** *n* 측면, 양상
- **exemplify** *v* ~의 좋은 예가 되다
- **separate** *a* 분리된

057 답 ①

더 많은 창의력이 요구되는 수리 작업

전문해석

물건을 고치고 복원하는 것은 흔히 최초 제작보다 훨씬 더 많은 창의력을 요구한다. 산업화 이전의 대장장이는 가까이에 사는 마을 사람들을 위해 주문에 따라 물건을 만들었고, 제품을 주문 제작하는 것, 즉 사용자에게 맞게 그것을 수정하거나 변형하는 일은 일상적이었다. 고객들은 뭔가 잘못되면 물건을 다시 가져다주곤 했고, 따라서 수리는 제작의 연장이었다. 산업화와 결국 대량 생산이 이루어지면서, 물건을 만드는 것은 제한된 지식을 지닌 기계 관리자의 영역이 되었다. 그러나 **수리에는 설계와 재료에 대한 더 큰 이해, 즉 전체에 대한 이해와 설계자의 의도에 대한 이해가 계속 요구되었다.** 1896년의 〈Manual of Mending and Repairing〉에서는 "제조업자들은 모두 기계나 방대한 분업으로 일하고, 말하자면 수작업으로 일하지는 않는다." "그러나 모든 수리는 손으로 '해야 한다.' 우리는 기계로 손목시계나 총의 모든 세부적인 것을 만들 수 있지만, 고장 났을 때 기계는 그것을 고칠 수 없으며, 탁상시계나 권총은 말할 것도 없다!"라고 설명했다.

정답풀이

산업화로 제품의 생산은 기계가 담당하게 되었지만 수리를 하는 사람은 여전히 필요하며, 산업화 이후에도 수작업으로 하는 수리의 필요성은 계속 존재한다는 내용의 글이다. 따라서 글의 제목으로 가장 적절한 것은 ① '현대 대장장이에게 여전히 남겨진 것: 수리의 기술'이다.

② 수리의 기술이 어떻게 발전했는가에 관한 역사적 개괄
③ 창의적 수리공이 되는 방법: 조언과 아이디어
④ 수리의 과정: 만들고, 수정하고, 변형하라!
⑤ 산업화가 우리의 부서진 과거를 고칠 수 있을까?

구문풀이

17행 [We can make every detail (of a watch) or (of a gun) by machinery], but [the machine cannot mend it {when broken}, much less a clock or a pistol]!

: [ ]로 표시된 두 개의 절이 등위접속사 but으로 연결된 문장으로, 첫 번째 절에서 두

번째 전치사구 ( ) 앞에는 반복되는 명사구 every detail이 생략되어 있다. 두 번째 절에서 { }는 분사구문으로 의미를 명확하게 하기 위해 접속사 when을 생략하지 않았으며, when과 broken 사이에 being이 생략되었다. it은 a watch or a gun을 대신하며, much less는 '더구나 ~은 아니다'의 의미이다.

어휘풀이

- mend *v* 수리하다
- preindustrial *a* 산업화 이전의
- customize *v* ~을 주문에 따라 만들다
- transform *v* 변형시키다
- extension *n* 확장
- province *n* 분야; 주, 지방
- grasp *n* 이해, 파악
- intention *n* 의도
- so to speak 말하자면
- restore *v* 복원[복구]하다
- blacksmith *n* 대장장이
- modify *v* 수정하다
- routine *a* 일상적인
- fabrication *n* 제작
- tender *n* 돌보는 사람
- comprehension *n* 이해, 이해력
- subdivision *n* 세분, 한 부분
- pistol *n* 권총

058 답 ②

📖 현대 사회가 직면한 문제에 대한 고고학의 영향력

전문해석

고고학자들은, 그 분야가 생존하고 번영하려면, 현대 세계에 적용할 수 있는 고고학 연구의 측면들을 만들고 대중들에게 이것을 더 잘 전달하기 위해 더 많은 일을 해야 한다. 한 고고학자는 이렇게 언급했다. "고고학 연구는 그것의 표면상으로는 아무리 매혹적일지라도, 경제적 불확실성과 널리 퍼져 있는 빈곤과 기근에 시달리는 세계에서 우리가 할 여유가 없는 사치처럼 보인다." 그는 계속해서 이렇게 말한다. "하지만 고고학을 그런 식으로 간주하는 것은 인류의 전체 문화유산을 우리 삶의 질과 무관하고 불필요한 것으로 취급하는 것일 것이다. 실제로는 그것이 필수적이다." 하지만, 많은 고고학자들은 고고학적인 연구의 결과가 현대 사회와 오늘날 세계가 직면하고 있는 주요 문제들에 크게 영향을 미치지 않는다고 주장할 것이다. **현재 상황에 대한 이러한 견해가 아마도 정확한 것이라는 것에는 동의하지만, 고고학 분야가 우리 행성의 지속 가능성과 같은 주요한 현대적인 문제들과 스스로를 관련 있게 만들 수 있는 이전보다 더 나은 위치에 있기 때문에, 나는 고고학자들이 그것을 바꿀 수 있다고 확신한다.**

정답풀이

경제적 불확실성, 빈곤과 기근처럼 현대 세계가 직면하고 있는 문제를 해결하는 데 고고학이 영향력을 가질 수 있는 것인가에 대해 비관적인 전망도 있지만, 지구의 지속 가능성과 같은 문제들과는 관련성을 가질 수 있어서 고고학의 효용성에 대한 대중들의 인식을 바꿀 수 있는 여지도 있다는 것이 필자의 견해이므로, 글의 제목으로 가장 적절한 것은 ② '고고학이 현대 사회에 영향력을 미칠 수 있을까?'이다.
① 고고학에서 지속 가능성을 이루기 위한 방법
③ 학문적 성과를 얻기 위한 고고학자들의 노력
④ 고고학의 미래는 의사소통에 달려있다
⑤ 학문적으로 명분이 없는 지식 분야로서의 고고학

구문풀이

5행 On the face of it, the study of archaeology, **however fascinating**, seems a luxury [we can ill afford in a world {beset by economic uncertainties and widespread poverty and famine}].

: however fascinating은 no matter how fascinating it is(그것이 아무리 매혹적일지라도)의 의미로 이해할 수 있으며, [ ]는 a luxury를 수식하는 관계절이고 { }는 a world를 수식하는 분사구이다.

어휘풀이

- archaeologist *n* 고고학자
- flourish *v* 번영[번성]하다
- applicable *a* 적용 가능한
- archaeology *n* 고고학

- fascinating *a* 매혹적인
- ill afford 여유가 없다
- poverty *n* 가난
- heritage *n* 유산
- integral *a* 필수적인
- significantly *ad* 크게, 중요하게
- concur *v* 동의하다
- sustainability *n* 지속 가능성
- luxury *n* 사치(품)
- uncertainty *n* 불확실성
- famine *n* 기근
- irrelevant *a* 무관한
- contend *v* 주장하다
- contemporary *a* 현대의
- accurate *a* 정확한

059 답 ⑤

📖 팀 문화를 형성하는 코치의 역할

전문해석

코치는 팀 문화를 형성하는 데 중요한 역할을 한다. 코치가 뇌진탕에 대해 보이는 태도와 행동은 선수가 그것을 보고할 의지에 영향을 미친다. 코치가 과거에 부상을 보고한 것에 대해 조롱하거나 부정적인 피드백을 준 적이 있다면 선수는 뇌진탕을 앓고 있는 상태에서 계속 경기에 출전해야 하는 더 많은 부담감을 느낄 수 있다. 코치는 출전 시간을 통제하며, 코치가 어떤 선수가 약하거나 팀을 위해 희생할 의지가 없다고 생각하면 그 선수를 경기에 출전시킬 가능성이 작아질 수 있다. 일부 코치는 뇌진탕이 다리 부러진 것만큼 심각하지 않거나 선수에게 증상이 있다고 믿지 않는 발언을 하기도 한다. 코치가 선수에게 명시적으로 보고하지 말라고 말하지 않더라도 코치가 조성하는 안전 문화(또는 안전 문화의 부족)와 다친 선수에 대한 코치의 전반적인 태도는 실제 여부와 관계없이 코치가 선수의 뇌진탕 보고를 지지하지 않을 것이라는 인식을 줄 수 있다. 반대로 코치가 뇌진탕 증상을 보고하는 데 도움을 준다고 느끼는 선수는 뇌진탕이 의심되는 경우 올바른 의료 치료 계획을 따를 가능성이 더 높다.

정답풀이

코치의 태도가 선수들이 다쳤을 때 대처하는 행동 방식에 영향을 미친다는 내용이다. 따라서 글의 제목으로 가장 적절한 것은 ⑤ '리더로서의 코치: 팀 문화 설정하기'가 가장 적절하다.
① 동료 코칭의 놀라운 영향력
② 코칭의 힘: 감성 지능
③ 성과가 좋은 업무팀을 개발하는 방법
④ 직장 내 코칭 및 피드백의 이점

구문풀이

13행 Even if the coach doesn't explicitly tell their athletes not to report, / the culture of safety (or lack of it) [that they create], and their overall attitudes toward injured players, can give the perception, real or not, [that the coach would not support the athlete in reporting a concussion].

: 부사절과 주절로 이루어진 문장으로, 주절에서 the culture of safety와 their overall attitudes가 A and B 구조의 주어이고 can give가 동사이다. 첫 번째 [ ]는 the culture of safety를 수식하는 관계절이고, 두 번째 [ ]는 the perception의 동격절이다.

18행 In contrast, athletes [who feel {the coach supports them in reporting their concussion symptoms}] are more likely to follow the right protocols / if they suspect they have a concussion.

: 주절과 부사절로 이루어진 문장이며, [ ]는 주절의 주어인 athletes를 수식하는 관계절이고, 그 안의 { }는 feel의 목적어 역할을 하는 명사절이다.

어휘풀이

- critical *a* 중요한
- influence *v* 영향을 주다
- display *v* 보이다
- willingness *n* 의사, 의지

- pressure *n* 부담, 압박감
- sacrifice *v* 희생하다
- explicitly *ad* 명시적으로
- perception *n* 인식
- ridicule *v* 조롱하다
- statement *n* 진술
- overall *a* 전반적인

060 답 ③

📖 다른 사람을 먼저 생각함으로써 스스로의 자신감 높이기

전문해석

인간은 천성적으로 이기적이다. 우리는 본능적으로 우리의 시간의 90퍼센트 넘게 우리 자신에 관해 생각하고 우리의 시간의 10퍼센트를 다른 사람에 관해 생각하면서 보낸다고 나는 기꺼이 장담한다. **최고의 자신감을 계발하는 비결은 우리 시간의 90퍼센트를 다른 사람에 관해 생각하고 우리 시간의 10퍼센트를 우리 자신에 관해 생각하면서 보냄으로써 그 수치를 뒤바꾸는 우리 자신의 능력에 있다.** 이런 사고방식은, 인간으로서 우리의 가장 큰 욕망이 지속적으로 자존감을 경험하는 것이기 때문에 완전히 순리를 거스르는 것이다. 우리는 인정받기 위해 산다. 그런데 우리 자신을 위해서만 사는 것은 자신감을 만드는 데 절대적으로 아무것도 하지 않는다. 우리의 자신감이 치솟는 것은 우리가 우리 자신에게서 눈을 떼고 그것을 굳건하게 다른 사람에 둘 때만이다. 우리가 어떻게든 '나는 어때?'라는 태도를 버리고 그것을 섬기는 자의 마음가짐으로 대체할 수 있다면 우리가 예전에 경험해본 적이 없는 내면으로부터의 힘을 느끼기 시작할 것이다.

정답풀이

자신에 관한 생각보다 다른 사람에 대한 생각을 더 많이 하고 남을 섬기는 마음가짐을 가질 때 나의 자신감이 고양될 수 있다는 내용이므로, 글의 제목으로 가장 적절한 것은 ③ '남들을 먼저 생각함으로써 여러분의 자신감을 세워라'이다.
① 여러분의 한계를 알라, 더 잘 이끌게 될 것이다
② 자신감: 우리의 창조적 성장의 기반
④ 이기심을 옹호하며: 자신을 희생시키지 말라
⑤ 자신을 남들과 비교하지 말고 여러분에게 집중하라

구문풀이

13행 It is [only when we take our eyes off ourselves and place them firmly on other people] **that** our confidence soars.

: 「It is ~ that ....」 강조구문으로 [ ]로 표시된 부분을 강조한다. take와 place는 병렬 구조를 이룬다.

어휘풀이

- human being 인간
- by nature 천성적으로, 본래
- instinctively *ad* 본능적으로
- confidence *n* 자신감
- go against the grain 순리를 거스르다
- continuously *ad* 계속해서
- firmly *ad* 단단하게
- servant mentality 섬기는 자의 마음가짐
- selfish *a* 이기적인
- bet *v* 장담[주장]하다
- supreme *a* 최고의
- reverse *v* 뒤집다, 뒤엎다
- recognition *n* 인정
- soar *v* 치솟다

061 답 ①

📖 자동차 구입 전과 구입 후의 생각의 변화

전문해석

당신이 자동차를 구입하려고 하는데 승합차와 소형차 사이에서 (어떤 것을 구입할지) 갈팡질팡한다고 가정해 보자. 당신은 각각이 장점과 단점을 가지고 있다는 것을 안다. 승합차는 편리할 것이다. 당신은 거기에서 잠을 잘 수도 있고 그것은 힘이 좋지만, 연비가 좋지 않고 주차하기가 어렵다. 소형차는 훨씬 좁고 당신은 그것의 안전성을 의심한다. 하지만 그것은 구입하고 운영하기에 덜 비싸다. 당신이 결정하기 전에 당신은 아마도 가능한 한 많은 정보를 얻을 것이다. 당신은 아마도 승합차나 소형차를 가지고 있는 친구들과 얘기하게 될 것이다. 당신은 아마도 각각이 어떤지 보기 위해서 차량들을 시운전하려고 자동차 판매원을 방문할 것이다. 이제 당신이 소형차를 구입하기로 결정한다고 가정해 보자. 그 다음에는 무슨 일이 일어날까? 당신은 세상에서 갤런당 마일 수(연비)가 가장 중요한 것처럼 그것에 대해서 점점 더 많이 생각하게 될 것이다. 동시에 당신은 당신의 소형차에서 잠을 잘 수 없다는 사실을 거의 확실히 무시할 것이다. 마찬가지로, 당신은 새 자동차가 충돌 시에 당신을 상당한 위협에 빠뜨릴 수 있다는 것을 거의 기억하지 않을 것이다.

정답풀이

자동차를 구입하기 전에는 각 자동차의 장단점을 모두 살피는 사람이 자동차를 구입한 후에는 구입한 자동차의 장점만을 생각하고 단점을 외면하면서 자신의 선택을 합리화한다는 인간의 심리를 설명한 글이므로, 글의 제목으로 가장 적절한 것은 ① '구매 이후의 합리화'이다.
② 당신에게 딱 맞는 차 고르기
③ 더 현명한 소비자가 되기 위한 조언
④ 어리석은 소비자의 행동 유형
⑤ 소형차를 구입하는 것의 이점

구문풀이

9행 **Chances are** you will talk with friends [who own a van or a subcompact].

: 「Chances are (that)+주어+동사」는 '아마 ~일 것이다'의 의미이며, [ ]는 friends를 수식하는 관계절이다.

14행 You will begin to think more and more about the number of miles to the gallon / **as though** it **were** the most important thing in the world.

: 「as though[if]+주어+과거동사」는 현재 상황을 반대로 가정하는 가정법 과거 구문으로 '마치 ~한 것처럼'이라고 해석한다.

어휘풀이

- be torn between A and B A와 B 사이에서 망설이다
- subcompact *n* 소형차
- mileage *n* 연비
- assume *v* 가정하다
- downplay *v* 무시하다
- collision *n* 충돌
- convenient *a* 편리한
- vehicle *n* 차량, 탈것
- simultaneously *ad* 동시에
- considerable *a* 상당한
- rationalization *n* 합리화

062 답 ①

📖 관찰 또는 실험 그 자체가 대상에 미치는 영향

전문해석

물리학자 John Archibald Wheeler는 "심지어 전자처럼 그렇게 아주 작은 물체를 관찰하기 위해서도 물리학자는 유리를 산산조각 내야 한다. 그는 안으로 도달해야 한다. 그는 그가 선택한 측정 장비를 설치해야 한다. 게다가, 측정은 전자의 상태를 변화시킨다. 우주는 그 후로는 결코 동일하지 않을 것이다."라고 언급했다. 다시 말해서, 어떤 사건을 연구하는 행위가 그것을 바꿀 수 있다. 사회과학자들은 종종 이 현상에 직면한다. 인류학자들이 어떤 부족을 연구할 때, 그들이 외부인에 의해 관찰되고 있다는 사실에 의해 그 구성원들의 행동이 바뀔 수 있다는 것을 그들(인류학자들)은 알고 있다. 심리학 실험의 피실험자들은 어떤 실험 가설을 시험하고 있는지 안다면 그들의 행동을 바꿀 수 있다. 이것이 심리학자들이 모르게 하는 통제장치와 이중으로 모르게 하는 통제장치를 사용하는 이유이다. 그러한 통제장치가 없는 것은 흔히 초자연적인 힘의 시험에서 발견되며, 사이비 과학에서 사고가 잘못되는 전형적

인 방법 중 하나이다. 과학은 관찰이 피관찰자의 행동에 미치는 영향을 최소화하고 인정하려고 노력하지만, 사이비 과학은 그렇지 않다.

정답풀이

전자를 측정하는 자체가 전자의 상태를 변화시켜 우주를 동일하지 않게 만든다고 하며, 연구나 실험을 실행하는 자체가 그 대상 또는 대상자에게 영향을 미칠 수 있다는 것을 설명하는 글이다. 따라서 글의 제목으로 가장 적절한 것은 ① '관찰자가 피관찰자를 변화시킨다'이다.

② 사이비 과학: 맹신의 산물
③ 왜 과정이 결과보다 더 중요한가
④ 관찰: 사물의 본질에 이르는 길
⑤ 실험에서 외부의 영향력을 배제하는 방법

구문풀이

9행 Anthropologists <u>know</u> [that {when they study a tribe}, the behavior of the members may be altered by <u>the fact</u> {they are being observed by an outsider}].

: [ ]는 know의 목적어 역할을 하는 명사절이며, 그 안의 첫 번째 { }는 목적절에 삽입된 부사절이며, 두 번째 { }는 the fact의 구체적인 내용을 설명하고 있는 동격절이다.

어휘풀이

- physicist *n* 물리학자
- electron *n* 전자
- install *v* 설치하다
- encounter *v* 직면하다
- anthropologist *n* 인류학자
- subject *n* 피실험자
- paranormal *a* 초자연적인
- acknowledge *v* 인정하다
- minuscule *a* 아주 작은
- shatter *v* 산산조각 내다
- equipment *n* 장비
- phenomenon *n* 현상
- alter *v* 바꾸다
- hypothesis *n* 가설
- minimize *v* 최소화하다
- external *a* 외부의, 밖의

063 답 ⑤

📖 문화적이자 생물학적인 성격을 가진 인간의 적응 과정

전문해석

인간은 문화 때문에 유전적 자질과 자연 환경의 제약을 넘어서 왔다. 적응에 대한 연구는 거주 환경과 인간의 관계뿐만 아니라 더욱 중요하게는 변화하는 거주 환경을 받아들이고 이용하는 능력도 다룬다. 문화를 이루는 인간의 역량은, 자연의 다른 그 어느 곳도 비교의 대상이 되지 않는데, 이것을 가능하게 했다. 그러나 문화를 이루는 인간의 역량이 변화하는 거주지에 적응하기 위한 가장 큰 잠재력을 담고 있기는 하지만, 그리고 인간이 체질의 유전적 변형을 기다릴 필요 없이 상이한 거주 환경에 적응할 수 있을지라도, 인간의 문화적 적응이 생물학적 적응을 대체했다고 가정하는 것은 심각한 오해일 것이다. **인간에게 있어서 적응 과정은 그것이 문화적인 만큼 생물학적이다.** 인간의 생물학적 진화는, 진화를 공부하는 학생들은 아마도 그것이 극히 느려졌다는 것에 동의하기는 하겠지만, 멈추지 않았다.

정답풀이

인간은 자연 세계의 다른 그 어느 곳에서도 찾아볼 수 없는 문화적 적응이라는 특성을 보이지만 그럼에도 불구하고 문화적 적응이 생물학적 적응을 대체한 것은 아니며 단지 인간에게 있어서 생물학적 진화는 그 속도가 현저히 느려졌을 뿐이라는 내용이므로, 글의 제목으로 가장 적절한 것은 ⑤ '인간의 적응 과정: 문화적일 뿐만 아니라 생물학적이다'이다.

① 인간이 아닌 존재에서의 문화적 적응의 증거
② 문화적 적응에 의한 생물학적 적응의 대체
③ 유전적 변형: 조만간 멈출 운명이다
④ 문화: 특정한 주거지에 대한 적응의 결과물

구문풀이

8행 But [**while** man's capacity for culture contains his greatest potential for adapting to changing habitats] and [**although** he is able to adapt himself to different habitats without having to await genetic modifications in his constitution], / [to <u>assume</u> {that man's cultural adaptations have replaced his biological adaptations}] would be a serious misconception.

: 첫 번째와 두 번째 [ ]는 and로 연결된 양보의 부사절로, 각각 '~이긴 하지만', '비록 ~일지라도'로 해석한다. 주절의 주어는 세 번째 [ ]로 표시된 to부정사구이고 그 안의 { }는 assume의 목적어 역할을 하는 명사절이다.

어휘풀이

- transcend *v* 넘어서다, 초월하다
- genetic *a* 유전의
- adaptation *n* 적응
- come to terms with ~을 받아들이다
- capacity *n* 능력
- potential *n* 잠재력
- constitution *n* 체질; 구조
- drastically *ad* 극단적으로, 대폭적으로
- cease *v* 멈추다, 끝내다
- limitation *n* 제한, 제약
- endowment *n* (천부적) 자질, 재능
- habitat *n* 거주지, 서식지
- exploit *v* 이용하다
- unmatched *a* 비할 바 없는
- modification *n* 변형
- misconception *n* 오해, 그릇된 생각
- destined *a* (~할) 운명인

<table>
<tr><td colspan="6">08 도표   본문 pp.048~053</td></tr>
<tr><td>064 ④</td><td>065 ④</td><td>066 ④</td><td>067 ②</td><td>068 ⑤</td></tr>
<tr><td>069 ④</td><td>070 ③</td><td>071 ④</td><td>072 ⑤</td><td></td></tr>
</table>

064 답 ④

📖 때때로 또는 자주 적극적으로 뉴스를 회피한 응답자의 비율

전문해석

위 도표는 2017년과 2019년, 2022년에 다섯 개 나라에서 때때로 또는 자주 적극적으로 뉴스를 회피한 응답자 비율을 보여준다. 세 해 각각에 대해, 도표에 있는 나라들 중에서 아일랜드는 때때로 또는 자주 적극적으로 뉴스를 회피한 응답자의 가장 높은 비율을 보여주었다. 독일의 경우, 세 해 각각에서 때때로 또는 자주 적극적으로 뉴스를 회피한 응답자 비율은 30%보다 낮았다. 덴마크의 경우, 2019년에 때때로 또는 자주 적극적으로 뉴스를 회피한 응답자 비율이 2017년의 비율보다 더 높았으나 2022년의 그것보다는 더 낮았다. 핀란드의 경우, 2019년에 때때로 또는 자주 적극적으로 뉴스를 회피한 응답자 비율이 2017년의 그것보다 더 낮았으며, 이는 일본도 마찬가지였다. 일본의 경우, 세 해 각각에서 때때로 또는 자주 적극적으로 뉴스를 회피한 응답자 비율이 15%를 초과하지 않았다.

065 답 ④

📖 미국인들이 선호하는 거주지 유형의 비율

전문해석

위의 그래프는 2020년 조사를 기반으로 한 연령별로 미국인이 선호하는 거주지 유형의 비율을 보여준다. 각기 세 연령대에서 읍내/시골 지역이 가장 선호되는 거주지 유형이었다. 18~34세 그룹에서는 대도시/소도시를 선호하는 사람들의 비율이 대도

시/소도시 근교를 선호하는 사람들의 비율보다 더 높았다. 35~54세 연령층에서는 대도시/소도시 근교를 선호하는 사람들의 비율이 대도시/소도시를 선호하는 사람들의 비율을 넘어섰다. 55세 이상 연령층에서는 세 가지 선호하는 거주지 유형 중에서 대도시/소도시(→ 대도시/소도시 근교)를 선택한 사람들의 비율이 가장 낮았다. 세 가지 선호하는 거주지 유형의 각각의 비율은 세 연령대에 걸쳐 20%보다 더 높았다.

정답풀이

55세 이상 연령층에서 대도시/소도시 근교를 선택한 사람들의 비율이 22%로 가장 낮았으므로, ④는 도표의 내용과 일치하지 않는다.

구문풀이

5행 In the 18-34 year-olds group, / the percentage of those [who preferred Big/Small City] was higher than that of those [who preferred Suburb of Big/Small City].

: 핵심 주어는 the percentage이고, 동사는 was이다. 두 개의 [ ]는 관계절로 각각 앞의 선행사 those를 수식한다. that은 앞에서 언급된 the percentage의 반복 사용을 피하기 위해 사용된 지시대명사이다.

어휘풀이

- prefer *v* ~을 선호하다
- based on ~에 기반하여
- survey *n* (설문) 조사
- rural *a* 시골의
- suburb *n* 근교, 교외
- exceed *v* 넘어서다, 능가하다

066 답 ④

2015년과 2025년의 지역별 세계 중산층의 점유율

전문해석

위의 그래프들은 지역별로 2015년 세계 중산층의 점유율과 2025년에 예상되는 점유율을 보여준다. 아시아 태평양 지역의 세계 중산층 점유율은 2015년에 46퍼센트에서 2025년에는 60퍼센트로 증가할 것으로 예상된다. 2025년의 아시아 태평양 지역의 예상 점유율은 여섯 개의 지역 중에서 가장 크며, 같은 해 유럽의 예상 점유율의 세 배보다 더 많다. 유럽과 북미 지역의 점유율은, 유럽은 2015년에 24퍼센트에서 2025년에 16퍼센트로, 북미 지역은 2015년에 11퍼센트에서 2025년에 8퍼센트로, 둘 다 감소할 것으로 예상된다. 중남미 지역은 세계 중산층 점유율에 있어서 2015년에서 2025년까지 변화하지 않을 것으로(→ 2퍼센트 포인트 감소할 것으로) 예상된다. 2015년에 그랬듯이, 2025년에 중동 및 북아프리카의 점유율은 사하라 사막 이남의 아프리카의 점유율보다 더 클 것이다.

정답풀이

중남미 지역의 세계 중산층 점유율은 2015년에 9퍼센트였고 2025년의 예상 점유율은 7퍼센트이므로, 2퍼센트 포인트 감소할 것이다. 따라서 2015년에서 2025년까지 변화하지 않을 것으로 예상된다고 한 ④는 도표의 내용과 일치하지 않는다.

구문풀이

3행 It is projected [**that** the share of the global middle class in Asia Pacific will increase from 46 percent in 2015 to 60 percent in 2025].

: It은 가주어이고, [ ]로 표시한 that절이 진주어이다. 이 that절에는 「from A to B」 구문이 쓰였다.

어휘풀이

- share *n* 점유율
- middle class 중산층
- region *n* 지역
- rounding *n* 반올림
- project *v* 예상하다

067 답 ②

전 세계 휴대전화 앱 사용 시간의 카테고리별 분포

전문해석

위 그래프는 2020년부터 2022년까지 전 세계 휴대전화 앱 사용 시간의 카테고리별 분포를 보여준다. 이 기간 동안 Social & Communication 앱은 항상 전 세계 사용자의 휴대전화 앱 사용 시간 중 42퍼센트 이상을 차지했다. Photo & Video 앱이 그다음으로 높은 비율을 차지했는데, 3개년 각각 휴대전화 사용자 시간의 25퍼센트(→ 24퍼센트) 이상을 차지했다. Games 앱 사용 시간은 2020년부터 2022년까지의 기간에 약간 변동이 있었으며, 2022년에는 휴대전화 사용자가 그들의 시간 중 8퍼센트를 Games 앱에 사용했다. 2020년부터 2022년까지 사람들이 Social & Communication 앱 사용에 소비한 시간은 Games 앱에 사용한 시간의 5배가 넘었다. 같은 기간 동안, 가장 적게 사용된 앱은 Shopping이며, 휴대전화 사용자들은 2021년과 2022년에 Shopping 앱에 그들의 시간의 2.7퍼센트를 사용했다.

정답풀이

Photo & Video 앱 항목은 2021년과 2022년에는 25퍼센트를 넘었지만, 2020년에는 24.2퍼센트이므로 ②가 도표의 내용과 일치하지 않는다.

구문풀이

3행 [During the period], Social & Communication apps always accounted for more than 42 percent of the time [users worldwide spent on mobile phone apps].

: 첫 번째 [ ]는 부사구이고, 두 번째 [ ]는 목적격 관계대명사가 생략된 관계절로 the time을 수식한다.

12행 From 2020 to 2022, the time [people spent using Social & Communication apps] was more than five times the time [they spent on Games apps].

: 첫 번째와 두 번째 [ ]는 각각 바로 앞의 the time을 수식하는, 목적격 관계대명사가 생략된 관계절이다.

어휘풀이

- distribution *n* 분포
- category *n* 카테고리, 부문
- account for ~을 차지하다
- slightly *ad* 약간, 가볍게
- fluctuate *v* 변동하다

068 답 ⑤

섭취한 당의 종류에 따른 입 속의 산도

전문해석

입 속의 pH 농도가 5.5 이상으로 유지되면, 충치가 발생할 위험이 없을 정도의 산도이다. 과당, 설탕, 꿀 중에서 설탕이 가장 오랜 시간 동안 pH 농도를 떨어뜨려서 가장 큰 충치의 위험성을 초래한다. 설탕 섭취 후 대략 5분이 지나면 pH 농도는 최하 3.5까지 떨어진다. 그러다가 pH 농도는 서서히 오르기 시작하지만, 최소한 30분이 지나야 pH 농도가 5.5 이상으로 올라간다. 이와는 대조적으로, 과당은 pH 4를 약간 넘는 수준까지 입 속의 pH 농도를 떨어뜨리는데, 더 짧은 시간 동안 위험성을 지니므로, 섭취한 지 20분이 지나면 충치가 발생할 가능성이 없어지게 된다. 꿀은 섭취한 지 5분 이내에 산도가 pH 4.75 정도까지 떨어지기는 하지만, 10분 이내에(→ 15분 이내에) 다시 pH 5.5 이상으로 회복된다.

정답풀이

꿀을 먹었을 경우 15분 약간 못 되는 시간이 지나면 입 속의 pH 농도가 5.5 이상으로 올라간다는 것을 알 수 있으므로 10분 이내라고 한 ⑤는 도표의 내용과 일치하지 않는다.

9행 By contrast, fruit sugar, [which causes the mouth's pH level to fall to just above pH 4], poses a danger for a shorter period: tooth decay is unlikely 20 minutes after consumption.

: fruit sugar가 주어, poses가 동사이며, [ ]는 주어인 fruit sugar에 대한 부연 설명을 하는 관계절이다. 이 관계절의 동사는 causes인데, cause는 목적격보어로 to부정사를 취해 '~가 …하도록 야기하다'의 의미를 나타낸다.

어휘풀이
- consumption *n* 소비, 소모
- acidity *n* 산도(酸度)
- cane sugar 사탕수수 설탕
- pH *n* 페하, 수소 이온 농도 지수
- decay *n* 부패, 부식
- approximately *ad* 대략, 거의

069 답 ④

📖📖 **2000년과 2013년 미국의 취학 아동 인구의 인종적/민족적 분포**

전문해석
위 그래프는 2000년과 2013년 미국의 취학 인구의 인종적/민족적 분포를 보여준다. 백인 취학 아동의 비율은 이 기간 동안 62퍼센트에서 53퍼센트로 감소했다. 또한 흑인 아동의 비율은 15퍼센트에서 14퍼센트로 감소했다. 이와는 대조적으로, 다른 인종/민족 집단의 취학 아동의 비율은 이 기간 동안 증가했는데, 히스패닉계는 16퍼센트에서 24퍼센트로, 아시아인은 3퍼센트에서 5퍼센트로, 두 개 이상 인종의 아동은 2퍼센트에서 4퍼센트로 증가했다. 2000년과 2013년에 히스패닉계 아동(→ 백인 아동)의 비율은 각각 최고였다. 미국 인디언/알래스카 원주민 취학 아동의 비율은 두 기간 모두 1퍼센트로 그대로였다.

정답풀이
2000년과 2013년에 가장 높은 것은 히스패닉계 아동의 비율이 아니라 백인 아동의 비율이므로, 도표의 내용과 일치하지 않는 것은 ④이다.

구문풀이
3행 [The percentage of school-age children {who were White}] decreased **from** 62 percent **to** 53 percent during this time period.

: { }는 school-age children을 수식하는 관계절이며, The percentage가 핵심 주어, decreased가 동사이다. 주어가 「the percentage of ~」 형태인 경우 the percentage에 동사의 수를 일치시켜 단수동사가 오고, 「a/수 percentage of ~」의 경우 of 이하에 나오는 명사에 동사의 수를 일치시킨다. 술부에는 「from A to B」 구문이 쓰였다.

어휘풀이
- racial *a* 인종의
- distribution *n* 분포
- respectively *ad* 각각
- ethnic *a* 민족의
- second to none 최고인
- remain *v* 여전히 ~인 채 남아 있다

070 답 ③

📖📖 **가톨릭교도의 세계 지역별 분포 변화**

전문해석
위 그래프는 1910년과 2010년의 세계 가톨릭교도의 지역적 분포를 보여주는데, 각 지역에 거주한 모든 가톨릭교도의 비율에 의해 표시되었다. 1910년에 세계 가톨릭교도의 거의 3분의 2가 유럽에 살았고, 라틴아메리카-카리브해 지역에 약 4분의 1이 살았다. 같은 해에 북아메리카와 아시아-태평양 지역에는 동일한 비율의 가톨릭교도가 있었는데, 둘 다 세계 가톨릭교도의 5%를 차지했다. 2010년에는 세계의 다른 어느 지역보다도 라틴아메리카-카리브해 지역에 더 많은 가톨릭교도가 살았는데, 세계 가톨릭교도의 5분의 3 이상을(→ 약 5분의 2를) 차지했다. 100년의 기간에 걸쳐, 유럽에서 세계 가톨릭교도의 비율에 극적인 감소가 일어났고, 2010년에 4분의 1 미만이 그곳에 살았다. 아시아-태평양 지역과 북아메리카의 세계 가톨릭교

도의 비율은 1910년에서 2010년 사이에 높아졌는데, 특히 전자는 두 배 이상 증가했다.

정답풀이
2010년에 라틴아메리카-카리브해 지역에 가장 많은 가톨릭교도가 산 것은 맞지만 그 비율이 39%로 5분의 2가 채 되지 않으므로, 5분의 3 이상이라고 한 ③은 도표의 내용과 일치하지 않는다.

구문풀이
9행 In 2010, **more** Catholics lived in Latin America-Caribbean **than any other region** in the world, [**accounting for** over three-fifths of the world Catholics].

: 「more ~ than any other+단수명사」는 '다른 어느 ~보다도 더'라는 뜻으로 최상급을 표현하는 비교구문이다. [ ]는 분사구문으로 and they accounted for ~의 절을 구로 표현한 것이다.

14행 **Both** the percentages of the world Catholics in Asia-Pacific and in North America went up from 1910 to 2010, [especially the former being more than doubled].

: both는 전치 한정사로 「both (of) the+명사」의 형태로 한정사 앞에 위치하며, 이러한 쓰임을 갖는 것에는 all, double, half, twice, three times 등이 있다. [ ]는 분사구문으로 앞 절의 주어와 분사구문의 주어가 달라 분사구문의 주어인 the former를 표시하고 있다.

어휘풀이
- distribution *n* 분포
- account for (~의 비율을) 차지하다
- decline *n* 감소
- double *v* 두 배가 되다
- Catholic *n* 가톨릭교도
- dramatic *a* 극적인
- the former 전자

071 답 ④

📖📖 **네 도시에서 사용되는 네 가지 쓰레기 처리 방법**

전문해석
위 그래프는 네 도시와 매립, 소각, 재활용, 그리고 퇴비화라는 네 개의 다른 쓰레기 처리 방법의 비율을 보여준다. Toronto와 Amman은 쓰레기 처리 방법으로 매립을 가장 많이 이용했는데, 이 도시들의 거의 4분의 3과 절반에 조금 못 미치는 정도의 쓰레기가 각각 매립으로 처리되었다. 소각은 Madrid와 Kuala Lumpur에서 가장 인기 있는 쓰레기 처리 방법으로, 각각 대략 40퍼센트와 약 55퍼센트였다. 재활용으로 쓰레기의 25퍼센트 이상을 처리한 도시는 없었으며, Toronto의 경우에는 8퍼센트 정도였다. Madrid와 Kuala Lumpur는 거의 같은 비율의 매립된 쓰레기(→ 재활용으로 처리된 쓰레기)를 갖고 있었다. 가장 인기가 적은 쓰레기 처리 방법은 퇴비화에 의한 것이었고 그것은 네 개의 도시 모두에서 10퍼센트 미만을 차지했다.

정답풀이
Madrid와 Kuala Lumpur가 거의 같은 비율인 것은 매립된 쓰레기가 아니라 재활용으로 처리된 쓰레기이므로, ④는 도표의 내용과 일치하지 않는다.

구문풀이
14행 The least popular method of waste disposal was by composting, / **which** accounted for less than 10% in all four cities.

: The least popular method of waste disposal이 주어, was가 동사이다. which는 계속적 용법으로 쓰인 관계대명사로 이 관계절은 앞 절의 composting을 부연 설명한다. 계속적 용법의 관계대명사는 '접속사+주어'로 바꿔 쓸 수 있으므로 and it ~으로 나타낼 수 있다.

어휘풀이
- waste disposal 쓰레기 처리
- landfill *n* 매립

- incineration *n* 소각
- respectively *ad* 각각
- approximately *ad* 대략, 어림잡아
- compost *n* 퇴비(화)
- dispose of ~을 처리하다
- account for (~의 비율을) 차지하다

072 답 ⑤

📖📖 전자 기기를 통한 온라인 거래의 지역별 시장 점유율

전문해석

위의 그래프는 2018년 3가지 기기(모바일 앱, 모바일 웹사이트, 데스크톱)를 기반으로 한 온라인 거래의 시장 점유율을 지역별로 나타낸다. 모바일 앱을 통한 온라인 거래에서는 아시아·태평양 지역이 가장 높은 활용도를 보였지만, 라틴 아메리카가 가장 낮은 활용도를 보였다. 온라인 거래를 위한 모바일 웹사이트 부문에서 라틴 아메리카가 그것에 가장 크게 의존했고, 반면에 북미 지역이 그것에 가장 적게 의존했다. 라틴 아메리카의 데스크탑을 이용한 온라인 거래의 시장 점유율은 아시아와 태평양 지역의 시장 점유율보다 정확히 두 배가 컸다. 유럽에서는 모바일 앱과 모바일 웹사이트 거래의 합친 시장 점유율이 데스크톱을 이용한 온라인 거래의 시장 점유율을 초과했다. 모바일 앱의 시장 점유율과 데스트톱의 시장 점유율 사이의 차이는 라틴 아메리카에서 가장 컸지만, 아프리카와 중동(→ 북미)에서 가장 작았다.

정답풀이

모바일 앱과 데스크톱을 이용한 온라인 거래의 시장 점유율의 격차가 가장 큰 곳은 35퍼센트 포인트로 라틴 아메리카가 맞지만, 가장 작은 곳은 14퍼센트 포인트를 나타낸 북미이므로, ⑤는 도표의 내용과 일치하지 않는다.

구문풀이

9행 [The share of online transactions {using a desktop} in Latin America] was exactly **twice as large as** that in Asia and the Pacific.

: [ ]가 문장의 주어이고 핵심 주어가 share이므로 단수동사 was가 쓰였다. 현재분사구인 { }는 앞의 명사 online transactions를 수식한다. 술부에는 「배수사+as+원급+as」 형태의 동등비교 구문이 쓰였고, 지시대명사 that은 the share of online transactions using a desktop을 대신한다.

어휘풀이

- share *n* 시장 점유율
- device *n* 기기, 장치
- when it comes to ~에 관해 말하자면
- rely on ~에 의존하다
- transaction *n* 거래
- region *n* 지역
- utilization *n* 활용(도)
- exceed *v* 초과하다, 넘다

09	**내용 불일치**			본문 pp.054~059
073 ②	**074** ⑤	**075** ③	**076** ④	**077** ③
078 ⑤	**079** ④	**080** ④	**081** ④	

073 답 ②

📖📖 미국의 물리학자 Charles H. Townes의 생애

전문해석

가장 영향력 있는 미국의 물리학자 중 한 사람인 Charles H. Townes는 South Carolina에서 태어났다. 어린 시절에 그는 하늘에 별들을 연구하면서 농장에서 성장했다. 그는 1939년에 California Institute of Technology에서 박사 학위를 받

았고, 그 후 뉴욕시에 있는 Bell Labs에서 일자리를 얻었다. 제2차 세계 대전 후에 그는 Columbia 대학교에서 물리학 부교수가 되었다. 1958년에 Townes와 그의 동료 연구자는 레이저의 개념을 제안했다. 레이저 기술은 산업과 연구에서 빠르게 인정받았다. 그는 1964년에 노벨 물리학상을 받았다. 그는 또한 달 착륙 프로젝트인 아폴로 계획에 관여했다. 인터넷과 모든 디지털 미디어는 레이저 없이는 상상할 수 없을 것이기 때문에 그의 공헌은 대단히 귀중하다.

074 답 ⑤

📖📖 사회학자 Niklas Luhmann의 생애

전문해석

20세기의 유명한 사회학자인 Niklas Luhmann은 1927년에 독일의 Lüneburg에서 태어났다. 제2차 세계 대전 후, 그는 Freiburg 대학교에서 1949년까지 법학을 공부했다. 경력 초기에 그는 State of Lower Saxony에서 일했는데, 그곳에서 그는 교육 개혁을 담당했다. 1960년에서 1961년 기간에 Luhmann은 Harvard 대학교에서 사회학을 공부할 기회가 있었는데, 그곳에서 그는 가장 유명한 사회 체계 이론가 중 한 명이었던 Talcott Parsons의 영향을 받았다. 나중에 Luhmann은 자기 자신의 사회 체계 이론을 개발했다. 1968년에 그는 Bielefeld 대학교에서 사회학 교수가 되었다. 그는 대중 매체와 법을 포함하여 다양한 주제를 연구했다. **그의 책들은 번역하기 어렵다고 알려져 있긴 하지만, 그것들은 사실 다른 언어들로 널리 번역되었다.**

정답풀이

마지막 문장에서 Luhmann의 책들은 번역하기 어렵다고 알려져 있다고 했으므로, ⑤는 글의 내용과 일치하지 않는다.

구문풀이

4행 Early in his career, / he worked for the State of Lower Saxony, [**where** he was in charge of educational reform].

: [ ]는 계속적 용법으로 쓰인 관계부사절로, where의 선행사는 the State of Lower Saxony이다.

6행 In 1960 — 1961, Luhmann had the chance [to study sociology at Harvard University], [where he was influenced by Talcott Parsons, {one of the most famous social system theorists}].

: 첫 번째 [ ]는 형용사적 용법으로 쓰인 to부정사구로, 앞의 the chance를 수식한다. 두 번째 [ ]는 계속적 용법으로 쓰인 관계부사절로, 선행사는 Harvard University이다. { }는 Talcott Parsons와 동격이다.

어휘풀이

- renowned *a* 유명한
- be in charge of ~을 담당하다[책임지다]
- reform *n* 개혁
- theory *n* 이론
- subject *n* 주제
- widely *ad* 널리
- theorist *n* 이론가
- a variety of 다양한
- translate *v* 번역하다

075 답 ③

📖📖 건축가이자 화가인 Donato Bramante의 생애

전문해석

이탈리아의 Fermignano에서 태어난 Donato Bramante는 인생에서 일찍이 그림을 그리기 시작했다. 그의 아버지는 그에게 그림을 공부하는 것을 권했다. 나중에 그는 Urbino에서 Piero della Francesca의 조수로 일했다. 1480년경, 그는 Milan에 몇 개의 교회들을 새로운 양식으로 건축했다. 그는 Leonardo da Vinci와 친밀한 관계를 맺었으며, 그들은 그 도시에서 함께 작업했다. **건축이 그의 주요 관심사가**

되었지만, 그는 그림을 포기하지 않았다. Bramante는 1499년에 Rome으로 이주해서 교황 Julius 2세의 Rome 재개발 계획에 참여했다. 그는 Rome의 성 베드로 대성당의 새로운 바실리카를 구상했는데, 그것은 인류 역사상 가장 야심 찬 건축 프로젝트 중 하나였다. Bramante는 1514년 4월 11일에 사망했고 Rome에 묻혔다. 그의 건축물들은 여러 세기 동안 다른 건축가들에게 영향을 끼쳤다.

정답풀이
글의 중반부에서 건축이 그의 주요한 관심사가 되었지만 그림을 포기하지 않았다고 했으므로, ③은 글의 내용과 일치하지 않는다.

구문풀이
1행 Donato Bramante, [**born** in Fermignano, Italy], began to paint early in his life. His father encouraged him to study painting.

: 첫 번째 문장은 Donato Bramante가 주어, began이 동사이다. [ ]는 주어를 부연 설명하는 분사구로 앞에 '주격 관계대명사+be동사'인 who was가 생략된 것으로 볼 수 있다. 두 번째 문장에는 「encourage+목적어+목적격보어(to부정사)」 구문이 쓰여 '~가 …하도록 권장하다'의 의미를 나타낸다.

어휘풀이
- encourage *v* 권장하다, 격려하다
- architecture *n* 건축
- pope *n* 교황
- basilica *n* 바실리카(끝 부분이 둥그렇고, 내부에 기둥이 두 줄로 서 있는 큰 교회나 회관)
- ambitious *a* 야심 찬
- influence *v* 영향을 끼치다
- assistant *n* 조수
- participate in ~에 참여[참가]하다
- renewal *n* 재개발
- bury *v* 묻다, 매장하다
- architect *n* 건축가

076 답 ④

📖📖 **육군 장교이자 작가였던 Robert Baden-Powell의 생애**

전문해석
Robert Baden-Powell은 영국 육군 장교이자 작가, 스카우트 운동의 창시자였다. 그는 1857년 런던에서 태어나 1876년 영국 육군에 입대했다. 그는 인도, 아프리카, 지중해에서 복무했으며 1879년 줄루족 전쟁 중 Rorke's Drift 전투에서 용맹함을 인정받아 빅토리아 십자 훈장을 받았다. 1908년, Baden-Powell은 젊은이를 위한 새로운 교육 프로그램을 기술한 〈Scouting for Boys〉라는 책을 출간했다. 이 책은 Baden-Powell이 군대에서 겪은 경험을 바탕으로 소년들에게 캠핑, 추적하기, 응급처치 등의 기술을 가르치기 위해 기획되었다. 이 책은 큰 성공을 거두었고 몇 년 만에 전 세계에 스카우트 단이 창설되었다. 1910년, **Baden-Powell은 스카우트 운동에 전념하기 위해 육군에서 전역했다.** 그는 여동생 Agnes와 공동 집필한 〈Scouting for Girls〉를 비롯해 스카우트 활동에 관한 많은 책을 저술했다. Baden-Powell은 1941년에 83세의 나이로 사망했고 케냐 Nyeri에 묻혔다.

정답풀이
1910년에 스카우트 운동에 전념하기 위해서 육군에서 전역했다고 했으므로 ④는 글의 내용과 일치하지 않는다.

구문풀이
4행 He [served in India, Africa, and the Mediterranean], and [was awarded the Victoria Cross for his bravery in the Battle of Rorke's Drift during the Zulu War of 1879].

: 두 개의 [ ]는 and로 연결되어 주어인 He에 이어지는 술부이다.

7행 In 1908, Baden-Powell published a book [called *Scouting for Boys*], [which described a new educational program for young men].

: 첫 번째 [ ]는 a book을 수식하는 분사구이고, 두 번째 [ ]는 a book called *Scouting for Boys*를 부가적으로 설명하는 관계절이다.

어휘풀이
- founder *n* 창시자, 설립자
- award *v* 수여하다
- describe *v* 기술하다, 설명하다
- retire *v* 전역하다, 은퇴하다
- the Mediterranean 지중해
- Cross *n* 십자 훈장
- first aid 응급처치
- devote *v* 전념하다

077 답 ③

📖📖 **노벨 평화상을 수상한 최초의 여성 Bertha Suttner**

전문해석
Bertha Suttner는 1843년 프라하에서 태어났고, 군인 가정에서 자랐으며 전쟁의 참혹한 결과를 직접 목격했다. 그녀는 어린 나이에 평화 운동에 관심을 갖게 되었다. 1876년에 그녀는 〈무기를 내려놓으라!〉라는 반전(反戰) 소설을 출판하였는데, 이 책은 널리 읽히며 평화의 메시지를 전파하는 데 큰 영향을 미쳤다. 곧 그녀의 이름은 평화의 이상과 전쟁에 반대하는 강력한 입장과 밀접한 관련이 있게 되었다. 남성 위주의 평화 회의에서 그녀는 자유롭고 강력한 지도자로 두각을 나타냈다. 1870년대에는 Alfred Nobel과 절친한 친구가 되어 평화를 주제로 수년간 서신을 주고받았다. 그녀는 노벨 평화상을 수상한 최초의 여성인데, 1905년에 평화와 국제 이해 증진을 위한 노력에 대한 것으로 수상했다.

정답풀이
1876년에 쓴 반전 소설은 널리 읽히면서 평화의 메시지를 전파했다는 부분에서 ③은 글의 내용과 일치하지 않는다.

구문풀이
4행 In 1876, she published an anti-war novel *Lay Down Your Arms!* [that was widely read and influential in spreading the message of peace].

: an anti-war novel과 *Lay Down Your Arms!*는 동격 관계이고 [ ]는 관계절로 앞에 나온 an anti-war novel *Lay Down Your Arms!*를 수식한다.

어휘풀이
- military *a* 군의, 군인의
- devastating *a* 파괴적인
- anti-war *a* 전쟁 반대의
- spread *v* 퍼지다, 확산되다
- liberal *a* 자유주의적인
- correspond *v* 편지를 주고받다, 서신을 교환하다
- promote *v* 증진하다, 촉진하다
- witness *v* 목격하다
- firsthand *ad* 직접
- influential *a* 영향력 있는
- congress *n* 회의
- forceful *a* 강력한, 결단력 있는

078 답 ⑤

📖📖 **최초의 텔레비전 방송에 공헌한 John Logie Baird**

전문해석
John Logie Baird는 시각적 이미지를 전송하는 것이 가능하다는 것을 보여준 최초의 사람이었고, 그래서 그의 이름은 항상 텔레비전 역사의 일부로 존재할 것이다. 엔지니어로서 Baird가 처음 했던 일들은 너무나 형편없어서 26살 때 그는 그 직업을 포기하고 발명가가 되기로 결심했다. 그의 초기 아이디어는 완전히 실패했고 35세가 될 무렵에 그는 모든 돈을 잃었다. 하지만 1923년에 그는 무선으로 소리뿐만 아니라 그림을 전송하는 기계에 대한 연구를 시작했다. 곧 그는 무선 송신기로 몇 피트 떨어진 수신기에 조잡한 영상을 보낼 수 있었다. 1926년 1월 그는 런던에 있는 Royal Institution(왕립 과학 연구소)에서 대중들에게 텔레비전을 시연했다. 이것은 텔레비전에 대한 최초의 시연이었다. 1929년에 BBC는 Baird의 장비를 사용하여 최초의 텔레비전 방송을 했다. 그러나 **그는 현대 텔레비전이 의존하는 브라운관을 사용하지 못해서 1933년경 그의 발명품은 이 상대 체제에게 밀려났다.**

정답풀이

마지막 문장에서 John Logie Baird는 브라운관을 도입한 현대적인 텔레비전과의 경쟁에서 졌다고 했으므로, ⑤는 글의 내용과 일치하지 않는다.

구문풀이

16행 But he failed to make use of the cathode-ray tubes [on which modern televisions depend] / and thus, by 1933, his invention had lost out to this rival system.

: 두 개의 절이 and로 연결되어 있다. [ ]는 '전치사+관계대명사'가 사용된 절로 the cathode-ray tubes를 수식한다.

어휘풀이

- transmit *v* 전송하다
- miserable *a* 형편없는
- profession *n* 직업
- crude *a* 조잡한
- demonstration *n* 시연, 시범 설명
- lose out to ~에게 밀리다
- visual *a* 시각적인
- abandon *v* 포기하다
- radio *n* 무선 통신
- wireless transmitter 무선 송신기
- equipment *n* 장비

079 답 ④

📖 Bauhaus를 설립한 Walter Gropius의 생애

전문해석

Walter Gropius는 건축가의 아들이었다. 경력 초창기부터 그는 단지 현대적인 재료만 사용한 건물들을 디자인했다. 1914년에 그는 오직 유리와 강철만으로 구성된 몇몇 공장들을 지었다. 그는 또한 이따금씩 추상화처럼 보이는 자신의 건물을 만들면서 현대 미술로부터 아이디어를 빌려왔다. 1919년에 그는 독일에 디자인 학교인 'Bauhaus'를 설립했다. Gropius는 자신이 직접 그 학교의 새 건물을 만들었다. 거기서 학생들은 자신들의 건물에 부드러운 표면, 밝은 색깔, 그리고 삼차원의 디자인을 사용하는 법을 배웠다. **1933년에 Bauhaus는 나치에 의해 문을 닫았다. 그 일이 있기 5년 전에 Bauhaus를 떠났던 Gropius는 나치 정부의 세력이 점점 증가하여 1934년에 영국으로 이주했다.** 영국에서 보다 더 멋있는 현대적 건물을 디자인한 후에 그는 마침내 미국에 정착했다.

정답풀이

Bauhaus가 1933년에 문을 닫았고 그 다음 해인 1934년에 Gropius가 독일에서 영국으로 떠났다고 했으므로 ④는 글의 내용과 일치하지 않는다.

구문풀이

12행 Gropius, [who **had left** the Bauhaus five years before that], moved to England in 1934 [**because of** the growing power of the Nazi government].

: Gropius가 주어, moved가 동사이다. 첫 번째 [ ]는 Gropius에 대한 추가적인 정보를 덧붙이고 있는 관계절로, 문맥상 주절의 시제인 과거보다 더 이전에 일어난 일이므로 「had p.p.」의 과거완료 형태로 표현하였다. because of 다음에는 명사구가 와서 '~ 때문에'의 의미를 나타낸다.

어휘풀이

- from early on 초기부터
- found *v* 설립하다
- close down 폐쇄하다
- settle *v* 정착하다
- abstract painting 추상화
- three-dimensional *a* 3차원의
- striking *a* 멋있는

080 답 ④

📖 기름쏙독새의 생태

전문해석

남미에 해안가를 따라 있는 산의 동굴에 기름쏙독새라고 불리는 새가 산다. 수세기 동안 어린 기름쏙독새의 지방은 깨끗한 노란색의 냄새가 없는 기름을 얻기 위해서 끓여져 왔다. 사람들은 요리를 하고 자신들의 집에 쓸 조명을 위해서 그것을 사용한다. 기름쏙독새는 대부분의 생애를 어둠 속에서 보낸다. 그것은 큰 푸른 눈, 짧은 다리, 약한 발 그리고 강하고 구부러진 부리를 가지고 있다. 그것이 날개를 펼치면 36인치까지 펼쳐진다. 기름쏙독새의 색은 적갈색으로 검은색과 흰색의 반점이 있다. 그 입 주변에는 길고 뻣뻣한 털이 나 있다. 어두운 동굴 속에서 날 때, **기름쏙독새는 딸깍거리는 소리를 내고, 그러면 메아리가 그 새에게 돌아온다. 이것은 기름쏙독새가 방해가 되는 어떤 것과 부딪치는 것을 피하는 것을 돕는다.** 그것은 접시 모양의 둥지에서 두 개에서 네 개까지의 흰색 알을 낳는다. 암컷과 수컷은 알들이 부화할 때까지 번갈아 가면서 알을 품는다. 밤에 그것은 먹이를 구하러 동굴을 떠난다. 그것은 세계에서 유일하게 밤에 날아다니는, 과일을 먹는 새이다.

정답풀이

기름쏙독새는 반사되는 소리를 이용해서 동굴에서 장애물을 피한다고 했으므로, ④는 글의 내용과 일치하지 않는다.

구문풀이

11행 As it flies around in the dark cave, / the guacharo gives off clicking sounds, [**echoes** coming back to the bird].

: [ ]는 분사구문으로 앞 절의 주어와 분사구문의 주어가 달라 분사구문의 주어를 표시한 독립 분사구문이다.

13행 This **helps** it **avoid** bumping into anything [**that** is in the way].

: help는 준사역동사로 목적격보어로 to부정사와 원형부정사 모두 취해 '~가 …하도록 돕다'의 의미를 나타낸다. avoid는 동명사를 목적어로 취하는 동사이므로 bumping이 쓰였다. anything과 같은 부정대명사가 선행사일 경우, 관계대명사는 주로 that을 쓴다. 이때, anything that은 whatever(~하는 것은 무엇이든지)로 바꿔 쓸 수 있다.

어휘풀이

- coast *n* 해안, 해변
- hooked *a* 굽은, 갈고리 모양의
- spread *v* 펴다, 뻗다
- stiff *a* 뻣뻣한
- click *v* 찰칵[딸깍] 소리가 나다
- bump into ~에 부딪치다
- saucer *n* 받침 접시
- odorless *a* 냄새가 없는
- bill *n* (새의) 부리
- spotted *a* 반점이 있는, 얼룩덜룩한
- give off (소리 등을) 내다, 방출하다
- echo *n* 메아리
- be in the way 방해가 되다
- hatch *v* 부화하다

081 답 ④

📖 Antonio Gramsci의 업적과 생애

전문해석

Antonio Gramsci는 1891년에 이탈리아의 Sardinia에서 태어났다. 그는 이탈리아 공산당의 공동 창설자였다. 그 당의 지도자로 활동하고 있는 동안, 그는 그 당시 이탈리아의 수상이자 독재자였던 Benito Mussolini에 의해 1928년에 20년 형을 선고받았다. Gramsci는 감옥에 있는 동안 왕성하게 글을 썼다. 그가 뛰어난 기억력을 가지고 있기는 했지만, 자주 방문을 했던 그의 친척인 Tania의 도움이 없었더라면 그의 사상은 빛을 보지 못했을 것이다. **이 지적인 작업은 제2차 세계 대전이 끝나고 몇 년 후에야 비로소 모습을 드러냈는데, 그때 그것은 〈Prison Notebooks〉라고 알려진 것으로 그의 사후에 출판되었다.** 1950년대 경에는 그가 감옥에서 쓴 저술들은 서구 유럽에서뿐만 아니라 소비에트 연합에서도 또한 흥미를 끌었다. 감옥에서 겪었던 열악한 식사, 질병, 그리고 안 좋은 건강 때문에 Gramsci는 겨우 46세의 나이에 감옥에서 뇌졸중으로 죽었다.

글의 중반부에서 〈Prison Notebooks〉는 제2차 세계 대전이 끝나고 몇 년 후에 Antonio Gramsci의 사후에 출판되었다고 했으므로 ④는 글의 내용과 일치하지 않는다.

구문풀이

6행 [Although he had an exceptional memory], **without** the help of his relative, Tania, [who was a frequent visitor], his ideas **would not have come** to light.

: 첫 번째 [ ]는 접속사 Although가 이끄는 양보의 부사절이다. without은 if it had not been for ~(~이 없었더라면)의 의미로 주절의 would not have come과 함께 과거의 사실에 반대되는 상황을 가정하는 가정법 과거완료를 이루고 있다. his relative와 Tania는 동격이며, 두 번째 [ ]는 관계절로 Tania를 수식한다.

어휘풀이

- cofounder *n* 공동 창설자
- sentence *v* (형을) 선고하다
- dictator *n* 독재자, 절대 권력자
- exceptional *a* 뛰어난, 예외적인
- Communist Party 공산당
- imprisonment *n* 구금, 투옥
- prolifically *ad* 왕성하게
- stroke *n* 뇌졸중

---

10 안내문 본문 pp.060~065

082 ③	083 ④	084 ④	085 ⑤	086 ③
087 ⑤	088 ③	089 ④	090 ③	

---

082 답 ③

📖 Turtle Island 보트 투어 안내문

전문해석

Turtle Island 보트 투어

환상적인 Turtle Island 보트 투어가 여러분을 아름다운 바다의 세계로 초대합니다.

날짜: 2024년 6월 1일부터 8월 31일까지

투어 시간

주중	오후 1시 ~ 오후 5시
주말	오전 9시 ~ 오후 1시
	오후 1시 ~ 오후 5시

※ 각 투어는 4시간 동안 진행됩니다.

표와 예약

- 투어별 1인당 50달러
  (17세 이상만 참가할 수 있습니다.)
- 예약은 늦어도 투어 당일 이틀 전에 완료되어야 합니다.
- 출발 시각 이후에는 환불 불가
- 각각의 투어 그룹 규모는 10명의 참가자로 제한됩니다.

활동

- 전문 다이버와 함께 하는 스노클링
- 열대어 먹이 주기

※ 저희 웹사이트인 www.snorkelingti.com을 마음껏 탐색하세요.

---

083 답 ④

📖 Valestown 재활용 포스터 대회 안내

전문해석

2022 Valestown 재활용 포스터 대회

올해의 Valestown 재활용 포스터 대회에 참가하여 여러분의 예술적 재능을 뽐내세요!

참가 기준
- Valestown의 고등학생만 참가할 수 있습니다.
- 참가자들은 '미래를 위한 재활용'이라는 주제를 사용해야 합니다.

출품작 형식
- 파일 형식: PDF만 가능
- 최대 파일 크기: 40MB

심사 기준
- 주제 활용   - 창의성   - 예술적 기술

세부 사항
- 출품작은 1인당 한 장의 포스터로 제한됩니다.
- 출품작은 12월 19일 오후 6시까지 웹사이트에 업로드되어야 합니다.
- 수상자는 12월 28일에 웹사이트에 발표될 것입니다.

더 많은 정보를 원하시면 www.vtco.org를 방문하십시오.

정답풀이

심사 기준은 주제 활용, 창의성, 예술적 기술이라고 했으므로, 안내문의 내용과 일치하는 것은 ④이다.

오답풀이

① Valestown의 고등학생만 참가할 수 있다.
② 참가자들은 '미래를 위한 재활용'이라는 주제를 사용해야 한다.
③ 출품할 파일 양식은 PDF만 가능하다.
⑤ 출품작은 1인당 한 장만 가능하다.

구문풀이

2행 Join this year's Valestown Recycles Poster Contest / and **show off** your artistic talent!

: 명령문으로서 동사 Join으로 시작하는 문장이며, 접속사 and가 두 절을 연결해 Join과 show는 병렬구조를 이룬다. show off는 '~을 뽐내다'의 의미이다.

어휘풀이

- show off ~을 뽐내다[자랑하다]
- participation *n* 참가
- criteria *n* 기준(criterion의 복수형)
- talent *n* 재능
- submission *n* 출품작, 제출(물)
- announce *v* 발표하다

---

084 답 ④

📖 Cornhill 종이컵 사용하지 않기 챌린지 참여 촉구

> **Cornhill 종이컵 사용하지 않기 챌린지**
>
> Cornhill 고등학교는 '종이컵 사용하지 않기 챌린지'에 여러분을 초대합니다. 이 행사는 여러분이 종이컵의 사용을 줄이도록 권장합니다. 함께 지구를 구합시다!
>
> **참여 방법**
> 1) 선택된 후, 여러분이 텀블러를 사용하는 것을 보여주는 동영상을 녹화하세요.
> 2) 동영상에서 그 사람의 이름을 말하여 다음 참가자를 선택하세요.
> 3) 24시간 이내에 우리 학교 웹사이트에 동영상을 업로드하세요.
> ※ 총학생회 회장이 2021년 12월 1일에 챌린지를 시작할 것입니다.
>
> **추가 정보**
> • 챌린지는 2주 동안 진행될 것입니다.
> • 모든 참가자는 티셔츠를 받을 것입니다.
>
> 챌린지에 관한 질문이 있으면 cornhillsc@chs.edu로 저희에게 연락해 주세요.

정답풀이

Cornhill 종이컵 사용하지 않기 챌린지는 2주 동안 진행될 거라고 했으므로 ④는 안내문의 내용과 일치하지 않는다.

구문풀이

3행 This encourages you to reduce your use of paper cups.

: '~가 …하도록 권장하다[부추기다]'라는 의미의 「encourage+목적어+목적격보어(to부정사)」 구문이 쓰였다.

어휘풀이
• challenge *n* 챌린지, 도전
• tumbler *n* 텀블러
• participant *n* 참가자
• student council 총학생회

085 답 ⑤

📖 Big Bookend 책 서평 대회 참가 안내

전문해석

> **Big Bookend 책 서평 대회**
>
> **지금 출품작을 받고 있습니다!**
> – 참가를 위해서는 Leeds에 있는 중학교 또는 고등학교에 다니고 있어야 합니다.
> – 책 서평은 여러분이 고른 어떠한 책에 대한 것이든 가능하나 500단어를 넘으면 안 됩니다.
> – 연령 부문은 12세~14세, 15세~16세, 그리고 17세~18세입니다. 각 연령 부문별로 하나의 상이 있을 것입니다.
> • 수상자들은 5월 16일에 발표될 것이고 시상은 6월 5일 저녁 Big Bookend 책 서평 파티에서 할 것입니다.
> • 수상자들의 책 서평은 Big Bookend 웹사이트에 게재될 것입니다.
> • 참가하려면 Big Bookend 웹사이트 www.theleedsbigbookend.com에서 이용 가능한 참가 신청서를 작성하여 여러분의 서평과 함께 그것을 5월 2일까지 info@bigbookend.co.uk로 보내시면 됩니다.

정답풀이

마지막 문장에서 참가 신청서는 서평과 함께 보내라고 했으므로, 안내문의 내용과 일치하는 것은 ⑤이다.

① Leeds에 있는 중·고등학교에 다니고 있어야 참가할 수 있다.
② 서평은 500단어를 넘으면 안 된다.
③ 연령 부문별로 각각 하나의 상이 있다.
④ 수상자는 5월 16일에 발표된다.

구문풀이

9행 The winners will be announced on May 16th / and prizes will be awarded at the Big Bookend Book Review Party on the evening of June 5th.

: 두 개의 절이 접속사 and로 연결된 문장이며, 각 절의 동사는 의미상 수동형으로 제시되어 있다.

어휘풀이
• review *n* 서평
• competition *n* 대회
• submission *n* 출품작
• category *n* 부문, 범주
• complete *v* 작성하다
• entry form 참가 신청서

086 답 ③

📖 2023년 Queen Mary Wasafiri New Writing Prize

전문해석

> **Queen Mary Wasafiri New Writing Prize 2023**
>
> **마감일**
> 2023년 5월 30일 오후 5시
>
> **참가 가능자**
> 이 대회는 책을 출간해본 적이 없는 사람이라면 누구나 참여할 수 있습니다.
>
> **간단한 설명**
> • 이 대회는 계간 영국 문학잡지인 〈Wasafiri〉가 주관합니다.
> • 소설, 시, 그리고 생활문 세 가지 부문의 상이 있습니다.
> • 단어 제한은 최대 3,000단어입니다.
> • 출품작은 이전에 어떤 형태로든 출판된 적이 없어야 합니다.
>
> **참가비**
> 출품작 하나는 10파운드이고, 출품작 두 개는 16파운드입니다.
>
> **상**
> 각 부문의 수상자는 1,000파운드를 받게 되며, 수상자의 작품은 〈Wasafiri〉 잡지에 게재될 것입니다.
>
> 더 자세한 내용을 원하시면 대회 공식 웹사이트를 방문하세요.

정답풀이

단어 수는 최대 3,000단어로 제한하고 있으므로 ③이 안내문의 내용과 일치하지 않는다.

구문풀이

6행 The competition is open to anyone [who has not published a book].

: [ ]는 anyone을 수식하는 관계절이다.

어휘풀이
• competition *n* 대회, 경쟁
• publish *v* 출판하다
• description *n* 설명, 묘사
• quarterly *a* 계간[연 4회]의
• literary *a* 문학의
• category *n* 부문, 범주

- entry _n_ 출품작
- previously _ad_ 이전에
- entry fee 참가비

---

087 답 ⑤

📖 **Hands Craft Store 상품권에 관한 안내문**

전문해석

> ### Hands Craft Store 상품권
>
> 다른 누군가를 위해 쇼핑하는데 그들에게 무엇을 줄지 확신하지 못하시나요? Hands Craft Store 상품권으로 그들에게 선택이라는 선물을 주세요!
>
> - \$10, \$25, \$50, 또는 \$100 상품권을 선택할 수 있습니다.
> - 한 번의 구매에 최소 한 장의 상품권 그리고 최대 다섯 장의 상품권을 구매할 수 있습니다.
> - 상품권은 이메일로 전송됩니다.
> - 상품권에는 저희 가게의 웹사이트에서 상품으로 바꿀 수 있는 코드가 있습니다.
> - 또는 수령인이 그것을 상품으로 바꾸기 위해서 이메일 상품권을 가게에 가져오셔도 됩니다.
> - 저희 상품권은 추가적인 수수료가 없습니다.
> - 일단 상품권 구매가 확정되면, 취소할 수 없으며 지불한 돈은 환불되지 않습니다.

정답풀이

일단 상품권 구매가 확정되면 취소할 수 없고 지불한 돈은 환불되지 않는다고 했으므로, 안내문의 내용과 일치하는 것은 ⑤이다.

오답풀이

① \$10, \$25, \$50, \$100의 총 4개 종류의 상품권이 판매되고 있다.
② 한 번에 최대 5장의 상품권을 구입할 수 있다.
③ 구입한 상품권은 이메일로 전송된다.
④ 상품권은 온라인과 오프라인 모두에서 사용할 수 있다.

구문풀이

17행 Once purchase of the voucher is confirmed, / it cannot be cancelled and the payment [you made] is not refundable.

: 접속사로 쓰인 Once는 '일단 ~하면'이라는 의미이다. and 이하 절의 주어인 the payment는 목적격 관계대명사가 생략된 관계절 [ ]의 수식을 받는다.

어휘풀이

- gift voucher 상품권
- redeem _v_ (상품권 등을) 상품으로 교환하다
- processing fee 취급 수수료
- refundable _a_ 환불할 수 있는
- recipient _n_ 수령인
- confirm _v_ 확인하다, 확정하다

---

088 답 ③

📖 **Manhattan 카메라 클럽 사진 전시회 안내**

전문해석

> ### Manhattan 카메라 클럽 사진 전시회
> Manhattan 문화회관에서
> 2018년 11월 15일 – 19일
> 오전 11시에서 오후 9시까지
>
> **11월 15일 수요일**
> - Royal 사진 협회장인 Robert Tyler가 지휘하는 개막 행사가 오후 7시에 열릴 것입니다.
> - 전시회 작품에 대한 해설이 개막 행사 후에 이어질 것입니다.
>
> **11월 19일 일요일**
> - 선도하는 신문사인 New York 신문사의 수석 사진작가인 Barnet Saidman이 자신의 작품에 대한 대중 강연을 할 것입니다.
> - 강연 후에 무료 치즈와 와인 행사가 있을 것입니다.
>
> 전시회에 방문하셔서 위에 안내된 행사에 참석하실 것을 진심으로 요청합니다.
> **입장료는 무료입니다**
> 더 궁금한 사항은 419–1199로 전화주십시오.

정답풀이

개막 행사 후에 전시회 작품에 대한 해설이 이어진다고 했으므로, ③은 안내문의 내용과 일치하지 않는다.

구문풀이

18행 You are cordially invited [to visit the Exhibition] and [to attend the functions announced above].

: 「invite+목적어+to부정사(~가 …할 것을 요청하다)」라는 뜻의 구문이 수동태가 된 문장으로, '~가 …할 것이 요청된다'의 의미를 나타낸다. 이때, 두 개의 to부정사구 [ ]가 등위접속사 and로 연결되어 있다.

어휘풀이

- exhibition _n_ 전시회
- community center 지역 문화회관, 지역 주민센터
- inaugural _a_ 개회의, 개시의
- society _n_ 협회
- commentary _n_ 해설, 주석
- give a lecture 강연하다
- function _n_ 행사
- conduct _v_ 실시하다, 지휘하다
- B be followed by A A가 B를 뒤따르다
- leading _a_ 일류의, 선도하는
- cordially _ad_ 진심으로

---

089 답 ④

📖 **티셔츠 디자인 경연 대회**

전문해석

> ### 티셔츠 디자인 경연대회
>
> BrandNew 스튜디오는 고등학교 학생들에게 현대 미술관에서 판매될 홍보 티셔츠 디자인을 창작할 것을 요청합니다.
>
> 수상자는 200달러 상당의 가치가 있는 좋은 품질의 헤드폰을 받게 될 것이며 그 디자인은 티셔츠에 인쇄되어 미술관에서 널리 홍보될 것입니다.
>
> 또한 모든 참가자들은 주로 지역 창작 사업 디자이너들로 구성된 심사위원들에게 자신들의 작품을 선보이게 되는 혜택을 얻습니다. 최상위 5개의 디자인들은 또한 2019년 8월 12일부터 17일까지의 포스터로 미술관에 전시될 예정입니다.
>
> **마감일: 2019년 8월 5일 오후 5시**
>
> **형식 관련 지침**
> - 디자인은 반드시 BrandNew 스튜디오 로고를 보여줘야 함
> - 색이 있는 티셔츠(흰색 아님)에 두 가지 색상의 디자인
> - 앞쪽에만 도판 작업
>
> tshirtcompetition@umbrella.org로 출품작을 제출하십시오.

디자인은 반드시 BrandNew 스튜디오 로고를 보여줘야 한다고 했으므로 ④는 안내문의 내용과 일치한다.

오답풀이

① 고등학생들이 출품할 수 있다.
② 참가자 전원에게 상금과 상품이 수여되는 것은 아니다.
③ 최상위 다섯 작품이 미술관에 전시된다.
⑤ 흰색이 아닌 티셔츠에 두 가지 색으로 디자인한 작품을 제출한다.

구문풀이

9행 All entrants also benefit from **having their designs seen** by the judging panel [mainly composed of local designers from creative business].

: All entrants가 주어, benefit이 동사이다. from 이하에 「have+목적어+과거분사」 구문이 쓰였는데, 문맥상 목적어인 their designs와 see의 관계가 수동이므로 having 의 목적격보어로 과거분사가 쓰였다. [ ]는 과거분사구로 the judging panel을 수식한다.

어휘풀이

- promotional *a* 홍보의
- valued *a* 가치를 가진
- entrant *n* 참가자
- judging panel 심사 위원단
- artwork *n* 도판, 그림
- entry *n* 출품작
- contemporary *a* 현대의
- promote *v* 홍보하다
- benefit from ~로부터 이익을 얻다
- exhibit *v* 전시하다
- submit *v* 제출하다

090 답 ③

📖 Peach Grove의 원스톱 건강 교육 행사 안내

전문해석

Peach Grove의 원스톱 건강 교육 행사

이것은 Peach Grove 주민을 위해 준비된 만족스럽고 교육적인 행사입니다. 건강 검사는 치료하기 더 용이할 때 조기에 질병과 질환을 발견할 수가 있습니다. 행사는 강연과 건강 검사를 포함합니다.

강연
- 어린이와 십 대 청소년을 위한 좋은 건강 습관 기르기
- 건강한 식단을 위해 영양가 있는 점심 만들기

건강 검사
- 눈 검사와 청력 검사 (무료)
- 치과 검사 (개인당 5달러; 65세 이상 노인에게는 무료)
- 당뇨병과 콜레스테롤을 위한 혈액 검사 (개인당 10달러)

면허가 있는 의사들이 모든 질문에 답하도록 자리할 것입니다.

– Peach Grove 병원에서 후원
– 9월 7일 토요일 오전 9시부터 오후 1시 30분까지
– Peach Grove 병원의 건강 교육 센터에 위치

더 많은 정보를 얻으려면 저희 웹사이트 www.peachhospital.com을 방문하십시오.

정답풀이

치과 검사는 5달러이지만 65세 이상 노인에게는 무료이므로, ③은 안내문의 내용과 일치하지 않는다.

구문풀이

2행 This is a fulfilling and informative event [arranged for Peach Grove residents].

: 문장의 동사는 is이며, [ ]는 과거분사구로 앞의 명사 event를 수식한다.

어휘풀이

- one-stop 한 곳에서 모든 일을 처리하는, 한 장소에 모든 것이 구비된
- fulfilling *a* 만족을 주는, 성취감을 주는
- informative *a* 교육적인
- arrange *v* 준비하다
- resident *n* 거주자
- health screening 건강 검사
- condition *n* 질환, (몸의) 이상
- lecture *n* 강의, 강연
- promote *v* 촉진하다, 고취하다
- nutritious *a* 영양가가 높은
- be on hand 참석하다

11 어법				본문 pp.066~071
091 ②	092 ②	093 ④	094 ③	095 ⑤
096 ④	097 ④	098 ③	099 ②	

091 답 ②

📖 사회적 자극에 차별적으로 반응하는 타고난 인간 성향

전문해석

많은 연구가 사회적 자극에 차별적으로 반응하는 타고난 인간 성향에 대한 상당한 증거를 제시한다. 태어날 때부터, 아기들은 사람의 얼굴과 목소리 쪽으로 우선하여 향하게 되는데, 이러한 자극이 자신들에게 특별하게 의미가 있다는 것을 알고 있는 것 같다. 게다가, 아기들은 혀 내밀기, 입술 다물기, 입 벌리기와 같이 자신들에게 보여지는 다양한 얼굴 제스처를 모방하면서 이러한 연결을 적극적으로 마음속에 새긴다. 심지어 그들은 자신들이 다소 어려워하는 제스처에 맞추려고 노력하고, 성공할 때까지 자기 자신의 얼굴로 실험한다. 그들은 정말 성공하면 눈을 반짝이면서 즐거움을 보여주고, 실패하면 괴로움을 나타낸다. 다시 말해, 그들은 운동감각적으로 경험한 그들 자신의 신체적 움직임과 시각적으로 지각되는 다른 사람의 그것들을 조화시키는 타고난 능력을 가지고 있을 뿐만 아니라, 그렇게 하려는 타고난 욕구도 가지고 있다. 즉, 그들은 자신들이 '나와 비슷하다'라고 판단하는 타인을 모방하려는 타고난 욕구를 가지고 있는 것 같다.

092 답 ②

📖 변화를 위한 기반으로서의 패션의 중요성

전문해석

유행은 개인이 자신을 재연출할 새로운 기회를 끊임없이 제시하며 변화의 계기를 나타낸다. 어떻게 유행이 궁극적으로 개인에게 힘과 자유를 줄 수 있는지를 이해하기 위해서는 먼저 변화를 위한 기반으로서의 패션의 중요성에 대해 논의해야 한다. 패션이 왜 그렇게 매력적인지에 대해 나의 정보 제공자들이 해 준 가장 흔한 설명은 그것이 일종의 연극적인 의상을 구성한다는 것이다. **옷은 사람들이 자신을 세상에 보여 주는 방식의 일부이고, 패션은 사회에서 일어나고 있는 일, 그리고 패션 자체의 역사와 관련하여 그들을 현재에 위치시킨다.** 표현의 한 형태로서 패션은 많은 모호함을 담고 있어서 사람들이 특정한 옷과 연관된 의미를 재창조할 수 있게 해 준다. 패션은 자기표현의 가장 단순하고 저렴한 방법 중 하나로, 옷은 싸게 구매할 수 있으

며, 부, 지적 능력, 휴식 또는 환경 의식에 대한 개념을, 비록 이것들 중 어느 것도 사실이 아니라고 해도, 전달하기 쉽게 해 줄 수 있다. 패션은 또한 다양한 방법으로 행동성을 강화하여 행동을 위한 공간을 열어 줄 수 있다.

정답풀이

② **재귀대명사**: how가 이끄는 의문사절에서 동사 present의 목적어는 주어와 동일한 people이므로 them은 재귀대명사인 themselves로 바꿔야 한다.

오답풀이

① **접속사 that**: 뒤에 완전한 절이 이어지고, is의 보어 역할을 하는 명사절을 이끌고 있으므로 접속사 that은 적절하게 쓰였다.

③ **분사의 태**: 수식을 받는 the meanings는 '연관되는' 대상이므로 수동의 의미를 지닌 과거분사 associated는 적절하다.

④ **부사**: 수동태를 이루는 과거분사 purchased를 수식하는 역할을 하는 부사 inexpensively는 적절하게 쓰였다.

⑤ **분사구문**: 앞 절 내용에 이어지는 결과를 보여주는 분사구문을 이끄는 현재분사 opening은 적절하다.

구문풀이

6행 [The most common explanation {offered by my informants as to (why fashion is so appealing)}] **is** [that it constitutes a kind of theatrical costumery].

: 첫 번째 [ ]가 주어이며, 핵심 주어인 explanation에 맞춰 단수동사 is가 왔다. { }는 The most common explanation을 수식하는 과거분사구이고, ( )는 전치사 as to의 목적어로 쓰인 의문사절이다. 두 번째 [ ]는 문장의 보어인 명사절이다.

16행 ~: clothes can be inexpensively purchased [while making **it** easy {to convey notions of wealth, intellectual stature, relaxation or environmental consciousness}], [even if none of these is true].

: 두 개의 [ ]는 각각 접속사 while과 even if가 이끄는 양보의 부사절이다. 첫 번째 [ ]에서 it은 형식상의 목적어이고, { }가 내용상의 목적어이다.

어휘풀이

- constantly *ad* 끊임없이, 계속
- occasion *n* 계기, 때
- informant *n* 정보 제공자
- constitute *v* 구성하다
- costumery *n* 의상, 복장
- relative to ~와 관련하여
- ambiguity *n* 모호함, 불분명함
- notion *n* 개념, 관념
- relaxation *n* 휴식
- restage *v* 재상연하다
- ultimately *ad* 궁극적으로
- appealing *a* 매력적인
- theatrical *a* 연극적인
- locate *v* 위치시키다
- a host of 다수의, 많은
- convey *v* 전달하다
- intellectual *a* 지적인
- agency *n* 행동성, 행동력

093 답 ④

📖 세포의 생명 주기

전문해석

개체 전체와 마찬가지로, 세포는 수명이 있다. 그것의 생명 주기(세포 주기) 동안에 세포의 크기, 형태 그리고 물질대사 활동은 급격하게 변할 수 있다. 세포는 모세포가 분열하여 두 개의 딸세포를 생성할 때 쌍둥이로 '탄생'한다. 각각의 딸세포는 모세포보다 더 작으며, 특이한 경우를 제외하고 각각은 모세포만큼 커질 때까지 자란다. 이 시간 동안에 세포는 물, 당, 아미노산 그리고 다른 영양소들을 흡수하고 그것들을 새로운 살아 있는 원형질로 조합한다. 세포가 적절한 크기로 자란 후에, 그것이 분열할 준비를 하거나 또는 다 자라 특화된 세포로 분화하면서 그것의 물질대사는 변한다. 성장과 발달 둘 다 모든 세포 부분을 포함하는 일련의 복잡하고 역동적인 상호 작용을 필요로 한다. 세포의 물질대사와 구조가 복잡할 것임은 놀라운 일이 아니지만, 실제로 그것들은 꽤 간단하고 논리적이다. 가장 복잡한 세포조차도 단지 적은 수의 부분만을 가지고 있는데, 각각은 세포 생명의 뚜렷하고 명확한 측면을 맡고 있다.

정답풀이

④ **접속사와 관계사**: What ~ complex의 명사절이 but 앞 절의 주어이며 동사는 would not be이다. What이 이끄는 절은 주어(cell metabolism and structure), 동사(should be), 보어(complex)를 모두 갖춘 완전한 구조를 이루므로 선행사를 포함하는 관계대명사 What은 명사절을 이끄는 접속사 That으로 바꿔야 한다.

오답풀이

① **분사구문의 태**: 의미상의 주어인 its mother cell이 생산하는 주체이고, 뒤에 목적어 two daughter cells가 있으므로 능동의 분사구문을 이끄는 현재분사 producing은 어법상 적절하다.

② **생략**: 원래 as the mother cell was large에서 보어인 large가 생략된 형태이다.

③ **병렬구조**: as절의 동사가 「either A or B」 구문으로 연결된 형태로 앞의 prepares와 병렬구조를 이루는 matures and differentiates는 어법상 적절하다.

⑤ **독립분사구문**: each를 의미상의 주어로 하는 분사구문 each being responsible ~에서 being이 생략된 형태로 responsible의 쓰임은 어법상 적절하다.

구문풀이

8행 During this time, the cell [absorbs water, sugars, amino acids, and other nutrients] and [assembles **them** into new, living protoplasm].

: [ ]로 표시된 두 부분이 문장의 주어 the cell에 이어지는 술부이며, absorbs와 assembles는 병렬구조를 이룬다. them은 water ~ other nutrients를 가리키는 대명사이다.

어휘풀이

- life span 수명
- except for ~을 제외하고
- amino acid 아미노산
- assemble A into B A를 조합하여 B를 만들다
- mature *v* 다 자라다
- dynamic *a* 역동적인
- logical *a* 논리적인
- responsible *a* ~을 담당하고 있는
- well-defined *a* 명확하게 규정된
- dramatically *ad* 극적으로, 급격하게
- absorb *v* ~을 흡수하다
- nutrient *n* 영양소, 영양분
- differentiate *v* 분화하다
- rather *ad* 꽤, 오히려
- distinct *a* 전혀 다른, 뚜렷이 구별되는

094 답 ③

📖 스키마의 역할

전문해석

자동적 사고는 새로운 상황을 우리의 사전 경험과 관련지음으로써 우리가 그것들을 이해하는 것을 돕는다. 우리가 새로운 누군가를 만날 때, 우리는 그가 어떤 사람인지를 알아내기 위해서 처음부터 시작하지 않는다. 우리는 그 사람을 '공학 전공 학생' 또는 '내 사촌 Helen과 같은' 사람으로 분류한다. 장소, 사물, 그리고 상황에도 동일한 것이 적용된다. 우리가 한 번도 가본 적이 없는 패스트푸드 식당에 들어갈 때, 우리는 생각하지 않고도 테이블에서 종업원과 메뉴를 기다리지 않는다는 것을 안다. 우리는 주문하기 위해서 계산대로 가야 한다는 것을 아는데, 이는 우리의 정신 '대본'이 자동적으로 우리에게 이것이 패스트푸드 식당에서 우리가 하는 것이라고 말해주기 때문이며, 그래서 우리가 이곳은 다르지 않다고 생각한다. 좀 더 공식적으로는, 사람들은 스키마를 사용하는데, 이는 사회적 세상에 관한 우리의 지식을 조직하는 정신 구조다. 이러한 정신 구조는 우리가 알아차리고, 생각하고 기억하는 정보에 영향

을 준다. 스키마라는 용어는 매우 일반적이다. 그것은 다른 사람들, 우리 자신, 사회적 역할 그리고 구체적인 사건 등과 같은 많은 것들에 관한 우리의 지식을 포함한다.

정답풀이

③ **관계부사와 관계대명사:** 선행사가 a fast-food restaurant이고 이어지는 절에서 been to의 목적어 역할을 해야 하므로, 목적격 관계대명사 that 또는 which가 와야 한다. 관계부사 뒤에는 모든 구성 요소를 갖춘 완전한 절이 온다.

오답풀이

① **help의 목적격보어:** help는 목적어 뒤에 동사원형 또는 to부정사를 목적격보어로 쓸 수 있다.
② **형용사의 후치 수식:** 형용사가 -one이나 -thing으로 끝나는 명사를 수식할 때는 후치 수식한다.
④ **접속사:** 뒤에 주어와 동사가 있는 절이 이어지므로 접속사 because가 쓰인 것은 어법상 적절하다.
⑤ **주어와 동사의 수 일치:** 주격 관계대명사절의 동사는 선행사와 수를 일치시켜야 하는데 선행사가 복수명사(mental structures)이므로 organize는 적절하다.

구문풀이

10행 We know [that we have to go to the counter to order] [because our mental "script" automatically **tells** us {that this is what we do in fast-food restaurants}], / and we assume that this one is no different.

: 두 개의 등위절이 접속사 and로 연결된 구조이며, 첫 번째 절은 다시 주절과 이유의 부사절로 나뉜다. 첫 번째 [ ]는 know의 목적어인 명사절이다. 두 번째 [ ]는 이유의 부사절이며 그 안의 { }는 tells의 직접목적어로, 'A에게 B를 말하다'의 의미인 「tell A B」의 구조가 쓰였다.

어휘풀이

- relate *v* 관련짓다, 연계시키다
- from scratch 완전히 처음부터
- categorize *v* 분류하다
- formally *ad* 공식적으로
- prior *a* 이전의, 사전의
- figure out 알아내다
- assume *v* 생각하다
- encompass *v* 포함하다, 아우르다

---

095 답 ⑤

📖 기술 진보에 발맞춘 입법

전문해석

제2차 세계 대전 후 기술 진보의 가속화와 더불어, 기술 제품 또는 사안과 관련된 입법이 최신을 유지하도록 확실히 해야 할 현실적인 난제가 있음이 명백해졌다. 한 가지 멋진 해결책이 1980년대에 유럽에서 발견되었는데, 그때 일부 EU 지침이 오직 '필수 요건'만 담도록 간소화되는 한편, 필요한 뒷받침 기준들을 만들어 내는 과제는 표준화 위원회가 하도록 넘겼는데, '조정된 기준들'이라 불렸다. 따라서 이 '필수 요건'은 매우 '안정적'이었으므로, 계속해서 입법을 개정할 필요가 없었고, 반면에 기준들은 더 신속하게 개선되고 기술 혁신에 적용될 수 있었다. 경험은 그런 절차의 커다란 이로움을 보여주었는데, 그것은 적용이 가능할 때마다 새로운 분야를 다루도록 유용하게 확대될 수 있었고, 또 그래야 했다! 모든 이해관계자가 이 기준들의 입안에 참여할 수 있다는 사실은 **이 기준들의 실용성과 이 지침과 규제의 수용성** 둘 다를 향상한다.

정답풀이

⑤ **문장의 구조 파악:** 문장의 주어 The fact의 구체적인 내용을 설명하는 동격의 명사절(that절) 다음에 문장의 술어 동사가 없으므로 to부정사인 to enhance를 문장의 동사 역할을 할 수 있는 enhances로 바꿔야 한다.

오답풀이

① **과거분사:** ensure의 목적어로 쓰인 명사절의 동사는 would remain이므로 명사절의 주어 legislation을 수식하도록 과거분사 related를 쓴 것은 어법상 적절하다. related 앞에는 which was가 생략되어 있다.
② **관계부사:** the 1980s를 수식하는 관계절이 주어(some EU Directives), 수동태 동사(were streamlined)의 문장 성분과 필요한 어구를 모두 갖추고 있으므로 관계부사 when은 어법상 적절하다.
③ **부사:** 수동태를 이루는 과거분사 improved and adapted를 수식하는 부사에 해당하므로 rapidly는 어법상 적절하다.
④ **관계대명사:** 선행사 such a procedure를 부가적으로 설명하는 관계절의 주어 역할을 하는 주격 관계대명사 which의 쓰임은 적절하다.

구문풀이

1행 [With the acceleration of technical progress after the Second World War], / **it** became evident / **that** there was a real challenge to ensure [that legislation {related to technical products or issues} would remain up to date].

: 첫 번째 [ ]는 '~와 더불어'라는 의미의 전치사구이다. it은 가주어이고, that 이하가 진주어이다. 두 번째 [ ]는 ensure의 목적어로 쓰인 명사절이고 그 안의 { }는 명사절 주어인 legislation을 수식하는 과거분사구이다.

어휘풀이

- acceleration *n* 가속화
- legislation *n* 입법
- streamline *v* 간소화하다
- stable *a* 안정된
- rapidly *ad* 신속하게
- procedure *n* 절차
- applicable *a* 적용할 수 있는
- have an input in ~에 참여하다
- practicability *n* 실용성
- regulation *n* 규제
- evident *a* 명백한
- up to date 최신의
- committee *n* 위원회
- amend *v* 개정하다
- adapt *v* 변경하다, 적응시키다
- expand *v* 확대하다
- stakeholder *n* 이해관계자
- draft *v* 입안하다, 기초하다
- acceptability *n* 수용성

---

096 답 ④

📖 요청의 이로움과 조직에서 그것의 중요성

전문해석

연구는 도움 요청하기의 많은 이로움을 보여 준다. 도움을 요청하는 것은 우리가 필요로 하는 것을 얻을 가능성을 높게 (우리가 생각하는 것보다 더 가능성 높게) 만들 뿐만 아니라, 우리가 상상하는 것보다 덜 가혹하게 판단되는 경향도 있으며, 심지어 도움을 청함으로써 우리의 관계를 강화시킬 수도 있다. 하지만 이것은 연구 결과가 '현실 세계'와 결코 맞지 않는 것 같은 영역이다. 도움 요청에 커다란 가치가 있을지라도, 그것의 잠재적 가치를 이해하는 듯 보이는 사람은 거의 없다. 전형적인 직원 근무 평가를 예로 들어 보자. 거의 모든 근무 평가가 직원들이 자신의 동료들에게 도움을 제공하는지의 여부를 측정한다. 반대로, 근무 평가는 필요할 때 도움을 요청하는 직원들의 능력을 거의 평가하지 않는다. 하지만 자신의 동료들의 전문성에 접근할 의지가 있고 능력이 있다는 것은 조직에서의 협력의 결정적인 동인인 듯 보인다.

정답풀이

④ **명사절 접속사:** 밑줄 친 부분은 동사 measures의 목적어 역할을 하는 명사절을 이끌고 있는데, 명사절이 주어(employees), 동사(offer), 목적어(help), 전치사구(to their co-workers)로 이루어진 완전한 구조이다. 따라서 관계대명사 what을 접속사로 바꿔야 한다. 문맥상 '~인지의 여부를 측정하다'라는 의미를 나타내는 whether로 바꿔야 한다.

오답풀이

① **도치 구문:** Not only가 문두에 쓰여 「조동사+주어+동사」로 어순이 도치된 형태이며, 주어가 동명사구(asking for help)이므로 단수형 조동사 does는 어법상 적절하다.

② **관계대명사:** 선행사 an area를 수식하는 관계절이 주어(research findings), 동사(seem), 보어(to fit ~)의 문장 성분을 모두 갖춘 완전한 구조이므로 관계대명사 which가 전치사 in을 수반한 것은 어법상 적절하다.

③ **주어와 동사의 수 일치:** few는 문맥상 few people을 의미하므로, 복수동사 seem을 쓴 것은 어법상 적절하다.

⑤ **문장의 구조 파악:** would seem이 동사인 문장에서 being은 주어 역할을 하는 동명사구를 이루고 있으므로 어법상 적절하다.

구문풀이

1행 **Not only** does asking for help make **it** likely [that we will get what we need (more likely than we think)], **but** we **also** tend to be judged less harshly than we might imagine — we may even strengthen our relationships by soliciting help.

: 「not only A but also B」의 상관접속사가 두 개의 절을 연결하면서 'A뿐만 아니라, B도'의 뜻을 나타내는데, 첫 번째 절은 Not only가 문두로 나오면서 「Not only+조동사+주어+동사」로 어순이 도치되었다. it은 가목적어이며, [ ]로 표시된 that절이 진목적어에 해당한다.

어휘풀이

- harshly *ad* 가혹하게, 모질게
- solicit *v* 간청하다
- appraisal *n* 평가
- expertise *n* 전문성, 전문 기술[지식]
- driver *n* 동인, 추진 요인
- strengthen *v* 강화하다
- potential *a* 잠재적인
- rarely *ad* 거의 ~하지 않는
- critical *a* 결정적인, 중대한
- collaboration *n* 협력; 공동 작업

097 답 ④

📖 자녀에게 다른 사람에 대해 좋게 말하는 것을 가르치기

전문해석

아이들이 어릴 때, 부모는 그들이 다른 사람에 대해 좋게 말하도록 가르침으로써 그들의 친절함을 발달시키기 시작할 수 있다. 말과 행동은 함께 간다. 아이가 다른 사람에 대해 좋게 말하도록 훈련시켜라, 그러면 시간이 흐르면서 그 아이는 그 사람을 더 잘 대할 것이다. 아이가 다르게 말하도록 훈련하는 것은 아이가 다르게 생각하게 할 것이다. 이 방법은 아주 잘 통한다. 예를 들어, 부모가 아이로 하여금 친구에 대해 부정적으로 말하는 것을 중단하라고 주장한다면, 시간이 흐르면서 아이는 그 친구의 나쁜 습관에 관해 잊어버리거나 실제로 그 친구를 좋아하는 법을 배울 것이다. 아이들이 불평하는 것이 금지되면, 그들은 더 행복해진다. 아이가 누군가에 대해 말하는 방식은 아이로 하여금 그 사람에 대해 같은 방식으로 생각하게 한다. 아이들은 자신들이 말하는 것에 관해 생각한다. 불평을 하면 부정적인 생각을 먼저 해서 불평을 하는 것도 있지만 (불평을 하고 나면) 부정적인 생각이 그 뒤에 이어지기도 한다. 그러면 아이는 매우 부정적인 사고 패턴을 형성한다. 이렇게 되면 아이는 더 많이 불평할 뿐만 아니라 불행하게 행동하기 시작한다.

정답풀이

④ **문장의 구조 파악:** The way a child talks about someone이 문장의 주어인데 동사가 없으므로 causing을 문장의 동사 역할을 할 수 있는 causes로 바꿔야 한다.

오답풀이

① **명령문:** 「명령문, and+주어+동사」는 '~하라, 그러면 …할 것이다'라고 해석한다. 동사원형 Train은 어법상 적절하게 사용되었다.

② **사역동사의 목적격보어:** 사역동사 make의 목적격보어로 동사원형 think가

사용되었는데 목적어와 목적격보어가 능동의 의미 관계이므로 어법상 적절하게 사용되었다.

③ **당위성을 가진 동사:** insist 다음에 이어지는 that절이 당위적인 의미를 가질 때 '(should+) 동사원형'을 써야 하므로 stop은 어법상 적절하다.

⑤ **관계대명사 what:** what은 선행사를 포함한 관계대명사로 '~인 것'이라는 의미를 가지며 여기서는 이어지는 절의 동사 say의 목적어 역할을 한다.

구문풀이

18행 When this happens, / he or she **not only** complains more **but** begins to act unhappy.

: 부사절과 주절로 이루어진 문장이다. 주절에는 'A뿐만 아니라 B도'라는 의미의 「not only A but (also) B」 구문이 사용되어 동사인 complains와 begins가 병렬구조를 이룬다.

어휘풀이

- kindness *n* 친절함
- over time 시간이 흐르면서
- discipline *v* 훈련하다, 훈육하다
- insist *v* 주장하다
- complain *v* 불평하다
- speak well of ~에 대해 좋게 말하다
- treat *v* 대하다
- differently *ad* 다르게
- prohibit *v* 금지하다
- precede *v* 앞서다, 선행하다

098 답 ③

📖 19세기 미국 경제를 지배한 면화 재배와 노예 노동력의 필요성

전문해석

1790년에 미국 인구 조사는 697,624명의 노예를 기록하였다. 남북전쟁 무렵에 그 숫자는 거의 4백만으로 증가했다. 19세기 남부의 주에서 노예 노동력에 대한 증가하는 의존은 주로 1793년 조면기의 발명 때문이었다. 이 기구는 목화 섬유에서 씨앗을 분리하는 과정을 자동화했다. 이 장치는 인간이 그 작업을 수행할 필요를 없애주었지만, 그것은 경작과 가공에 있어서 인간 노동력에 대한 전반적인 필요성을 크게 증가시켰다. 미국의 면화 생산량은 1790년 2백만 파운드에서 1860년 10억 파운드로 증가하여, 세기의 중반 무렵에 세계 시장을 지배하게 되었다. 이 무렵 (단지 남부의 경제뿐만 아니라) 국가의 경제는 면화에 상당히 의존적이었는데, 이것은 남부 사람들의 노예를 포기하는 것에 대한 반감과 북부 사람들이 (노예) 제도에 손을 대는 것을 꺼려하는 것 둘 다를 설명하는 데 도움을 준다.

정답풀이

③ **대명사의 수 일치:** 글의 흐름으로 보아, 앞에 나오는 단수명사 the device를 가리키는 대명사를 써야 하므로 they를 it으로 바꿔야 한다.

오답풀이

① **시제:** 남북전쟁 이전부터 남북전쟁 무렵까지 일어난 일을 표현하기 위한 과거완료시제 had grown은 어법상 적절하다.

② **주어와 동사의 수 일치:** 문장의 핵심 주어인 reliance가 단수이므로 단수형 be동사 was를 쓴 것은 어법상 적절하다.

④ **분사구문:** '~해서, …했다'라는 결과의 의미를 표현하기 위해 사용된 분사구문이다.

⑤ **to부정사와 전치사 to의 구분:** aversion to ~는 '~에 대한 혐오감'이라는 뜻인데, 여기서 to는 전치사이므로 동명사 giving을 쓴 것은 어법상 적절하다.

구문풀이

7행 **While** the device eliminated the need [for humans to perform that task], / it vastly increased the overall need for human labor in cultivation and processing.

: 부사절과 주절로 이루어진 문장으로 접속사 While은 '~이긴 하지만'의 의미로 쓰여 양보의 부사절을 이끌고 있다. [ ]는 the need를 수식하는 형용사적 용법의 to부정사구

이며, for humans가 의미상의 주어이다. 부사인 vastly는 주절의 동사인 increased 를 수식한다.

어휘풀이
- census *n* 인구 조사, 공적인 조사
- slave *n* 노예
- reliance *n* 의존
- automate *v* 자동화하다
- eliminate *v* 없애다, 제거하다
- cultivation *n* 경작
- dominate *v* 지배하다
- aversion *n* 반감, 혐오
- reluctance *n* (~하는 것을) 꺼림, 싫어함
- tamper with (변화시키기 위해서) ~에 손을 대다

099 답 ②

📖 의무 규정 위반이 정당화될 수 있는 이유

전문해석
우리는 유용한 지침이기는 하지만 받아들여졌을 때조차도 그 자체로 행동에 대한 이유를 제시하지 못하는 '경험 법칙'을 '의무 규정'과 구분해야 한다. 의무 규정은 받아들여졌을 때 그것들이 규정'으로서' 존재한다는 이유만으로 행동에 대한 이유를 제공하며, 따라서 규정의 저변에 깔려 있는 타당한 이유(근거)가 반대의 결과를 나타내는 경우에도 규범적 압력을 발생시킨다. 이것은 모든 것을 고려해 볼 때, **의무 규정을 위반하는 것이 반드시 '잘못된' 일이라고 말하는 것은 아니다. 모든 것을 고려해 볼 때, 우리가 해야 할 이유가 있는 것은 우리가 '해야' 할 것과 다르다.** 규칙이 지시하는 것을 따라야 할 이유를 의무 규정이 제공할 때에도, 그 상황의 다른 특성들은 어떤 다른 방식으로 행동해야 할 이유를 제공할 수 있다. 중상을 입은 사람을 급히 병원으로 이송하기 위해 제한 속도를 초과하는 것은 여전히 제한 속도를 '위반하는' 것이지만, 행동에 대한 다른 이유들이 그것을 위반하는 것을 정당화할 수 있다.

정답풀이
② 관계대명사: 선행사는 those cases이고, 뒤에 완전한 구조의 절이 왔으므로 which를 in which 또는 관계부사 where로 바꿔야 한다.

오답풀이
① 동사의 부정: 앞에 which가 주격 관계대명사로 쓰였으므로, which의 선행사 *rules of thumb*이 주어이고, 문맥상 뒤에 나오는 일반동사 provide를 부정하므로 do는 어법상 적절하다.
③ 가주어와 진주어: 앞에 나오는 가주어 it에 대한 진주어 역할을 하는 to부정사이므로 to violate는 어법상 적절하다.
④ 관계대명사 what: what은 선행사를 포함하는 관계대명사로 전치사 from 의 목적어 역할을 하는 명사절을 이끌며, 동시에 그 절에서의 동사 do의 목적어 역할을 하고 있다.
⑤ 대명사의 수 일치: 가리키는 대상인 the speed limit이 단수이므로 it을 쓴 것은 어법상 적절하다.

구문풀이
`4행` Mandatory rules, when accepted, furnish reasons for action simply by virtue of their existence *qua* rules, **and** thus generate normative pressure even in those cases [**where** the justifications (rationales) underlying the rules indicate the contrary result].

: 주어 Mandatory rules에 두 개의 동사 furnish와 generate가 등위접속사 and로 연결되어 있다. [ ]는 those cases를 수식하는 관계절로, 관계부사 where는 '전치사 + 관계대명사'인 in which로 바꿔 쓸 수 있다.

어휘풀이
- distinguish A from B A와 B를 구별하다
- rule of thumb 경험 법칙, 어림 계산
- mandatory *a* 의무적인
- furnish *v* 제공하다
- by virtue of ~라는 이유로
- existence *n* 존재
- generate *v* 발생시키다
- normative *a* 규범적인
- justification *n* 타당한 이유
- rationale *n* 근거, 이유
- underlying *a* 밑에 놓인, 근본적인
- violate *v* 위반하다
- conform to ~을 따르다[지키다]
- feature *n* 특성, 특징

<table>
<tr><td colspan="2">**12 어휘**</td><td colspan="3" style="text-align:right">본문 pp.072~077</td></tr>
<tr><td>**100** ④</td><td>**101** ⑤</td><td>**102** ③</td><td>**103** ②</td><td>**104** ①</td></tr>
<tr><td>**105** ③</td><td>**106** ②</td><td>**107** ③</td><td>**108** ③</td><td></td></tr>
</table>

100 답 ④

📖 상점가 경제의 유연한 가격 설정 메커니즘

전문해석
상점가 경제는 공유되는 문화라는 보다 지속적인 유대 위에 자리 잡은, 겉보기에 유연한 가격 설정 메커니즘을 특징으로 한다. 구매자와 판매자 둘 다 서로의 제약을 알고 있다. 델리의 상점가에서, 구매자와 판매자는 대체로 다른 행위자들이 그들의 일상생활에서 가지는 재정적인 압박을 평가할 수 있다. 특정 경제 계층에 속하는 각 행위자는 상대방이 무엇을 필수품으로 여기고 무엇을 사치품으로 여기는지를 이해한다. 비디오 게임 같은 전자 제품의 경우, 그것들은 식품과 같은 다른 가정 구매품과 같은 수준의 필수품이 아니다. 따라서 델리의 상점가에서 판매자는 비디오 게임에 대해 곧바로 매우 낮은(→ 높은) 가격을 요구하지 않도록 주의하는데, 구매자가 비디오 게임 소유를 절대적 필수 사항으로 볼 이유가 전혀 없기 때문이다. 이러한 유형의 지식에 대한 접근은 비슷한 문화적, 경제적 세상에 속한 것에서 비롯된 서로의 선호와 한계를 관련지어 가격 일치를 정립한다.

101 답 ⑤

📖 우리의 일상생활로 들어와야 할 신기술인 '사이버공간'

전문해석
우리가 고개를 돌리는 곳 어디서든 우리는 전능하신 '사이버공간'에 대해 듣는다! 과대광고는 우리가 지루한 삶을 떠나 고글과 보디 슈트를 착용하고, 어떤 금속성의, 3차원의, 멀티미디어로 만들어진 다른 세계로 들어갈 것이라고 약속한다. 위대한 혁신 모터와 함께 산업 혁명이 도래했을 때, 우리는 어떤 멀리 떨어진 모터 공간으로 가기 위해 우리의 세상을 떠나지 않았다! 반대로, 우리는 모터를 자동차, 냉장고, 드릴 프레스, 연필깎이와 같은 것들로 우리 삶으로 가져왔다. 이 흡수는 매우 완전해서 우리는 그것들의 '모터성'이 아니라 그것들의 사용을 분명하게 밝히는 이름으로 이 모든 도구를 지칭한다. 이러한 혁신품들은 정확히 우리의 일상생활에 들어와서 깊이 영향을 미쳤기 때문에 주요한 사회경제적 운동으로 이어졌다. **사람들은 수천 년 동안 근본적으로 변하지 않았다. 기술은 끊임없이 변화한다. 우리에게 적응해야 하는 것은 바로 기술이다.** 그것이 바로 인간 중심의 컴퓨터 사용 하에서 정보 기술과 그 장치들에 일어날 일이다. 컴퓨터가 우리를 마법 같은 신세계로 데려다줄 것이라고 계속해서 더 오래 믿을수록 컴퓨터와 우리 삶의 자연스러운 융합이 더 오래 유지될(→ 지연될) 것인데, 이[융합]는 사회경제적 혁명이라고 불리기를 열망하는 모든 주요 운동의 특징이다.

정답풀이
⑤ 새로운 기술이 발달할 때 우리가 그 기술에 적용하는 것이 아니라, 그 기술이 우리의 삶으로 들어와야 하고 우리에게 적용해야 한다는 내용의 글이다.

따라서 컴퓨터가 우리를 마법 같은 신세계로 데려다줄 것이라고 더 오래 믿을수록 컴퓨터와 우리 삶의 자연스러운 융합은 더 '지연될' 것임을 추론할 수 있다. 따라서 maintain은 delay로 바꿔야 한다.

오답풀이

① 산업 혁명 때 우리는 '떨어져 있는' 모터 공간으로 가기 위해 세상을 떠나지 않았다는 문맥이므로 remote의 쓰임은 적절하다.
② 모터를 자동차와 냉장고 등에 적용시킨 것을 의미하므로 '흡수'라는 의미의 absorption의 쓰임은 적절하다.
③ 모터를 사용한 혁신품들이 우리 삶에 들어와 크게 '영향을 미쳤다'는 문맥이므로 affected의 쓰임은 적절하다.
④ 우리는 변하지 않았고 기술은 계속 변하므로 기술이 우리에게 '적응해야' 한다는 문맥이므로 adapt의 쓰임은 적절하다.

구문풀이

10행 This absorption has been **so** complete [**that** we refer to all these tools with names {that declare their usage, not their "motorness."}]

: '너무 ~해서 …하다'라는 의미의 「so ~ that …」 구문이 쓰였으며 부사절인 [ ]는 '결과'를 나타낸다. { }는 관계절로 선행사 names를 수식한다.

19행 **The longer** we continue to believe [that computers will take us to a magical new world], / **the longer** we will delay their natural fusion with our lives, / the hallmark of every major movement [that aspires to be called a socioeconomic revolution].

: '~할수록 점점 더 …하다'라는 의미의 「the 비교급 ~, the 비교급 …」 구문이 쓰였다. 첫 번째 [ ]는 believe의 목적어인 명사절이며, 두 번째 [ ]는 관계절로 선행사는 every major movement이다.

어휘풀이

- almighty *a* 전능한, 대단한
- revolution *n* 혁명
- refrigerator *n* 냉장고
- complete *a* 완전한
- usage *n* 사용
- profoundly *ad* 깊이
- constantly *ad* 끊임없이
- fusion *n* 융합
- dimensional *a* 차원의
- innovation *n* 혁신
- absorption *n* 흡수
- declare *v* 분명하게 밝히다
- precisely *ad* 정확히
- fundamentally *ad* 근본적으로
- adapt *v* 적응하다
- aspire *v* 열망하다

102 답 ③

📖 유기농 경작 방식의 한계와 그 보완책

전문해석

천연 생성물만 투입물로 사용될 수 있는 방식으로 정의되는 '유기농' 방식은 생물권에 해를 덜 끼친다고 시사되어 왔다. 그러나 '유기농' 경작 방식의 대규모 채택은 많은 주요 작물의 수확량을 감소시키고 생산비를 증가시키게 된다. 무기질 질소 공급은 많은 비(非)콩과 작물 종에 있어서 중상 수준의 생산성을 유지하는 데 필수적인데, 질소성 물질의 유기적 공급이 무기질 질소 비료보다 자주 제한적이거나 더 비싸기 때문이다. 게다가 거름이나 '친환경 거름' 작물로 콩과 식물을 광범위하게 사용하는 데는 이점(→ 제약)이 있다. 많은 경우, 화학 물질이 사용될 수 없으면 잡초 방제가 매우 어렵거나 많은 수작업을 필요로 하는데, 사회가 부유해짐에 따라 더 적은 사람들이 이 작업을 기꺼이 하려고 한다. 그러나 돌려짓기의 합리적인 사용과 경작과 가축 경영의 특정한 조합과 같은 '유기농' 경작에서 사용되는 몇몇 방식들은 농촌 생태계의 지속 가능성에 중요한 기여를 할 수 있다.

정답풀이

③ 유기농 경작 방식을 대규모로 채택하면 주요 작물의 수확량이 감소하고 생

산비가 증가한다는 내용 다음에 또 다른 단점을 덧붙이는 흐름이다. 그러므로 거름이나 콩과 식물을 광범위하게 사용하는 것에는 잡초 방제의 어려움이 따른다는 문맥이 되어야 한다. 따라서 benefits(이점)를 constraints(제약)로 바꿔야 한다.

오답풀이

① 유기농 방식을 대규모로 채택하는 것의 단점에 대해 언급하는 문장으로 주요 작물의 수확량이 '줄고(reduce)' 생산비가 증가한다는 문맥은 적절하다.
② 유기농 방식을 대규모로 채택할 경우 생산비가 증가하는 이유를 밝히는 문장이다. 따라서 무기 질소 공급은 많은 비콩과 작물 종의 생산성을 유지하는 데 '필수적(essential)'인데, 질소성 물질의 유기적 공급이 제한적이고 비싸기 때문이라는 문맥은 적절하다.
④ 화학 물질을 쓰지 않으면 잡초 방제를 수작업으로 해야 하는데, 사회가 부유해짐에 따라 그런 일을 할 사람들이 '더 적을(fewer)' 것이라는 문맥은 적절하다.
⑤ 유기농 경작 방식의 단점을 극복할 수 있는 방법을 소개하는 문장으로 돌려짓기 등의 방식을 통해 농촌 생태계의 지속 가능성에 '기여(contributions)'할 수 있다는 문맥은 적절하다.

구문풀이

1행 **It** has been suggested [**that** "organic" methods, {defined as those (in which only natural products can be used as inputs)}, would be less damaging to the biosphere].

: It은 가주어이고 [ ]로 표시된 that절이 진주어이다. that절에서는 "organic" methods가 주어, would be가 동사이다. { }는 "organic" methods를 부연 설명하는 과거분사구로, 앞에 being 또는 which are가 생략된 것으로 볼 수 있다. ( )는 선행사 those(= methods)를 수식하는 관계절이다.

17행 Some methods [used in "organic" farming], however, **such as** [the sensible use of crop rotations] and [specific combinations of cropping and livestock enterprises], can make important contributions to the sustainability of rural ecosystems.

: 첫 번째 [ ]는 문장의 핵심 주어인 Some methods를 수식하는 과거분사구이며, 문장의 동사는 can make이다. and로 연결된 두 번째와 세 번째 [ ]는 such as에 이어져서 주어 Some methods ~ farming의 구체적인 예를 제시한다.

어휘풀이

- organic *a* 유기농의
- biosphere *n* 생물권
- yield *n* 수확량, 산출량
- moderate *a* 보통의, 중간의
- extensive *a* 광범위한
- crop rotation 윤작, 돌려짓기
- livestock *n* 축산, 가축
- sustainability *n* 지속 가능성
- ecosystem *n* 생태계
- define *v* 정의하다
- adoption *n* 채택
- inorganic nitrogen 무기 질소
- productivity *n* 생산성
- sensible *a* 합리적인, 현명한
- combination *n* 조합
- enterprise *n* 사업 (경영)
- rural *a* 농촌의

103 답 ②

📖 최초의 특허권 발급과 그것의 효과

전문해석

시장의 탁월함은 그것이 다른 사람이 소중하게 여기는 물건을 생산한 노동자에게 보상한다는 것이다. 그것의 시작 이후 곧, 시장은 다른 사람이 소중하게 여기는 아이디어를 생산한 혁신가에게 보상하는 것으로 확장되었다. 1449년에 세계 최초의 특허권이 베네치아 유리 제조인 John Utyman에게 그의 색유리 제조 과정에 대해 발급되었다. Utyman은 영국에서 20년 동안 그 기술에 대한 독점권을 부여받았고, 그 대

가로 그는 그의 기술을 견습생들에게 가르쳐야 해서 그 지식이 확산될 것을 <u>막았다</u> (→ 보장했다). 거기서부터 특허가 확립되었다. 이런 특허법이 시행되면서, 발명가는 새로운 발명품으로 많은 돈을 벌 수 있는 더 큰 기회를 가졌다. 더 많은 <u>이윤</u>이 창출될 것이기 때문에, 더 많은 교육받은 계층들은 자신의 노력을 혁신으로 돌렸다. 처음 몇 개의 증기 엔진, 백열등, 기계 베틀, 조면기, 그리고 자동차의 발명가들은 모두 적어도 부분적으로 특허의 가용성에 의해 동기 부여가 되었다. 그리고 **특허 시스템에 의한 발명가에 대한 보상은 새로운 아이디어의 창조를 가속화했다.**

정답풀이

② John Utyman에게 그의 색유리 제조 기술에 대해 특허권이 발급되어 20년간 그 기술에 대한 독점권을 부여받았지만 그 대가로 견습생들에게 그 기술을 가르쳐야 했다고 했으므로 그 지식의 확산을 막은 것이 아니라 보장했다는 맥락이 되어야 한다. 따라서 preventing(막다)을 guaranteeing(보장하다)으로 바꿔야 한다.

오답풀이

① 최초의 특허권에 관한 내용의 글로, 물건 생산자에 대한 보상이 아이디어 생산자에게 보상하는 것으로 '확장되었다(extended)'는 문맥은 적절하다.
③ 발명가는 많은 돈을 벌 수 있는 기회를 가졌다고 했으므로 더 많은 '이윤(profits)'이 창출될 것이다.
④ 더 많은 이윤이 창출될 수 있다고 했으므로, 특허권의 '가용성(availability)'이 많은 발명가들에게 동기 부여가 되었을 것이다.
⑤ 이러한 특허에 의한 보상, 즉 많은 이윤은 발명가로 하여금 새로운 아이디어를 창조하는 것을 '가속화시켰을(accelerated)' 것이다.

구문풀이

7행 Utyman was granted a twenty-year monopoly on the technique in England, in exchange for **which** he was required to teach his technique to apprentices, [guaranteeing that the knowledge would spread].

: grant는 목적어를 두 개 가지는 4형식 동사로, 수동태가 되면서 직접목적어(a twenty-year ~ technique)가 수동태 동사 뒤에 남은 형태이다. in exchange for는 '~에 대한 대가로'로 해석한다. which는 앞 절의 내용을 선행사로 받는 목적격 관계대명사이고, [ ]는 결과를 나타내는 분사구문이다.

어휘풀이

- brilliance *n* 탁월함
- extend *v* 확장하다
- patent *n* 특허(권)
- glassmaker *n* 유리 제조인
- monopoly *n* 독점
- in exchange for ~에 대한 대가로, ~와 교환하여
- apprentice *n* 견습생, 도제
- make a fortune 많은 돈을 벌다, 재산을 모으다
- incandescent light bulb 백열등
- reward *v* 보상하다
- innovator *n* 혁신가
- issue *v* 발급하다, 발행하다
- grant *v* 부여하다, 수여하다
- take hold 확립되다
- accelerate *v* 가속화하다

104 답 ①

📖📖 과학 분야에서 패러다임의 개념과 역할

전문해석

Khun에 따르면, 과학 분야는 패러다임이 확립되고 우세해질 때 일정한 성숙도에 도달한 것이다. 그런 다음 시작되는 정상 과학 단계는 기존의 패러다임 내에서 당분간 모든 문제가 해결될 수 있다는 무조건적인 자신감을 특징으로 한다. 따라서 Khun에 따르면, **정상 과학에서 과학자들은 기본 법칙의 반증(기본 법칙을 뒤엎을 증거)을 찾지 않고, 패러다임에 의해 제공된 수용된 틀 내에서 작업한다. 이 틀은 학교 및 대학 교육과정에서도 반영된다.** 이것은 과학자들의 배경지식과 접근 방식을 크게 형성한

다. 학생들은 자연스럽게 주류 패러다임과 더불어 성장하며, 확립된 과학 원리를 받아들인다. 패러다임의 채택은 따라서 과학 사회화의 일부이며 공통된 세계관을 형성한다. 그것의 개방성과 복잡성 때문에 패러다임은 결코 과학자에게 완전히 의식되지 않는다. 일반적으로, 그것은 교과서에 반영되지 않지만 그럼에도 불문율처럼 과학계에 영향을 미치는 무수한 <u>암묵적인</u> 가정과 형이상학적인 해석을 포함한다.

정답풀이

(A) 앞에서 정상 과학의 단계에서 과학자들은 기본 법칙의 반증을 찾지 않고, 당분간은 모든 문제가 해결될 수 있다는 믿음을 갖는다고 했으므로 패러다임에 의해 '받아들여진' 틀 안에서 작업할 거라는 것을 추론할 수 있다. 따라서 accepted가 적절하다. (disputed: 반박을 받은, 논쟁이 되는)
(B) 패러다임이 과학계에 의해 '채택'되는 것이므로 adoption이 적절하다. (adaptation: 적응, 변경)
(C) 패러다임이 과학자에게 완전히 의식되지 않는다고 했고 무수한 가정과 형이상학적 해석이 불문율처럼 과학계에 영향을 미친다고 했으므로 '암묵적인' 가정을 포함하고 있음을 추론할 수 있다. 따라서 implicit이 적절하다. (explicit: 명시적인)

구문풀이

3행 The phase of normal science [that then begins] is characterized by unconditional confidence [that all problems can be solved within the existing paradigm for the time being].

: 첫 번째 [ ]는 관계절로 문장의 주어인 The phase of normal science를 수식한다. 두 번째 [ ]는 unconditional confidence와 동격을 이루는 명사절이다.

19행 As a rule, it contains numerous implicit assumptions and metaphysical interpretations [that are not reflected in the textbooks, but nevertheless influence the scientific enterprise like unwritten laws].

: [ ]는 관계절로 선행사 numerous ~ interpretations를 수식한다.

어휘풀이

- discipline *n* (학문의) 분야, 학과
- establish *v* 확립하다, 구축하다
- confidence *n* 자신(감)
- fundamental *a* 근본적인, 기본적인
- curricula *n* 교육과정(curriculum의 복수형)
- significantly *ad* 상당히, 크게
- complexity *n* 복잡성
- numerous *a* 무수히 많은
- metaphysical *a* 형이상학의
- influence *v* 영향을 미치다
- maturity *n* 성숙
- dominant *a* 지배적인
- for the time being 당분간은, 당장은
- framework *n* 틀, 체제
- prevailing *a* 우세한
- as a rule 일반적으로
- assumption *n* 가정, 추정
- interpretation *n* 해석
- enterprise *n* 사업 (활동)

105 답 ③

📖📖 인간의 이동 수단 발달사

전문해석

크게 보면, 이동의 변화하는 특성은 운송 시스템의 변화하는 특성과 밀접하게 연결되어 있다. 인류 역사의 초기 단계 내내, 인간의 이동 수단은 도보에 한정되었다. 이것은 이동이 인간의 지구력의 한계에 의해 제약되었다는 것을 의미했다. 가축화의 도래와 특정 기술의 발달(예를 들면, 마구)과 더불어, 축력의 사용은 사람들의 이동을 증가시키는 수단이 되었다. 따라서 활동의 범위는 말과 다른 동물들이 인간이 갖고 있는 것보다 더 큰 신체적 지구력을 갖고 있기 때문에 축소되었다(→ 확대되었다). 20세기가 시작될 무렵, 사람들의 이동은 자동차('말 없는 마차')의 발명에 의해 다시 한 번 변화되었다. 이 발달에 더하여, 철도, 선박 회사, 항공사가 개인 이동의 지리적 범위를 확대시켰고, 잠재적으로 사람들이 지구촌 시민이 되도록 하였다.

③ 인간의 이동 수단이 초기 단계의 도보에서 축력을 이용하는 것으로 발달하게 되었는데, 말 등의 동물이 인간보다 신체적 지구력이 더 강하다고 했으므로 인간의 이동이 증가하고 활동의 범위도 확대되었음을 추론할 수 있다. 따라서 shrunk(줄어들다)를 enlarged(확대하다)로 바꿔야 한다.

오답풀이

① 인간의 이동 및 '운송(transportation)' 수단의 발달에 대해 설명하는 글이다.
② 가축화의 '도래(advent)'로 인해, 마구와 같은 특정 기술이 발달하고 축력의 사용이 사람들의 이동을 증가시키는 수단이 되었을 것이다.
④ 20세기 시작 무렵 새로운 운송 수단인 자동차가 발명됐으므로 사람들의 이동이 '변화되었을(transformed)' 것이다.
⑤ 철도, 선박 회사, 항공사는 사람들을 지구촌 시민이 되도록 했다고 했으므로 이동의 '지리적(geographic)' 범위를 확대시켰을 것이다.

구문풀이

15행 In addition to these developments, [railroads, shipping lines, and airplanes] have expanded the geographic scope of personal mobility, [potentially **allowing** individuals **to become** global citizens].

: 첫 번째 [ ]가 주어, have expanded가 동사이다. 두 번째 [ ]는 결과를 나타내는 분사구문으로 and they potentially allowed ~로 풀어 쓸 수 있으며, 「allow+목적어+목적격보어(to부정사)」 구문이 쓰여 '~가 …하도록 해주다'의 의미를 나타낸다.

어휘풀이

- mobility *n* 이동(성)
- constrain *v* 제약하다
- advent *n* 도래, 등장
- harness *n* 마구(馬具)
- shrink *v* 축소시키다, 줄어들게 하다
- shipping line 선박 회사
- scope *n* 범위, 한계
- transportation *n* 운송, 교통 기관
- endurance *n* 지구력, 인내력
- domestication *n* 가축화
- animal power *n* 축력
- carriage *n* 마차, 탈것
- expand *v* 확대시키다
- potentially *ad* 잠재적으로

106 답 ②

📖📖 설득의 상대방이 느끼는 반발 (심리)

전문해석

저항은 설득의 줄다리기 상대방이다. 줄다리기 경기를 위해서는 상대팀이 필요한 것처럼 저항과 설득은 서로 대립하지만 설득력 있는 상호작용의 필수적인 부분들이다. 다가오는 설득 시도에 관해서 아는 것은 우리로 하여금 그 메시지가 무엇이든 저항하도록 동기를 준다. 이것은 '반발 (또는 부메랑 효과)'이라고 불린다. 반발은 사람들의 자유가 위협을 받아서 그들이 그 자유를 포기하기(→ 유지하기)를 원할 때 갖는 감정을 가리킨다. 만일 여러분의 부모님이 여러분의 데이트 상대를 정말로 싫어해서 헤어지게 하려고 한다면 여러분은 어떻게 반응할 것인가? 여러분은 부모님이 여러분의 자유를 제한하게 하는 것을 피하는 방법으로서 이 사람에 대해 더 애착을 느끼게 될 것이다. 이러한 경우에 설득은 역효과를 낸다. 반발은 왜 TV 폭력물을 금지하거나 특정한 TV 프로그램이나 영화에 경고 딱지를 붙이는 것이 이러한 프로그램을 보는 사람들의 흥미를 증가시키는지를 설명할 수 있다.

정답풀이

② 뒤에 이어지는 예시인 부모님이 자신의 데이트 상대를 싫어해서 헤어지게 할 때 상대에 더 애착을 느낀다는 것을 통해, 자신의 자유가 위협받을 때 그 자유를 유지하기를 원할 것임을 추론할 수 있다. 따라서 abandon(포기하다)을 preserve(유지하다)로 바꿔야 한다.

① 저항과 설득은 서로 대립하지만 상호작용의 필수적인 부분이라고 하였으므로, 누군가 설득하려 한다면 그것에 저항하려는 '동기가 생길(motivates)' 것이다.
③ 부모님이 자신의 데이트 상대를 싫어한다면 그에 대한 반발이 일어나서 부모님이 여러분의 자유를 제한하는 것을 '피하는(avoiding)' 방법으로 그 사람에 대해 더 애착을 느끼게 될 것이다.
④ 부모님이 싫어하는 데이트 상대에게 더 애착을 느끼는 경우, 설득이 '역효과를 내는(backfires)' 것이다.
⑤ 어떤 행동을 금지하는 것이 오히려 관심을 더 증가시키는 예시가 언급되었으므로, 특정 TV 프로그램이나 영화에 경고 딱지를 붙이는 것은 사람들의 흥미를 '증가시킬(increase)' 것이다.

구문풀이

4행 [Knowing about an upcoming persuasion attempt] motivates us to resist **whatever** the message is; ~.

: 동명사구인 [ ]가 주어, motivates가 동사이다. whatever는 양보 부사절을 이끌며 '어떤 ~이든(no matter what)'의 의미를 나타낸다.

어휘풀이

- resistance *n* 저항
- persuasion *n* 설득
- integral *a* 필수적인, 불가결한
- attached *a* 애착을 느끼는
- backfire *v* 역효과를 내다
- violence *n* 폭력, 범죄
- tug-of-war *n* 줄다리기
- competition *n* 경기, 경쟁
- abandon *v* 포기하다
- restrict *v* 제한하다
- ban *v* 금지하다

107 답 ③

📖📖 미디어 업계에서의 규모의 경제

전문해석

규모의 경제는 잡지 출판에서 라디오 방송, 음악 출판에 이르기까지 사실상 미디어의 모든 분야에서 존재한다. 따라서, 수평적 확장은 대부분의 미디어 회사에 이로운 전략이다. 예를 들어, 신문 출판의 경우 동일한 판형의 신문을 한 부 더 판매하는 데 드는 한계 비용이 상대적으로 낮아서, 발행 부수가 확대될수록 제품별 규모의 경제가 발생할 것이다. 한계 비용은 (방송과 달리) 인쇄 및 배포 비용이 일부 포함되는 유형(有形)의 형태로 제품이 전달되기 때문에 양(플러스)이다. 그러나 편집 간접비는 인쇄 매체 출판 업자의 지출에서 가장 큰 단일 구성 요소인 경향이 있으며, 이는 제품 소비가 확대되거나 축소되더라도 반드시 변하지는 않는다. 특정 이름의 신문 발행과 관련된 편집 간접비는 실제 발행 부수의 양과 관계없이 고정되어있는 경향이 있어서, 더 큰 수준의 독자층이 더 많은 수익으로 변환됨에 따라 규모의 경제를 달성할 수 있다.

정답풀이

(A) 뒤에 이어지는 예에서 동일한 판형의 신문을 한 부 더 판매하는 데 드는 한계 비용이 상대적으로 낮아 발행 부수가 확대될수록 제품별 규모의 경제가 발생한다고 했으므로 advantageous(이로운)가 적절하다. (disadvantageous: 불리한)
(B) 신문 출판에서는 특정한 형태를 가진 제품이 인쇄되고 배포되어 구매자에게 전달되므로 tangible(유형의)이 문맥상 적절하다. (intangible: 무형의)
(C) 앞 문장에서 편집 간접비는 제품 소비가 확대되거나 축소되더라도 반드시 변하지는 않는다고 했으므로 fixed(고정된)가 문맥상 적절하다. (changed: 변하는)

구문풀이

5행 In newspaper publishing, for example, [the marginal costs {involved in selling one additional copy of the same edition of a newspaper} are relatively low], / **so** [product-specific economies of scale will arise {as circulations expand}].

: 두 개의 [ ]는 접속사 so로 연결된 절이다. 첫 번째 { }는 첫 번째 절의 주어인 the marginal costs를 수식하는 분사구이고, 두 번째 { }는 두 번째 절에 포함된 부사절이다.

17행 The editorial overheads [associated with publishing any given newspaper title] tend to be fixed, [regardless of actual circulation volume], / **and so** economies of scale can be gained [as larger levels of readership are translated into more revenue].

: 두 개의 절이 and so로 연결된 구조이다. 첫 번째 [ ]는 첫 번째 절의 주어인 The editorial overheads를 수식하는 과거분사구이고, 두 번째 [ ]는 전치사구이다. 세 번째 [ ]는 두 번째 절에 포함된 부사절이다.

어휘풀이

- virtually *ad* 사실상
- expansion *n* 확장
- specific *a* 특유한
- positive *a* 양[플러스]의, 0보다 많은
- editorial *a* 편집의
- expenditure *n* 지출
- regardless of ~에 관계없이
- translate *v* 변환시키다
- horizontal *a* 수평의
- marginal cost 한계 비용
- circulation *n* 발행 부수
- distribution *n* 배포
- component *n* 구성 요소
- contract *v* 축소되다
- readership *n* 독자층
- revenue *n* 수입

108 답 ③

📖 진화적 관점에서 본 시기심(envy)의 기능

전문해석

시기심은 한 사람이 다른 사람이 가진 재능, 기술, 성취, 또는 소유물이 없는데 그것을 열망하거나 상대방이 그것을 가지고 있지 않았기를 소망할 때 일어나는 감정이다. 왜 이 감정이 그토록 널리 퍼져 있는 범문화적 감정인지를 이해하기는 쉽다. 가치 있는 특성이 우월한 사람은 더 높은 자긍심뿐만 아니라 더 큰 권력과 관심을 수확한다. 열등함은 더 낮은 자긍심뿐만 아니라 더 작은 권력과 관심으로 이어진다. **다른 사람들의 결과적인 유리함이 우리에게 아무런 감정적 영향을 미치지 않는다면 이상할 것이다.** 게다가 진화적인 관점에서 볼 때, 진화심리학자인 Sarah Hill과 David Buss가 주장하듯이, 다른 사람의 유리함이 완전히 <u>만족스러운</u> 결과라고 느끼는 경향이 있는 것은 거의 적응에 도움이 되기 어려울 것이다. 이런 의미에서, **시기심을 느끼는 능력은**, 비록 그것이 그것에 불유쾌한 구석이 있기는 하지만, **필수적인 진화적 기능을 수행한다.** 만일 우리가 진화하는 존재로서 사회적 지위가 비슷비슷한 사람들과 보조를 맞추는 것을 돕도록 고안된 감정을 발달시키는 데 <u>실패했다면</u>, 아마도 우리는 진화의 덩굴에서 시들어 사라졌을 것이다.

정답풀이

(A) 앞에서 우월성이 자긍심, 권력, 관심에 긍정적 효과를 가져온다고 했으므로, 부정적 효과를 언급하는 내용을 고려하면 Inferiority(열등함)가 문맥상 적절하다. (excellence: 탁월함)

(B) 앞에서 다른 사람들이 유리한 상황에 대해 별다른 감정을 느끼지 않는 것은 비정상적이라고 했으므로, 시기심이 없으면 진화론적으로 바람직하지 않다는 것을 추론할 수 있다. 따라서 hardly를 고려하면 satisfactory(만족스러운)가 적절하다. (unsatisfactory: 불만족스러운)

(C) 앞에서 시기심은 필수적인 진화적 기능을 수행한다고 했으므로, 우리가 진화의 덩굴에서 시들어 사라지는 상황은 그런 감정이 없을 때일 것임을 추론

할 수 있다. 따라서 인간이 시기심을 발달시키지 못한 상황을 기술하는 failed(실패했다)가 문맥상 적절하다. (manage to *do*: 용케도 ~하다)

구문풀이

1행 Envy is an emotion / **which** occurs [when a person lacks another's quality, skill, achievement, or possession **and either** desires it **or** wishes {that the other lacked it}].

: which 이하는 문장의 보어인 an emotion을 수식하는 관계절이다. [ ]는 시간의 부사절로 lacks, desires, wishes 이 세 개의 동사가 and와 either ~ or로 연결되어 주어 a person에 이어지고 있다. { }는 wishes의 목적어 역할을 하는 명사절이다.

어휘풀이

- quality *n* 재능, 능력
- prevalent *a* 널리 퍼져 있는
- superior *a* 우월한
- reap *v* 수확하다
- inferiority *n* 열등함
- evolutionary *a* 진화적인
- argue *v* 주장하다
- be inclined to *do* ~하는 경향이 있다
- keep up with ~와 보조를 맞추다
- vine *n* 덩굴 (식물), 포도나무
- possession *n* 소유(물)
- pan-cultural *a* 범문화적인
- attribute *n* 특성
- self-esteem *n* 자긍심
- consequential *a* 결과적인
- perspective *n* 관점
- adaptive *a* 적응할 수 있는, 적응성의
- outcome *n* 결과
- wither *v* 시들다, 약해지다

01~12 어휘 REVIEW 본문 pp.078~083

01 글의 목적

01 전문가 02 기사, 글 03 ~에 가입하다 04 활기찬 05 우연히 ~하다 06 열정적인 07 ~에 의존하다 08 특권, 영광 09 즉각적인, 신속한 10 후한 11 전문성 12 insight 13 현재 14 등록하다 15 해 나가다 16 고급의, 엄청난 17 열광적인 18 상환 19 loan 20 기부(금)

02 심경 변화

01 잔인한 02 다가가다, 접근하다 03 짜증이 난 04 깜짝 놀라게 하다 05 자갈 06 확신시키다, 납득시키다 07 열등감 08 희귀한 09 헤매다 10 제출하다 11 대회, 시합, 경쟁 12 dramatically 13 comment 14 (곰·사자·여우 등의) 새끼 15 부족, 집단 16 두드러지게, 눈에 띄게 17 비난하는 (듯한), 고발하는 (듯한) 18 뛰어오르다 19 thigh 20 죄수

03 필자의 주장

01 직관 02 해결하다 03 이행, 충족 04 막연한 05 나타내다, 내비치다 06 감소 07 대단히 08 오로지, 독점적으로 09 배열하다 10 강력한, 강한 11 목적지 12 철저한 13 임의적인 14 practice 15 우선순위를 정하다 16 분석하다 17 적절히 18 의존, 의지 19 수반, 동반 20 드러내 보이다, 보여주다

04 함축 의미 추론

01 다수의 02 적용 03 purchase 04 나타나다, 등장하다 05 붕괴, 와해 06 영역, 분야 07 자격이 있는 08 (개미·벌 등의) 집단, 군체 09 분산시키다, 흩뜨리다 10 직업 11 평가 12 괜찮은 13 신속, 속도 14 ~을 바치다 15 어려운, 힘든 16 erosion 17 편향된 18 감소 19 ~을 지정하다 20 지나친, 과도한

13 빈칸 추론(1)

본문 pp.084~089

| 109 ② | 110 ② | 111 ① | 112 ② | 113 ⑤ |
| 114 ④ | 115 ① | 116 ① | 117 ① | |

109 답 ②

▣▣ 단어 인식을 넘어서는 텍스트성의 본질

전문해석

지난 10년 동안 어떻게 어린이들이 읽게 되는지에 관한 관심은 '텍스트성'의 본질과 모든 연령의 독자들이 텍스트를 의미하게 하는 다양하고 상호 연관된 방식의 본질을 전면으로 불러왔다. 이제 '읽기'는 과거의 어느 때보다 훨씬 더 많은 표현 형식에 적용되는데, 그림, 지도, 화면, 디자인 그래픽과 사진이 모두 텍스트로 여겨진다. 새로운 인쇄 공정에 의해 그림책에서 가능해진 혁신에 더해, 시집이나 정보 텍스트와 같은 다른 종류에서도 디자인적 특징이 두드러진다. 따라서, 읽기는 어린이들의 주의가 인쇄된 텍스트에 집중되고 스케치나 그림이 부속물이었을 때보다 더 복잡한 종류의 해석이 된다. 이제 어린이들은 그림책을 통해 글과 삽화가 서로를 보완하여 향상한다는 것을 배운다. 읽기는 단순히 단어 인식이 아니다. 심지어 가장 쉬운 텍스트에서도, 문장이 '말하는' 것은 종종 그 문장이 의미하는 것이 아니다.

110 답 ②

▣▣ 전문적인 지위를 누리지 못하는 스포츠 신문 기자

전문해석

스포츠 저널리즘의 전문적인 지위에 관해, 특히 인쇄 매체에서 매우 역설적인 것이 있다. 기자들이 자신들의 통상 업무인 설명과 논평을 수행할 때 스포츠 팬들은 스포츠 경기에 관한 기자들의 설명을 열심히 찾아보는 한편, 다양한 형식으로 스포츠를 취재하는 그들의 더 폭넓은 저널리스트의 역할에서, 스포츠 기자들은 동시대의 모든 작가들 중에서 가장 눈에 띄는 사람 중 하나이다. 엘리트급 '유명인' 스포츠 기자들의 생각은 주요 신문에서 많이 원하며, 그들의 수익성 있는 계약은 저널리즘의 다른 '분야' 동료들의 선망의 대상이다. 그러나 스포츠 기자는 그들의 독자 수나 급여 액수의 크기에 상응하는, 자신들의 전문직에서의 지위를 누리지 못하며, 스포츠는 스포츠 기자들이 하는 일의 가치를 묵살하는 말로 여전히 쉽게 건네지는 (이제는 상투적인 문구의 지위에 이르는) '뉴스 매체의 장난감 부서'라는 옛말이 따라붙는다. 이렇게 스포츠 저널리즘을 진지하게 여기기를 꺼리는 것은 **스포츠 신문 기자들이 많이 읽히지만 거의 존경받지 못하는 역설적인 결과를 낳는다.**

정답풀이

스포츠 기자들은 독자층도 많고 신문사들도 많이 원하며 돈도 많이 벌지만 뉴스 매체에서는 장난감 부서 취급을 받아 전문적인 지위를 누리지 못한다는 내용이므로 빈칸에 들어갈 말로 가장 적절한 것은 ② '존경받지'이다.

① 돈을 받지   ③ 검열되지
④ 도전받지   ⑤ 논의되지

구문풀이

13행 Yet sports journalists do not have a standing in their profession [that corresponds to the size of their readerships or of their pay packets], [with the old saying (now reaching the status of cliché) {that sport is the 'toy department of the news media' still readily to hand as a dismissal of the worth of (what sports journalists do)}].

: 문장의 주어는 sports journalists이고 동사는 do not have이다. 첫 번째 [ ]는 관계

절로 앞에 나온 명사구 a standing in their profession을 수식하며, 두 번째 [ ]는 앞에 나온 내용을 부연 설명하는 전치사구이다. 그 안에 { }는 the old saying의 동격 구문으로 the old saying의 내용을 포함한다. ( )는 선행사를 포함하는 관계대명사 what이 이끄는 명사절로 전치사 of의 목적어이다.

어휘풀이
- **paradoxical** *a* 역설적인
- **medium** *n* 매체
- **account** *n* 설명
- **cover** *v* 취재하다
- **celebrity** *n* 유명인사
- **contract** *n* 계약
- **standing** *n* 지위
- **correspond to** ~에 상응하다
- **pay packet** 급여 액수
- **dismissal** *n* 묵살
- **censor** *v* 검열하다
- **status** *n* 지위
- **commentary** *n* 논평
- **consult** *v* 찾아보다
- **contemporary** *a* 동시대의
- **sought after** 많은 사람들이 원하는
- **discipline** *n* 부문, 분야
- **profession** *n* 전문직
- **readership** *n* 독자 수
- **cliché** *n* 상투적인 문구
- **reluctance** *n* 꺼림

111 답 ①

📖 **정확함보다는 즐거움을 제공하는 유머의 기능**

전문해석
유머는 실용적인 해방뿐만 아니라 인식의 해방도 포함한다. 어떤 것이 재미있기만 하다면, 우리는 그것이 진짜인지 허구인지, 참인지 거짓인지에 대해서는 당장은 신경 쓰지 않는다. 그렇기 때문에 우리는 재미있는 이야기를 하는 사람들에게 상당한 여지를 제공한다. 상황의 우스꽝스러움을 과장하거나 약간의 세부 사항을 지어내서라도 웃음을 더 얻는다면, 우리는 그들에게 일종의 시적 허용인 코믹 허용을 기꺼이 허락한다. 실제로 재미있는 이야기를 듣고 있는 사람이 '아니요, 스파게티를 키보드와 모니터에 흘린 것이 아니라 키보드에만 흘린 거예요'라며 이야기하는 사람을 정정하려고 하면 아마도 이야기를 듣는 다른 사람으로부터 끼어들지 말라는 말을 듣게 될 것이다. **유머를 창조하는 사람은 정확한 정보를 제공하는 것이 아니라 그 아이디어가 가져올 즐거움을 위해 사람들의 머릿속에 아이디어를 집어넣고 있는 것이다.**

정답풀이
유머가 현실과 허구, 참과 거짓과는 별개로 웃음과 즐거움을 제공하는 경험에 대한 것이라는 내용의 글이며, 구체적인 예로 재미있는 이야기를 듣고 있는 사람이 이야기의 내용을 정확하게 정정하려고 하면 다른 사람으로부터 끼어들지 말라는 말을 듣게 될 것이라고 했다. 따라서 유머를 창조하는 사람의 목적은 정확한 정보를 제공하는 것이 아니라 즐거움을 위한 것임을 추론할 수 있으므로 빈칸에는 ① '정확한'이 들어가는 것이 가장 적절하다.

② 자세한 ③ 유용한
④ 추가적인 ⑤ 대안적인

구문풀이
6행 [If they are getting extra laughs {by exaggerating the silliness of a situation} or {even by making up a few details}], we are happy to grant them comic licence, [a kind of poetic licence].

: 첫 번째 [ ]는 조건의 의미인 부사절이고, 그 안에 두 개의 { }는 or로 연결된 전치사구이다. 두 번째 [ ]는 바로 앞의 comic licence와 동격인 어구이다.

9행 Indeed, [someone {listening to a funny story} {who tries to correct the teller}]—['No, he didn't spill the spaghetti on the keyboard and the monitor, just on the keyboard']—[**will** probably **be told** by the other listeners to stop interrupting].

: 첫 번째 [ ]는 문장의 주어로, 그 안의 두 개의 { }는 각각 someone을 수식하는 분사구와 관계절이다. 두 번째 [ ]는 주어에 대한 구체적 말의 예시이며, 세 번째 [ ]는 수동태인 술부이다.

어휘풀이
- **practical** *a* 실용적인, 실제적인
- **for the moment** 당장은, 지금은
- **fictional** *a* 허구적인
- **exaggerate** *v* 과장하다
- **grant** *v* 허락하다, 승인하다
- **correct** *v* 정정하다
- **alternative** *a* 대안적인
- **disengagement** *n* 해방, 자유
- **be concerned with** ~에 신경 쓰다
- **considerable** *a* 상당한
- **make up** 지어내다
- **poetic licence** 시적 허용
- **interrupt** *v* 끼어들다, 방해하다

112 답 ②

📖 **다양성을 무시한 나치가 독일 과학계에 끼친 부정적 영향**

전문해석
경제학자인 Fabian Waldinger는 제2차 세계 대전 전에 독일 대학의 유대인 교수들의 숙청의 영향을 조사했고 놀라운 사실을 발견했다. Waldinger의 연구 전략은 다양한 대학 학과가 매우 다른 해고 비율을 겪었다는 사실에 기초했다. 예를 들어, 영향력 있는 수학자인 Hilbert가 사랑했던 Göttingen에서는, 수학자의 60퍼센트가 강제 해고되었지만, 화학과에서는 아무도 해고되지 않았다. 이러한 무작위 변이를 이용하여, Waldinger는 독일 전역에서, 예를 들어, 한 학과에서 과학자의 10퍼센트를 잃었을 때 그 영향이 얼마나 심각한지 보여줄 수 있었다. 그런 다음 그는 그것을 전쟁 중 대학 학과에 대한 폭격의 영향과 비교했다. 그는 유대인 또는 반체제 과학자를 잃은 피해가 사무실이나 실험실 시설에 대한 피해보다 훨씬 더 크고 오래 지속된다는 사실을 발견했다. **인종적으로 순수한 과학 기관을 고집하는 것은 연구 성과와 최고의 멘토 몇 명을 잃은 젊은 박사 과정 학생들의 생산성 모두에 영구적인 피해를 입혔다.** 다양성을 박탈당한 독일 대학은 회복할 수 없었다.

정답풀이
독일 대학에서 유대인과 반체제 과학자를 추방한 것이 전쟁 중 폭격으로 인한 시설 피해보다 연구 성과와 생산성에 훨씬 더 큰 영향을 미쳤다는 연구에 대한 글로, 후반부에서 인종적으로 순수한 과학 기관을 고집하는 것이 연구 성과와 최고의 멘토를 잃은 학생들의 생산성 모두에 영구적인 피해를 입혔다고 말하고 있으므로, 빈칸에 들어갈 말로 가장 적절한 것은 ② '다양성'이다.

① 재정 지원 ③ 권위
④ 신뢰 ⑤ 평판

구문풀이
10행 [Using such random variations across Germany], Waldinger was able to show [how serious the impact was of losing, say, {10 per cent of the scientists in a department}].

: 첫 번째 [ ]는 문장의 주어인 Waldinger를 의미상의 주어로 하는 분사구문이며, 두 번째 [ ]는 show의 목적어 역할을 하는 명사절이다. say는 '예를 들어, 가령'으로 해석하며, { }는 of losing에 연결되어 the impact의 구체적인 예를 제시한 것이다.

15행 He found [the damage from losing Jewish or dissident scientists {was far greater and longer lasting than the damage to offices or laboratory facilities}].

: [ ]는 앞에 접속사 that이 생략된 명사절로 found의 목적어이고, { }는 그 안의 술부이다. 여기에는 비교구문이 쓰여 두 가지 피해를 비교하고 있다.

어휘풀이
- **striking** *a* 놀라운
- **influential** *a* 영향력 있는
- **variation** *n* 변이
- **bombing raid** 폭격
- **racially** *ad* 인종적으로
- **establishment** *n* 기관, 조직
- **dismissal** *n* 해고
- **random** *a* 무작위의
- **impact** *n* 영향
- **insist on** ~을 고집하다
- **pure** *a* 순수한
- **inflict** *v* 입히다, 가하다

- permanent *a* 영구적인 　　　　• mentor *n* 멘토
- strip ~ of ... ~에게서 …을 박탈하다 　• bounce back 회복하다

113 답 ⑤

📖 자녀를 일관성 있게 지도해야 할 필요성

전문해석

부모로서 우리는 모두 자녀에게 요구하는 받아들일 수 있는 것으로 허용하는 행동에 대한 서로 다른 기준을 갖고 있다. 걸음마를 배우는 여러분의 아이가 여러분의 규칙들과 경계선을 알고 있고 여러분이 그것들을 고수하는 한, 아이는 여러분의 일관성에 의해 안정감을 갖고 안심을 할 것이다. 여러분은 이따금 "Jane이 사탕을 먹고 있어요, 나도 좀 먹으면 안 될까요?"와 같은 말을 들을 것이다. 여러분의 대답이 '안 된다'는 것이라면 주장을 굽히지 말라. 그렇게 해버리면 걸음마를 배우는 여러분의 아이는 그것을 기억하고 다음번에는 여러분이 다시 굴복할 때까지 계속해서 줄기차게 요구할 것이다. 사회적인 상황에서, 다른 사람들이 있기 때문에, 여러분의 아이에게 평상시에는 하지 않는 어떤 것을 하게 해주어야 하는 압력을 느낀다면, 계속적인 압력을 받은 결과로 허락해 주기보다는 요청을 받자마자 바로 '그래'라고 말해주는 것이 더 좋다. 예를 들어, 단 것을 먹겠다고 조르는 경우에, 그것이 특별한 대우라는 것을 아이에게 알게 하라. "좋아, 우리가 특별한 외출을 한 상황이기 때문에 엄마가 너에게 단 것을 먹게 해주겠지만, 보통 때에는 단 것을 점심식사 '후에' 먹는거야, 알지?" 상기시켜 주는 그 작은 말이 여러분의 평상시 규칙을 강화시킬 것이며 걸음마를 배우는 아이의 압력에 의해서가 아니라 여러분이 결정을 내리는 것이라는 의미를 갖게 해줄 것이다.

정답풀이

아이에게 사탕을 주는 것과 관련하여 사탕을 주지 않기로 결심했으면 그것을 반드시 지키되, 사회적인 상황으로 인해 예외적으로 사탕을 주어야 하는 일이 발생하더라도 평상시의 규칙을 상기시킴으로써 그것을 강화하는 방법으로 자녀를 지도해야 한다는 내용이다. 따라서 빈칸에는 ⑤ '일관성'이 들어가고, 이것이 아이들에게 안정감을 준다는 문맥이 되어야 한다.

① 정직성 　　　　　② 인내심
③ 근면성 　　　　　④ 정확성

구문풀이

11행 If you feel pressure [to let your child do something {he wouldn't normally do in a social situation}, because others are], / then **it** is better [**to say** *yes* as soon as you are asked], rather than as a result of continued pressure.

: If가 이끄는 부사절과 then 이하의 주절로 이루어진 문장이다. 부사절에서 목적어 pressure는 to부정사구의 수식을 받으며, 이 to부정사구 내의 something은 { }로 표시된 목적격 관계대명사가 생략된 관계절의 수식을 받는다. 주절에는 「가주어 it – 진주어(to부정사구)」 구문이 사용되었다.

어휘풀이

- toddler *n* 걸음마를 배우는 아이 　• boundary *n* 경계, 한계
- reassured *a* 안심한 　　　　• back down 포기하다, 후퇴하다
- determined *a* 완강한, 단호한 　• persevere *v* 굴하지 않고 계속하다
- reminder *n* 상기시키는 것 　　• reinforce *v* 강화하다

114 답 ④

📖 동물보다 오히려 재순환을 더 많이 하는 식물

전문해석

재순환하는 것은 큰 동물의 경우에 우리 눈에 가장 잘 띄지만, 게다가 가장 극적이고 장관이겠지만, 사실은 가장 많은 생물량이 집중된 식물에게서 훨씬 더 많이 벌어진다. 식물은 흙과 공기에서 화학물질의 형태로 영양분을 취하지만 — 모든 생물은 함께 결합된 탄소들로 만들어졌고, 이는 나중에 분해되어 이산화탄소로 배출된다 — 그럼에도 불구하고 식물 역시 다른 생명에 "의지하여 산다." 식물이 자신들의 몸을 생장하는 데 쓰는 이산화탄소는 세균과 균류의 작용에 의해 이용가능하며, 과거와 현재의 생명이라는 거대한 집합체로부터 막대한 규모로 흡수되었다. 데이지꽃이나 나무를 이루는 탄소 구성 덩이들은 여러 곳에서 공급되는데, 일주일 전에 아프리카에서 죽어 썩어가는 코끼리로부터, (지금은) 멸종한 석탄기의 식물로부터, 한 달 전에 흙으로 돌아간 북극 양귀비로부터 말이다. 바로 전날에 공중으로 배출된 분자라도, 분자 자체는 수백만 년 전에 살았던 동식물에게서 왔다.

정답풀이

빈칸에는 덩치가 큰 동물에게서 잘 보일 수 있지만 실제로는 식물에게 훨씬 더 많이 벌어지고 있는 것에 대한 내용이 들어가야 한다. 중반부의 but 이하의 문장에서 '식물이 다른 생명에 의지하여 산다'고 언급한 후, 동식물이 죽어서 이루어지는 세균과 균류의 작용으로 이산화탄소가 발생되고, 식물들이 이를 흡수하여 자신의 몸을 생장시킨다고 했다. 즉, 죽은 동식물들로부터 살아있는 식물이 생장한다는 내용을 언급하고 있으므로 빈칸에는 ④ '재순환하는 것'이 들어가는 것이 가장 적절하다.

① 파괴하는 것 　　　　② 진화하는 것
③ 다양화하는 것 　　　⑤ 조화시키는 것

구문풀이

8행 [The carbon dioxide {**that** plants take up to build their bodies}] is made available through the agency of bacteria and fungi and is sucked up massively from the enormous pool of past and present life.

: { }는 관계절로 문장의 주어인 The carbon dioxide를 수식한다. 두 개의 동사구 is made ~와 is sucked ~는 병렬구조를 이룬다.

어휘풀이

- spectacular *a* 장관의, 구경거리의 　• biomass *n* 생물량, 생물자원
- concentrate *v* 응집하다 　　• nutrient *n* 영양소 *a* 영양이 되는
- chemical *n* 화학물질 　　　• carbon *n* 탄소
- disassemble *v* 분해하다, 해체하다 • carbon dioxide 이산화탄소
- live off ~에 의지해서 살다 　• agency *n* 작용, 기능
- fungi *n* 균류(fungus의 복수형) • suck up 빨아올리다
- massively *ad* 거대하게, 엄청나게 • enormous *a* 거대한, 막대한
- decay *v* 부패하다 　　　　• extinct *a* 멸종한, 끊어진
- Arctic poppy 북극 양귀비 　• molecule *n* 분자

115 답 ①

📖 정신병학 진단에서 개인의 복지를 고려하는 적절성 기준

전문해석

적절성 기준은 정신병학 진단에 중요하다. 예를 들어, 주우울증의 진단은 '그 사람의 증세가 가정, 직장, 또는 다른 중요한 분야에서 직분을 다하는 것에 커다란 고통이나 어려움의 원인일 것'을 요구한다. 우리 모두는 어느 정도 분별 있고 어느 정도 불합리한 두려움을 가지고 있다. 두려움은 '두려운 상황에 대한 회피, 걱정 또는 고통이 한 사람의 삶에서 다음 영역, 즉 보통의 일상 활동, 직장의 (또는 학업의) 직분, 사회 활동 또는 개인적 관계 중 하나 또는 그 이상을 크게 방해할 경우에만 비정상, 다시 말해서 공포증으로 분류된다. 이런 종류의 요소를 진단에 도입하는 것은 매우 도움이 되는데, 그 이유는 그것이 유별난 것과 비정상인 것 사이의 구분점이 어디인지를 정하고, 우리가 사회적 기준 이외에 개인의 복지를 고려하는 것을 보장하기 때문이다.

정답풀이

빈칸은 어떠한 요소를 (정신병학) 진단에 도입하는 것이 개인의 '어떠한 측면'을 보장하는지에 관해 묻고 있다. 적절성 기준은 정신병학 진단에 중요하다고 하며, 주우울증 진단의 기준은 '우울증이 직분을 다하는 것에 고통이나 어려움을 느끼는 원인일 경우'이고, 두려움의 진단 기준은 '두려움이 보통의 일상 활동, 직분 활동, 사회활동, 개인적 관계 등을 방해할 경우'라고 언급하였다. 즉, 진단의 기준이 개인이 심리적 고통 없이 건강하고, 안락한 일상생활을 하는지에 관심을 두는 것이므로, 이는 개인의 복지를 고려한다고 연결할 수 있다. 따라서 빈칸에는 ① '복지'가 들어가는 것이 가장 적절하다.

② 도덕성 ③ 유전적 특질
④ 자신감 ⑤ 배경

구문풀이

12행 [Introducing these sorts of elements to diagnosis] is very helpful [**because** it defines {where the cut-off points should be between unusual and abnormal}], and [**because** it ensures {we take into account the welfare of the person as well as social norms}].

: 첫 번째 [ ]는 문장의 주어 역할을 하는 동명사구로 단수 취급하므로 단수동사 is가 왔다. 두 번째와 세 번째 [ ]는 이유를 나타내는 부사절로 and에 의해서 대등하게 연결되고 있다. 첫 번째 { }는 defines의 목적어인 의문사절이고 두 번째 { }는 ensures의 목적어인 명사절인데 접속사 that이 생략되었다.

어휘풀이

- adequacy *n* 적절성
- psychiatric diagnosis 정신병학 진단
- symptom *n* 증상
- sensible *a* 분별 있는, 현명한
- classify *v* 분류하다
- phobia *n* 공포증
- daily routine 일상 업무
- cut-off point 구분점
- norm *n* 기준
- criterion *n* 기준
- depression *n* 우울증
- distress *n* 고통
- irrational *a* 비이성[비논리]적인
- abnormal *a* 비정상적인
- avoidance *n* 회피
- occupational *a* 직업의
- take into account ~을 고려하다

116 답 ①

📖 칭찬을 시간대의 관점에서 고려하기

전문해석

칭찬을 시간대의 관점에서 고려하는 것은 유용하다. 우리가 어떤 소년을 '격려할' 때, 우리의 초점은 미래에 있는데, 우리는 그가 후에 성공하기 위해 현재의 어떤 어려움이라도 극복하도록 그를 설득하려고 한다. 따라서 우리는 믿음, 희망, 그리고 자신감을 만들어주고 그에게 마음을 주는 것이다. 우리가 그와 함께 있는 것과 그의 성취를 분명히 '즐길' 때, 우리는 현재의 그의 사람됨에 대한 우리의 행복과 즐거움을 표시한다. 우리가 그의 행동, 세상에 대한 그의 견해, 배움에 대한 그의 접근방식, 그리고 그의 감정을 '지지할' 때, 우리는 그의 과거에 의해 만들어진 그의 그러한 일부를 받아들이고 있는 것이다. 소년들이 과거의 행동과 경험이 어려웠을지라도 (지금) 그것들이 편안하다면, 그들은 미래를 낙관적으로 더 잘 볼 수 있을 것이다. 부모나 다른 중요한 사람들이 소년이 자신의 과거에 대해 부끄러워하거나 죄책감을 느끼도록 만들거나, 다시 초점을 맞추어 다시 출발하고자 하는 어떤 시도로 그것을 완전히 없애버리려고 하는 것은 도움이 되지 않는다.

정답풀이

빈칸에는 칭찬할 때의 고려점이 무엇인지에 대한 내용이 들어가야 한다. 이어지는 내용에서 칭찬의 일종인 '격려'의 초점은 '현재를 극복하고, 미래에 대한 희망을 주는 것'이고, 그를 '지지'할 때의 초점은 '과거를 인정해 미래를 더 낙관적으로 볼 수 있게 하는 것'이라고 했으므로, 빈칸에는 ① '시간대'가 들어가는 것이 가장 적절하다.

② 간접적인 경고 ③ 행동 교정
④ 성격 차이 ⑤ 목표 추구

구문풀이

15행 **It** is not helpful for parents or significant others [**to make** a boy feel either ashamed of or guilty about his past] or [**to wipe** it out in any attempt to refocus and start again].

: It이 가주어이고 or로 연결된 두 개의 to부정사구 [ ]가 진주어이며, for parents or significant others는 to부정사의 의미상의 주어이다. 첫 번째 [ ]에는 「make+목적어+목적격보어(~가 …하도록 하다)」 구문과 「either A or B」 구문이 쓰였다.

어휘풀이

- in terms of ~의 관점에서
- convince *v* 설득하다
- achievement *n* 성취
- endorse *v* (사람을) 지지하다
- optimistically *ad* 낙관적으로
- wipe out 완전히 없애다
- focus *n* 초점
- confidence *n* 자신감
- indicate *v* 표시하다
- fashion *v* 만들다, 형성하다
- significant *a* 중요한

117 답 ①

📖 현대 기업이 아이들을 대하는 방식

전문해석

"한 사회가 아이들을 다루는 방법보다 사회의 정신에 대해 더 날카롭게 드러내는 것은 없다."라는 Nelson Mandela의 분별력 있는 의견은, 거대 기업이 이윤을 내기 위해 고안된 관행으로 무자비하게 어린 시절을 갈취하는 때에, 우리 사회의 정신에 대한 우려를 일으킨다. 기업의 이기적인 시각으로부터 어린이들은 이용해야 할 기회, 예를 들어 패스트푸드나 표준화된 수험을 위한 시장과 같은 기회에 지나지 않는다. 그리고 기업이 아이들과 부모의 삶에서 지배적인 힘이 되었기 때문에, 도덕적으로 근시안적인 시각과 그것이 고취시키는 관행들이 우리가, 사회로서, 어린 시절에 관하여 생각하고 행동하는 것을 점점 더 규정한다. 아이들을 돌보고, 양육하고, 보호하고, 후원하며 어린 시절의 가치를 명백히 하고자 하는 우리의 사회적 열망은 결국 아이들의 경제적 가치를 극대화하고자 고안된 전략들에 의해 밀려나게 된다.

정답풀이

빈칸 이하의 문장에서 기업은 이기적인 시각에서 아이들을 패스트푸드 시장이나 표준화된 수험 시장에서의 기회로 여긴다고 언급하였고, 같은 맥락의 내용들이 이어지다가 글의 마지막 부분에서 아이들을 양육하고 보호하고자 하는 우리의 사회적 열망이 결국 아이들의 경제적 가치를 극대화하려고 만들어진 전략들에 의해 밀려난다고 정리하고 있다. 따라서 빈칸에는 ① '이윤을 내기'가 들어가는 것이 가장 적절하다.

② 도덕을 가르치기 ③ 정보를 공유하기
④ 가난을 극복하기 ⑤ 지식을 향상시키기

구문풀이

1행 Nelson Mandela's sage observation [**that** "there can be no keener revelation of a society's soul than the way {in which it treats its children,"}] invites concern about our own society's soul / [**as** big business ruthlessly squeezes childhood into practices {designed to yield profits}].

: 주절과 부사절로 이루어진 문장이다. 주절에서 핵심 주어인 observation은 동격절인 첫 번째 [ ]의 수식을 받고 있으며, 동사는 이에 수 일치하여 단수동사 invites가 쓰였다. 두 번째 [ ]는 '~할 때'라는 의미의 시간 부사절이며 그 안의 { }는 앞의 practices를 수식하는 과거분사구이다.

어휘풀이

- sage *a* 분별력 있는, 현명한
- observation *n* (관찰에 의한) 의견

- keen *a* 날카로운
- invite *v* 일으키다, 야기하다
- squeeze *v* 갈취하다
- self-interested *a* 이기적인
- corporation *n* 기업
- dominant *a* 지배적인
- define *v* 규정하다, 정의하다
- manifest *v* 명백히 하다
- end up -ing 결국 ~하게 되다
- devise *v* 고안하다

- revelation *n* 드러내는 것, 폭로
- ruthlessly *ad* 무자비하게
- practice *n* 관행
- perspective *n* 시각
- exploit *v* 이용하다
- inspire *v* 고취시키다
- aspiration *n* 열망
- nurture *v* 양육하다
- push aside 옆으로 옮기다
- maximize *v* 극대화하다

13 빈칸 추론(2) - 유형 연습 문제(1) · 본문 pp.090~095

| 118 ④ | 119 ⑤ | 120 ② | 121 ④ | 122 ② |
| 123 ④ | 124 ② | 125 ③ | 126 ⑤ | |

118 답 ④

📖📖 교통 사용자들이 교통을 바라보는 개인 중심적 태도

전문해석

도시에서 차를 몰거나 걸어 다니거나 판독기에 교통 카드를 통과시키는 모든 사람은 현관문을 나서는 순간부터 자신을 교통 전문가로 여긴다. 그리고 그 사람이 거리를 바라보는 방식은 그 사람이 돌아디니는 방식과 매우 긴밀하게 맞아떨어진다. 그것이 바로 우리가 선의와 시민 의식을 가진 매우 많은 사람이 서로를 지나치며 언쟁하는 것을 보게 되는 이유이다. 학교 강당에서, 그리고 도서관과 교회의 뒷방에서 열리는 지역 회의에서, 전국의 지역 주민들이 모여 도시의 거리를 바꿀 교통 제안에 대해 흔히 논쟁적인 토론을 벌인다. 그리고 모든 정치와 마찬가지로, 모든 교통은 지역적이고 지극히 개인적이다. 수만 명의 이동 속도를 높일 수 있는 교통 프로젝트는 몇 개의 주차 공간 상실에 대한 반대나 프로젝트가 효과가 없을 것이라는 단순한 두려움에 의해 중단될 수 있다. 그것은 데이터, 교통 공학 또는 계획상의 난제가 아니다. 거리에 대한 대중 토론은 보통 변화가 개인의 통근, 주차 능력, 안전한 것과 안전하지 않은 것에 대한 믿음, 또는 지역 사업체의 순익에 어떤 영향을 미칠지에 대한 감정적인 추정에 뿌리를 두고 있다.

119 답 ⑤

📖📖 시간에 대한 우리의 인식과 책임 문제

전문해석

우리는 우리의 의식을 현재, 과거, 미래로 분리하는 것이 허구이며 또한 이상하게도 자기 지시적인 틀이라는 것을 이해하는데, 여러분의 현재는 여러분 어머니의 미래의 일부였고, 여러분의 아이의 과거는 여러분의 현재의 일부일 것이라는 것이다. 시간에 대한 우리의 의식을 이러한 전통적인 방식으로 구조화하는 것에는 일반적으로, 잘못된 것이 없으며 그것은 흔히 충분히 효과적이다. 그러나 기후 변화의 경우에는, 시간을 과거, 현재, 미래로 분명하게 구분하는 것은 심하게 사실을 오도해 왔고 가장 중요하게는, 지금 살아 있는 우리들의 책임 범위를 시야로부터 숨겨왔다. 시간에 대한 우리의 의식을 좁히는 것은 사실 우리의 삶이 깊게 뒤얽혀 있는 과거와 미래의 발전에 대한 책임으로부터 우리를 분리시키는 길을 닦는다. 기후의 경우에는, 우리가 사실을 직면하면서도 우리의 책임을 부인하는 것이 문제가 아니다. 문제는 시간

을 나눔으로써 현실이 시야에서 흐릿해져서 과거와 미래의 책임에 관한 질문이 자연스럽게 생기지 않는 것이다.

정답풀이

시간을 분리하여 인식하는 것과 기후 변화에 대한 책임 문제에 관해 언급한 글로, 우리가 시간에 대한 의식을 현재, 과거, 미래로 분리하거나 자기 생각대로 의식을 구조화하는 것은 일반적으로 잘못된 것이 없지만 기후 변화의 경우에는 시간을 현재, 과거, 미래로 나누는 것이 우리의 책임 범위를 숨겨왔다고 말하고 있다. 빈칸 앞에는 부정어 not이 있으므로 빈칸에는 이와 반대되는 내용이 들어가야 한다. 따라서 빈칸에는 ⑤ '우리가 사실을 직면하면서도 우리의 책임을 부인하는'이 들어가는 것이 가장 적절하다.
① 모든 우리의 노력이 효과적으로 밝혀지고 따라서 장려되는
② 충분한 과학적 증거가 우리에게 제공되어 온
③ 미래의 우려가 현재의 필요보다 더 시급한
④ 우리의 조상들이 다른 시간적 틀을 유지한

구문풀이

1행 We understand [that {the segregation of our consciousness into present, past, and future} is both a fiction and an oddly self-referential framework]; / [your present was part of your mother's future], and [your children's past will be in part your present].

: [ ]로 표시한 that절은 동사 understand의 목적절이며, 이 that절에서는 명사구인 { } 부분이 주어, is가 동사이다. 세미콜론(;) 이하의 문장에는 두 개의 절 [ ] 부분이 and로 연결되어 있다.

12행 [The narrowing of our consciousness of time] smooths the way to divorcing ourselves from responsibility for developments in the past and the future [with which our lives are in fact deeply intertwined].

: 첫 번째 [ ]가 주어, smooths가 동사이다. 두 번째 [ ]는 '전치사+관계대명사' 형태의 관계절로 바로 앞의 명사구 the past and the future를 수식한다.

어휘풀이

- consciousness *n* 의식, 인식
- oddly *ad* 이상하게
- framework *n* 틀
- conventional *a* 전통적인
- desperately *ad* 심하게, 극도로
- misleading *a* (사실을) 오도[호도]하는
- extent *n* 범위
- divorce *v* 단절시키다, 분리하다

- fiction *n* 허구
- self-referential *a* 자기 지시적인
- structure *v* 구조화하다
- division *n* 구분, 분할
- smooth *v* 평탄하게 하다
- partition *v* 나누다, 분할하다

120 답 ②

📖📖 과학 발전과 대비되는 역사적 통찰의 발전

전문해석

정확성과 확정성은 모든 의미 있는 과학 토론을 위해 없어서는 안 될 필요조건이고, 과학에서의 발전은 상당 부분 점점 더 높은 정확성을 달성하는 진행 중인 과정이다. 그러나 역사적 진술은 진술의 증식을 중요시하는데, 이는 한 가지 진술의 정제가 아니라 더 다양한 일련의 진술의 생성을 중요시하는 것이다. 역사적 통찰은 이전에 선택한 것들을 지속적으로 '좁혀 가는' 것의 문제, 즉 진리에 대한 근접함의 문제가 아니라, 반대로 가능한 관점들의 '폭발적 증가'이다. 따라서 그것은 이전의 진술들에서 무엇이 옳고 그른지에 대한 주의 깊은 분석에 의해 진리를 획득하는 것이 아니라, 새롭고 대안적인 진술의 생성에 의해 확정성과 정확성에 대한 이전의 환상의 정체를 밝혀내는 것을 목표로 한다. 그리고 이러한 관점에서 볼 때, 역사적 통찰의 발전은 과학에서처럼 진리에 점점 더 많이 근접함보다는, 점점 더 큰 혼란을 만들어 내는 과

정, 즉 이미 획득된 것으로 보이는 확실성과 정확성에 대한 지속적인 의문 제기로 외부인에게 정말로 여겨질 수도 있다.

정답풀이

정확성과 확정성이 중요한 과학과 달리 역사적 진술에서는 한 가지 진술을 정제하는 것이 아니라 더 다양한 일련의 진술을 생성하는 것이 중요하다는 내용이다. 역사적 통찰은 진리에의 근접함이 아니라 가능한 관점들의 '폭발적 증가'로, 이전에 확실하다고 여겨졌던 것의 정체를 드러내는 것을 목표로 한다는 점에서 외부인에게 역사적 통찰의 발전은 ② '이미 획득된 것으로 보이는 확실성과 정확성'에 지속적으로 의문을 제기하는 것으로 보일 수 있다고 할 수 있다.
① 역사적 진술을 평가하는 기준
③ 어떤 사건에 대한 대안적 해석의 가능성
④ 역사 저술에서 다수의 관점의 공존
⑤ 수집된 역사적 증거의 정확성과 신뢰성

구문풀이

16행 And from this perspective, the development of historical insight may indeed be **regarded** by the outsider [**as** {a process of creating ever more confusion}, {a continuous questioning of certainty and precision (seemingly achieved already)}], **rather than**, [as in the sciences, an ever greater approximation to the truth].

: the development of historical insight가 주어, may be regarded가 동사이며, 「regard A as B(A를 B로 여기다)」 구문이 수동태로 쓰였다. 두 개의 [ ]는 「A rather than B(B라기보다는 A)」 구문의 A와 B에 해당한다. 첫 번째 [ ]에서 두 개의 { }는 동격 관계를 이루며, ( )는 certainty and precision을 수식하는 과거분사구이다.

어휘풀이

- precision *n* 정확성
- requirement *n* 필요조건
- to a large extent 상당한 정도로
- representation *n* 진술, 설명
- refinement *n* 정제, 개선
- on the contrary 반대로
- unmask *v* ~의 정체를 밝혀내다
- alternative *a* 대안적인
- confusion *n* 혼란
- seemingly *ad* 겉보기에
- determinacy *n* 확정성, 결정성
- debate *n* 토론, 논쟁
- ongoing *a* 진행 중인, 지속적인
- put a premium on ~을 중요시하다
- approximation *n* 근접, 근사
- explosion *n* 폭발적 증가
- illusion *n* 환상
- analysis *n* 분석
- question *v* ~에 대해 의문을 제기하다

121 답 ④

📖 창의력에 도움을 주는 비유의 사용

전문해석

일반적으로, 정신의 연상 능력을 더 잘 활용하는 것은 창의적인 과정에 매우 도움이 될 수 있다. 예를 들어, 16세기와 17세기에 지구가 움직이지 않는다는 것을 증명하기 위해 사람들이 사용한 한 가지 주장은 탑에서 떨어진 돌이 그 기둥 아래에 떨어진다는 것이었다. 그들은 지구가 움직인다면 그것이 다른 곳에 떨어져야 한다고 주장했다. 습관적으로 비유의 관점에서 생각했던 갈릴레오는 그의 마음속에서 지구를 일종의 우주 공간을 항해하는 배로 여겼다. 지구의 움직임에 대한 의심을 표시한 사람들에게 그가 설명했듯이, 움직이는 배의 돛대에서 떨어진 돌은 여전히 그 아래에 떨어진다. 이러한 비유는 Isaac Newton이 정원의 나무에서 떨어지는 사과와 우주 공간에서 떨어지는 달을 비교한 것처럼 엄밀하고 논리적일 수 있다. 또는 재즈 음악가 John Coltrane이 자신의 작품을 그가 짓고 있는 소리의 대성당으로 생각한 것처럼 그것들은 다소 느슨하고 비이성적일 수도 있다. 어쨌든, 비유와 은유의 관점으로 생각하는 것은 당신의 아이디어를 확장할 수 있다.

정답풀이

지구의 움직임(공전)을 설명하기 위해서 지구를 항해하는 배로 생각한 것이나, 나무에서 떨어지는 사과와 우주 공간에서 떨어지는 달을 연결한 것은 정신의 연상 작용을 사용한 예에 해당한다. 따라서 빈칸에 들어갈 말로 가장 적절한 것은 ④ '정신의 연상 능력을 더 잘 활용하는 것'이다.
① 의심하는 사람들에게 그들의 비이성적인 주장을 납득시키는 것
② 보통의 언어로 논란의 여지가 없는 아이디어를 설명하는 것
③ 느슨한 비유와 은유를 엄밀한 논리로 발전시키는 것
⑤ 위대한 예술가들뿐 아니라 과학계의 훌륭한 인물들을 인용하는 것

구문풀이

2행 For instance, an argument [people used {in the sixteenth and seventeenth centuries} to prove {that Earth does not move}] was to say [that a rock {dropped from a tower} lands at its base].

: [ ]는 문장의 주어인 an argument를 수식하는 관계절로, 앞에 목적격 관계대명사 that[which]이 생략되었다. 여기서 첫 번째 { }는 삽입구이고, 두 번째 { }는 to prove의 목적어인 명사절이다. 두 번째 [ ]는 to say의 목적절이며, 그 안의 { }는 a rock을 수식하는 과거분사구이다.

어휘풀이

- extremely *ad* 매우, 극도로
- habitually *ad* 습관적으로
- comparison *n* 비교, 비유
- composition *n* 작곡
- in any event 어쨌든, 아무튼
- expand *v* 확대하다
- uncontroversial *a* 논란의 여지가 없는
- take advantage of ~을 활용[이용]하다
- associative *a* 연상의, 연상 작용의
- argument *n* 주장, 논쟁
- in terms of ~의 관점에서
- irrational *a* 비이성적인, 비합리적인
- cathedral *n* 대성당
- metaphor *n* 은유
- convince *v* 설득하다

122 답 ②

📖 귀납 추리가 틀리기 쉽다는 것에 관한 사례

전문해석

미래가 과거와 흡사할 것이라고 잘못 가정하는 실제 사례는 항생제의 도래와 더불어 발견될 수 있는데, 그것은 1940년대 후반 페니실린의 생산과 함께 시작하였다. 페니실린이 치료 목적으로 인간에 처음 사용되었을 때, 박테리아가 일으키는 일부 전염성 질병에 걸린 환자들에 대한 페니실린 투여가 그 박테리아를 죽이는 데 일률적으로 효능이 있음이 관찰되었다. 혹자는 일반 원칙을, 즉 페니실린이 그 박테리아를 죽인다는 결론을 내리고 싶은 마음이 생길 수도 있을 것이다. 사실, 이것은 실제적인 진실로 받아들여졌고, 페니실린은 의학계에 의해 그 질병들에 대한 결정적인 치료제로 등재되었다. 하지만 널리 퍼진 페니실린 사용의 선택압을 고려할 때, 그 박테리아의 일부 변종이 진화 과정을 통해 페니실린에 대한 저항력을 얻었다. 그래서 예전에는 그 박테리아의 100%가 기본적으로 페니실린에 민감하다고 관찰되었지만, 그런 경우가 현재에는 해당하지 않는 것인데, 앞날을 예측할 수 있는 것에서의 귀납 추리가 틀리기 쉽다는 것에 관한 명확한 사례가 된다.

정답풀이

페니실린이 박테리아가 일으키는 일부 전염성 질병에 투여되었을 때 그 박테리아를 죽이는 데 효능이 있다는 것이 관찰되자 의학계에서 그것의 효과를 100% 인정했지만, 선택압에 의해 변종이 생겨나면서 그 효과는 점차 사라지게 되었다는 내용이다. 결국 페니실린의 약효가 미래에도 통할 것이라고 잘못 가정한 귀납 추리의 오류를 설명하는 내용이므로, 빈칸에 들어갈 말로 가장 적절한 것은 ② '미래가 과거와 흡사할 것'이다.
① 만병통치약은 없을 것

③ 진화는 순식간에 일어날 수 있을 것
④ 발견이 우연히 이루어질 수 있을 것
⑤ 오늘은 어제와 다를 것

구문풀이

4행 When penicillin was first used therapeutically in humans, / **it** was observed [**that** the administration of penicillin in <u>patients</u> {infected with <u>some contagious diseases</u> (caused by bacteria)} <u>was</u> uniformly efficacious in killing off the bacteria].

: 부사절(When절)과 주절로 이루어진 문장이다. 주절에서 it은 가주어이고 [ ]가 진주어이다. 이 진주어 that절에서 핵심 주어는 administration이고 동사는 was이다. { }는 patients를 수식하는 분사구이고, ( )는 some contagious diseases를 수식하는 분사구이다.

어휘풀이

- practical *a* 실제적인
- antibiotics *n* 항생제
- infect *v* (병에) 걸리게 하다, 감염시키다
- uniformly *ad* 일률적으로, 동일하게
- selective pressure <생물학> 선택압
- strain *n* 변종
- sensitive *a* 민감한
- advent *n* 도래, 출현
- administration *n* 투여, 투약
- contagious *a* 전염성의
- definitive *a* 결정적인, 최후의
- widespread *a* 널리 퍼진
- resistance *n* 저항(력)
- induction *n* 귀납 추리

123 답 ④

📖 얼굴 표정에 의해 만들어질 수 있는 감정

전문해석

얼굴 표정과 느껴지는 감정 사이의 관계를 고려해 보라. 우리는 자주 우리가 감정을 느끼고 그다음 어울리는 표정이 우리의 얼굴 도처에 재생된다고 추정한다. 실제로는 그 관계의 방향이 반대로도 진행될 수 있음을 보여주는 증거가 있다. 미소를 짓는 것이 일부 사람들로 하여금 더 행복함을 느끼게 하고 기억으로부터 더 많은 긍정적인 사건들을 찾아내는 쪽으로 기울어지게 하는 것으로 나타났다. 한 연구는 참가자들이 만화를 보는 동안 그들의 이 사이에 펜을 물고 있는 것을 수반하였는데, 이는 그들이 웃는 얼굴을 모방하도록 하였다. 이 미소 짓는 자세로 얼굴 표정을 한 사람들은 펜이 입술 사이에 유지된 자세를 취했던(그것은 미소를 방해했다) 다른 참가자들보다 그 만화를 더 재미있다고 평가했다. 미용을 목적으로 보톡스를 사용하는 것이 사람들의 감정 경험을 방해할 수 있다는 증거까지도 있는데, 아마도 그들이 얼굴을 당겨서 적절한 얼굴 표정을 만들 수 없고, 이것이 결국 <u>얼굴로부터 뇌로의 피드백 결핍</u>을 초래하기 때문일 수 있다.

정답풀이

사람들의 흔한 생각과는 반대로, 표정을 지은 후 감정을 느끼는 경우도 있을 수 있다고 하며, 웃는 얼굴을 하게 한 피실험자가 웃지 못하게 한 피실험자보다 더 긍정적인 평가를 했다는 실험 결과를 언급하고 있다. 이를 보톡스 사용과 연결하여, 얼굴 표정을 지을 수 없는 것이 초래하는 결과를 빈칸에서 묻고 있으므로, 빈칸에 들어갈 말로 가장 적절한 것은 ④ '얼굴로부터 뇌로의 피드백 결핍'이다. 이때, 얼굴은 얼굴 표정을 의미하고, 뇌는 감정을 느끼게 하는 주체로 볼 수 있으므로 감정을 의미한다고 볼 수 있다.
① 신체 언어의 발달
② 다양한 감정들 사이의 혼란
③ 몸 전체의 일시적인 마비
⑤ 뇌에서 오는 신호의 잘못된 전달

구문풀이

11행 [Those {with their face in this smiling position}] <u>rated</u> the cartoons as funnier than <u>other participants</u> [who posed **with** the

pen **held** between their lips (which prevents smiling)].

: 첫 번째 [ ]가 주어, rated가 동사이다. 핵심 주어인 Those는 { }로 표시한 전치사구의 수식을 받아 '~하는 사람들'의 의미를 나타내고 있다. 이 문장은 전체적으로 Those와 other participants를 비교하고 있으며, 관계절인 두 번째 [ ]가 other participants를 수식하고 있다. 여기에는 「with+명사+분사」 구문이 쓰였는데 명사와 분사의 의미 관계가 수동이므로 과거분사가 쓰여 '~가 …이 된 채로'의 의미를 나타낸다.

어휘풀이

- assume *v* 추정하다
- pull *v* (표정을) 짓다
- retrieve *v* 되찾아오다
- participant *n* 참가자
- rate *v* 평가하다
- Botox *n* 보톡스(근육 수축 주사제)
- presumably *ad* 아마도
- paralysis *n* 마비
- appropriate *a* 어울리는, 적절한
- biased *a* 편향된
- pertinent *a* 관련 있는
- imitate *v* 모방하다
- cosmetic *a* 미용의
- interfere with ~을 방해하다
- temporary *a* 일시적인

124 답 ②

📖 유전적 한계를 설정하고 그것에 맞추어 사는 것의 잘못

전문해석

우리 자신과 다른 사람들이 우리의 유전자에 의해 울타리 안에 갇혀있는 죄수라고 상상하는 것은 잘못된 것이다. 과학은 우리가 어떤 유전적 한계를 가지고 있든지 간에, 이 한계들의 특정한 경계가 우리에게 알려져 있지 않다는 것을 그 어느 때보다도 보다 분명하게 지금 우리에게 보여주고 있다. 따라서, 우리가 이러한 감옥의 벽을 안다고 가정하고 그에 맞춰 우리의 삶을 항해하는 것은 이치에 맞지 않다. 물론, 유전적인 유산은 지적 잠재력의 큰 요소이다. 사람들이 아무리 열심히 노력하건 혹은 아무리 많은 기회를 가지건 간에 결코 노벨상을 탈 만한 공적을 이루지 못할 두뇌를 실제로 가지고 태어난다는 것은 확실하다. 하지만 누가 어떤 범주에 속하는지 우리가 어떻게 정확히 알 수 있을까? 우리가 할 수 있는 전부는 현재의 능력을 측정하는 것이다. 우리는 있었을지도 모르는 지능이나 있을 수도 있는 지능을 결정할 수 없다. 따라서, 우리는 우리의 지능에 대해 알려진 유전적 한계라는 거짓말이 개인이나 집단, 또는 종으로서의 우리를 결코 억압하도록 해서는 안 된다.

정답풀이

지능에 대한 알려진 유전적 한계를 거짓말이라고 표현하며 이것이 우리를 억압하게 해서는 안 된다고 하고 있다. 따라서 사람들이 잘못 상상하고 있는 내용이 들어가야 하는 빈칸에는 유전자로 우리 능력에 한계를 둔다는 맥락이 와야 하므로, ② '우리의 유전자에 의해 울타리 안에 갇혀있는 죄수'가 들어가는 것이 가장 적절하다.
① 먹이 사슬에 있는 최상위 소비자
③ 다른 종들과의 서툰 협력자
④ 음식 사용에 있어서 비능률의 표본
⑤ 무한한 진화 능력을 가진 생물

구문풀이

9행 Sure, people really are born with <u>brains</u> [**that** will never produce Nobel Prize-winning achievements **no matter** {**how** hard they work} or {**how** many opportunities they have}].

: [ ]는 관계절로 brains를 수식한다. 이 관계절 내에는 「no matter+의문사」 형태로 양보의 뜻을 나타내는 표현이 쓰였으며, 여기서는 no matter 이하에 의문사 how로 시작하는 두 개의 절 { }이 연결되어 있다.

어휘풀이

- limitation *n* 한계
- pretend *v* 가정하다
- accordingly *ad* 그에 맞춰
- boundary *n* 경계(선)
- navigate *v* 항해하다, (길을) 찾다
- inheritance *n* 유산

- potential *n* 잠재력
- hold back ~을 억압하다[저지하다]
- infinite *a* 무한한
- fall into ~에 속하다
- specimen *n* 견본, 표본

125 답 ③

📖 다른 사람의 입장이 되어봄으로써 그들과 공감하기

전문해석
사람들은 자신이 되기를 원하는 사람처럼 행동함으로써 새로운 의미의 정체성을 만들어 낼 수 있다. 동일한 원리는 또한 사람들에게 세상이 다른 사람들에게 어떻게 보이는지 알게 함으로써 그들의 마음을 한 데 모으는 데 도움이 될 수 있다. 예를 들어, 한 연구에서 한 집단의 학생들에게 최근에 교통사고를 당해 몸이 마비되어 이제는 휠체어를 타게 된 것처럼 행동하라고 요청했다. 학생들은 휠체어를 타고 미리 정해진 길을 다니면서 20분을 보냈으며 그래서 몇 개의 엘리베이터, 경사로, 문을 이용하고 다녀야만 했다. 다른 한 집단의 학생들은 휠체어 뒤에서 걸어 다니면서 일어나는 모든 일을 목격하였다. 그런 다음에 두 집단 모두는, 예를 들어, 새로운 재활 센터에 공적 자금이 투입되어야 하는지를 포함하는, 장애인과 관련된 문제에 대한 그들의 입장에 대해서 질문받았다. 집단들 사이에 놀랄 만한 차이가 나타났는데, 휠체어를 타고 시간을 보낸 사람들이 장애인들에 대해 훨씬 더 큰 공감을 보여주었다.

정답풀이
빈칸 앞 문장은 주제문으로 사람들은 자신이 되기를 원하는 사람처럼 행동함으로써 새로운 의미의 정체성을 만들어 낸다고 했고, 빈칸 이하에서는 휠체어를 타고 장애인이 되어본 경험을 한 학생들이 장애인 문제에 대해 더 많이 공감하게 되었다는 실험이 소개되고 있다. 이 두 내용 사이에 들어가는 빈칸 문장은 주제와 관련하여 사람들의 마음을 모으는 방법에 대한 것으로, 내용상 다른 사람의 입장이 되어보는 것에 대한 내용이 들어가야 함을 알 수 있다. 따라서 빈칸에는 ③ '세상이 다른 사람들에게 어떻게 보이는지 알게'가 들어가는 것이 가장 적절하다.
① 동등한 기회를 갖게
② 자원봉사 활동을 하는 날을 계획하게
④ 어떤 멋진 야외 활동 계획을 세우게
⑤ 문화적 차이를 고려하게

구문풀이
16행 A remarkable difference emerged between the groups, [**with those** {who had spent time in a wheelchair} **showing** far greater empathy for the disabled].

: 「with+목적어+분사」 구문이 사용된 문장으로, 관계절인 { }의 수식을 받는 those와 show가 능동의 관계이므로 현재분사 showing이 쓰였다. 「the+형용사」는 '~한 사람들'이라는 뜻을 나타낸다.

어휘풀이
- identity *n* 정체성
- confined to ~에 제한된[갇힌]
- navigate *v* (길을) 찾아다니다
- ramp *n* 경사면
- the disabled 장애인
- remarkable *a* 놀랄 만한
- empathy *n* 공감, 감정이입
- paralyze *v* 마비시키다
- prespecified *a* 미리 정해진
- lift *n* 엘리베이터, 승강기
- witness *v* 목격하다
- rehabilitation *n* 재활
- emerge *v* 나타나다

126 답 ⑤

📖 잡지 구독료 인상 또는 광고비 인상의 효과

전문해석
상업 잡지에 있어서 판매 부수와 광고가 그것들이 인쇄이든 디지털이든, 대부분의 수입원을 차지한다는 것은 명백하다. 독자들로부터의 구독료와 광고 수입 모두에 의존하는 매체로서, 잡지는 그 두 가지 주요 수입원들 사이의 상호의존 관계를 반드시 인식해야 한다. 제작과 홍보 둘 다에 수반되는 비용의 증가에 직면할 때, 출판사는 더 높아진 비용을 상쇄하기 위해서 구독료를 올리려는 충동을 느끼게 된다. 인상된 구독료는 결국 판매 부수를 감소시키고, 따라서 광고 수입을 낮추며, 구독료 상승으로부터의 이익을 상쇄하는 결과를 낳는다. 더 높은 제작비와 홍보비에 대한 동일한 문제를 해결하고자 하는 시도로 광고비를 올리는 것에서 해결책을 찾는 출판사에서 같은 종류의 시나리오가 발생한다. 많은 독자들이 비상업적인 내용뿐만 아니라, 광고, 특히 가격이나 다른 특정한 정보를 제공하는 것들을 가치 있게 평가하기 때문에, 광고료의 인상으로 발생하는 광고의 감소는 판매 부수를 줄이게 되고, 또 다시 더 비싼 광고료로부터 오는 이익을 상쇄한다.

정답풀이
상업 잡지에 있어 주요 수입원인 구독료와 광고 수입 사이의 의존 관계에 대한 글로, 제작비와 홍보비가 증가할 경우, 이를 상쇄하기 위해 구독료를 인상하는데, 이는 판매 부수 감소로 이어지고, 이는 다시 광고 수입을 낮춤으로써 구독료 상승의 효과가 없어지게 한다. 이어지는 내용에서 같은 목적으로 '광고료를 인상'할 때 벌어지는 결과에 대해 언급하고 있는데, 많은 독자들이 몇몇 광고들을 가치 있게 평가하는 특징으로 인해, 광고료 인상으로 광고가 감소되면 판매 부수가 줄게 되므로, 결과적으로 '광고료 상승의 효과가 없다'는 내용으로 전개되는 것이 적절하다. 따라서 빈칸에는 ⑤ '더 비싼 광고료로부터 오는 이익을 상쇄한다'가 들어가야 한다.
① 출판사로 하여금 다른 해법을 찾도록 촉진한다
② 정교하게 균형을 맞춘 수익-비용 분석을 유도한다
③ 가능한 곳마다 생산 비용 축소를 필요로 한다
④ 독자와 출판사 사이의 긴장을 만든다

구문풀이
17행 Because many members of the audience may value **advertisements**, [especially **those** {with pricing and other specific information}], as well as noncommercial content, / a reduction in advertising [resulting from higher prices for advertisements] reduces circulation, [again canceling out the gains from more expensive advertising].

: 부사절(Because절)과 주절로 이루어진 문장이다. 부사절의 those는 반복되는 명사 advertisements를 대신하며, 첫 번째 [ ]는 앞서 언급된 advertisements를 부연 설명한다. 전치사구인 { }는 those를 수식한다. 주절의 핵심 주어인 a reduction in advertising은 두 번째 [ ]로 표시한 현재분사구의 수식을 받으며, 주절의 동사는 reduces이다. 세 번째 [ ]는 분사구문으로 앞 절의 내용에 대한 부연 설명을 제시한다.

어휘풀이
- circulation *n* 판매 부수, 유통
- revenue *n* 수입, 수익
- dependent *a* 의존하는
- entail *v* 수반하다
- hike *v* (가격 등을) 기습적으로 올리다
- resolve *v* 해결하다
- induce *v* 유발하다, 일으키다
- analysis *n* 분석
- account for ~을 차지하다
- commercial *a* 상업적인
- subscription *n* 구독
- promotion *n* 홍보
- offset *v* 상쇄하다
- prompt *v* 자극하다, 재촉하다
- delicately *ad* 조심스럽게, 신중하게
- cancel out ~을 상쇄하다

13 빈칸 추론(2) - 유형 연습 문제(2)				본문 pp.096~099
127 ③	128 ①	129 ②	130 ①	131 ①
132 ④	133 ①	134 ⑤		

127 답 ③

📖 초기 부족 집단에서 쫓겨나지 않고 남아 있어야 할 필요성

전문해석

우리 조상들의 마음 맨 앞에 있는 것은 '오늘 무엇을 하든 잡아먹히지 말라'였다. 무엇보다도 제일 중요한 것은 끝내 그 구역의 사자와 호랑이의 메뉴에 오르게 되지 않는 것이었다. 하지만 두 번째는 부족 내에 남아있는 것이었다. 초기 부족들은 기여하지 않거나, 탐욕스럽거나 게으른 사람들을 특히 용서하지 않았는데, 부족의 생존을 위해 그럴 형편이 못 되었다. 이런 구성원들은 집단에서 쫓겨났는데, 이빨이 없고, 발톱이 없고, 털이 없는 포유동물에게, 이것은 확실한 죽음을 의미했다. 이로 인한 결과는 우리 조상들 중 살아남은 사람들은 조금도 방심하지 않는 자들이었다는 것이다. 그들은 조심스러웠고 사자와 호랑이를 경계했다. 또한, 그들은 부족 내에서 조심스러웠고, 자신들이 <u>자신의 임무를 다하지 못하고 있다는</u> 신호들에 대해 조금도 방심하지 않았다. 느긋하고, 안일하고, 조금은 태평하고, 다른 사람들이 자신들에 대해 어떻게 생각하는지 신경 쓰지 않는 경향이 있는 사람들은 자신들의 유전자를 성공적으로 물려줄 수 있을 만큼 충분히 오랫동안 머물지 못하는 경향이 있었다.

정답풀이

빈칸 앞에서는 원시 부족들이 기여하지 않거나 탐욕스럽거나 게으른 사람들을 쫓아냈고 살아남은 자들은 조금도 방심하지 않는 자들이었다고 언급한 후, 빈칸 뒤에서는 태평하고 타인이 자신을 어떻게 생각하는지 신경 쓰지 않는 사람들은 오래 머물지 못했다고 했다. 빈칸에는 부족 내에서 조심스러웠던 사람들이 경계하고 신경 썼던 부분에 대한 내용이 들어가야 하므로, ③ '자신의 임무를 다하지 못하고 있다는'이 적절하다.
① 쫓기고 있다는
② 건강을 유지하기 위해 노력하고 있지 않다는
④ 음식을 다른 사람들로부터 숨기고 있다는
⑤ 자신들의 짝을 쫓고 있다는

구문풀이

14행 [Those {who tended to be (relaxed, easy-going, a little carefree, and not bothered about what others thought of them)}], tended not to stick around <u>long enough to</u> successfully <u>pass</u> on their genes.

: [ ]는 문장의 주어이고 { }는 Those를 수식하는 관계절이다. 이 관계절에는 be의 보어로 ( )로 표시한 네 개의 형용사(구)가 「A, B, C, and D」의 구조로 연결되어 있다. tended가 문장의 동사이며 술부에는 「부사+enough+to부정사」 구조가 쓰여 '~하기에 충분히 …하게'의 의미를 나타낸다.

어휘풀이
- forefront *n* 맨 앞, 선두
- ancestor *n* 조상
- first and foremost 무엇보다도 제일 중요한
- greedy *a* 탐욕스러운, 욕심 많은
- eject *v* 쫓아내다
- mammal *n* 포유동물
- vigilant *a* 조금도 방심하지 않는
- cautious *a* 조심스러운
- look out for ~을 경계하다, ~에 주의하다
- easy-going *a* 안일한, 느긋한
- pull one's weight 자기 임무를 다하다

128 답 ①

📖 광고 시장에서 발생하는 '죄수의 딜레마'

전문해석

이제 '죄수의 딜레마'라고 불리는 매우 다른 모델을 생각해보자. 그것은 수학자들의 연구에 그 기원을 두고 있지만, 경제학에서의 많은 현대적인 연구의 초석이다. 두 개

의 경쟁하는 회사들이 많은 광고 예산을 편성할지를 결정해야 한다고 가정해 보자. 광고는 한 회사가 다른 회사 고객들 일부를 빼내도록 할 것이다. 하지만 두 회사 모두 광고를 하면 고객 수요에 미치는 영향은 상쇄된다. 그 회사들은 결국에는 쓸데없이 돈을 지출하게 된다. 우리는 어느 회사도 광고에 많은 돈을 소비하는 선택을 하지 **않을 것으로 예상할지 모르지만**, 그 모델은 **이 논리가 완전히 틀렸다는** 것을 보여준다. 회사들이 독립적으로 선택을 하고 그들이 자신의 이익만 신경을 쓸 때, **각자는 상대 회사가 하는 것과 관계 없이 광고를 할 동기를 갖게 된다**. 상대 회사가 광고를 하지 않을 때, 당신이 정말로 광고를 하면 당신은 그 회사로부터 고객을 빼올 수 있다. 상대 회사가 광고를 할 때, 당신은 고객을 뺏기지 않기 위해서 광고를 해야만 한다. 그래서 두 회사는 모두 자원을 낭비해야 하는 나쁜 균형에 도달하게 된다. 이런 시장은 전혀 효율적이지 않다.

정답풀이

빈칸 앞에는 두 회사가 모두 광고를 하면 그 효과가 상쇄되므로 두 회사 모두 광고를 하지 않을 것으로 예상하겠지만, 빈칸 뒤에서는 결국에는 두 회사 모두 광고를 하게 된다고 했다. 따라서 빈칸에는 이러한 내용의 간극을 연결할 수 있는 표현이 들어가야 하므로, ① '이 논리가 완전히 틀렸다'고 언급한 후, 예상에 반하는 내용으로 글을 전개하는 것이 적절하다.
② 광고가 최상의 전략이다
③ 경쟁은 효율성에서 이익을 가져온다
④ 협력은 전반적인 이익을 증가시킨다
⑤ 합리적인 결정은 좋은 균형을 가져온다

구문풀이

12행 When [the firms make their choices independently] and [they care only about their own profits], / each one has <u>an incentive</u> [to advertise], regardless of {**what** the other firm **does**}.

: 부사절과 주절로 이루어진 문장으로 when절에는 [ ]로 표시한 두 개의 절이 and로 연결되어 있다. each 이하의 주절에서 to advertise는 형용사적 용법으로 쓰여 an incentive를 수식한다. 전치사구 regardless of의 목적어로 선행사를 포함한 관계대명사 what이 이끄는 절이 왔으며, 이때 what은 the thing which로 바꾸어 쓸 수 있다. 또한 이 관계절 내의 does는 대동사로 앞에 나온 동사 advertises를 대신한다.

어휘풀이
- contemporary *a* 현대의
- budget *n* 예산
- cancel out ~을 상쇄하다
- end up -ing 결국 ~로 끝나다
- needlessly *ad* 불필요하게
- independently *ad* 독립적으로
- regardless of ~에 관계없이
- prevent *v* 막다
- equilibrium *n* 균형
- efficient *a* 효율적인
- off base 완전히 빗나간

129 답 ②

📖 수메르 경제에서 문자의 사용 용도와 발달을 보여주는 점토판

전문해석

수메르 경제의 대표적 모델에서 사원은 상품의 생산, 수집, 그리고 재분배를 관장하는 관리 당국으로서 기능했다. Uruk의 사원 단지에서 나온 관리용 (점토)판의 발견은, 상징의 사용과 그에 따른 글자가 중앙 집권화된 경제 관리의 수단으로서 발달했다는 것을 시사한다. Uruk 시기 가정집의 터에서 나온 고고학적 증거가 부족하다는 점을 고려하면, 개인들도 개인적 합의를 위해 그 체계를 사용했는지의 여부는 명확하지 않다. 그 문제와 관련하여, 읽고 쓰는 능력이 그것의 초기에 얼마나 널리 퍼져 있었는지 명확하지 않다. 초기의 판에서 식별 가능한 기호와 그림 문자의 사용은 관리자들이 읽고 쓸 줄 아는 측과 읽고 쓸 수 없는 측이 서로 이해할 수 있는 어휘 목록을 필요로 한 것과 일치한다. 쐐기 문자가 더욱 추상적으로 되어감에 따라, 읽고 쓰는 능력은 자신이 하기로 합의했던 것을 이해하고 있다는 것을 확실히 하기 위해 점점 더 중요해졌음이 틀림없다.

빈칸 앞에서는 상징과 글자가 수메르 경제에서 중앙 집권화된 경제 관리의 수단으로 발달했고, 빈칸 이하에서는 개인들도 자신이 하기로 합의한 것을 이해하고 있다는 것을 확실히 하기 위해 읽고 쓰는 능력이 중요해졌다고 언급하고 있으므로, 이들 사이에 위치한 빈칸 문장에는 개인들이 자신들이 한 합의 내용을 확인할 목적으로 상징이나 문자 체계를 사용했다는 내용이 들어가야 적절하다. 따라서 빈칸에는 ② '개인적 합의'가 들어가야 한다.

① 종교 행사   ③ 공동 책임
④ 역사적 기록   ⑤ 권력 이동

구문풀이

7행 [Given the lack of archaeological evidence from Uruk-period domestic sites], **it** is not clear [whether individuals also used the system for personal agreements].

: 첫 번째 [ ]는 '~을 고려하면'이라는 의미의 전치사 given이 이끄는 전치사구이고, 두 번째 [ ]는 가주어 it에 대한 진주어이다.

12행 [The use {of identifiable symbols and pictograms (on the early tablets)}] is consistent with [**administrators** needing a lexicon {that was mutually intelligible by literate and nonliterate parties}].

: 첫 번째 [ ]는 문장의 주어로, 핵심 주어가 use이므로 단수동사 is가 쓰였다. 전치사구인 ( )는 앞의 명사구 identifiable symbols and pictograms를 수식한다. 두 번째 [ ]는 with의 목적어인 동명사구로, administrators가 동명사 needing의 의미상의 주어이다. { }는 needing의 목적어인 a lexicon을 수식하는 관계절이다.

어휘풀이

- administrative *a* 관리의, 행정의
- authority *n* 권위, 권한
- commodity *n* 상품, 물품
- redistribution *n* 재분배, 재배포
- tablet *n* 판
- complex *n* (건물) 단지, 복합 건물
- token *n* (개별적이고 구체적인 표식으로서의) 상징, 대용 화폐, 기념물
- consequently *ad* 그 결과, 따라서
- governance *n* 관리, 통치
- domestic *a* 가정의, 집안의, 국내의
- identifiable *a* 식별 가능한
- pictogram *n* 그림 문자
- consistent with ~와 일치하는
- mutually *ad* 서로, 상호 간에, 공통으로
- intelligible *a* (쉽게) 이해할 수 있는
- literate *a* 읽고 쓸 수 있는
- party *n* 당사자, 측
- abstract *a* 추상적인

130 답 ①

📖 감정적인 상태에서 이성적인 상태로 옮겨가게 하는 질문

전문해석

친구가 문제가 있을 때 질문을 하는 가장 중요한 이유는 '사람들이 동시에 완전하게 생각하고 느낄 수 없기' 때문인데, 그것은 뇌의 두 가지 서로 다른 영역을 포함한다. 여러분이 화가 났을 때 내가 여러분에게 수학 문제를 준다면, 여러분은 다음 두 가지 중 하나의 행동을 할 것이다. 분노가 뒷전으로 물러났기 때문에 그 문제를 해결하거나, 아니면 여러분의 감정이 그것에 대해 충분히 생각하는 것을 방해하기 때문에 그 문제를 풀 수 없을 것이다. 그 둘 중 어느 하나가 지배할 것이다. 상처받은 감정을 단계적으로 완화하는 가장 좋은 방법은 감정(감정적인 논리)에서 사고(합리적인 논리)로 전환하는 것이다. 그러므로 여러분이 질문을 한다면, 특히 어떤 자기 분석을 필요로 하는 질문을 한다면, **여러분은 여러분의 친구가 반응하는 것을 지나서, 무슨 일이 일어나고 있는지, 즉 '왜 그것이 실제로 마음을 아프게 했을까?'에 대해 '생각하는 것'으로 옮겨가도록 도와주고 있는 것이다.** 여러분이 아직도 친구의 감정에 대해 묻고 있는 것이 사실이지만, 여러분은 그것을 객관적인 수준에 가져다 놓고 있다. 여러분은 여러분의 친구가 그 문제를 해결하기 위해 그 문제로부터 일정한 감정적인 거리를 찾도록 돕고 있으며, 동시에 긴장을 단계적으로 완화하고 있다.

빈칸 앞 문장에서는 여러분이 친구에게 질문을 하면, 친구가 (단지) 반응하는 단계를 지나서 자신이 무엇으로 마음이 아픈지를 생각하도록 해준다고 했고, 빈칸 뒤 문장에서는 여러분이 친구가 그 문제를 해결하기 위해 문제로부터 일정한 감정적인 거리를 두도록 돕게 하고 있다고 했다. 따라서 '여러분이 질문을 하는 것'은 감정적 반응을 하는 것에서 벗어나 문제에 대해 사고를 하게 만들어준다는 것을 알 수 있으므로, 빈칸에는 ① '그것을 객관적인 수준에 가져다 놓고'가 적절하다.

② 그나 그녀의 노여움에 기름을 붓고
③ 여러분 자신의 실수를 감추려고 애쓰고
④ 그나 그녀의 감정에 동정하고
⑤ 감정과 사고의 차이를 깨닫고

구문풀이

11행 So, [if you ask a question, especially one {that requires some self-analysis}], you're **helping** your friend **move** past reacting, and **on to** *thinking* about [what's going on] — *Why did that actually hurt?*

: [ ]는 조건의 부사절로 이 절 내의 부정대명사 one은 a question을 가리키며, { }로 표시한 관계절의 수식을 받고 있다. 부정대명사가 선행사일 경우, 주로 관계대명사는 that을 쓴다. 주절의 동사로 준동사 help가 쓰여 목적격보어로 원형부정사 move가 쓰였으며, on to 앞에 반복되는 동사 move가 생략된 것으로 볼 수 있다. 두 번째 [ ]는 전치사 about의 목적어인 간접의문문이다.

어휘풀이

- take a back-seat (다른 사람[것]에게 더 중요한 위치를 주고) 뒷자리에 서다
- get in the way of ~을 방해하다
- dominate *v* 지배하다
- de-escalate *v* 단계적으로 완화하다
- transition *n* 전환
- logic *n* 논리
- rational *a* 합리적인
- self-analysis *n* 자기 분석
- resolve *v* 해결하다
- tension *n* 긴장
- objective *a* 객관적인

131 답 ①

📖 좌절–공격성 이론 실험

전문해석

좌절–공격성 이론을 시험한 한 연구에서, 참가자들이 다양한 상점, 은행, 음식점, 매표소, 그리고 공항 여객 탑승 수속대의 긴 줄에 서서 기다리고 있었는데, 비밀리에 연구자를 위해 일하는 누군가인 비밀 조력자가 줄을 서 있는 그들 앞에 끼어들었다. 참가자들은 심지어 자신들이 연구에 참여하고 있다는 것조차 몰랐다. 동전 던지기로, 그 비밀 조력자는 줄에서 두 번째에 서 있는 사람 또는 줄에서 열두 번째에 서 있는 사람 앞에 끼어들었다. 좌절–공격성 이론에 따르면, 사건은 여러분이 목표에 더 가까이 있는 경우에 더 좌절감을 준다. 그러고 나서 비밀 조력자는 참가자의 반응을 기록했다. 결과는 줄에서 두 번째에 있던 참가자들이 그들 앞에 끼어든 비밀 조력자에게 줄에서 열두 번째에 있던 참가자들보다 더 공격적으로 반응했다는 것을 보여주었는데, 그것은 좌절–공격성 이론과 부합한다. 진정, 여러분이 '거의 그것을 맛볼' 수 있는데 누군가가 여러분을 방해한다면 그것은 분명 매우 좌절감을 줄 것이다.

정답풀이

빈칸 앞에서는 '좌절–공격성 이론'과 관련한 실험의 내용에 대해 언급하였고, 빈칸 뒤에서는 이 실험의 결과에 대해 언급하고 있다. 실험의 내용은 대기하고 있는 줄에서 두 번째에 있는 사람과 열두 번째에 있는 사람 앞에 누군가 새치기를 하는 것이고, 이에 대한 결과는 열두 번째에 있던 사람보다 두 번째에 있던 사람이 더 공격적으로 반응했다는 것이다. 따라서 빈칸에는 좌절–공격

성 이론에 따라 어떤 경우에 더 좌절감을 느끼는지에 대한 내용이 들어가야 하므로, ① '목표에 더 가까이 있는'이 적절하다.
② 양보할 용의가 없는
③ 특히 서두르고 있는
④ 오래 기다릴 것으로 예상하는
⑤ 사건과 아무 관계가 없는

구문풀이

13행 The results <u>showed</u> [that {participants (2nd in line)} responded more aggressively to <u>the confederate</u> {**who** crowded in front of them} **than did participants** (12th in line)], **which** is consistent with the frustration-aggression theory.

: 문장의 동사 showed의 목적어로 [ ]의 명사절이 쓰였다. 이 절에는 비교급이 쓰였고 2nd in line의 수식을 받는 participants와 12th in line의 수식을 받는 participants 를 비교하고 있다. 여기서 접속사 than 이하에는 '동사+주어'의 도치가 일어났는데, 비교급 접속사 than 뒤에는 종종 주어와 동사를 도치하여 쓰기도 하며, 여기서 did는 responded를 대신한다. { }로 표시한 주격 관계대명사 who절은 the confederate를 수식하고, which 이하는 앞 절 전체를 선행사로 취해 이를 부연 설명한다.

어휘풀이

- frustration *n* 좌절(감)
- aggression *n* 공격(성)
- confederate *n* (흔히 몰래 혹은 불법적인) 공모자
- crowd *v* 끼어들다, 밀고 들어가다
- the flip of a coin 동전 던지기
- consistent *a* 부합하는, 일치하는
- frustrating *a* 좌절감을 주는
- get in one's way ~을 방해하다

132 답 ④

📖 도시에서 교외로 이주하면서 변화된 삶의 형태

전문해석

1945년 이후 제2차 세계 대전 이후 시절에 유례없는 경제 성장은 건축 붐과 중심 도시에서 새로운 교외 지역으로의 대규모 이주를 부채질했다. 교외 지역은 자동차에 훨씬 더 많이 의존했고, 대중교통에 대한 주된 의존에서 자가용으로의 전환을 알렸다. 이것은 곧 더 나은 고속도로와 초고속도로의 건설과 대중교통의 감소, 심지어 쇠퇴까지로 이어졌다. 이러한 모든 변화와 함께 여가의 사유화가 이루어졌다. 더 많은 사람이 내부 공간은 더 넓어지고 외부 정원은 더 아름다운 자신의 집을 소유하면서 그들의 휴식과 여가 시간은 점점 더 집이나 기껏해야 이웃에 집중되었다. 이러한 가정에 기반한 여가의 한 가지 주요 활동은 TV를 시청하는 것이었다. 더 이상 영화를 보기 위해 전차를 타고 극장까지 갈 필요가 없었고, 유사한 오락(물)이 텔레비전을 통해 무료로 그리고 더욱 편리하게 이용할 수 있게 되었다.

정답풀이

유례없는 경제 성장이 이루어지면서 사람들의 주거 지역이 도시에서 새로운 교외 지역으로 이동되고 자신들이 원하는 형태의 집을 소유하게 되면서 여가나 오락을 즐기는 양상도 집에서 누리는 형태로 바뀌었다는 내용이므로 빈칸에는 ④ '사유화'가 들어가는 것이 가장 적절하다.
① 몰락
② 획일성
③ 회복
⑤ 맞춤화

구문풀이

4행 The suburbs <u>were</u> far more <u>dependent</u> on the automobile, [signaling <u>the shift</u> {**from** primary dependence on public transportation **to** private cars}].

: be dependent on은 '~에 의존하다'라는 의미이며, far는 비교급 more를 강조하는 부사로 쓰였다. [ ]는 앞 절의 내용을 부연 설명하는 분사구문이며, 「from A to B」 구문 이 쓰인 전치사구 { }는 the shift를 수식한다.

어휘풀이

- fuel *v* 부채질하다
- massive *a* 대규모의
- migration *n* 이주
- suburban *a* 교외의
- signal *v* 신호로 알리다
- shift *n* 전환, 변화
- primary *a* 주된
- freeway *n* 초고속도로
- decline *n* 감소
- loss *n* 쇠퇴, 상실
- available *a* 이용할 수 있는

133 답 ①

📖 다른 사람들이 모으고 저장한 지식을 공유함으로써 알게 된 지식

전문해석

사람이 달 위를 걸었다는 것을 여러분은 어떻게 아는가? 여러분은 직접 달에 가본 적도 없고, 최초로 인간이 달에 착륙하는 것을 자신의 눈으로 목격하기 위해 아폴로 11호에 탑승하지도 않았다. 그렇다면 우리가 달 착륙에 대해 여러분이 기억하는 것을 우리에게 말해달라고 여러분에게 요청하고, 여러분이 우리에게 1969년 7월 20일에 아폴로 11호의 임무의 일환으로 달 착륙선인 'Eagle'이 달에 착륙했다는 것과 Neil Armstrong이 달에 인류의 첫발을 내딛으면서, '한 사람에게는 작은 한 걸음이지만 인류에게는 하나의 거대한 도약'이라는 기억에 남을 만한 묘사로 그 행사를 유명하게 기념했다고 말할 때, 여러분은 다른 사람들이 모으고 기록한 정보를 기억하고 있다. 어쩌면 여러분에게는 텔레비전에서 달 착륙을 본 것을 기억하는 친척이 있을 것이다. 어쩌면 여러분은 그 동영상 장면을 본 적이 있을 것이다. 어쩌면 역사책에서 그 사건에 관해 읽었거나, 그 당시 뉴스 기사를 본 적이 있을 것이다. 달 착륙에 관한 여러분의 지식은 여러분이 그것을 개인적으로 알고 있다는 점에서 개인적인 것이지만, 그것은 또한 다른 사람들과 공유되어 있다. 다시 말하자면, 여러분이 달 착륙에 대해 알고 있는 이유는, 다른 사람들이, 그들 중 대다수는 여러분이 만나본 적도 없는 사람들인데, 우리의 문화적 기억 속에 그것을 기록했고 저장했기 때문이다.

정답풀이

빈칸에는 달 착륙에 관한 우리가 갖고 있는 지식이 개인적인 것일 수도 있지만, 그 외 가지고 있는 특성 또는 의미가 무엇인지에 대한 내용이 들어가야 한다. 빈칸 앞에서는 우리가 직접 겪지도 목격하지도 않은 달 착륙과 같은 사건을 다른 사람이 모으고 기록한 정보를 통해 알게 된 것이라고 했고, 빈칸 뒤에는 앞의 내용을 재진술함을 나타내는 연결어구 That is(즉, 다시 말해)를 사용하여 우리가 달 착륙에 대해 알고 있는 이유가 다른 사람들이 우리의 기억 속에 그것을 기록하고 저장했기 때문이라고 했다. 따라서 달 착륙에 대한 우리의 지식은 다른 사람들이 모은 것을 공유받은 것임을 알 수 있으므로 빈칸에 가장 적절한 것은 ① '다른 사람들과 공유되어'이다.
② 행동을 통해 발달된
③ 개인적 해석에 열려 있는
④ 그것이 피상적일 때 위험한
⑤ 어떤 세속적인 쾌락보다 우수한

구문풀이

18행 Your knowledge of the moon landing is personal, [**in that** you personally know it], / but it is also shared with other people.

: 크게 두 개의 절이 접속사 but으로 연결되어 있으며, in that은 '~라는 점에서'라는 의미로 이유의 부사절을 이끈다.

어휘풀이

- personally *ad* 직접, 개인적으로
- witness *v* 목격하다
- manned *a* 유인(有人)의, 사람을 실은
- lunar *a* 달의
- landing *n* 착륙
- mark the occasion 행사를 기념하다
- memorable *a* 기억에 남을 만한
- description *n* 묘사, 설명
- leap *n* 도약, 비약

- amass *v* 모으다, 축적하다
- footage *n* (특정한 사건을 담은) 장면
- document *v* 기록하다
- superficial *a* 피상적인, 표면상의
- relative *n* 친척
- article *n* 기사
- interpretation *n* 해석
- superior *a* 우수한, 상급의

134 답 ⑤

📖 부족 사회에서 선물을 소비해야 할 도덕적 의무

전문해석

부족민들은 보통 선물과 자본 사이를 구분한다. 그들은 "한 사람의 선물은 다른 사람의 자본이 되어서는 안 된다."고 말한다. 영국의 사회 인류학자인 Wendy James는 북동부 아프리카의 Uduk족 사이에서는 "소(小)부족으로부터 다른 소부족으로 인도된 부는, 그것이 짐승이든 곡물이든 아니면 돈이든, 선물의 성격이며, 소비되어야지 증식을 위해 투자되어서는 안 된다. 그런 인도된 부가, 이 경우에는 소인데, 그 소부족의 자본에 더해지고 증식과 투자를 위해 보유되면, 그 소부족은 원래의 선물을 준 사람에게 비도덕적인 채무 관계에 있는 것으로 간주된다."고 우리에게 말한다. 가령 다른 소부족으로부터 선물로 받은 한 쌍의 염소가 번식하기 위해서나 소를 사기 위해 보유된다면, "아무개가 다른 누군가의 비용으로 부유해지고 있고, 선물을 비축하고 투자함으로써 도의를 저버리고 행동하고 있으며, 따라서 심각한 채무 상태에 있다는 일반적인 불평이 있을 것이다. 그들은 곧 폭풍 피해를 볼 것으로 예상될 것이다."

정답풀이

빈칸 앞에서 아프리카의 한 부족이 다른 부족에게 선물을 받으면 선물이 반드시 소비되어야 한다고 했고, 빈칸 뒤에서는 선물로 받은 염소가 소비되지 않고 새끼를 낳거나 소를 사는 등의 목적으로 보유(부의 증식)되면 이는 도의를 저버리는 것이고 채무 상태(빚을 진 상태)에 있게 되는 것이라고 했다. 따라서 빈칸 문장은 선물 받은 소를 증식과 투자를 위해 보유하면 '도의에 어긋나고 심각한 채무 상태에 있게 된다'는 내용이 되어야 하므로, 빈칸에는 ⑤ '원래의 선물을 준 사람에게 비도덕적인 채무 관계에 있는'이 적절하다.

① 그 선물을 자신의 뜻대로 이용할 수 있는 입장에 있는
② 선물에 내재되어 있는 선물을 준 사람의 의도에 부합하는
③ 그 선물을 증식을 위해 투자하여 더 부유해져야 할 도덕적 의무가 있는
④ 자신의 선물이 자본이 되기를 기대하는 선물을 준 사람에게 반하는

구문풀이

12행 If [a pair of goats {received as a gift from another subclan}] is kept to breed or to buy cattle, / "there will be general complaint [**that** the so-and-sos are getting rich at someone else's expense, {behaving without regard for morality by hoarding and investing gifts}, and therefore {being in a state of severe debt}].

: 조건절과 주절로 이루어진 문장으로, 첫 번째 [ ]는 조건절의 주어로 핵심 주어인 a pair of goats가 과거분사구 { }의 수식을 받고 있다. 두 번째 [ ]는 주절의 주어인 general complaint와 동격을 이루는 명사절인데, 이 절 내에는 { }로 표시한 두 개의 분사구문이 and로 연결되어 부대상황을 나타내고 있다.

어휘풀이

- tribal *a* 부족의, 동족의
- capital *n* 자본
- transfer *v* 인도하다, 넘겨주다
- morality *n* 도의, 도덕(성)
- in accordance with ~에 부합하는
- obligation *n* 의무, 책임
- distinguish *v* 구별하다
- anthropologist *n* 인류학자
- so-and-so *n* 아무개
- severe *a* 심각한, 심한
- embed *v* 내재시키다, 안에 넣다
- in opposition to ~에 반대하여

13 빈칸 추론(2) - 유형 연습 문제(3)   본문 pp.100~103

| 135 ③ | 136 ③ | 137 ② | 138 ② | 139 ① |
| 140 ② | 141 ① | 142 ③ | | |

135 답 ③

📖 전시 맥락에 따라 좌우되는 예술품 전시 여부

전문해석

미술관에 전시되기도 하고 안 되기도 하는 예술품에 관한 선택은 미술사의 정전에 의해 형성되고 결국 미술사의 정전을 다시 형성한다. 미술사는 이러한 점에서 아주 영향력이 있어서 Donald Preziosi는 그것을 'museography', 즉 미술관이 보여주는 것에 관한 기록이라고 부르기까지 한다. 무엇이 전시되고 무엇이 창고에 보관되는가에 관한 결정은 몇 가지 관심사를 고려함에 의해 영향을 받는다. 큐레이터가 똑같은 유형의 많은 작품에 직면하고 전시할 하나의 작품을 선택해야 할 때, 그 사람의 결정은 미학에 의해 유도될 가능성이 높아 보일지도 모른다. 하지만 이런 종류의 큐레이터의 결정조차도, 몇 가지 유형의 박물관만 언급하더라도, 미술관, 일상용품 박물관, 그리고 과학 기술 박물관, 자연사 박물관, 인류학 박물관 또는 지역사 박물관에서 서로 다르다. 미술 큐레이터에 의해 이류 작품이고 전시할 가치가 없다고 거부될 청동 조각이 미술 큐레이터는 관심 밖인 합금의 그 특별한 특성들을 강조하고 싶은 과학 큐레이터에 의해 전시될지도 모른다. 그래서 무엇이 전시할 가치가 있고 무엇이 아닌지는 전시의 맥락에 크게 달려 있다.

정답풀이

미술관에서 어떤 예술품이 전시되고 안 되는지는 전시 주제와 관련된 맥락과 크게 관련이 있다는 내용으로, 미술 큐레이터는 가치가 없다고 거부할 청동 조각이 합금의 특성을 강조하고 싶은 과학 큐레이터에 의해 전시될 수 있다는 예를 들고 있다. 따라서 빈칸에 들어갈 말로는 ③ '맥락'이 가장 적절하다.

① 비용   ② 공간
④ 기간   ⑤ 인기

구문풀이

6행 Decisions about [what goes on show and what stays in storage] are affected by the taking into consideration of a few concerns.

: [ ]는 about의 목적어인 명사절이며, Decisions가 문장의 핵심 주어, are affected가 동사이다.

16행 A bronze sculpture [that would be rejected as second-rate and unworthy of showing by an art curator], might be displayed by a science curator [who wishes to highlight those exceptional qualities of the alloy {that the art curator is unconcerned about}].

: 첫 번째 [ ]는 문장의 주어인 A bronze sculpture를 수식하는 관계절이고, 수동태인 might be displayed가 문장의 동사이다. 두 번째 [ ]는 a science curator를 수식하는 관계절이며, 그 안의 { }는 those exceptional qualities of the alloy를 수식하는 관계절이다.

어휘풀이

- display *n* 전시 *v* 전시하다
- in this respect 이런 점에서
- take into consideration of ~을 고려하다
- confront *v* 직면하다, 맞서다
- anthropology *n* 인류학
- highlight *v* 강조하다
- in turn 결국, 결과적으로
- aesthetics *n* 미학
- sculpture *n* 조각품, 조각
- exceptional *a* 특별한, 우수한

136 답 ③

전문해석

현대 과학이 우리에게 제공하는 중요한 메시지는 <u>진화된 설계가 의도치 않은 결과를 가져올 수 있다는 것</u>이다. 어떤 전략이나 특성이 진화하려면 그것은 다른 것과 경쟁해 이기면 된다. 다음과 같은 오래된 농담이 있다. '늑대보다 더 빨리 달릴 필요는 없다. 그저 여러분의 친구보다 더 빨리 달리기만 하면 된다.' 물론, 그래서 그것이 우정에는 아무런 도움이 되지 않지만, 그것은 진화가 한 영역에서 동물들에게 이점을 주기 위해 부여한 것들 중 일부가 다른 영역에서 그들의 능력을 손상시킬 수 있다는 것을 정말로 입증한다. 이러한 거래는 공작의 꼬리에서 볼 수 있는데, 이것은 짝을 유혹하는 데는 좋지만 포식자로부터 도망치려 할 때는 불리한 여건이다. 또한 기린이 물을 마시려고 목을 숙이기 위해 어떻게 고군분투해야 하는지 생각해 보라. 이 행성을 방문하는 어떤 외계인이든 그들을(기린들을) 다소 이상한 동물로 여길 것이다. 어떻게 그런 동물이 진화할 수 있었을까? 그러고 나서 우리는 긴 목이 실제로 기린이 보다 높은 나뭇가지의 잎을 먹을 수 있게 해주는 하나의 적응이라는 것을 발견한다. 그래서 한 분야의 이점은 실제로 또 다른 분야에서 심각한 단점을 만들어 낼 수 있다.

정답풀이

진화의 한 영역에서 동물들에게 이점을 부여하는 특성이 다른 영역에서는 단점이 될 수 있음을 설명하면서 공작의 꼬리와 기린의 긴 목을 예로 들고 있다. 짝짓기에 장점이 되는 공작의 꼬리와 높은 나뭇가지의 잎을 먹게 해주는 기린의 목은 모두 진화의 결과로 생긴 적응이지만 포식자로부터 도망을 가거나 물을 마시는 데는 불리하게 작용한다는 것이다. 따라서 빈칸에 들어갈 말로 적절한 것은 ③ '진화된 설계가 의도치 않은 결과를 가져올 수 있다'이다.
① 노력과 고통이 없이는 아무것도 설계되지 않는다
② 경쟁의 과정이 늘 공정한 것은 아니다
④ 과정이 최종 결과보다 더 중요하다
⑤ 진화에는 늘 큰 우연의 요소가 있다

구문풀이

6행 Okay – so it does nothing for friendship, but it **does** **demonstrate** [that some of the things {that evolution has bestowed on animals to give them an advantage in one area} can compromise their abilities in another].

: does는 동사 demonstrate를 강조하는 조동사로 쓰였다. [ ]는 demonstrate의 목적어 역할을 하는 명사절이고, 그 안의 { }는 the things를 수식하는 관계절이다.

16행 Then we discover [that the long neck is actually an adaptation {that allows giraffes to eat leaves from the higher branches of trees}].

: [ ]는 문장의 동사인 discover의 목적어 역할을 하는 명사절이며, 그 안의 { }는 an adaptation을 수식하는 관계절이다.

어휘풀이

- strategy *n* 전략
- out-compete *v* 경쟁에서 이기다
- compromise *v* 손상시키다
- peacock *n* 공작
- predator *n* 포식자
- alien *n* 외계인
- competition *n* 경쟁
- element *n* 요소
- trait *n* 특성
- demonstrate *v* 입증하다
- trade-off *n* 거래, 교환
- handicap *n* 불리한 여건
- struggle *v* 고군분투하다
- adaptation *n* 적응
- consequence *n* 결과

137 답 ②

전문해석

우리가 진화론적 관점에서 우리 자신을 바라볼 때, 우리는 우리가 아주 최근에 지구에 도착했을 뿐 아니라 지구상의 새로운 종으로서 우리의 출현이 원래 사물의 전체 체계에 특별한 중요성이 없는 사건이었다는 것을 이해한다. 지구는 우리가 나타나기 오래전부터 생명체로 가득 차 있었다. 요점을 은유적으로 표현하자면, 우리는 상대적으로 새롭게 온 존재로, 수억 년 동안 다른 것들의 거주지였고 이제 우리 모두가 함께 공유해야 하는 집에 들어온 것이다. <u>지구상의 인간 생명체의 상대적인 짧음은 공간적인 측면에서 지질학적 시간 척도를 상상함으로써 생생하게 묘사될 수 있다.</u> 우리가 적어도 6억 년 동안 존재해 온 조류로부터 시작한다고 가정해 보자. 조류가 여기에 있었던 시간이 축구장의 길이(300피트)로 표현된다면, 상어가 세계의 대양에서 헤엄치고 거미가 거미집을 지어온 기간은 축구장 길이의 4분의 3을 차지할 것이고, 파충류는 축구장의 거의 중앙에서 나타날 것이고, 포유류는 축구장의 마지막 3분의 1에 걸치고, 유인원은 마지막 2피트에, 그리고 호모 사피엔스 종은 마지막 6인치에 걸칠 것이다.

정답풀이

우리가 다른 생명체에 비해 지구라는 집에 늦게 도착한 존재임을 설명하는 글이다. 지구에 6억 년 동안 있었던 조류의 존재 기간을 300피트 길이의 축구장으로 표현할 때 현재의 우리 인간에 해당하는 호모 사피엔스 종은 마지막 6인치에 걸쳐 있다는 내용을 통해 우리가 지구상에 아주 짧게 존재한 생명체임을 이야기하고 있는데, 이것은 다양한 생명체가 존재한 지질학적 시간을 축구장이라는 공간을 가정해 비교한 것이므로 빈칸에 들어갈 말로 가장 적절한 것은 ② '공간적인'이다.
① 인과 관계의
③ 추상적인
④ 경쟁적인
⑤ 포괄적인

구문풀이

7행 [Putting the point metaphorically], we are relative newcomers, [entering **a home** {that has been the residence of others for hundreds of millions of years}, **a home** {that must now be shared by all of us together}].

: 첫 번째 [ ]는 we가 의미상의 주어인 분사구문이다. 두 번째 [ ]는 relative newcomers를 의미상의 주어로 하면서 부가적인 설명을 하는 분사구문이다. 그 안에 있는 두 개의 a home은 각각 주격 관계대명사 that이 이끄는 관계절의 수식을 받으며 서로 동격 관계를 이룬다.

어휘풀이

- evolutionary *a* 진화론적인
- emergence *n* 출현
- metaphorically *ad* 은유적으로
- comparative *a* 상대적인
- geological *a* 지질학적인
- occupy *v* 차지하다
- hominid *n* 유인원(인류의 조상)
- competitive *a* 경쟁적인
- point of view 관점
- scheme *n* 체계, 계획
- residence *n* 거주지
- depict *v* 묘사하다
- alga *n* 조류(藻類)(*pl.* algae)
- reptile *n* 파충류
- abstract *a* 추상적인

138 답 ②

전문해석

우리는 모퉁이에 있는 가격이 지나치게 높은 편의점에서 물건을 사는데 왜냐하면 그것이 가격이 더 낮은 가게까지 차를 타고 운전해 가는 것보다 더 쉽기 때문이다. 우리는 식기 세척기 대신 싱크대에 우리 접시를 두는데 왜냐하면 한 단계가 덜 요구되기 때문이다. 우리는 우리의 십 대 아이가 저녁 식사 내내 문자 메시지를 주고받는 것을 그대로 두는데 전화 금지 규칙을 시행하려고 애씀으로써 말다툼을 자초하는 것보다 그것이 더 쉽기 때문이다. 우리는 어떤 주제에 관해 우리가 온라인에서 찾는 첫 번째, 최소한으로 믿을 만한 정보를 받아들이는데 왜냐하면 그것이 우리 질문에 대답하게 하는 가장 쉬운 방법이기 때문이다. 기타 등등. **진화의 관점에서 쉬운 것을 향한 이런 편향은 유용하다.** 대부분의 인류 역사 동안 그것은 우리의 생존과 진보에 중요했다. 만약 인간이 가장 어려운 가능한 방법으로 일을 하는 것에 대한 편향이 있었으면 어땠을지 상상만 해보라. 만약 우리 조상들이 "먹을 것을 얻는 가장 어려운 방법이 뭐지? 우리 가족을 위한 주거지를 제공하는 가장 어려운 방법은? 우리 부족 내에서 좋은 관계를 유지하는 가장 어려운 방법은?"이라고 묻도록 설정되어 있었다면 어땠을까? 그들은 살아남지 못했을 것이다! 하나의 종으로서 우리의 생존은 <u>가장 적은 저항이 있는 경로를 취하는 것</u>에 대한 우리의 타고난 선호에서 비롯된다.

정답풀이
어려운 길보다 쉬운 길을 선택하려는 인간의 편향이 진화의 관점에서 보면 오히려 생존에 도움이 되었다는 내용이므로, 빈칸에 들어갈 말로는 ② '가장 적은 저항이 있는 경로를 취하는 것'이 가장 적절하다.
① 전쟁보다는 평화를 선택하는 것
③ 고독보다는 교우 관계를 추구하는 것
④ 우리 주변의 세상에 관해 파악하는 것
⑤ 고된 난관에도 불구하고 성공하기 위해 노력하는 것

구문풀이
1행 We buy something [at the overpriced convenience store on the corner] / because it's easier than <u>getting</u> in the car and <u>driving</u> to the store [where prices are lower].

: 주절과 이유의 부사절로 이루어진 문장으로, 첫 번째 [ ]는 주절에 포함된 부사구이다. 이유의 부사절에서 than의 목적어인 동명사 getting과 driving은 병렬구조를 이루며, 두 번째 [ ]는 the store를 수식하는 관계부사절이다.

7행 We accept <u>the first, minimally credible information</u> [we find online about a subject] / because it's <u>the easiest way</u> [to get our questions answered].

: 첫 번째 [ ]는 the first, minimally credible information을 수식하는 관계절이고, 두 번째 [ ]는 the easiest way를 수식하는 to부정사구이다.

어휘풀이
- overpriced *a* 가격이 지나치게 높은
- convenience store 편의점
- argument *n* 말다툼
- enforce *v* 시행하다
- credible *a* 믿을 만한
- perspective *n* 관점
- bias *n* 편향
- crucial *a* 중요한
- wire *v* 설정하다, 연결하다
- tribe *n* 부족
- innate *a* 타고난
- preference *n* 선호
- solitude *n* 고독
- strive for ~을 얻으려고 노력하다

139 답 ①

📖 사회 체계 내의 역할 수행을 통해 정립되는 사회 정체성

전문해석
인간은 일생의 과정을 거치면서 많은 다른 역할을 맡는다. 이 역할들은 어디에서 나오는가? 흔히 그것들은 사회 체계의 일부분이다. 만약 여러분이 역사적으로 대부분의 사람들이 살았던 작은 소작농촌에 산다면, 여러분은 많은 역할을 할 수 없을 것이다. 그 마을 사회 체계의 제한된 기회는 여러분이 예컨대 농구 코치나 소프트웨어 상담원, 또는 인기 영화배우가 될 수 없다는 것을 의미하는데, 여러분이 만날 수 있는 다른 사람이라고는 시골 농부들뿐이기 때문이다. **대부분의 역할은 한 문화 체계 내**에서 다른 사람들과 관계를 맺는 방법이다. 여러분이 숲에 홀로 산다면, 자신을 경찰관, 바텐더, 학교 선생님, 또는 텔레마케팅 회사의 부회장이라고 기술하는 것은 어리석을 것이다. **한 사람의 사회 정체성은 따라서 개인과 더 큰 문화 체계 사이의 상호작용을 보여 주는데** 즉, 사회는 역할을 만들어 내고 정의하며, 개별적인 사람들은 그 역할을 추구하며, 채택하며, 때때로 자기 자신의 스타일을 그 역할에 도입한다. 사회가 없으면, <u>자아는 온전히 존재하지 않을 것이다</u>.

정답풀이
글의 도입부에서 작은 소작농촌에 살 경우, 우리는 시골 농부들만 볼 수 있으므로 이 외의 다른 역할을 할 수 없다고 언급하며, 대부분의 역할은 한 문화 체계 즉, 사회에서 다른 사람들과 관계를 맺는 방법이라고 언급했다. 이어지는 내용에서도 앞의 내용과 같은 맥락으로 숲에 홀로 사는 경우를 가정하고 있으므로, 빈칸에는 '사회가 없으면 자신의 역할을 형성하고 발전시키지 못한다'는 맥락이 와야 한다. 따라서 빈칸에는 ① '자아는 온전히 존재하지 않을 것이다'가 적절하다.
② 분쟁은 전혀 없을 것이다
③ 어떤 기술도 발전하지 않을 것이다
④ 개인적인 역할이 더 큰 중요성을 띨 것이다
⑤ 자연과 조화를 이루며 사는 것은 불가능할 것이다

구문풀이
6행 [The limited opportunities {in that village's social system}] <u>mean</u> [that you could not be a basketball coach, for example, or a software consultant, or a movie star {because <u>the only other people</u> (you ever meet) are peasant farmers}].

: 첫 번째 [ ]는 주어로 핵심 주어인 The limited opportunities가 전치사구의 수식을 받고 있으며, 문장의 동사는 mean이다. 두 번째 [ ]는 mean의 목적절로, 이는 { }로 표시한 이유의 부사절을 포함하고 있다. 이 부사절의 주어 the only other people은 목적격 관계대명사가 생략된 ( )로 표시한 관계절의 수식을 받는다.

어휘풀이
- peasant *n* 소작농
- relate to ~와 관계를 맺다
- vice president 부회장
- interplay *n* 상호작용
- adopt *v* 채택하다
- impose *v* 도입하다
- conflict *n* 갈등, 분쟁

140 답 ②

📖 인지적 지도를 만들 수 있는 동물의 능력을 부인하는 행동주의자들

전문해석
동물이 자신이 달린 미로의 인지적 '지도'를 만드는 것처럼 보인다는 것을 심리학자들이 처음 보여주었을 때, **회의론자들은 아마도 그 동물이 미로를 통과해 달릴 때 자신의 연속적인 반응의 기록을 남기는 것이라고 주장했다.** 이 '행동주의자들'은 이 연속적인 행동의 각 구성 요소들을 '부분 예기 목표 반응'이라고 불렀는데, 그것은 그들이 우리를 포함해 어떤 동물이든 정신적 삶을 가지고 있다고 인정하는 정도까지였다. 이런 이유로, 내 마음에는 내 의자와 Nassau 거리 사이의 공간적 관계에 대한 묘사가 들어 있지 않다. 그것이 담고 있는 것이라고는 일련의 '단편적인' 반응이 전부인데, 좌회전하고, 10피트 전진하고, 거실문을 통과하고, 좌회전하고, 현관문으로 나가고 등등이다. 반대로 쥐가 내부 지도를 정말로 만든다는 것을 보여 주기란 쉬웠다. 그들은 먹이를 담은 상자로 가는 급커브 길을 배웠다. 실험자가 이 경로를 차단했을 때, 그들은 음식 상자로 가는 직행 경로를 선택할 수 있었다. 만약 <u>그들이 가지고 있는 모든 것이 반응 기록이라면</u> 그들은 이런 전환을 할 수 없었을 것이다. 먹이를 찾는 동물에 대한 연구도 회의론자들을 반박하고 있는데, 침팬지와 새들은 그들에게 그 은닉처를 보여 주었던 순서와는 다른 순서로 다양한 은닉처로부터 먹이를 되찾을 수 있다.

행동주의자들은 동물들이 연속적인 반응의 기록으로 미로를 통과할 수 있다고 했음을 언급하고, 이를 쥐의 경우를 예로 들어 반박하고 있다. 쥐는 '내부 지도'를 만든다고 하며, 그 근거로 학습된 먹이 경로가 차단되자 먹이로 가는 직행 경로를 선택할 수 있었다고 했다. 이를 토대로 다음에 이어지는 빈칸 문장에서는 그들(쥐들)이 단편적 반응을 기록하는 것에 그치는 것이라면, 이러한 전환(직행 경로를 선택하는 것)을 할 수 없었을 것이라는 문맥이 되어야 한다. 따라서 빈칸에는 ② '그들이 가지고 있는 모든 것이 반응 기록이다'가 들어가는 것이 가장 적절하다.

① 그들이 도구를 사용하는 법을 알지 못한다
③ 먹이의 유혹이 강렬하지 않다
④ 그들의 방향 감각이 매우 예민하지 않다
⑤ 미로의 구조가 그들에게 알려져 있지 않다

1행 When psychologists first showed [that animals appeared to construct cognitive "maps" of the mazes {in which they ran}], / skeptics argued [that perhaps the animals laid down a record of their sequence of responses {as they ran through a maze}].

: 부사절과 주절로 이루어진 문장으로, 첫 번째 [ ]는 showed의 목적어 역할을 한다. 이때, 이 목적절 내의 the mazes는 '전치사+관계대명사' 형태인 관계절의 수식을 받는다. 두 번째 [ ]는 argued의 목적절로 이 절에는 접속사 as가 이끄는 시간 부사절이 포함되어 있다.

- construct *v* 만들다, 건설하다
- maze *n* 미로
- sequence *n* 연속
- component *n* 구성 요소
- anticipatory *a* 예상의
- account *n* 이유
- experimenter *n* 실험자
- forage *v* 먹이를 찾다
- cognitive *a* 인지의
- skeptic *n* 회의론자
- behaviorist *n* 행동주의자
- fractional *a* 부분적인, 단편적인
- concede *v* 인정하다
- representation *n* 묘사, 표현
- switch *n* 변화, 전환
- refute *v* 반박하다

141 답 ①

📖📖 **친환경 대체 기술 개발을 위한 핵심 재료 공급 확충의 필요성**

첨단 기술 제품의 미래는 우리 생각의 한계에 놓여 있는 것이 아니라, 그것을 생산하기 위한 재료를 확보할 수 있는 우리의 능력에 놓여 있을지도 모른다. 철기 시대와 청동기 시대와 같은 이전 시대에, 새로운 요소의 발견은 끝이 없을 것 같은 무수한 새로운 발명품들을 낳았다. 이제 그 조합은 정말로 끝이 없을 수도 있다. 우리는 이제 자원 수요에 있어서 근본적인 변화를 목격하고 있다. 인류 역사의 어느 지점에서도, 우리는 (지금보다) '더 많은' 조합으로, 그리고 점차 정밀한 양으로, '더 많은' 요소를 사용한 적은 없었다. 우리의 창의력은 곧 우리의 물질 공급을 앞지를 것이다. 이 상황은 세계가 화석 연료에 대한 의존을 줄이려고 분투하고 있는 결정적인 순간에 온다. 다행히, 희금속들이 전기 자동차, 풍력발전용 터빈, 그리고 태양 전지판과 같은 친환경 기술의 핵심 재료이다. 그것들은 태양과 바람과 같은 천연 자유재를 우리의 생활에 연료를 공급하는 동력으로 전환하는 데 도움을 준다. 하지만 오늘날의 제한된 공급을 늘리지 않고서는, 우리는 기후 변화를 늦추기 위해 우리가 필요로 하는 친환경 대체 기술을 개발할 가망이 없다.

현재 우리는 자원 수요에서 근본적인 변동 현상을 목격할 수 있는데, 곧 인간의 창의력이 재료의 공급을 추월하게 될 것이고, 이는 세계가 화석 연료 의존

도를 감소시키기 위해 애쓸 때 온다고 언급했다. 이어지는 내용에서 친환경 제품들을 생산하기 위해서는 핵심 재료들의 공급이 중요한데, 이것의 공급이 제한되어 있다고 했다. 이러한 내용을 토대로 첨단 기술 제품의 미래는 이러한 재료를 확보하는 것에 있음을 알 수 있으므로, 빈칸에 들어갈 말로 가장 적절한 것은 ① '그것을 생산하기 위한 재료를 확보할 수 있는 우리의 능력'이다.

② 그것을 가능한 한 친환경적으로 만들기 위한 우리의 노력
③ 혁신 기술의 보다 광범위한 보급
④ 자원 공급을 제한하지 않는 정부의 정책
⑤ 그것들의 기능의 지속적인 업데이트와 개선

8행 [At **no** point in human history] have we used *more* elements, in *more* combinations, and in increasingly refined amounts.

: 부정어구 At no point in human history가 문두에 위치하며, 주어 we와 조동사 have가 도치되었다.

- bring forth ~을 낳다
- combination *n* 조합
- fundamental *a* 근본적인
- refined *a* 정밀한, 정제된
- defining *a* 결정적인
- ingredient *n* 재료, 요소
- alternative *a* 대체의, 대안의
- numbers of 무수한, 수많은
- witness *v* 목격하다
- shift *n* 변화
- outpace *v* 앞지르다
- reliance *n* 의존
- convert *v* 전환하다
- distribution *n* 보급, 분배

142 답 ③

📖📖 **직무에 태만한 팀원이 다른 팀원들에게 미치는 영향**

내 경험으로는 공짜로 빌붙는 사람, 즉, 다른 사람들만큼 (업무에) 전념하지 않는 사람이 팀에 들어오고 관료적인 정책 때문에 거부될 수 없을 때, **다른 열심히 일하는 팀원들은 즉각적으로, 그리고 대폭 자신의 업무량 수준을 낮추고 삶의 다른 부분에 주의를 돌리고 정신을 쏟는다.** 왜 그럴까? 이것은 팀원들이 그들의 노력을 최대화하고 싶은 것이 인간의 본성이기 때문이다. 특히 시간이 제한적일 때, 우리들 각자는 우리의 주의를 가장 커다란 결과를 일구어낼 것에 사용하기를 원한다. 우리가 큰 소리로 말하든 그렇지 않든, **모든 이는 공짜로 빌붙는 사람이 우리의 노력을 위쪽이 아니라 아래쪽으로 향하도록 영향을 준다는 것을 안다.** 따라서 불편한 진실은 **팀이 (업무에) 가장 적게 투자한 동료 직원의 수준으로 업무를 수행할 것이라는 것이다.** 총명한 팀장과 눈치 빠른 팀원은 이 원리를 이해하고 동기 부여의 문제를 쉽게, 직접적으로, 그리고 주기적으로 다룬다. 일을 덜 하는 것이 팀원들에게 더 수월한 듯하지만, 결국에는 그것이 팀의 소멸을 초래할 수 있다.

공짜로 빌붙는 사람이 팀에 들어오면 열심히 일하는 팀원들이 자신의 업무 수준을 낮추는데, 그 이유가 자신의 노력을 최대화하고 싶기 때문이라고 했다. 또한 빈칸 바로 앞 문장에서 공짜로 빌붙는 사람이 우리의 노력을 위쪽이 아니라 아래쪽으로 향하도록 영향을 준다고 했고, 이어지는 빈칸 문장이 결과를 나타내는 Thus(따라서)로 시작하고 있으므로, 전체적으로 팀원들이 일을 많이 하지 않게 된다는 내용이 들어가야 한다. 따라서 빈칸에는 ③ '팀이 (업무에) 가장 적게 투자한 동료 직원의 수준으로 업무를 수행할 것이다'가 가장 적절하다.

① 팀이 (업무에) 가장 덜 전념하는 구성원들을 묵인해야 할 것이다
② 상사가 각 구성원의 업무 수행을 평가할 수 없을 것이다
④ 상사가 다른 열심히 일하는 구성원들에게 더 많은 일을 부여할 것이다
⑤ 팀장이 몇몇 팀원들을 평소보다 일을 덜 하게 할 것이다

1행 In my experience, [when a freeloader, {a person not as committed as others}, comes into a team and can't be rejected because of bureaucratic policy], / the other hard-working members of the team immediately and drastically reduce their work level and channel their attention and commitment to other parts of their lives.

: [ ]로 표시한 부사절과 주절로 이루어진 문장으로 부사절의 주어 a freeloader는 동격 어구 { }에서 부연 설명되고 있다. 부사절의 동사 comes와 can't be rejected는 병렬 구조를 이루고, 주절에서도 동사 reduce와 channel이 병렬구조를 이룬다.

어휘풀이
- freeloader *n* 공짜로 빌붙는 사람
- committed *a* 전념하는
- bureaucratic *a* 관료적인, 관료주의의
- drastically *ad* 대폭, 과감하게
- channel *v* (돈, 생각 등을) ~에 쏟다[돌리다]
- commitment *n* 전념, 몰두
- maximize *v* 최대화하다
- savvy *a* 눈치 빠른
- address *v* 다루다
- motivation *n* 동기 부여
- in the long run 결국
- demise *n* 소멸, 종말
- tolerate *v* 용인하다, 참다

14	**무관한 문장**			본문 pp.104~109
143 ③	**144** ③	**145** ④	**146** ④	**147** ②
148 ④	**149** ④	**150** ④	**151** ④	

143 답 ③

📖 빠르게 말하는 것의 언어적 위험 부담

전문해석

빠르게 말하는 것은 위험 부담이 큰 일이다. 입이 제한 속도를 훨씬 넘어서 움직일 때 설득력 있고, 말을 잘하며, 효과적인 이상적 상태를 유지하는 것은 거의 불가능하다. 우리는 우리의 정신이 항상 최고의 효율로 좋은 결정을 내릴 수 있을 정도로 예리하다고 생각하고 싶겠지만, 그것은 정말 그렇지 않다. 실제로 뇌는 말할 가능성이 있는 것들 4~5가지가 교차하는 지점에 도달하면 몇 초 동안 빈둥거리며 선택지를 고려한다. (좋은 결정을 내리는 것은 응답을 생각해 낼 시간이 더 많아지기 때문에 여러분이 더 빠르게 말하는 데 도움을 준다.) 뇌가 입에 향해 지시를 다시 보내는 것을 멈추었는데 입이 너무 빨리 움직여 중단할 수 없을 때, 이때가 바로 여러분이 가벼운 언어적 장애, 또는 필러라고도 하는 것을 겪게 되는 때이다. '음, 아, 알다시피, 그러니까'는 입이 갈 곳이 없을 때 하는 것이다.

144 답 ③

📖 교사의 목소리 사용 기술 개발

전문해석

배우, 가수, 정치가, 그 외의 무수한 사람들은 사용된 낱말들의 단순한 해독을 넘어서는 의사소통 수단으로서의 사람 목소리의 힘을 인정한다. 따라서 **여러분의 목소리를 통제하고 그것을 다양한 목적을 위해 사용하는 것을 배우는 것은 경력 초기의 교사로서 개발해야 할 가장 중요한 기술 중 하나이다.** 여러분이 더 자신 있게 수업할수록, 학급의 긍정적 반응이 나올 확률은 더 높다. 목소리를 크게 내보낼 수 있는 것은

이 학교에서 일할 때 매우 유용할 때가 있고, 여러분이 시끄러운 교실, 구내식당이나 운동장을 (목소리로) 가를 수 있다는 것을 아는 것은 갖출 훌륭한 기술이다. (학교 내의 심각한 소음 문제에 대처하려면 학생, 학부모, 교사가 함께 해결책을 찾아야 한다.) 하지만, 나는 항상 여러분이 여러분의 가장 큰 목소리는 놀랍도록 드물게 쓰고 가능한 한 고함치는 것을 피해야 한다고 조언하고자 한다. 조용하면서도 권위가 있으며 침착한 어조는 다소 당황한 고함보다 참으로 훨씬 더 큰 효과가 있다.

정답풀이

교사는 의사소통 수단인 목소리를 여러 목적을 위해 유용하게 사용할 줄 알아야 한다는 내용의 글로, 큰 목소리를 내야 할 때도 있지만 조용하고 차분한 목소리를 내는 것도 중요하다고 말하고 있다. 따라서 학교 소음 문제에 대한 해결 관련된 내용인 ③은 글의 흐름과 관계가 없다.

구문풀이

9행 There are times [when being able to project your voice loudly will be very useful {when working in school}], / and [knowing {that you can cut through a noisy classroom, dinner hall or playground}] is a great skill to have.

: 두 개의 등위절이 and로 연결된 구조이다. 첫 번째 [ ]는 times를 수식하는 관계절이고, 두 번째 [ ]는 두 번째 절의 주어로 사용된 동명사구이다. 첫 번째 { }는 관계절에 포함된 시간 부사절이고 두 번째 { }는 knowing의 목적어인 명사절이다.

어휘풀이
- politician *n* 정치가
- countless *a* 무수한
- decode *v* (암호 등을) 해독하다
- purpose *n* 목적
- instruction *n* 지시
- project *v* 내지르다
- address *v* 대처하다, 다루다
- incredibly *ad* 놀랍도록, 엄청나게
- sparingly *ad* 드물게, 인색하게
- authoritative *a* 권위가 있는
- measured *a* 침착한
- tone *n* 어조
- slightly *ad* 다소, 약간
- panicked *a* 당황한

145 답 ④

📖 정보 시스템 도입으로 인한 사업 수행 방식의 변화

전문해석

정보 시스템은 도입 이래로 사업이 수행되는 방식을 상당히 변화시켰다. 이는 다수의 부문에 걸쳐 가치 사슬의 통합을 수반하는 기업 간의 협력의 형태와 유형의 사업에 특히 해당된다. 그 결과로 나타나는 네트워크는 단일 기업의 사업 부문을 포함할 뿐만 아니라 일반적으로 서로 다른 기업의 여러 부문을 포함하기도 한다. 결과적으로, 기업은 지속 가능한 사업 성과를 보장하기 위해 그들 내부 조직에 주의를 기울일 필요가 있을 뿐만 아니라, 그들은 자신들을 둘러싸고 있는 부문들의 전체 생태계를 고려할 필요도 있다. (많은 주요 기업들은 수익성이 있는 부문에는 집중하고 수익성이 낮은 부문은 잘라냄으로써 자신들의 사업 모델을 근본적으로 변화시키고 있다.) 이 서로 다른 부문들이 성공적으로 협력할 수 있도록 하기 위해서는 공동 플랫폼의 존재가 매우 중요하다.

정답풀이

정보 시스템(information systems) 도입 이후 기업이 사업을 수행하는 방식을 상당히 변화시켰다는 내용의 글로, 수익성이 있는 부문에 집중하고 수익성이 낮은 부문은 제거하는 기업의 사업 모델을 설명하는 ④는 이러한 핵심과 무관하다.

구문풀이

6행 The resulting networks do **not only** [cover the business units of a single firm] **but** typically **also** [include multiple units from different firms].

: do는 강조의 조동사로 쓰였으며, 두 개의 [ ]는 'A뿐만 아니라 B도'라는 의미의 「not only A but also B」 구문의 A와 B에 해당한다. 이때 A와 B는 문법적 자격과 형태가 같아야 하므로 여기서는 각각 동사구가 사용되었다.

어휘풀이

- **substantially** *ad* 상당히
- **value chain** 가치 사슬
- **sustainable** *a* 지속 가능한
- **ecosystem** *n* 생태계
- **profitable** *a* 수익성이 있는
- **integration** *n* 통합
- **business unit** 사업 부문
- **take into account** ~을 고려하다
- **fundamentally** *ad* 근본적으로

146 답 ④

📖📖 인간이 맥락을 적용하는 방식

전문해석

맥락을 적용하는 것은 인간에게 자연스러운 일이다. 그것은 우리의 뇌가 의식적으로 끊임없이 상황을 파악하지 않고 수많은 데이터를 처리하는 한 가지 방법이다. 우리의 뇌는, 거의 숨을 쉬는 것만큼이나 쉽게, 어떠한 두드러진 노력 없이도 눈에 띄지 않는 곳에서 작업을 수행한다. 체스를 매우 잘 두는 사람은 특정 위치에서 특정 유형의 움직임이 좋다는 것을 한눈에 알아차리고, 여러분은 자신이 특정 모양으로 생긴 페이스트리를 즐길 것이라는 것을 안다. (직접 체스를 두든 온라인에서 체스를 두든, 여러분은 그 과정에서 의사소통, 스포츠맨십, 협업을 포함한 많은 사회적 기술을 향상시킬 수 있다.) 물론 이러한 눈에 띄지 않는 곳의 직관 과정은 때때로 틀려서, 그 결과 (체스에서의) 포지션을 잃거나 2류 과자를 갖게 해, 결과적으로 여러분이 다음번에 그러한 상황에 처할 때 의식적인 마음이 아마도 조금 더 자기주장을 하고 직관을 재고하게 될 것이다.

정답풀이

이 글은 인간의 뇌가 맥락을 적용하는 방식이 얼마나 자연스럽고 효율적인지에 대해 말하고 있다. 따라서 체스가 사회적 기술 향상에 끼치는 영향에 대해 말하는 ④는 글의 흐름과 관계가 없다.

구문풀이

6행 A strong chess player knows in a glance [that a certain type of move is good in a certain type of position] / and you know [you will enjoy a pastry {that looks a particular way}].

: 두 개의 절이 and로 연결된 구조이다. 첫 번째 [ ]는 knows의 목적절이며, 두 번째 [ ]는 know의 목적절이다. { }는 a pastry를 수식하는 관계절이다.

13행 Of course, these background intuition processes are sometimes wrong, [leaving you with a lost position or a second-rate snack], / and as a result your conscious mind will probably [assert itself a little more next time you are in that situation] and [second-guess your intuition].

: 두 개의 절이 and로 연결된 구조이다. 첫 번째 [ ]는 these background intuition processes를 의미상의 주어로 하는 분사구문이고, 두 번째 절에서 and로 연결된 두 번째와 세 번째 [ ]는 will에 이어지는 술부이다.

어휘풀이

- **apply** *v* 적용하다
- **handle** *v* 처리하다, 다루다
- **background** *n* 눈에 띄지 않는 곳
- **effortlessly** *ad* 쉽게
- **particular** *a* 특정한
- **collaboration** *n* 협업
- **assert** *v* 주장하다
- **context** *n* 맥락
- **figure out** 알아내다, 이해하다
- **noticeable** *a* 두드러진
- **in a glance** 한눈에
- **in person** 직접
- **intuition** *n* 직관
- **second-guess** *v* 재고하다

147 답 ②

📖📖 욕망을 만들어 내는 광고

전문해석

물자가 더 풍부해지고 그것들이 기본적인 육체적 그리고 사회적 필요와 더 동떨어질수록, 우리는 심리에 근거를 둔 호소에 더 마음이 열린다. 가게와 슈퍼마켓에서 전시되는 상품이 우리의 긴급한 욕구와 주로 관련이 없더라도, 그럼에도 불구하고 우리는 그것들을 갈망한다. 광고의 중심 기능은 전에는 존재하지 않았던 갈망을 만드는 것이다. (선진국의 경험은 광고가 사람들의 생활수준을 올리는 데 커다란 역할을 한다는 것을 보여준다.) 따라서 광고는 상품과 더 많은 상품을 선호하는 우리의 관심과 감정을 불러일으키고, 그것이 충족시키고자 하는 욕망을 실제로 만들어 낸다. 우리의 욕망은 사회나 개인의 욕구에 의해서가 아닌, 생산 시스템의 요구에 의해서 자극되고 형성된다. 따라서 정보를 제공하는 것이라기보다 설득하려고 노력하는 것이 광고자의 업무이다.

정답풀이

광고는 우리를 감정적으로 자극하여 전에는 존재하지 않았던 갈망을 만들어 낸다는 내용의 글이다. 따라서 광고가 사람들의 생활수준을 올리는 역할을 한다는 내용인 ②는 전체 흐름과 무관하다.

구문풀이

1행 [The more abundant goods become] and [the more removed they are from basic physical and social needs], [the more open we are to appeals {which are psychologically grounded}].

: 세 개의 「the 비교급 ~, the 비교급 …(~하면 할수록 더 …하다)」 구문이 연결되어, 'A하고 B할수록, 더욱 C하다'의 의미를 나타낸다. { }는 관계절로 앞의 명사 appeals를 수식한다.

어휘풀이

- **abundant** *a* 풍부한
- **psychologically** *ad* 심리적으로
- **relate to** ~과 관계가 있다
- **in favour of** ~을 선호하는, ~에 찬성하여
- **persuade** *v* 설득하다
- **removed** *a* 떨어진, 먼
- **grounded** *a* 근거를 둔
- **arouse** *v* (느낌·태도를) 불러일으키다

148 답 ④

📖📖 청소년기의 또래 인정 욕구

전문해석

13세에서 20세 연령 사이의 대다수 아이들에게 있어서 남자든 여자든 간에, 또래들의 인정은 대단히 중요하다. 이것의 이유는 집단의 일원으로 받아들여지고자 하는 욕구만큼 우정 그 자체에 대한 욕구에 있는 것은 아니다. 유년기과 성인기 사이의 어색한 과도기에 갇혀서, 십 대들은 개인으로서는 심리적으로 불안정한데 그것은 대략 6세에서 12세 연령 사이까지 걸쳐있는 이른바 잠재연령기 동안보다 훨씬 더 그렇다(불안정하다). 특정한 또래 집단의 구성원이 된다는 것은 한 사람으로서 가치 있고, 사회적 힘을 가지고 있으며, 가족 외의 세상 어느 곳에 속해 있다는 귀중한 느낌을 준다. (사춘기의 주요한 신체 발달 이정표가 모든 사람에게 일어나지만, 어떤 청소년들은 또래들보다 더 빨리 성숙하는 신체적인 징후를 보이고, 또 어떤 청소년들은 그것들을 더 나중에 보여준다.) 사실 인기가 있는 것은 일반적으로 십 대에게는 주요한 문제라서 그것은 각각의 십 대가 특정 동료 집단에 치열하게 포함된 구성원이 아니라면 자주 정서적 문제의 징후가 된다.

정답풀이

청소년기에서 나타나는 동료 집단에 받아들여지는 것을 중시하는 특성과 그 이유를 설명하는 글이다. 따라서 청소년기의 신체적 발달을 언급한 ④는 글 전체 흐름과 무관하다.

6행 [**Caught** in an awkward transition period between childhood and adulthood], teenagers are psychologically insecure as individuals — much more so <u>than</u> [during <u>the so-called latency</u> <u>period</u> {that extends roughly from age six to age twelve}].

: 첫 번째 [ ]는 Being이 생략된 분사구문으로 As they(= teenagers) are caught in ~으로 바꿔 쓸 수 있다. 두 번째 [ ]는 than의 목적어인 전치사구이며, { }로 표시한 관계절은 앞의 명사구 the so-called latency period를 수식한다.

어휘풀이

- vast *a* 막대한, 방대한
- approval *n* 인정, 승인
- awkward *a* 어색한, 힘든
- psychologically *ad* 심리적으로
- worthy *a* 가치 있는
- adolescence *n* 청소년기, 사춘기
- fiercely *ad* 치열하게, 지독히
- peer *n* 동료
- enormously *ad* 대단히
- transition period 과도기
- insecure *a* 불안정한, 자신이 없는
- milestone *n* 이정표, 획기적인 사건
- maturity *n* 성숙

149 답 ④

📖 우주의 행성들 간에 실시간 대화가 불가능한 이유

전문해석

모든 인간을 이웃으로 만들면서 전 세계를 하나로 묶어준 경이로운 전화와 텔레비전 네트워크는 우주로 확장될 수 없다. '다른 행성의 누구와도 대화하는 것은 결코 불가능할 것이다.' 이 말을 오해하지 말라. 오늘날의 무선 통신 장비로도, 다른 행성으로 말을 전송하는 문제는 거의 사소한 것이다. 하지만 전파와 광파가 초당 186,000마일의 동일한 제한된 속도로 이동하므로 이 메시지들이 도달하는 데 몇 분, 때로는 몇 시간이 걸릴 것이다. 앞으로 20년 후에는 화성에 있는 친구의 말을 들을 수 있게 되겠지만, 여러분이 듣는 말은 적어도 3분 전에 그의 입을 떠났을 것이며, 여러분의 답변이 그에게 도달하려면 그에 상응하는 시간이 걸릴 것이다. (오늘날의 기술로 만들 수 있는 어떤 우주선도 화성에 도달하는 데 6개월에서 9개월이 걸릴 것이다.) 그런 상황에서, 구두 메시지의 교환은 가능하지만 대화는 가능하지 않다.

정답풀이

행성들 간에 말을 전송하는 것은 가능하지만 전파가 도달하는 데 시간이 걸리므로 행성들 간에 실시간 대화를 하는 것은 불가능하다는 내용의 글이다. 따라서 오늘날의 기술로 만들 수 있는 우주선이 화성에 도달하는 데 걸리는 시간에 관한 내용의 ④는 글 전체 흐름과 무관하다.

구문풀이

1행 The marvellous telephone and television network [**that** enmeshed the whole world], [making all human beings neighbours], cannot be extended into space.

: 첫 번째 [ ]는 문장의 주어 The marvellous telephone and television network를 수식하는 관계절이고, 두 번째 [ ]는 부대상황을 나타내는 분사구문으로 문장의 주어와 동사 사이에 삽입되었다.

어휘풀이

- marvellous *a* 경이로운, 경탄할 만한
- statement *n* 진술
- radio wave 전파
- corresponding *a* 상응하는
- verbal *a* 말의, 구두의
- converse with ~와 대화하다
- trivial *a* 사소한, 하찮은
- light wave 광파
- spacecraft *n* 우주선

150 답 ④

📖 상호 호혜적인 멘토와 지도를 받는 사람의 관계

전문해석

당신이 멘토를 찾을 때 진실되고, 목적 의식이 있으며, 여분의 것을 기꺼이 돌려주려 한다면, 당신은 대부분의 사람들이 당신이 목표에 도달하는 것을 기꺼이 도울 만큼 충분히 친절하다는 것을 알게 될 것이다. **당신이 멘토를 찾기 위한 첫 걸음을 떼는 것이 두렵다면, 멘토링은 쌍방향적인 관계임을 명심하라.** 도움을 청할 때, 당신은 당신이 표현하는 감사와 경력 성장에 따라 당신이 제공할 수 있는 정보, 연락처 또는 지원 모두에서 모든 기회마다 당신의 멘토에게 기꺼이 보답을 해야 한다. 쌍방향적인 멘토 관계에서 당신 자신의 성취는 당신의 멘토의 성공을 입증하는 데 도움이 될 수 있고, 당신이 당신의 멘토에게 다른 연령 집단에 대한 귀중한 통찰력을 제공해줄 수 있다는 것을 잊지 마라. (멘토는 자문을 받는 사람보다 더 나이가 들 수도 더 어릴 수도 있지만, 멘토는 어떤 분야의 전문지식을 가지고 있어야 한다.) 그러니 제발 "그녀는 나와 이야기하기에는 너무나 바쁘고 중요한 사람이야."라고 생각함으로써 멈추지 마라.

정답풀이

멘토링은 멘토와 지도를 받는 사람의 상호 호혜적 관계이므로 멘토를 찾아 자문을 요청하는 것을 꺼리지 말라는 것이 글의 요지이다. 따라서 멘토의 자격에 대해 언급한 ④는 전체의 흐름과 무관하다.

구문풀이

10행 Don't <u>forget</u> [that in a two-way mentor relationship, {your own achievements can help validate your mentor's success}, and {you can provide your mentor with valuable insights into a different age group}].

: [ ]로 표시된 that절은 동사 forget의 목적어 역할을 하는 명사절이고, 그 안에 { }로 표시된 두 개의 절이 and로 연결되어 있다.

어휘풀이

- sincere *a* 진실한, 성실한
- be willing to *do* 기꺼이 ~하다
- appreciation *n* 감사
- validate *v* 입증하다, 확인하다
- expertise *n* 전문지식
- focused *a* 목적 의식이 있는, 집중한
- mentor *n* 멘토 *v* 조언하다, 지도하다
- assistance *n* 도움
- insight *n* 통찰력

151 답 ④

📖 음악에 대한 흥미와 음악적 재능 사이의 불일치

전문해석

음악적 재능은 복합적이며, 언제나 같은 사람에게서 모두 발견되는 것은 아니다. **음악적 흥미와 음악적 재능 사이에는 커다란 불일치가 자주 존재한다.** 음악이 매우 중요한 사람들 중 많은 사람들은 보람도 없이 여러 해 동안 작곡가나 연주자로 자신을 표현하려고 애쓴다. 음악 적성 검사에 의해서 보이듯이, 청각적으로 재능이 있는 다른 사람들이 반드시 음악에 많은 관심이 있는 것은 아니다. 흥미와 재능 사이의 이런 불일치는 다른 과목보다 음악에서 더 자주 맞닥뜨린다. (음악은 그것을 공부하는 사람들의 성격을 변화시켜 내적인 질서와 조화를 지향하도록 하는 강력한 교육적 도구로 여겨진다.) 예를 들어서, 수학적으로 재능이 없는 사람은 거의 수학자가 되기를 갈망하지 않지만, 음악에 열광하는 사람들은 자신의 음악적 재능의 부족이 자신의 가장 커다란 실망이라고 자주 고백한다.

정답풀이

음악은 수학 등의 과목과 달리 흥미와 재능 사이에 불일치가 크게 존재한다는 내용의 글이다. 따라서 음악이 교육적 도구로 여겨진다는 내용인 ④는 전체 흐름과 무관하다.

구문풀이

4행 Many [of those {**to whom** music is immensely important}] struggle for years [to express themselves as composers or executants] in vain.

: 첫 번째 [ ]는 핵심 주어인 Many를 수식하는 전치사구이고 그 안의 { }는 those를 수식하는 관계절이다. 전치사 to 뒤에는 목적어가 나오므로 목적격 관계대명사 whom이 왔다. 문장의 동사는 struggle이며, 두 번째 [ ]는 목적을 나타내는 부사적 용법의 to부정사구로 '~하기 위해'로 해석한다.

어휘풀이

- multiple *a* 복합적인
- immensely *ad* 대단히
- in vain 헛되이, 보람 없이
- aptitude *n* 적성, 소질
- alter *v* 바꾸다
- enthusiast *n* 열광자
- discrepancy *n* 불일치
- composer *n* 작곡가
- auditorily *ad* 청각적으로
- encounter *v* 마주치다, 직면하다
- incline *v* (마음을) 내키게 하다
- confess *v* 고백하다

---

15 글의 순서 파악 - 유형 연습 문제[1] 본문 pp.110~115

| 152 ④ | 153 ② | 154 ② | 155 ⑤ | 156 ⑤ |
| 157 ⑤ | 158 ③ | 159 ⑤ | 160 ④ | |

---

152 답 ④

📖 집단의 규범에 대한 순응

전문해석

규범은 사람들이 다른 사람들의 행동에 순응하는 결과로 집단들 내에 생겨난다. 따라서 한 사람이 특정 상황에서 자신이 그래야만 한다고 생각하기 때문에 특정 방식으로 행동할 때 규범의 시작이 발생한다. (C) 그런 다음 다른 사람들은 여러 가지 이유로 이 행동에 순응할 수도 있다. 최초의 행동을 한 사람은 다른 사람들이 이러한 유형의 상황에서 자신이 행동하는 것처럼 행동해야 한다고 생각할 수도 있다. (A) 따라서 그 사람은 지시하는 방식으로 규범 진술을 함으로써 그들에게 행동을 지시할 수도 있다. 다른 방식으로는 몸짓과 같은 것으로 순응이 요망된다는 것을 전달할 수도 있다. 더군다나 그 사람은 자신이 원하는 대로 행동하지 않으면 그들에게 제재를 가하겠다고 겁을 줄 수도 있다. 이것은 일부 사람들이 그 사람의 바람에 순응하고 그 사람이 행동하는 대로 행동하는 것을 초래할 것이다. (B) 그러나 일부 다른 사람들은 그 행동이 자신에게 지시되게 할 필요가 없을 것이다. 그들은 행동의 규칙성을 관찰하고 자신이 순응해야만 하는가를 스스로 결정할 것이다. 그들은 이성적이나 도덕적 이유로 그렇게 할 수도 있다.

---

153 답 ②

📖 물벼룩의 적응 가소성

전문해석

물벼룩이라는 흥미로운 종은 진화 생물학자들이 '적응 가소성'이라고 부르는 일종의 유연성을 보여준다. (B) 새끼 물벼룩이 물벼룩을 잡아먹는 생물의 화학적 특징을 포함한 물에서 성체로 성장하고 있으면, 그것은 포식자로부터 자신을 방어하기 위해 투구와 가시 돌기를 발달시킨다. 그것 주변의 물에 포식자의 화학적 특징이 포함되

어 있지 않으면 물벼룩은 이러한 보호 장치를 발달시키지 않는다. (A) 이것은 영리한 묘책인데, 왜냐하면 에너지의 관점에서 가시 돌기와 투구를 만드는 데는 에너지 비용이 많이 들고, 에너지를 절약하는 것은 유기체의 생존과 번식 능력에 필수적이기 때문이다. 물벼룩은 필요할 때만 가시 돌기와 투구를 만드는 데 필요한 에너지를 소비한다. (C) 따라서 이러한 가소성은 아마도 적응일 것인데, 즉 그것이 번식 적합성에 기여했기 때문에 종에 존재하게 된 특성인 것이다. 많은 종에 걸쳐 적응 가소성의 사례가 많이 있다. 가소성은 환경에 충분한 변화가 있을 때 적합성에 도움이 된다.

정답풀이

물벼룩의 '적응 가소성'을 일종의 유연성이라고 소개하는 주어진 글 다음에는, 새끼 물벼룩이 자신을 잡아먹는 생물의 화학적 특징을 포함한 물에서 성체로 성장할 경우 투구와 가시 돌기를 발달시킨다고 하며 주어진 글의 개념을 설명하는 (B)가 온다. 그리고 물벼룩이 투구와 가시 돌기를 발달시키는 것을 영리한 묘책(a clever trick)이라 지칭하며 에너지 절약의 관점에서 설명하는 (A)가 오고, 앞서 설명한 가소성을 '적응(adaptation)'이라고 말하며 많은 종에 적응 가소성의 사례가 있다고 마무리하는 (C)가 오는 것이 가장 적절하다.

구문풀이

4행 That's a clever trick, / because [{producing spines and a helmet} is costly, in terms of energy], and [{conserving energy} is essential for an organism's ability to survive and reproduce].

: 주절과 이유의 부사절로 이루어진 문장이다. 두 개의 [ ]는 부사절 내에서 and로 병렬 연결된 절이며, 두 { } 부분이 각 절의 주어인 동명사구이다.

10행 If the baby water flea is developing into an adult in water [that includes the chemical signatures of creatures {that prey on water fleas}], / it develops a helmet and spines [to defend itself against predators].

: It절과 주절로 이루어진 문장이다. 첫 번째 [ ]는 water를 수식하는 관계절이며, 그 안의 { }는 creatures를 수식하는 관계절이다. 두 번째 [ ]는 부사적 용법으로 쓰인 to부정사구이다.

어휘풀이

- fascinating *a* 흥미로운, 매력적인
- water flea 물벼룩
- evolutionary *a* 진화의
- trick *n* 묘책
- in terms of ~의 관점에서
- reproduce *v* 번식하다
- defend *v* 방어하다
- adaptation *n* 적응
- fitness *n* 적합성
- species *n* 종
- flexibility *n* 유연성
- adaptive plasticity 적응 가소성
- costly *a* 비용이 많이 드는
- conserve *v* 절약하다, 보존하다
- signature *n* 특징
- predator *n* 포식자
- reproductive *a* 번식의, 생식의
- variation *n* 변화, 변이

---

154 답 ②

📖 소비자에게 환경 비용을 부담하게 하는 것의 효과

전문해석

시장 반응 모형에 따르면, 공급자가 새로운 공급원을 찾게 하고, 혁신가가 대용하게 하고, 소비자가 아껴 쓰게 하고, 대안이 생기게 하는 것은 바로 가격 인상이다. (B) 특정 재화나 서비스에 과세하고, 그래서 가격을 인상하면 이러한 자원의 사용이 줄게 하거나 새로운 공급원 또는 선택 사항의 창조적 혁신을 가져올 것이다. 세금을 통해 조성된 돈은 정부가 직접 서비스를 공급하거나 대안을 찾는 데 사용될 수 있다. (A) 그러한 '환경세'의 많은 사례가 존재한다. 예를 들어, 쓰레기 매립 비용, 인건비, 음식물 찌꺼기 처리기를 공급하는 데 관련된 비용에 직면한 일부 도시는 가정이 모든 폐기물을 소비자가 직접 구입한, 보통 개당 1달러 또는 그 이상의 비용이 드는 특

정한 쓰레기봉투에 담아 처리하도록 요구해 왔다. (C) 그 결과 재활용이 크게 늘었고, 소비자가 포장과 폐기물에 더 세심한 주의를 기울이게 되었다. 소비자에게 쓰레기 비용을 자기 것으로 만들게 함으로써, 가정에서 나오는 쓰레기 흐름에서 눈에 띄는 감소가 있었다.

정답풀이

가격을 인상하면 공급자는 새로운 공급원을 찾고, 혁신가는 대용하고, 소비자는 아껴 쓰고, 대안이 생기게 된다는 내용의 주어진 글 다음에는, 특정 재화나 서비스에 대한 과세로 가격이 인상되면 자원 사용이 줄거나 새로운 공급원 또는 선택 사항을 창조적으로 혁신하게 된다고 부연 설명하는 (B)가 와야 한다. 그리고 특정 재화나 서비스에 부과되는 세금을 such "green taxes"로 받아서 가정 폐기물을 소비자가 직접 구입한 쓰레기봉투를 사용하여 처리하도록 한 예를 제시하는 (A)가 오고, 마지막으로 (A)에서 제시한 사례의 결과로 재활용이 늘고 가정 쓰레기가 줄었다는 내용의 (C)가 이어지는 것이 적절하다.

구문풀이

5행 [Facing landfill costs, labor expenses, and related costs in the provision of garbage disposal], for example, some cities have **required** households **to dispose** of all waste in special trash bags, [**purchased** by consumers themselves], and [often **costing** a dollar or more each].

: 첫 번째 [ ]는 some cities를 의미상의 주어로 하는 분사구문으로 some cities의 상황을 설명한다. 「require+목적어+목적격보어(to부정사)(~가 …할 것을 요구하다)」 구문이 쓰였으며, and로 연결된 두 번째와 세 번째 [ ]는 special trash bags를 의미상 주어로 하는 분사구문으로 which are purchased ~ and often cost ~로 이해할 수 있다.

어휘풀이

- drive v ~하게 내몰다
- substitute v 대체하다, 대용하다
- alternative n 대안
- green tax 환경세
- labor expense 인건비
- garbage disposal 음식물 찌꺼기 처리기
- internalize v ~을 자기 것으로 하다, ~을 내면화하다
- observed a 눈에 띄는, 관찰되는
- innovator n 혁신가
- conserve v 절약하다, 보존하다
- emerge v 나오다, 나타나다
- landfill n 쓰레기 매립(지)
- provision n 준비, 공급

155 답 ⑤

📖 생명의 역사에서 다세포성의 등장

전문해석

생명의 역사에서 가장 지대한 변이 중 하나는 다세포 진핵생물의 진화였다. (C) 다세포성의 명확한 증거는 조류(藻類) 종의 형태로 약 12억 년 전 시작한 화석 기록에 나타난다. 다세포성의 발달로 이어진 실제 사건은 신비에 싸여있지만, 그것이 발생했던 방식은 상상하기 쉽다. (B) 아마도 어느 한 특정 종의 개별 세포 무리가 뭉쳐서 군체를 형성했거나, 아니면 단일 세포가 분열한 결과로 생긴 두 개의 세포가 분리되지 않았을 것이다. 가장 단순한 다세포 유기체에서는 모든 세포가 구조적으로, 기능적으로 자율적(독자적)이다. (A) 이것은 더 진보한 다세포 유기체의 핵심 특성의 길을 열었는데, 분업이다. 시간이 흐르면서 세포는 구조적, 기능적으로 구별되게 되었다. 예를 들어, 일부 세포는 에너지를 거두어들이는 데 특화되었을 것이고 반면에 다른 것은 유기체의 이동성과 관련된 역할을 발달시켰을 것이다.

정답풀이

다세포 진핵생물의 진화가 생명의 역사에서 중요한 사건이었다는 내용의 주어진 글 다음에는, 이와 관련하여 그러한 진화의 시기와 방식을 언급하는 내용의 (C)가 이어져야 한다. 그리고 (C)에서 언급한 방식과 관련하여 구체적인 정보를 제공하는 내용의 (B)가 온 다음에, (B)에서 언급한 세포의 구조적, 기능적 자율성을 This로 받으며 그러한 자율성이 낳은 결과에 관해 설명하는 내용의 (A)로 마무리되는 것이 글의 순서로 가장 적절하다.

구문풀이

18행 The actual events [that led to the development of multicellularity] are a mystery / but **it** is easy [**to envision** {how it may have occurred}].

: 접속사 but이 두 절을 연결하는 구조이다. 첫 번째 [ ]는 첫 번째 절의 주어 The actual events를 수식하는 관계절이다. 두 번째 절에서 it은 가주어이고 to부정사구인 [ ]가 진주어이다. { }는 envision의 목적어 역할을 하는 명사절이다.

어휘풀이

- profound a 지대한, 엄청난
- multicellular a 다세포의
- distinct a 구별되는, 별개의
- harvest v 거두어들이다, 수확하다
- separate v 분리되다
- evidence n 증거
- appear v 나타나다, 등장하다
- envision v 상상하다, 마음속에 그리다
- transition n 변이(變移), 변천
- division of labour 분업
- specialize in ~에 특화되다
- colony n 군체
- autonomous a 자율적인
- alga n 조류(藻類)(pl. algae)
- fossil n 화석 a 화석의

156 답 ⑤

📖 일상에서 경험하게 되는 반동 효과

전문해석

직접 반동 효과는 난방, 조명 및 냉장과 같은 개별 에너지 서비스와 관련이 있으며 그러한 서비스를 제공하는 데 필요한 에너지로 국한된다. (C) 에너지 효율성이 향상되면 관련 서비스를 제공하는 한계 비용이 감소하므로 해당 서비스의 소비 증가로 이어질 수 있다. 예를 들어, 연료 효율적인 자동차를 구매한 후에는 킬로미터당 연비가 감소했기 때문에 소비자는 더 멀리 그리고/또는 더 자주 운전하는 것을 선택할 것이다. (B) 마찬가지로, 다락 단열재를 설치한 후에는 제곱미터당 운영 비용이 감소했기 때문에 소비자는 집을 더 오랜 기간 동안 그리고/또는 더 높은 온도로 난방하는 것을 선택할 것이다. 이러한 현상이 발생하는 정도는 에너지 서비스 간, 상황 간 및 시기 간에 따라 매우 다양할 것으로 예상된다. (A) 그러나 에너지 서비스 소비의 증가는 에너지 효율성 향상으로 달성한 '에너지 절약'을 감소시킬 것이다. 일부 상황에서는 그러한 절약을 완전히 상쇄시킬 수 있다.

정답풀이

직접 반동 효과를 언급한 주어진 글 다음에는, 연비가 좋은 자동차를 구입한 후에 연료를 더 많이 소비하게 되는 예를 설명한 (C)가 이어지고, 비슷한 예로(Similarly) 단열재를 설치한 후 더 많은 에너지를 소비하게 된다는 내용의 (B)가 와야 한다. 그러나(But) 반동 효과로 인해 에너지 효율의 증가가 에너지 절약 효과를 완전히 상쇄시킬 수 있다는 내용의 (A)는 이 글의 결론에 해당하므로 마지막에 오는 것이 가장 적절하다.

구문풀이

13행 The extent [to which this occurs] may be expected to vary widely {from one energy service to another}, {from one circumstance to another} and {from one time period to another}.

: The extent가 핵심 주어, may be expected가 동사이다. [ ]는 관계절로 선행사 The extent를 수식한다. 세 개의 전치사구 { }는 병렬구조로 연결되어 있다.

어휘풀이

- rebound effect 반동 효과
- refrigeration n 냉장
- efficiency n 효율성
- offset v 상쇄하다
- relate to ~와 관계가 있다
- confine v 한정하다, 국한하다
- circumstance n 상황
- temperature n 온도

- installation *n* 설치
- insulation *n* 단열(재), 단열 처리
- relevant *a* 관련된
- attic *n* 다락방
- marginal cost 한계 비용
- consumption *n* 소비

157 답 ⑤

📖 오늘날 음식 섭취로 인한 질병 문제를 해결할 수 있는 조상들의 자연 식품

전문해석

우리의 조상이 무엇을 먹었는지 더 많이 조사할수록 무엇이 우리 건강에 좋은지에 관해 더욱 더 많이 알게 된다. (C) 예를 들어, 우리는 조만간 미국인의 약 90퍼센트에게 고혈압이 생기게 될 것이라는 것을 이제 깨닫는다. 고혈압의 원인으로는 과도한 체중, 신체활동 부족, 신장병, 그리고 가공식품의 염분을 과다 섭취하거나 식사시간에 남용하는 것이 있다. (B) 석기시대에는 소금을 쉽게 구할 수 없었다. 우리의 식단에서 소금을 과다 섭취하면 혈압이 높아질 수 있는 반면 음식으로 높은 수준의 칼륨을 먹으면 혈압이 낮아질 수 있다. 이것을 알고 있는가? (A) 칼륨은 미국식 식단에서 너무 흔히 부족한 과일과 채소에서 발견된다. 자연으로 다시 돌아감으로써 우리는 수천 년에 걸쳐 만들어진 많은 문제들을 해결할 수 있다. 우리는 너무 오랜 세월 동안 몇몇 일을 잘못 해 와서 따라야 할 올바른 방향을 잊어버렸다.

정답풀이

조상이 먹었던 것을 조사해 보면 무엇을 먹는 것이 건강에 좋은지 더 많이 알 수 있다는 주어진 글 다음에는, 그 사례로 많은 미국인에게 고혈압이 생길 것을 알 수 있고 그 원인 중 하나가 염분 과다 섭취라는 내용의 (C)가 이어져야 한다. 그리고 조상들이 살았던 석기 시대에는 소금을 쉽게 구할 수 없었다고 하면서 칼륨을 먹으면 혈압이 낮아질 수 있다고 하는 (B)가 오고, 칼륨은 과일과 채소에 많이 들어있으므로 조상들처럼 자연으로 돌아가면 많은 건강 문제가 해결될 수 있다고 하는 (A)가 마지막에 이어지는 것이 가장 적절한 순서이다.

구문풀이

6행 We've been doing some things wrong for **so** many years we have forgotten the correct course [to follow].

: 「so ~ (that) ...(너무 ~해서 ...하다) 구문이 쓰인 문장으로, that 이하의 절은 앞의 절에 대한 결과의 의미를 나타낸다. [ ]는 the correct course를 수식하는 형용사적 용법의 to부정사이다.

어휘풀이

- investigate *v* 조사하다
- lacking *a* (~이) 없는[부족한]
- readily *ad* 손쉽게
- blood pressure 혈압
- sooner or later 조만간
- kidney disease 신장병
- processed food 가공식품
- ancestor *n* 조상
- diet *n* 식단
- excess *a* 초과의, 여분의
- ingest *v* (음식을) 먹다, (약을) 삼키다
- excessive *a* 과도한
- intake *n* 섭취
- overuse *n* 남용, 과용

158 답 ③

📖 눈을 마주치는 행동을 통해 사람의 마음을 읽는 것의 어려움

전문해석

우리 인간은 한 사람의 눈이 '마음의 창'이라고 오랫동안 생각해 왔고 우리는 어떤 사람이 대화를 하는 동안에 눈을 계속 마주치거나 마주치는 것을 피하는 것에 의미를 부여하는 경향이 있다. '마음을 읽는 것'이 약간 까다로울 수 있는 부분이 바로 여기이다. (B) 어떤 사람들은 눈을 많이 마주치지 않고 자주 다른 곳을 보는 경향이 있다. 이것이 그런 사람들은 보통 기만적이라고 말하는 일반 통념을 반드시 지지하는 것은 아니다. (C) 그 사람들은 단지 수줍어 할 수도 있다. 한편으로는, 어떤 사람이

단지 말할 때 끊임없이 당신을 뚫어지게 바라본다고 해서 그것이 이 사람이 반드시 정직의 본보기라는 것을 의미하는 것은 아니다. (A) 반면에 속이는 사람들은 그들이 진실하고 흥미가 있다는 것을 당신에게 확신시켜 주기 위해 사실 의식적으로 눈을 마주치도록 스스로를 강요하고 있을 수 있다. 아니면 그들이 어떤식으로든 확고하고 동요되지 않는 응시로 당신을 조정하려고 하는지도 모른다.

정답풀이

눈을 마주치고 마주치지 않는 행동을 통해 마음을 읽는 것이 까다로울 수 있다는 주어진 글의 내용 다음에는, 이에 대한 예시로 어떤 사람들은 눈을 마주치는 것을 꺼리지만 그것이 그들이 반드시 기만적임을 의미하는 것은 아니라고 하는 (B)가 와야 한다. 그리고 그들이 그저 수줍어 할 수도 있다는 (C)가 이어져야 하는데 (C)의 They는 (B)에서 언급한 눈을 마주치지 않는 경향이 있는 사람들을 가리킨다. 그리고 눈을 마주치는 것이 정직을 의미하는 것은 아니라는 (C)의 마지막 부분에 이어, 눈을 마주치는 행동이 상대를 속이거나 조정하려는 의도로 이루어질 수 있다고 부연하는 (A)가 오는 것이 가장 적절한 순서이다.

구문풀이

6행 On the contrary, deceivers **may** actually be consciously **forcing** themselves **to maintain** eye contact [to convince you {that they are truthful and interested}].

: deceivers가 주어, may be forcing이 동사이다. 여기에는 「force+목적어+to부정사」 구문이 쓰여 '~에게 …하도록 강제하다'의 의미를 나타낸다. [ ]는 목적을 나타내는 to부정사구이고, 그 안의 { }는 convince의 직접목적어로 쓰인 that절이다.

어휘풀이

- hold *v* (생각 등을) 지니다, 품다
- consciously *ad* 의식적으로
- unwavering *a* 동요하지 않는, 확고한
- be inclined to ~하고 싶어지다, ~하는 경향이 있다
- conventional wisdom 일반적 통념, 속된 지혜
- deceitful *a* 기만적인, 사람을 속이는
- integrity *n* 정직, 청렴결백
- tricky *a* 하기 까다로운, 신중을 요하는
- manipulate *v* 조종하다, 조작하다
- gaze *n* 응시, 시선
- unceasingly *ad* 끊임없이

159 답 ⑤

📖 서로 보완해주는 특성을 가진 사람들끼리 만날 때 유사성을 이기는 상이성

전문해석

대부분의 경우에 (타인에게) 끌림에 관한 한 유사성은 상이성을 이긴다. 사람들은 일반적으로 비슷한 다른 사람들과 사귀며, 그들은 그들과 다른 사람들에 의해서 배척된다. (C) 1:1의 관계에서 사람들은 때때로 아주 바람직한 자질을 가진 개인들에게 끌리지만, 집단을 평가할 때 사람들은 그 집단과 자신들 사이의 유사성의 정도에 선호의 토대를 둔다. (B) 그러나 만일 사람들의 자질이 서로 보완해주면 — 그들은 상이하지만 서로 잘 맞는다 — 이러한 독특한 형태의 상이성은 사람들이 서로 사귀도록 장려한다. 예를 들어, 만일 Claude가 집단을 이끄는 것을 좋아하면, 그는 역시 집단을 이끌려고 하는 다른 개인들에게 끌리지 않을 것이다. (A) 대신에, 그는 자신의 지도를 받아들이는 사람들에게 더 적극적으로 반응할 것이다. 마찬가지로, 하나의 집단을 만드는 개인들은 그 집단이 성공하려면 그 구성원들의 기술과 능력이 서로 보완해야 한다는 것을 깨달을 것이다. 이러한 사례들은 사람들이 그들 자신의 개인적 특성을 보완해주는 특성을 가진 사람들에게 끌린다는 것을 시사한다.

정답풀이

사람들이 일반적으로 비슷한 사람들과 사귄다는 주어진 글에 이어서, 사람들은 유사성에 기반해서 집단을 평가한다고 주어진 글의 내용을 부연하는 (C)가 이어져야 한다. 그리고 however로 글의 흐름을 전환시켜서 서로 상이하지만 보완 관계에 있는 경우에는 서로 잘 사귀게 된다는 (B)가 오고, 그것의

구체적인 사례를 소개하는 (A)가 오는 것이 가장 적절한 순서이다. (A)의 he
가 지칭하는 것은 (B)의 Claude이다.

구문풀이

9행 These cases <u>suggest</u> [that people are attracted to <u>those</u> {who
possess <u>characteristics</u> (that complement their own personal
characteristics)}].

: [ ]는 문장의 동사 suggest의 목적어 역할을 하는 명사절이다. 그 안의 { }는 those를
수식하는 관계절이고, ( )는 characteristics를 수식하는 관계절이다.

어휘풀이

- similarity *n* 유사성
- trump *v* 앞지르다, 능가하다
- dissimilarity *n* 상이성
- when it comes to ~에 관한 한
- associate with ~와 교체하다
- repulse *v* (제의자를) 거절하다, 물리치다
- dissimilar *a* 같지 않은, 다른
- complement *v* 보완하다
- strive *v* 노력하다, 애쓰다
- desirable *a* 바람직한
- evaluate *v* 평가하다

---

160 답 ④

📖 **인간의 뇌 속에 남아 있는 목소리에 끌리는 성향**

전문해석

우리 인간이 속한 사람 속(屬)은 200만 년 동안 진화했다. 뇌의 진화는 수천, 수백만
년에 걸쳐 일어나지만, 인간이 문명사회에 살게 된 것은 그 기간의 1퍼센트도 채 되
지 않는다. (C) 그것은 곧 우리 머릿속에 21세기의 지식이 가득 들어 있을지라도 두
개골 속 그 기관(뇌)은 여전히 석기시대의 뇌라는 뜻이다. **우리는 스스로를 문명화된
종으로 여기지만, 우리 뇌는 지나간 시대의 과제를 충족시키도록 설계되었다.** (A) 인
간과 다른 많은 동물들 중에서, 목소리는 짝을 선택하는 것과 같은 그러한 요구들 중
하나를 충족시키는 역할을 하는 것 같다. 우리가 목소리의 중요성을 이해할 수 있는
한 가지 방법은 한 성이 다른 성을 평가할 때 목소리의 어떤 측면이 가장 높게 평가
되는지를 조사하는 것이다. (B) 예를 들어, 여자들은 턱수염이 있는 검은 피부의 남
자, 깔끔하게 면도한 금발의 남자 또는 스포츠카의 운전석에 앉은 모습의 남자 중 어
느 쪽을 더 선호하는지에 관해 의견이 다를 수 있다. 하지만 그들이 들을 수 있으나
볼 수 없는 남자들을 평가하라고 요청받았을 때, 여자들은 신기하게 깊은 목소리를
가진 남자가 더 매력적이라는 것에 동의하는 경향이 있다.

정답풀이

인간의 뇌의 발전 기간 동안 문명사회에 산 기간은 1퍼센트도 안된다는 주어
진 글의 내용 다음에는 That means로 시작하여 주어진 글의 내용을 부연하
는 (C)가 와야 한다. 그리고 (C)에서 언급한 지나간 시대의 과제를 those
demands로 받으며 그러한 요구들 중 하나를 충족시키는 데 목소리가 중요
한 역할을 한다는 (A)가 오고, 인간과 동물들이 목소리에 끌린다는 (A)의 내
용을 예를 들어(For example) 뒷받침하는 내용의 (B)가 오는 것이 가장 자
연스러운 순서이다.

구문풀이

7행 One way [we can understand the importance of voice] is [to
<u>examine</u> {which aspect of it is most highly valued by one sex when
evaluating the other sex}].

: 첫 번째 [ ]는 핵심 주어인 One way를 수식하는 관계부사절이다. 두 번째 [ ]는 is의
보어 역할을 하는 명사적 용법의 to부정사구이고, 그 안의 { }는 examine의 목적어 역
할을 하는 명사절(의문사절)이다.

어휘풀이

- genus Homo 사람 속(屬), 인류
- evolve *v* 진화하다

- civilized *a* 문명화된, 교양 있는
- evaluate *v* 평가하다
- miraculously *ad* 신기하게, 기적적으로
- organ *n* 기관, 조직, 장기
- skull *n* 두개골, 두뇌
- challenge *n* 도전, 과제
- era *n* 시대, 시기

---

15 글의 순서 파악 - 유형 연습 문제(2)   본문 pp.116~119

161 ③	162 ②	163 ③	164 ⑤	165 ⑤
166 ②	167 ②	168 ④		

---

161 답 ③

📖 **뇌의 대사 활동**

전문해석

뇌는 흔히 적절한 행동 반응을 생성하기 위해 외부로부터 정보를 처리하는 입력/출
력 시스템으로 여겨지며, 대부분의 뇌 스캔 연구는 특정 행동이나 지각 중에 어떤 영
역이 활성화되는지, 즉 '불이 켜지는지'를 조사한다. (B) 그러나 특히 흥미로운 것은
뇌의 대사 활동이다. 뇌는 몸무게의 2%를 차지하는 것에 불과하지만 신체 에너지의
약 20%를 소비하는 굶주린 기관이다. (C) 그러나 뇌가 과제를 수행하기 위해 활발
하게 활동할 때는 그것의 대사 활동은 거의 변하지 않는다. 다시 말해, **뇌는 우리가
아무것도 하지 않을 때에도 계속 활동하며, 대부분의 에너지를 소모하는 내재적 활
동 패턴을 가지고 있다.** (A) 이 '기본' 활동은 우리가 무엇을 하든 거의 변하지 않는
채로 배경에서 지속적으로 실행된다. 이것은 뇌의 '기본 모드', 즉 뇌가 깨어 있지만
쉬고 있을 때 온라인 상태가 되는 뇌 영역의 네트워크이다.

정답풀이

뇌의 일반적 특성을 언급한 주어진 글 다음에는 뇌의 대사가 특히 흥미롭다는
내용으로 시작되는 (B)가 와야 한다. 뇌가 신체 에너지의 약 20%를 소비한다
는 (B)의 내용 다음에는, 역접의 접속사(Yet)로 시작하면서 뇌의 대사 활동의
독특한 점을 설명하기 시작하는 (C)가 온다. 그리고 (C)의 마지막에 뇌가 아
무 과제를 수행하지 않을 때를 언급했으므로 이에 대한 부연으로 뇌가 쉬고
있는 기본 모드를 언급하는 (A)가 마지막에 오는 흐름이 자연스럽다.

구문풀이

9행 This is [the brain's 'default mode'], [a network of brain regions
{that comes online when the brain is awake but resting}].

: 두 개의 [ ]는 동격 관계로 두 번째 [ ]는 문장의 보어인 the brain's 'default mode'
를 부연 설명한다. { }는 관계절로 앞에 나온 명사구 a network of brain regions를
수식한다.

어휘풀이

- appropriate *a* 적절한
- response *n* 반응
- active *a* 활성화된
- particular *a* 특정한
- perception *n* 지각, 인식
- baseline *n* 기준(선)
- default mode 기본 모드, 평상시 모드
- particularly *ad* 특히
- intriguing *a* 흥미를 자아내는
- metabolic *a* 대사의
- account for (부분·비율을) 차지하다
- mass *n* 질량
- intrinsic *a* 내재하는, 본질적인
- use up 소모하다

162 답 ②

전문해석

일부 연구에서, 한 엄마가 생후 몇 개월 된 아기를 카시트에 앉혀 안전띠를 맨 후 아기와 보통 잠깐 동안 상호작용을 한다. 그러고 나서 엄마는 시선을 돌리는데, 몇 분 후 무표정한 얼굴로 아기를 향해 다시 돌아선다. (A) 이는 아기를 당황하게 하고, 아기는 보통 먼저 미소를 지으며 엄마의 관심을 끌기 위해 노력한다. 이것이 실패하고 엄마가 지시에 따라 냉담한 표정을 유지하면 아기는 엄마를 돌아오게 하려는 시도를 확대하여 애원하듯이(간절히) 울부짖는다. (C) 아기가 웃었다가 울면, 아기는 엄마의 **자신에 대한 무관심한 행동을 바꾸도록 강요하려 하면서, 문제 중심적 대처 방식을 사용하고 있다.** 이것이 성공적이지 않으면 아기는 전략을 바꾸어 시선을 돌리거나 손가락이나 팔 또는 발가락을 빨면서 자신에게로 물러난다. (B) 이것은 **아기가 엄마의 도움 없이는 자신이 할 수 있는 것이 자신을 달래는 것뿐이라는 것을 깨닫기 때문에 감정에 초점을 맞춘 대처**이다. 아기는 겉으로는 도움이나 해결책을 찾는 것을 포기하는 것처럼 보이지만, 자신을 구하기 위해 내면으로 탈출한다.

정답풀이

(A)의 첫 문장의 주어인 This는 주어진 글에 언급된 시선을 돌렸다가 다시 무표정한 얼굴로 아기를 향해 돌아서는 엄마의 행동을 가리키므로 주어진 글 다음에는 (A)가 와야 한다. 아기가 우는 것이 문제 중심적 대처 방식이라는 (C)의 첫 문장은 (A)의 내용을 요약해서 언급하므로 (A) 다음에는 (C)가 와야 한다. (B)의 This는 (C)에서 언급된 시선을 돌리거나 손가락이나 팔 또는 발가락을 빠는 아기의 행동을 가리키므로 (C) 다음에 (B)가 와야 한다.

구문풀이

6행 This is disconcerting for the baby, [who attempts to engage her, {usually first by smiling}].

: [ ]는 the baby를 부연 설명하는 관계절이고 그 안의 { }는 앞에 나온 절의 주어(baby)의 행동을 부연 설명하는 부사구이다.

11행 This is emotion-focused coping / as the baby realizes [that, without help from the mother, all {he can do} is soothe himself].

: 주절과 as가 이끄는 부사절로 이루어진 문장이다. [ ]는 부사절의 동사 realizes의 목적어 역할을 하는 명사절이다. 이 that절의 주어는 all이며, { }는 all을 수식하는 관계절이다. soothe 앞에는 to가 생략되었는데 주어를 수식하는 관계절에 do가 있을 경우 주격보어로 원형부정사를 쓸 수 있다.

어휘풀이

- strap *v* 매다
- interact *v* 상호작용하다
- engage *v* (관심을) 끌다, 사로잡다
- escalate *v* 확대하다
- compel *v* 강요하다
- withdraw *v* 물러나다, 중단하다
- infant *n* 아기, 유아
- normally *ad* 보통, 정상적으로
- stony *a* 냉담한, 냉랭한
- soothe *v* 달래다
- strategy *n* 전략

163 답 ③

전문해석

정치는 포트와인의 역사에 있어서 도움이 되었으며, 그 와인의 발달에 있어서 계속해서 중요한 역할을 했다. 1678년에 영국이 프랑스에 전쟁을 선포하고 모든 항구를 봉쇄하자, 즉시 와인이 부족해졌다. (B) 포르투갈과 영국은 14세기부터 긴밀한 무역 관계를 유지했기에, 영국은 더 이상 프랑스에서 수입할 수 없는 와인을 포르투갈이 제공할 거라고 논리적으로 기대했다. (C) 하지만 그들은 곧 포르투갈의 와인이 프랑스와 같은 품질이 아니라는 것을 깨달았으며, 영국인들이 익숙해져 있는 품질을 보

장하기 위해서 와인의 생산을 감독할 필요가 있었을 것이다. Douro Valley가 질 좋은 와인에 꼭 필요한, 더 진한 풍미와 짙은 색을 가진 포도를 생산할 이상적인 기후를 갖고 있다는 것이 밝혀졌다. (A) 와인은 영국으로 수출하기 위해서 Douro River를 따라서 운반되었다. 그러나 이 와인들은 장거리 운송이 힘들었기에, 영국으로 가는 운송을 위해 발효 과정을 멈추고 안정제 역할을 하도록 브랜디가 첨가되었다. **이것은 달콤하고 포도 맛이 강하며 독한 와인을 탄생시켰고, 포트와인의 기원이 되었다.**

정답풀이

영국과 프랑스의 전쟁으로 영국에서 와인이 부족해졌다는 주어진 글 다음에는, 영국이 긴밀한 관계인 포르투갈로부터 와인을 얻기를 기대했다는 (B)가 이어져야 한다. 그리고 포르투갈의 와인의 품질이 떨어진다는 사실을 깨달은 영국이 Douro Valley가 와인 생산에 이상적인 기후임을 알아냈다는 (C)가 오고, 마지막으로 Douro Valley에서 생산된 포르투갈 와인이 영국으로 수입되는 과정에서 포트와인이 탄생했다는 (A)가 오는 것이 자연스럽다.

구문풀이

3행 In 1678, Britain declared war on France and blocked all its ports, [creating an immediate wine shortage].

: 문장의 동사인 declared와 blocked가 병렬구조로 연결되어 있으며, [ ]는 결과를 나타내는 분사구문이다.

16행 But they soon realized [that Portuguese wines were not of the same quality as the French], / and they would need to oversee its production to ensure the quality [to which they had become accustomed].

: 두 개의 절이 and로 연결된 구조이다. 첫 번째 [ ]는 realized의 목적어 역할을 하는 명사절이고, 두 번째 [ ]는 the quality를 수식하는 관계절이다.

어휘풀이

- instrumental *a* (~하는 데에) 도움이 되는
- declare *v* 선언하다
- shortage *n* 부족
- fermentation *n* 발효
- shipment *n* 운송, 선적
- oversee *v* 감독하다
- intense *a* 강렬한
- immediate *a* 즉각의, 당면한
- ship *v* 배에 싣다
- stabilizer *n* 안정제
- logically *ad* 논리적으로
- accustomed *a* 익숙한
- flavor *n* 맛

164 답 ⑤

전문해석

대부분의 경제학자들은 자신들을 사람들이 행동하는 방식에 대한 진실을 추구하는 과학자로 본다. 그들은 경제적인 행동에 대해 추측을 하고, 그 다음 이상적으로 인간의 경험에 기초해 그러한 예측의 타당성을 평가한다. (C) 그들의 작업은 사람들이 어떻게 행동'해야 하는지' 보다는 사람들이 '정말로' 어떻게 행동하는지를 강조한다. 과학자의 역할에서, 경제학자는 행동의 유형을 그 행동의 적절성이나 비적절성에 대한 언급 없이 객관적으로 관찰하려고 한다. (B) 과학적인 방법에 기초를 둔, 이런 객관적이고 주관이 개입되지 않은 접근법은 실증적인 분석이라고 불린다. 실증적인 분석에서 우리는 변수 A가 변수 B에 미치는 영향을 알기를 원한다. 우리는 가설을 검사할 수 있기를 원한다. (A) 예를 들어, 다음의 진술은 실증적인 진술이다. 집세 통제가 시행되면 공실률은 떨어질 것이다. 이 진술은 검증할 수 있다. 실증적인 진술이 올바른 진술일 필요는 없지만, 그것은 검증할 수 있는 진술이어야 한다.

정답풀이

경제학자들은 스스로를 사람들의 행동에 대한 진실을 추구하는 과학자로 본다는 주어진 글 다음에는, 경제학자들이 과학자들처럼 사람들의 행동 유형을

객관적으로 관찰한다고 부연하는 (C)가 와야 한다. (C)의 Their가 가리키는 것은 주어진 글의 경제학자들이다. 그리고 (B)의 This objective, value-free approach는 (C)에서 언급된 경제학자들의 객관적인 관찰을 의미하므로 그런 관찰이 실증적인 분석이라고 하는 (B)가 오고, 실증적인 분석에 대한 예시인 (A)가 이어지는 것이 적절한 순서이다.

구문풀이

1행 Most economists **view** themselves **as** scientists [seeking the truth about the way {people behave}].

: 「view A as B」 구문이 쓰여 'A를 B로 여기다[간주하다]'의 의미를 나타낸다. [ ]는 scientists를 수식하는 현재분사구이고 그 안의 { }는 the way를 수식하는 관계부사절이다.

어휘풀이

- speculation *n* 추측
- assess *v* 평가하다
- validity *n* 타당성
- prediction *n* 예측
- impose *v* 시행하다, 부과하다
- vacancy rate 공실률(비어 있는 방의 비율)
- testable *a* 검증할 수 있는
- objective *a* 객관적인
- value-free *a* 주관이 개입되지 않은
- analysis *n* 분석
- variable *n* 변수
- hypothesis *n* 가설
- emphasize *v* 강조하다, 중시하다
- reference *n* 언급
- appropriateness *n* 적절성
- inappropriateness *n* 비적절성

165 답 ⑤

우리가 영화를 재미있게 즐기는 이유

전문해석

영화는 지배적인 문화를 지지하고 시간이 지남에 따라 그것의 재생산을 위한 수단의 역할을 한다고 말할 수 있다. (C) 그러나 영화가 하는 일의 전부가 적절한 삶에 대한 문화적 지시와 처방을 전달하는 것뿐이라면 관객들이 왜 그러한 영화가 즐겁다고 생각하는지에 대해 질문할 수 있다. 우리들 대부분은 그러한 교훈적인 영화에는 싫증이 나게 될 것이고, 아마도 그것들을 소련 그리고 다른 독재 사회에서 흔했던, 문화적 예술 작품과 유사한 선전용으로 보게 될 것이다. (B) 이 질문에 대한 간단한 대답은 영화가 책임 있는 행동에 관한 두 시간짜리 국민 윤리 교육이나 사설을 제시하는 것 이상을 한다는 것이다. 그것들은 또한, 결국 우리가 만족스럽다고 느끼는 이야기를 한다. (A) 나쁜 사람들은 보통 벌을 받고, 낭만적인 커플은 진정한 사랑에 이르는 길에서 그들이 만나는 장애물과 어려움에도 불구하고 거의 항상 서로 만나게 되며, 우리가 소망하는 세상의 모습이 영화 속에서는 대개 결국 그런 모습이 되고 만다. 우리가 왜 그렇게 많이 영화를 즐기는지를 설명해 주는 것은 바로 영화의 이 이상적인 측면임이 틀림없다.

정답풀이

영화가 지배적인 문화를 지지하고 재생산하는 수단이 될 수 있다는 내용의 주어진 글 다음에는, 그렇다면 관객들은 왜 영화가 즐겁다고 생각하는지에 대한 의문이 생길 수 있다고 하는 (C)가 오는 것이 적절하다. 그리고 관객들이 왜 영화가 즐겁다고 생각하는지에 대한 대답으로 영화가 우리에게 만족스러운 이야기를 해서라고 설명하는 (B)가 그 다음에 오고, 만족스러운 이야기의 구체적인 사례들을 제시하는 (A)가 마지막에 오는 것이 적절한 순서이다.

구문풀이

4행 The bad guys are usually punished; / the romantic couple almost always find each other [**despite** the obstacles and difficulties {they encounter on the path to true love}]; / and the way [we wish the world to be] is [how, in the movies, it more often than not winds up being].

: 첫 번째 [ ]는 despite가 이끄는 전치사구이고, 그 안에 { }는 the obstacles and difficulties를 수식하는, 목적격 관계대명사가 생략된 관계절이다. 두 번째 [ ]는 the way를 수식하는 관계부사절이고, 세 번째 [ ]는 be동사 is의 보어 역할을 하는 명사절이다. more often than not은 '대개'로 해석한다.

9행 No doubt [**it is** this utopian aspect of movies **that** accounts for why we enjoy them so much].

: [ ]로 표시된 절은 「no doubt (that): ~임에 틀림없다」에 연결되는, that이 생략된 명사절(진주어)이며, 이 안에 「it is ~ that …」 강조구문이 사용되어 this utopian aspect of movies를 강조하고 있다.

어휘풀이

- dominant *a* 지배적인
- serve as ~의 역할을 하다
- reproduction *n* 재생산
- punish *v* 처벌하다
- encounter *v* 만나다 *n* 만남, 조우
- path *n* 길, 통로
- more often than not 대개, 대체로
- wind up -ing 결국 ~로 끝나다
- account for ~을 설명하다
- civics lesson 국민 윤리 교육
- editorial *n* 사설
- satisfying *a* 만족스러운
- directive *n* 지시, 명령
- prescription *n* 처방
- grow tired of ~에 싫증 나다
- propaganda *n* 선전

166 답 ②

영장류 사회에서 미소의 의미

전문해석

여러분이 공공장소에 앉아 있다가 여러분을 지켜보는 누군가의 시선을 눈치챘다고 가정하자. 여러분이 되받아 응시했을 때 상대방이 미소를 지으면, 여러분은 그 시선 교환에 기분이 좋아질 것이다. 그러나 상대가 웃을 기색 없이 계속 빤히 바라보면 여러분은 아마도 불편한 기분이 들 것이다. (B) 미소의 통화를 교환할 때 우리는 우리의 많은 영장류 사촌들이 경험하는 기분을 공유한다. 인간이 아닌 영장류 사회에서 정면 응시는 공격적인 신호이다. 그것은 공격에 앞서는 행위일 때가 많고, 따라서 공격을 야기할 수 있다. (A) 그 결과, 예를 들어 복종하는 원숭이는 서열이 높은 원숭이를 확인하고 싶을 때 평화의 신호로서 이빨을 드러낸다. 원숭이 언어에서 드러낸 이빨은 "내 시선을 용서해주세요. 사실 내가 쳐다보고 있지만 공격하겠다는 뜻이 아니니까 제발 나를 먼저 공격하지는 마세요."라는 뜻이다. (C) 침팬지 사이에서는 미소가 다른 뜻으로도 통한다. 우위에 있는 개체가 복종하는 개체에게 미소를 보이는데, 그것은 "걱정하지 마. 너를 공격하려는 것은 아니니까"와 유사한 뜻이다. 그러므로 복도에서 지나친 낯선 사람이 우리에게 설핏 미소를 비칠 때, 우리는 영장류의 전통 깊숙이 뿌리 내린 의사 교환을 경험하는 것이다.

정답풀이

공공장소에서의 시선 교환에 미소가 있느냐의 여부에 따라 기분이 좋을 수도 있고 불편할 수도 있다는 주어진 글 다음에는, 미소를 주고 받을 때 우리는 인간 이외의 영장류와 같은 기분을 공유한다고 하며 영장류 사회에서의 경우를 설명하는 (B)가 나와야 한다. 그리고 정면 응시는 공격을 야기할 수 있다는 (B)의 내용에 이어, 복종하는 원숭이는 공격을 받지 않도록 이빨을 드러낸다는, 즉 미소를 띤다는 (A)가 나와야 한다. 그리고 침팬지 사회에서는 미소가 다른 뜻이며 인간도 이와 유사하게 타인에게 미소를 지을 때가 있다는 (C)가 결론으로 나오는 것이 적절하다.

구문풀이

20행 So when [you pass a stranger in the corridor] and [that person flashes a brief smile], / you're experiencing an exchange with roots deep in our primate heritage.

: 시간을 나타내는 부사절과 주절로 이루어진 문장이다. 두 개의 [ ]는 부사절 내에 and로 병렬 연결된 절이다.

어휘풀이

- gaze *n* 응시, 시선
- submissive *a* 복종하는, 유순한
- bare *v* 드러내다
- currency *n* 유통, 통용
- aggressive *a* 공격적인
- analogously *ad* 비슷하게, 유사하게
- flash *v* (잠깐) 비치다
- stare *v* 응시하다, 빤히 보다
- dominant *a* 지배적인, 우세한
- pardon *v* 용서하다
- primate *n* 영장류의 동물
- precede *v* ~에 선행하다[앞서다]
- corridor *n* 복도
- heritage *n* 유산

167 답 ②

📖 결국 틀린 것으로 입증된 데카르트의 반사 작용의 개념

전문해석

데카르트는 그가 반사 작용의 개념을 만들어 냈을 때 행동의 이해에 매우 중요한 기여를 했다. 행동이 (반응을) 유발하는 자극을 반사할 수 있다는 기본적인 생각은 행동 이론의 중요한 구성 요소로 남아 있다. (B) 하지만, 데카르트는 반사 작용의 세부 사항들에 대한 그의 믿음에 있어서 실수를 했다. 그는 감각 기관에서 뇌로 가는 감각 메시지와 뇌에서 근육으로 가는 운동신경의 메시지가 동일한 신경을 따라 이동한다고 믿었다. (A) 그는 신경이 비어있는 관이고, 신경 전달은 동물 정기(精氣)라고 불리는 기체의 이동을 수반한다고 생각했다. 송과선에 의해 분출되는 동물 정기는 신경의 관을 통해 흘러 근육으로 들어가 그것을 부풀게 해 움직임을 만들어 내는 것으로 생각되었다. (C) 덧붙여 데카르트는 모든 반사적인 움직임은 타고난 것이고 신경계의 조직에 의해 고정되어 있는 것으로 여겼다. 데카르트가 죽고 난 이후로 몇백 년에 걸쳐서 반사 작용에 관한 이런 모든 생각은 틀렸음이 입증되었다.

정답풀이

데카르트가 반사 작용의 개념을 만들어 냈을 때 행동의 이해에 중요한 기여를 했다는 주어진 글 다음에는, 그가 실수를 했다고 하며 그것에 대해 설명하기 시작하는 (B)가 와야 한다. 그리고 데카르트가 감각 메시지와 운동신경의 메시지가 동일한 신경을 따라 이동한다고 믿었다는 (B)의 내용을 부연 설명하는 (A)가 오고, 마지막으로 그의 생각들이 틀렸음이 입증되었다고 결론 내리는 (C)가 오는 것이 적절한 순서이다.

구문풀이

13행 He believed [that sensory messages {going from sense organs to the brain} and motor messages {going from the brain to the muscles} traveled along the same nerves].

: [ ]는 동사 believed의 목적어 역할을 하는 명사절이다. 그 안의 { }는 각각 명사절의 주어인 sensory messages와 motor messages를 수식하는 현재분사구이며, 이 두 명사구가 명사절 동사인 traveled에 연결된다.

어휘풀이

- significant *a* 중요한
- formulate *v* 만들어 내다
- trigger *v* 유발하다, 일으키다
- building block 구성 요소
- neural transmission 신경 전달
- release *v* 분출하다
- motor *a* 운동(신경)의
- anatomy *n* (동식물의) 조직, 구조
- contribution *n* 기여
- reflex *n* 반사 작용
- stimulus *n* 자극
- hollow *a* 비어 있는
- animal spirits 동물 정기(精氣)
- swell *v* 부풀다
- innate *a* 타고난

168 답 ④

📖 사회적 태만의 정의

전문해석

사회적 태만은 사람들이 집단 결과물을 만들어 내기 위해 자신들의 노력을 결합할 때 발견되는 동기와 노력의 감소를 의미한다. 사람들은 개별적으로 일할 때보다 기여가 결합된 작업을 집단적으로 수행할 때 더 적은 생산량을 내거나 노력을 덜 기울이는 경향이 있다. (C) 그 결과, 사람들은 개인적으로 일할 때보다 집단의 일부로서 일할 때 생산성이 떨어진다. 사회적 태만은 사람들이 그들의 기여가 없어도 된다고 인식할 때 집단적 노력에 덜 기여하는 '무임승차 효과'와 비슷하다. (A) 이것은 또한 다른 집단 구성원들의 사회적 태만이나 무임승차 시도의 희생양이 되는 것을 피하기 위해 집단에 대한 기여를 억제하는 '편승 효과'와도 유사하다. (B) 그러나, '무임승차 효과'와 '편승 효과'는 사회적 태만의 구체적인 원인을 일컫는 더 좁은 용어들이다. 사회적 태만은 기여가 결합되지 않은 경우와 비교하여 결합되었을 때 발생하는 동기와 노력에 있어서의 모든 감소를 일컫는 더 넓은 구성개념이다.

정답풀이

사회적 태만을 설명하며 사람들이 집합적으로 일할 때 노력을 덜 기울인다고 한 주어진 글 다음에는, 그 결과로 생산성이 떨어진다고 하며 이는 '무임승차 효과'와 비슷하다고 하는 (C)가 이어져야 한다. 그리고 (C)에서 설명한 현상을 This로 받아 이것이 '편승 효과'와도 비슷하다고 하는 (A)가 이어지고, '무임승차 효과'와 '편승 효과'가 사회적 태만의 개념과 다른 점을 설명하는 (B)로 마무리되는 것이 적절한 순서이다.

구문풀이

3행 People tend to generate **less** output or to contribute **less** effort [when working on a task collectively {**where** contributions are combined}] **than** [when working individually].

: to generate와 to contribute는 or로 병렬 연결되어 tend에 이어진다. 두 개의 [ ]가 비교되고 있는 비교 구문으로, { }는 a task를 수식하는 관계절이다.

어휘풀이

- decline *n* 감소
- output *n* 생산(량)
- collectively *ad* 집합적으로
- withhold *v* 억제하다, 보류하다
- construct *n* 구성개념
- pool *v* (공동으로 이용할 자금·정보 등을) 모으다
- consequence *n* 결과
- perceive *v* 인식하다
- generate *v* 생성시키다
- contribute *v* 기여하다
- individually *ad* 개인적으로
- free riding 무임승차
- collective *a* 집단적인
- dispensable *a* 없어도 되는, 불필요한

16	문장 삽입 - 유형 연습 문제[1]			본문 pp.120~125
169 ③	**170** ⑤	**171** ④	**172** ④	**173** ③
174 ④	**175** ⑤	**176** ④	**177** ④	

169 답 ③

📖 과학을 승자독식 대회로 보는 견해의 극단성

전문해석

과학은 때때로 승자독식 대회로 묘사되는데, 이는 2등이나 3등인 것에 대한 보상이 없다는 뜻이다. 이는 과학 대회의 본질에 대한 극단적인 견해이다. 과학 대회를 그렇게 설명하는 사람들조차도 그것이 다소 부정확한 설명이라고 말하는데, 반복과 입증이 사회적 가치를 지니고 있으며 과학에서는 일반적이라는 것을 감안할 때 그렇다. 그것은 단지 소수의 대회만 존재한다는 것을 보여 줄 경우에 또한 부정확하다. 물론,

힉스 입자의 확인 또는 고온 초전도체 개발과 같은 몇몇 대회는 세계적인 수준으로 여겨진다. 하지만 다른 많은 대회에는 다양한 부분이 있고, 그런 대회의 수는 증가하고 있을 것이다. 예를 들어, 여러 해 동안 암에 대해 '하나'의 치료법만 있다고 생각되었지만, 암은 여러 가지 형태를 띠고 치료를 제공하기 위해 다양한 접근 방식이 필요하다고 이제 인식된다. 승자는 한 명이 아니라 여러 명이 있을 것이다.

170 답 ⑤

📖 **자연과 도시의 관계에 대한 생각을 드러내고 구현하는 도시 공원**

전문해석

공원은 그것이 속한 시대의 문화적 관심사가 요구하는 형태를 취한다. 일단 공원이 자리 잡으면, 그것은 결코 비활성 단계가 아니며 그것의 목적과 의미는 계획한 사람과 공원 이용자에 의해 만들어지고 개조된다. 그러나 공원을 조성하는 시기는 특히 의미가 있는데, 그것(공원을 조성하는 시기)이 자연과 자연이 도시 사회와 갖는 관계에 관한 생각을 드러내고 실현하기 때문이다. 실제로 **공원을 더 넓은 범주의 공공 공간과 구별하는 것은 공원이 구현하려는 자연의 표상이다.** 공공 공간에는 공원, 콘크리트 광장, 보도, 심지어 실내 아트리움도 포함된다. 일반적으로 공원에는 그것의 가장 중요한 특징으로 나무, 풀, 그리고 여타 식물이 있다. 도시 공원에 들어갈 때, 사람들은 흔히 거리, 자동차, 그리고 건물과의 분명한 분리를 상상한다. 그것에 대한 이유가 있는데, 전통적으로 공원 설계자들은 공원 경계에 키가 큰 나무를 심고, 돌담을 쌓고, 그 밖의 다른 경계벽의 수단을 건축하여 그런 느낌을 만들어 내려고 했다. 이 생각의 배후에는 미적으로 시사하는 바가 큰 공원 공간을 설계하려는 조경가의 욕망뿐만 아니라, 도시와 자연을 대조적인 공간이자 대립하는 세력으로 상상하는 서구 사상의 훨씬 더 오래된 역사도 있다.

정답풀이

주어진 문장의 such a feeling은 ⑤ 앞 문장에 언급된 공원과 도시의 사물이 분리되는 느낌을 의미하고, ⑤ 다음 문장의 this idea는 주어진 문장에 언급된 공원을 지을 때 나무나 돌담으로 경계벽을 세우는 것을 의미하므로 주어진 문장은 ⑤에 들어가는 것이 가장 적절하다.

구문풀이

12행 Indeed, [**what** distinguishes a park from the broader category of public space] is the representation of nature [that parks are meant to embody].

: 첫 번째 [ ]는 선행사를 포함한 관계대명사 what이 이끄는 명사절로 문장의 주어 역할을 한다. 두 번째 [ ]는 문장의 보어인 the representation of nature를 수식하는 관계절이다.

20행 What's behind this idea is **not only** [landscape architects' desire to design aesthetically suggestive park spaces], **but** [a much longer history of Western thought {that envisions cities and nature as antithetical spaces and oppositional forces}].

: 두 개의 [ ]는 '~뿐만 아니라 …도'라는 의미의 「not only ~ but (also) …」 구문으로 연결되어 있다. { }는 a much longer history of Western thought를 수식하는 관계절이다.

어휘풀이

- partition *n* 경계벽, 칸막이
- reveal *v* 드러내다
- distinguish *v* 구별하다
- representation *n* 표상, 표현
- concrete *a* 콘크리트로 된
- suggestive *a* 시사하는 바가 큰
- oppositional *a* 대립하는
- inert *a* 비활성의, 불활성의
- actualize *v* 실현하다
- category *n* 범주
- embody *v* 구현하다, 상징하다
- separation *n* 분리
- envision *v* 상상하다, 마음속에 그리다

171 답 ④

📖 **영화의 기술 혁신 도입으로 인한 영화적 환상 파괴**

전문해석

영화는 우리 현실의 숨겨진 윤곽을 보이게 만드는 그것의 능력 때문이 아니라 현실 자체가 가리고 있는 것, 즉 환상의 차원을 드러내는 그것의 능력 때문에 가치가 있다. 이것이 최초의 위대한 영화 이론가들이 영화를 사실주의 쪽으로 밀어붙였던 소리와 (색채 같은) 다른 기술 혁신의 도입을 한 목소리로 공공연히 비난한 이유이다. 영화는 전적으로 환상적인 예술이므로 이러한 혁신은 완전히 불필요했다. 그리고 설상가상으로 그것들은 잠재적으로 영화를 현실 묘사를 위한 단순한 전달 장치로 변형시키면서 영화 제작자와 관객을 영화의 환상적인 차원에서 멀어지게 할 수 있을 뿐이었다. 무성의 흑백 영화의 비사실주의가 지배하는 한, 영화적인 환상을 현실의 표현으로 받아들일 수 없었다. 그러나 **소리와 색채는 바로 그러한 착각을 만들겠다고 위협하여 영화 예술의 바로 그 본질을 파괴했다.** Rudolf Arnheim이 표현한 것처럼 "예술가의 창의적 힘은 현실과 표현 매체가 일치하지 않는 곳에서만 발휘될 수 있다."

정답풀이

④를 중심으로, 소리와 색채의 도입으로 영화가 현실 묘사를 위한 단순한 전달 장치로 변형되어 영화 제작자와 관객을 영화의 환상적인 차원에서 멀어지게 했다는 내용과, 소리와 색채가 영화 예술의 본질을 파괴했다는 같은 맥락의 내용이 역접(But)으로 이어지고 있어 어색하다. 또 ④ 뒤에 나오는 문장의 such an illusion은 주어진 문장에서 언급한 영화적인 환상을 현실의 표현으로 받아들이는 것을 가리키므로, 주어진 문장은 ④에 들어가야 한다.

구문풀이

4행 Cinema is valuable **not** [for its ability {**to make** visible the hidden outlines of our reality}], **but** [for its ability {**to reveal** what reality itself veils}] — [the dimension of fantasy].

: 첫 번째와 두 번째 [ ]가 「not A but B」의 상관접속사로 연결되면서 for와 함께 'A 때문이 아니라 B 때문에'라는 뜻을 나타내고 있다. 두 개의 { }는 각각 바로 앞의 its ability를 수식하는 형용사적 용법의 to부정사구이다. 첫 번째 { }에서는 to부정사구에 「make+목적어+목적격보어(~를 …로 만들다)」 표현이 사용되었는데, 목적어가 길어서 목적격보어 뒤로 이동한 형태가 되었다. 세 번째 [ ]는 what reality itself veils의 내용을 구체적으로 제시하는 동격어구이다.

어휘풀이

- predominate *v* 우세하다, 지배적이다
- take A for B A를 B라고 생각하다
- dimension *n* 차원
- nothing but 단지 ~일 뿐인
- transform *v* ~을 변형시키다
- come into play 작동하기 시작하다
- veil *v* ~을 가리다
- entirely *ad* 전적으로
- potentially *ad* 잠재적으로
- illusion *n* 환상, 착각
- coincide *v* 일치하다

172 답 ④

📖 **예방 원칙에 대한 찬성과 반대 입장**

전문해석

예방 원칙의 모든 판본에는 한 가지 공통 공리가 담겨 있다. 기술은 받아들이기 전에 해를 입히지 않는 것으로 입증되어야 한다. 그것은 전파되기 전에 안전한 것으로 증명되어야 한다. **안전성이 증명되지 않으면, 그것은 금지되거나 제한되거나 수정되거나 내버려지거나 무시되어야 한다.** 다시 말해, 새로운 아이디어에 대한 첫 번째 반응은 그것의 안전성이 확립될 때까지 무반응이어야 한다. 어떤 혁신이 이루어질 때 우리는 멈추어야 한다. 과학적 확실성에 의해 새로운 기술이 괜찮다고 승인받은 후에만 우리는 그것과 함께 살려고 해야 한다. 표면적으로 이 접근 방식은 합리적이고 신중해 보인다. 피해는 예견되고 선제적으로 예방되어야 한다. 후회하는 것보다 안전한 것이 더 낫다. 불행하게도, 예방 원칙은 이론적으로는 좋지만 실제로는 잘 작동하지 않는다. "예방 원칙은 정말 아주 잘하는 것이 하나 있는데, 기술 발전을 멈추는 것이다."라고 철학자이자 컨설턴트인 Max More는 말한다. 그 원칙의 실상을 폭로하는 책을 쓴 Cass R. Sunstein은 **"우리는 예방 원칙이 우리를 나쁜 방향으로 이끌기 때문이 아니라, 그것이 어떤 방향으로도 이끌지 않기 때문에 그것에 이의를 제기해야 한다."**라고 말한다.

정답풀이

주어진 문장은 Unfortunately(불행하게도)로 시작하면서, 예방 원칙이 이론적으로는 좋지만 실제로는 잘 작동하지 않는다고 했으므로 예방 원칙의 좋은 점이 소개되고 난 뒤, 이 원칙에 어떤 문제나 한계가 있는지를 설명하는 내용 앞에 위치해야 한다. 따라서 주어진 문장은 예방 원칙이 기술 발전을 멈춘다는 내용 앞인 ④에 들어가는 것이 가장 적절하다.

구문풀이

11행 [**Only** after a new technology has been confirmed okay by the certainty of science] should we try to live with it.

: Only가 한정하는 부사절이 문장 앞으로 나오면서 도치 구문이 되어 조동사 should와 주어 we가 도치되었다.

어휘풀이

- precautionary *a* 예방의
- embrace *v* 받아들이다
- restrict *v* 제한하다
- junk *v* 버리다, 폐기하다
- innovation *n* 혁신
- confirm *v* 승인하다, 확인하다
- prudent *a* 신중한
- preempt *v* ~에 선수를 치다, 선취하다
- devote A to B A를 B에 쏟다[전념하다]
- principle *n* 원리, 원칙
- prohibit *v* 금지하다
- modify *v* 수정하다, 바꾸다
- establish *v* 확립하다
- pause *v* 잠시 멈추다
- reasonable *a* 합리적인, 타당한
- anticipate *v* 예상하다
- progress *n* 진보, 발전

---

173 답 ③

📖 인간에게 고유한 인과 관계에 대한 이해

전문해석

인과적 이해는 인간에게 고유한데, 떨어지는 바위의 무게는 분명히 통나무가 쪼개지게 '강제한다.' 동물들은 그러한 믿음을 가지고 있지 않은데, 인과적 믿음을 가질 수 있는 이 능력은 어떻게 진화했을까? 물론 인간과 포유류, 그리고 특히 영장류의 인식 사이에는 인지적 유사성이 있다. 영장류는 자기의 지역적 환경을 기억하고, 새로운 우회로를 택하며, 사물의 움직임을 쫓고, 유사한 점들을 인식하며, 문제 해결에 대한 어떤 통찰력을 지닌다. 그것들은 또한 개체를 인식하고, 그것들의 행동을 예측하며, 동맹을 형성한다. 하지만 그것들은 생명이 없는 사물 사이의 인과 관계에 관한 이해가 거의 없다. 그것들은 인간의 사고에 기본적인 근원적 '힘'이라는 견지에서 세상을 보지 않으며 의도적 또는 인과적 견지에서 세상을 이해하지 못한다. 인간이 아닌 영장류는 자기 행동과 자신이 경험하는 결과 간의 인과 관계를 이해하지 못한다. 예를 들어, 유인원은 대대적인 교육 없이는 단순한 물리적 조작을 위한 적절한 도구를 선택할 수 없다.

정답풀이

주어진 문장은 글의 흐름을 전환하는 연결사 However로 시작하면서 그것들(인간이 아닌 영장류)의 인식에는 사물 사이의 인과 관계에 관한 이해가 거의 없다는 내용을 담고 있다. 따라서 그것들의 인식이 인간의 인식과 비슷한 점이 있다는 진술이 끝나는 문장 다음, 그리고 그것들의 인과 관계 이해 결여에 관한 부연이 이어지는 문장 앞인 ③에 들어가는 것이 가장 적절하다.

구문풀이

9행 Primates [remember their local environment], [take novel detours], [follow object movement], [recognise similarities] and [have some insight into problem solving].

: and로 연결된 다섯 개의 [ ]는 주어 Primates에 이어지는 술부이다.

어휘풀이

- causal *a* 인과의
- cognitive *a* 인지의
- mammalian *a* 포유류의
- novel *a* 새로운
- alliance *n* 동맹
- appropriate *a* 적절한
- extensive *a* 대대적인, 광범위한
- splinter *v* 쪼개지다
- similarity *n* 유사성
- primate *a* 영장류의
- insight *n* 통찰력
- underlying *a* 근원적인
- manipulation *n* 조작

---

174 답 ④

📖 여러 요인에 의해 사람마다 서로 다른 맛보기 능력

전문해석

모든 사람들이 애플파이의 맛을 같은 방식으로 인지하는 것은 아니다. 사람들 간에 기본적 맛에 대한 민감성에 상당한 유전적 다양함이 존재한다. 맛보기 능력은 또한 여러 외부 영향에 따라 사람들 안에서도 다양하다. 맛에 영향을 미치는 한 가지 그러한 요소는 음식이나 음료의 온도이다. 미뢰는 약 30℃의 온도에서 가장 잘 작동한다. 음식이나 음료의 온도가 20℃ 미만이나 30℃ 초과가 되면, 그것들의 맛을 정확히 구별하는 것은 더 어려워진다. 외양이나 비슷한 음식에 대한 이전 경험에 기반을 둔 미리 생각한 아이디어와 같은 심리적 요인들 또한 사람의 맛 인지에 영향을 미친다. 예를 들어, 체리 맛 음식은 빨간색일 것으로 기대되지만 그것이 노란색이면 그것을 체리로 식별하기가 어려워진다. 또한 음식과 관련된 불쾌한 경험이 미래에 그 음식에 대해 인지되는 맛에 영향을 줄 수 있다.

정답풀이

맛에 대한 유전적인 민감성, 온도와 같은 외부 요인, 그리고 심리적 요인에 따라 맛보기 능력이 달라진다는 내용의 글이다. 주어진 문장은 음식의 외양이나 선입견 같은 심리적 요인이 맛의 인지에 영향을 끼친다는 내용이므로, 체리 맛 음식이 빨간색일 거라고 기대된다고 하며 음식의 외양에 따른 심리적 요인과 맛의 인지 사이의 관계에 대해 구체적으로 예를 드는 문장 앞인 ④에 들어가는 것이 적절하다.

구문풀이

1행 Psychological factors, such as preconceived ideas [based {on appearance} or {on previous experiences with a similar food}], also affect a person's perception of taste.

: 주어는 Psychological factors이고 동사는 affect이다. [ ]는 preconceived ideas를 수식하는 과거분사구이며, { }로 표시된 두 전치사구는 병렬구조를 이룬다.

어휘풀이

- preconceive *v* 미리 생각하다
- genetic *a* 유전의
- sensitivity *n* 민감도
- taste bud 미뢰
- perception *n* 인식, 인지
- variation *n* 다양함, 변화
- vary *v* 다르다, 다양하다
- identify *v* 확인하다, 식별하다

---

175 답 ⑤

📖 유명인의 목소리 배역 출연과 성우들의 일자리 문제

전문해석

성우들과 관련한 좀 더 최근의 문제는 유명인의 목소리를 사용하는 것이다. 사업가들은 잘 알려진 유명인의 이름이 특히 영화에 관객을 불러 모을 것이라고 느낀다. 팬들은 유명인을 직접 보지는 못하더라도 유명인의 작품을 보러 갈 것이다. 그리고 유명인은 TV 토크 쇼 순회를 함으로써 그리고 그 영화에 대해서 얘기함으로써 영화를 대중에게 알릴 수 있다. Jeff Bridges는 그의 이름뿐만 아니라 그의 걸걸한 목소리 때문에, 그리고 그 자신이 서핑을 하는 사람으로서 그 등장인물과 아주 잘 부합하기 때문에 (애니메이션 영화) 〈Surf's Up〉의 Big Z 목소리를 위해서 선택되었다. 물론, 유명인의 목소리가 더 많이 사용될수록 직업 성우들의 일자리는 더 줄게 된다. 유명인들이 자주 그들 자신의 목소리를 내기 위해서 캐스팅되긴 하지만, 유명인 자신이 너무 바쁘거나 출연료가 너무 적을 때 (그래서 출연을 하지 않을 때) 유명인의 목소리를 모사할 수 있는 성우들을 위한 성장하는 시장이 있다. 그래서 유명인의 사용은 때때로 일자리를 빼앗아 갈뿐만 아니라 실제로 일자리를 가져올 수도 있다.

정답풀이

주어진 문장은 유명인의 목소리를 흉내 내는 성우들을 위한 시장이 커지고 있다는 내용이므로, 유명인 때문에 일자리를 잃고 있는 성우에 관한 진술과 유명인의 사용이 일자리를 가져올 수도 있다는 진술 사이인 ⑤에 들어가는 것이 적절하다. ⑤ 뒤의 문장의 결과를 나타내는 접속사 So가 단서가 된다.

구문풀이

13행 Jeff Bridges was chosen for the voice of Big Z in *Surf's Up*, **not only** for his celebrity name, **but also** [**because of** this gravelly voice and, **because** (as a surfer himself), he was a close match for the character].

: 'A뿐만 아니라 B도'의 의미인 「not only A but also B」 구문이 쓰였다. [ ]에는 전치사구 「because of+명사(구)」와 부사절 「because+주어+동사 ~」가 and로 연결되어 있다. himself는 강조 용법으로 쓰인 재귀대명사이다.

어휘풀이
- celebrity *n* 유명인
- imitate *v* 흉내 내다
- circuit *n* 순회
- voice-over artist 성우
- give publicity 널리 알리다

176 답 ④

📖 반복적으로 듣는 메시지를 믿게 되는 타당성 효과

전문해석

설득적 의사소통의 매우 놀라운 한 측면은 우리가 메시지를 반복적으로 들었을 때 그것들을 더 사실인 것으로 인식하는 경향이 있다는 것이다. 이것은 타당성 효과로 알려져 있으며, 연구자들은 그것이 어떤 주장에 대한 실제 증거와 관계없이 작동한다는 것을 보여주었다. 다시 말해서, 우리는 그 진술을 뒷받침하는 아무런 증거가 제시되지 않았을 때에도, 우리가 반복적으로 들은 진술이 우리가 덜 자주 들었거나 전혀 듣지 못한 진술보다 더 진실하다고 인식한다. 우리가 슈퍼마켓에서 쇼핑을 하면서 탄산음료의 한 브랜드가 다른 브랜드보다 우수하다고 생각할 때, 우리는 우리의 믿음이 그 특정 브랜드를 광고하는 반복적인 광고 방송을 들은 데서 비롯된 것임을 깨닫지 못한다. 타당성 효과는 정치적 선전에서도 한몫을 한다. 한 지도자가 처음에 터무니없는 것처럼 들리고 사람들이 일반적으로 사실이 아니라고 알고 있는 주장을 할 수 있다. 하지만 그 지도자가 시간이 흐르면서 같은 주장을 반복적으로 함에 따라, 사람들은 흔히 점차로 그 진술이 사실이라고 믿는다. 비록 어떤 것이 사실이라고 말하는 것이 그것을 사실로 만드는 것은 아니지만, 그렇게 하는 것은 사람들의 마음속에서 그것이 사실인 것 같아 보이게 만들 수 있다.

정답풀이

어떤 메시지를 반복적으로 들으면 그것을 사실로 인식할 가능성이 더 높다는 타당성 효과를 상업적인 광고 방송과 정치적 선전 두 가지의 예를 들어 설명하는 글이다. 따라서 한 지도자가 처음에 터무니없는 주장을 한다는 주

어진 문장은 그러한 주장도 반복적으로 들으면 믿게 된다는 문장 앞인 ④에 들어가야 한다. ④ 앞 문장에서 상업적인 광고 방송의 경우에서 정치적 선전의 경우로 글의 흐름이 전환되는 것도 단서가 된다.

구문풀이

8행 In other words, we **perceive** a statement [that we have heard repeatedly] **as more** true **than** a statement [we have heard less often or not at all] — [**even when** no evidence {supporting the statement} has been offered].

: 「perceive A as B」는 'A를 B로 인식하다'의 의미이며 「more ~ than ...」의 비교구문이 쓰였다. 첫 번째와 두 번째 [ ]는 각각 앞의 a statement를 수식하는 관계절이다. 세 번째 [ ]는 시간 부사절로, 그 안의 { }는 evidence를 수식하는 현재분사구이다. even when은 '~할 때에도'로 해석한다.

어휘풀이
- initially *ad* 처음에
- persuasive *a* 설득적인
- repeatedly *ad* 반복적으로
- statement *n* 진술
- stem from ~에서 생겨나다
- absurd *a* 터무니없는
- perceive *v* 인지하다, 이해하다
- validity *n* 타당성
- superior to ~보다 우수한
- commercial *n* 광고 방송

177 답 ④

📖 짝 선호의 진화

전문해석

어느 곳에서도 사람들이 이성의 모든 구성원에게 동등한 욕구를 가지고 있지 않다. 어느 곳에서나 일부의 잠재적 짝이 선호되며, 다른 짝들은 회피된다. 오래 전에 우리의 조상들이 그랬던 것처럼 사는 것을 상상해 보라. 그들은 불 옆에서 몸을 따뜻하게 하기 위해 애썼고, 친족을 위해서 고기를 사냥했고, 견과류, 베리, 그리고 허브를 채집했고, 위험한 동물들과 적대적인 인간들을 피했다. 만일 우리가 약속한 자원을 갖다 주지 못하고, 게으르고, 사냥 기술이 부족하고, 또는 우리에게 신체적 학대를 많이 하는 짝을 선택한다면, 우리의 생존은 보잘것없고 번식이 위기에 처할 것이다. 대조적으로, 풍부한 자원을 제공하고 우리와 우리의 아이들을 보호하고, 우리의 가족에게 시간과 에너지와 노력을 바치는 짝은 큰 자산이 될 것이다. 짝을 현명하게 선택했던 우리 조상들에게서 받은 강력한 생존과 생식의 이득의 결과로 많은 특수한 욕구가 진화하게 되었다. 진화의 제비뽑기에서 성공을 거둔 사람들의 후손들로서 현대인들은 특정한 일련의 짝 선호를 물려받았다.

정답풀이

주어진 문장이 대조를 나타내는 In contrast로 시작하며 능력이 있고 헌신적인 배우자가 커다란 자산이 될 것이라는 내용이므로, 주어진 문장 앞에는 무능한 배우자를 선택했을 경우에 생길 수 있는 일이 언급되어야 한다. 따라서 주어진 문장이 들어가기에 가장 적절한 곳은 ④이다.

구문풀이

12행 If we **were to** select a mate [**who** failed to deliver the resources promised, **who** was lazy, **who** lacked hunting skills, or **who** heaped physical abuse on us], / our survival **would be** tenuous, our reproduction (being) at risk.

: 불가능한 일을 상상하는 가정법 미래 구문으로, 조건절에는 「were to+동사원형」이 사용되었고, 주절에는 「would+동사원형」이 사용되었다. [ ]에는 선행사 a mate를 수식하는 관계절이 병렬로 연결되어 있다. our reproduction (being) at risk는 and our reproduction would be at risk로 풀어쓸 수 있다.

어휘풀이
- abundant *a* 풍부한
- asset *n* 자산
- devote *v* (노력·시간 등을) 바치다
- potential *a* 잠재적인

- shun *v* 피하다
- kin *n* 친족
- heap *v* (모욕 등을) 여러 번 주다
- tenuous *a* 미약한, 보잘것없는
- at risk 위험한 상태로
- descendant *n* 후손
- inherit *v* 물려받다, 상속받다
- struggle *v* 애쓰다, 분투하다
- hostile *a* 적대적인, 적의가 있는
- abuse *n* 학대, 혹사
- reproduction *n* 번식
- reap *v* (노력·행동의 결과로) 받다, 얻다
- lottery *n* 복권, 제비뽑기

- unacceptably *ad* 받아들일 수 없을 정도로
- severity *n* 극심함, 심각함
- extreme *a* 극도의, 심한
- bushfire *n* (야산에 난) 산불, 들불
- fast-track *v* (법안 등을) 신속하게 처리하다
- prone *a* ~하기 쉬운
- property *n* 재산
- permit *n* 허가
- proactively *ad* 선제적으로
- pose *v* (위험 등을) 제기하다
- locale *n* 장소, 현장
- aftermath *n* 여파, 영향
- assessment *n* 평가
- obtain *v* 얻다
- construction *n* 건축

---

16 문장 삽입 - 유형 연습 문제[2]　본문 pp.126~129

178 ⑤	179 ②	180 ③	181 ⑤	182 ⑤
183 ③	184 ④	185 ③		

178　답 ⑤

📖 산불 피해에 선제적으로 대응하기 위한 호주의 이주 및 재정착 정책

전문해석

더욱 극심한 폭풍, 더 큰 산불, 더 높아진 해수면에 의해서 제기되는 위험의 극심함은 일부 지역에 대해 '더 이상 안 돼'는 진정으로 '더 이상 안 돼'를 의미해야 한다는 것을 요구한다. 사람들은 (자연재해의) 위해로부터 벗어나야만 할 것이다. 호주의 '더 이상 안 돼'의 순간은 2009년의 어느 한 토요일에 빅토리아주에서 400여 건의 산불이 났을 때 찾아왔다. 소위 '검은 토요일' 산불은 수천 채의 집을 파괴했고, 200여 명을 숨지게 했으며, 100만 에이커 이상을 불태웠다. 화재로 인한 파괴의 여파로 호주는 산불에 취약한 지역을 위한 새로운 건축 규정을 신속하게 처리했다. 규범은 이제 산불지역 밖에 있는 재산을 포함해서 모든 재산에 대한 위험성 평가를 요구하며, 고위험 지역의 건축가들은 새로운 건축에 대해서 특별 허가를 얻어야 한다. 하지만 그때 호주는 한 단계 더 나아갔다. 빅토리아 주정부는 정부가 받아들일 수 없을 정도로 화재 위험이 높은 토지를 구입하는 것을 허용하는 자발적인 되사주기 프로그램을 만들어서 '이주 및 재정착' 전략을 또한 추구했다. 그 순간, 호주는 '어떻게'뿐만 아니라 '어디에 지을 것인지'를 재고려함으로써 증가하는 산불 위험에 대비하여 선제적으로 준비를 했다.

정답풀이

주어진 문장에 also가 쓰였으며 빅토리아 주정부가 추구한 전략을 추가로 소개하고 있으므로, 주어진 문장은 빅토리아 주정부가 산불 피해에 대응하기 위해 한 일을 설명한 후 한 단계 더 나아간 대응을 언급한 문장 다음에, 그리고 주어진 문장에서 언급한 전략을 부연 설명하는 문장 앞에 와야 한다. 따라서 주어진 문장이 들어가기에 가장 적절한 곳은 ⑤이다.

구문풀이

5행 [The severity of the risks {posed by more extreme storms, bigger wildfires, and higher sea levels}] requires [that "no more" must truly mean "no more" for some locales]: ~.

: 첫 번째 [ ]가 문장의 주어이고 핵심 주어는 The severity이며, 문장의 동사는 requires이다. { }는 the risks를 수식하는 과거분사구이며, 두 번째 [ ]는 requires의 목적어로 쓰인 명사절이다.

어휘풀이

- pursue *v* 추구하다
- resettlement *n* 재정착
- voluntary *a* 자발적인
- retreat *n* 후퇴, 물러남, 철수
- strategy *n* 전략

179　답 ②

📖 서로 연결된 마음과 몸의 관계

전문해석

철학자 데카르트는 몸과 마음의 이중성 또는 분리성의 개념을 가지고 있었다. 몸만 진통제로 치료하는 전통적인 의학은 그 개념을 지속시킨다. 그것들은 흔히 증상만 치료하지 원인은 치료하지 않는다. 하지만 마음과 몸이 너무 깊이 얽혀 있어 더 이상 그렇게 분리할 수 없다는 늘어나는 증거가 있다. 심지어 마음에서 생기는 고통도 분명히 몸에 영향을 미친다. 이러한 몸과 마음의 혼합을 보여주는 고통의 유형은 '환상 사지 통증'이다. 환상 사지 통증은 절단 수술을 받았지만 없어진 사지에서 여전히 몹시 고통스러운 감각을 느끼는 사람들이 경험한다. 한때 사지의 잘리고 남은 부분에서 손상된 신경 말단이 이 통증의 원인이라고 여겨졌으나, 이 이론은 증거와 일치하지 않는다.

정답풀이

몸과 마음이 분리되어 있다는 개념을 설명한 뒤, 몸과 마음은 서로 연결되어 있다는 것을 환상 사지 통증을 근거로 들어 설명하는 글이다. 역접을 나타내는 접속사 However로 시작하는 주어진 문장은 마음과 몸이 분리되어 있다는 견해에 대한 설명에서 마음과 몸이 서로 얽혀 있다는 견해로 전환되는 자리인 ②에 들어가는 것이 가장 적절하다.

구문풀이

11행 Phantom limb pain is experienced by people [who {have had an amputation}, but {still feel often excruciating sensations in the missing limb}].

: [ ]는 people을 수식하는 관계절이고, but으로 연결된 두 개의 { }는 주격 관계대명사 who 다음에 이어지는 술부이다.

어휘풀이

- interweave *v* 엮다, 뒤섞다
- separateness *n* 분리, 단독
- perpetuate *v* 지속시키다
- demonstrate *v* 보여주다
- phantom *a* 환영의
- excruciating *a* 몹시 고통스러운, 극심한
- nerve *n* 신경
- duality *n* 이중성
- conventional *a* 전통적인
- symptom *n* 증상
- blending *n* 혼합
- limb *n* 사지, 수족
- be consistent with ~와 일치하다

180　답 ③

📖 오늘날 더 많이 생산된 농산물의 더 적어진 영양가

전문해석

오늘날 식품 산업은 이전 어느 때보다 더 많은 헥타르당 식품을 만들어 낸다. 그러나 이러한 증가한 농작물은 품질을 희생시킨다. 같은 토양에서 같은 작물을 계속 재배하는 것은 영양분을 없앤다. 결국 이 고갈된 토양은 더 적은 영양을 가진 작물로 이어진다. 기업적 농업은 미량 영양소를 가진 비료를 주어서 토양 고갈을 바로잡으려

고 한다. 이것은 건강한 토양의 초소형 생태계를 무시했기 때문에 단기 해결책이고 장기적으로는 효과가 없다. USDA(미국 농무성)는 1950년대 이후 지속적으로 추적했던 43개의 작물을 연구했다. 평균적으로 오늘날의 작물에서 비타민 C 함유량은 20퍼센트 내려갔고, 철분은 15퍼센트 내려갔으며, 리보플라빈은 38퍼센트, 그리고 칼슘은 16퍼센트 내려갔다. 구체적인 예로서 1940년대 사과는 오늘날의 사과 중 하나보다 세 배 정도 더 많은 철분을 포함했다.

정답풀이

주어진 문장에서 이것은 단기 해결책이고 장기적으로는 효과가 없다고 했으므로 단기적인 해결책에 대한 내용이 나온 뒤, 그리고 장기적인 해결책이 되지 않는 이유 앞에 나와야 한다. 따라서 주어진 문장은 단기적인 해결책인 비료를 주어서 토양 고갈을 바로잡으려 했다는 문장 뒤, 그리고 USDA의 연구에서 오늘날 작물의 영양소가 줄어들었다는, 즉 비료를 주는 것이 효과가 없다는 문장 앞인 ③에 들어가야 한다.

구문풀이

1행 This is a short-term fix and doesn't work in the long term / because the micro-ecosystems of healthy soils are ignored.

: 주절과 이유 부사절로 이루어진 문장이며, 주절에는 동사 is와 doesn't work가 병렬 구조를 이룬다.

어휘풀이

- fix *n* 해결책
- generate *v* 발생시키다, 일으키다
- yield *n* 농작물, 산출고
- continuous *a* 끊이지 않는
- deplete *v* 고갈시키다
- fertilize *v* 비료를 주다, 기름지게 하다
- consistently *ad* 지속적으로
- micro-ecosystem *n* 초소형 생태계
- hectare *n* 헥타르(면적의 단위)
- expense *n* 손실, 대가
- nutrient *n* 영양소
- depletion *n* 고갈, 결핍
- micro-nutrient *n* 미량 영양소
- track *v* 추적하다, 지켜보다

181 답 ⑤

📖 상관관계 연구에서 유의할 점

전문해석

만일 한 연구원이 두 개의 변수들 사이에서 상관관계가 있다는 것을 발견한다면, 그것은 이러한 변수들 사이에 세 개의 가능한 인과 관계가 있다는 것을 의미한다. 예를 들어, 연구원들이 아이들의 TV 폭력물 시청 시간과 그들의 공격성 사이의 상관관계를 발견했다. 이 상관관계에 대한 한 가지 설명은 TV 폭력물의 시청이 아이들이 더 폭력적이 되도록 야기한다는 것이다. 그러나 그 역이 마찬가지로 진실일 수도 있다. 처음부터 폭력적인 아이들이 TV 폭력물을 시청할 가능성이 더 높다. 또는 이 두 변수들 사이에 전혀 인과 관계가 없을 수도 있다. 대신에, TV 시청과 폭력적인 행동은 모두 자녀에게 많은 관심을 두지 않는 무관심한 부모의 존재와 같은 제3의 변수에 의해 야기될 수도 있다. 상관관계는 인과 작용을 입증하기 않기 때문에 상관관계 기법을 사용할 때 하나의 변수가 다른 변수를 야기한다고 성급하게 결론에 도달하는 것은 잘못이다.

정답풀이

두 가지 변수 사이에 상관관계가 있을 경우에 세 가지의 인과 관계가 있을 수 있다는 첫 문장의 내용에 이어서 각각의 인과 관계를 설명하고 있는데, 주어진 문장에서는 제3의 변수를 언급하고 있다. 따라서 주어진 문장은 앞서 언급된 두 가지 변수 사이에 전혀 인과 관계가 없을 수 있다는 내용 뒤인 ⑤에 들어가는 것이 가장 적절하다.

구문풀이

17행 [When using the correlational method], / it is wrong [**to jump** to the conclusion {that one variable is causing the other to occur}] because a correlation does not prove causation.

: 첫 번째 [ ]는 When we are using ~의 시간 부사절에서 '주어+be동사'가 생략된 형태이다. 주절에서 it은 가주어이고 두 번째 [ ]로 표시한 to부정사구가 진주어이다. { }는 동격절로 the conclusion의 내용을 구체적으로 설명한다.

어휘풀이

- variable *n* 변수
- correlation *n* 상관관계
- aggressive *a* 공격적인
- probable *a* 있음직한
- causation *n* 인과 작용
- neglectful *a* 소홀한, 무관심한
- causal relationship 인과 관계
- violence *n* 폭력 (행위)
- reverse *n* 역, 반대

182 답 ⑤

📖 일관되어야 하는 문장에서의 시제 사용

전문해석

문장에서 동사를 사용할 때마다, 여러분은 특정한 시제를 사용하고 있다. 시제에 대해 기억해야 할 가장 중요한 것은 일관성이 있어야 한다는 것이다. 한 시제에서 다른 시제로 임의로 바꿀 수 없다. 예를 들어, 여러분이 작년 여름 휴가 때 여러분에게 생겼던 일에 대한 이야기를 하고 있다면 여러분은 과거 시제를 유지할 것이다. 반면에 여러분이 저먼 셰퍼드와 아이리시 세터의 차이점을 설명하고 있다면 여러분은 현재 시제를 유지할 것이다. 물론 다른 시제로 옮겨가야 할 때도 있을 것이다. 예를 들어 옛 남자친구의 운전 습관과 새 남자친구의 운전 습관을 대조하고 있다면, 옛 남자친구에 대한 기록 부분은 과거 시제로 쓰일 것이고, 새 남자친구에 대한 부분은 현재 시제로 쓰일 것이다. 그러나 타당한 이유가 없는 한 다른 시제로 옮겨가서는 안 된다. 그러므로 여러분의 기록을 면밀하게 교정해서 글에 불필요한 시제 변화가 없도록 확인하라.

정답풀이

문장에서 동사를 사용할 때 일관된 시제를 사용해야 한다는 내용의 글이다. 주어진 문장은 글에서 다른 시제를 쓰는 예외의 경우에 대한 예시이므로, 다른 시제로 옮겨가야 할 때가 있다는 문장 다음인 ⑤에 들어가는 것이 가장 적절하다. ⑤ 뒤의 문장은 타당한 이유가 없는 한 다른 시제로 옮겨가서는 안 된다는 내용이므로 타당한 이유에 해당하는 주어진 문장 다음에 위치해야 한다.

구문풀이

18행 You should not move to a different tense, however, [unless you have a good reason], so proofread your papers carefully and make sure [your writing contains no unnecessary shifts in tense].

: 첫 번째 [ ]는 삽입절로 '~ 않다면'의 의미인 unless가 이끄는 부사절이다. so 이하 절에서 명령문을 이루는 동사 proofread와 make sure가 병렬구조를 이루며, 두 번째 [ ]는 make sure의 목적절이다.

어휘풀이

- contrast *v* 대조시키다
- consistent *a* 일관된
- shift *v* 바꾸다 *n* 변화
- proofread *v* 교정을 보다
- tense *n* 시제
- randomly *ad* 임의로, 되는대로
- German Shepherd (견종) 저먼 셰퍼드

183 답 ③

📖 온라인 설문조사의 대표성 한계

전문해석

온라인 설문조사의 주된 단점은 응답자들의 대표성과 관련이 있다. 이 단점은 가난하거나 나이가 많은 사람들을 대상으로 하는 사회 복지 설문조사와 관련이 있다. 인터넷을 사용하고 온라인 설문조사에 가장 답변을 할 것 같은 사람들은 아마도 대상

이 되는 모집단의 나머지보다 더 젊고, 더 부유하고, 더 교육을 받은 사람들이다. 그러나 이러한 문제는 점점 더 많은 사람들이 인터넷에 접속함에 따라서 줄어들 것이다. 사실, 일부는 온라인 설문조사가 조만간 다른, 좀 더 전통적인 설문 조사 방법들을 대체할 것으로 믿는다. 대상이 되는 응답자의 유형에 따라서, 특히 온라인 설문조사가 응답자들의 참여를 장려하는 우편엽서를 동반할 때 온라인 설문조사의 응답률이 우편 설문조사와 비슷할 수도 있다는 것을 보여주는 증거가 나타나고 있다. 이러한 온라인 설문조사와 우편 설문조사를 결합하는 '혼합 방법'은 주로 Don Dillman에 의해서 개발되었다. 그럼에도 불구하고, 가난한 사람들과 노인들은 예상되는 미래에 온라인 사회 복지 설문조사에서 덜 대표되는 상태로 머물 것이다.

정답풀이

주어진 문장은 온라인 설문조사가 기존의 다른 설문조사 방법을 대체한다는 내용이므로 온라인 설문조사의 문제점을 언급한 문장 바로 뒤에 올 수는 없다. 따라서 주어진 문장이 들어가기에 가장 적절한 곳은 온라인 설문조사의 문제점이 줄어들 것이라는 문장 이후, 온라인 설문조사가 우편과 결합하여 기존의 문제점을 극복하고 있다는 문장 앞인 ③이다.

구문풀이

12행 Depending on the type of <u>respondents</u> [being targeted], <u>evidence</u> is emerging [to suggest {that online survey response rates may be comparable to mail surveys, / especially when the online survey is accompanied by <u>a postcard reminder</u> (encouraging respondents to participate)}].

: 첫 번째 [ ]는 respondents를 수식하는 현재분사구이고, 두 번째 [ ]는 evidence를 수식하는 형용사적 용법으로 쓰인 to부정사구이다. 그 안의 { }는 suggest의 목적어 역할을 하는 명사절이고, ( )는 a postcard reminder를 수식하는 현재분사구이다.

어휘풀이

- representativeness *n* 대표성
- relevant *a* 관련 있는
- affluent *a* 부유한
- emerge *v* 나타나다
- postal *a* 우편의
- respondent *n* 응답자
- be apt to *do* ~하는 경향이 있다
- wane *v* 줄어들다
- comparable *a* 비슷한, 필적하는
- foreseeable *a* 예상되는

184 답 ④

📖 양질의 식품을 선택하는 전략의 필요성

전문해석

어떤 음식의 칼로리 값은 그것이 배고픔의 갈망을 줄이고 식사 간의 간격을 증가시킬 수 있는 방법으로 음식이 얼마나 포만감을 주는지와 어떻게 우리의 영양적 필요를 충족시킬 수 있는지를 우리에게 말해주지는 않는다. 포만감의 문제는 에너지 균형 방정식과는 무관하지만, 우리가 먹는 음식의 양의 측면에서 실질적인 의미를 갖는다. 만약 칼로리 값이 식사를 하거나 음료수를 마신 후에 우리가 얼마나 배부르게 느끼는지를 결정하지 못한다면, 저칼로리 음식을 선택하는 것이 반드시 체중 감량을 위한 최선의 전략은 아니다. 우리는 또한 음식을 선택하기 위한 다른 전략이 필요한데, 그것은 때때로 칼로리와 그에 수반되는 '더 적게 먹는' 메시지에 대해 좁게 초점을 맞추는 것과는 상반될 수도 있다. 고도로 가공된 일부 음식들은 더 쉽게 또는 더 빠르게 섭취할 수 있고, 잠재적으로 신체의 포만감 메커니즘을 무효화할 수 있다. 반면에 견과류나 전지유와 같은 일부 자연 식품은 비교적 에너지 밀도가 높지만 궁극적으로 포만감을 촉진하고 과도한 식품 섭취를 제한하는 많은 유익한 영양 성분을 가질 수 있다. 양질의 음식을 더 많이 먹으라는 말을 듣는 것이 더 적은 칼로리를 섭취하는 것보다 더 효과적인 공중 보건 메시지가 되는 것으로 판명될 수 있다.

정답풀이

포만감을 결정하지 못하는 칼로리 값에만 초점을 맞추는 대신 음식 선택을 위

한 다른 전략이 필요하다는 내용 뒤에, 역접의 연결어 On the other hand와 함께 견과류와 전지유와 같은 자연 식품에 대한 예가 나와 흐름이 단절되었다. 자연 식품과 대조되는 가공식품의 경우를 설명하는 주어진 문장이 ④에 들어가야 글의 흐름이 자연스럽다.

구문풀이

4행 The caloric value of a food <u>does not tell</u> us [how satiating a food is] and [how it might meet our nutritional needs in <u>a way</u> {that may reduce hunger cravings and increase the gap between meals}].

: The caloric value of a food가 주어, does not tell이 동사이다. 두 개의 [ ]는 tell의 직접목적어 역할을 하는 의문사절이고, { }는 a way를 수식하는 관계절이다.

어휘풀이

- processed food 가공식품
- consumable *a* 섭취할 수 있는, 소비할 수 있는
- potentially *ad* 잠재적으로
- satiety *n* 포만감
- caloric value 칼로리 값
- nutritional *a* 영양의
- independent of ~와는 관계없이
- practical *a* 실질적인, 현실적인
- contradict *v* 모순되다
- whole food 자연 식품, 무첨가 식품
- promote *v* 촉진시키다
- override *v* 무효화하다
- mechanism *n* 메커니즘, 기제
- satiate *v* 포만감을 주다, 만족시키다
- craving *n* 갈망
- equation *n* 방정식
- significance *n* 의미, 중요성
- accompanying *a* 수반되는
- dense *a* 밀도가 높은
- turn out 판명되다, 드러나다

185 답 ③

📖 기업의 환경성과 이윤의 상관관계

전문해석

우리는 우리가 이상적인 사회에 살고 있지 않으므로 경제적인 측면이 많은 결정에 그림자를 드리운다는 것을 깨달아야만 한다. 산업에서는 지속 가능성과 성장이 수익성에 묶여 있다. 사업을 지속하고 이윤을 유지하거나 늘리기 위해서, 무엇보다 앞서 기업은 비용 효율이 높은 방식으로 환경적인 의무 사항을 충족시켜야만 한다. 법적 요구를 넘어 필요 이상으로 환경을 보호하기 위해 돈을 더 많이 쓰는 기업은, 있다손 치더라도, 극히 드물다. 일부 산업 관련 글을 읽는 독자들은 이러한 진술에 동의하지 않고 진정 '(법의) 준수를 넘어가는' 기업이 있다는 것을 지적할지도 모른다. 하지만 이런 기업조차도 사실 그들의 수익성을 향상시키는 경제적 힘에 의존하고 있는 것이다. 환경 성과를 능가하는 쪽으로 더 많은 기금을 할당하는 기업은 경쟁적 이점을 주는 여론과 투자자들의 신뢰도 같은 분야로부터 재정적 혜택을 거둔다. 이러한 영향들은 궁극적으로 이윤에 긍정적 결과를 낳는다.

정답풀이

주어진 문장은 법의 준수를 넘는 기업이 있다는 내용으로, ③ 뒤의 문장의 these businesses가 주어진 문장에서 언급된 기업을 받아 그런 기업도 수익성을 향상시키기 위해 그렇게 하는 것이라는 내용으로 이어지는 것이 자연스럽다. 주어진 문장의 this statement는 ③ 앞의 법적 요구를 넘어 환경에 돈을 쓰는 기업은 드물다는 내용을 가리킨다. 따라서 주어진 문장이 들어가기에 가장 적절한 곳은 ③이다.

구문풀이

14행 Companies [that allocate more funds toward exceeding environmental performance] <u>reap</u> financial benefits from **such** areas **as** public opinion and investor confidence [that provide them competitive advantages].

: 첫 번째 [ ]는 문장의 주어인 Companies를 수식하는 관계절이고 문장의 동사는

reap이다. 「such ~ as ....」는 '…와 같은 ~'의 의미이며, 두 번째 [ ]는 앞의 명사구 public opinion and investor confidence를 수식하는 관계절이다.

어휘풀이
- statement *n* 진술
- utopian *a* 이상향의
- sustainability *n* 환경 지속 가능성
- profit margin 이윤
- cost-effective *a* 비용 효율이 높은
- enhance *v* 향상시키다
- exceed *v* 능가하다
- compliance *n* (법의) 준수
- overshadow *v* 그늘을 드리우다
- profitability *n* 수익성
- obligation *n* 의무, 책임
- requirement *n* 요구
- allocate *v* 할당하다
- reap *v* (좋은 결과 등을) 거두다, 받다

17 요약문 완성

본문 pp.130~135

| 186 ① | 187 ① | 188 ① | 189 ⑤ | 190 ③ |
| 191 ② | 192 ⑤ | 193 ⑤ | 194 ② | |

186 답 ①

📖 과학 탐구의 진행 방식

전문해석
평균적인 재능을 가진 사람들도, 한 번에 다양한 과학 분야 모두를 수용하려고 하지 않으면, 다양한 과학 분야에서 주목할 만한 작업을 만들어 낼 수 있다. 그러는 대신에, 비록 나중의 작업이 다른 영역에서의 더 이전의 성취를 약화시킬지라도, 그들은 한 주제 다음에 다른 주제로 (즉, 서로 다른 기간에) 집중해야 한다. 이것은 뇌가 보편적인 과학에 '시간'속에서 적응하는 것이지 '공간'속에서 적응하는 것이 아니라고 말하는 셈이다. 사실, 대단한 능력을 가진 사람들도 이런 식으로 나아간다. 따라서, 우리가 서로 다른 과학 분야에서 출판물을 가진 사람에게 놀랄 때, 각 주제는 특정 기간 동안 탐구되었다는 것을 깨달아라. 더 이전에 얻은 지식은 확실히 저자의 마음에서 사라지지 않았을 것이지만 그것은 공식이나 크게 축약된 기호로 응축되어 단순화되었을 것이다. 따라서 대뇌 칠판에 새로운 이미지를 인식하고 학습할 수 있는 충분한 공간이 남아 있다.
→ 하나의 과학 주제를 탐구한 다음에 다른 주제를 탐구하는 것은 과학 전반에 걸친 주목할 만한 작업을 (A)가능하게 하는데, 이전에 습득된 지식은 뇌 속에서 단순화된 형태로 유지되며 이는 새로운 학습을 위한 공간을 (B)남겨두기 때문이다.

187 답 ①

📖 장인정신의 개념과 특성

전문해석
'장인정신'은 산업 사회의 도래와 함께 쇠퇴한 삶의 방식을 나타낼 수도 있지만 이것은 오해를 불러일으킨다. 장인정신은 지속적이고 기본적인 인간의 충동, 즉 일 자체를 위해 그것을 잘하고 싶은 욕망을 말한다. 장인정신은 숙련된 육체노동보다 훨씬 더 넓은 구획을 가르는데, 그것은 컴퓨터 프로그래머, 의사, 그리고 예술가에게 도움이 되고, 시민정신과 마찬가지로 그것이 숙련된 기술로서 실행될 때 양육은 향상된다. 이 모든 영역에서 장인정신은 객관적인 기준, 즉 그 자체의 것에 초점을 맞춘다. 그러나 사회적, 경제적 조건은 종종 장인의 수련과 전념을 방해하는데, 학교는 일을 잘하기 위한 도구를 제공하지 못할 수도 있고, 직장은 품질에 대한 열망을 진정으로 가치 있게 보지 않을 수도 있다. 그리고 장인정신이 일에 대한 자부심으로 개인에게

보상을 줄 수 있지만, 이 보상은 간단하지 않다. **장인은 흔히 뛰어남에 대한 상충되는 객관적 기준에 직면하며, 어떤 일 그 자체를 위해 그것을 잘하려는 욕망은 경쟁적 압력에 의해, 좌절에 의해 또는 집착에 의해 약화될 수 있다.**
→ 다양한 상황에서 시간이 지남에 따라 (A)존속되어 온 인간의 욕망인 장인정신은 흔히 그 완전한 발전을 (B)제한하는 요소들과 마주친다.

정답풀이
장인정신은 산업 사회의 도래와 함께 쇠퇴한 것이 아니라 여러 분야에서 도움을 주는 것으로서 존재해 왔지만, 그것은 장인의 수련과 전념을 방해하는 사회적 경제적 조건, 뛰어남에 대한 상충되는 객관적 기준 등으로 인해 약화될 수 있다는 내용이다. 따라서 (A)에는 persisted(존속되었다)가, (B)에는 limit(제한하다)가 들어가야 한다.
② 존속되었다 – 양성하다　　③ 발달했다 – 가속화하다
④ 줄어들었다 – 형성하다　　⑤ 줄어들었다 – 제한하다

구문풀이
1행 "Craftsmanship" may suggest a way of life [that declined with the arrival of industrial society] – but **this** is misleading.
: [ ]는 a way of life를 수식하는 관계절이며, this는 앞부분의 내용 전체를 가리킨다.

3행 Craftsmanship names [an enduring, basic human impulse], [the desire to do a job well for its own sake].
: 첫 번째 [ ]가 문장의 동사 names의 목적어이며, 두 개의 [ ]는 동격 관계이다.

어휘풀이
- craftsmanship *n* 장인정신
- enduring *a* 지속적인
- for one's own sake ~ 자체를 위한
- serve *v* 도움이 되다
- craft *n* 기술
- domain *n* 영역
- standard *n* 기준
- discipline *n* 수련, 규율
- aspiration *n* 열망
- obsession *n* 집착
- misleading *a* 오해를 일으키는
- impulse *n* 충동
- manual *a* 육체노동의, 손으로 하는
- parenting *n* 양육, 육아
- citizenship *n* 시민정신
- objective *a* 객관적인
- stand in the way of ~을 방해하다
- commitment *n* 전념
- conflicting *a* 상충되는
- context *n* 상황, 맥락

188 답 ①

📖 설명에 대한 두 가지 철학적 이론

전문해석
Philip Kitcher와 Wesley Salmon은 **설명의 철학적 이론 중 두 가지 가능한 대안이 있다고 제안했다.** 하나는 과학적 설명이 최소한으로 적은 수의 일반화 아래 광범위한 많은 현상들을 '통합'하는 데 있다는 견해이다. 이 견해에 따르면, 과학의 목표 (혹은, 어쩌면 한 가지 목표)는 모든 관측 가능한 현상을 포함할 수 있는 법칙이나 일반화의 경제적인 틀을 구축하는 것이다. 과학적 설명은 경험적 세계에 대한 우리의 지식을 조직하고 체계화하는데, 체계화가 더 경제적일수록, 설명되는 것에 대한 우리의 이해는 더 깊어진다. 다른 관점은 '인과 관계적/기계론적' 접근이다. 그것에 따르면, 어떤 현상에 대한 과학적인 설명은 관심 있는 그 현상을 발생시킨 메커니즘을 밝히는 것으로 구성된다. 이 관점은 개별 사건에 대한 설명을 일차적으로 보고, 일반화에 대한 설명이 그것으로부터 흘러나온다고 본다. 즉, **과학적 일반화에 대한 설명은 규칙성을 생산하는 인과적 메커니즘에서 나온다.**
→ 과학적 설명은 모든 관찰에 적용되는 (A)최소한의 원리를 찾거나 개별적인 현상들로부터 도출된 일반적인 (B)패턴을 발견함으로써 이루어질 수 있다.

정답풀이
설명에 대한 철학적 이론 중 두 가지 가능한 대안에 대해 설명하는 글이다. 하

나는 과학적 설명이 '최소한으로 적은 수의' 일반화 아래에 광범위하게 많은 현상들을 통합하는 것에 있다는 관점이고, 다른 관점은 개별적인 사건에 대한 설명을 일차적인 것으로 보고 그것들로부터 '일반화'에 대한 설명이 나온다고 보는 인과 관계적/기계론적 접근이다. 따라서 (A)에는 least(최소한의)가, (B)에는 patterns(패턴)가 들어가야 한다.

② 고정된 – 특징   ③ 제한된 – 기능
④ 고정된 – 규칙   ⑤ 최소한의 – 가정

구문풀이

6행 According to this view, the (or perhaps, a) goal of science is [to construct an economical framework of laws or generalizations {that are capable of subsuming all observable phenomena}].

: [ ]는 문장의 보어 역할을 하는, 명사적 용법으로 쓰인 to부정사구이며, 그 안의 { }는 laws or generalizations를 수식하는 관계절이다.

어휘풀이

- alternative *n* 대안
- body *n* 많은 양
- generalization *n* 일반화
- framework *n* 틀
- systematize *v* ~을 체계화하다
- mechanical *a* 기계적인
- mechanism *n* 메커니즘, 구조
- regularity *n* 규칙성, 규칙적임
- unification *n* 결합, 통합
- minimal *a* 최소한의, 아주 적은
- construct *v* ~을 구성하다
- be capable of ~할 수 있다
- causal *a* 인과 관계의
- uncover *v* ~을 밝혀내다, ~을 알아내다
- primary *a* 일차적인, 주요한

---

189 답 ⑤

📖 디드로 효과

전문해석

디드로 효과는 1769년에, 프랑스 철학자 Denis Diderot의 에세이 〈Regrets on Paining with My Old Dressing Gown(나의 오래된 가운을 버림으로 인한 후회)〉에 처음으로 기술되었다. 그 논문에서 그는 아름다운 주홍색 실내복 선물이 어떻게 뜻하지 않은 결과로 이어져, 결국 자신을 빚더미 속으로 던져 넣었는지를 말한다. 처음에는 그 선물이 흡족해서, Diderot는 자신의 새로운 의복을 안쓰럽게 생각하게 되었다. 자신의 우아한 새 실내복과 비교했을 때, 자신의 나머지 소유물들이 저급한 듯 보이기 시작했고, 그는 그것들이 자신의 새로운 소유물의 우아함과 스타일에 부응하지 못한다는 것에 불만족스러워하기 시작했다. 예를 들어 그는 자신의 옛 밀짚 의자를 모로코산 가죽이 덮인 안락의자로 대체했고, 그의 옛 책상은 값비싼 새 집필 탁자로 대체되었으며, 그의 이전에 사랑받던 인쇄용지는 더 값비싼 인쇄용지로 대체되는 등등이었다. "나는 나의 옛 실내복의 절대적인 주인이었지만, 나의 새로운 실내복의 노예가 되었다. … 갑작스러운 부의 오염을 경계하라. 가난한 자는 자신의 겉모습을 생각하지 않고 편하게 있겠지만, 부유한 자는 항상 긴장 상태에 있다."라고 Diderot는 쓴다.
→ 현재 가지고 있는 물품의 질보다 더 좋은 품질의 물품을 얻는 것은 옛날 소유물들에 대한 (A)불만족스러운 감정을 느끼게 해 더 좋은 물품의 후속적인 (B)취득으로 이어진다.

정답풀이

18세기 프랑스 철학자 Denis Diderot가 고급 실내복을 선물로 받자 그 의복의 수준에 어울리도록 자신의 소유물을 새것으로 교체하기 시작했다는 내용으로, 디드로 효과라고 알려진 현상을 설명하는 글이다. (A)에는 자신의 옛 물건이 새로운 실내복의 우아함과 스타일에 부응하지 못한 것이 불만족스러웠다는 점을 나타내도록 discontentment(불만족)가, (B)에는 실내복 선물을 받은 이후에 자신의 옛 물품들을 계속 새로운 것들로 대체했다는 점을 나타내도록 acquisition(취득)이 들어가는 것이 적절하다.

---

① 애정 – 구매   ② 애정 – 거부
③ 부족 – 배제   ④ 불만족 – 기피

구문풀이

11행 [He replaced his old straw chair, for example, with an armchair {covered in Moroccan leather}], [his old desk was replaced with an expensive new writing table]; [his formerly beloved prints were replaced with more costly prints], and so on.

: 세 개의 등위절 [ ]가 콤마와 세미콜론으로 연결된 구조이다. { }는 an armchair를 수식하는 과거분사구이다.

어휘풀이

- scarlet *a* 주홍색의
- plunge *v* 던져넣다
- garment *n* 의복
- armchair *n* 안락의자
- costly *a* 값비싼
- beware *v* 경계하다, 주의하다
- take one's ease 편하게 있다
- strain *n* 긴장
- affection *n* 애정, 사랑
- inadequacy *n* 부족
- dressing gown 실내복
- debt *n* 빚, 부채
- live up to ~에 부응하다
- formerly *ad* 이전에
- absolute *a* 절대적인
- contamination *n* 오염
- appearance *n* 겉모습
- subsequent *a* 후속의, 차후의
- rejection *n* 거부, 거절

---

190 답 ③

📖 불안 장애 치료에 도움이 되는 치료 환경

전문해석

노출은 치료 관계의 복잡성을 가중시킬 수 있는데, 불안 장애 환자들이 어떤 치료적 환경 내에서든 특히 안전하다고 느낄 필요가 있기 때문이다. **신뢰할 수 있고 안전한 관계는 환자들이 불안을 유발하는 것들과 그것이 일으킬 수 있는 결과로서의 불편과 불확실성에 대한 노출의 위험을 스스로가 무릅쓰도록 허용해 주는 정서적 기반을 형성한다.** 불안은 위험의 느낌을 만들어 내고, 그리고 그 위험은 치료사와의 긍정적인 관계의 상황 속에서 가장 잘 용인된다. 어떤 치료사이든 환자가 위험에 처한 것처럼 느끼기 시작하도록 의도적으로 자극하면서 치료 관계 내에서 안전함의 인식을 유지하는 것이 난제인데, 치료사로서 우리의 본능은 환자가 불편할 때마다 환자를 안심시키고 편안하게 해주도록 우리를 밀어붙인다. 불안 장애 치료는 우리가 이러한 본능에 자주 저항해야 한다고 요구한다.
→ 불안 장애 치료 동안, 환자가 자신의 문제를 (A)드러내도록 돕기 위해, 치료사는 환자가 안전과 (B)불안 둘 다를 느끼는 치료 환경을 만들어야만 한다.

정답풀이

불안 장애 환자들은 신뢰할 수 있는 관계의 치료사와의 치료 상황에서, 불안을 유발하는 것의 노출과 그로 인한 불편의 위험을 무릅쓸 수 있어야 하고, 이에 따른 불안으로 인한 위험의 느낌 속에서도 안전하다고 느껴야 한다고 했다. 따라서 (A)에는 reveal(드러내다), (B)에는 uneasy(불안한)가 들어가는 것이 적절하다.

① 숨기다 – 긍정적인   ② 구분하다 – 편안한
④ 내면화하다 – 열등한   ⑤ 없애다 – 외로운

구문풀이

4행 A trusting and safe relationship forms the emotional platform [upon which patients **allow** themselves **to risk** exposure to the triggers of their anxiety, and the resultant discomfort and uncertainty {that it can bring}].

: 문장의 동사는 forms이다. [ ]는 '전치사+관계대명사'가 이끄는 절로 문장의 목적어인 the emotional platform을 수식한다. allow는 「allow+목적어+목적격보어(~가

…하도록 허용하다)」의 5형식 구조에서 목적격보어로 to부정사를 취하는 동사이다. { } 는 the resultant discomfort and uncertainty를 수식하는 관계절이다.

어휘풀이

- exposure *n* 노출
- therapeutic *a* 치료의
- platform *n* 토대
- resultant *a* 결과로서 생기는
- therapist *n* 치료사
- undertake *v* 착수하다, 시작하다
- resist *v* 저항하다
- internalize *v* 내면화하다
- complexity *n* 복잡성
- anxiety disorder 불안 장애
- trigger *n* 유발하는 것
- tolerate *v* 용인하다
- deliberately *ad* 고의로
- instinct *n* 본능, 자연적인 충동
- conceal *v* 숨기다
- inferior *a* 열등한

191 답 ②

📖 사회적 배제에 대한 대응으로서의 행동 모방

전문해석

소속되는 것에 대한 필요는 가장 강력한 핵심 동기 부여 중 하나이며, 그것은 사람들의 생각, 감정, 행동에 빈번하게 영향을 미친다. 따라서 한 사회 집단으로부터 배제되었을 때, 사람들은 자신이 호감을 생성하는 데 도움이 되고 그 집단에 다시 진입할 수 있게 해주는 행동을 할 것이라는 점은 놀라운 일이 아니다. Lakin과 Chartrand가 수행한 최근 연구는 집단 구성원들의 비언어적 행동을 흉내 내는 것이 그런 한 가지 전략이 될 수 있다는 것을 보여 주었다. 참가자들이 컴퓨터화된 공던지기 게임에서 배제된 후 다른 상황에서 실험 보조자와 상호작용할 때, 그들은 그 공던지기 게임 동안 배제되지 않았을 때보다 더 많이 실험 보조자의 행동을 흉내 냈다. 다시 말해서, 호감과 연대를 생성하려고 노력하던 참가자들은 다른 사람을 흉내 내는 것을 통해 이 목적을 추구할 수 있었다. Lakin과 Chartrand의 연구 결과는 사람들이 다른 이들의 행동을 무의식적으로 모방함으로써 친밀한 관계나 호감을 발전시키는 목적을 추구할 수 있다는 것을 보여 준다.
→ 한 사람이 경험한 최근의 사회적 (A)소외는 그 사람이 자신의 행동적 (B)모방을 증가시키도록 유도할 가능성이 있다.

정답풀이

인간은 사회적 소속에 대한 강한 필요를 느끼는데, 한 사회 집단에서 배제되는 경험을 한 사람은 다시 배제되지 않도록 호감과 연대를 생성하기 위해 다른 사람의 행동을 흉내 내는 전략을 사용한다는 내용의 글이다. 따라서 (A)에는 사회적으로 배제되는 것을 의미하는 alienation(소외)이, (B)에는 다른 사람의 행동을 흉내 낸다는 점을 나타내도록 imitation(모방)이 들어가는 것이 적절하다.

① 수용 – 융통성
③ 상호작용 – 일탈
④ 수용 – 모방
⑤ 소외 – 일탈

구문풀이

3행 **It** is therefore not surprising [**that** {when people have been excluded from a social group}, they will engage in behaviors {that **help** them **to create** liking and **allow** them **to reenter** the group}].

: It은 가주어이고 [ ]로 표시한 that절이 진주어에 해당한다. 이 that절 안에서 첫 번째 { }는 부사절이고, 두 번째 { }는 behaviors를 수식하는 관계절이다. 이 관계절 내에는 「help+목적어+목적격보어(~가 …하도록 돕다)」와 「allow+목적어+목적격보어(to부정사)(~가 …하도록 하다)」 구문이 쓰였으며, help와 allow는 관계절의 동사로 병렬구조를 이룬다.

9행 [When participants {were excluded from a computerized ball-tossing game} and then {interacted with a confederate in a different context}], they mimicked the behaviors of the confederate

more than [when they had not been excluded during the ball-toss game].

: 첫 번째 [ ]는 부사절로, 이 절 내에 두 개의 { }가 and로 연결되어 주어 participants의 술어 역할을 하고 있다. 이 문장을 전체적으로 볼 때 more than의 비교급 표현이 쓰였고, 이는 [ ]로 표시된 두 개의 부사절을 비교하여 '~일 때보다 …일 때 더 많이'의 뜻을 나타낸다.

어휘풀이

- core *a* 핵심적인
- frequently *ad* 빈번히
- liking *n* 호감
- nonverbal *a* 비언어적인
- alienation *n* 소외
- motivation *n* 동기 부여
- engage in ~을 하다
- mimic *v* 흉내 내다
- toss *v* 던지다
- deviance *n* 일탈

192 답 ⑤

📖 운송 기술의 발달이 건축에 미친 영향

전문해석

승강기 그리고 강철과 같은 자재의 확산인 새로운 기술은 이제는 우리 사회의 한 부분으로서 어디에나 있으며 계속 확대되고 있는 초고층 건물의 건축을 가능하게 했다. 하지만, 건축 산업과 직결되지 않은 기술 또한 건물 설계에 막대하게 영향을 미쳤다. 증기 기관, 그 다음에는 자동차가 한때 극복할 수 없었던 지리적 거리를 지워 버렸다. 이제는 자재와 기술이 전 세계로 운반될 수 있고 지역적으로 건축한다는 생각은 과거의 것이 되었다. 건축 자재는 더 이상 지역의 이용 가능한 석재, 벽돌, 목재 또는 흙에 한정되지 않았고 지역의 건축 특성은 지역적 한계에 의해 더 이상 제한되지 않기 때문에 크게 변화하였다. 자재가 변함에 따라 형태 또한 변했으며, 건물 설계가 문화 및 기후와 관계없이 전 세계적으로 수출되었다. 기술이 이제는 우리의 모든 편안함에 대한 요구를 다룰 수 있으므로, 지역주의는 많은 이들에 의해 부적절한 것으로 간주되었다. 건물들은 이제 그것들이 알래스카 주의 앵커리지에 위치하고 있든 하와이 주의 힐로에 위치하고 있든 관계없이 동일해 보일 수 있었다.
→ (A)운송에서의 기술적 진보는 건축에 막대한 영향을 미쳤고, 건축 자재와 디자인에서의 지역적 특색을 (B)감소시켰다.

정답풀이

증기 기관, 자동차와 같은 운송 기술의 발달은 건축 자재 및 기술이 전 세계적으로 두루 확산되는 것을 가능하게 하였고, 이로 인해 건축에서 자재와 디자인의 지역적 특색이 의미를 잃고 점차 사라져가게 되었다는 내용의 글이므로, (A)에는 transportation(운송), (B)에는 diminishing(감소시키다)이 들어가는 것이 적절하다.

① 통신 – 최소화하다
② 통신 – 강조하다
③ 제조 – 반영하다
④ 운송 – 촉진하다

구문풀이

1행 New technologies, [the elevator and the proliferation of materials {like steel}] allowed [the construction {of ever-escalating high-rise buildings (**that** now are a ubiquitous part of our society)}].

: 첫 번째 [ ]는 문장의 주어인 New technologies를 부연 설명하는 동격어구이며, 두 번째 [ ]는 문장의 동사 allowed의 목적어이다. 첫 번째와 두 번째 { }는 각각의 앞에 있는 명사 materials와 the construction을 수식하며, 관계절인 ( )는 ever-escalating high-rise buildings를 수식한다.

어휘풀이

- proliferation *n* 확산, 급증
- escalate *v* (단계적으로) 확대되다
- erase *v* 없애다, 지우다
- insurmountable *a* 극복할 수 없는
- construction *n* 건축
- ubiquitous *a* 어디에나 있는
- geographic *a* 지리적인
- brick *n* 벽돌

- confine *v* 한정하다
- regionalism *n* 지역주의
- irrelevant *a* 부적절한, 부당한
- highlight *v* 강조하다
- architectural *a* 건축(학)의
- deem *v* 간주하다, 생각하다
- distinction *n* (구별되는) 특색
- diminish *v* 줄이다, 적게 하다

193 답 ⑤

📖 인간이 향신료를 먹는 이유

전문해석

향신료는 꽃, 뿌리, 씨앗, 관목 그리고 열매 같은 식물에서 나온다. 향신료는 '2차 화합물'이라고 불리는 화학 물질 때문에 독특한 향을 내며 특별한 맛이 난다. 이러한 화합물은 대개 식물에서 거대 생물(초식동물)과 미생물(병원균)이 식물을 공격하지 못하게 하는 방어 기제로 작용한다. 인간들 사이에서 향신료 식물의 사용은 수천 년 전으로 거슬러 올라간다. 마르코 폴로와 크리스토퍼 콜럼버스와 같은 탐험가들은 향신료가 풍부한 땅을 찾기 위해서 엄청난 모험을 감행했다. 오늘날의 요리책에서 향신료가 들어가지 않은 요리를 찾기는 매우 어렵다. 왜 인간들은 향신료와 섭취하는 음식에 양념을 넣는 것에 그토록 신경을 쓸까? 항균 가설에 따르면, 향신료는 미생물을 죽이거나 성장을 억제하고, 우리가 먹는 음식물에서 독소가 생성되는 것을 막아 그러한 식으로 인간이 생존이라는 중요한 문제를 해결하는 것을 돕는다. 우리가 확실한 자료를 가지고 있는 향신료 30가지에서, (그것들) 모두 그것들이 실험됐던 식품에서 생기는 세균 중 많은 종류를 죽였다. 어떤 양념이 박테리아를 죽이는 데 가장 강력한지 추측할 수 있겠는가? 그것들은 양파, 마늘, 올스파이스, 그리고 꽃박하이다.

→ 식품에서의 향신료의 사용은 우리가 먹는 음식에 있는 위험과 (B)싸우기 위해서 인간들이 사용해온 한 가지 잠재적인 (A)해법이다.

정답풀이

인간이 향신료를 먹게 된 이유로 항균 가설을 소개하고 있다. 이 가설에 따르면 인간들은 식품 안에 있는 박테리아나 독소를 없애기 위해서 음식에 양념을 넣어 먹었다. 따라서 향신료의 사용은 음식에 있는 위험 요소들과 싸우기 위한 하나의 해법임을 알 수 있으므로 (A)에는 solution(해법), (B)에는 combat(~와 싸우다)가 들어가야 한다.

① 전통 – ~와 싸우다
② 전통 – 최소화하다
③ 위험 – 숨기다
④ 해법 – 숨기다

구문풀이

18행 [**Of** the thirty spices {for which we have solid data}], all killed many of the species of food-borne bacteria [on which they were tested].

: 첫 번째 [ ]는 전치사구로 Of는 '~ 중에'로 해석한다. all이 문장의 주어, killed가 동사이며, 두 번째 [ ]는 the species of food-borne bacteria를 수식하는 관계절이다.

어휘풀이

- spice *n* 향신료, 양념
- emit *v* 방출하다
- defense mechanism 방어 기제
- macroorganism *n* 육안으로 보이는 생물
- herbivore *n* 초식 동물
- pathogen *n* 병원균
- hypothesis *n* 가설
- toxin *n* 독소
- combat *v* (~와) 싸우다
- shrub *n* 관목
- compound *n* 화합물
- microorganism *n* 미생물
- abundant *a* 많은, 풍부한
- inhibit *v* 억제하다
- food-borne *a* 식품으로 옮겨지는

194 답 ②

📖 질병 치료에 대한 Frederick의 기여

전문해석

수세기 동안, 의사들은 질병을 오로지 신체 밖에서 생겨나서 그것(신체)을 공격하는 어떤 것, 즉 전염성이 있는 병균, 차가운 공기 바람, 유독한 증기 등으로만 여겼다. 치료는 이러한 환경적인 병원균들의 해로운 영향력에 맞설 수 있는 어떤 종류의 약을 발견하는 데 달려 있었다. 그런데, 20세기 초에, 생화학자인 Frederick Gowland Hopkins가 괴혈병의 결과를 연구하다가 이런 관점을 역전시키는 생각을 했다. 이 특별한 질병에서 문제를 일으켰던 것은 외부로부터 공격을 하고 있는 것이 아니라 신체 그 자체의 내부에 없는 것, 즉, 이 사례에서는 비타민 C라고 알려진 것이라고 그는 생각했다. 독창적으로 생각한 것이 그가 그 문제를 해결하는 것을 도왔다. 이것은 비타민에 대한 그의 획기적인 작업으로 이어졌고 건강에 대한 우리의 관념을 완전히 바꾸었다.

→ Frederick Gowland Hopkins는 (B)외부적인 병원균이 아니라 신체에 (A)없는 것에 초점을 맞춤으로써 질병 치료에 대한 새 장을 열었다.

정답풀이

Frederick Gowland Hopkins는 괴혈병을 연구하다가 이 병의 원인을 외부적인 병원균에서 찾은 것이 아니라 신체 내부에 결핍되어 있는 것에서 찾음으로써 질병 연구에 새 장을 열었다는 내용이므로, (A)에는 absent(없는), (B)에는 external(외부적인)이 들어가야 한다.

① 없는 – 일시적인
③ 발전된 – 일시적인
④ 회복한 – 외부적인
⑤ 회복한 – 내부적인

구문풀이

10행 [What caused the problem {in this particular disease}], [he speculated], was [**not** {**what** was attacking from the outside}, **but** {**what** was missing from within the body itself – in this case **what** came to be known as vitamin C}].

: 첫 번째 [ ]는 관계대명사 what이 이끄는 관계절로 문장의 주어 역할을 하며, 동사는 밑줄 친 was이다. 두 번째 [ ]는 삽입절이고, 세 번째 [ ]가 문장의 보어인데 { }로 표시한 두 개의 what절이 상관접속사 「not A but B(A가 아니라 B인)」 구문으로 연결되어 있다. 이때, B에 해당하는 부분은 대시(–) 이하의 부연 설명을 받는다.

어휘풀이

- exclusively *ad* 오로지, 배타적으로
- stem from ~에서 생겨나다, ~에서 기인하다
- contagious *a* 전염성이 있는
- poisonous *a* 유독한
- counteract *v* 대응하다
- perspective *n* 관점
- think outside the box 고정관념을 벗어나다, 독창적으로 생각하다
- groundbreaking *a* 획기적인
- agent *n* 매개물
- draft *n* 바람, 통풍
- vapor *n* 증기
- biochemist *n* 생화학자
- speculate *v* 생각하다, 추측하다
- alter *v* 바꾸다

18	장문(1지문 2문항)			본문 pp.136~141
195 ②	196 ⑤	197 ①	198 ④	199 ⑤
200 ③	201 ④	202 ⑤	203 ⑤	204 ③

195~196 답 ② / ⑤

📖 언론 소통에 관한 과학자의 개인적 선택

전문해석

이야기를 과대광고하는 것에 기여하는 것을 피하는 한 가지 방법은 아무 말도 하지

않는 것이다. 그러나 그것은 대중과 정책 입안자에게 정보를 전하고/전하거나 제안을 제공해야 한다는 강한 책임감을 느끼는 과학자들에게는 현실적인 선택 사항이 아니다. 언론 구성원들과 이야기를 나누는 것은 메시지를 알리고 아마 호의적인 인식을 받는다는 점에서 이점이 있지만, 오해를 일으키고 반복적인 해명이 필요하며 끝없는 논란에 얽힐 위험이 있다. **따라서 언론과 대화할지 여부는 아주 개인적으로 결정되는 경향이 있다.** 수십 년 전에 지구과학자들이 언론의 흥미를 끄는 연구 결과를 발표하는 것은 드문 일이었고, 따라서 언론과의 접촉을 기대하거나 권장하는 것은 거의 없었다. 1970년대에는, 언론과 자주 대화하는 소수의 과학자들은 흔히 그렇게 한 것에 대해 동료 과학자들로부터 <u>비난</u>을 받았다. 지금은 상황이 아주 다른데, 많은 과학자들이 지구 온난화와 관련 문제의 중요성 때문에 공개적으로 말해야 한다는 책임감을 느끼고 있고, 많은 기자들이 이런 감정들을 공유하고 있기 때문이다. 게다가, 많은 과학자들은 자신이 언론의 주목과 그에 따른 대중의 인정을 즐기고 있다는 사실을 알아가고 있다. 동시에, 다른 과학자들은 기자들과의 대화하기를 계속해서 거부하며, 그렇게 함으로써 자신의 과학을 위해 더 많은 시간을 유지하고, 언론 보도와 관련하여 잘못 인용되는 위험과 다른 불쾌한 상황들을 <u>감수한다(→ 피한다)</u>.

구문풀이

6행 Decades ago, [**it** was unusual **for** Earth scientists **to** have results {that were of interest to the media}], and [consequently few media contacts were expected or encouraged].

: 두 개의 절 [ ]가 and로 연결되어 있고, 첫 번째 절에는 「it(형식상의 주어) ~ for (의미상 주어) to부정사(내용상의 주어)」의 표현이 쓰였다. { }는 results를 수식하는 관계절이다.

197~198   답 ① / ④

📖 **예측 능력에 있어 알고리즘의 장점과 체크리스트의 효과**

전문해석

매우 간단한 알고리즘조차도 간단한 예측 문제에 대한 전문가의 판단을 능가할 수 있다는 증거가 있다. 예를 들어, 가석방으로 풀려난 죄수가 계속해서 다른 범죄를 저지를 것인지 예측하거나, 잠재적인 후보자가 장차 직장에서 일을 잘할 것인지를 예측하는 데 알고리즘이 인간보다 더 <u>정확</u>하다는 것이 입증되었다. 많은 다른 영역에 걸친 100개 이상의 연구에서, 모든 사례의 절반은 간단한 공식이 인간 전문가보다 중요한 예측을 더 <u>잘</u>하고, 그 나머지(아주 적은 소수를 제외하고는)는 둘 사이의 무승부를 보여준다. 관련된 많은 다른 요인들이 있고 상황이 매우 불확실할 때, 가장 중요한 요소에 초점을 맞추고 일관성을 유지함으로써 간단한 공식이 승리할 수 있는 반면, 인간의 판단은 특히 두드러지고 아마도 <u>관련이 없는</u> 고려 사항에 의해 너무 쉽게 영향을 받는다. 사람들이 편안하다고(→ 일이 너무 많다고) 느낄 때 중요한 조치나 고려 사항을 놓치지 않도록 함으로써 **'체크리스트'가 다양한 영역에서 전문가의 결정의 질을 향상할 수 있다**는 추가적인 증거가 유사한 아이디어를 뒷받침한다. 예를 들어, 집중 치료 중인 환자를 치료하려면 하루에 수백 가지의 작은 조치가 필요할 수 있으며, 작은 실수 하나로 생명을 잃게 할 수 있다. 어떠한 중요한 조치라도 놓치지 않기 위해 체크리스트를 사용하는 것은 당면한 감염을 예방하는 것에서부터 폐렴을 줄이는 것에 이르기까지 다양한 의학적 상황에서 매우 <u>효과적</u>이라는 것이 입증되었다.

197

정답풀이

간단한 예측 문제에 있어 알고리즘이 인간보다 더 나을 수 있고, 복잡한 문제 해결 시에 체크리스트를 이용하는 것이 전문가의 결정의 질을 향상할 수 있다는 내용의 글이다. 따라서 글의 제목으로는 ① '의사 결정을 할 때의 간단한 공식의 힘'이 가장 적절하다.
② 항상 우선순위를 결정하라: 빅 데이터 관리 요령
③ 알고리즘의 실수: 단순함의 신화

④ 준비하라! 만일의 경우에 대비해 체크리스트를 만들어라
⑤ 인간의 판단이 알고리즘을 이기는 방법

198

정답풀이

④ 뒤에 예로 제시된 내용을 보면, 집중 치료 중인 환자에게 하루에 수백 가지의 작은 조치가 필요한 상황처럼 사람들이 '할 일이 너무 많을' 때 중요한 것을 놓치지 않도록 하는 체크리스트가 효과적일 수 있다는 문맥이 되어야 하므로, (d)의 relaxed는 overloaded와 같은 어휘로 바꿔야 한다.

오답풀이

①, ② 알고리즘이 전문가의 판단을 능가할 수 있다는 증거에 대한 예이므로 인간보다 더 '정확하다'는 문맥과 간단한 공식이 중요한 예측을 '더 잘'한다는 문맥은 적절하다.
③ 불확실한 상황에서 간단한 공식은 일관성을 유지하지만 그에 반해 인간은 '관련이 없는' 고려 사항에 쉽게 영향을 받는다는 문맥이다.
⑤ 체크리스트 사용이 중요한 의학적 상황에서 매우 '효과적'이라는 것이 입증되었다는 문맥이다.

구문풀이

12행 When [there are a lot of different factors involved] and [a situation is very uncertain], / simple formulas can win out {by focusing on the most important factors and being consistent}, [**while** human judgement is too easily influenced by particularly salient and perhaps irrelevant considerations].

: 크게 부사절(When절)과 주절로 이루어진 문장이며, 주절에는 while절이 포함되어 있다. When절에는 [ ]로 표시된 두 절이 병렬 연결되어 있으며, 주절의 주어는 simple formulas, 동사는 can win out이다. '~함으로써'라는 의미의 「by -ing」 구문이 쓰였으며 focusing과 being은 병렬구조를 이룬다. 접속사 while은 '~인 반면'의 의미로 쓰였으며, while절의 주어는 human judgement, 동사는 수동형인 is influenced 이다.

어휘풀이

- evidence *n* 증거
- accurate *a* 정확한
- commit *v* (범죄를) 저지르다
- candidate *n* 후보
- remainder *n* 나머지
- consistent *a* 일관성이 있는
- intensive care 집중 치료
- crucial *a* 중요한
- context *n* 상황, 맥락
- infection *n* 감염
- outperform *v* ~을 능가하다
- release *v* 풀어주다, 석방하다
- potential *a* 잠재적인
- domain *n* 영역
- handful *n* 소수, 소량
- irrelevant *a* 관련이 없는
- cost *v* 잃게 하다, 희생시키다
- remarkably *ad* 현저하게, 매우
- live *a* 당면한, 생생한

199~200   답 ⑤ / ③

📖 **방어적 비관주의**

전문해석

프로 음악가인 내 고객의 사례를 생각해보자. 일부 사람들이 그러는 것처럼 내 고객은 부정적인 생각을 하는 경향이 있으며, 정신적으로 자책하는 습관이 있다. 일에서의 성공에도 불구하고 그는 끊임없이 자기 의심으로 고전한다. 우리는 그의 창의력을 풀어놓고 새 앨범을 위한 아이디어를 만들기 위해서 함께 일했다. 아이디어가 악보와 그의 기타줄 위로 흘러넘칠 때에도 나는 그가 자주 "이 노래는 어쨌든 잘 안 될 거야." 또는 "사람들은 이 독특한 노래를 많이 좋아하지 않을 거야."와 같은 것들을 말하는 것을 들었다. **이것은 방어적 비관주의가 작동하고 있는 것이다. 실패를 예측함으로써 그것(실패)이 찾아왔을 때 놀라지 않을 것이며,** 성공하게 되는 희박한 가능

성에 기뻐하게 될 것이다. 용기에 관한 한, 방어적 비관주의는 막다른 길이다. 그것은 전형적으로 사람들에게 기운을 불어넣으며(→ 에너지를 빼앗으며) 우리가 종종 용기와 연관 짓는 열정적이고 자동적인 반응을 막는다.

길 잃은 등산객들을 발견하지 못할 것을 두려워하는 산악 구조 대원을 상상해 보자. 이것은 정확히 구조 작업을 위해서 요구되는 견해와 정반대의 것이다. 응급 (구조) 대원은 심지어 희박한 성공의 가능성에도 열정적으로 매달리는 굳건한 사고방식을 가질 필요가 있다. 그들이 인내하도록 돕고 위험에 맞서기 위해서 필요한 에너지를 제공하는 것은 바로 이러한 낙관주의이다.

199

정답풀이

필자의 고객인 프로 음악가와 구조 대원들의 경우를 사례로 들어서 실패가 두려워 스스로를 의심하고 비관적으로 생각하는 방어적 비관주의를 설명하고 있으므로 글의 제목으로 가장 적절한 것은 ⑤ '방어적 비관주의: 정신의 준비 전략'이다.

① 낙관주의와 자기 확신
② 부정적인 사고의 긍정적인 힘
③ 낙관주의: 구조 대원들이 가장 필요로 하는 것
④ 낙관론자들이 성공할 때 왜 비관론자들은 실패하는가

200

정답풀이

③ 이 문장의 주어 It은 앞에 언급한 방어적 비관주의(defensive pessimism)이고, 이는 사람들에게 일을 추진할 용기, 즉 에너지를 주는 것이 아니라 오히려 '빼앗아가는' 것이다. 따라서 (c)의 energizes를 반대의 의미인 deenergizes로 바꿔야 한다.

오답풀이

① 고객이 정신적으로 자책하는 습관이 있다고 했으므로 '부정적인(negative)' 생각을 하는 경향이 있을 것이다.
② 실패가 찾아왔을 때 놀라지 않으려면 실패를 '예측(predicting)'해야 할 것이다.
④ 실패를 두려워하는 산악 구조 대원의 경우는 앞에서 설명한 방어적 비관주의가 구조 작업에 요구되는 것과 '정반대의 경우(opposite)'에 해당한다.
⑤ 응급 구조 대원이 인내하고 위험에 맞서게 하는 것이 낙관주의라고 했으므로 그들은 '희박한(slim)' 성공의 가능성에도 열정적으로 매달릴 것이다.

구문풀이

12행 This is defensive pessimism at work: / (**by predicting failure**) you won't be surprised [when it comes], / and you will be delighted on the off chance [**that** you are successful].

: 콜론(:) 이하는 두 개의 절을 and가 연결하는 구조이다. 첫 번째 절에서 「by -ing」는 '~함으로써'의 의미이고 it은 앞의 failure를 대신한다. the off chance는 두 번째 [ ]로 표시한 동격절의 수식을 받고 있으며, 이때 that은 접속사이므로 뒤에 완전한 절이 나온다는 것에 유의한다.

24행 **It is** this optimism / **that** helps them persevere and gives them the energy [they need {to face danger}].

: 「It is ~ that ....」 강조구문이 쓰인 문장으로 '…하는 것은 바로 ~이다'의 뜻을 나타낸다. [ ]는 the energy를 수식하는 관계절로, 앞에 목적격 관계대명사가 생략되었다. { }는 부사적 용법으로 쓰인 to부정사구이다.

어휘풀이

- beat oneself up 자책하다
- tumble forth 굴러 떨어지다
- defensive pessimism 방어적 비관주의
- off chance 희박한 가능성
- struggle *v* 애를 쓰다, 고전하다
- dead end 막다른 곳, 가망 없는 상황

- hold back from ~를 방해하다
- bravery *n* 용기, 용감
- robust *a* 강건한, 튼튼한
- cling to ~에 매달리다
- slim *a* (가능성이) 희박한
- persevere *v* 인내하다, 견디다
- enthusiastic *a* 열정적인
- outlook *n* 견해, 견지, 시야
- mindset *n* 사고방식
- feverishly *ad* 열광적으로
- optimism *n* 낙관주의

201~202 답 ④ / ⑤

📖 인간의 손실 회피 성향

전문해석

협상은 (그들이 그것을) 만들었거나 이미 소유하고 있어서 무엇인가를 포기하는 사람들이 구매자가 이익을 느끼는 것보다 그 손실을 언제나 더 크게 느끼기 때문에 일어난다. 한 연구에서 참가자들은 최근에 복권을 구매한, 거리에 있는 사람들에게 접근했다. 그들은 이 사람들에게 그들이 지불했던 것보다 8배의 금액을 받고 그들의 복권을 팔 기회를 제공했다. 물론 이런 판매는 복권 구매자가 이미 그들이 구매했던 것보다 2배에서 8배 많은 복권을 구매할 수 있게 하고, 명백히 그들의 복권 당첨 기회를 증가시켰을 것이다. 쉬운 계산으로 보인다. 그렇지 않은가? 인간의 마음은 합리적이지 않다는 것을 기억하라. 복권 구매자들은 자신들이 당첨 복권을 가지고 있다고 믿을 이유가 전혀 없었지만, 대체로 여전히 훨씬 더 비싼 가격에 그들의 복권을 판매하는 것을 거절했다. 이것은 손실 회피의 좋은 예다. 만약 그들이 당첨 복권을 팔았다면, 감정적인 대가가 실제로 복권에 당첨될 확률을 높여 얻을 수 있는 잠재적인 감정적인 안도감보다 훨씬 더 높을 것이라는 것을 그들은 알았다. 아무런 이유도 없이 이들은 이미 가지고 있는 복권에 특별한 가치를 부여했고, 그들이 얻을 수 있는 8장의 복권이 가지고 있는 잠재적인 가치를 일축했다. 이것은 합리적으로(→ 비합리적으로) 작동하는 인간 뇌의 완벽한 예다. 벼룩시장의 그 여성이 당신에게 바가지를 씌우려고 하는 것이 아님을 명심하라. 사실, 그녀는 당신처럼 그녀가 구매하는 것보다 그녀가 팔고 있는 것에 언제나 더 높은 가치가 있다고 여길 것이다.

201

정답풀이

사람들은 잃는 것의 가치를 얻은 것의 가치보다 높게 평가하기 때문에 손실 회피 경향이 있다는 것을 복권의 예를 들어 설명하고 있는 내용이므로, 글의 제목으로 가장 적절한 것은 ④ '손실 회피의 심리적 기제'이다.

① 복권: 할 가치가 있는가?
② 언제 이익이 손실보다 더 커 보이는가?
③ 사람들이 복권을 구매하는 이유
⑤ 협상: 양측 모두 이길 수 있는 유일한 방법

202

정답풀이

⑤ 자신이 소유한 복권이 당첨될 것이라는 기대를 해서 그 복권을 다른 복권 8장을 구매할 수 있는 가격에 팔지 않으려고 하는 것은 '합리적인' 행동이 아니라 '비합리적인' 행동이다. 따라서 (e)의 rationally를 irrationally와 같은 말로 바꿔야 한다.

오답풀이

① 어떤 물건을 만들었거나 소유하고 있는 사람은 그것의 손실을 '크게(heavily)' 생각하는 손실 회피를 설명하는 글이다.
② 한 장의 복권을 팔아서 8장의 복권을 구매하면 당첨 가능성은 '늘어나게(increasing)' 될 것이다.
③ 사람들은 잃어버린 것의 가치를 더 크게 여기므로 팔아버린 복권이 당첨된 것을 알게 된다면 새로 구매한 복권이 당첨되었을 때 느낄 수 있는 만족감보다 '더 큰(higher)' 상실감을 느낄 것임을 추론할 수 있다.

④ 8장의 복권을 살 수 있는 가격을 제안받았음에도 자신이 이미 구매한 복권을 판매하는 것을 거절했다고 했으므로, 8장의 복권이 가지고 있는 잠재적인 가치를 '일축한(dismissed)' 것이다.

구문풀이

8행 Of course, this sale **would have allowed** the lottery ticket buyers **to buy** two to eight times as many tickets as they'd already bought, [obviously increasing their chances of winning the lottery].

: would have p.p.는 과거의 추측을 나타내며, 「allow+목적어+목적격보어(to부정사)」 구문이 쓰였다. 「배수사+as+원급+as …」는 '…보다 ~배 더 −한'의 의미이다. [ ]는 this sale을 의미상의 주어로 하는 분사구문으로 앞 절의 내용을 부연 설명하며 and it(= this sale) would obviously have increased ~로 풀어 쓸 수 있다.

어휘풀이

- negotiation *n* 협상
- rational *a* 합리적인
- astronomically *ad* 천문학적으로
- potential *a* 잠재적인
- ascribe A to B A를 B에게 돌리다
- rip off 바가지를 씌우다
- lottery ticket 복권
- refuse *v* 거절하다
- aversion *n* 반감, 혐오
- odds *n* 가망, 가능성
- dismiss *v* 무시하다, 일축하다

203~204 답 ⑤ / ③

📖 사회적 상황에 따른 사람들의 상호 작용 방식

전문해석

인상 관리(자기표현)는 자기 자신의 이익이나 이미지에 가장 유리한 방식으로 다른 이들에게 자신을 나타내려는 사람들의 노력을 일컫는다. 예를 들어, 한 교수가 학급에 성적이 매겨진 시험지를 되돌려 주었다고 가정하자. 여러분은 그 시험과 여러분의 성적을 학급의 다른 이들과 의논하겠는가? 여러분이 대부분의 사람과 같다면, 아마도 여러분은 자신이 누구와 이야기하게 되는가와 여러분이 그 시험에서 어떤 성적을 받았는가에 따라 여러분의 학생 역할을 <u>다르게</u> 하게 될 것이다. 여러분의 '표현'은 다른 사람(여러분의 '청중')이 받은 성적에 따라 다를 수 있을 것이다. 한 연구에서, 모두 높은 성적을 받은 학생들은 ('최고 성적을 거둔 두 학생의 만남') 기꺼이 자신의 성적을 서로 이야기했고 때로는 자신들이 어떻게 그 시험에서 '최고 성적을 거두었는지'에 대해 다소 자랑하기도 했다. 하지만 높은 성적을 거둔 학생과 저조하거나 낙제 성적을 받은 학생의 만남('최고 성적을 거둔 학생과 성적이 엉망인 학생의 만남')은 불편했다. 최고 성적을 거둔 학생들은 마치 자신들이 자기 자신의 성적을 <u>과장해야(→ 낮게 평가해야)</u> 하는 것처럼 느꼈다. **결과적으로, 그들은 자신의 성공을 '행운' 탓으로 돌리는 경향이 있었고** 재빨리 성적이 엉망인 학생들에게 격려의 말을 건넸다. 반면에, 성적이 엉망인 학생들은 최고 성적을 받은 학생들을 <u>칭찬해야</u> 하고 자기 자신의 좌절감과 실망감을 감춰야 한다고 생각했다. 저조하거나 낙제 성적을 받은 학생들은 ('성적이 엉망인 두 학생의 만남') 자신들의 부정적인 감정을 공유할 수 있었으므로 서로 이야기할 때 더 <u>편안했다</u>. 그들은 흔히 자기 동정에 빠졌고 자신들의 저조한 수행 결과에 대해 (병이나 불공평한 시험 같은) 체면을 세우는 변명에 의존했다.

203

정답풀이

우수한 성적을 거둔 학생끼리 시험에 관해 이야기할 때, 우수한 성적을 거둔 학생과 성적이 엉망인 학생이 시험에 관해 이야기할 때, 그리고 성적이 엉망인 학생끼리 이야기할 때, 스스로를 표현하고 상대방을 대하는 방식이 달라지는 것을 통해 사람들은 자신과 상대의 상대적인 사회적 상황을 고려하여 자신의 인상을 관리할 수 있도록 상호 작용하는 방식을 달리하게 된다는 점을 이야기하는 글이다. 따라서 글의 제목으로 가장 적절한 것은 ⑤ '사회적 상황: 상호 작용하는 핵심 결정 요인'이다.

① 첫인상은 흔히 틀린 것으로 드러난다
② 최고 성적을 거둔 학생은 좋은 청중이 될 수 있지만, 성적이 엉망인 학생은 그럴 수 없다
③ 여러분이 시험을 망쳤을 때도 시험에 대해 의논하라
④ 발표 기술: 점점 더 중요해지고 있다

204

정답풀이

③ 최고 성적을 거둔 학생이 성적이 엉망인 학생과 시험에 관해 이야기할 때는 자신의 뛰어난 성적을 '행운' 탓으로 돌리는 경향을 보였고 서둘러 상대방에게 격려의 말을 건넸다고 했다. 따라서 자신의 성적에 대해 상대방에게 '과장하는' 것이 아니라 '낮게 평가하는' 모습을 보인다는 문맥이 되어야 하므로, (c)의 exaggerate는 minimize 정도로 바꿔야 한다.

오답풀이

① 이어지는 문장에서 상대방이 받은 성적에 따라 표현이 달라질 것이라고 했으므로 어떤 성적을 받았는지에 따라 역할을 '다르게(differently)' 하게 될 것이다.
② 최고 성적을 거둔 학생끼리는 자신들의 성적을 자랑하기도 한다고 했으므로, '기꺼이(willingly)' 자신의 성적을 서로 이야기했을 것이다.
④ 최고 성적을 거둔 학생들이 격려의 말을 건넨 것에 대해 성적이 엉망인 학생은 자기 자신의 좌절감과 실망감을 감추며 최고 성적을 받은 학생들을 '칭찬했을(praise)' 것이다.
⑤ 성적이 엉망인 두 학생은 자신들의 부정적인 감정을 공유할 수 있었다고 했으므로 서로 이야기할 때 '편안했을(comfortable)' 것이다.

구문풀이

1행 Impression management (presentation of self) refers to people's efforts [to present themselves to others] in ways [that are most favorable to their own interests or image].

: 첫 번째 [ ]는 people's efforts를 수식하는 형용사적 용법의 to부정사구이고, 두 번째 [ ]는 ways를 수식하는 관계절이다.

11행 In one study, [students {who all received high grades ("Ace-Ace encounters")}] willingly talked with one another about their grades and sometimes engaged in a little bragging about [how they had "aced" the test].

: 첫 번째 [ ]는 문장의 주어로 { }로 표시한 관계절이 핵심 주어 students를 수식한다. 두 개의 동사 talked와 engaged가 이끄는 술부가 and에 의해 병렬 연결되어 있으며, 두 번째 [ ]는 about의 목적어로 쓰인 명사절이다.

어휘풀이

- presentation *n* 표현, 발표
- favorable *a* 유리한, 호의적인
- encounter *n* 만남
- engage in ~을 하다
- attribute A to B A를 B의 탓으로 돌리다
- encouragement *n* 격려
- indulge in ~에 빠지다, ~을 탐닉하다
- face-saving *a* 체면을 세우는
- determinant *n* 결정 요인
- refer to ~을 일컫다
- vary *v* 다르다
- willingly *ad* 기꺼이
- brag about ~에 대해 자랑하다
- frustration *n* 좌절
- self-pity *n* 자기 동정
- excuse *n* 변명, 핑계

19 복합 장문 (1지문 3문항)

본문 pp.142~146

205 ⑤	**206** ③	**207** ③	**208** ⑤	**209** ⑤
210 ④	**211** ②	**212** ④	**213** ⑤	**214** ⑤
215 ⑤	**216** ③			

205~207 답 ⑤ / ③ / ③

📖 해변 도로를 따라 자전거를 타는 Emma와 Clara

전문해석

(A) Emma와 Clara는 끝없이 펼쳐진 바다에 시선을 고정한 채, 해변 도로에 나란히 서 있었다. 그들을 둘러싸고 있는 숨 막히는 풍경은 말로 표현할 수 없을 정도였다. 일출 직후에, 그들은 해변 도로를 따라 자전거를 탈 준비를 마쳤다. Emma는 Clara를 돌아보며, "이것이 네 인생 최고의 라이딩이 될 거라고 생각해?"라고 물었다. Clara의 얼굴이 환한 미소로 밝아지며 고개를 끄덕였다. "물론이지! (a) 나는 저 아름다운 파도를 보면서 어서 자전거를 타고 싶어!"

(D) Emma와 Clara는 자전거에 올라타서 해변 도로가 끝나는 하얀 절벽을 향해 페달을 밟기 시작했다. 속도를 높여 넓고 푸른 바다를 즐기면서, Emma는 자신의 흥분을 감추지 못하고 "Clara, 경치가 정말 멋져!"라고 외쳤다. 하지만, Clara의 침묵은 그녀가 자기 생각에 잠겨 있다는 것을 말하는 것 같았다. Emma는 그녀의 침묵의 의미를 이해했다. 자기 옆에서 자전거를 타고 있는 Clara를 바라보며, Emma는 지금은 (e) 그녀가 극복한 것처럼 보이는, Clara의 과거 비극에 대해 생각했다.

(C) Clara는 재능 있는 수영 선수였지만, 어깨 부상으로 인해 올림픽 수영 메달리스트가 되겠다는 자신의 꿈을 포기해야만 했다. 하지만 그녀는 그 고난에 건설적인 방식으로 대응했다. 수년간의 고된 훈련 끝에, 그녀는 믿어지지 않을 정도의 회복을 이뤄냈고 자전거 타기에 대한 새로운 열정을 발견했다. Emma는 고통스러운 과거가 그녀를 어떻게 더 성숙하게 만들어 주었는지, 그리고 그것이 결국에는 (d) 그녀를 어떻게 더 강하게 만들어 주었는지를 보았다. 한 시간 후에, Emma보다 앞서 달리던 Clara가 뒤를 돌아보며 "저 하얀 절벽을 봐!"라고 소리쳤다.

(B) 그들의 목적지에 도착했을 때, Emma와 Clara는 자전거를 멈췄다. Emma는 Clara에게 다가가 "자전거 타기는 수영과는 다르지, 그렇지 않니?"라고 말했다. Clara는 미소를 지으며 대답했다. "사실은, 꽤 비슷해. 수영과 꼭 마찬가지로 자전거 타기는 나에게 진정으로 살아있다는 느낌이 들게 해 줘." "그것은 (b) 나에게 인생의 힘든 도전에 직면하면서 산다는 것이 어떤 의미인지 보여줘."라고 그녀는 덧붙였다. Emma는 동의하면서 고개를 끄덕이고, "너의 첫 번째 해변 자전거 타기는 정말 대성공이었어. 내년 여름에 다시 오는 건 어때?"라고 제안했다. Clara는 "(c) 너와 함께라면, 물론이지!"라고 기뻐하면서 대답했다.

구문풀이

1행 Emma and Clara stood side by side on the beach road, [with their eyes fixed on the boundless ocean].

: 문장의 주어는 Emma and Clara이고 동사는 stood이다. 「with+명사+분사」의 구조인 [ ]는 동시상황을 나타내는 분사구로 '~한 채로'라는 의미이다. their eyes와 fix가 수동의 의미이므로 과거분사 fixed가 쓰였다.

13행 Emma saw [how the painful past made her maturer] and [how it made her stronger in the end].

: 주어는 Emma이고 동사는 saw이다. 의문사절인 두 개의 [ ]는 문장의 목적어로 병렬 구조를 이루고 있다.

어휘풀이

- boundless *a* 끝없는
- breathtaking *a* 숨이 (턱) 막히는, 깜짝 놀랄 만한

- beyond description 말로 표현할 수 없는
- hardship *n* 고난
- exclaim *v* 외치다
- tragedy *n* 비극
- incredible *a* 믿을 수 없을 정도의
- be lost in thought 생각에 잠기다

208~210 답 ⑤ / ⑤ / ④

📖 아빠에게 드리는 딸의 선물

전문해석

(A) "Hailey, 조심해!" Camila는 동생이 테이블로 거대한 케이크를 들고 오는 것을 보며 걱정되어 소리쳤다. "걱정 마, Camila." Hailey는 미소 지으며 답했다. Camila는 Hailey가 파티 테이블에 케이크를 무사히 올려 두었을 때 비로소 안심했다. "아빠가 곧 여기 오실 거야. 아빠 생신을 위해 (a) 너는 무슨 선물을 샀니?" Camila는 호기심에서 물었다. "그게 뭔지 알면 아빠는 깜짝 놀라실 거야!" Hailey는 윙크하며 대답했다.

(D) "틀림없이 (d) 너는 아빠를 위해 지갑이나 시계를 샀을 거야."라고 Camila가 말했다. 대꾸하면서 Hailey는 "아니. 난 훨씬 더 개인적인 것을 샀어. 그건 그렇고 (e) 언니가 아빠에 대해 알아야 할 게 있어…"하고 답했다. 초인종이 울리면서 그들의 대화는 갑자기 중단되었다. 그들의 아빠가 왔고 그들은 그를 보고 매우 기뻤다. "우리 사랑하는 아가씨들, 내 생일에 너희들 집에 날 초대해 줘서 고마워." 그는 기쁨에 차서 걸어 들어와서 그의 딸들을 껴안았다. 그들은 모두 식당으로 들어갔고, 그곳에서 그는 무지개색 생일 케이크와 50송이의 빨간 장미로 환영받았다.

(C) "생신 축하드려요! 오늘 쉰 살이세요, 아빠. 사랑해요!"라고 Camila가 말하고 나서 (c) 그녀의 동생이 그에게 작은 꾸러미를 드렸다. 그것을 열었을 때 그는 안에서 안경을 발견했다. "Hailey, 아빠에게 시력 문제는 없어."라고 Camila가 어리둥절해하며 말했다. "사실은 Camila, 난 아빠가 오랫동안 색맹을 앓고 있다는 것을 최근에 알게 되었어. 아빠는 우리를 걱정시키지 않으려고 그것을 비밀로 해왔어."라고 Hailey가 설명했다.

(B) "아빠, 이 안경은 적록색맹을 교정하는 데 도움이 될 수 있어요."라고 Hailey가 말했다. 그는 천천히 그것을 쓰고, 테이블 위에 있는 생일 선물을 바라보았다. 지금껏 처음으로 선명한 빨간색과 초록색을 보고 그는 울기 시작했다. "믿을 수가 없구나! 저 경이로운 색깔들을 보렴!" 그는 놀라서 소리쳤다. Hailey는 눈물을 흘리며 그에게 말했다. "아빠, 난 아빠가 이제 마침내 무지개와 장미의 진정한 아름다움을 즐길 수 있어서 기뻐요. 빨간색은 사랑을 나타내고 초록색은 건강을 나타내요. 아빠는 둘 다 누릴 자격이 있으세요." Camila는 고개를 끄덕였고, (b) 그녀의 안경 선물이 아빠를 얼마나 행복하게 했는지 알게 되었다.

정답풀이

208

Camila와 Hailey가 아빠의 생신 선물에 관해 이야기하는 내용인 (A) 다음에는, 아버지가 두 딸의 집에 와서 무지개색 생일 케이크와 빨간 장미를 받는 (D)가 오고, 아빠가 오랫동안 색맹을 앓고 있다는 것을 비밀로 했고 Hailey가 최근에 그것을 알게 되어 안경을 준비했다는 내용의 (C)가 온다. 그리고 아빠가 안경을 쓰고 기뻐하는 내용인 (B)가 마지막에 오는 순서가 가장 적절하다.

209

(e)는 Camila를 가리키고, 나머지는 모두 Hailey를 가리킨다.

210

(D)에서 아빠는 Camila와 Hailey의 집에 자신을 초대해 주어 고맙다고 했으므로 ④는 글의 내용으로 적절하지 않다.

구문풀이

1행 Camila yelled uneasily, [watching her sister carrying a huge cake to the table].

: [ ]는 주어 Camila의 동작을 설명하는 분사구문으로, her sister는 watch의 목적어이고 carrying 이하는 목적격보어이다. 진행형이므로 지각동사 watch의 목적격보어로 현재분사가 왔다.

36행 They all walked into the dining room, [where he was greeted with a rainbow-colored birthday cake and fifty red roses].

: [ ]는 the dining room을 부연 설명하는 관계절이다.

어휘풀이
- uneasily *ad* 걱정이 되어
- out of interest 호기심에서
- color blindness 색맹
- in amazement 놀라서
- deserve *v* 받을 만하다
- eyesight *n* 시력
- suffer from ~을 앓다
- interrupt *v* 중단하다
- greet *v* 환영하다, 맞이하다
- shortly *ad* 곧
- correct *v* 교정하다
- vivid *a* 선명한
- represent *v* 나타내다, 의미하다
- parcel *n* 꾸러미, 소포
- puzzled *a* 어리둥절하는
- personal *a* 개인적인
- overjoyed *a* 매우 기뻐하는

211~213 답 ② / ④ / ⑤

📖 다친 참새를 보살핀 후 떠나보낸 Jenny 자매

전문해석

(A) 6월의 어느 화창한 오후 언니 Jenny와 나는 학교에서 집으로 오고 있었는데, 그때 우리는 연석에 있는 빈 쓰레기통 속에서 나는 시끄러운 새 울음소리를 들었다. 우리는 그곳으로 가서 안을 들여다보았다. 슬퍼 보이는 작은 참새 한 마리가 쓰레기통 바닥에 앉아 애처롭게 울고 있었다. 그녀의 오른쪽 날개는 몸통에서 이상한 각도로 튀어나와 있었다. Jenny는 그것이 부러진 것 같다고 말했다. 그녀는 안으로 손을 뻗어 양손을 오므려 감쌌고 (a)그녀가 겁먹지 않도록 '구구' 소리를 냈다. 그 참새는 우리 집으로 오는 내내 짹짹거렸다.

(C) 엄마는 그 작은 새를 한 번 보시고, "절대 안 돼! 집 안에 다른 동물을 키우지 않을 거야."라고 말씀하셨다. 하지만 엄마가 그 크고 슬픈 눈을 가까이서 보고 애처롭게 우는 소리를 들었을 때, (d)그녀의 마음은 녹아내렸다. 우리는 그것을 믿고 있었다. 엄마는 새의 오른쪽 날개가 분명히 부러졌다고 말했고, 그녀는 아이스크림 막대기로 부목을 만들어 그것을 조심스럽게 날개에 테이프로 붙였다.

(B) 일단 부목을 대고, 우리는 그 새에게 물과 빵조각을 먹였다. 처음에는 먹으려고 하지 않았지만, 잠시 후에 (b)그녀는 (먹는 것을) 멈추려 하지 않았다. 그 작은 새는 Peep이라는 이름을 얻게 되었다. 우리는 그녀를 빈 새장에 넣었다. 얼마 후에 Peep의 날개는 좋아졌고 우리는 부목을 제거했다. 엄마는 그 새를 보내줄 때가 된 것 같다고 말했다. 다음 날 아침 우리가 새장의 문을 열었을 때, 그 새는 공중으로 50피트 정도 날았다가 다시 돌아왔다. 그때부터 Peep은 매일 아침 더 멀리 날아갔지만 (c)그녀는 늘 다시 돌아왔다.

(D) 2주 후 어느 일요일 아침에 Jenny가 Peep을 새장에서 내보냈을 때, 그녀는 계속 날았다. 우리는 문을 열어둔 채 새장을 밖에 두었지만 그녀는 그날 종일 집으로 돌아오지 않았다. 밤에 우리는 Peep이 돌아오지 않을 것이라는 진실과 마주했다. 엄마는 (e)그녀가 아마도 몇몇 다른 참새들을 발견하고 그들과 함께 있을 때라고 결정했을 것이라고 말했다. 내 눈에는 눈물이 고였고 Jenny도 역시 그랬다.

정답풀이

211

하굣길에 다친 참새를 발견하고 집으로 데려오는 내용인 (A)에 이어, 집에서 엄마가 다친 새를 치료해주는 내용인 (C)가 오고 참새가 회복되는 과정을 보여 주는 (B)가 온다. 그리고 마지막에 완치된 새가 날아가버려 슬퍼하는 내용

인 (D)가 오는 것이 자연스럽다.

212

(d)는 엄마를 가리키고, 나머지는 모두 다친 참새를 가리킨다.

213

Peep이 부상에서 완치한 후에는 새장 밖으로 날아갔다가 다시 돌아오곤 했으며, 2주가 지나서야 완전히 날아갔으므로 ⑤는 글의 내용으로 적절하지 않다.

구문풀이

8행 She reached in and cupped the bird in her hands, [cooing to her {so she wouldn't be scared}].

: [ ]는 분사구문으로 and she cooed ~의 의미이다. { }는 목적을 나타내는 부사절이다.

22행 But [**once** she got a closer look at those big, sad eyes and heard **that** pathetic chirping], her heart melted.

: [ ]는 접속사 once가 이끄는 시간을 나타내는 부사절이며, 이 절의 동사인 got과 heard가 and에 의해 병렬구조로 연결되어 있다. that은 지시형용사로 이어지는 명사구 pathetic chirping을 수식한다.

어휘풀이
- chirp *v* (새가) 짹짹거리다
- peer *v* 들여다보다
- stick out from ~에서 튀어나오다
- cup *v* (컵 모양처럼) 손을 오목하게 만들다
- pathetic *a* 애처로운, 측은한
- definitely *ad* 분명히, 확실히
- curb *n* (인도와 차도 사이의) 연석
- sparrow *n* 참새
- count on 믿다, 기대하다

214~216 답 ⑤ / ⑤ / ③

📖 선수로서의 올바른 자세를 가르쳐준 마이너리그 코치 George Kissell

전문해석

(A) 내가 Cardinal의 마이너리그 코치들 중 한 명인 George Kissell을 처음 만났을 때, 나는 Sarasota에 있는 야구장에 막 도착했었다. 첫날 아침, 나는 여러분이 'B급'이라고 부를 것이라 생각되는 경기에 있었다. 나는 그것이 무엇이었는지 정말 모른다. 하지만 그 경기가 대략 오후 3시 30분경에 끝나자 나는 호텔로 돌아갔고 그때 (a)그 코치는 "야간 경기를 위해 5시에 되돌아가게."라고 말했다.

(D) 나는 Sacramento에서 와 거의 이틀 동안 잠을 자지 못해서 방으로 가 늦잠을 잤다. 나는 4시 45분에 깨서, 택시에 올라탔다. 나는 우리가 낮 경기를 했던 야구장에 도착했고, 야구 장비들을 모아 버스로 달려갔다. 그것은 정확하게 5시에 우리가 야간 경기를 하는 야구장으로 떠날 예정이었다. 내가 버스에 승차하고 있을 때, 매니저인 Ray Hathaway가 내게 다가왔다. (e)그가 내게 한 유일한 말은, "절대 늦지 말게." 그게 다였다.

(C) 우리는 야구장에 도착했고 경기가 시작되었다. 우천으로 인한 지연이 있었고, 나는 심지어 출전을 하고 있지도 않았으며, 무엇보다도 이틀 동안 잠을 자지 못했었다. 선수 대기석 중간에 커다란 조명 기둥이 있었고, 나는 그 뒤에 좀 앉아 있었다. (c)이 남자가 내 바로 앞으로 걸어오더니 "볼카운트가 어떻게 되고, 몇 아웃인가?"라고 말했다. 나는 (d)그가 원하는 답을 알아보는 편이 나을 거라 생각했다.

(B) 나는 조명 기둥 주위에 기대어 득점판을 보고 그가 나에게 물은 것에 관한 것을 읽어주었다. 나는 "이 사람은 득점판도 볼 수 없는 건가."라고 생각하고 있었다. (b)그는 내게 "볼카운트와 아웃이 몇인지도 모르고 벤치에 앉아 있지는 말게. 항상 경기에 가담하고 있어야 하네. 그곳에 앉아 있으려면 뭔가를 알고 있게!"라고 말했다. 나는 이곳에 온 지 하루가 되었고, "장난하시나요? 나는 이곳에 있기도 싫어요."라고 생각하고 있었다. 하지만 이제 나는 그가 옳았다는 것을 안다. George는 항상 옳았다!

214

필자가 처음 George Kissell을 만나고 그가 야간 경기 시간에 맞춰 오라고 한 (A)의 상황 다음에, 늦잠을 자서 경기장에 늦게 도착한 (D)의 상황이 이어지고, 야구장에 도착했지만 피로로 경기에 집중하지 않고 있던 필자를 묘사한 (C)가 그 다음에 온다. 그리고 그런 필자에게 George Kissell이 충고를 하고 필자가 결국 그가 옳다는 것을 깨닫는 (B)가 오는 것이 적절하다.

215

(e)는 매니저인 Ray Hathaway를 가리키고, 나머지는 모두 코치인 George Kissell을 가리킨다.

216

볼카운트를 물어보는 George를 이상하게 생각했지만 대답을 해주었으므로 그의 질문을 무시했다는 ③은 윗글의 내용으로 적절하지 않다.

구문풀이

9행 I [leaned around the light pole] and [looked at the scoreboard] and [read him the stuff {he asked me about}].

: [ ]로 표시한 3개의 동사구가 접속사 and로 연결된 구조이고, 세 번째 [ ]에서 read의 직접목적어인 the stuff는 목적격 관계대명사가 생략된 { }의 수식을 받는다.

어휘풀이

- ballpark *n* 야구장
- lean *v* 기대다
- scoreboard *n* 스코어보드, 득점판
- delay *n* 지연
- report back (근무 장소로) 돌아가다
- pole *n* 기둥
- be involved in ~에 개입되다
- dugout *n* 대기석

13~19 어휘 REVIEW 본문 pp.147~152

13 빈칸 추론

01 만들다, 형성하다 02 귀납 추리 03 해고 04 상대적인 05 상당한 06 기준 07 부문, 분야 08 강화하다 09 비정상적인 10 장관의, 구경거리의 11 굴하지 않고 계속하다 12 (사람을) 지지하다 13 멸종한, 끊어진 14 ~에 의지해서 살다 15 응집하다 16 분별 있는, 현명한 17 명백히 하다 18 고통 19 해방, 자유 20 적절성 21 ~의 관점에서 22 수반하다 23 놀라운 24 쫓아내다 25 결정적인, 최후의 26 양육하다 27 마비 28 수입, 수익 29 무한한 30 그에 맞춰 31 ~와 일치하는 32 경사면 33 관리, 통치 34 이주 35 판매 부수, 유통 36 유발하다, 일으키다 37 조심스럽게, 신중하게 38 depression 39 변종 40 전염성의 41 관료적인, 관료주의의 42 예산 43 결국 ~로 끝나다 44 균형 45 가정의, 집안의, 국내의 46 심하게, 극도로 47 witness 48 손상시키다 49 끼어들다, 밀고 들어가다 50 도입하다 51 대규모의 52 신호로 알리다 53 ~에 제한된[갇힌] 54 ~을 상쇄하다 55 친척 56 피상적인, 표면상의 57 서로, 상호 간에, 공통으로 58 내재시키다, 안에 넣다 59 의무, 책임 60 부채질하다 61 특별한, 우수한 62 직면하다, 맞서다 63 탐욕스러운, 욕심 많은 64 부분적인, 단편적인 65 재료, 요소 66 상품, 물품 67 추상적인 68 묘사하다 69 solitude 70 시행하다 71 먹이를 찾다 72 반박하다 73 소작농 74 전환, 변화 75 (돈, 생각 등을) ~에 쏟다[돌리다] 76 다루다 77 파충류 78 ~을 낳다 79 요소 80 공모자

14 무관한 문장

01 수익성이 있는 02 주장하다 03 풍부한 04 어색한, 힘든 05 sustainable 06 사소한, 하찮은 07 입증하다, 확인하다 08 침착한 09 인정, 승인 10 불일치 11 적성, 소질 12 말의, 구두의 13 한눈에 14 드물게, 인색하게 15 ~을 생각해 내다 16 청소년기, 사춘기 17 경이로운, 경탄할 만한 18 intuition 19 당황한 20 헛되이, 보람 없이

15 글의 순서 파악

01 조종하다, 조작하다 02 쓰레기 매립(지) 03 번식의, 생식의 04 보완하다 05 skull 06 ~에 선행하다[앞서다] 07 유발하다, 일으키다 08 절약하다, 보존하다 09 바람직한 10 corridor 11 지대한, 엄청난 12 정직, 청렴결백 13 손쉽게 14 기만적인, 사람을 속이는 15 노력하다, 애쓰다 16 ~을 설명하다 17 상쇄하다 18 상상하다, 마음속에 그리다 19 적절성 20 흥미를 자아내는 21 끊임없이 22 attic 23 처방 24 과도한 25 내재하는, 본질적인 26 물러나다, 중단하다 27 구별되는, 별개의 28 primate 29 강요하다 30 (동식물의) 조직, 구조 31 평가하다 32 era 33 타당성 34 비어 있는 35 공격적인 36 배에 싣다 37 자극 38 강렬한 39 감소 40 infant

16 문장 삽입

01 구현하다, 상징하다 02 예방의 03 유명인 04 ~에서 생겨나다 05 모순되다 06 소수의 07 순회 08 ~하는 경향이 있다 09 진술 10 dimension 11 흉내 내다 12 비활성의, 불활성의 13 부유한 14 원리, 원칙 15 쪼개지다 16 소홀한, 무관심한 17 터무니없는 18 적대적인, 적의가 있는 19 genetic 20 예상하다 21 (법의) 준수 22 고갈, 결핍 23 대대적인, 광범위한 24 해결책 25 신중한 26 satiety 27 드러내다 28 할당하다 29 (위험 등을) 제기하다 30 변수 31 일치하다 32 농작물, 산출고 33 극심함, 심각함 34 새로운 35 descendant 36 무효화하다 37 환상, 착각 38 후퇴, 물러남, 철수 39 (좋은 결과 등을) 거두다, 받다 40 작동하기 시작하다

17 요약문 완성

01 육체노동의, 손으로 하는 02 주홍색의 03 초식 동물 04 놀라게 하다 05 ~ 자체를 위한 06 확산, 급증 07 충동 08 착수하다, 시작하다 09 억제하다 10 의복 11 obsession 12 긴장 13 축약된 14 소외 15 고정관념을 벗어나다, 독창적으로 생각하다 16 상충되는 17 ~에 부응하다 18 영역 19 성취, 성과 20 생각하다, 추측하다

18 장문(1지문 2문항)

01 열광적으로 02 (범죄를) 저지르다 03 determinant 04 ~에 대해 자랑하다 05 가망, 가능성 06 (언론의) 보도 07 당연한, 생생한 08 ~에 매달리다 09 반감, 혐오 10 사고방식 11 해명 12 무시하다, 일축하다 13 ~에 빠지다, ~을 탐닉하다 14 애를 쓰다, 고전하다 15 release 16 강건한, 튼튼한 17 A를 B에게 돌리다 18 ~을 일컫다 19 (가능성이) 희박한 20 논란

19 복합 장문(1지문 3문항)

01 들여다보다 02 tragedy 03 중단하다 04 ~에 개입되다 05 연석 06 환영하다, 맞이하다 07 분명히, 확실히 08 고난 09 (새가) 짹짹거리다 10 받을 만하다 11 ~에서 튀어나오다 12 애처로운, 측은한 13 parcel 14 참새 15 기둥 16 (근무 장소로) 돌아가다 17 목적지 18 선명한 19 믿다, 기대하다 20 기대다

적중 예상 문제 1회

본문 pp.154~159

217 ⑤	218 ②	219 ⑤	220 ④	221 ④
222 ⑤	223 ③	224 ④	225 ⑤	226 ⑤
227 ②	228 ③			

217 답 ⑤

📖 방갈로 공사가 지연된 이유와 완공 예정일을 알림

전문해석

Watson 씨께,

저희는 귀하의 방갈로 완성을 위한 예상 기간이 이미 초과되었다는 것을 알고 있습니다. 불행히도, 유난히 혹독한 겨울이었다는 것을 기억하실 겁니다. **여러 번의 장기적인 폭설 기간 동안 귀하의 건물에 대한 작업은 정말 불가능했습니다.** 건축 자재, 특히 벽돌과 목재의 전국적인 부족도 있었고 그로부터 거래가 이제야 회복되고 있습니다. 이 두 가지 어려움 모두 예견될 수 없었습니다. 그것들이 없었다면, 예상 완성 기간인 6개월이 확실히 지켜졌을 것입니다. 날씨가 좋아져서 이제 일이 매우 잘 진행되고 있습니다. 예상치 못한 지연이 발생하지 않는다면, **방갈로는 8월 말까지 귀하를 위해 준비될 것이라고 틀림없이 약속할 수 있습니다.**

Tom Peters 드림

정답풀이

방갈로 공사가 예정된 기간을 넘긴 것은 겨울의 장기적인 폭설과 건축 자재 부족 사태 때문이었다고 이해를 구하면서 이제 순조롭게 일이 진행되어 8월 말에 완공될 것임을 알리는 내용이므로, 글의 목적으로는 ⑤가 가장 적절하다.

구문풀이

12행 **Without** them, / the estimated completion period of six months **would have** definitely **been met**.

: Without은 '~이 없었다면'이라는 의미로, 주절의 「조동사의 과거형+have p.p.」와 함께 과거의 사실에 반대되는 상황을 가정하는 가정법 과거완료 구문을 이룬다. 이때, Without은 If it had not been for로 바꾸어 쓸 수 있다.

어휘풀이

- bungalow *n* 방갈로, 작은 주택
- recall *v* 기억하다
- severe *a* 혹독한
- prolonged *a* 장기적인
- building material 건축 자재
- now that ~ 때문에, ~한 이상
- exceed *v* 초과하다
- exceptionally *ad* 유난히
- property *n* 건물
- shortage *n* 부족
- foresee *v* 예견하다

218 답 ②

📖 양분법적인 사고방식을 벗어날 필요성

전문해석

어쩌면 여러분은 자기 직업에 매우 불만족스러워하는 친구가 있었을 것이다. 그는 자신의 불만족에 대해 어떻게 해야 할지 고민하면서, 자신이 그만두거나 그저 끝까지 계속할 수 있다고 빠르게 결론을 내린다. 우리 삶에서 우리는 몇 번이나 중요한 결정이나 의견을 두 가지 선택사항으로 줄이는가? 두 가지 극단 중 하나에 걸려 꼼짝 못 하게 되기는 매우 쉽다. 우리는 좋은/나쁜, 옳은/틀린, 흑/백의 관점에서 생각하도록 훈련되어 왔다. 하지만 삶의 방식은 그렇지가 않다! 흑백 사고는 우리 자신이 **선택할 수 있는 것들을 감소시킬 뿐만 아니라, 또한 우리가 더 비판적이게 만드는데,** 내가 옳다면, 그들은 틀렸음에 틀림없다. 편협한 사고는 우리 사회의 많은 현재의 갈등에서 명백하다. 항상 두 가지보다 더 많은 측면이 있다. 색깔로 생각해 보라. 여러분과 다른 사람들에게 개방적이고, 여러분의 선택사항을 탐구하며, 일반적인 것 바깥으로 한 걸음 나와 **이것 아니면 저것이라는 해결 방안의 덫을 피하라.**

정답풀이

이것 아니면 저것이라는 식의 양분법적인 사고방식을 벗어나 개방적인 마음으로 다양하게 인생의 선택사항을 생각해 보라는 내용의 글이다. 따라서 필자가 주장하는 바로는 ②가 가장 적절하다.

구문풀이

14행 **Be** open to those [who are different than you], **explore** your options, **step** outside the norm and **avoid** the trap of either/or solutions.

: 명령문으로, 동사원형인 Be, explore, step, avoid가 「A, B, C and D」의 구조로 연결되어 병렬구조를 이룬다. [ ]는 앞의 those를 수식하는 관계절이다.

어휘풀이

- agonize *v* 고민하다
- conclude *v* 결론을 내리다
- stick ~ out ~을 끝까지 계속하다
- judgmental *a* 비판적인, 판단적인
- evident *a* 명백한
- norm *n* 일반적인 것
- dissatisfaction *n* 불만, 불평
- quit *v* 그만두다
- get stuck at ~에 걸려 꼼짝 못 하다
- intolerant *a* 편협한
- conflict *n* 갈등
- trap *n* 덫

219 답 ⑤

📖 좋은 글쓰기의 시작

전문해석

많은 사람들은 그들이 그들의 주제를 먼저 완벽하게 생각할 때까지 어떤 것을 쓸 수 없다고 생각한다. 그것은 큰 판돈을 거는 도박 글쓰기이다. 적은 판돈을 거는 글쓰기를 해라. **완벽하게 되려는 것을 내려 놓고 그냥 글을 써라.** 적은 판돈을 거는 글쓰기를 할 때 여러분은 문법, 구두점, 문장 구조, 심지어 아이디어의 흐름에 대해 걱정하지 않고도 종이에 펜을 (또는 키보드에다 손을) 갖다 댈 수가 있다. 그것은 스스로와 하는 브레인스토밍이다. 그리고 그것은 재미있을 수가 있다! 그것이 잡동사니 같아 보이더라도 그냥 쓰기 시작하라. 그것은 여러분이 들었던 (의) 한 행일 수 있다. 그것은 할아버지의 틀니, 지난 6월의 라일락의 향기가 어땠는지, 여덟 살 때의 새들 슈즈처럼 갑자기 떠오른 기억일 수 있다. 그것은 당신이 언제든지 적어두는 어떤 주제일 수 있다. 여러분이 어떤 것을 생각할 때마다 목록에 추가하라. 그러면 여러분이 글을 쓰기 위해 앉았을 때 여러분은 목록으로부터 그저 하나의 주제를 잡아 (글쓰기를) 시작할 수 있다.

정답풀이

글의 주제가 완벽하게 잡힐 때까지 기다리지 말고 자유롭게 글쓰기를 시작하면 좋은 주제를 잡아 좋은 글을 쓸 수 있다는 내용이다. 그러므로 ⑤가 요지로 가장 적절하다.

구문풀이

1행 A lot of people think [they **can't** write something {**until** they have first thought their topic out perfectly}].

: [ ]는 문장의 동사인 think의 목적어 역할을 하는 명사절로 앞에 접속사 that이 생략되었다. until은 not과 함께 쓰여 '~해야 비로소 …하다'의 의미를 나타낸다.

- stake *n* 내기에 건 돈
- let go of (쥐고 있던 것을) 내려 놓다
- punctuation *n* 구두점
- brainstorming *n* 브레인스토밍, 창조적 집단 사고
- junk *n* 쓰레기, 잡동사니
- flash *n* 번쩍임, 갑자기 떠오름
- false teeth 틀니, 의치
- saddle shoes 새들 슈즈(구두끈 있는 등 부분을 색이 다른 가죽으로 씌운 캐주얼 슈즈)
- jot down ~을 적다

220 답 ④

📖 한국의 가구당 평균 보육비와 교육비 지출의 변화

전문해석

위의 도표는 2016년 3월과 2017년 3월의 한국의 가구당 보육비와 교육비 (유치원에서 고등학교까지) 평균 지출의 변화를 보여준다. 2017년 3월의 전반적인 평균 지출은 2016년 3월의 평균 지출과 비교할 때 상당히 증가한 것으로 나타났다. 2017년 3월에 유치원생을 교육하는 데 지출한 금액은 보육에 지출한 금액보다 조금 더 많았다. 가구당 중학생을 교육하는 데 쓰인 평균 지출 금액은 다섯 개의 항목 중에서 가장 큰 상승을 기록했다. 보육 시설에 지불한 지출의 증가액은 고등학생을 교육하는 데 지불한 지출액의 증가액보다 조금 많았다(→ 적었다). 고등학생을 교육하는 데 쓰인 지출의 상승률은 모든 항목 중에서 가장 적었다.

정답풀이

보육 시설에 지불한 지출의 증가액 17만원은 고등학생을 교육하는 데 지불한 지출의 증가액 18만원보다 조금 적으므로 ④가 도표의 내용과 일치하지 않는다.

구문풀이

12행 [The increased amount of the expenditure on day care facilities] was a little more than **that** of the expenditure on paying education fee for high school students.

: [ ]가 주어, was가 동사이다. 지시대명사 that은 앞에 나온 the increased amount를 대신한다.

어휘풀이
- average *a* 평균의 *n* 평균
- expenditure *n* 지출
- household *n* 가구
- massive *a* 엄청나게 큰
- facility *n* 시설

221 답 ④

📖 영국의 법학자, 철학자, 정치학자이자 경제학자인 Jeremy Bentham

전문해석

Jeremy Bentham은 1748년에 런던에서 태어났다. 그는 영재였는데, 세 살 때 역사책과 다른 '진지한' 책들을 읽고, 다섯 살 때 바이올린을 연주했으며, 겨우 여섯 살이었을 때 라틴어와 프랑스어를 공부했다. 열두 살 때, 그는 옥스퍼드에 있는 Queens College에 입학하여 법을 공부했다. 십 대 후반에 Bentham은 자신의 저술에 집중하기로 결정했다. 부친의 재정적 뒷받침을 받아, 그는 철학, 경제학, 정치학에 관한 일련의 책을 저술했다. 그는 흔히 하루 8시간에서 12시간 동안 글을 쓰곤 했는데, 평생 계속된 습관이었으며, 학자들에게 향후 여러 해 동안 편집할 자료를 남겼다. 그의 저작물 대부분은 그가 사망하고 한 세기가 훌쩍 지나서야 출판되었다. 경제학에 대한 그의 가장 유명한 기여는 유용성과 어떻게 그것이 경제적, 사회적 행동에서 원동력이 되는지에 관한 개념이었다.

정답풀이

Jeremy Bentham의 저작물 대부분은 그가 사망하고 한 세기가 훌쩍 지나서야 출판되었다고 했으므로, 대부분의 저작물이 사망하기 전에 출판되었다는 ④는 글의 내용과 일치하지 않는다.

구문풀이

9행 He would often write for 8 to 12 hours a day, [a practice {that continued through his life}], [**leaving** scholars material to compile for years to come].

: 첫 번째 [ ]는 앞 절의 내용과 동격을 이루는 명사구이고, 이 명사구 내의 { }는 a practice를 수식하는 관계절이다. 두 번째 [ ]는 분사구문으로 and he left ~의 절로 바꾸어 쓸 수 있다.

어휘풀이
- gifted child 영재
- philosophy *n* 철학
- politics *n* 정치(학)
- practice *n* 습관, 버릇
- compile *v* 편집[편찬]하다
- contribution *n* 기여
- utility *n* 유용(성)
- driving force 원동력

222 답 ⑤

📖 선택에 대한 후회를 줄여주는 선택의 과정에 대한 생각

전문해석

한 과학자가 동료들이 열띤 토론을 벌이고 있는 학술지에 실린 논문을 읽지 않은 것 때문에 한심한 기분을 느끼고 있다고 생각해 보자. 어리석은 뒤늦은 깨달음이 그를 이렇게 느끼게 했다. 그는 자신이 그 중요한 논문을 읽을 것인지 읽지 않을 것인지 두 가지 중 하나를 선택할 수 있었는데, 어리석게도 잘못된 선택을 했다고 생각한다. 그러나 이것은 잘못된 비교의 한 예이다. 그가 그 선택의 결과에 좀 덜 집착했다면, 사실은 자신이 논문을 읽는 것과 아무것도 하지 않는 것 사이에서 선택한 것이 아니라, 논문을 읽는 것과 연구실에서 실험을 하는 것 또는 꼭 필요한 휴식을 취하거나 딸에게 책을 읽어주는 것 사이에서 선택했음을 깨달았을 것이다. **이 예는 실제 선택을 하는 과정을 인식하는 것은 우리가 회고할 때 죄의식을 덜 느낄 것이라는 것을 보여준다.** 때때로 선택의 결과를 알고 난 후에 우리는 우리가 다르게 선택했더라면 좋았을 것이라고 바랄 수도 있지만, 왜 우리가 어떤 선택을 했는지 그리고 대신 무엇을 했는지를 알 때 우리 자신에 대해 아주 까다롭지 않은 경향이 있다.

정답풀이

예시로 나온 과학자는 자기가 논문을 읽지 않은 결과에 집착을 해서 자신을 탓했지만, 그렇게 결정을 내린 과정을 살피면 자신이 그런 결정을 한 것이 이해가 될 것이다. 그러므로 빈칸에는 ⑤ '실제 선택을 하는 과정'을 인식하는 것이라는 말이 들어가야 가장 적절하다.

① 선택하는 자유
② 결정을 내리는 것을 피하는 것
③ 무시되고 있는 선택지
④ 우리의 선택의 부정적인 영향

구문풀이

7행 **Had** he **been** less **fixated** on the outcome of the choice, / he **might have realized** that the choice had not been between reading the article and doing nothing, but rather between reading the article and working in the lab, taking a much-needed rest, or reading to his daughter.

: 과거의 사실에 대한 반대를 가정하는 가정법 과거완료 문장으로, 「if+주어+had p.p. ~, 주어+조동사의 과거형+have p.p. ....」의 조건절에서 if가 생략되어 주어와 동사가 도치된 형태이다. 따라서 Had he been less fixated on ~은 If he had been less fixated on ~으로 바꾸어 쓸 수 있다.

어휘풀이

- heatedly *ad* 열띠게
- hindsight *n* 뒤늦은 깨달음
- faulty *a* 불완전한
- fixate *v* 고정시키다, 집착하다
- guilty *a* 유죄의, 죄의식의
- on occasion 가끔
- mindless *a* 어리석은, 무지한
- stupidly *ad* 어리석게
- comparison *n* 비교
- outcome *n* 결과, 과정
- in retrospect 되돌아보면
- hard on ~에 엄한

---

223 답 ③

📖 유대관계를 통해 가능한 천재의 재능 개발

전문해석

대단한 재능을 가진 사람들이 종종 눈에 띄지 않는 학생이라는 것은 흔히 발견되는 일이다. 예를 들어, 아무도 아인슈타인의 위대한 업적을 그의 평범한 학교 성적을 바탕으로 예측할 수 없었을 것이다. 평범함의 이유가 능력의 부재는 분명 아니다. 대신, 그것은 자기 몰두나 당면한 평범한 과제에 집중하지 못했던 것에 원인이 있을 수 있다. 한 개인이 몰입이나 몰두 같은 공상을 벗어날 수 있는 가장 확실한 방법은 **위대한 스승, 또는 그 천재적 인물을 이해하고 그와 대화할 줄 아는 능력을 가진 사람과의 깊은 유대관계를 형성하는 것이다.** 천재적 인물들이 일대일의 관계에서 자신이 필요로 하는 것을 발견하는 것의 여부는 자신의 재능을 계발하는 법을 아는 스승을 만나느냐의 여부에 달려있다. 다행히 이런 일이 일어나게 되면, 우리는 어떻게 리더를 만들어 내고 어떻게 다른 세대의 천재들이 서로에게 영향을 미치는가를 더 많이 알게 된다.

정답풀이

천재들이 학교에서 평범해 보이는 것은 자기 몰입이나 몰두 같은 공상 때문일 수 있으며, 이러한 공상을 벗어날 수 있는 방법은 훌륭한 스승과의 깊은 유대관계 형성이라고 했으므로, 빈칸에는 이와 유사한 개념인 ③ '자신의 재능을 계발하는 법을 아는 스승을 만나느냐의 여부'가 적절하다.
① 그들의 특출난 자질이 얼마나 일찍 발견되는가
② 그들의 부모가 그들을 위한 특별 교육을 해줄 여유의 여부
④ 당면한 과제에서 주의를 빼앗기지 않으려는 의지
⑤ 그들에게 주어진 학교 과제의 난이도

구문풀이

13행 [**Whether** gifted individuals <u>find</u> {what they need in one-to-one relationships}] <u>depends on</u> [the availability of <u>teachers</u> {who know (**how to** cultivate their talents)}].

: 첫 번째 [ ]는 문장의 주어 역할을 하는 명사절이고 문장의 동사는 depends이다. Whether(~인지 아닌지)절 내의 { }는 find의 목적어 역할을 하는 관계절이며, 두 번째 [ ]는 on의 목적어 역할을 하는 명사구이다. 이 명사구 내에서 { }는 teachers를 수식하는 관계절이고, 이 관계절의 동사 know의 목적어로 「how+to부정사」가 쓰였는데, 이는 '~하는 방법'의 뜻을 나타낸다.

어휘풀이

- observation *n* 관찰 (결과)
- at hand 당면한, 수중의
- preoccupation *n* 몰두, 열중
- gifted *a* 천부의 재능이 있는, 유능한
- cultivate *v* 키우다, 함양하다
- distract *v* 집중이 안 되게 하다, 산만하게 하다
- self-absorption *n* 자기 몰두
- daydreaming *n* 몽상, 공상
- attachment *n* 애착, 유대관계
- extraordinary *a* 비범한, 보통이 아닌

---

224 답 ④

📖 다국적 기업들의 하도급 업체를 이용한 관리 감독 회피 행태

전문해석

노동 착취 공장이나 국제 노동 기준을 이해하는 사람이라면 누구나 이제는 공급망의 투명성과 그것을 감시하는 것의 중요성에 익숙할 것이다. **최근 거대 다국적 기업들은 좀처럼 직접 자신의 공장을 소유하지 않는다.** 대신 그들은 도급업자와 하도급업자의 뒤얽힌 망을 통하여 자신들의 제품을 생산한다. 이러한 방식의 사업은 회사들이 제품의 각 구성요소에 대한 가능한 최저 가격을 얻도록 하며, 오래된 공장을 폐쇄시키거나 새로운 공장을 세워야 할 필요 없이 신속하게 생산 시설을 이전시킬 수 있게 한다. (도급업자들과 하도급업자들 사이의 관계가 새로운 공장 건설 성공의 관건 중의 하나이다.) 불행히도, 그것은 또한 노동 감시자들이 어느 회사가 아동 노동을 이용하고 있거나 노동자들을 기만하여 초과근무를 하도록 시키고 있는지 감시하는 것을 매우 어렵게 한다.

정답풀이

다국적 기업들이 하도급업체를 이용해 관리 감독을 피하는 것에 대한 글인데, ④는 새로운 공장 건설의 성공 요인에 관해 언급하는 문장이므로 글의 전체 흐름과 무관하다.

구문풀이

7행 This way of doing business **allows** companies [**to get** the lowest price {possible for each component of their product}], and [**shift** production swiftly without having to shut down an old factory or build a new one].

: allow는 「allow+목적어+목적격보어(~가 …하도록 허락하다)」의 형태에서 목적격보어로 to부정사를 취하는 동사이다. 이 문장에서는 to get과 (to) shift가 병렬로 연결되어 있다. { }는 the lowest price를 수식하는 형용사구이다.

어휘풀이

- by now 지금쯤은, 이제
- monitor *v* 감시하다
- via *p* ~을 통해서, 경유하여
- contractor *n* 도급업자, 계약자
- component *n* 성분, 구성요소
- swiftly *ad* 신속하게, 빨리
- cheat *v* 속이다, 기만하다
- transparency *n* 투명성
- supply chain 공급망
- tangled *a* 뒤얽힌, 복잡한
- subcontractor *n* 하도급업자
- shift *v* 이동시키다, 옮기다
- shut down 폐쇄하다, 중단하다
- overtime *n* 초과근무

---

225 답 ⑤

📖 쌀 연구를 통한 빈곤 문제 완화

전문해석

쌀 연구는 몇 가지 경로를 통해 가난을 완화하는 데 기여하며, 이러한 기여는 생산자와 소비자 모두에게 도움이 된다. 직접적인 경로는 농부를 위한 더 높은 생산성과 더 높은 이윤을 초래한다. 간접적인 경로는 어느 특정한 수준의 수요에 대한 더 높은 농업 생산성의 필연적 결과인 소비자들을 위한 더 낮은 가격으로부터 비롯된다. 단기적으로, 소비자들을 위한 더 낮은 가격은 가난을 줄이는데, 이는 많은 가난한 사람들이 쌀의 최종 구매자여서, 더 낮은 가격이 그들의 실질적인 수입을 증가시키기 때문이다. 장기적으로는, 소비자를 위한 더 낮은 가격이 노동자를 고용하는 고용자들에게 비용을 절감시킨다. 이것은 경제의 더 높은 생산성의 산업 부문과 서비스 부문에서 일자리 창출을 자극해 결국 노동력을 농업 밖으로 끌어낸다. 이러한 경제의 구조적 변화는 장기적 가난 완화에 필수적이다.

정답풀이

주어진 문장의 This는 고용을 위한 비용이 덜 든다는 ⑤ 앞 문장의 내용을 가리키고, 주어진 문장의 농업에서 산업과 서비스 분야로 노동력이 이동된다는 내용을 ⑤ 다음 문장에서 This structural transformation of the economy(이러한 경제의 구조적 변화)로 지칭하고 있으므로 주어진 문장은 ⑤에 들어가는 것이 가장 적절하다.

4행 Rice research <u>contributes to</u> poverty alleviation through several pathways, / and these contributions <u>benefit</u> **both** producers **and** consumers.

: 두 개의 절이 and로 연결된 구조이다. contribute to는 '~에 기여하다'의 의미이며, 두 번째 절에는 동사 benefit의 목적어가 상관접속사 「both A and B(A와 B 둘 다)」에 의해 연결되어 있다.

어휘풀이

- stimulate *v* 자극하다
- productivity *n* 생산성
- alleviation *n* 경감, 완화
- lead to ~로 이어지다
- arise *v* 비롯되다, 발생하다
- demand *n* 수요
- net *a* 최종의, 순
- in the long run 장기적으로
- transformation *n* 변화
- job creation 일자리 창출
- contribute to ~에 기여하다
- benefit *v* 도움이 되다
- profit *n* 이윤
- inevitable *a* 불가피한
- in the short run 단기적으로
- effective *a* 실질적인, 효과적인
- structural *a* 구조적인
- essential *a* 필수적인

226 답 ⑤

📖📖 기존 이론을 통합하며 개발되는 새로운 이론

전문해석

과학은 일반적으로 이전의 이론들을 전면적으로 거부함으로써가 아니라 그것들을 확장함으로써 진보한다. 새로운 이론이 옛 이론을 반드시 부정하는 것은 아니다. 오히려 그것은 옛 이론을 특정 상황에만 국한된 것으로 재구상한다. 새로운 이론은 더 많은 조건이 설명될 수 있도록 옛 이론을 다른 영역으로 확장시킨다. 예를 들어, 갈릴레오의 낙하하는 물체들에 관한 (그것들이 전부 같은 속도로 낙하한다는) 이론은 진공에서 작용하지만, 뉴턴의 법칙은 진공에서 작용하고 진공이 아닌 곳으로 확장된다. 뉴턴의 역학이 (빛의 속도에 근접하는) 매우 빠르게 움직이는 물체들이나 (블랙홀처럼) 육중한 물체들을 충분히 설명하지 못한다는 점이 20세기에 분명해졌다. 뉴턴의 물리학은 이러한 경우들에서 상당한 오류를 발생시켜서, 이러한 조건들로 확장되는 더 넓은 이론이 필요했는데, 이것이 바로 아인슈타인의 특수 상대성 원리가 고속에 대하여 한 일이며 그의 일반 상대성 원리가 중력에 대하여 한 일이었다.

→ 과학 이론이 새로운 상황에 (A) 적용될 수 없는 것으로 판명될 때, 새로운 이론이 개발되고, 그것은 기존의 이론을 (B) 통합한다.

정답풀이

기존의 과학 이론이 적용될 수 없는 새로운 상황이 나올 때, 과학은 기존 이론을 폐기하기보다는 특정 영역에 국한하여 적용되는 것이라고 보고, 이들이 새로운 영역으로 확장 적용될 수 있도록 새로운 이론을 발달시켜왔다는 내용이다. 그러므로 (A)에는 inapplicable(적용될 수 없는), (B)에는 integrates(통합하다)가 가장 적절하다.

① 효과적인 – 대체하다
② 효과적인 – 통합하다
③ 비슷한 – 보완하다
④ 적용할 수 없는 – 대체하다

구문풀이

15행 ~, so broader theories were needed [that extended to these conditions], [**which** is exactly {what Einstein's special theory of relativity did for high speeds and his general theory of relativity did for gravity}].

: 첫 번째 [ ]는 문장의 주어인 broader theories를 수식하는 관계절이고, 두 번째 [ ]는 계속적 용법의 관계대명사 which가 이끄는 절로 여기서 which는 앞부분 전체를 가리킨다. { }는 관계절의 동사 is의 보어인 명사절이다.

어휘풀이

- progress *v* 진보하다
- contradict *v* 부정하다
- reconceive *v* 새롭게 생각하다, 재구상하다
- domain *n* 영역
- mechanics *n* 역학
- massive *a* 무거운, 육중한
- theory of relativity 상대성 원리
- outright *ad* 노골적으로, 전면적으로
- vacuum *n* 진공
- adequately *ad* 적당히, 충분히
- significant *a* 상당한

227~228 답 ② / ③

📖📖 미디어가 자녀에게 미치는 부정적인 영향

전문해석

James Steyer는 〈다른 하나의 부모: 미디어가 우리의 아이들에게 미치는 영향에 대한 내막〉이라는 제목의 진지하게 생각을 하게 하는 책을 썼다. 불행하게도, 미디어는 아이들의 마음과 현실을 형성하고, 행동에 영향을 미치고, 기대를 설정하고, 자아상을 정의하며, 관심, 선택, 그리고 가치를 지배하는 힘이 됨으로써 또 다른 부모로서의 역할을 한다. 실제로, 이 다른 부모는 Time Warner, News Corporation, Disney, Viacom, Vivendi, Sony와 같은 거대 기업들을 포함하는 소수의 거대 미디어 기업들로 구성되어 있다. 슬프게도, 이 기업들은 아이들의 복지에 관해 관심을 두지 않는다. 오히려, 그들은 이익을 극대화하기 위해 영업을 한다. 돈, 즉 단기 수익에만 관심을 둔다.

이러한 미디어 거대 복합 기업들이 수익을 극대화하는 한 가지 방법은 영화, TV 쇼, 비디오, 상품, 테마 공원, 책, 잡지, 음악 등의 브랜드화된 재산과 상품 간의 상호 촉진 광고를 통해서이다. 이것은 그 누구도 감히 거대 구조화된 기업 집단 내에서 누군가가 생산하는 것의 품위와 가치를 인정하지(→ 에 대해 의문을 제기하지) 않는다는 것을 의미한다. 그 거대 복합 기업들은 또한 자신들의 이익을 보호하고 홍보하기 위해 자체 네트워크 뉴스 프로그램과 잡지 기사를 비난한다. 일반적인 관행은 광고주들을 불쾌하게 할 수도 있는 이야기를 최소화하거나 없애는 것이다. 미디어 기업 CEO들이 자신들의 아이들에 대해 취하는 태도를 살펴보는 것은 흥미롭다. 역설적이게도, 많은 이들이 다른 사람들의 아이들을 위해 자신들이 제작하고 판매하는 작품들을 자신들의 아이들이 보거나 듣는 것을 허락하지 않을 것이다. 우리의 아이들이 다른 하나의 부모의 좋은 영향과 나쁜 영향에 건전하게 대처하도록 도움을 주기 위해, 초등학교부터 시작해서 모든 학교에서 미디어 정보 해독력 교육이 제공되어야 한다.

227

정답풀이

수익 창출만을 목적으로 하는 미디어 기업들이 아이들에게 미치는 부정적인 영향에 대해 경각심을 갖고 관련 대책을 마련해야 할 필요성을 설명하는 글이다. 첫 문장에서 미디어가 아이들에게 큰 영향을 미치기 때문에 다른 하나의 부모라고 불린다고 했고, 미디어 기업들은 아이들에게 유익을 주는 것보다는 기업의 이익 극대화에 더 관심이 있으므로 그들이 제공하는 것들을 비판적으로 받아들이고 주체적으로 이용할 수 있는 능력을 갖추어야 한다는 내용이 이어진다. 따라서 글의 제목으로 가장 적절한 것은 ② "다른 하나의 부모'를 조심하라'이다.

① 미디어의 바다에 빠져라
③ 나쁜 독서 습관은 고치기 어렵다
④ 여러분의 아이들에게 역할 모델이 돼라
⑤ 미디어 사용이 교육에 미치는 효과

228

정답풀이

미디어 거대 복합 기업 내에서 자신의 기업의 이익을 보호하려고 한다는 흐름

이므로, 어느 누구도 그러한 기업에서 생산하는 것의 품위와 가치를 '인정하지' 않는 것이 아니라 '의문을 제기하지' 않는다는 흐름이 되어야 한다. 따라서 (c) admit을 question 또는 challenge 정도로 바꿔야 한다.

오답풀이

① 미디어는 또 다른 부모로서 역할을 한다고 했으므로 아이들의 마음과 현실을 형성하고 행동에 '영향을 미칠(influences)' 것이다.

② 기업들은 아이들의 복지에 관심을 두지 않고 단기 수익에만 관심을 갖는다고 했다. 따라서 이익을 '극대화하는(maximize)' 것이 목적일 것이다.

④ 거대 복합 기업들은 또한 자신들의 이익을 보호하고 홍보하기 위해 자체 네트워크 뉴스 프로그램과 잡지 기사를 비난한다고 했으므로 광고주들을 '불쾌하게(offend)' 할 수 있는 이야기를 없앨 것이다.

⑤ 역설적이게도 아이들을 위한 작품을 판매하는 미디어 기업 CEO들은 자신의 자녀에게는 그러한 작품을 '허락하지(allow)' 않을 것이라는 흐름이다.

구문풀이

3행 Unfortunately, the media **serve as** another parent [**by being a force** {that (shapes children's minds and reality), (influences behavior), (sets expectations), (defines self-image), and (dictates interests, choices, and values)}].

: serve as는 '~의 역할을 하다'라는 의미이며, [ ]는 전치사구로 「by -ing」는 '~함으로써'의 의미를 나타낸다. a force는 동명사 being의 보어로 { }로 표시한 관계절의 수식을 받으며, 이 관계절 내에는 다섯 개의 동사구가 나열되어 있다.

어휘풀이

- thought-provoking *a* (어떤 문제에 대해) 진지하게 생각을 하게 하는
- expectation *n* 기대
- dictate *v* ~을 좌우하다, ~에 영향을 끼치다
- corporation *n* 기업
- maximize *v* 극대화하다
- merchandise *n* 상품, 물품
- decency *n* 품위
- censure *v* 비난하다, 질책하다
- media literacy 미디어 정보 해독력(각종 미디어 정보를 주체성을 갖고 해독할 수 있는 능력)

적중 예상 문제 2회
본문 pp.160~165

229 ②	230 ③	231 ①	232 ③	233 ⑤
234 ③	235 ⑤	236 ③	237 ④	238 ②
239 ②	240 ③			

---

229 답 ②

📖 아이들을 생각하면서 삶을 헤쳐나갈 수 있는 용기를 얻음

전문해석

어느 날 저녁 나는 연구실에 앉아 있었다. 해가 막 지자, 달이 바다 위로 떠오르고 있었다. 일을 할 정도로 밝지는 않았다. 나는 방을 나와서 문을 잠갔다. 그리고 해변으로 갔다. 나는 혼자였다. 나를 돕거나 위로해 줄 사람은 아무도 없었다. 몇 시간이 흘렀다. 나는 바다를 응시한 채 그곳에 남아 있었다. 바다는 거의 움직이지 않는 것처럼 보였다. 바람은 아무 소리도 내지 않았으며, 만물이 달의 조용한 눈길 아래 쉬고 있는 것처럼 보였다. 어선 몇 척이 물 위에 떠 있었다. 갑자기 나는 바람결에 실려 온

목소리를 들었다. 그것은 따뜻하고 부드러웠다. 나는 고개를 돌려서 엄마와 함께 걷고 있는 몇몇 아이들을 보았다. 그때 나 역시 집에서 나를 기다리고 있는 아이들이 있다는 것을 깨달았다. 그것은 내가 계속 나아갈 수 있는 용기를 주었다. 나는 마음속의 모든 생각을 떨치고, 서둘러 집으로 갔다.

정답풀이

필자는 혼자 해변에서 자신을 돕거나 위로해 줄 사람이 아무도 없다고 느꼈지만, 자신의 아이들을 떠올리고는 용기를 얻어 아이들이 기다리고 있는 집으로 갔다. 따라서 'I'의 심경 변화로 가장 적절한 것은 ② '외로운 → 기운이 나는'이다.

① 화난 → 침착한   ③ 기쁜 → 슬픈
④ 걱정하는 → 질투하는   ⑤ 흥분한 → 당황한

구문풀이

6행 I remained there [gazing at the sea].

: [ ]는 분사구문으로 '~하면서'로 해석하며, as I gazed at ~으로 바꿔 쓸 수 있다.

어휘풀이

- laboratory *n* 실험실, 연구실
- seashore *n* 해변, 해안
- comfort *v* 위안을 주다
- gaze at ~을 응시하다
- motionless *a* 움직이지 않는
- carry on 계속 가다[움직이다]
- sorrowful *a* 슬픈
- embarrassed *a* 당황스러운

---

230 답 ③

📖 타인을 배려하는 비판

전문해석

다른 사람의 문법, 발음 또는 단어의 잘못된 사용을 고쳐주는 것이 필요한 때가 있다. 만일 당신의 직원들이나 자녀가 다른 사람들에게 주는 인상에 나쁜 영향을 줄 방식으로 단어를 사용한다면, 당신은 그들을 재치 있게 고쳐줌으로써 그들의 인상을 좋게 만드는 것을 도와줄 동기를 가지며, 심지어 종종 그럴 책임이 있다. 하지만 당신의 행동이 (상대방의) 창피함을 초래할 것이라면, 당신이 공개적으로 그렇게 할 필요는 거의 없다. 당신이 고쳐줄 이유가 없는 누군가와 대화를 할 때, 만일 그가 말을 잘못한다면 왜 꼭 그를 고쳐줘야 한다고 느끼는가? 왜 그냥 내버려 두지 않는가? 그의 실수를 지적하는 것이 당신을 더 현명하게 보이게 만드는 정도까지, 그것은 그를 더 바보처럼 느끼게 만들 것이다. 때로 당신은 친구, 연인, 직원, 동료 또는 부모로서 비판적일 필요가 있다. 하지만 얼마나 자주 그러한 비판이 공개적으로 표현될 필요가 있을까? 최악의 창피함은 다른 사람이 없는 곳에서는 존재할 수 없다. 그것은 목격자를 필요로 한다.

정답풀이

다른 사람의 잘못을 고쳐줄 필요가 있을 때일지라도 공개적으로 비판을 하게 되면 상대방이 창피함을 느낄 수 있으므로 불필요하고 공개적인 비판을 삼가라는 내용의 글이다. 따라서 필자의 주장으로 가장 적절한 것은 ③이다.

구문풀이

3행 If your employees or children use words in ways [that will adversely affect the impression {they make on others}], / you have an incentive, and often even a responsibility, [to **help** them **improve** their impression (by correcting them tactfully)].

: 부사절과 주절로 이루어진 문장이다. 첫 번째 [ ]는 ways를 수식하는 관계절이고, { }는 목적격 관계대명사가 생략된 관계절로 the impression을 수식한다. 두 번째 [ ]는 형용사적 용법으로 쓰인 to부정사구로 앞의 명사구 an incentive와 a responsibility를 수식한다. 여기에는 「help+목적어+목적격보어(~가 …하도록 돕다)」의 구문이 사용되었는데, help는 목적격보어로 동사원형이나 to부정사를 둘 다 취할 수 있다.

- pronunciation *n* 발음
- misuse *n* 오용[악용]
- adversely *ad* 불리하게, 반대로
- tactfully *ad* 재치 있게, 요령 있게
- embarrassment *n* 난처함, 창피함
- feel compelled to *do* 꼭 ~을 해야 할 것 같다
- dumb *a* 바보 같은, 멍청한
- in private 다른 사람이 없는 데서
- witness *n* 목격자, 증인

231 답 ①

📖 현실에 안주하는 것의 위험성

전문해석

현실에 안주하는 것에 있어서, 사람들이 뭐라고 말을 하든지, 그들이 하는 행동을 살펴보면, 그들이 현재의 상태에 일반적으로 만족하고 있음이 분명하다. 그들은 멋진 새로운 기회와 무서운 새로운 위험에 대해 불충분한 관심을 기울인다. 그들은 과거에 기준이 되었던 것을 계속한다. 외부인의 입장에서 여러분은 내부의 현실 안주가 위험하다는 것, 즉 과거의 성공이 나태와 오만을 가져왔다는 것을 올바르게 볼 수 있겠지만, 현실에 안주하는 내부자들은, 심지어 아주 똑똑한 사람들조차도 그러한 시각을 갖지 못한다. 그들은 해결하기 어려운 문제가 있다는 사실을 인정하기는 하지만, 그 난제가 저기 다른 사람의 부서에 존재한다고 여길 것이다. 그들은 어떻게 해야 하는지 알고 있다고 생각하며 그렇게 한다. 서서히 움직이며 여러분이 강력한 지위를 차지하고 있는 세상에서, 이러한 태도는 분명히 문제가 되지만, 다른 많은 문제들보다 더 심각한 것은 아니다. 빠르게 움직이며 변화하는 세상에서 활기가 없거나 변화 없이 현재 상태에 만족하는 것은 재앙, 글자 그대로 재앙을 만들어 낼 수 있다.

정답풀이

현재 상태에 안주하면서 빠른 변화에 적절하게 대처하지 않는다면 심각한 문제를 초래하게 된다는 내용의 글이므로 글의 요지로 가장 적절한 것은 ① 이다.

구문풀이

1행 With complacency, **no matter what** people say, if you look at [what they do] **it** is clear [**that** they are mostly content with the status quo].

: no matter what은 '~하는 것은 무엇이든지'의 의미로 whatever로 바꿔 쓸 수 있다. 첫 번째 [ ]는 선행사를 포함하는 관계대명사 what절로, if절의 동사인 look at의 목적어 역할을 한다. 두 번째 [ ]는 가주어 it에 대한 진주어 역할을 하는 that절이다.

어휘풀이

- complacency *n* 현 상태에 만족함, 안주
- be content with ~에 만족하다
- insufficient *a* 불충분한
- hazard *n* 위험
- sluggishness *n* 게으름, 나태
- arrogance *n* 오만
- perspective *n* 관점, 시각
- steadfast *a* 변함없는
- contentment *n* 만족

232 답 ③

📖 쇠똥구리로 덤불파리 문제를 해결한 과학자 George Bornemissza

전문해석

호주의 과학자 George Bornemissza는 호주에서 소똥 문제를 다루기에 가장 적합한 쇠똥구리의 종을 찾기 위해 32개국의 토종 쇠똥구리를 조사했다. 소똥은 매우 성가신 덤불파리의 이상적인 번식지였기 때문에 호주에서 실로 심각한 문제였다. 유충이 파리로 변한 후 덤불파리는 땀, 콧물, 침, 혈액, 그리고 눈물과 같은 체액에 끌리기 때문에 인간을 공포에 떨게 한다. 결과적으로, 사람들이 파리가 자신들의 몸에 착지하거나, 코나 입으로 들어가는 것을 막기 위해 정기적으로 얼굴 앞에서 손을 흔

들어야 한다. 이러한 행동을 설명하기 위해 그런 제스처를 뜻하는 '호주 경례'라는 말이 생겼다. 마침내 Bornemissza는 소똥을 재활용할 수 있는 쇠똥구리를 발견하여 55종의 쇠똥구리를 호주로 들여와 단번에 문제를 해결했다. 이제 호주의 경례는 점점 줄어드는 제스처가 되었다.

정답풀이

호주에서 소똥에 번식하는 덤불파리를 쫓아내기 위해 얼굴 앞에서 손을 흔들다가 그러한 제스처를 뜻하는 '호주 경례'라는 말이 생겼다고 했고 George Bornemissza는 소똥을 재활용할 수 있는 쇠똥구리를 외국에서 들여와 덤불파리의 문제를 해결했다고 했으므로, 밑줄 친 부분이 의미하는 바로는 ③ 'Bornemissza의 행동이 덤불파리의 수를 감소시켰다'가 가장 적절하다.
① 호주에서 토종 쇠똥구리가 급격히 사라졌다.
② 호주의 경례는 호주에 대한 충성을 표시하는 데 쓰인다.
④ 덤불파리는 호주 경례의 직접적인 원인이다.
⑤ 소똥 문제로 성가신 덤불파리가 증가했다.

구문풀이

9행 As a result, people have to wave their hands in front of the face at regular intervals / in order to **prevent** the flies **from** [**landing** on their body], or [**entering** their nose or mouth].

: in order to 이하는 '~하기 위해'라는 의미의 부사구이다. or로 연결되어 있는 두 개의 동명사구 [ ]는 「prevent+목적어+from -ing(~가 …하는 것을 막다[방지하다]」 구문에 쓰인 전치사 from의 목적어이다.

어휘풀이

- dung beetle 쇠똥구리
- breeding *n* 번식
- pesky *a* 성가신, 귀찮은
- fluid *n* 분비액
- saliva *n* 침, 타액
- wave one's hand 손을 흔들다
- interval *n* 간격, 거리
- salute *n* 인사, 경례
- coin *v* (신조어를) 만들어 내다
- in one stroke 딘빈에
- dwindling *a* 줄어드는

233 답 ⑤

📖 Ashokashtami 축제의 유래

전문해석

Ashokashtami는 매년 인도 동부와 인도 중부 전역에서 열리는 힌두교 신 Shiva에게 바치는 축제이다. 이것은 고대 힌두교 성전인 Puranas에 나오는 이야기에 바탕을 둔 것으로, 악마 Ravana를 죽이려는 Rama 경의 시도에 관한 것이다. Ravana가 Kali 여신의 총애와 보호를 받았기 때문에 그의 노력은 좌절되고 있었다. 그는 Ravana를 이기는 방법은 Kali를 숭배하고 기쁘게 하여 그녀의 신의를 그 악마에게서 멀어지게 바꾸는 것이라는 조언을 들었다. Rama는 이후 7일간의 공들인 의식을 치렀고, 이로 인해 Kali는 Ravana에 대한 자신의 지원을 거둬들였고, Rama는 그를 그 후 쉽게 죽였다. Rama는 자신의 전차에 자신이 Ravana를 무찌르는 데 도움을 주었던 두 신인 Shiva와 Durga를 태움으로써 자신의 승리를 축하했다. 현대의 Ashokashtami 축제는 Rama, Shiva, 그리고 Durga가 전차를 타고 달린 것을 극적으로 재현한 것으로 운영된다. 그리고 Rama는 Ravana에게 포로로 잡혀있던 자신의 아내인 Sita와 재회했다.

정답풀이

악마 Ravana를 죽인 후 Rama는 자신의 아내인 Sita와 재회했다고 했으므로, ⑤는 글의 내용과 일치하지 않는다.

구문풀이

7행 He was advised [**that** {the way (to defeat Ravana)} was {to worship and please Kali and thus change her allegiance away from the demon}].

: 「advise+목적어+that절」이 수동태로 바뀐 구조이다. that은 목적절을 이끄는 접속사로, [ ]는 능동태 문장에서 advised의 직접목적어 역할을 한다. 첫 번째 { }가 이 목적절의 주어 역할을 하고, to부정사구인 두 번째 { }가 보어 역할을 한다. ( )는 앞의 명사구 the way를 수식하는 형용사적 용법으로 쓰인 to부정사구이다.

어휘풀이
- deity *n* 신
- concerning *p* ~에 관한
- favor *n* 총애
- allegiance *n* 신의, 충성
- elaborate *a* 공들인
- withdraw *v* (~에서) 거둬들이다, 철회하다
- subsequently *ad* 이후, 그 후
- be held captive 포로로 잡히다
- annually *ad* 해마다
- demon *n* 악마
- worship *v* 숭배하다
- engage in ~을 하다
- ritual *n* 의식
- reenactment *n* 재현

234 답 ③

📖 **Smoky Mountains 국립공원 이용 안내**

전문해석

Smoky Mountains 국립공원

위치: 노스캐롤라이나주 개틀린버그시 Headquarters Road 107 Park

개방: 일년 내내. 운영시간은 계절에 따라 다릅니다.
   3월–5월: 오전 9시부터 오후 6시까지
   6월–10월: 오전 8시부터 오후 7시까지
   11월–2월: 오전 8시부터 오후 6시까지
   방문센터는 매일 엽니다.

전화: 녹음된 정보임 (865) 436-1232

웹사이트: http://www.nps.gov/grsm

비용: 캠핑 요금은 1박에 5달러입니다.

Smoky Mountains 국립공원은 가족을 데려와 경치를 즐기기에 좋은 곳입니다. 바구니를 챙겨, 장소를 고르고, 놀랄 만한 경치를 보며 세차게 흐르는 시냇가에서 식사나 간식을 즐기세요. 이 공원은 송어 낚시와 더운 여름에는 수영하기 좋은 수 마일에 걸쳐 있는 깨끗한 산골짜기 시냇물의 고향입니다. 공원의 많은 곳을 여러분의 차량으로 즐길 수 있습니다.

주의: Smoky Mountains 국립공원의 대부분의 산길은 가파르고 험합니다.

정답풀이

great for both trout fishing and swimming on a hot summer day라는 말로 보아, 시냇물에서 수영과 낚시를 할 수 있다는 것을 알 수 있다. 그러므로 ③은 본문의 내용과 일치한다.

구문풀이

[18행] The park is home to miles and miles of clear mountain streams, / great for **both** trout fishing **and** swimming on a hot summer day.

: great 이하는 주절을 부연 설명하며, 앞에 being 또는 which are가 생략되어 있다. 여기에는 「both A and B」의 구조가 쓰였다.

어휘풀이
- operation *n* 운용, 가동
- spot *n* 장소
- pack *v* (꾸러미를) 싸다
- breathtaking *a* 놀랄 만한

- trout *n* 송어
- steep *a* 가파른
- trail *n* 오솔길, 산길
- rugged *a* 바위투성이의, 험한

235 답 ⑤

📖 **평소에 인간관계를 구축해야 할 필요성**

전문해석

인생의 중요한 규칙은 부탁할 일이 생길 때까지 기다렸다가 우정을 쌓지 말라는 것이다. 업무상의 위기 중에는 조직 외부에 있는 사람에게 도움을 구하는 것이 흔히 중요하고/하거나 바람직하다. 많은 경우 공동체에 속한 조직의 도움이 필요할 수 있다. 사건 발생 이전에 이러한 실체들과 관계를 맺는 것은 그들과 함께 작업하고 그들이 대응하는 것을 더 쉽게 만들어 줄 것이다. 누구에게 전화해야 하는지 파악한 다음 자신과 자신의 조직에 대한 모든 것을 그들에게 설명해야 한다면, 도움을 받는 데 시간이 훨씬 더 오래 걸릴 것이며 시간이 오래 걸릴수록 여러분의 조직에 가해지는 피해는 더 크다. 외적인 관계를 구축하는 것이 중요할 뿐만 아니라, 내적인 관계를 구축하는 것도 그에 못지않게 중요하다. 업무 지원 센터의 관리자, 법무부, 홍보부와 업무상 관계를 맺고 있으면, 사고가 발생한 동안에 그들의 도움을 요청하는 것이 훨씬 더 쉽고 원활할 것이다.

정답풀이

업무상 문제가 생겨 부탁할 일이 생기기 전에 미리미리 평소에 도움을 청할 수 있는 사람들과 인간관계를 형성해 놓아야 한다는 내용의 글이다. 따라서 빈칸에 들어갈 말로 가장 적절한 것은 ⑤ '부탁할 일이 생길 때까지 기다렸다가 우정을 쌓지 말라'이다.
① 어느 누구에게도 불법적인 선물을 받지 말라
② 개인의 이익에 앞서 공공의 이익을 우선하라
③ 여러분의 조직의 결점을 드러내지 말라
④ 자연 재해가 발생할 경우에 대비하여 대피 계획을 세워라

구문풀이

[13행] **Not only** is building external relationships important, **but also** building internal relationships is just as critical.

: 「Not only A but also B」 구문이 쓰인 문장으로, 부정어를 포함한 표현인 Not only가 문두로 나오면서 주어와 동사의 어순이 도치되었다.

어휘풀이
- critical *a* 중요한
- assistance *n* 도움, 거듦
- responsive *a* 반응하는
- internal *a* 내적인, 내부의
- flaw *n* 결점, 약점
- desirable *a* 바람직한
- entity *n* 실체, 독립체
- external *a* 외적인, 외부의
- illegal *a* 불법의
- evacuation *n* 피난, 퇴거

236 답 ③

📖 **'정족수 감지' 현상을 이용한 탈모 치료법의 실마리**

전문해석

2015년 논문에서 Southern California 대학(USC)의 한 연구팀이 실험실 동물을 대상으로 한 실험을 통해 인간의 탈모에 대한 치료법을 발견한 것 같다고 밝혔다. 이상하게 들리겠지만, 그들은 머리카락을 뽑는 것이 실제로는 새로운 머리카락 성장을 자극할 수 있다는 것을 발견했다. USC 과학자들은 그들의 주장을 '정족수 감지'라고 알려진 미생물 현상에 대한 그들의 연구에 토대를 두고 있다. (머리가 벗겨지기 시작한 아빠를 둔 남자는 자기 자신도 대머리가 될 가능성이 높은 것으로 밝혀졌으므로, 대머리의 위험성을 결정하는 것은 사람들이 엄마로부터 물려받은 유전자일리가 없다.) 이 현상은 새로운 발견이 아닌데, 40년 전에 이것은 한 무리의 하버드 과학자들

에 의해 박테리아 군체에서 발견되었다. 박테리아가 공격을 받을 때, 건강한 개체 밀도를 유지하기 위해서 서로에게 신호를 보낸다는 것이 관찰되었다.

정답풀이

머리카락을 뽑는 것이 '정족수 감지'라고 알려진 미생물 현상으로 인하여 새로운 머리카락 성장을 자극할 수 있다는 연구 결과를 설명하는 글이다. 따라서 부계의 대머리 유전자에 대해 설명하는 ③은 글의 흐름과 관계 없다.

구문풀이

4행 **As** strange **as** it sounds, / they found [**that** pulling hairs out could actually stimulate new hair growth].

: 부사절과 주절로 이루어진 문장이다. as가 접속사(~이긴 하지만)로 쓰여 양보의 뜻을 나타낼 때 보어를 문장의 맨 앞에 두어 강조하는데, 이 경우 보어 앞에 '~듯이'의 뜻을 나타내는 부사 as를 붙여서 표현하기도 한다. 주절에서 접속사 that이 이끄는 [ ]는 found의 목적절이며, pulling hairs out이 주어, could stimulate가 동사이다.

어휘풀이

- article *n* 논문, 기사
- laboratory *n* 실험실
- investigation *n* 조사, 연구
- phenomenon *n* 현상
- gene *n* 유전자
- colony *n* 군체
- density *n* 밀도
- reveal *v* 드러내다, 밝히다
- stimulate *v* 자극하다
- microbiological *a* 미생물학의
- bald *v* (머리가) 벗겨지다
- inherit *v* 물려받다
- observe *v* 관찰하다

237 답 ④

📖 철학적, 정치적 가치관에 따른 환경보호론자의 구분

전문해석

종교와 영적 가치관이 환경에 대한 우리의 태도에 영향을 미치는 유일한 요인은 아니다. 철학적 그리고 정치적 가치관 또한 강력한 영향력을 가질 수 있다. O'Riordan은 환경보호론자를 크게 두 집단으로 나누는데, 기술중심주의자와 환경중심주의자이다. **기술중심주의자는 과학과 기술에 더 많은 신념을 가지고 있다. 그들은 자연에 대한 인간의 우위를 믿으며,** 더 나아가 미래의 과학적, 기술적 발달이 우리로 하여금 환경적 문제와 제약을 극복하도록 해줄 것이라는 것에 더 낙관적이다. 반면에, 환경중심주의자는 인간과 자연 사이의 평등을 더 높은 정도로 믿으며, 심지어 자연에 대한 인간의 예속을 믿는다. 그와 같은 믿음에서, **그들은 우리가 단지 세계적인 생태계의 일부이며, 그것이 존중되어야만 한다고 믿는다.** 어느 한 사람이 기술중심적인가 환경중심적인가의 범위를 결정하는 중요한 쟁점에는 환경 문제를 해결하는 과학과 기술의 능력에 대한 신념과 과학과 기술을 경제 발전의 원동력이라고 여기는 믿음 또는 회의론이 포함된다.

정답풀이

주어진 문장은 on the other hand라는 대조의 의미를 나타내는 연결어를 포함하며 환경중심주의자에 대한 설명을 담고 있으므로 기술중심주의자에 대한 설명이 끝나는 부분이자 환경중심주의자에 대한 설명이 시작되는 부분인 ④에 들어가야 한다. 또한 ④ 다음에 나온 문장의 they가 문맥상 주어진 문장의 Ecocentrics를 가리켜야 한다는 점도 중요한 단서가 된다.

구문풀이

10행 They believe in man's dominance over nature, and furthermore are more optimistic [**that** future scientific and technological developments will **enable** us **to overcome** environmental problems and constraints].

: believe와 are는 문장의 동사로 병렬구조이다. 접속사 that이 이끄는 [ ]는 형용사(optimistic)의 의미를 보충해 주는 명사절로 주로 의견이나 감정을 나타내는 형용사가

쓰인 경우, that절을 동반하는 형태로 사용된다. 이 절 내에 동사로 사용된 enable은 목적격보어로 to부정사를 취해 '~가 …할 수 있게 해주다'의 의미를 나타낸다.

어휘풀이

- ecocentric *n* 환경중심주의자 *a* 환경 중심적인
- subordination *n* 예속, 종속
- technocentric *n* 기술중심주의자 *a* 기술 중심적인
- dominance *n* 우위, 우세
- constraint *n* 구속, 제약
- extent *n* 범위, 한계, 정도
- philosophical *a* 철학적인
- optimistic *a* 낙관적인
- ecosystem *n* 생태계
- resolve *v* 해결하다

238~240 답 ② / ② / ③

📖 지뢰를 밟아 심하게 다쳤지만 불굴의 의지로 살아남은 소녀

전문해석

(A) 약 15년 전에, 한 어린 소녀가 모잠비크의 수도 Maputo의 중앙 병원 밖에서 녹슨 휠체어에 앉아 있었다. 그녀는 다리가 없었고, 아마도 10살 정도였을 것이다. 나는 지나가다 멈추어 서서 그녀와 몇 마디를 나눴다. 나는 여전히 그 이유를 모르겠다. 그녀의 이름은 Sofia였다. 몇 년이 지난 오늘, (a)그녀는 나의 가장 친한 친구 중 한 명이다.

(C) Sofia에게 일어난 일은 그녀와 그녀의 언니가 마을 가까이에 있는 작은 도로를 따라 달리고 있었다. Sofia는 그녀와 그녀의 언니가 도로에서 벗어나지 말아야 한다는 것을 잘 알고 있었다. 도로 옆에는 땅속에 묻힌 그녀가 '땅 악어'라고 부르는 것이 있었다. Sofia는 그녀의 오른발로 우연히 도로의 옆을 디뎠다. (c)그녀는 지뢰를 발로 밟았다. 그러나 뒤따라오는 폭발의 대부분은 그녀의 언니인 Maria를 향했다. 그녀는 그 자리에서 죽었으며, Sofia는 병원으로 이송되었다.

(B) 그녀의 이야기를 듣고 나서, 나는 그녀가 병원에 도착했을 때 그녀를 돌본 의사와 이야기를 했다. 그 의사는 "저는 이제 어떤 의사도 해서는 안 될 말을 당신에게 할게요. 그럼에도 불구하고, 이 어린 소녀의 놀라운 힘을 당신이 완전히 이해할 수 있도록 제가 그렇게 하려고요." 그리고 (b)그녀는 계속해서 말하기를, "그녀는 너무 심각하게 다쳤기에, 우리는 Sofia가 그녀의 언니와 함께 죽기를 바랐어요. 그녀의 다리는 찢겼으며, 가슴은 산산조각이 났었죠."라고 했다.

(D) 그러나 Sofia는 이런 심각한 피해에도 불구하고 살아났다. 비록 (d)그녀는 언니의 죽음으로 깊게 좌절했지만, 그녀의 목숨을 빼앗으려 했던 전체 군산 복합체보다 더 강한 힘을 갖고 있었다. 그녀의 몸과 마음속에서, Sofia는 전 세계 가난한 사람들의 강한 저항력을 갖고 있었다. 그리고 그녀는 극복했다. 현재, Sofia에게는 두 명의 아이가 있다. 그녀는 매우 훌륭한 여자 재봉사이며, 공부를 하고 있으며, 교사가 되기를 원한다. 그러나 이것 이상으로, **그녀는 지뢰 사용을 반대하는 전 세계적인 상징이 되었다. 많은 젊은이들에게, (e)그녀는 영웅이 되었다.**

정답풀이

238

15년 전에 한 병원에서 Sofia를 만났다는 주어진 글 다음에, Sofia가 자신의 언니와 함께 당한 지뢰 사고에 대해 이야기하는 (C)가 이어지고, 당시 심각한 부상으로 병원에 옮겨진 Sofia를 담당한 의사와의 대화에 대한 내용 (B)가 온다. 그리고 그녀가 심각한 부상과 상처를 극복하고 지뢰 사용을 반대하는 전 세계적인 상징이 된 현재의 모습에 대해 언급하는 (D)로 이어지는 흐름이 적절하다.

239

(b)는 의사를 가리키고 나머지는 모두 Sofia를 가리킨다.

240

지뢰를 밟은 것은 Maria가 아닌 Sofia이므로, ③은 글의 내용으로 적절하지 않다.

15행 Her legs were torn apart, / and her chest **blown** to pieces.

: and 이하의 blown 앞에는 be동사 was가 생략되어 있다.

20행 There was something [she called "earth crocodiles" {buried in the ground by the side of the road}].

: [ ]는 something을 수식하는 관계절로 she 앞에 목적격 관계대명사 that이 생략되어 있다. { }로 표시한 과거분사구는 앞의 earth crocodiles를 수식한다.

어휘풀이

- rusty *a* 녹이 슨
- comprehend *v* 이해하다
- blow to pieces 산산조각으로 폭파하다
- crocodile *n* 악어
- accidentally *ad* 우연히
- landmine *n* 지뢰
- explosion *n* 폭발
- direct *v* 향하게 하다
- frustrated *a* 좌절한
- military industrial complex 군산 복합체
- will to resist 저항의지
- seamstress *n* 여자 재봉사
- resistance *n* 저항
- heroine *n* 여자 영웅

적중 예상 문제 3회			본문 pp.166~171	
241 ①	242 ④	243 ③	244 ③	245 ②
246 ③	247 ②	248 ③	249 ③	250 ④
251 ③	252 ②			

241 답 ①

물질적 자산의 소유 없이 이용이 가능해진 서비스

전문해석

〈TechCrunch〉의 한 기자가 최근에 말하기를, "세계 최대 택시회사인 Uber는 차량을 소유하지 않고 있다. 금전적 가치가 가장 높은 소매상인 Alibaba는 재고품이 없다. 그리고 세계 최대의 숙박시설 제공업체인 Airbnb는 부동산을 소유하고 있지 않다. 재미있는 일이 벌어지고 있다." 실제로 디지털 미디어도 비슷한 부재를 보인다. 세계 최대의 비디오 허브인 Netflix는 내가 영화를 소유하지 않고도 그것을 볼 수 있게 해준다. 가장 큰 음악 스트리밍 회사인 Spotify는 내가 원하는 어떤 음악도 소유하지 않고 들을 수 있게 해준다. Amazon의 Kindle Unlimited는 내가 책을 소유하지 않고도 그것의 80만 권의 도서 목록에서 어떤 책이든 읽을 수 있게 해주고, PlayStation Now는 내가 게임을 구매하지 않고도 게임을 할 수 있게 해준다. 매년 나는 내가 소비하는 오락 상품을 덜 소유하는데 왜냐하면 이런 대여점을 이용함으로써 내가 바라는 것은 무엇이든 소비할 수 있기 때문이다. 왜 요즘 누가 어떤 것을 소유하려고 하겠는가? 보거나 듣고 싶은 것은 무엇이든지 빠르고 쉽게 빌릴 수 있다. 즉각적인 대여는 여러분에게 소유의 혜택의 대부분을 주고 그것의 단점은 거의 주지 않는다. 당신은 청소하고, 수리하고, 보관하고, 정리하고, 보험에 들고, 업그레이드를 하고, 유지 보수를 할 책임이 없다.

정답풀이

오늘날 성공적인 사업체인 Uber, Alibaba, Airbnb는 물질적인 자산을 소유하지 않은 채 서비스를 제공하고 있고, 문화 산업에서의 이용자들 역시 영화, 음악, 독서, 게임 등 오락 서비스를 Netflix, Spotify, Amazon, PlayStation Now를 통해 제품을 구매하지 않고도 이용할 수 있다고 한다. 따라서 밑줄 친

'비슷한 부재(a similar absence)'가 의미하는 바로는 ① '우리는 소유하지 않고 오락 상품에 접근할 수 있다'이다.

② 작은 신규 기업이 대기업의 주요한 경쟁자가 될 수 있다
③ 새로운 회사를 위해 혁신적인 생각에 더 많은 투자가 있어야 한다
④ 지식 기반 경제에서 지식의 부족은 문제일 수 있다
⑤ 우리는 온라인 사회생활과 오프라인 사회생활 간의 균형을 찾을 필요가 있다

구문풀이

11행 Amazon's Kindle Unlimited **enables** me **to read** any book in its 800,000-volume library without owning books, / **and** PlayStation Now **lets** me **play** games without purchasing them.

: 등위접속사 and로 두 개의 절이 연결되어 있다. 첫 번째 절에는 '~가 …할 수 있게 해주다'의 의미인 「enable+목적어+to부정사」 구문이 쓰였고, 두 번째 절에서 let은 사역동사이므로 목적격보어로 동사원형 play가 왔다.

어휘풀이

- observe *v* (소견으로서) 말하다
- retailer *n* 소매상
- inventory *n* 재고(품)
- accommodation *n* 숙박시설
- real estate 부동산
- exhibit *v* 보이다, 나타내다
- absence *n* 부재
- hub *n* 허브, 중심(지)
- rental store 대여점
- insure *v* 보험에 들다
- investment *n* 투자

242 답 ④

지구 생태계를 통해 전 세계적으로 상호 연결된 사회

전문해석

점차적으로 도시화되고 있는 전 세계의 사회는 중요한 생태계 서비스로 도시 생활을 지원하기 위해 전 세계 모든 종류의 생태계의 역량에 의존하고 있는데, 비록 사람들이 이런 지원을 인지하지 못하거나 이것이 귀중하다고 믿지 않는다고 할지라도 그렇다. 예를 들어서, 산업 국가의 도시에 수출하기 위해서 태국의 연못에서 양식된 새우는 전 세계적인 바다 생태계에서의 물고기 수확으로 얻어진 물고기 먹이로 길러진다. 또는 식량 생산, 무역, 이주, 그리고 어쩌면 사회 정치적인 안정성에 영향을 주는 가뭄, 화재, 폭풍 그리고 홍수의 빈도, 강도 그리고 기간에 변화를 초래할 수 있을 강수 패턴의 변동성에서 서서히 전개되는 변화를 고려해 보라. 기록적인 온도와 여름 가뭄으로 촉발된 2010년 러시아 들불이 러시아 밀 수확의 많은 부분을 태워버렸고 수출을 중단시켰는데, 아랍의 봄을 일으킨 원인 중 하나로 여겨지는 식량 가격의 상승에 기여했다는 주장이 제기됐다.

정답풀이

한 지역에 사는 사람들의 먹고 사는 행동은 그 지역 생태계의 영향만을 받는 것이 아니라, 전세계적인 생태계의 영향도 받고 있다는 내용으로, 그 예로 태국에서 양식되어 다른 국가로 수출되는 새우는 전세계적인 바다 생태계에서 얻은 물고기 먹이로 길러지고, 2010년 러시아에서 일어난 들불은 아랍의 식량 가격의 상승을 일으켰다고 말하고 있으므로 글의 주제로 가장 적절한 것은 ④ '지구 생태계를 통해 전 세계적으로 상호 연결된 사회'이다.

① 세계 통상과 무역의 중요성
② 경제적이고 정치적인 개입의 해로운 영향
③ 기술 혁신이 식량 공급에 미치는 영향
⑤ 환경 정책을 위해 일하는 국제기구

구문풀이

5행 For example, shrimp [farmed in ponds in Thailand for export to cities in industrial countries] are fed with fish meal [derived from the harvests of fish in marine ecosystems worldwide].

: 첫 번째 [ ]는 문장의 주어 shrimp를 수식하는 과거분사구이고, are fed가 동사이다. 두 번째 [ ]는 앞의 명사구 fish meal을 수식하는 과거분사구이다.

어휘풀이

- urbanized *a* 도시화된
- derive from ~에서 유래하다
- trigger *v* 촉발하다
- magnitude *n* 강도, 크기
- stability *n* 안정성
- halt *v* 중단하다
- intervention *n* 중재, 조정, 개입
- pond *n* 연못
- variability *n* 변동성
- frequency *n* 빈도
- migration *n* 이주
- wildfire *n* 들불
- contribute *v* 기여하다

243 답 ③

📖📖 경제 성장과 환경 규제의 관계

전문해석

환경 규제가 경제에 부정적인 영향을 미친다는 널리 퍼져있는 믿음은, 성장의 심각한 둔화가 환경 규제의 출현에 기인했던 1970년대로 거슬러 올라갈 수 있다. 반면에, 중국에서 급속한 경제 성장은 광범위한 대기와 수질 오염과 함께 조기 사망, 질병, 건강 문제를 야기하면서 심각한 환경 악화를 초래했다. 환경 규제는 성장을 저해하지만 환경을 유지하고 생명을 살리기 때문에, 정책 입안자들은 그들의 딜레마가 환경 악화와 경제 성장 사이에서의 선택이라고 생각한다. 이것이 흔히 갖는 견해이지만, 성장과 환경의 질은 반드시 상호 배타적인 것은 아니며 환경적 목표와 경제적 목표 사이에서의 선택이 반드시 어떤 종류의 교환에 의해 지배되는 것은 아니라고 믿는 사람들이 있다.

정답풀이

흔히 사람들은 환경 보호를 위한 규제가 경제 성장을 저해한다고 생각하지만, 환경 보호를 위한 규제와 경제 성장이 공존할 수 있다고 생각하는 의견도 있다는 내용의 글이다. 따라서 글의 제목으로는 ③ '환경 보호와 경제 성장이 공존할 수 있을까?'가 가장 적절하다.

① 환경오염의 주요 원인은 무엇인가?
② 환경 정화를 위한 중국의 고된 노력
④ 산업 발전과 경제 성장의 어두운 면
⑤ 환경에 관한 사람들의 잘못된 생각은 어떻게 형성되는가?

구문풀이

1행 The widespread belief [that environmental regulation has an adverse effect on the economy] can be **traced back to** the 1970s [**when** a significant slowing down of growth was attributed to (the advent of environmental regulation)].

: 첫 번째 [ ]는 핵심 주어인 belief를 설명하는 동격절로 '~라는 믿음'으로 해석한다. trace back to는 '~로 거슬러 올라가다'의 의미이다. 두 번째 [ ]는 관계부사절로 선행사 the 1970s를 수식하며, ( )는 앞의 전치사 to의 목적어 역할을 하는 명사구이다. be attributed to는 '~에 기인하다'의 의미이다.

어휘풀이

- regulation *n* 규제
- be attributed to ~에 기인하다
- degradation *n* 악화
- mutually *ad* 상호간에, 서로
- trade-off *n* 교환
- misconception *n* 오해
- adverse *a* 부정적인
- advent *n* 출현
- premature *a* 너무 이른
- exclusive *a* 배타적인
- strenuous *a* (일·직책 등이) 힘든

244 답 ③

📖📖 상근 정규직 남녀 근로자의 연간 평균 소득 변화 추이

전문해석

위 그래프는 1955년부터 2005년까지 성별 간 상근 정규직 근로자의 평균 수입을 2005년 기준 달러화로 보여준다. 남성 근로자의 평균 수입은 1970년대까지 급격히 증가했으나, 그 이후로는 보합세를 보이는데 몇몇 해에는 실제로 감소했다. 여성 근로자의 평균 수입은 같은 시기 전체에 걸쳐 꾸준한 증가세를 보여준다. 제시된 시기의 처음 부분에서 여성 근로자의 평균 수입은 남성 근로자의 평균 수입의 절반 이하(→ 이상)였지만, 그 수치는 제시된 시기의 끝 부분에서 거의 5분의 4로 올라갔다. 남녀 근로자의 평균 수입에서 가장 큰 격차는 1970년대 초반에 기록되었는데, 여성 근로자가 남성 근로자가 번 것의 60% 정도를 벌었다. 2005년에 남녀 근로자의 임금에 여전히 20% 정도의 격차가 지속되었는데, 사회가 보수에 있어서 성적 형평에 더 근접했었음에도 불구하고 그러했다.

정답풀이

50년에 걸친 상근 정규직 남녀 근로자의 연평균 수입액과 수입액의 성별 간 격차 비율을 보여주는 그래프이다. 제시된 시기의 처음, 즉 1955년에 남성 근로자의 평균 수입 대비 여성 근로자의 평균 수입의 비율은 약 65%로 절반 이상이므로 절반 이하라고 한 ③은 도표의 내용과 일치하지 않는다.

구문풀이

7행 (At the start of the time period), the average income for female workers <u>was</u> less than half of the average income for male workers, / but the figure <u>rose</u> to almost <u>four-fifths</u> by the end of the time period.

: ( )는 부사구이며, 두 개의 절이 but으로 연결된 구조의 문장이다. was와 rose가 각 절의 동사가 된다. 분수를 표기할 때는 분자를 기수, 분모를 서수로 표현하되 분자가 2 이상이면 분모에 -s를 붙인다. (ex. 1/3: one-third (a third), 2/3: two-thirds)

어휘풀이

- gender *n* 성, 성별
- level off 보합세가 되다, (변화 없이) 안정을 유지하다
- steady *a* 꾸준한
- persist *v* 지속되다
- equity *n* 형평, 공정
- figure *n* 수치, 숫자
- wage *n* 임금

245 답 ②

📖📖 영어를 제2언어로 사용하는 학생들에 대한 모국어 교육 필요성에 관한 쟁점

전문해석

일부 교육학자들은 영어를 제2언어로 사용하는 학생들이 그들의 모국어로도 교육을 받아야 한다고 믿는 반면에, 비평가들은 그러한 접근법이 효과가 없을 것이라고 주장한다. 그 비평가들은 대부분의 경우에 소수 언어 학생들이 학업성취로 가는 가장 좋은 길은 영어를 배우고 그것을 빨리 배우는 것이라고 믿는다. 그들은 너무나 많은 이중 언어 프로그램들이 제한된 영어 능력을 갖춘 학생들을 충분한 영어를 배우지 못하고 결코 나올 수 없는 느린 학습 과정에 놓이게 한다고 믿는다. 이 비평가들은 기본적으로 2개 언어 교육의 몰입 모델은 지지하지만 과도기·유지 모델은 반대한다. 하지만 과도기·유지 모델의 지지자들은 학생들이 영어를 배우는 동안에 적어도 부분적으로 그들의 모국어를 배우게 되면, 학업적으로 영어를 말하는 또래들을 가장 잘 따라잡을 수 있다고 주장한다.

정답풀이

② **주어와 동사의 수 일치**: 주어가 the best path로 단수이므로 are는 is로 바꿔야 한다.

오답풀이

① **동사**: insist가 당위성이나 소망 등을 나타내는 것이 아니라 사실을 주장하는 경우 that절의 동사는 '(should+)동사원형'이 아니라, 인칭과 시제에 맞는

형태가 되어야 한다. 주어가 such an approach로 단수이므로 doesn't work는 올바르게 사용되었다.

③ **관계부사**: 선행사가 slower learning tracks이며 뒤에 완전한 구조의 절이 이어지므로 장소를 나타내는 관계부사 where는 적절하다.

④ **병렬구조**: 앞의 동사 support와 병렬구조로 이어지므로 oppose는 올바르게 사용되었다. 주어는 These critics이다.

⑤ **생략**: 접속사 while 뒤에 they are가 생략된 형태이다. 부사절의 주어가 주절의 주어와 같은 경우에 부사절의 '주어+be동사'는 생략이 가능하다.

구문풀이

13행 But supporters of transitional and maintenance models argue [that students can best **keep up** academically **with** their English-speaking peers {if they are taught at least partly in their native languages (while learning English)}].

: 핵심 주어가 supporters이고 argue가 동사이다. [ ]는 argue의 목적어 역할을 하는 명사절이고 그 안의 { }는 조건을 나타내는 부사절이다. keep up with는 '~을 따르다, ~에 뒤지지 않다'라는 의미이며, ( )에서 접속사 while 뒤에는 '주어+be동사'인 they are가 생략된 것으로 볼 수 있다.

어휘풀이

- insist *v* 주장하다
- academic achievement 학업성취 • bilingual *a* 2개 언어를 구사하는
- sufficient *a* 충분한
- emerge from ~에서 벗어나다[나오다] • immersion *n* 몰입
- transitional *a* 과도기의, 전환기의 • maintenance *n* 유지
- keep up with ~에 뒤지지 않다

246 답 ③

📖 **우리의 행복을 위해 작동하는 심리적 면역 체계**

전문해석

우리는 Gilbert와 Wilson이 '심리적 면역 체계'라고 부르는 것 때문에 고통스런 좌절에 반응하는 데 있어서 자주 놀랄만하게 회복력이 있는데, **그것(심리적 면역 체계)은 우리가 스트레스로 가득 찬 경험과 트라우마를 넘어설 수 있게 해준다.** 우리의 생물학적 면역 체계가 우리를 독소와 질병으로부터 보호해주는 것과 꼭 마찬가지로, 우리의 심리적 면역 체계는 우리를 심리적인 고통으로부터 보호해 준다. 우리는 고통스런 좌절과 외상 경험에 직면해서도 밝은 희망, 유머, 통찰과 성장을 위한 잠재력을 발견하는 대단한 능력을 가지고 있다. 그리고 이러한 '면역과 관련된' 과정은 우리가 부정적인 경험에 직면해서도 만족감을 주는 삶으로 돌아가는 것을 막는다(→ 허용한다). 하지만 때때로 우리는 우리의 심리적 면역 체계를 과대평가한다. 그래서 우리는 이별이나 일에서의 실패와 같은 대단히 충격적인 사건의 영향을 추정할 때, 우리는 그것들이 얼마나 효과적으로 강력해지느냐 혹은 얼마나 빨리 그것들이 영향력을 행사하느냐를 고려하는 데 실패한다. 그 결과 우리는 우리의 미래 행복을 부정확하게 예측한다.

정답풀이

③ '심리적 면역 체계' 때문에 고통스런 좌절과 외상 경험에 직면해서도 놀랄 정도로 회복력이 있다고 했으므로 이것은 부정적인 경험에 직면해서도 우리가 만족감을 주는 삶으로 돌아갈 수 있게 '허용해 줄' 것이다. 따라서 forbid는 allow로 바꿔야 한다.

오답풀이

① 심리적 면역 체계는 스트레스로 가득 찬 경험과 트라우마를 넘어설 수 있게 해준다고 했으므로, '회복력이 있다(resilient)'는 것은 문맥상 적절하다.

② 우리의 생물학적 면역 체계가 우리를 독소와 질병으로부터 보호해주는 것과 마찬가지라고 했으므로, 심리적 면역 체계는 우리를 심리적인 '고통(distress)'

에서 보호해 줄 것이다.

④ 때때로 심리적 면역 체계를 과대평가한다고 했으므로, 그것이 얼마나 강력해지는지 또는 얼마나 빨리 영향력을 행사하는지 고려'하지 못할(fail)' 것이다.

⑤ 심리적 면역 체계를 과대평가하여 그것의 영향을 고려하지 못한다고 했으므로, 미래의 행복을 '부정확하게(inaccurately)' 예측할 것이다.

구문풀이

1행 We are often remarkably resilient **in** respond**ing** to painful setbacks, largely because of [**what** Gilbert and Wilson call the "psychological immune system,"] [**which** enables us to get beyond stressful experiences and traumas].

: 「in -ing」는 '~에 있어서'로 해석된다. 첫 번째 [ ]는 because of의 목적어 역할을 하는, 선행사를 포함한 관계대명사 what절이고, 두 번째 [ ]는 the "psychological immune system"을 부연 설명하는 관계절이다.

어휘풀이

- remarkably *ad* 주목할 만하게 • resilient *a* 회복력이 있는
- setback *n* 좌절, 실패 • immune system 면역 체계
- trauma *n* 트라우마, 정신적 외상 • distress *n* 고통, 괴로움
- silver lining 밝은 희망 • potential *n* 잠재력
- breakup *n* 이별 • take hold 강력해지다
- exert *v* (권력·영향력을) 행사하다 • inaccurately *ad* 부정확하게

247 답 ②

📖 **언어에 반영되는 고정관념**

전문해석

언어는 종종 집단의 정체성을 주장하기 위해서 사용된다. 흥미롭게도 집단들은 때때로 다른 집단과의 차이를 강조하기 위해서 고의적으로 단어를 바꾼다. 전형적으로 십 대들은 그 차이를 두드러지게 하기 위해서 부모님들이 이해할 수 없는 단어를 사용한다. 언어의 이러한 사용은 매우 흔하다. 하지만 그것은 기대를 벗어난 결과를 갖는다. 일부 방언이나 악센트는 단지 언어나 악센트에 기반해서 여러 범주로 화자들을 분류할 수 있다. 고정관념이 언어를 만나는 지점이 바로 이곳이다. Kinzler와 DeJesus는 미국의 북부와 남부의 악센트에 관해서 5~6세의 아이들을 인터뷰했다. 그들은 실제로 눈에 띄는 차이를 발견하지 못했다. 아이들은 악센트에 따라서 사람들을 범주화하기에는 그저 너무 어렸다. 그들은 10세경의 아이들과 함께 그 실험 절차를 반복했다. 이때는 그 아이들은 '착한'이라는 꼬리표를 남부 억양에, '똑똑한'이라는 꼬리표를 북부 억양에 돌렸다. **여기에서 우리는 언어 속성(악센트)이 아이들로 하여금 화자의 기질을 판단하도록 초래한 개념('착한' 대(對) '똑똑한')과 연관되었다는 것을 알 수 있다.**

정답풀이

다른 사람이 사용하는 언어의 악센트를 듣고 화자의 기질에 대한 판단을 내린다는 빈칸 뒤의 예시를 통해 언어가 고정관념을 형성할 수 있음을 추론할 수 있다. 따라서 빈칸에 들어갈 말로 가장 적절한 것은 ② '고정관념'이다.

① 오류   ③ 능력
④ 특징   ⑤ 해석

구문풀이

4행 Typically, teenagers use words [**that** will not be understood by their parents] [to mark the difference].

: 첫 번째 [ ]는 words를 수식하는 관계절이고, 두 번째 [ ]는 목적을 나타내는 부사적 용법의 to부정사구이다.

어휘풀이

- identity *n* 정체성 • purposefully *ad* 의도적으로
- accentuate *v* 강조하다 • distinction *n* (뚜렷한) 차이

- dialect *n* 방언
- noticeable *a* 눈에 띄는, 두드러지는
- attribute A to B A의 원인을 B에 돌리다
- property *n* 속성
- temperament *n* 기질
- competency *n* 능력
- classify *v* 분류[구분]하다
- associate *v* 연관시키다, 연상하다
- stereotype *n* 고정관념
- interpretation *n* 해석, 해설

248 답 ③

📖 색의 특성

전문해석
무채색은 흰색, 검은색, 회색이다. 그들은 색조와 음영을 만들지만 어떤 색의 색깔에도 영향을 주지 않는다. (B) 예를 들어, 아무리 많은 검정, 흰색 또는 회색이 파란색에 혼합된다 하더라도 그것을 보라색으로 바꿀 수 없다. 그러나 무채색은 혼합된 색깔의 명암도를 바꾼다. (C) 명암도란 색의 상대적인 밝음이나 어두움을 의미한다. 그것은 색의 강도와는 다르며, 특정 색깔의 선명도를 가리킨다. 예를 들어, TV에서 색 설정을 불러올 때 색의 강도를 높인다. 색 사이의 상대적 명암도는 동일하게 유지된다. (A) 어둠은 여전히 어둠이고, 빛은 여전히 빛이다. 가장 높은 강도의 색은 때로는 채도가 높다고 표현된다. 무채색을 추가하면 색상의 강도를 감소시킬 것이다. 달리 말하면, 분홍색은 순수한 빨간색보다 명암도가 밝지만, 그만큼 강렬하지는 않다.

정답풀이
주어진 글에서 무채색은 색조와 음영을 만들지만 색상 변화에 영향을 주지 않는다고 했으므로, 구체적 예를 들어 부연 설명하는 (B)가 그 뒤에 와야 한다. 그리고 무채색이 명암도를 바꾼다고 한 (B)의 마지막 부분을 (C)가 명암도를 구체적으로 설명하며 받는다. (C)의 마지막 부분에서 색 사이의 상대적 명암도는 동일하게 유지된다고 했으므로, 어둠은 여전히 어둠이고, 빛은 여전히 빛이라고 하는 (A)가 이어지는 흐름이 적절하다.

구문풀이
12행 Neutral colors **do**, however, **change** the value of any hue [with which they are mixed].

: do가 쓰여 문장의 동사 change를 강조하고 있으며, 그 사이에 연결사 however가 삽입되었다. [ ]는 선행사 any hue를 수식하는 관계절이다.

어휘풀이
- neutral color 무채색
- shade *n* 음영, 명암의 정도
- intensity *n* 강도
- diminish *v* 감소시키다
- vividness *n* 선명도
- tint *n* 색조, 엷은 색
- hue *n* 색깔
- addition *n* 첨가
- value *n* 명암도

249 답 ③

📖 온라인 커뮤니티에서 마케팅을 위한 소비자 정보 얻기

전문해석
온라인 공간에 모이는 사람들 수의 증가는 소셜 미디어라고 불리는 현상을 창조하였다. 10억 명이 넘는 사람들이 이제 다양한 형태의 소셜 미디어에 참여하고 있는데, 그 새로운 사회적 세계가 온라인이기 때문(에 가능한 일)이다. 사람들은 관계를 형성하고 유지하는 것뿐만 아니라 사회적 증진, 여흥, 즐거움이라는 이유로 온라인 커뮤니티에 합류한다. 온라인 커뮤니티는 소비자들뿐만 아니라 마케터들에게도 풍부한 정보의 출처가 될 잠재력을 지닌다. 온라인 커뮤니티에서의 회원 기고와 토론은 소비자의 필요, 가치, 규범, 그리고 행동을 드러낸다. 따라서 마케터들은 소비자들이 어떻게 상품을 사용하고, 그 상품에 대해 무엇을 좋아하고 무엇을 싫어하는지를 알 수 있다. 게다가, 그 상품이 그 커뮤니티와 다양한 소비자 집단에게 무엇을 의미하는지를 알 수 있다. 이와 같이 마케터들은 소비자들에 의해 생성된 온라인 내용물을 분석함으로써 구매 행동의 토대를 이루는 과정을 더 잘 이해할 수 있다.

정답풀이
주어진 문장은 온라인 커뮤니티에서 사람들이 소비자로서의 정보를 드러낸다는 내용이므로, 주어진 문장 뒤에는 이러한 정보가 마케터들에게 어떤 영향을 주는지에 관한 내용이 이어져야 한다. 따라서 주어진 문장은 온라인 커뮤니티가 마케터들에게도 정보의 출처라고 마케팅에 대해 언급한 문장 뒤, 그러한 정보로 마케팅에 필요한 여러 가지를 알 수 있다는 내용이 시작되기 전인 ③에 들어가는 것이 가장 적절하다.

구문풀이
4행 Increasing number of people [gathering in cyberspace] has created the phenomenon [called social media].

: 첫 번째 [ ]는 people을 수식하는 현재분사구이고, 두 번째 [ ]는 문장의 동사 has created의 목적어인 the phenomenon을 수식하는 과거분사구이다.

어휘풀이
- contribution *n* 기고, 투고
- phenomenon *n* 현상
- retain *v* 유지하다, 보유하다
- underlie *v* 기저를 이루다
- generate *v* 생성하다
- norm *n* 규범
- enhancement *n* 증진, 고양
- potential *n* 잠재력
- analyze *v* 분석하다

250 답 ④

📖 같은 정당 소속의 판사가 동석할 때 판결에 주는 영향력

전문해석
3인 재판부에서 판사가 보수적인 혹은 진보적인 동료와 함께 앉았는지 여부에 영향을 받을 것 같은가? 이것이 전혀 문제가 되지 않는다고 완곡히 말하는 것이 더 마음에 끌린다. 어쩌면 판사는 그들이 법을 볼 때 단순히 그것을 따를 수도 있다. 그러나 이 말은 잘못된 것으로 드러났다. 공화당원 대통령이 지명한 두 명의 다른 판사와 함께 동석하면, **공화당 지명 판사는** 보수적인 **고정관념에 따라** 환경 법규를 무효화하고, 소수집단 우대정책이나 선거자금 법을 폐지하고, 여성들이나 장애인들이 제기한 차별에 대한 청구를 거부하는 데 특히 투표하기 쉽다. 같은 것을 민주당 지명 판사에 대해서도 말할 수 있는데, 두 명의 다른 **민주당 피임명자와 함께 동석한다면** 진보적 **고정관념에 따라** 투표하기가 훨씬 더 쉽다.
→ 법정에서 판사의 이념적 성향은 (B) 동일한 정당에 속한 다른 판사와 함께 동석함으로 (A) 극대화된다.

정답풀이
3명의 판사가 판결을 할 때 보수 정당인 공화당 임명 판사는 같은 정당이 임명한 판사와 동석할 때 보수적 고정관념에 따라 투표를 하고, 같은 상황에서 민주당 임명 판사는 진보적 이념에 따라 투표를 한다고 했다. 따라서 판사의 이념적 성향은 같은 정당의 판사와 동석할 때 극대화되는 것임을 알 수 있으므로 (A)에는 magnified(극대화된), (B)에는 identical(동일한)이 들어가는 것이 가장 적절하다.

① 무시된 – 동일한
② 중화된 – 다른
③ 감소된 – 중립적인
⑤ 유지된 – 다른
④

구문풀이
6행 [If accompanied by two other judges appointed by a Republican president,] a Republican-appointed judge is especially likely to vote according to conservative stereotypes — [to invalidate environmental regulations, to strike down affirmative action programs or campaign finance laws, and to reject claims of discrimination

made by women and handicapped people].

: 첫 번째 [ ]는 접속사가 생략되지 않은 분사구문으로, If와 accompanied 사이에 he or she(= a Republican-appointed judge) is가 생략되었다고 보면 된다. 주절의 주어는 a Republican-appointed judge, 동사는 is이며, conservative stereotypes를 —(대시) 이하에서 예를 들어 보충 설명하고 있다.

어휘풀이
- judge panel 재판부
- liberal *a* 진보적인, 자유주의의
- turn out ~인 것으로 드러나다[밝혀지다]
- appoint *v* 지명하다, 임명하다
- invalidate *v* 무효로 하다
- strike down ~을 폐지하다
- affirmative action (소수 민족과 여성의 교육 기회와 고용에 있어) 소수집단 우대정책
- campaign finance 선거자금
- discrimination *n* 차별
- the same hold for 같은 것을 ~에 대해 말할 수 있다
- Democrat *n* 민주당원
- ideological *a* 이념적인, 사상적인
- conservative *a* 보수적인
- tempting *a* 솔깃한, 마음을 끄는
- Republican *a* 공화당의 *n* 공화당원
- regulation *n* 법규, 조례
- claim *n* (보상·배상의) 청구, 주장
- appointee *n* 지명된 사람, 피임명자
- inclination *n* 성향, 경향

251~252 답 ③ / ②

📖 학교 교육 목표의 진전 상황을 주기적으로 점검하는 것의 필요성

전문해석
너무 자주, 가르치는 것과 관련된 목표를 세우는 데 아주 많은 에너지가 투입되지만, **목표를 향한 진전을 어떻게 추적 관찰할 수 있는지에 대해서는 훨씬 적은 관심이 주어진다.** 일단 목표 설정이 완료되면, 당해 연도의 학사 일정의 속도가 우리를 압도하고, 우리는 어떤 진전이 이루어지고 있고, 우리의 전략에서 어떤 수정을 해야 하는지에 대해 충분한 관심을 기울이지 않는다. 가을에 목표가 정해지고 봄까지 무시되면 학생과 교사의 배움의 기회는 사라진다. 이 함정을 만드는(→ 피하는) 가장 좋은 방법은 당해 연도의 학사 일정 내내 주기적으로 개인들이 접촉하고 자신의 진전을 공유하는 시간을 계획하는 것이다. 목표가 세워지는 가을에 일정이 계획되는 이러한 상호작용은 교사와 관리자 사이의 공식적인 일대일 만남이 될 수도 있고, 또는 교직원 회의나 이메일 교환을 통해 교사 간의 소규모 그룹 대화가 될 수도 있다. 우리 학교에서는 가끔 목표 진전에 대한 최신 정보를 위해 교직원 회의를 지정한다. 교사들도 목표의 유사성에 따라 토론 그룹에 배치되며, 이 모임들은 1년 간 몇 차례 만난다. 소규모 환경과 공통의 초점은 교사가 자신의 진전을 공유하고 유사한 문제를 다루기 위해 다른 사람들이 하고 있는 것으로부터 배울 수 있게 해준다. 수업과 관련한 목표에 초점을 맞춘 교사와 관리자 간의 적어도 한 번의 얼굴을 맞댄 회의는 매년 있어야 한다. 결국, 관리자가 목표에 대해 교사와 이야기를 나누는 시간을 들이지 않는다면, 우리가 그것의 중요성에 관해 주는 메시지는 무엇인가?

251

정답풀이
학교 교육 목표를 세우는 것으로 끝나는 것이 아니라 주기적으로 목표를 향한 진전 상황을 확인하고 수정할 수 있도록 교사 모임 등의 일정을 세워야 한다는 내용이다. 따라서 글의 제목으로는 ③ '학교에서 목표와 관련된 진전을 추적 관찰할 필요성'이 가장 적절하다.
① 교육 개혁에서의 관리자의 역할
② 교사나 관리자가 아니라 학생을 위한 목표를 세워라
④ 학생의 학업 성취도 향상시키기: 최고의 목표
⑤ 교사 협업은 학생 학습 향상으로 이어질 수 있다

252

정답풀이
개인들이 연락하고 진전을 공유하며 주기적으로 시간을 계획하는 것은 가을에 목표를 세우고 봄까지 방치하는 함정을 만드는 것이 아니라 '피하기' 위한 가장 좋은 방법이라는 흐름이므로 (b)의 construct를 avoid와 같은 단어로 바꿔야 한다.

오답풀이
① 목표 설정이 완료되면 목표로 가는 중간 과정에는 '충분한(sufficient)' 관심을 갖지 않는다는 흐름이다.
③ 일대일 만남 또는 소규모 그룹 대화는 '상호작용(interactions)'이라고 할 수 있다.
④ 목표의 유사성에 따른 교직원 회의와 소규모 모임은 교사가 자신의 진전을 공유하고 다른 사람들로부터 배울 수 있게 '해줄(allow)' 것이다.
⑤ 결국, 관리자가 목표에 대해 교사와 회의할 시간을 갖지 않는다면, 우리가 그것의 '중요성(importance)'에 관해 주는 메시지는 의미가 없다는 흐름이다.

구문풀이
13행 [Scheduled in the fall when the goals are developed], these interactions could be formal, one-on-one meetings [between a teacher and an administrator], / or **they** could be small-group conversations [among teachers at faculty meetings or through e-mail exchanges].

: 두 개의 절이 접속사 or로 연결된 구조이다. 첫 번째 [ ]는 뒤에 이어지는 절의 주어인 these interactions를 의미상의 주어로 하는 분사구문이다. 두 번째와 세 번째 [ ]는 전치사구로 각각 앞의 명사구 formal, one-on-one meetings와 small-group conversations를 수식한다. or 뒤의 절의 주어인 they는 앞 절의 these interactions를 가리킨다.

어휘풀이
- progress *n* 진전, 진행
- pace *n* 속도
- overwhelm *v* 압도하다
- modification *n* 수정
- touch base 접촉[연락]하다
- formal *a* 공식적인
- faculty meeting 교직원 회의
- update *n* 최신 정보
- address *v* (문제 등을) 다루다
- monitor *v* 추적 관찰하다
- school year 1년간의 학업, 학년
- sufficient *a* 충분한
- periodic *a* 주기적인
- interaction *n* 상호작용, 교류
- administrator *n* 관리자
- designate *v* 지정하다
- setting *n* 환경, 설정
- take place 일어나다, 발생하다

적중 예상 문제 4회				본문 pp.172~177
253 ②	254 ④	255 ③	256 ④	257 ④
258 ③	259 ①	260 ②	261 ②	262 ③
263 ④	264 ④			

253 답 ②

📖 친구들과 함께 있다 혼자 남겨진 Hannah

전문해석
병원에서의 마지막 주 동안, Hannah는 다시 고형 식품을 먹기 시작했다. 어느 오후에 그녀의 친한 친구들이 그녀를 보러왔다. 그들은 그녀의 휠체어를 밀어서 2층 라

운지로 데려갔는데, 그곳의 바깥 테라스에서는 공원과 호수가 내려다보였다. 테라스에서 그들 모두는 길에 있는 Hannah의 남편인 Kenneth를 지켜보았다. 그는 신형의 빨간색 Jetta에 기댄 채로 그들에게 손을 흔들었다. 그 차 둘레에 우스꽝스러운 커다란 금색 나비매듭 리본이 묶여 있었다. 모두 손뼉을 쳤다. **Hannah는 자신의 멋진 새 차를 보면서 미소 지었다.** Kenneth는 테라스에서 그들과 만났다. 그는 샴페인 한 병과 종이컵을 가져왔다. 모두 Hannah의 놀라운 회복에 건배했다. 축하는 오래 지속되지 않았다. 그녀의 친구들과 Kenneth는 일하러 돌아가야 했다. 몇 분 동안 Hannah는 간호사와 함께 테라스에 꼼짝 못하고 있었다. Hannah는 자신의 휠체어에 앉아서 물결이 이는 회색 물을 응시하였다. 하늘은 어두워지고 있었다. 그때 Hannah는 울기 시작했다. 그녀는 또다시 혼자 남겨졌다는 갑작스러운 깨달음 때문에 울었다.

정답풀이

친구들이 병문안을 오고 그녀의 남편이 멋진 차를 선물하여 Hannah는 그들과 함께 샴페인을 마시고 즐거워했지만, 그들이 모두 떠나자 그녀는 다시 혼자 남겨진 것을 깨닫고 눈물을 흘렸다. 따라서 Hannah의 심경 변화로 가장 적절한 것은 ② '기쁜 → 외로운'이다.

① 지루한 → 슬픈
③ 우울한 → 감동받은
④ 들뜬 → 초조한
⑤ 안도한 → 후회스러운

구문풀이

8행 Tied around the car was a ridiculous large gold bow.

: 보어가 문장 앞으로 나오면서, 주어와 동사가 도치되었다.

어휘풀이

- solid food 고형 식품
- overlook *v* 내려다보다
- ridiculous *a* 우스꽝스러운
- applaud *v* 손뼉을 치다
- remarkable *a* 놀랄 만한, 주목할 만한
- gaze *v* 응시하다
- wheel *v* (바퀴 달린 것을) 밀어 움직이다
- wave *v* (손·깃발 등을) 흔들다
- bow *n* 나비매듭 리본
- toast *v* 건배하다
- celebration *n* 축하
- choppy *a* 물결이 이는

---

254 답 ④

📖 식물의 생명 주기 조정 능력

전문해석

1년생 식물의 수명은 상대적으로 고정되어 있고 짧지만, **많은 다른 식물종의 수명은 상대적으로 유동적이다.** 보통 꽃을 피워 씨앗을 남긴 후 두 번째 성장 시기가 끝난 뒤에 죽는 많은 2년생 종들조차, 계절을 통해 정상적인 진행을 알리는 환경적인 단서를 얻지 않으면 (꽃을 피우지 않고) 여러 해를 살 것이다. 많은 다른 종에서 생명 주기를 통한 진행의 시기 선택은 매우 유동적이어서, 한 식물이 성장하고 발달하는 조건에 좌우된다. 번식은 자원이 제한되었을 때 일반적으로 지연되고, 빛이 잘 들고 영양소가 풍부한 장소에서 자라는 식물에서는 더 빨리 일어난다. 조직(예를 들어, 잎)과 전체 식물 수준 둘 다에서 전반적인 발달은 일반적으로 자원이 풍부한 조건에서 빨라진다.

정답풀이

식물은 그것이 처한 환경 조건에 따라 생명 주기를 유동적으로 조절할 수 있다는 내용이므로, 글의 주제로 가장 적절한 것은 ④ '생명 주기를 조절하는 식물의 능력'이다.

① 식물 번식의 다양한 방법
② 식물 서식지의 전 세계적인 감소
③ 식물종에서 다양성의 중요성
⑤ 성장 시기에서 유동성의 부재

구문풀이

3행 Even many biennial species, [**which** normally die at the end of the second growing season {after flowering and leaving seeds}], will live for years (without flowering) / **if** they do not receive the environmental cues [**that** signal the normal progression through the seasons].

: 주절과 if절로 이루어진 문장이다. 첫 번째 [ ]는 주절의 주어인 many biennial species를 부연 설명하는 관계절로 계속적 용법으로 사용되었으며, 주절의 동사는 will live이다. if 이하의 조건 부사절에서 [ ]는 the environmental cues를 수식하는 관계절이다.

어휘풀이

- lifespan *n* 수명
- flexible *a* 유동적인, 유연한
- progression *n* 진행, 진전
- nutrient *n* 영양소
- diversity *n* 다양성
- absence *n* 부재, 없음
- annual *a* (식물) 1년생의
- biennial *a* (식물) 2년생의
- reproduction *n* 번식
- accelerate *v* 빨리하다, 가속하다
- adjust *v* 조절[조정]하다

---

255 답 ③

📖 혁신적인 사고를 하는 사람들의 남의 의견을 경청하는 태도

전문해석

아이디어가 결코 고갈되지 않을 것으로 보이는 혁신적인 사람들에 대해 생각할 때 여러분의 마음 속에 떠오르는 첫 번째 일은 무엇인가? 내 마음에 즉시 떠오르는 것은 그들이 그들의 부하 직원들의 이야기를 듣는 데 명성이 나 있다는 것이다. 〈Restaurants and Institutions〉 잡지에 따르면 Romano's Macaroni Grill은 전국에서 가장 운영이 뛰어난 음식 체인점 중 하나이다. 식당 메뉴의 거의 80%는 지점 지배인들의 제안으로부터 만들어졌다. 효율적인 회사에게 좋은 것은 개인에게도 좋다. 당신이 남의 말을 시종일관 잘 들어주면, 당신은 절대 아이디어 때문에 고통받지 않을 것이다. **당신이 만약 사람들에게 그들의 생각을 공유할 기회를 주고, 열린 마음으로 경청하면, 문제에 신선한 통찰력을 얻고 좋은 결정을 내릴 것이다.** 그리고 당신이 비록 효과가 나지 않을 아이디어를 들었을 때도, 단지 그것을 듣는 것만으로 종종 당신과 다른 사람들에게 혁신적인 생각을 불러일으킬 수가 있다.

정답풀이

혁신적인 아이디어를 가진 사람들의 특징은 남의 말을 잘 경청하는 사람이라는 내용의 글이다. 따라서 ③ '듣는 것이 혁신의 근육을 강화한다'가 글의 제목으로 가장 적절하다.

① 의사소통이 어떻게 혁신을 이끄는가
② 먼저 들으려 하고, 다음에 이해를 받아라
④ 지도력의 중요한 원칙: 다른 사람들의 이야기를 경청하라
⑤ 혁신적인 조직의 몇 가지 중요한 특징들

구문풀이

7행 Almost 80 percent of its restaurants' menu items have come from suggestions [made by unit managers].

: Almost 80 percent of 다음에 셀 수 있는 명사의 복수형(items)이 나왔기 때문에 복수형 동사 have come이 왔다. [ ]는 과거분사구로 앞의 명사 suggestions를 수식한다.

어휘풀이

- innovative *a* 혁신적인
- immediately *ad* 즉시
- consistently *ad* 시종일관하여
- insight *n* 통찰력
- run out of ~을 다 써버리다, ~이 없어지다
- reputation *n* 명성
- suffer *v* 괴로워하다
- spark *v* 불러일으키다

256 답 ④

📖 자동화된 직조기를 만든 Joseph-Marie Jacquard

전문해석

Joseph-Marie Jacquard는 1752년 7월 7일 프랑스 Lyon에서 태어났다. 양친 모두 직물업에 종사했기 때문에, 어릴 때 Jacquard가 그 산업에 참여하는 것은 단지 시간 문제일 뿐이었다. 10살 때부터 Jacquard는 18세기 후반 직물업의 단조로운 환경에서 일했다. 1790년에 Jacquard는 자동화된 직조기라는 창의적인 개념을 생각해냈다. 하지만 자동화된 직조기를 개발하려는 그의 노력은 프랑스 혁명으로 중단되었다. 프랑스를 사로잡은 내전 동안, Jacquard는 혁명군의 편에서 싸웠고 그의 고향인 Lyon을 방어하는 데 참여했다. 혁명 이후, Jacquard는 프랑스의 직물업을 자동화하는 데 도움이 될 장치를 개발하기 위한 자신의 노력을 재개했다. 1801년에 그는 카펫이 직조기로 만들어질 때 그것의 무늬를 프로그래밍하기 위한 천공 카드 시스템을 도입했다. 프랑스의 나폴레옹 정부는 Jacquard의 장치의 가치를 빠르게 인정했다. 그는 메달과 평생 연금을 받았다.

정답풀이

Joseph-Marie Jacquard는 프랑스 혁명으로 인한 내전 동안 혁명군의 편에서 싸웠다고 했으므로, 반혁명군 편에서 싸웠다고 한 ④는 글의 내용과 일치하지 않는다.

구문풀이

11행 During the civil conflict [that gripped France], / Jacquard fought on the side of the revolutionaries and participated in the defense of his home city of Lyon.

: 부사구와 절로 이루어진 문장으로, 첫 번째 [ ]는 the civil conflict를 수식하는 관계절이다. 이어지는 절에는 주어인 Jacquard에 두 개의 동사 fought와 participated가 and로 연결되어 있다.

어휘풀이

- weaving industry 직물업
- textile industry 직물업, 섬유 산업
- interrupt *v* 중단시키다
- grip *v* 사로잡다
- defense *n* 방어
- device *n* 장치
- monotonous *a* 단조로운
- come up with ~을 생각해내다
- civil conflict 내전
- revolutionary *n* 혁명군
- resume *v* 재개하다, 다시 시작하다
- pension *n* 연금

257 답 ④

📖 세상에서 긍정적인 면을 찾아보아야 할 필요성

전문해석

"멈추어서 장미의 향기를 맡아보라." 이것은 여러분이 자주 듣지만, 아마도 이해하는지 아주 확신하지는 못하는 경구일 것이다. 그것은, 비록 그 실행이 해를 줄 수는 없겠지만, 여러분이 장미를 볼 때마다 멈추어서 실제로 그것들의 향기를 맡아보는 것을 의미하는 것은 아니다. 그것이 나에게 의미하는 것은 세상이 여러분에게 던지는 것 같아 보이는 모든 시련과 역경에도 불구하고, 세상은 또한 아름다움과 평온도 제공한다는 것이다. 그러나 그것을 알아차리는 것은 여러분에게 달려있다. 여러분은 그것이 세상에 존재한다는 것을 알게 되겠지만, 세상이 모든 범죄, 폭력, 가난으로 얼마나 끔찍한지 줄곧 불평하면서 많은 이들이 그것을 그냥 지나쳐버린다. 나는 범죄, 폭력, 가난이 존재하지 않는다고 말하는 것은 아니지만, 사랑, 후원, 풍요로움 또한 마찬가지다(존재한다). 많은 경우에 세상에 존재하는 부정성은 피할 수 없는 것처럼 보이며, 많은 경우에 그것은 사실일 수 있다. 그 경우에 행해져야만 하는 것은 우리가 동료의 사랑과 후원을 보여주는 사례를 찾아내는 것이다.

정답풀이

④ **대동사**: 일반동사 exist를 대신하는 자리이므로 are를 do로 고쳐 써야 한다.

오답풀이

① **접속사**: 뒤에 주어와 동사가 있는 절이 왔으므로 접속사 although를 쓴 것은 어법상 적절하다.

② **대명사의 수 일치**: 가리키는 대상인 the world가 단수이므로 단수 대명사 it을 쓴 것은 어법상 적절하다.

③ **분사구문**: complaining ~은 분사구문으로, '~하면서'라고 해석한다. 분사구문의 의미상 주어는 주절의 주어인 so many people이다.

⑤ **지시대명사**: that은 앞에서 말한 the negativity out there seems impossible to avoid를 가리키는 지시대명사이다.

구문풀이

15행 [**What** must be done in that instance] is [for us **to seek** out an example {demonstrating love and support of our fellow man}].

: 첫 번째 [ ]로 표시한, 선행사를 포함한 관계대명사 what이 이끄는 절이 주어, is가 동사이다. 두 번째 [ ]는 be동사 is의 보어 역할을 하는 to부정사구이고, for us는 to seek의 의미상 주어이다. { }는 an example을 수식하는 현재분사구이다.

어휘풀이

- phrase *n* 경구, 짤막한 말
- hurt *v* 해를 주다, 상처를 주다
- adversity *n* 역경
- complain *v* 불평하다
- poverty *n* 가난, 빈곤
- instance *n* 사례
- demonstrate *v* 보여주다
- practice *n* 실행, 실천
- trial *n* 시련
- serenity *n* 평온, 고요함
- violence *n* 폭력
- abundance *n* 풍요로움, 풍부
- negativity *n* 부정성, 부정적 성향

258 답 ③

📖 농약 사용을 옹호하는 농업 관행이 지속되는 이유

전문해석

농업 시스템은 이제 살충제에 의존하도록 적응하였다. 농부, 농사 조사 기관, 농업 정책, 그리고 농업 연구 시스템이 살충제 사용에 의존하고 그것을 지원하기 때문에 이런 일이 발생했다. 이것은 관련 당사자들을 변화에 저항하게 만들어 새로운 기술들이 발판을 얻는 것을 어렵게 만든다. 예를 들어, 벨기에에서 질병에 저항력이 있는 밀 품종의 더딘 채택은 빈약한 기술적 특성의 결과가 아니라 농부부터 자원 공급자, 정책 입안자에 이르기까지 식량 공급망의 모든 수준에서의 저항의 결과이다. 지배적인 밀 시스템은 화학적인 투입물 사용을 찬성하는 시스템을 중심으로 조직되었고, 현존 업자들은 질병에 저항력이 있는 밀 품종과 같은 새로운 진입자들과 새로운 기술이 기존의 식품 재배 관행을 파괴하는 것을 어렵게 만들었다. 민간 이해관계자는 세 가지 농작물 보호 관행을 바꾸는 데 집중할 수 있었는데, 종자 판매보다는 농약을 지지하는 공급업체의 내부 편향, 공급업체 영업사원들의 농화학 약품 적용을 향한 편향, 그리고 종자 회사에서 병충해 저항성을 위한 육종에 부여된 낮은 우선순위이다.

정답풀이

(A) 농부를 비롯해서 농업 관련 기관과 정책이 살충제 사용을 지원하기 때문에 변화가 어렵다는 맥락이므로 resistant(저항하는)가 적절하다. (vulnerable: 취약한)

(B) 현존 업자들의 영향력으로 인해 질병에 저항력이 있는 품종이 기존의 관행을 깨기가 어렵다는 맥락이므로 disrupt(파괴하다)가 적절하다. (maintain: 유지하다)

(C) 종자 회사에 병충해 저항성을 위해 부여된 우선순위가 낮아 기존의 농작물 재배 방식이 유지된다는 맥락이므로 low(낮은)가 적절하다. (high: 높은)

2행 This has occurred / because [farmers, extension services, agricultural policies, and agricultural research systems] depend on and support the use of pesticides.

: 주절과 이유의 부사절로 이루어진 문장이다. [ ] 부분이 부사절의 주어이며, the use of pesticides는 부사절의 동사인 depend on과 support의 공통 목적어이다.

5행 This makes the parties involved resistant to change, / **making it difficult** [for new technologies to gain a foothold].

: 문장의 술부에는 「make + 목적어 + 목적격보어」 구문이 쓰였고 making 이하는 앞 절을 부연 설명하는 분사구문이다. it은 형식상의 목적어, difficult가 목적격보어, [ ]로 표시한 to부정사구가 내용상의 목적어이며, for new technologies는 to부정사의 의미상 주어를 나타낸다.

어휘풀이

- pesticide *n* 농약, 살충제
- adoption *n* 채택
- input supplier (생산에 들어가는) 자원 공급자
- policymaker *n* 정책 입안자
- entrant *n* 진입자, 참가자
- stakeholder *n* 이해관계자
- in favor of ~을 지지하는
- application *n* 적용
- breeding *n* 육종
- foothold *n* 발판
- characteristic *n* 특성, 특징
- dominant *a* 지배적인, 우세한
- practice *n* 관행, 관습
- bias *n* 편향
- agrochemical *n* 농약, 농화학 약품
- priority *n* 우선순위
- pest *n* 해충

259 답 ①

📖 사업적인 명령에 의해 움직이고 있는 저널리즘

전문해석

저널리즘은 흥미롭고 논쟁적인 산업이고 늘 그래왔으며, 수세기 동안 그것의 목적, 관행 및 기준에 대한 집중적이고 치열한 검토의 대상이었던 산업이었다. 저널리즘은 많은 다양하고 때로는 상충되는 기능과 이익에 기여한다. 뉴스 제공자의 역할은 공공의 이익에 관한 사실들을 밝혀내 그들의 청중들을 위해 중립적인 방법으로 그것을 전달하는 것이다. 따라서 대중은 다른 사람의 행동에 대해 정보에 입각한 판단과 의견을 만들 수 있고, 이는 결국 사회 전체에 이익이 될 수 있다. 하지만 이 다양하고 역동적인 산업의 엄청난 대다수가 강력한 사업적 명령에 의존한다는 사실을 잊어서는 안 된다. 뉴스는 주주들을 위해 이익을 내고 광고주들에게 고객을 전달하는 상품이다. 저널리즘이 상품을 팔지 않는다면, 다음의 보도 사이클에 자금을 댈 충분한 돈이 없을 것이다. **그래서 저널리즘은 그것의 청중들에게 매력적이어야 하고, 판매 부수를 극대화해 그것의 비용에 대한 수익을 보장해야 한다.**

정답풀이

빈칸 앞에서는 뉴스가 공공의 이익들에 관련한 사실을 발견해 대중에게 중립적으로 그것들을 전달하며, 그 결과(Thus) 대중들이 이를 토대로 판단과 의견을 만듦으로 이것이 사회 전체에 이익이 될 수 있다고 했고, 빈칸 이하에서는 뉴스가 주주들을 위해 이익을 내고 광고주에게 고객을 전달하는 상품이 된다고 했다. 따라서 이들 두 내용 사이에 위치한 빈칸 문장은 역접의 접속사 Yet이 이끌고 있으므로, 앞의 내용과 반대되고 뒤의 내용과 같은 맥락을 이루어야 한다. 즉, 빈칸 이하가 뉴스가 수익을 내는 상품과 같은 성격이 있다는 것에 관해 언급하고 있으므로, 빈칸에는 이와 같은 맥락인 ① '강력한 사업적 명령에 의존한다'가 들어가는 것이 적절하다.

② 그것의 직원으로부터 낮은 생산성을 얻는다
③ 디지털 기술에 의해 위협을 받고 있다
④ 사회 정의의 실현을 위해 노력한다
⑤ 사회 갈등과 분열을 크게 조장한다

1행 Journalism is, and always has been, an exciting and controversial industry and **one** [**which** for centuries has **been subject to** intense scrutiny of its purposes, practices and standards].

: is와 has been 두 개의 동사가 보여 an exciting and controversial industry를 공통으로 취하고 있다. 부정대명사 one은 앞에 나온 명사 an industry를 대신하며, [ ]로 표시한 관계절의 수식을 받고 있다. 선행사가 부정대명사인 경우, 주로 관계대명사 that을 사용하지만 which 또한 사용 가능하다. be subject to는 '~의 대상이다'라는 의미이다.

어휘풀이

- controversial *a* 논쟁적인, 논란이 많은
- intense *a* 집중적인
- conflicting *a* 상충하는
- mediate *v* 전달하다, 중재하다
- bulk *n* 대부분, 태반
- commodity *n* 상품
- maximize *v* 최대화하다
- guarantee *v* 보장하다
- imperative *n* 명령, 요청
- threaten *v* 위협하다
- be subject to ~의 대상이다
- scrutiny *n* 치열한 검토
- unearth *v* 밝히다, 발굴하다
- neutral *a* 중립적인
- dynamic *a* 역동적인
- shareholder *n* 주주
- circulation *n* 발행 부수
- return *n* 수익
- productivity *n* 생산성
- strive for ~을 얻으려고 노력하다

260 답 ②

📖 집단적 인간 협력의 공통적 이유

전문해석

현대 국가나, 중세 교회, 고대 도시 혹은 태곳적 부족이든 간에 어떠한 대규모의 인간의 협력도 사람들의 집단적 상상력에서만 존재하는 공동의 신화에 뿌리를 둔다. **교회는 공동의 종교적 신화에 뿌리를 두고 있다.** 만난 적이 전혀 없는 두 가톨릭교도가 그들 모두 신이 우리의 죄를 구원하려고 인간 육체의 모습을 하고 자신을 십자가에 못 박히게 했다고 믿기 때문에, 그럼에도 불구하고 성전에 함께 하거나 가톨릭 교회 건립을 위한 기금을 모을 수 있다. **국가는 공동의 국가적 신화에 뿌리를 둔다.** 전혀 만난 적이 없는 두 명의 세르비아인이 모두 세르비아 국가와, 세르비아 조국, 세르비아 국기의 존재를 믿기 때문에 서로를 구하기 위해 자신의 삶을 위태롭게 할 수 있다. **사법 제도는 공동의 법적 신화에 뿌리를 둔다.** 만난 적이 없는 두 변호사가 그럼에도 불구하고 그들 모두 법, 정의 그리고 인권의 존재를 믿기 때문에 완전한 낯선 사람을 변호하기 위해 협력할 수 있다.

정답풀이

종교인은 같은 종교적 신화를 믿기 때문에, 한 국가의 국민은 공동의 국가적 신화를 믿기 때문에, 법조인은 공동의 법적 신화를 믿기 때문에 서로 협력한다고 했는데, 이러한 협력의 이유는 어떤 집단의 사람들이 집단 내에서 공유하는 믿음 때문이라는 것을 알 수 있다. 따라서 빈칸에 들어갈 말로 가장 적절한 것은 ② '사람들의 집단적 상상력에서만 존재하는'이다.

① 우리가 실패를 두려워하도록 잘못 야기하는
③ 종교적 근본주의자들을 보다 극단적이게 하는
④ 집단주의에 기반하여 인간의 행동을 조종하는
⑤ 우리가 동료애의 중요성을 깨닫도록 돕는

5행 Two Catholics [who have never met] can nevertheless go together on a crusade or pool funds to build a Catholics church / because they both believe [that God {was incarnated in human flesh} and {allowed Himself to be crucified} to redeem our sins].

: 주절과 이유 부사절로 이루어진 문장이다. 첫 번째 [ ]는 주절의 주어인 Two Catholics를 수식하는 관계절이며, 두 개의 동사 can go와 (can) pool이 병렬로 연결되었다. 두 번째 [ ]는 이유 부사절의 동사 believe의 목적어 역할을 하는 명사절이고, 두 개의 { }는 이 절의 주어 God에 병렬로 연결된 술부이다.

어휘풀이

- cooperation *n* 협력
- archaic *a* 고대의, 태곳적의
- myth *n* 신화, (근거 없는) 통념
- incarnate *v* 인간의 모습을 하다
- crucify *v* 십자가에 못 박다
- risk *v* 위태롭게 하다
- defend *v* 변호하다, 방어하다
- collectivism *n* 집단주의
- medieval *a* 중세의
- be rooted in ~에 뿌리를 두고 있다
- crusade *n* 성전, 십자군
- flesh *n* 육체
- redeem *v* 구원하다, 보완[만회]하다
- judicial *a* 사법의
- collective *a* 집단적인
- companionship *n* 동료애

261 답 ②

📖 다른 의사의 의견을 구하는 것의 필요성

전문해석

마스터스 러너들은 자기 자신의 판단력에 대한 자신감을 갖고 있다. 자신의 코치, 팀 동료, 친구들을 포함한 다른 사람들의 견해는 예전에 그랬던 것보다 덜 중요하다. (B) 마스터스 러너들은 또한 건강 전문가들의 조언과 진단이 옳은 것처럼 느껴지는지 아닌지에 대해 더 많이 식별하고 있다. **어떤 전문가가 옳지 않은 것처럼 느껴지는 어떤 말을 하면, 그들은 다른 견해를 구할 가능성이 더 크다.** (A) 다른 견해가 나를 포함한 많은 마스터스 러너들을 구해 주었다. 한 유명한 정형외과 의사가 내가 40대 후반일 때 나에게 관절염이 있으므로 앞으로는 한 주에 2마일(3.2킬로미터)만 달려야 한다고 말했다. 나는 다른 의사로부터 다른 견해를 구했다. (C) 그는 나의 뼈가 서른 살 먹은 사람들의 뼈여서 내가 계속 한 주에 30~40마일(48~64킬로미터)을 달릴 수 있다고 말했다. 그 두 번째 의사의 진단이 옳은 것처럼 느껴졌다. 그것이 8년쯤 전인데 나는 그때 이후로 계속해서 달리기를 해 오고 있다.

정답풀이

마스터스 러너(미국에서 아마추어 마라톤 참가자를 통칭하는 말)는 자신의 판단에 자신감을 지닌다는 내용의 주어진 글 다음에는, 그들은 또한 건강 전문가들의 판단에 식별력을 가지고 있어서 어떤 전문가의 견해가 옳지 않다고 느껴지면 다른 전문가의 견해를 찾는다고 부연하는 (B)가 와야 한다. 그리고 그런 다른 견해가 많은 마스터스 러너들을 구해 주었다고 하며 자신이 실제 경험했던 일을 소개하는 (A)가 온 다음에, 두 번째 의사의 의견을 구체적으로 이야기하는 (C)가 마지막에 오는 것이 가장 적절하다.

구문풀이

14행 He said [{my bones were **those** of a 30-year-old} and {I could continue to run 30 to 40 miles (48 – 64 km) a week}].

: [ ]는 문장의 동사 said의 목적어 역할을 하는 명사절로, 접속사 that이 생략되어 있다. [ ]에는 { }로 표시한 두 개의 절이 and에 의해 병렬로 연결되어 있다. 대명사 those는 앞의 bones를 대신한다.

어휘풀이

- confidence *n* 자신감
- second opinion 다른 의견
- specialist *n* 전문가
- henceforth *ad* 앞으로, 지금부터
- discerning *a* 식별력이 있는
- diagnosis *n* 진단

262 답 ③

📖 태도가 지속적인 것인지 아니면 임시적인 것인지에 관한 논쟁

전문해석

많은 학파의 심리학자들이 태도를 영구적인 것, 성격의 '지속되는' 측면, '인성의 통합된 부분'으로 여기는 것을 선호한다. 그래서 태도는 고정되어 있고 일관적이다. 태도는 예측 가능한 것이 되는데 왜냐하면 개인이 자신의 환경에서 동일한 사물과 사람들과 상호작용할 때 태도를 형성하기 때문이다. 개인은 정신적인 짜임새를 만드는데, 이것은 Eysenck가 '프로그램되어진다'고 부르는 것이자 다른 사람들이 습관이라고 부르기를 좋아하는 것이다. **하지만 Newcomb과 같은 이론가들은 태도의 임시적인 성격을 강조했고, 개인은 새로운 상황을 새롭게 평가할 것이고 즉석에서 그것에 관한 어떤 태도를 형성할 거라고 지적했다. 그런 이론가들에게 개인은 충동적이고 자발적인 존재인데,** 자아에 관한 이론가와 사회학자들이 이런 사고 학파에 속한다. 저명한 사회 심리학자인 Allport는 성격에는 어떠한 내면의 일관성도 없다고 지적하는 사람들 가운데 한 명이다. 우리는 어떤 상황에서 경향성들의 다발이기 때문에 주어진 상황에서 특징적인 행동을 이끌어내는 것은 오직 우리가 움직이는 환경이다.

정답풀이

태도를 지속적이고 예측 가능한 것으로 보는 입장과 충동적이고 일관성 없는 것으로 보는 입장을 설명하는 글이다. 주어진 문장은 태도가 일관되고 지속적인 것이라고 보는 주장에서 임시적이고 충동적인 것이라고 보는 주장으로 내용이 전환되는 자리인 ③에 들어가는 것이 가장 적절하다.

구문풀이

19행 ~, it is [only the environments {in which we move}] **that** elicit characteristic behaviour in given situations.

: 「it is ~ that ....」 강조구문이 사용되어 [ ]로 표시된 부분을 강조한다. { }는 the environments를 수식하는 관계절이다.

어휘풀이

- theorist *n* 이론가
- tentative *a* 임시적인
- afresh *ad* 새로이, 다시
- school *n* 학파
- enduring *a* 지속적인
- personality *n* 성격
- consistent *a* 일관된
- interact with ~와 상호작용하다
- spontaneous *a* 자발적인
- eminent *a* 고명한
- elicit *v* 이끌어내다
- stress *v* 강조하다
- nature *n* 성격, 본성
- on the spot 즉석에서
- permanent *a* 영구적인
- integral *a* 통합된
- anchored *a* 닻을 내린, 고정된
- predictable *a* 예측 가능한
- impulsive *a* 충동적인
- sociologist *n* 사회학자
- bundle *n* 다발, 묶음

263~264 답 ④ / ④

📖 뇌에 의한 과도한 에너지 사용을 막기 위해 인간이 발달시킨 무의식적 사고

전문해석

우리의 뇌는 탐욕스러운 에너지를 많이 소비하는 장기이다. 우리의 몸무게 중 단지 2퍼센트만 차지함에도 불구하고, 그것은 우리 몸의 에너지의 25퍼센트까지 사용한다. 분명히, 뇌가 더 적은 에너지원을 사용하기 위해 할 수 있는 어떤 것이든 도움이 될 것인데, 그것이 사람의 에너지가 고갈되어 굶주리는 것을 멈출 것이기 때문이다. **오랜 시간에 걸쳐서, 우리 조상들의 뇌는 에너지를 절약할 수 있는 사고의 지름길을 진화시켰다.** 우리의 뇌에 의식적이고, 이성적이고, 신중한 사고와 같은 포도당 간식 거리를 주는 것이 전혀 없어서, 우리는 '에너지 절약' 사고방식이 필요했다. 마찬가지로, 위협이 있을 수 있는 상황에서, 만약 우리의 수렵·채집인 조상들이 시간을 내

어 그들 눈의 구석에서 본 움직임이 사자일 가능성에 대해 의식적, 이성적으로 가늠해 보았다면, 그들은 그리 오래 살아남지 못했을 것이다. 요점을 강조하자면, 우리의 뇌가 들어오는 감각 정보를 소화하고 우리의 의식적인 마음에 의미 있는 경험을 제시하는 데 보통 0.5초 또는 그 이상이 걸린다. 이것은 빠르게 보일지 모르지만, 포식자를 피하는 데 있어서 그것의 결과는 치명적일 수 있다. 심지어 오늘날에도, 우리의 의식은 변함없이 실제보다 0.5초 뒤지는데, 이것은 운동에서부터 걷기 그리고 심지어 말하기까지 대부분의 활동이 주로 우리의 무의식적인 정신에 의해 처리되고 있다는 것을 의미하는데, 비록 우리의 의식이 완전히 자율상태에(→ 통제되고) 있다는 기이한 환상을 뇌가 만들어 냄에도 불구하고 그러하다! 그러므로, 대자연은 수백만 년 동안 빠른 지름길 사고에 대한 선호를 가진 우리의 뇌를 조각해 왔다.

263
정답풀이
우리의 뇌는 에너지를 많이 소비하는 기관이고 이러한 뇌의 에너지 사용을 줄일 수 있는 것이 우리의 생존과 직결된 상황에서, 우리 인간은 에너지 절약을 위한 사고의 지름길을 발달시켜 대부분의 활동을 의식적인 사고의 개입 없이 무의식적으로 처리하도록 진화해 왔다는 내용이다. 따라서 글의 제목으로 적절한 것은 ④ '에너지 절감을 위한 무의식적 사고: 우리의 생존 도구'이다.
① 왜 우리의 뇌는 그렇게 많은 에너지를 필요로 하는가?
② 진화: 에너지를 확보하기 위해 고군분투한 역사
③ 생존 전략: 그것을 뇌의 안이 아니라 밖에서 발견하라
⑤ 잠재적 위협에 대비해 의식적 사고를 확대하라

264
정답풀이
우리의 의식은 실제보다 보통 0.5초 이상 뒤져있고 걷기와 말하기 같은 많은 활동이 무의식적인 정신에 의해 처리되고 있다고 했으므로, 이러한 상태에서 우리의 뇌가 만들어 내는 잘못된 환상은 우리의 의식이 무의식적인 정신에 의해 치러지는 것이 아니라 우리의 의식의 통제를 받고 있다는 내용일 것이다. 따라서 (d)의 autonomy(자율상태)는 control(통제)과 같은 어휘로 바꿔야 한다.

오답풀이
① 앞에서 뇌가 우리 몸의 에너지의 25퍼센트나 사용한다고 했으므로 적은 에너지원 사용은 '도움이 될(advantage)' 것이라는 문맥이다.
② 뒤에서 사자의 움직임을 본 것을 예로 들고 있으므로 이는 '위협(threat)'이 있는 상황일 것이다.
③ 뇌가 정보를 인식하는 0.5초 또는 그 이상의 시간은 빠르게 느껴지지만 포식자를 피하는 상황에서는 '치명적일(fatal)' 수 있다는 문맥이다.
⑤ 우리의 뇌는 빠른 지름길 사고에 대한 '선호(preference)'가 있기 때문에 에너지를 절약하기 위해 진화했을 것이다.

구문풀이
3행 Clearly, anything [that the brain can do to use less power] will be of advantage, / as it would **stop** the person **running** out of energy and **starving**.

: 주절과 부사절로 이루어진 문장으로, [ ]는 주절의 주어인 anything을 수식하는 관계절이다. as절에는 '(목적어)가 ~하는 것을 막다'라는 의미의 「stop+목적어+(from) -ing」 구문이 사용되었으며, running과 starving은 병렬구조를 이루고 있다.

11행 Equally, in situations of possible threat, / if our hunter-gatherer ancestors **had taken** the time to consciously, rationally weigh up the chances [that the movement they saw in the corner of their eye was a lion], / they **may** not **have survived** for very long.

: if절에 「had p.p.」를 사용하고 주절에 「조동사+have p.p.」를 사용해 과거의 사실과 반대되는 상황을 가정하고 있다. [ ]는 the chances의 구체적인 내용을 설명하는 동격

절이다.

16행 To underscore the point: **it** typically **takes** up to half a second or more **for** our brains **to digest** incoming sensory information and present a meaningful experience to our conscious mind.

: 「it takes+시간+for ~+to부정사 …」 구문을 사용해 '~가 …하는 데 (~의 시간)이 걸리다'의 의미를 나타내고 있다.

어휘풀이
- greedy *a* 탐욕스러운
- energy-hungry *a* 에너지를 많이 소비하는
- comprise *v* 차지하다, 구성하다
- shortcut *n* 지름길
- deliberative *a* 신중한
- underscore *v* 강조하다
- digest *v* 소화하다
- predator *n* 포식자
- take care of ~을 처리하다, ~을 돌보다
- sculpt *v* 조각하다
- starve *v* 굶주리다
- rational *a* 합리적인
- weigh up 가늠하다, 무게를 재다
- take up 차지하다
- implication *n* 결과, 영향
- fatal *a* 치명적인
- autonomy *n* 자율(성)
- preference *n* 선호

적중 예상 문제 5회				본문 pp.178~183
265 ④	**266** ③	**267** ①	**268** ⑤	**269** ④
270 ④	**271** ③	**272** ④	**273** ⑤	**274** ②
275 ⑤	**276** ⑤			

265 답 ④

📖 지인의 구직 추천
전문해석
관계자분께,
저는 John Brown을 여러 해 동안 알고 지내왔습니다. John이 고등학생일 때, 그는 제가 지역의 9세에서 10세 소년들의 축구팀을 지도하는 것을 도왔습니다. 인내심과 전략을 명쾌하게 설명하고 보여주는 능력으로, 그는 이 소년들로부터 최선을 발휘하게 했고, 그들은 결국 그를 존경했습니다. 저는 John이 믿을 수 있고, 책임감이 있으며, 정직하고, 예의 바르다는 것을 알고 있습니다. 그는 현재 자신이 일하고 있는 식당에서 단연 가장 인기 있는 웨이터입니다. 그 식당에서 식사를 하는 동안, 저는 우연히도 손님들이 그가 담당하는 구역에 앉게 해달라고 요청하는 것을 자주 들었습니다. John은 어떤 조직에서든지 자산이 될 사람입니다. 저는 자신 있게 귀사에 어느 자리에든지 그를 추천할 수 있습니다. 제가 위에서 언급한 것에 대해 더 논의하고 싶으시다면 주저 말고 저에게 전화해주세요.
Fred Miller 드림 (303) 444-1313

정답풀이
자신감과 친분이 있는 사람인 John Brown의 긍정적 자질을 열거하면서 회사에 채용될 수 있도록 추천하고 있는 글이므로 글의 목적으로 가장 적절한 것은 ④이다.

구문풀이
5행 [With patience and an ability to explain and demonstrate strategy clearly], he drew out the very best from these boys, [**who**, {in turn}, looked up to him].

: 첫 번째 [ ]는 부사구이고, 두 번째 [ ]는 계속적 용법으로 쓰인 관계대명사 who가 이끄는 관계절로 앞에 나온 these boys를 부연 설명한다. 여기에 부사구 in turn이 주격 관계대명사 who와 동사 looked 사이에 삽입되어 있다.

어휘풀이
- community *n* 지역 사회
- demonstrate *v* 입증하다
- strategy *n* 전략
- draw out the best from ~로부터 최선을 발휘하게 하다
- in turn 결국
- look up to ~을 존경하다
- dependable *a* 믿을 만한
- responsible *a* 책임감 있는
- courteous *a* 예의 바른, 공손한
- by far 단연코, 틀림없이
- dine *v* 식사를 하다
- overhear *v* 우연히 듣다
- asset *n* 자산
- confidently *ad* 자신 있게
- hesitate *v* 주저하다

266 답 ③

📖 자신의 일에 한계를 설정하는 것의 필요성

전문해석
어떤 내과의사는 진단하기 어려운 사례에 대해 그의 전문지식에 대한 한계를 설정한다. "테스트가 문제가 X라는 것을 보여주면, 저는 당신의 약물치료를 도와 줄 수 있습니다. 그러나 엑스레이가 Y를 나타내면, 저는 더 많은 테스트를 받도록 당신을 전문가에게 보내야 할 것입니다." 당신은 그 의사가 경계를 설정한다고 해서 조금이라도 덜 존경하지 않는다. 오히려 당신은 그가 실험을 하기보다는 그의 전문지식의 한계에 대해 정직한 것에 대해 기뻐한다. 당신은 전문지식의 결핍 때문이거나 혹은 단지 당신이 대답을 하고 싶지 않기 때문에 유사한 한계를 둘 수 있다. (그렇다면) 그렇게 말하라. "이번 회의에서 저는 비용 문제까지 들어가고 싶지 않습니다. 저는 시스템이 어떻게 작동하는지에 대한 기술적인 문제에 응답을 하기 위해 여기에 참석했습니다." 그리고 비용에 관한 어떤 문제가 나중에 표면화되면, 당신의 한계를 고수하라. "이전에 언급했던 것처럼, 저는 비용에 대해 토론할 준비가 되어 있지 않습니다." 당신이 직접 그렇게 한다면 사람들은 당신의 한계를 존중할 것이다.

정답풀이
자신의 전문지식이나 자신이 할 일에 있어서 한계를 설정하고 그 한도 내에서 일을 처리하면 타인들도 그 한계를 존중할 것이라는 내용이다. 따라서 필자의 주장으로 적절한 것은 ③이다.

구문풀이
8행 You may have similar limits, **either because of** a lack of expertise **or** simply **because** you prefer not to answer.

: 「either A or B(A이거나 혹은 B)」 구문이 사용되었다. because of 다음에는 명사(구)가 이어지고 because 다음에는 절이 이어진다.

어휘풀이
- set a limit on ~에 한계를 설정하다
- expertise *n* 전문지식
- diagnose *v* 진단하다
- medication *n* 약물치료
- boundary *n* 한계, 경계선
- if anything 오히려
- surface *v* 표면에 떠오르다
- stick to ~을 고수하다[지키다]

267 답 ①

📖 완벽을 요구하지 않음으로써 후회 줄이기

전문해석
완벽을 요구하는 것에 유리한 점이 존재할까? 여러분은 이것이 여러분으로 하여금 최상의 해결책을 찾도록 동기를 부여할 거라고 생각할지 모른다. 하지만 그것이 과연 최상의 해결책으로 이어질까? 대안들이 완벽하지 않다고 하여 그것들을 모두 거절하는 것은 그 어떤 해결책도 보장하지 못한다. 아니면 여러분은 완벽을 요구하는 것이 후회를 할 가능성을 줄여줄 것이라고 생각할지 모른다. 다시 말하지만, 완벽주의는 사실 정반대로 이어진다. 완벽을 요구한다면, 여러분은 가능한 최상의 결과를 내지 못하는, 여러분이 내리는 결정을 되돌아보며 그것을 후회의 이유로 여길 것이다. 완벽을 바라는 여러분의 요구에 의해 여러분의 후회는 확대될 것이다. 이에 반해, 여러분 자신에게 실수에 대한 약간의 여지를 허용한다면, 여러분은 일부 결정이 부정적인 결과를 가져올 수 있다는 것을 받아들일 것이고, 이것이 (그러한 상황에서) 일상적인 일이라고 여길 것이다.

정답풀이
완벽을 요구하는 것은 좋은 해결책을 이끌어내는 데 도움이 되지 않고 그것은 후회로 이어지므로, 완벽을 요구하는 태도를 버리면 후회를 줄일 수 있다고 말하는 내용의 글이다. 따라서 글의 요지로 가장 적절한 것은 ①이다.

구문풀이
7행 Again, perfectionism actually leads to the opposite — **if** you demand perfection, **then** you will **look back on** [any decisions {**that** you make} {**that** do not lead to the best possible outcome}] **as** [a reason for regret].

: lead to는 '~로 이어지다, ~을 초래하다'의 의미이고, 「if ~, then ....」은 '~하면, …하다'의 의미이다. 「look back on A as B」는 'A를 되돌아보며 B로 여기다'라고 해석한다. 이 구문의 A에 해당하는 첫 번째 [ ]에서 두 개의 { }로 표시된 관계절이 any decisions를 수식하는데, 첫 번째 that은 목적격 관계대명사이고 두 번째 that은 주격 관계대명사이다.

어휘풀이
- demand *v* 요구[요청]하다
- perfection *n* 완벽
- motivate *v* 동기를 부여하다
- reject *v* 거절하다
- alternative *n* 대안
- guarantee *v* 보장하다
- whatsoever *ad* 전혀, 어떤 것도(whatever의 강조형)
- regret *n* 후회
- perfectionism *n* 완벽주의
- opposite *n* 반대(의 것)
- magnify *v* 확대하다
- come with the territory (어떤 상황에서) 일상적인 일이다, 보통이다

268 답 ⑤

📊 2005년과 2011년 사이 유럽 4개국의 가정용 포장 재활용 비율

전문해석
위 도표는 2005년과 2011년 사이에 선택된 유럽 4개국의 가정용 포장 재활용 비율을 보여준다. 벨기에는 이 기간 동안에 가장 높은 가정 재활용 비율을 차지했고, 2011년에는 약 80%의 가정용 포장을 재활용했다. 2011년에 네덜란드와 아일랜드는 거의 같은 재활용 비율을 차지했다. 2005년과 2006년 사이에 네덜란드는 벨기에 다음으로 높은 재활용 비율을 보였는데, 그 재활용 비율에서 10%의 급격한 증가를 했다. 2006년부터 2011년까지 아일랜드에서 가정용 포장 재활용 비율은 꾸준히 증가했다. 2006년에 영국(→ 아일랜드)의 재활용 비율은 이 4개의 유럽 국가들 중에서 가장 낮았다.

정답풀이
2006년에 가정용 포장 재활용 비율이 가장 낮은 나라는 아일랜드이므로, 영국의 재활용 비율이 가장 낮았다는 ⑤는 도표의 내용과 일치하지 않는다.

구문풀이
3행 Belgium [had the highest household recycling rate (during this period)] and [recycled about 80% of its packaging in 2011].

: [ ]로 표시한 두 개의 동사구가 주어에 병렬로 연결되어 있다. ( )는 첫 번째 술부에 포함된 부사구이다.

어휘풀이

- household *a* 가정의, 가구의
- recycling *n* 재활용
- steadily *ad* 꾸준히
- packaging *n* 포장
- drastic *a* 급격한

269 답 ④

📖 지질학자 Charles Lyell의 업적과 생애

전문해석

스코틀랜드의 Kinnordy에서 상당한 문학적 취향을 가진 식물학자인 아버지에게서 태어난 Charles Lyell은 1821년에 옥스퍼드 대학을 졸업했고 1825년에 변호사가 되었다. 그는 곧 자신의 포부가 과학을 더 향한다는 것을 깨달았고, 그래서 1827년에 마침내 그는 법보다 지질학을 선택했다. 그의 전설적인 책 〈Principles of Geology〉의 첫 권은 1830년에 출간되었다. 세 번째이자 마지막 권은 3년 후에 출간되었다. 그의 다른 작품인 〈Antiquity of Man〉은 1863년에 출간되었고, 지구상에 인간이 오래 존재했다는 증거에 대해 논의했다. Lyell의 지질학적 접근은 더 넓은 의미에서의 진화론에 대한 평가인 경향이 있다. **그는 생물학에서 Darwin의 자연 선택설을 받아들인 최초의 사람들 중 한 명이었다.** 1866년에 Charles Lyell은 스웨덴 왕립 과학원의 외국인 구성원이 되었다. Lyell은 1875년 2월 22일에 죽었다. 그는 77세였다. 그는 웨스트민스터 수도원에 안장되었다.

정답풀이

생물학에서 Darwin의 자연 선택설을 받아들인 최초의 사람들 중 한 명이라고 했으므로, ④는 글의 내용과 일치하지 않는다.

구문풀이

1행 [Born at Kinnordy, Scotland to a botanist father {who possessed considerable literary tastes}], Charles Lyell graduated from Oxford in 1821 and joined the bar in 1825.

: [ ]는 앞에 Having been이 생략된 분사구문으로, 이 안의 { }는 a botanist father를 수식하는 관계절이다. 주어인 Charles Lyell에 두 개의 동사 graduated와 joined가 and로 연결되어 있다.

어휘풀이

- botanist *n* 식물학자
- considerable *a* 상당한
- taste *n* 취향
- geology *n* 지질학
- principle *n* 원리
- assessment *n* 평가
- embrace *v* (생각·제안 등을) 받아들이다
- theory of natural selection 자연 선택설
- abbey *n* 수도원
- possess *v* 가지고 있다, 소유하다
- literary *a* 문학의
- ambition *n* 포부, 야망
- legendary *a* 전설적인
- antiquity *n* 오래됨
- evolutionism *n* 진화론

270 답 ④

📖 교육이 나아가야 할 방향

전문해석

시인 William Yeats가 쓴 것처럼, "교육은 들통을 채우는 것이 아니라 불을 지피는 것이다." 생각하고, 정보에 입각하고, 영감을 받고, 자기를 실현하는 개인과 시민을 만들며 그 불을 지피는 것이 고등 보통 교육의 목적이다. 그 이상은 개인이 자신의 잠재력에 도달하도록 도울 뿐만 아니라 민주주의가 생존하고 번성하는 것을 돕기 위해 지난 세기에 민주 사회에 의해 수용되어 왔다. 민주주의는 친절하고 사려 깊은 시민만큼 유식하고 생각하는 시민을 필요로 한다. 달리 말해, **교육은 단지 우리가 아이들을 위해 제공하는 것에 관한 것만은 아니다. 그것은 또한 우리 아이들이 세상에**

제공할 가능성이 있는 것에 관한 것이다. 우리의 젊은이들을 어떻게 교육하는가, 그들의 마음을 어떻게 개발하는가, 어떻게 그들의 사회적, 도덕적 발달을 안내할 것인가와 같은 것들은 그들이 개인으로서 누가 그리고 무엇이 될 것인가에 있어 뿐만 아니라 사회로서의 우리가 어떻게 미래와 공동의 운명을 만들어 갈 것인가에 있어서도 핵심 부분이다. 진부할 수도 있지만 젊은이가 우리의 미래라는 것과 내일의 세계의 운명은 우리 아이들에게 달려있다는 것도 완전히 진실이다.

정답풀이

④ 문장의 구조 파악: 「not only A but also B」 구문에서, B에 해당하는 how절 안의 주어 we에 이어지는 동사가 필요하므로 creating은 create가 되어야 한다.

오답풀이

① 주어와 동사의 수 일치: 동명사구 Lighting that fire가 문장의 주어이므로 단수동사 is는 적절하다.
② 병렬구조: 「not only A but also B」 구문에서, A와 B에 해당하는 to help ~ their potentials와 to help ~ thrive가 병렬로 연결된 구조이다.
③ 관계대명사: 앞의 전치사 about의 목적어 역할을 하는 선행사를 포함한 관계대명사 what절이므로 올바르게 사용되었다.
⑤ 도치: 부사구가 문장의 앞으로 나오면서 '동사+주어'의 어순으로 도치된 경우이다. the fate of tomorrow's world가 주어이므로 동사 rests는 어법상 적절하다.

구문풀이

18행 It may be cliché, / but **it** is also profoundly true [**that** youth are our future] and [**that** upon our children rests the fate of tomorrow's world].

: 크게 두 개의 절이 but으로 연결되어 있다. 두 번째 절에서 it은 가주어이고 이에 대한 진주어는 [ ]로 표시된 두 개의 that절이다.

어휘풀이

- pail *n* 들통, 원통형 용기
- liberal education 고등 보통 교육
- potential *n* 잠재력
- considerate *a* 친절한, 사려 깊은
- moral *a* 도덕적인
- destiny *n* 운명
- profoundly *ad* 완전히, 깊게
- fate *n* 운명
- self-actualized *a* 자기를 실현하는
- embrace *v* 수용하다
- thrive *v* 번성하다
- cultivate *v* 개발하다
- collective *a* 공동의, 단체의
- cliché *a* 진부한
- rest upon[on] ~에 의존하다

271 답 ③

📖 다수와 소수의 설득 기술의 차이

전문해석

사람들의 동의를 얻는 것은 기술, 즉 설득의 기술이다. 대다수는 엄청난 이점을 가지고 있는 것으로 밝혀졌다. 그들은 우리를 설득하려고 노력할 필요가 별로 없다. 그들이 다수라는 단순한 사실은 사람들이 그 의견에 동의하거나 그들을 따르게 하는 데 거의 항상 충분하다. 다수는 현실을 왜곡할 수 있는 능력을 가지고 있다. 사실, 그들의 힘은 매우 즉각적이고 강력해서 우리 자신의 감각이 틀렸다고 말할 때조차도 우리는 그들을 따른다. 반면에 소수의 견해는 우리를 설득하기 위해 힘겨운 싸움을 벌여야 한다. 우리는 쉽게 (그들에게) 동의하지 않는다. 사실, 우리는 동의에 저항하는 많은 이유를 발견한다. 그것은 체계적인 설득 방법을 통해 시간을 두고 행해져야 한다. 그러나 이러한 계획적인 설득 과정은 궁극적으로 소수의 견해에 대한 우리의 지지가 정말 진정성 있는 것임을 보장하는 것이다. 우리가 소수의 견해에 동의할 때, 그것은 대개 태도의 진정한 변화를 기반으로 한다. 즉, 우리는 납득이 되었기 때문에 그 견해에 이제 따르거나 동의한다는 의미이다.

정답풀이

(A) 뒤의 문장에서 다수의 힘은 매우 강력해서 우리 자신이 그것이 틀렸다고 말할 때조차도 그들을 따른다는 내용으로 보아 다수는 현실을 '왜곡할' 수 있을 것이다. 따라서 bend가 적절하다. (comprehend: 이해하다)

(B) 소수의 설득이 체계적인 설득 방법을 통해 시간을 두고 행해져야 한다는 말은 그 설득이 '계획적'으로 행해져야 한다는 말이다. 따라서 deliberate가 적절하다. (random: 무작위의, 우연한)

(C) 소수의 견해에 동의할 때 그것이 대개 태도의 진정한 변화를 기반으로 한다는 말은 태도를 변화한 사람이 '납득이 되었다'는 의미이므로 convinced가 적절하다. (conditioned: 조건화된, 훈련된)

구문풀이

4행 The simple fact [that they are the majority] is almost always enough for people **to agree** with them or **to follow** them.

: 문장의 주어는 The simple fact이고 동사는 is이다. [ ]는 The simple fact의 내용을 담고 있는 동격절이다. 두 개의 부정사 to agree와 to follow가 의미상의 주어인 for people에 이어져 병렬구조를 이루고 있다.

14행 However, this deliberate process of persuasion is [**what** ultimately ensures {that our support for a minority view is truly genuine}].

: [ ]는 선행사를 포함하는 관계대명사 what이 이끄는 명사절로 문장에서 보어 역할을 하고, { }는 명사절의 동사 ensures의 목적어이다.

어휘풀이

• persuasion *n* 설득
• majority *n* 다수, 대다수
• compelling *a* 설득력 있는, 강력한
• uphill *a* 힘든, 오르막의
• ultimately *ad* 궁극적으로, 결국
• turn out ~인 것으로 드러나다[밝혀지다]
• enormous *a* 거대한, 엄청난
• minority *n* 소수, 소수 집단
• deliberate *a* 계획적인, 의도적인
• genuine *a* 진정한, 진실한

272 답 ④

📖 최고의 성과를 내는 사람들의 자기 관찰 능력

전문해석

최고의 성과를 내는 사람들이 업무 중에 사용하는 가장 중요한 자기 조절 기술은 자기 관찰에 대한 자신의 생각을 통제하는 것이다. 예를 들어, 엘리트 경기자는 자신에게 열심히 집중하고, 무엇보다도 특정 비율을 유지하기 위해 그들의 호흡을 세고 동시에 발걸음을 센다. 반면에, 경기에 참가하는 일반 지구력 경기자는 자신이 하고 있는 일 외에 다른 것에 대해 생각하는 경향이 있으며, 고통스럽고 그래서 그들은 그것에서 마음을 돌리기를 바란다. 우리들 대부분은 그렇게 대단한 육체적인 방법으로 노력하지는 않지만, 순전히 정신적인 작업에도 동일한 원리가 적용된다. 최고의 성과를 내는 사람들은 자신을 면밀히 살펴본다. 그들은 사실상 자기 자신을 벗어나 자신의 마음속에서 일어나는 일을 살펴보고 그것이 어떻게 진행되고 있는지 물어볼 수 있다. 연구자들은 이것을 메타인지, 즉 자신의 지식에 대한 지식, 자신의 사고에 대한 사고라고 부른다. 최고의 성과를 내는 사람들은 다른 사람들이 하는 것보다 훨씬 더 체계적으로 이것을 수행하며, 이는 그들의 일과에서 확립된 부분이다.

정답풀이

엘리트 경기자는 경기 중에 자신에게 집중해서 호흡을 세고 동시에 발걸음을 세는 자기 관찰을 하고, 최고의 성과자는 업무를 진행할 때 자신의 마음에서 일어나는 일을 살핀다는 내용의 글이다. 따라서 빈칸에는 ④ '자기 관찰'이 들어가는 것이 가장 적절하다.

① 자기 방어
② 자기 표현
③ 자기 확신
⑤ 자기 만족

구문풀이

13행 They are in effect able to [step outside themselves], [monitor {what is happening in their own minds}], and [ask {how it's going}].

: [ ]로 묶인 3개의 동사구가 to에 병렬구조로 연결되어 있다. 두 개의 { }는 각각 앞의 동사 monitor와 ask의 목적절이다.

어휘풀이

• self-regulatory *a* 자기 조절의
• simultaneously *ad* 동시에
• ratio *n* 비율, 비
• endurance runner 지구력 경기자, 장거리 주자
• take one's mind off ~에서 마음을 돌리다, ~의 일을 잊다
• exert *v* 노력하다
• metacognition *n* 메타인지, 자신의 사고에 대한 인식
• systematically *ad* 체계적으로
• intensely *ad* 강렬하게, 열심히
• stride *n* 발걸음
• significant *a* 상당한, 중요한
• established *a* 확립된

273 답 ⑤

📖 여러 가지 일을 동시에 하는 것의 효율성

전문해석

순차적인 문화권 출신 사람들은 순서대로 진행하는 것이 질서 있고 효율적이며 최소한의 노력이 들기 때문에 합리적이라고 주장할 것이다. (C) 그러나 이런 일렬 사고는 어떤 일을 하는 데 언제나 가장 좋은 방법은 아닐 수 있는데, 그 이유는 어떤 공유된 행위의 효율성과 상호연관을 보지 못하기 때문이다. 때때로 많은 서로 다른 일을 같은 시간에 잘 처리하는 것이 사실은 가장 시간 효율적일 수 있다. (B) Trompenaars와 Hampden-Turner는 이탈리아(순차적인 문화권)의 정육점의 예를 든다. 그 가게에서는 정육점 주인이 포장을 풀고 한 고객에게 줄 살라미의 주문 분량을 자른 후에 "내가 살라미를 재포장하기 전에 살라미를 원하는 사람이 있나요?"라고 외친다. (A) 비록 각 고객은 순서대로 응대받지는 못하지만, 전체 과정은 더 효율적인데, 그 이유는 다양한 종류의 고기를 훨씬 덜 풀었다 재포장하기 때문이다.

정답풀이

순차적으로 일을 처리하는 것이 합리적이라고 주장할 수 있다는 주어진 글 다음에는, 이런 일렬적인 사고는 효율적이지 않다고 역접의 연결사 However로 시작하여 반박하는 (C)가 이어져야 한다. 그리고 서로 다른 일을 같은 시간에 하는 것이 효율적일 수 있다는 (C)의 마지막 부분에 대한 구체적인 예시로 이탈리아 정육점에서의 경우가 제시되는 (B)가 오고, 그 예시의 결론을 내리는 (A)가 마지막으로 오는 것이 가장 적절한 순서이다.

구문풀이

1행 People from a sequential culture would argue [that proceeding in a straight line is reasonable {because it is orderly, efficient, and involves a minimum of effort}].

: People from a sequential culture가 문장의 주어, would argue가 동사이다. [ ]는 argue의 목적어 역할을 하는 명사절이고, 그 안의 { }는 이유를 나타내는 부사절이다.

어휘풀이

• sequential *a* 순차적인, 잇따라 일어나는
• proceeding *n* 진행
• unwrap *v* 포장을 풀다
• butcher shop 정육점
• efficiency *n* 효율
• juggle *v* 여러 가지 일을 잘 처리하다, 저글링을 하다
• orderly *a* 질서 있는
• cite *v* 언급하다, 예증하다
• be blind to ~을 알지 못하다
• interconnection *n* 상호연관성

274~276 답 ② / ⑤ / ⑤

📖📖 **가난한 집의 막내딸인 Ginger의 아름다운 선행**

전문해석

(A) 나는 최저임금을 지불하는 직장에서 일하면서 네 명의 어린 자녀를 홀로 키우는 부모였다. 항상 돈에 쪼들렸으나, 우리는 거처할 집이 있고 먹을 음식과 입을 옷이 있었는데, 많지는 않더라도 항상 충분했다. 나의 아이들은 나에게 그 당시에 우리가 가난했다는 것을 알지 못했다고 말했다. 그들은 그저 엄마가 인색하다고 생각했다. (a)나는 항상 그런 사실에 대해 고맙게 생각해 왔다. 크리스마스 철이 되어서 비록 많은 선물을 살 돈은 없었지만, 우리는 교회와 가족, 파티와 친구들과 함께 축하하고, 차를 타고 시내에 가서 크리스마스 조명을 보고, 특별한 저녁식사를 하기로 계획했다.

(C) 하지만 아이들에게 큰 흥분은 쇼핑몰에서 크리스마스 쇼핑을 하는 즐거움이었다. 그들은 서로에게 그리고 조부모에게 크리스마스 선물로 무엇을 원하는지 물으면서, 그 전부터 몇 주 동안 이야기를 하고 계획을 세웠다. 나는 그것이 두려웠다. (d)나는 우리 다섯 명 모두가 나눌 선물을 사기 위한 돈으로 120달러를 모아 두었다. 그 중요한 날이 왔고 우리는 일찌감치 출발했다. 나는 네 명의 아이들에게 각각 20달러짜리 지폐를 주고 각각 4달러 정도 되는 선물을 찾아보라고 그들에게 일깨워 주었다. 그런 다음에 모두가 흩어졌다. 우리는 두 시간 동안 쇼핑을 하고 나서 '산타의 작업장' 전시장에서 다시 만나기로 했다.

(B) 다시 차를 타고 집으로 오는 길에, 모두들 크리스마스 기분에 고조되어, 서로에게 무엇을 샀는지에 대해 힌트와 단서를 가지고 서로 웃고 장난을 쳤다. 나의 여덟 살짜리 막내딸 Ginger는 평소와 달리 조용했다. (b)나는 그녀가 선물 쇼핑을 하고 난 후에 작고 납작한 봉지 하나만을 갖고 있는 것을 발견했다. 나는 그 비닐봉지를 통해 그녀가 50센트짜리 초코바들을 샀다는 것을 충분히 알 수 있었다! 나는 무척 화가 났다. 나는 그녀에게 소리를 지르고 싶었지만, 집에 도착할 때까지 아무 말도 하지 않았다. 나는 그녀를 내 방으로 불러서 방문을 닫고, (c)내가 그녀에게 그 돈을 어떻게 했느냐고 물었을 때 다시 화를 낼 준비를 했다.

(D) 그녀는 나에게 다음과 같이 말했다. "저는 무엇을 살까 생각하면서 둘러보다가 멈추어 서서 구세군의 '기부 나무들' 중 하나에 달려 있는 작은 카드들을 읽었어요. 그 카드들 중 하나는 네 살짜리 작은 소녀를 위한 것이었는데, 그녀가 크리스마스 선물로 원하는 것은 오직 옷을 입힌 인형과 머리빗뿐이래요. 그래서 (e)저는 그 나무에서 카드를 떼어내고 그녀를 위해서 인형과 머리빗을 사서 그것들을 구세군 부스에 갖다 주었어요. 저는 겨우 우리를 위해서 초코바를 살 돈만 남았어요."라고 하며 Ginger는 말을 계속했다. "하지만 우리는 아주 많은 것을 갖고 있고 그녀는 아무것도 갖고 있지 않아요." 나는 이제껏 그날만큼 부유하게 느낀 적이 결코 없었다.

정답풀이

274

네 명의 자녀를 데리고 크리스마스 준비를 위해 시내로 가기로 했다는 (A) 뒤에는, 쇼핑몰에서 크리스마스 선물 쇼핑을 하기로 했다는 (C)가 와야 한다. 그리고 쇼핑이 끝나고 딸 Ginger가 산 선물을 보고 화가 나서 자초지종을 물었다는 (B)가 오고, Ginger가 한 선행을 알게 되었다는 (D)가 오는 것이 가장 적절한 순서이다.

275

(e)는 구세군 부스에 선물을 갖다 준 Ginger를 가리키고 나머지는 모두 Ginger의 어머니인 필자를 가리킨다.

276

인형과 머리빗을 사서 구세군에게 선물로 준 것은 필자가 아니라 필자의 딸 Ginger~이므로 ⑤는 글의 내용으로 적절하지 않다.

구문풀이

32행 I [gave each of the four kids a twenty-dollar bill] and [reminded them to look for gifts {that cost about four dollars each}].

: [ ]로 표시한 두 개의 동사구가 and로 연결된 구조이다. each of the four kids와 a twenty-dollar bill은 각각 gave의 간접목적어와 직접목적어이다. 두 번째 [ ]에서 them은 reminded의 목적어, to look ~은 목적격보어이고, { }는 주격 관계대명사 that이 이끄는 관계절로 앞의 gifts를 수식한다.

어휘풀이

- roof over one's head 거처할 집
- tease *v* 놀리다, 장난하다
- shopping spree 물건을 (왕창) 사들임
- scatter *v* (황급히) 흩어지다
- cheap *a* 인색한
- flat *a* 납작한, 편평한
- dread *v* 두려워하다, 몹시 무서워하다

독해 실전 모의고사 1회				본문 pp.184~197
277 ⑤	278 ③	279 ④	280 ③	281 ④
282 ④	283 ③	284 ⑤	285 ③	286 ⑤
287 ④	288 ③	289 ④	290 ①	291 ①
292 ①	293 ③	294 ④	295 ③	296 ②
297 ⑤	298 ③	299 ④	300 ①	301 ⑤
302 ②	303 ③	304 ⑤		

---

277 답 ⑤

📖📖 **홍보 기사 작성을 문의하는 편지글**

전문해석

Hamilton 씨께,

귀사와 인터뷰할 기회와 흥미로운 투어를 제공해 주셔서 감사합니다. 저는 우리의 유익한 논의가 즐거웠고 귀사의 새 애니메이션은 정말 멋졌습니다. 제가 지역 주간 컴퓨터 신문인 'The Web-Byter'에 그것에 관한 기사를 써서 귀사의 곧 출시될 비디오 게임을 홍보해도 될까요? 저는 매달 새로운 소프트웨어나 컴퓨터 비디오 게임을 검토하고 추천하는 칼럼을 편집자에게 보내는 자원봉사를 하고 있습니다. 또한 저는 최근에 귀사의 소프트웨어로 전환한 고객들에 대한 이야기를 쓰고 싶습니다. 독자들은 그들이 전환한 이유를 알게 되는 것이 흥미로울 것입니다. 관심이 있으시다면, 귀사의 마케팅 커뮤니케이션 담당자에게 제 이메일 주소나 전화번호를 알려주시기를 바랍니다. 편하신 시간에 답변해 주시기를 바랍니다.

Brian Adams 드림

정답풀이

지역 주간 컴퓨터 신문인 'The Web-Byter'에 곧 출시될 비디오 게임을 홍보하고 신규 전환한 고객에 관한 기사를 작성하고 싶으니 관심이 있으면 연락을 달라고 제안하는 내용의 글이므로, 글의 목적으로는 ⑤가 가장 적절하다.

구문풀이

14행 If you are interested, / please make my email address or phone number available to your marketing communications representative.

: 부사절과 명령문으로 이루어진 문장으로, 명령문은 「make+목적어+목적격보어」인 5형식 문장이다.

어휘풀이

- informative *a* 유익한
- publicize *v* 홍보하다
- volunteer *v* 자원봉사를 하다
- representative *n* 대행자, 대표자
- breathtaking *a* 멋진, 대단한
- forthcoming *a* 곧 출시되는
- column *n* 칼럼, (신문의) 기고(란)

278 답 ③

📖📖 **이사 온 새 집에 만족했다가 집 주변 소음을 알게 된 Susan**

전문해석

Susan이 새 집으로 이사 왔을 때, 그녀는 그것이 자신이 지금까지 원했던 전부임을 알았다. 그녀는 새 부엌, 그리고 뒤뜰에 정원을 가꾸기 시작할 충분한 공간이 있는 곳을 찾기 위해 여러 곳을 둘러보고 있었다. 첫 주는 흥미진진했다. Susan은 Byron Bay에 산다는 생각을 좋아했다. 오랫동안 그녀는 신선한 유기농 지역 농산물에 대한 손쉬운 접근은 말할 것도 없이 해변, 햇빛 가까이 살면서 생활방식이 얼마나 편안할 수 있는지에 대해 들어 왔다. 그러나 평온하게 살겠다는 Susan의 꿈은 거의 시작하자마자 산산조각이 났다. 그녀가 시끌벅적한 웃음소리, 유리잔이 쨍그랑하는 소리, 그리고 브라스 밴드의 연주처럼 들렸던 소리에 반복해서 잠에서 깼을 때 그녀는 새 집에 겨우 2주 정도 짧게 있었을 때였다. 자신의 집이 크고 시끄러운 호텔 결혼식장 바로 근처에 있다는 것을 알고 그녀는 가슴이 철렁 내려앉았다.

정답풀이

Susan은 새 집에 이사 와서 꿈꿔오던 평온하고 자연 친화적인 삶의 방식을 이룰 수 있을 것 같아 신이 났다가, 그녀의 집 인근에 있는 호텔의 결혼식장에서 나는 소음을 깨닫고 가슴이 내려앉았다고 했으므로, Susan의 심경 변화로는 ③ '기쁜 → 속상한'이 가장 적절하다.
① 자랑스러운 → 질투가 나는
② 지루한 → 신이 난
④ 좌절한 → 안심한
⑤ 화가 난 → 무관심한

구문풀이

14행 Her heart sank in her chest [when she realized {her house was right near a big, loud hotel wedding venue}].

: [ ]는 when이 이끄는 시간 부사절이고 그 안의 { }는 realized의 목적절로 앞에 접속사 that이 생략되어 있다.

어휘풀이

- backyard *n* 뒤뜰
- not to mention ~은 말할 것도 없이
- produce *n* 농산물
- repeatedly *ad* 반복해서
- clinking *n* 쨍그랑하는 소리
- brass band 브라스 밴드(금관악기들로 구성된 악단)
- sink *v* 내려앉다, 낙담하다
- relaxing *a* 편안한
- access *n* 접근, 이용
- shatter *v* 산산조각 나다
- roaring *a* 시끌벅적한
- venue *n* (경기·회담 등의) 장소

279 답 ④

📖📖 **상사가 효과적으로 부하 직원을 칭찬하는 방법**

전문해석

상사로부터의 칭찬은 직원이 칭찬이 진실하다고 믿는다면 훨씬 더 효과적이다. 의심할 여지없이, 많은 요소가 진실성을 결정할 수 있지만 두 가지가 특히 중요하다. **첫 번째는 칭찬이 주어지는 빈도와 관련이 있다.** 만약 상사가 계속해서 그들의 부하 직원을 칭찬한다면, 이 칭찬의 동기유발 가치는 시간이 지나면서 아마 줄어들 것이다. 반면, 칭찬이 매우 드물게 주어진다면, 부하 직원은 정말 칭찬을 받는 그 드문 경우를 매우 의심하게 될 것이다. 따라서 칭찬이 효과적이려면, 상사는 너무 많이 하는 것 또는 너무 적게 하는 것 사이의 균형을 잡아야 한다. **못지않게 중요한 관련된 문제는 칭찬을 받기 위해서 성취되어야 하는 성과의 수준이다.** 만약 상사가 평범한 성과에 대해서 부하 직원에게 아낌없는 칭찬을 듬뿍 한다면, 이것은 높은 수준의 성과가 실제로 이루어졌을 때 칭찬의 가치를 감소시킬 것이다.

정답풀이

상사가 부하 직원을 칭찬할 때 중요한 두 가지가 있는데, 첫 번째는 칭찬의 빈도이고 두 번째는 칭찬하는 성과의 수준이라고 했다. 칭찬을 너무 많이 또는 너무 드물게 하지 말고, 칭찬받을 만한 수준의 성과를 이루었을 때 칭찬을 하라고 했으므로, 필자가 주장하는 바로 가장 적절한 것은 ④이다.

구문풀이

12행 A related issue, [though no less important], is the level of performance [that must be achieved {in order to receive praise}].

: 첫 번째 [ ]는 양보의 부사절에서 접속사 though 다음에 it is가 생략된 형태로 볼 수 있다. 두 번째 [ ]는 문장의 보어인 the level of performance를 수식하는 관계절이며, { }는 부사구이다.

어휘풀이

- supervisor *n* 상사
- sincere *a* 진실된, 진정한
- undoubtedly *ad* 의심할 여지 없이, 확실히
- sincerity *n* 진실성
- frequency *n* 빈도
- motivational *a* 동기유발의
- rarely *ad* 드물게, 좀처럼 ~하지 않는
- strike a balance between ~ 사이에서 균형을 유지하다
- heap *v* ~을 듬뿍 주다, ~을 쌓아올리다
- ordinary *a* 평범한, 보통 수준의
- effective *a* 효과적인
- have to do with ~와 관련이 있다
- subordinate *n* 부하, 하급자
- diminish *v* 감소하다
- suspicious *a* 의심하는
- lavish *a* 아낌없는, 후한

280 답 ③

📖📖 **관객과 상호작용하는 연극**

전문해석

스크린을 볼 때 의사소통은 단지 한 방향으로만 흐르는데, TV 화면에서 당신의 안락의자로, 또는 대형 스크린에서 당신을 사로잡는 복합상영관의 당신의 좌석으로 말이다. 당신은 토마토를 화면에 던질 수 있지만 그것은 그 쇼를 전혀 바꾸지 않을 것이다. 관객은 볼 것인지 보지 않을 것인지의 두 개의 선택을 가지고 있다. 이것은 연극에서 보다 아주 다른 차원의 관객 참여를 가져온다. 예를 들어, 끝에 관객이 박수를 치는 영화를 마지막으로 본 것이 언제인가? 당신이 TV를 시청할 때, 당신은 거실에서 일어나서 박수를 치는가? 연기가 아무리 뛰어나고, 영화나 TV가 아무리 많이 당신에게 영향을 끼쳤더라도, 당신은 대개 박수를 치지 않는다. 왜? 연기자들이 당신의 소리를 들을 수 없기 때문이다. **당신과 그들 사이에는 의사소통이 없다.** 나이지리아의 서부 지역인 Yoruba에서는 TV가 'ero asoro maghese'라고 불리는데, 이는 '말을 하지만 반응을 받아들이지 않는 기계'를 의미한다. **반면에 연극은 반응을 받아들인다.** 요약하면, 연극에서의 연기는 <u>가장 완전한 형태의 연기이다.</u>

정답풀이

TV나 영화에서는 의사소통이 일방적이어서 반응을 받아들이지 못하는 반면, 연극에서는 관객과 배우가 상호작용을 한다는 의미에서 연극에서의 연기가 가장 완전한 형태의 연기라고 한 것이므로 밑줄 친 부분이 의미하는 바로 가장 적절한 것은 ③ '배우들과 관객들이 상연하는 내내 상호작용한다'이다.

① 무대에서 배우들은 실제로 다른 배우들을 쳐다보지 않는다
② 관객의 참여는 배우들에 의해 적극적으로 요청된다
④ 연기는 가면을 쓰는 것이라기보다는 가면을 벗는 것이다
⑤ 배우들은 즉흥적으로 하면서 그들의 캐릭터에 새로운 것을 더하는 것을 좋아한다

구문풀이

11행 [**No matter how brilliant** the acting], [**no matter how much** the film or television show affected you], / you don't usually applaud.

: 양보의 의미를 갖는 두 개의 [ ]로 표시한 부사절과 주절로 이루어진 문장으로 no matter는 의문사와 함께 쓰일 때, 접속사의 역할을 한다. 「no matter how+형용사/부사」는 '아무리 ~하더라도'의 의미다. 첫 번째 [ ]에서 주어인 the acting 다음에는 be동사 was가 생략되었는데 이때, 주어가 대명사이면 be동사를 생략하지 않는다.

어휘풀이

- easy chair 안락의자
- megaplex *n* 초대형 복합상영관
- applaud *v* 박수를 치다
- pure *a* 완전한, 순전한
- improvise *v* (노래·연설 등을) 즉석에서 짓다[하다]
- sticky *a* 들러붙는, (사람을) 사로잡는
- make for (특정 결과를) 가져오다
- brilliant *a* 탁월한, 눈부신
- actively *ad* 적극적으로, 활발히

281 답 ④

🔲🔲 시골 생활이 환경에 미치는 악영향

전문해석

우리는 많은 사람들이 자연과 가까이 살고 자급자족하는 것이 이상적으로 단순한 시골 생활 방식의 중요한 요소라는 것을 보아왔다. 하지만 David Owen이 〈Green Metropolis〉에서 주장하듯이 진실이 직관에 어긋날 때가 있다. **시골에서 산다는 것은 보통 단독주택을 의미하는데 이것은 일반적으로 더 작고 한 면을 제외한 모든 면이 다른 아파트로 둘러싸여 있는 도시 아파트보다 난방하는 데 훨씬 더 많은 에너지를 필요로 한다.** 그것은 또한 광범위한 대중교통이 있고 흔히 걷는 것이 운전보다 오히려 더 나은 대도시에서의 삶에 비해 보통 훨씬 더 많은 운전을 포함한다. 시골에서 자급자족하는 것의 일부가 여러분이 자른 나무로 집을 난방하는 것이라면 이것은 아마 가스로 난방하는 것보다 환경에 더 나쁠 것이다. 심지어 나무를 적절히 건조해서 미국 환경청이 승인한 형태의 효율적인 현대식 난로에서 태울 때조차도 나무를 태우는 것은 여전히 석유나 가스 화로로 가열하는 것보다 훨씬 많은 미세 입자 오염 물질을 발생시킬 것이다.

정답풀이

자연친화적일 것으로 생각되는 시골의 생활 방식이 난방에 에너지가 많이 들고 이동할 때 걷거나 대중교통을 이용할 수 없어서 많은 운전을 해야 하는 등 오히려 밀집된 도시의 삶보다 환경에 더 나쁜 영향을 준다는 내용의 글이다. 따라서 글의 요지로는 ④가 가장 적절하다.

구문풀이

5행 Living in the countryside usually means a detached house, [**which** takes a lot more energy to heat than a city apartment {**that** is typically more compact and surrounded on all sides but one by other apartments}].

: [ ]는 a detached house를 부연 설명하는 계속적 용법으로 쓰인 관계절이고, { }는 앞의 명사구 a city apartment를 수식하는 관계절이다.

어휘풀이

- self-sufficient *a* 자급자족하는
- rural *a* 시골의, 지방의
- counterintuitive *a* 반직관적인, 직관에 어긋나는
- component *n* 구성요소

- detached house 단독주택
- extensive *a* 광범위한
- preferable *a* 오히려 더 나은
- give off (냄새·열·빛 등을) 내다, 발하다
- fine-particle *n* 미세 입자
- compact *a* 작은, 소형의
- public transport 대중교통
- efficient *a* 효율적인

282 답 ④

🔲🔲 유전자 변형 식품[작물]이 가지는 환경적 이점

전문해석

유전자 변형 식품의 옹호자들은 일반적인 믿음과는 반대로 유전자 변형 식품이 그렇지 않은 식품보다 환경 피해를 덜 야기한다고 주장한다. 일부 작물들의 경우, 경작과 같은 물리적인 수단으로 잡초를 제거하는 것이 비용적 측면에서 효과적이지 않기 때문에 농부들은 잡초를 제거하기 위해 종종 여러 종류의 제초제를 대량으로 뿌릴 것인데, 이는 제초제가 작물이나 환경을 해치지 않도록 주의가 요구되는 시간이 오래 걸리고 비싼 과정이다. 하나의 아주 강력한 제초제에 내성을 가지도록 유전자 변형된 작물은 필요로 하는 제초제의 양을 줄임으로써 환경 피해를 막는 것을 도울 수 있을 것이다. 예를 들어, Monsanto사는 자사의 제초제인 Roundup에 의해서 영향을 받지 않도록 유전적으로 변형된 콩 변종을 만들었다. 농부는 여러 번 제초제를 사용하는 대신 단지 한 번 제초제를 사용하는 콩을 재배해서 생산비를 줄이고 땅에 살포된 제초제가 땅에 흐르게 되는 위험을 줄인다.

정답풀이

유전자 변형 식품이 환경 피해를 덜 야기한다는 주장이 있는데, 유전자 변형된 작물은 필요로 하는 제초제의 양을 줄임으로써 환경 피해를 막을 수 있기 때문이라고 했다. 따라서 글의 주제로 가장 적절한 것은 ④ '유전자 변형 식물의 환경적 이점'이다.

① 작물을 위한 최고의 제초제
② 제초제가 작물에 미치는 불리한 점들
③ 농약이 장기적으로 건강에 미치는 영향
⑤ 유전자 조작 식품의 잠재적인 건강 위험 요소

구문풀이

4행 For some crops, **it** is not cost-effective [**to remove** weeds by physical means such as tilling], so farmers will often spray large quantities of different herbicides to destroy weeds, [a time-consuming and expensive process {that requires care **so that** the herbicide doesn't harm the crop plant or the environment}].

: 첫 번째 [ ]는 가주어 it에 대한 진주어 역할을 하는 to부정사구이다. 두 번째 [ ]는 앞 절의 내용을 부연 설명하는 동격어구이며, 그 안의 { }는 a time-consuming and expensive process를 수식하는 관계절로, so that은 '~하도록'의 의미이다.

어휘풀이

- advocate *n* 옹호자
- counterpart *n* 대응물
- weed *n* 잡초
- herbicide *n* 제초제
- resistant *a* 저항하는
- application *n* 적용, 응용
- run-off *n* 흘러가 버리는 것
- contrary to ~와는 반대로
- crop *n* 농작물, 수확량
- till *v* 경작하다, (밭을) 갈다
- engineer *v* 유전자를 조작하다
- strain *n* 변종, 품종
- agricultural *a* 농업의
- pesticide *n* 농약, 살충제

283 답 ③

🔲🔲 소수가 다수의 마음을 바꾸는 방법

실제 생활은 영화 속 세계만큼 극적인 경우가 거의 없고 배심원실과 같은 상황에서 소수가 승리하는 경우는 거의 없다. 그럼에도 불구하고 소수가 때로는 다수를 변화시킨다. 소수의 성공은 관련된 개인의 행동 방식에 달려있다. **소수가 일관되고 융통성이 있으며 그들의 주장이 유의미하다면 그들은 결국 다수의 의견을 이길 수도 있다.** 이런 요소들 중 첫 번째로, 그 집단이 자신의 입장을 방어하고 옹호하는 일관성이 가장 중요하다. 이런 일관성은 소수집단 간에도 그리고 시간이 흘러도 유지되어야 한다. 만약 소수집단 구성원들이 자기들 간에 의견이 일치하고 계속 그렇게 한다면 그들은 다수가 자신의 가정을 의심해 보고 소수의 가정을 진지하게 고려하도록 설득할 수도 있을 것이다. 성공하기 위해서 소수집단에 속한 사람들은 완고하고 독단적이게 보여서는 안 되고 자신들의 접근에서 융통성이 있고 자기들이 다수의 의견에 동의하지 않는 이유를 기꺼이 토론해야 한다.

정답풀이

소수가 다수의 마음을 얻기 위한 방법에 대한 글로, 소수가 성공하기 위해서는 의견이 일관되며 지속적이고 유의미한 주장을 펼치되 독단적이게 보여서는 안된다고 했으므로 글의 제목으로는 ③ '어떻게 소수가 다수에게 영향을 미칠 수 있는가?'가 가장 적절하다.
① 태도가 전부인 것은 아니다!
② 다수결 제도로서의 민주주의
④ 실제 삶은 스크린에 나타나는 삶과 다르다
⑤ 정치 개혁이 소수 권리에 미친 영향

구문풀이

8행 The first of these factors, the consistency [**with which** the group defends and advocates its position], is the most crucial.

: 문장의 주어인 The first of these factors와 the consistency는 동격 관계이며, [ ]는 the consistency를 수식하는 관계절이다.

어휘풀이

- dramatic *a* 극적인
- minority *n* 소수, 소수집단
- win the day 이기다
- majority *n* 다수
- argument *n* 주장
- advocate *v* 옹호하다
- persuade *v* 설득하다
- assumption *n* 가정
- dogmatic *a* 독단적인
- cinematic *a* 영화의
- jury room 배심원실
- convert *v* 바꾸다
- consistent *a* 일관된
- relevant *a* 유의미한, 관련 있는
- crucial *a* 중요한
- question *v* 의심하다
- rigid *a* 완고한

284 답 ⑤

📖 직장에서 인공지능(AI)에 노출된 미국 노동자의 비율

전문해석

위 그래프는 2022년 직장에서 인공지능(AI)에 노출된 미국 노동자의 비율을 보여준다. 2022년에 거의 미국 노동자 5명 중 1명(19%)이 AI에 노출된 직종에 종사하고 있었다. 여성은 남성보다 4퍼센트 포인트 더 높은 비율로 직장에서 AI에 노출되었다. 백인 노동자는 흑인 노동자보다 5퍼센트 포인트 더 높은 노출 비율을 가지고 있었지만, 아메리칸 인디언 또는 태평양 섬 주민 노동자는 히스패닉 노동자보다 3퍼센트 포인트 더 높은 노출 비율을 가지고 있었다. 아시아계 노동자의 거의 4분의 1이 직장에서 AI에 노출되어 모든 인종 집단 중 가장 높은 AI 노출 수준을 보였다. 학사 학위 이상의 학력을 가진 노동자는 고등학교 졸업장만 가진 노동자에 비해 약 3배(→약 2배), 고등학교 졸업장이 없는 노동자들보다는 9배 이상 직업 내 AI 노출 수준이 높았다.

정답풀이

학사 학위 이상의 학력을 가진 노동자가 AI에 노출된 비율은 27%이고, 고등학교 졸업장만 가진 노동자의 노출 비율은 12%이므로, 학사 학위 이상의 학력을 가진 노동자는 고등학교 졸업장만 가진 노동자와 비교하여 두 배가 약간 넘는 수준이다. 따라서 약 3배라고 기술한 ⑤는 도표의 내용과 일치하지 않는다.

구문풀이

13행 Workers [with a bachelor's degree or higher] had about three times the AI exposure level in their professions compared to those [with only a high school diploma] and [nine times more than those without a high school diploma].

: 첫 번째와 두 번째 [ ]는 각각 앞에 있는 Workers와 those를 수식하는 전치사구이다. 세 번째 [ ] 앞에는 동일 어구의 반복을 피하기 위해 workers with a bachelor's degree or higher had가 생략되었다.

어휘풀이

- be exposed to ~에 노출되다
- bachelor's degree 학사 학위
- diploma *n* 졸업증

285 답 ③

📖 랭커셔를 세계 면화 산업의 중심지로 만드는 데 기여한 Richard Arkwright

전문해석

Richard Arkwright는 13명의 자녀들 중 막내였다. 그는 학교에 전혀 다니지 않았고 중년이 되어서야 비로소 읽고 쓰는 것을 배웠다. 10살의 나이에 그는 한 이발소에 일을 하도록 보내졌다. 거기서 일을 하는 동안에 그는 색이 바래지지 않게 머리를 염색하는 방법을 발견했으며, 부유하고 성공적인 이발사이자 가발 제조업자가 되었다. 하지만, Arkwright가 유명한 진짜 이유는 면화를 잣는 기계인 '정방기'를 그가 발명한 것이다. **그는 숙련된 시계 기술자인 John Kay의 도움을 받아 그것을 만들었다.** Arkwright는 더 나아가 직물 제조에 사용되는 다른 기계들을 발명하고 향상시켰다. 많은 노동자들은 자신들의 일을 새로운 기계가 떠맡는 것을 알게 되었다. 그들은 매우 화가 났고 그래서 기계를 파괴하고 심지어 Arkwright를 위협하기도 했다. 그러나 그는 단호한 사람이었고 그의 공장들은 그의 고향 지역인 랭커셔가 세계 면화 산업의 중심지가 되는 데 도움을 주었다.

정답풀이

Arkwright는 John Kay의 도움을 받아 면화를 잣는 기계인 정방기를 발명했다고 했으므로, John Kay의 정방기 발명을 도왔다는 ③은 글의 내용과 일치하지 않는다.

구문풀이

15행 But he was a determined man / and his factories **helped** his home county of Lancashire **become** the centre of the world's cotton industry.

: 두 개의 절이 and로 연결되어 있으며, 두 번째 절에는 helped가 쓰여 목적격보어 자리에 원형부정사 become이 사용되었다. 이때, to become을 써도 되며, 둘 사이의 의미 차이는 없다.

어휘풀이

- dye *v* 염색하다
- wigmaker *n* 가발 제작업자
- invention *n* 발명
- watchmaker *n* 시계 기술자
- determined *a* 단호한
- fade *v* 색이 바래다
- claim to fame 유명한 이유
- spin *v* (실을) 잣다
- textile *n* 직물

286 답 ⑤

📖 **2024 춘계 직업 박람회 안내**

전문해석

2024년 춘계 직업 박람회

2024년 4월 6일 토요일

오후 2시 ~ 오후 6시

Bayshore 지역 문화회관

작년의 취업 박람회는 80명 이상의 고용주와 1,000명 이상의 구직자가 참여한 것으로 이 지역에서 개최된 것 중 가장 규모가 컸습니다. 올해, 우리는 모든 참석자들을 위한 충분한 공간을 갖춘 훨씬 더 큰 장소로 옮겨갈 것입니다.

고용주를 위한 향상된 서비스
• 테이블이 있는 가로 세로 5미터의 부스
• 무료 와이파이
• 탁 트인 공간과 인터뷰 공간
• 고용주 전용 라운지와 다과

등록 비용은 50달러이며, 그것이 올해의 행사를 위해 제공되는 향상된 이벤트와 서비스를 충당하는 데 도움이 될 것입니다.

지금 등록하세요! (여기를 클릭하세요)

이 직업 박람회는 Grey 카운티, Georgian 대학 및 4개 카운티 노동 시장 계획 위원회의 후원을 받는 협력 행사입니다.

더 많은 정보를 원하시면, P_Kalina@jobfair.org로 Peter Kalina에게 이메일을 보내시거나 541-2345-4321로 전화주세요.

정답풀이

Grey 카운티, Georgian 대학 및 4개 카운티 노동 시장 계획 위원회가 후원하는 행사라고 했으므로 지역 대학에서 단독 후원하는 행사라는 ⑤는 안내문의 내용과 일치하지 않는다.

구문풀이

5행 Last year's Job Fair was the largest [ever held in this area] [with more than 80 employers and over 1,000 job seekers].

: the largest의 최상급 표현이 두 개의 [ ]의 수식을 받고 있으며, 첫 번째 [ ]는 과거분사구이고, 두 번째 [ ]는 전치사구이다. 이때, the largest 다음에는 반복되는 앞에 나온 명사구 job fair가 생략된 것으로 볼 수 있다.

어휘풀이
• fair *n* 박람회
• attendee *n* 참석자
• offset *v* 상쇄하다, 벌충하다
• support *v* 후원하다
• job seeker 구직자
• refreshments *n* 다과
• collaborative *a* 협력의

---

287 답 ④

📖 **George 호수에서의 자전거 대여**

전문해석

George 호수 자전거 대여

멋지고 편안한 휴가를 위해 오셨건 George 호수가 제공하는 모든 것을 적극적으로 발견하기를 원하셨건 간에 자전거로 지역을 경험하는 것보다

더 좋은 방법은 없습니다. 여러분은 저희 대여 가게 중 한 곳에서 저렴한 가격에 자전거를 빌리실 수 있습니다.

대여 가게 운영 시간
– 오전 9시 ~ 오후 6시 (3월~10월)
– 모든 자전거는 오후 5시 45분까지 반납해야 합니다.

대여료
– 일반 자전거: 시간당 5달러, 하루에 20달러
– 트레일러가 부착된 자전거: 시간당 10달러, 하루에 30달러
– 헬멧 대여료는 자전거 대여료에 포함되어 있습니다.

안전 점검
– 자전거 탑승자들은 포장된 자전거용 도로에서만 타야 합니다.
– 모든 자전거 탑승자는 헬멧을 착용해야 합니다.
– 자전거를 빌린 사람만 그것을 타도록 허용됩니다.
– 트레일러당 아이 한 명만 가능

예약은 필요 없습니다.
선착순 원칙입니다.

정답풀이

자전거 탑승자들은 포장된 자전거용 도로에서만 타야 한다고 했으므로 ④가 안내문의 내용과 일치한다.

오답풀이
① 3월부터 10월까지 하루 9시간 영업을 한다.
② 트레일러가 부착된 자전거의 대여료는 시간당 10달러이다.
③ 헬멧 대여 비용은 자전거 대여료에 포함되어 있다.
⑤ 예약은 필요 없고 선착순이다.

구문풀이

2행 **Whether** you [have come for a nice relaxing vacation] or [want to actively discover all {Lake George has to offer}], / there is no better way to experience the area than on a bike.

: 접속사 Whether(~이든)가 이끄는 부사절과 주절로 이루어진 문장이다. [ ]로 표시한 두 동사구는 or로 연결되어 병렬구조를 이룬다. { }는 목적격 관계대명사 that이 생략된 관계절로 앞의 all을 수식한다.

어휘풀이
• operating hours 운영 시간
• attach *v* 부착하다
• paved *a* 포장된
• return *v* 반납하다
• include *v* 포함하다
• first-come, first-served 선착순

---

288 답 ③

📖 **열역학 제2법칙인 에너지 점감 원칙**

전문해석

열역학의 제2법칙은 유효 에너지가 하나의 상태에서 다른 상태로 전환될 때마다, 항상 첫 번째 상태에 있던 것보다 두 번째 상태에 이용 가능한 유효 에너지가 더 적다고 명시한다. 예를 들어 백열전구의 경우에, 전기 에너지는 쓸모없는 얼마간의 열에너지 뿐만 아니라 '유효' 빛 에너지로도 전환되는데, 이것(쓸모없는 얼마간의 열에너지)은 여러분이 몇 분간 켜져 있는 전구를 만져 봄으로써 알아차릴 수 있다. 백열광의 경우에는 대략 5퍼센트의 전기 에너지가 빛이 되고 95퍼센트가 열이 되어, 에너

지 효율성은 5퍼센트이다. 마찬가지로, 자동차를 움직이는 일을 하는 데 사용된 화석 연료 에너지는 '냉각 시스템'을 통해 흩뜨려져야만 하고 그렇지 않으면 모터를 망칠 상당한 양의 쓸모없는 열을 발생시킨다. 그러므로 어떤 에너지의 변환에서도 에너지의 질(유효 에너지)이라는 면에서 이용 가능한 에너지의 분명한 손실이 있다. 이 현상은 에너지 점감 원칙이라 일컬어지며, 보편적으로 적용될 수 있다.

정답풀이
③ 문장의 구조 파악: the fossil fuel energy가 문장의 주어이고, used to do the work of moving an automobile은 주어를 수식하는 분사구이다. a substantial amount of useless heat이 목적어, 그리고 그 뒤의 that 이하가 목적어를 수식하는 관계절이다. 따라서 generating을 generates로 바꾸어 문장의 동사 역할을 하도록 해야 한다.

오답풀이
① 비교급: 앞에 비교급 형용사 lesser가 쓰였으므로 than을 써서 비교급 구문을 구성한 것은 적절하다.
② 관계대명사: some useless heat를 선행사로 하는 목적격 관계대명사이므로 적절하다.
④ 한정사: 긍정문에 쓰여 '어떤 ~이라도'의 뜻을 나타내고 있으므로 적절하다.
⑤ 수동태: 「refer to A as B(A를 B라고 일컫다)」 구문에서 A를 주어로 하여 수동태로 전환된 형태로, This phenomenon이 refer to가 나타내는 동작의 주체가 아니라 대상이다.

구문풀이
5행 For example, [**in the case of** an incandescent light bulb], electrical energy **is converted to** ['useful' light energy] **as well as** [some useless heat], [**which** you can detect by touching a light bulb {**that** has been turned on for a few minutes}].

: 첫 번째 [ ]는 '~의 경우에'의 의미인 부사구이다. 주절에는 「convert A to B(A를 B로 전환하다)」 구문이 A를 주어로 하여 수동태로 전환되었는데, B에 해당하는 두 번째와 세 번째 [ ]가 as well as로 연결되었다. which가 이끄는 계속적 용법의 관계절인 네 번째 [ ]는 some useless heat에 대한 부가적인 설명을 위해 쓰였고, that이 이끄는 관계절인 { }는 a light bulb를 수식하고 있다.

어휘풀이
- convert *v* 전환하다
- detect *v* 탐지하다
- substantial *a* 상당한
- transformation *n* 변환
- phenomenon *n* 현상
- energy degradation 에너지 점감[열화]
- applicable *a* 적용할 수 있는
- incandescent light bulb 백열전구
- approximately *ad* 대략
- dissipate *v* 흩뜨리다
- apparent *a* 분명한
- refer to A as B A를 B라고 일컫다

289 답 ④

📖 진화 지향적 측면에서 바라본 비만의 기원

전문해석
진화 지향적인 연구원들은 비만의 만연이 극적으로 증가한 것에 대한 그럴듯한 설명을 가지고 있다. 그들은 역사의 과정 내내 대부분의 동물과 인간이 제한되고 불확실한 식량 자원에 대한 치열한 경쟁이 있고 굶주림이 매우 실제적인 위협이 되는 환경에서 살았다는 것을 지적한다. 그 결과, 식량을 찾는 온혈동물들은 기회가 나타났을 때 후에 식량이 이용 가능하지 않을 수도 있으므로 즉각적으로 필요한 것보다 더 많은 식량을 소비하는 성향을 진화시켰다. 초과 칼로리는 식량 부족에 대비하여 체내에 저장되었고, 몸에 여분의 지방을 보유한다는 것은 실제로 매력 없는(→ 매력적인) 것으로 여겨졌다. 먹는 것에 대한 이러한 접근방식은 예측 불가능한 식량 공급의 성쇠와 끊임없이 싸워야 하는 대부분의 동물 종들에게 여전히 적응성이 있는 채로 남아 있다.

정답풀이
④ 진화 지향적 연구에서 볼 때 비만은 환경에 대한 적응의 한 형태라는 내용이다. 식량 확보가 보장되지 않는 상황에서 기회가 있을 때 초과 칼로리를 저장해 여분의 지방을 보유하는 것은 생존을 위해 바람직하므로 '매력적인' 것으로 여겨졌을 것이다. 따라서 unappealing(매력 없는)은 appealing(매력적인)으로 바꿔야 한다.

오답풀이
① 글 전체의 내용을 종합해 볼 때 진화적 측면에서 비만의 '만연(prevalence)'이 증가한 것을 설명하는 내용이다.
② 불확실한 식량 자원에 대한 치열한 경쟁이 있다고 했으므로, '굶주림(starvation)'이 위협이 되는 환경이었을 것이다.
③ 나중에 식량이 없을 수도 있다고 하였으므로 식량을 찾는 동물이 기회가 생겼을 때 필요한 것보다 더 많이 '소비할(consume)' 것이다.
⑤ 식량이 부족할 때를 대비해서 초과 칼로리를 저장했다고 했으므로, 식량 공급은 '예측 불가능한(unpredictable)' 것일 것이다.

구문풀이
3행 They point out [that over the course of history, most animals and humans have lived in environments {**in which** there was fierce competition for limited, unreliable food resources and starvation was a very real threat}].

: [ ]는 문장의 동사인 point out의 목적어 역할을 하는 명사절이고, 그 안의 { }는 environments를 수식하는 관계절이다.

어휘풀이
- plausible *a* 그럴듯한
- obesity *n* 비만
- foraging *a* 먹이를 찾는, 수렵 채집의
- adaptive *a* 적응성이 있는
- the ebb and flow 성쇠
- prevalence *n* 만연, 창궐
- starvation *n* 기아, 굶주림
- shortage *n* 부족
- struggle *v* 싸우다, 고투하다
- unpredictable *a* 예측 불가능한

290 답 ①

📖 교사가 채점에 사용해야 하는 지표의 종류

전문해석
성장 마음가짐을 가진 교사는 학생들이 학업적으로 성장하기 위해 열심히 공부하거나 노력하도록 격려한다. 그 격려는 성공에 있어 노력이 중요한 역할을 한다는 점에서 충분히 근거가 있다. 그러나 성적과 관련해서는 어휘를 조금 바꿔야 한다. 노력을 정확하게 관찰하는 것은 불가능하며, 관찰할 수 없는 것을 채점할 수도 없다(채점하려고 시도해서는 안 된다). 그래서 '노력'에서 '과정'으로 어휘의 전환이 필요하다. 우리는 학생이 과제물의 질을 개선하기 위해 기꺼이 수정하는 것을 관찰할 수 있다. 우리는 학생이 작업의 어떤 측면에서 막혔을 때 도움을 구하는 것을 관찰할 수 있다. 우리는 학생이 복잡한 과제를 완료하기 위한 시간표를 세우고 이를 고수하는 것을 관찰할 수 있다. 이러한 종류의 '마음과 일의 습관'은 성공한 사람들과 관련된 일종의 '지적인 과정'을 나타내는 지표이다. 좋은 채점 관행을 위해서는 눈에 보이는 지표를 사용해야 한다.

정답풀이
교사가 성적을 매길 때는 관찰할 수 있는, 즉 눈으로 확인할 수 있는 과정을 대상으로 삼아야 한다는 내용이므로 교사가 사용할 지표로서 빈칸에는 ① '눈에 보이는'이 들어가는 것이 가장 적절하다.
② 상호의
③ 기술의
④ 학문의
⑤ 질적인

1행 Teachers [with a growth mind-set] **encourage** students **to work** hard, or **to make** an effort, / in order to grow academically.

: [ ]는 문장의 주어인 Teachers를 수식하는 전치사구이다. 동사구에는 「encourage +목적어+to부정사」 구문이 쓰여 '~가 …하도록 격려하다'의 의미를 나타내며, to work와 to make는 병렬구조이다. 「in order+to부정사」는 목적의 의미를 나타내는 to부정사구이다.

14행 Those sorts of "habits of mind and work" are indicators of the sorts of "intelligent processes" [**that** are associated with successful people].

: [ ]는 주격 관계대명사 that이 이끄는 관계절로 앞에 나온 "intelligent processes"를 수식한다.

어휘풀이

- mind-set *n* 마음가짐, 정신 자세
- in terms of ~ 면에서
- shift *v* 바꾸다, 전환하다 *n* 전환
- be stuck 막히다
- indicator *n* 지표
- found *v* ~의 기반을 두다
- critical *a* 중요한
- revise *v* 수정하다
- adhere to ~을 고수하다

291 답 ①

📖 꾸준하게 인내하고 훈련하는 사람에게 오는 승리

전문해석

Napoleon이 말했듯이, 승리는 가장 많이 참는 사람의 것이다. 대부분의 사람들은 가치 있는 것을 성취하기 위해서 드는 시간을 과소평가하는 경향이 있지만 성공하기 위해서 여러분은 요금을 기꺼이 지불해야 한다. James Watt는 20년을 그의 증기 기관을 완성하기 위해 애쓰면서 보냈다. William Harvay는 혈액이 인간의 몸에서 어떻게 순환되는가를 증명하려고 8년 동안 밤낮 노력을 하였다. 그리고 의학계가 그가 옳았다는 것을 인정하는 데 또 다른 25년이 걸렸다. 과정을 생략하는 것은 조바심과 부족한 자기 훈련의 증후이다. 그렇지만 여러분이 시작한 일을 다 끝내려고 한다면, 여러분은 획기적인 성공을 거둘 것이다. 그런 이유로 Albert Gray는 "성공의 공통 분모는 실패자들이 하려고 하지 않는 일을 하는 습관을 형성하는 데 있다"고 말한다. 자기 훈련은 연습을 통해서 얻어지는 특질이다. 심리학자 Joseph Mancusi는 "진정으로 성공하는 사람들은 자연적으로 오지 않는 것을 하는 것을 배웠다. 진정한 성공은 두려움 또는 반감을 경험하고 그럼에도 불구하고 행동하는 데 있다"고 말했다.

정답풀이

성공한 사람들의 공통된 특징은 강한 자기 훈련으로 오랜 시간이 걸리더라도 성공할 때까지 꾸준하게 노력한 것이라는 것을, 빈칸 뒤에서 증기 기관을 발명한 James Watt, 혈액의 순환을 증명한 William Harvey 등의 여러 예시를 들어 설명하고 있다. 따라서 빈칸에 들어갈 말로 가장 적절한 것은 ① '가장 많이 참는 사람의 것이다'이다.

② 열렬히 갈망할 때 온다
③ 강함, 지혜, 기술을 필요로 한다
④ 기회와 가능성의 산물이다
⑤ 도달이 아니라 과정에 있다

구문풀이

2행 Most people tend to underestimate the time [it takes to achieve something of value], / but {to be successful}, you have to **be willing to pay** your dues.

: 두 개의 절이 접속사 but으로 연결되었다. 첫 번째 절에서 [ ]는 the time을 수식하는, 목적격 관계대명사가 생략된 관계절이다. 두 번째 절에서 { }는 부사적 용법으로 사용된

to부정사구로, '~하기 위해서'로 해석하며, 뒤의 주절 동사에 쓰인 「be willing+to부정사」는 '기꺼이 ~하다'의 의미이다.

어휘풀이

- underestimate *v* 과소평가하다
- labor *v* 일하다, 애쓰다
- the medical profession 의료계, 의료업
- acknowledge *v* 인정하다
- cut corners (일을 쉽게 하려고) 절차를 무시하다, 과정을 생략하다
- self-discipline *n* 자기 훈련, 자기 통제
- follow through (이미 시작한 일을) 다 끝내다
- breakthrough *n* 획기적인 성공, 큰 발전
- aversion *n* 혐오, 반감
- eagerly *ad* 열망하여
- dues *n* 부과금, 요금
- circulate *v* 돌다, 순환하다
- persevere *v* 참다, 견디다
- attainment *n* 성취, 도달

292 답 ①

📖 모호함을 피하기 위한 추가 맥락의 제시

전문해석

모호한 진술에서조차 ('일'의 다양한 의미에서와 같이) 각 단어는 명확하면서도 별개의 뜻을 갖고 있다. 우리는 어떤 의미를 의도된 것으로 받아들여야 하는지 알지 못할 뿐이다. 예를 들어 '회계 감사관의 일이 끝났다'라는 예문에서, 화자는 전체적인 회계 감사가 완료되었다는 것 또는 회계 감사관이 그날의 일을 끝내고 귀가할 것이라는 것을 의미할 수 있다. 여기서 '일'과 '끝났다' 둘 다 명료화되어야 한다. 화자가 "회계 감사관의 회계 기록에 대한 오늘의 검토가 끝났다"라고 말했다면 잠재적인 혼동은 제거될 것이다. 의미의 모호함은 어의적 모호함이라 불리는데 모호한 단어나 구 대신 모호하지 않은 단어나 구를 씀으로써 피할 수 있다. 또는 어의적 모호함은 오직 한 가지 해석만을 가능하게 하는 명료한 정보를 제공함으로써 잘 설명될 수 있다. 예를 들어 우리는 "회계 감사관의 일이 끝났다. 그는 다음해까지 돌아올 필요가 없다."라고 말함으로써 모호함을 피할 수 있다. 이와 같이, 추가적인 맥락은 모호함을 피한다.

정답풀이

명확하면서도 별개의 뜻을 가진 단어들도 맥락에 따라 여러 가지 의미로 받아들여질 수 있으므로 이러한 모호함을 피하기 위해서는 맥락을 알려주는 정보를 추가적으로 제공할 필요가 있다는 내용이다. 따라서 빈칸에 들어갈 말로 가장 적절한 것은 ① '추가적인 맥락은 모호함을 피한다'이다.

② 은유는 애매모호한 것을 분명히 하기 위해 사용된다
③ 모호한 단어들은 이해를 늦춘다
④ 모호한 진술은 명료하게 진술될 수 없다
⑤ 단어를 단순화하는 것은 흔히 모호함을 제거하는 데 실패한다

구문풀이

4행 For example, [in {the sample sentence}, {"The auditor's work is done,"}] the speaker could <u>mean</u> [that {the entire audit has been completed} or {the auditor is done for the day and is going home}].

: 첫 번째 [ ]는 전치사구로, 그 안에 두 개의 { }는 동격 관계이다. 두 번째 [ ]는 mean의 목적어인 명사절인데, 그 안에 { }로 표시된 두 개의 등위절이 or로 연결되어 있다.

어휘풀이

- ambiguous *a* 모호한, 불명료한
- distinct *a* 별개의, 뚜렷한
- clarify *v* 명료화하다
- potential *a* 잠재적인
- ambiguity *n* 모호함
- substitute A for B B 대신 A를 쓰다
- statement *n* 진술, 말
- audit *n* 회계 감사
- accounting *n* 회계
- confusion *n* 혼란
- explain away ~을 잘 해명하다

- interpretation *n* 해석
- comprehension *n* 이해(도)
- metaphor *n* 은유(법)

293 답 ②

📖 프랑스 혁명의 파괴적 성격

전문해석

감정에 기반을 둔 개혁이, 특히 그 개혁이 사회를 뒷받침하는 전통과 제도를 공격할 때, 얼마나 사회의 건강에 위험한지에 대한 아주 좋은 실례는 프랑스 혁명에서 발견될 수 있다. **완전히 새로운 질서를 창조하려는 시도에서, 프랑스의 혁명가들은 무력과 테러를 통해 모든 사회적, 정치적 제도를 파괴하기를 추구했다.** 전통적인 가족 제도, 재산에 대한 권리, 그리고 종교적 권위를 훼손하면서, 혁명은 사회의 과거와 사회적 전통을 파괴하고, 상속되어 온 프랑스 문명의 근간, 즉 예술, 도덕적 관념, 과학, 이성을 공격함으로써 사회를 개조하려고 노력하였다. 그 결과는 대량 학살과 권위의 완전한 붕괴였고, Napoleon Bonaparte의 독재로 정점에 이르렀다. 보다 제한적이었던 미국 독립 혁명과 달리, 프랑스 혁명은 <u>과거로부터의 파괴적 단절이라는 특징을 보였다.</u>

정답풀이

혁명가들은 완전히 새로운 질서를 창조하기 위해 무력과 테러를 통해 모든 사회적 정치적 제도를 파괴하고자 했고, 이어지는 내용에서 기존의 것들을 훼손하며, 과거를 파괴하고 전통적 프랑스 문명의 근간들을 공격하여 사회를 개조하려고 했다고 했다. 이러한 내용을 토대로 프랑스 혁명은 기존의 모든 것을 파괴하며 이루어졌음을 알 수 있으므로, 빈칸에는 ② '과거로부터의 파괴적 단절이라는 특징을 보였다'가 들어가는 것이 가장 적절하다.

① 이성적이고 신뢰할 수 있는 지도자들이 이끌었다
③ 자유와 질서 사이의 균형을 가져왔다
④ 더 큰 독립과 민주주의를 허용했다
⑤ 오래된 권위의 놀랄 만한 생존으로 이어졌다

구문풀이

8행 [**Undermining** the traditional family, the right to property, and religious authority], the Revolution tried to refashion society [**by destroying** its past and its social traditions], and [**by attacking** the inherited foundations of French civilization — its art, moral ideas, science, and reason].

: 첫 번째 [ ]는 '~하면서'라는 동시동작을 나타내는 분사구문인데, 여기에 밑줄 친 세 개의 명사구가 「A, B, and C」의 구조로 연결되어 Undermining의 목적어 역할을 하고 있다. 두 번째와 세 번째 [ ]는 전치사구로, 「by -ing」는 '~함으로써'의 뜻을 나타낸다.

어휘풀이

- prime *a* 아주 좋은[적절한]
- reform *n* 개혁
- revolutionary *n* 혁명가
- property *n* 재산, 부동산
- refashion *v* 개조하다
- foundation *n* 근간, 토대
- mass murder 대량 학살
- culminate *v* 정점을 이루다
- the American Revolution 미국 독립 혁명
- credible *a* 신뢰할 수 있는
- democracy *n* 민주주의
- illustration *n* 실례
- institution *n* 제도
- undermine *v* 훼손하다
- authority *n* 권위
- inherit *v* 상속하다
- reason *n* 이성, 사고력
- breakdown *n* 붕괴, 와해
- dictatorship *n* 독재
- independence *n* 독립

294 답 ④

📖 이슬람 세계에서의 천문학의 발달

전문해석

이슬람 세계에서 부족들과 민족들은 별을 연구하는 자신들만의 오랜 역사를 갖고 있다. 처음에 이것은 부분적으로는 그들이 사는 사막을 건너기 위한 것이었는데, 그곳은 땅에는 주요 지형지물이 거의 없지만 맑고 별이 많은 하늘에는 머리 위로 셀 수 없이 많은 표시가 있었다. 그러나 나중에 그것은 이슬람의 기도 시간을 위한 정확한 시간과 향할 방향을 판단하기 위한 것이었다. 이슬람 학자들은 고대 그리스의 저술들을 번역했고 자기들만의 달력과 별자리표를 만들기 위해 그들의 생각과 도구를 응용했다. (이슬람과 비이슬람 집단 간의 정치적 갈등은 특정한 문명 또는 사회와 다른 집단의 상호 작용에 영향을 미쳤다.) Abd Allah Muhammad Ibn Jabir Sinan al-Battani와 같은 학자들은 점성술에 관한 많은 중요한 작품을 쓰고 고쳐썼고 점을 치는 데 사용된 점성술과 '하늘' 그 자체에 대한 순수하고 정확한 연구로서의 천문학 사이의 차이점을 끌어내기 시작했다.

정답풀이

이슬람 세계에 별을 연구하는 자신들만의 오랜 역사가 있다는 내용이다. 따라서 이슬람과 비이슬람 간의 정치적 갈등이 집단 간의 상호 교류에 영향을 미쳤다는 ④는 글의 흐름과 무관하다.

구문풀이

13행 Scholars [like Abd Allah Muhammad Ibn Jabir Sinan al-Battani] <u>wrote and rewrote</u> many important works on astrology, and <u>started</u> to draw out the **differences between** [astrology, {used for fortune-telling}], **and** [astronomy {as a pure and accurate study of 'the heavens' for its own sake}].

: 첫 번째 [ ]는 문장의 주어인 Scholars를 수식하는 전치사구이며, 두 개의 동사구 wrote and rewrote ~와 started ~가 and로 연결된 술부이다. 「difference between A and B」는 'A와 B의 차이'라는 의미이고, 첫 번째 { }는 astrology를 수식하는 과거분사구, 두 번째 { }는 astronomy를 수식하는 전치사구이다.

어휘풀이

- tribe *n* 부족
- navigate *v* (장소를) 지나다, 통과하다
- countless *a* 셀 수 없이 많은
- translate *v* 번역하다
- star-chart *n* 별자리표
- interaction *n* 상호 작용
- fortune-telling *n* 점치기
- for its own sake 그 자체를 위해
- stargazing *n* 별 연구하기
- landmark *n* 주요 지형지물
- prayer *n* 기도
- adapt *v* 응용하다
- conflict *n* 갈등
- astrology *n* 점성술
- astronomy *n* 천문학

295 답 ③

📖 텍스트나 비텍스트적인 창작과 문화적 경험이 청중에게 수용되는 현상의 연구

전문해석

청중에 초점을 맞춘 접근법과 관련된 용어는 '수용'이다. 수용에 대한 연구는 텍스트, 문화적 대상 또는 경험이 특정 청중에 의해 어떻게 받아들여지는지에 초점을 맞춘다. (B) 수용 연구는 작가와 텍스트 사이의 관계에 초점을 맞추기보다는 **텍스트와 청중 사이의 관계를 살펴본다. 수용 접근법은 비텍스트적인 미학적 창작과 문화적 경험에도 적용된다.** (C) 누군가가 텍스트를 읽을 때 어떤 일이 일어나는지 우리가 고려하는 것과 꼭 마찬가지로, 우리는 누군가가 그림을 보거나 영화를 볼 때, 또는 누군가가 한 곡의 음악을 들을 때도 어떤 일이 일어나는지 물어볼 수 있다. 종교적인 텍스트, 이미지, 건축 그리고 의식은 모두 이런 방식으로 '읽힐' 수 있다. (A) 이러한 종류의 접근 방식은 다른 청중들이 다른 방식으로 동일한 미학적 경험을 읽거나 받

아들인다고 인식한다. 이러한 것들이 원래의 청중들에게 무엇을 의미했을지에 대한 질문과 함께, 우리는 오늘날 그것들을 '읽는' 사람들에게 그것들이 무엇을 의미하는지 탐구할 수 있다.

정답풀이

텍스트나 비텍스트적인 창작과 문화적 경험이 청중에게 수용되는 현상의 연구에 관한 글로, 주어진 글에서 언급된 수용 접근법을 보다 구체적으로 설명하면서 그것이 작가와 텍스트의 관계보다는 텍스트와 청중의 관계에 집중하며 나아가 비텍스트적인 미학적 창작과 문화적 경험에도 적용된다는 것을 언급하는 (B)가 가장 먼저 온다. 그리고 비텍스트와 관련해 보다 구체적으로 그림, 영화, 음악, 종교적인 텍스트나 의식, 건축 등의 예를 들어 설명하는 (C)가 온 후, 앞에서 설명한 접근 방식이 어떤 의미를 가지며 어떠한 탐구에 도움이 되는지 설명한 (A)가 마지막에 오는 순서가 가장 적절하다.

구문풀이

7행 Alongside the question of [what these things may have meant to the original audiences], we can explore [what they mean to those {who "read" them today}].

: 첫 번째 [ ]는 of의 목적어 역할을 하는 명사절이고, 두 번째 [ ]는 explore의 목적어 역할을 하는 명사절이다. { }는 앞의 those를 수식하는 관계절이다.

어휘풀이

- term *n* 용어
- focus on ~에 초점을 맞추다
- esthetic *a* 미학적인
- author *n* 작가, 저자
- gaze *v* 응시하다
- architecture *n* 건축(술)
- reception *n* 수용
- recognize *v* 인식하다
- explore *v* 탐구하다
- non-textual *a* 비텍스트적인
- religious *a* 종교적인
- ritual *n* 의식

296 답 ②

📖📖 동물 실험이 의학적 치료법 발전에 기여했다는 주장에 대한 반박

전문해석

논증 없이 실험실 동물에 대한 연구 결과가 인간에게 확대 적용할 수 있다고 그저 가정하는 것은 잘못된 정보를 주는 것이기는 하지만, 많은 동물 실험 옹호자들은 바로 그렇게 하는 것으로 보인다. 그들이 그 관행을 정말 옹호할 때 그들은 일반적으로 실험 성공 사례들을 언급함으로써 그렇게 한다. (B) 예를 들어, 'Ben Franklin and Open Heart Surgery'라는 이제는 고전이 된 1974년의 논문을 고려해 보라. 이 논문은 아마도 동물 실험이 새로운 의학적 치료법 개발에서 얼마나 널리 퍼져 있고 얼마나 중요했는지 보여줄 뿐이었다. 논문 저자들은 이런 주장을 뒷받침할 때 어떤 증거를 제공했는가? (A) 기본적으로 그들은 그저 자신들의 권위를 근거로 동물 실험이 다양한 생체 의학적 발견에 중요했다고 말했을 뿐이었다. 그들이 제공한 증거는 그저 역사적일 뿐이었는데, 특정 생체 의학적 발견이 있기 전에 일부 동물 실험의 존재는 그 실험이 그 발견의 원인이었음을 보여준다고 전해졌다. (C) 하지만 전자가 후자를 유발했다고 우리가 주장하기 전에 더 많이 주의해야 한다. 사례들이 상관관계를 이룰지는 모르지만, 상관관계와 원인 사이에는 커다란 간극이 있다. 그리고 이것은 특히 동물 실험에 대해 그렇다.

정답풀이

동물 실험 옹호자들이 동물 실험 결과가 인간에게 확대 적용할 수 있다고 주장한다는 주어진 글 다음에는, 그 사례로 'Ben Franklin and Open Heart Surgery'를 들며 그것은 동물 실험이 의학적 치료법 개발에서 중요했다는 것뿐 증거가 불충분하다는 내용의 (B)가 온다. 그리고 (B)의 마지막에 언급된 논문 저자들을 they라고 칭하며 증거는 의학적 발견 이전에 어떤 동물 실험이 있었음을 보여줄 뿐이었다는 내용의 (A)가 오고 마지막으로 어떤 일이 앞

서 있었다는 것이 뒤에 일어난 일과 상관관계가 있을 수는 있지만 그것이 반드시 인과 관계인 것은 아니라는 내용의 (C)가 오는 순서가 가장 적절하다.

구문풀이

1행 Although **it** is misleading simply [**to assume**, without argumentation, {that findings on laboratory animals are extrapolable to humans}], / many defenders of animal experimentation appear to do just that.

: 부사절과 주절로 이루어진 문장으로, Although가 이끄는 부사절에서 it은 가주어이고 to부정사구인 [ ]가 진주어이다. { }는 assume의 목적어 역할을 한다.

어휘풀이

- misleading *a* 잘못된 정보를 주는
- findings *n* 연구 결과
- experimentation *n* 실험
- typically *ad* 일반적으로, 보통
- state *v* 말하다
- crucial *a* 중요한
- presumably *ad* 추정되기를, 아마
- medical treatment 의학적 치료법
- gulf *n* 간극, 틈
- argumentation *n* 논증
- defender *n* 옹호자
- practice *n* 관행
- cite *v* 언급하다
- authority *n* 권위
- biomedical *a* 생체 의학적
- pervasive *a* 널리 퍼진
- correlation *n* 상관관계

297 답 ⑤

📖📖 식사의 재료로서 고기와 채소의 비교

전문해석

고기는 풍부하고 비싸서 엄숙한 의식에 사용하기 좋으며, 예전에는 비교적 드물게 그리고 보통 특별한 경우에만 먹었다. 최근까지 고기는 저장성이 매우 좋지 않았는데, 이것은 그것을 빨리 먹어야 함을 의미했다. 수천 년 동안 고기는 남성의 사업과 승리의 결과로 가족 앞에 놓였다. 그리고 남성들은 칼을 들고 그것을 썰고 심지어 기대하고 감탄하는 군중 앞에서 그것을 요리하기를 고집했다. 반면에 채소는 대부분 밭에서 채소를 수확하고 가꾸는 데 필요한 꾸준하고 협동적이며 종종 주로 여성 노동의 결과였다. 그것들은 큰 노력과 정성이 들지만, 동물을 잡거나 도살할 때 드는 것보다 훨씬 덜한 죄책감, 극적 긴장감, 그리고 강도를 수반한다. 저녁 식사에 고기를 함께 제공하는 것은 또한 초대 손님 수가 제한되지만, 채식 식사는 쉽게 나누고 연장할 수 있어서 훨씬 더 탄력적으로 준비할 수 있다.

정답풀이

동물을 잡을 때와 비교해서 They가 가진 장단점에 대해 설명하는 주어진 문장에서 주어 They는 채소(Vegetables)를 지칭하므로 주어진 문장은 채소에 대해 언급한 문장 바로 다음인 ⑤에 들어가는 것이 가장 적절하다.

구문풀이

7행 (Until recent times), meat has had exceptionally poor storage qualities, [which meant {that it had to be eaten quickly}].

: ( )는 부사구이며, 문장의 동사는 has had로 현재완료가 쓰였다. [ ]는 앞에 나온 절을 부연 설명하는 관계절이고 그 안의 { }는 meant의 목적어 역할을 하는 명사절이다.

14행 Vegetables, on the other hand, were most often the result of the steady, cooperative, and often mainly female work [required for collecting and tending them in the fields].

: Vegetables가 주어, were가 동사이다. [ ]는 the steady, cooperative, and often mainly female work를 수식하는 과거분사구이다.

어휘풀이

- accompany *v* 동반[수반]하다
- intensity *n* 강도
- drama *n* 극적인 상황
- attend *v* 수반하다

- slaughter *v* 도살하다
- storage *n* 저장, 보관
- triumph *n* 승리
- expectant *a* 기대하는
- joint *n* 구운 고기
- elastic *a* 탄력적인
- solemn *a* 엄숙한
- enterprise *n* 사업
- carve up 조각하다
- steady *a* 꾸준한
- vegetarian *a* 채식의
- extend *v* 연장하다

298 답 ⑤

📖 영장류의 환경적 도전에 대한 혁신적인 대응

전문해석

많은 영장류는 단지 먹이 획득 이외에도 환경의 도전을 받을 때 혁신을 일으킨다. 오랑우탄은 비가 올 때 큰 나뭇잎을 가져다가 머리에 이고 다니고, 침팬지는 장내 기생충이 있을 때 작은 강모로 덮인 맛이 안 좋은 특정 나뭇잎을 먹는데, 이 나뭇잎은 신체를 청소하는 데 도움이 된다. 많은 다른 동물들도 주변에서 흔히 볼 수 있는 물건을 가져다가 새로운 용도로 사용함으로써 생태학적 도전에 대처한다. 이러한 행동에는 호기심도 포함되어 있지만, 거의 모든 이러한 혁신은 굶주림, 갈증, 질병, 안락함 등의 기능적인 목표에 의해 주도된다. 진화의 과정은 세상의 도전에 대한 많은 종의 대응을 놀랍고 혁신적인 능력으로 연마해 왔다. 그들의 해결책은 대개 어느 정도의 학습과 다른 종의 관찰, 수많은 시행착오 실험을 통해 얻어진다. 하지만 어린 침팬지가 바위를 효과적으로 사용하여 견과류를 깨서 여는 방법을 배우는 데는 몇 년은 아니더라도 수개월이 걸리는 반면, 어린 인간에게는 하루 만에 같은 기술을 가르칠 수 있다는 점을 기억하라.

정답풀이

영장류는 환경의 도전을 극복하기 위해 혁신적인 행동을 보인다고 하며 여러 동물들의 예를 들고 그중에서도 인간은 그 학습의 속도가 침팬지에 비해 월등히 빠르다고 말하고 있다. 주어진 문장의 Their는 ⑤ 앞 문장의 many species'를 가리키고, 주어진 문장의 해결책이 학습과 다른 종의 관찰, 수많은 시행착오 실험을 통해 얻어진다는 내용이 ⑤ 다음 문장의 침팬지와 인간의 학습 속도는 인간이 월등하다는 내용으로 이어지는 것이 글의 흐름상 적절하므로 주어진 문장이 들어가기에 가장 적절한 곳은 ⑤이다.

구문풀이

4행 Many primates innovate [**when challenged** by the environment outside of just food acquisition].

: [ ]는 주절에 이어지는 부사절이며, when과 challenged 사이에 they(= many primates) are 정도가 생략되었다.

18행 But remember, [**it takes** a young chimpanzee many months, {if not years}, **to learn** how to effectively use a rock to crack open nuts, {whereas the same skill can be taught to a young human in a day}].

: 동사 remember로 시작하는 명령문이며, [ ]는 remember의 목적어인데 여기에는 「it takes+시간+to부정사구」 구문이 쓰였다. 첫 번째 { }는 양보의 의미를 갖는 부사절이고, 두 번째 { }는 대조의 의미를 갖는 부사절이다.

어휘풀이

- obtain *v* 얻다
- experimentation *n* 실험
- innovate *v* 혁신하다
- acquisition *n* 획득
- rise to ~에 잘 대처하다
- via *p* ~함으로써, ~을 통해
- curiosity *n* 호기심
- capacity *n* 능력
- trial-and-error *a* 시행착오의
- primate *n* 영장류
- outside of ~ 이외에
- system *n* 신체, 조직
- ecological *a* 생태학적인
- novel *a* 새로운
- functional *a* 기능적인
- crack *v* 깨다

299 답 ④

📖 문자적인 의미를 중시하는 좌반구와 맥락을 중시하는 우반구

전문해석

어느 날 밤 여러분과 여러분의 배우자가 저녁 식사를 준비하고 있다고 가정해 보자. 또한, 준비 도중에 여러분의 배우자가 저녁 식사의 가장 중요한 재료를 잊어버리고 사지 않았다는 것을 알게 된다고 가정해 보자. 그래서 여러분의 배우자가 자동차 키를 움켜잡고, 입술을 비죽거리고, 여러분을 노려보고, "나 가게에 가요."라고 낮게 말한다고 가정해 보자. 온전한 뇌를 가진 거의 모든 사람들은 방금 한 말에 대해 두 가지를 이해할 것이다. 첫째, 여러분의 배우자는 Safeway(미국의 슈퍼마켓 체인)로 향하고 있다. 둘째, 여러분의 배우자는 화가 나 있다. **여러분의 좌뇌는 첫 번째 부분을 파악했는데, 즉 여러분 배우자가 한 말의 소리와 구문을 해독하고 그것들의 문자적인 의미에 도달했다. 하지만 여러분의 우뇌는 이 대화의 두 번째 측면, 즉 일반적으로 중립적인 "나 가게에 가요"라는 말이 전혀 중립적이지 않다는 것을 이해했다.** 노려보는 눈과 화난 낮은 목소리는 여러분의 배우자가 화가 나 있다는 것을 나타낸다.

→ 뇌의 좌반구는 (A)내용에 더 많은 주의를 기울이는 반면, 우반구는 (B)맥락에 대해 더 많이 생각한다.

정답풀이

저녁 식사를 준비하는 부부의 상황을 예로 들어 좌뇌와 우뇌의 차이를 설명하고 있다. 중요한 식사 재료를 사 오지 않아 배우자가 그 재료를 사러 가게에 가겠다고 낮은 목소리로 말하는 상황에서 좌뇌는 '가게에 간다'는 문자적인 의미에 집중하지만, 우뇌는 '가게에 간다'는 말이 중립적인 표현이 아니라 맥락상 상대방에 대한 화난 감정을 표출하는 말임을 파악한다는 내용이므로, (A)에는 content(내용), (B)에는 context(맥락)가 들어가는 것이 적절하다.

① 내용 – 번역
② 과정 – 결과
③ 공감 – 논리
⑤ 과정 – 효율

구문풀이

5행 Suppose then [that your spouse {grabs the car keys}, {curls a lip}, {glares at you}, and {hisses, "I'm going to the store."}]

: [ ]는 Suppose의 목적어 역할을 하는 명사절이며, 네 개의 동사구 { }가 병렬구조로 연결되어 있다.

어휘풀이

- ingredient *n* (요리의) 재료, 요소
- curl *v* 비죽거리다
- intact *a* 온전한
- hemisphere *n* 뇌반구
- decipher *v* 해독하다
- literal *a* 문자적인
- neutral *a* 중립적인
- grab *v* 움켜잡다
- glare *v* 노려보다
- utter *v* 말하다
- figure out ~을 알아내다
- syntax *n* 구문
- exchange *n* 대화, 논쟁

300~301 답 ① / ⑤

📖 과학과 관련된 글이 잘 읽히도록 만드는 방법

전문해석

만약 과학 기사가 읽히기 위해 쓰여지는 것이라면, 필자로서 여러분은 독자가 될 가능성이 있는 사람의 종류와 그들이 어떻게 읽기 시작하는지에 대해 현실적으로 생각하는 것이 중요하다. 실제로, 잠재적 독자들이 여러분보다 크게 다르게 동기 부여를 받을 것 같지는 않다. 그것은 그들이 바쁘고, 게으르고, 참을성이 없고, 기분이 언짢고, 여러분과 꼭 마찬가지로 다른 것들에 몰두하고 있을지도 모른다는 것을 의미한다. 그들은 자신들의 일상 목록에 과학 기사를 읽는 것보다는 다른 것들을 가지고 있고 자신들의 책상이나 컴퓨터 화면을 스쳐 지나가는 학술지 속의 많은 기사를 읽을 필

요가 없다는 것을 스스로에게 기쁘게 납득시킬 것이다. 분명히 그들은 혹시나 기사들이 어떤 불명확한 단락에 숨겨져 있는 어떤 예기치 못한 그러나 유용한 자료를 포함하고 있을 때를 대비해 읽고 있지는 않을 것이다. 그래서, 여러분의 첫 번째 과제는 그들의 관심을 끌고 다음에는 마지막에 완전히 멈출 때까지 그 주의를 유지하려고 하는 것이다. 그것이 여러분의 목표가 되어야 하지만, 잘 써진 글일지라도, 여러분은 흔히 그것을 성취할 것 같지 않다. 처음부터, 독자들은 기사와 그것이 그들에게 제공하기 위해 가지고 있는 것에 대한 느낌을 가질 때까지 선택적이다. 그리고 나서, 만약 그것이 정말로 그들에게 흥미있다면, 그들은 돌아와서 전체 기사를 주의 깊게 그리고 과학적인 관심을 가지고 세심히 살필 것이다. 난제는, 비록 그들이 단지 잠깐의 시간을 내어 여러분의 기사를 정독한다고 할지라도, 그것이 말하려고 하는 내용의 핵심을 이해하도록 확실히 하는 것이다. 이것은 그들이 **가장 중요한 부분이 명확히 제시되어 있다는 것을 발견하고 찾을 것으로 예상하는 장소에서 찾아야만 한다**는 것을 의미한다. 만약 그들이 **'결과(항목)'의 이질적인 정보 덩어리에 묻혀있는 여러분의 가장 흥미로운 자료를 찾거나 '토론(항목)'에 있는 일련의 문제점 논평들 중에서 여러분의 가장 훌륭한 영감을 찾도록 강요받는다면**, 여러분은 여러분의 글을 인정받거나 올바르게 이해받게 할 가능성을 많이 가질(→ 거의 가지지 못할) 것이다.

300
정답풀이

과학적인 글이 독자들에게 잘 읽히게 만들기 위한 방법에 관한 글로, 내용의 핵심을 분명하게 제시하고 독자들이 그것을 발견할 것으로 예상되는 곳에 배치하라는 내용이다. 따라서 글의 제목으로 가장 적절한 것은 ① '과학적인 글이 읽히게 만드는 데 대한 조언'이다.
② 신뢰성: 과학적인 글의 중요한 요소
③ 왜 과학적인 글은 많은 검증을 필요로 하는가
④ 과학적인 연구의 중요한 부분으로서의 글쓰기
⑤ 과학적인 글과 일반적인 글의 차이점

301
정답풀이

과학적인 글에서 독자들은 자신들이 예상하는 장소에서 핵심적인 내용을 찾아야 하며, 그것을 엉뚱한 곳에서 찾도록 강요를 받으면 자신의 작업을 이해받을 가능성을 '거의 가지지 못할' 것이다. 따라서 (e) much는 little과 같은 어휘로 고쳐 써야 한다.

오답풀이

① 우리가 쓴 과학적인 글을 읽게 될 독자도 우리와 크게 '다르지(differently)' 않게 바쁘고, 게으르고, 다른 일에 몰두해 있을 가능성이 크다는 문맥이다.
② 독자들은 과학 기사를 읽는 것 외 다른 할 일도 가지고 있고 학술지의 기사들을 다 읽을 필요는 없다고 생각하므로, 불명확한 단락 속의 '예기치 않은 (unforeseen)' 정보를 위해 과학 기사를 읽지는 않을 거라는 문맥이다.
③ 관심을 끌고 주의를 유지하는 것을 목표로 해야 하지만, 잘 쓰인 글이라도 그 목표를 성취할 '것 같지 않다(unlikely)'는 흐름이 되어야 한다.
④ 독자들이 전체 글을 주의 깊고 세심하게 살피는 것은 글이 독자의 '흥미를 끄는(interests)' 경우일 것이다.

구문풀이

1행 If scientific articles are written {to be read}, / then **it** is important (for you as a writer) [**to have** a realistic impression {of the sort of person (who is likely to be a reader) and how they go about reading}].

: 부사절과 주절로 이루어진 문장으로, 첫 번째 { }는 부사적 용법으로 쓰인 to부정사구이다. 주절에는 「가주어 it − 진주어(to부정사)」 구문이 쓰였으며, 첫 번째 ( )는 to부정사구의 의미상 주어이다. [ ]로 표시한 부분이 진주어 역할을 하는 to부정사구이고, to have의 목적어로 쓰인 a realistic impression은 전치사구인 { }의 수식을 받는다. 이 안에 전치사 of의 목적어로 명사구 the sort ~ a reader와 명사절 how ~

reading이 접속사 and로 연결되어 있다. ( )는 앞의 person을 수식하는 관계절이다.

어휘풀이

- impression *n* 생각, 인상
- potential *a* 잠재적인
- impatient *a* 참을성이 없는
- agenda *n* 목록, 의제
- just in case 혹시나 ~할까 봐, ~할 경우를 대비하여
- unforeseen *a* 예기치 않은
- scrutinise *v* 세심히 살피다
- pick up 이해하다
- heterogeneous *a* 이질적인
- problematical *a* 문제의, 문제가 되는
- go about ~을 시작하다
- motivate *v* 동기를 부여하다
- preoccupied with ~에 몰두한
- convince *v* 확신시키다
- obscure *a* 불명확한
- challenge *n* 난제, 도전
- bury *v* 묻다
- inspiration *n* 영감

302~304 답 ② / ③ / ⑤

📖 야생화된 돼지를 다시 잡은 노인

전문해석

(A) 여러 해 전에, Tennessee주의 Smokey 산맥에서 일부 길들인 돼지들이 농부의 우리에서 탈출했다. 돼지들이 여러 세대를 거치는 기간 동안, 이 돼지들은 점점 더 야생화되어서 그들과 마주친 누구에게라도 그들은 위협이 되었다. 많은 숙련된 사냥꾼들이 (a)그것들을 찾아내서 죽이려고 했지만, 돼지는 너무 쉽게 찾을 수 없는 것으로 밝혀졌다. 어느 날 짐마차를 끄는 작은 당나귀를 이끄는 노인이 이 야생 돼지들의 서식지에 가장 가까운 마을로 들어왔다.

(C) 그 짐마차에는 목재와 곡물이 실려 있었다. 그 지역 시민들은 그가 무엇을 할지에 관해 궁금해 했다. 그는 (c)그들에게 '야생 돼지를 잡으러 왔다'고 말했다. 그들은 그 노인이 지역 사냥꾼들이 할 수 없었던 일을 해낼 수 있다는 것을 믿지 못하면서 웃었다. **두 달 후 그 노인은 그 마을로 돌아와 시민들에게 그 돼지들이 산 정상 근처의 우리에 갇혔다고 말했다.**

(B) 그 마을 사람들은 그가 어떻게 그런 위업을 달성했는지 자신들에게 말하도록 그를 구슬렸다. "처음 한 일은 돼지들이 먹기 위해 오는 장소를 찾는 것이었습니다. 그런 다음 저는 공터 한가운데에 약간의 곡물을 두었습니다. 돼지들은 처음에 무서워 했지만 결국 호기심이 (b)그것들에게 영향을 미쳤고 늙은 수퇘지가 냄새를 맡기 시작했습니다. 그 돼지가 처음 한 입을 베어 물자, 다른 돼지들이 가담했고, 저는 바로 그때 거기서 제가 그들을 잡았다는 것을 알았습니다."

(D) "다음날 저는 곡식을 조금 더 놓고, 판자 하나를 몇 피트 떨어진 곳에 두었습니다. 그 판자는 그들을 한동안 겁먹게 했지만, 그 공짜 점심은 강력한 매력이었습니다. 머지않아 (d)그것들은 다시 와서 먹고 있었습니다. 저는 매일 두어 개의 판자를 추가하기만 하면 되었고 마침내 저의 덫에 필요한 모든 것을 갖추었습니다. 그런 다음 저는 구멍을 파고 첫 번째 모서리 기둥을 세웠습니다. 제가 뭔가를 할 때마다 그들은 한동안 피하곤 했습니다. **하지만 그들은 항상 먹기 위해 돌아왔습니다.** 마침내 우리가 만들어졌고 함정문이 설치되었습니다. 다음에 (e)그것들이 먹으려고 왔을 때, 그들은 우리로 곧장 들어갔고 저는 덫이 찰칵 닫히게 했습니다."

정답풀이

302

우리를 탈출한 돼지들이 여러 세대가 지나면서 야생화되어 사람들에게 위협이 되었는데 한 노인이 그 마을에 왔다는 내용인 (A) 다음에는, 돼지를 잡으러 왔다는 그 노인이 두 달 후에 돼지들을 우리에 가뒀다고 말하는 내용인 (C)가 와야 한다. 그리고 마을 사람들이 어떻게 그 일을 해냈느냐고 말해달라고 하자 노인이 돼지들이 먹으러 오는 장소에 곡물을 두고 그것을 먹기를 기다렸다고 말하는 내용인 (B)가 이어지고, 돼지들이 곡물을 먹는 데 익숙해지고 반복하는 동안 조금씩 판자와 기둥을 세워 우리를 완성했다고 말하는 내용인 (D)가 마지막에 이어지는 것이 가장 자연스러운 글의 순서이다.

303

(c)는 그 지역의 시민들을 가리키고, 나머지는 모두 돼지들을 가리킨다.

304

노인이 조금씩 울타리와 기둥을 세우는 동안 돼지들은 계속 먹이를 먹으러 돌아왔다고 했으므로 ⑤는 글의 내용으로 적절하지 않다.

구문풀이

31행 [All {I had to do}] was [add a couple of boards each day until I had everything I needed for my trap].

: 첫 번째 [ ]가 문장의 주어이고, 두 번째 [ ]는 보어이다. 첫 번째 [ ]에서 핵심 주어는 All이며, 목적격 관계대명사가 생략된 관계절 { }의 수식을 받는다. All, The (one/first) thing, What ~ do의 형태가 주어로 쓰이고 동사로 be동사가 쓰인 경우, 보어로 to부정사가 아닌, 동사원형이 올 수 있다.

어휘풀이

- domesticated *a* 길들인
- menace *n* 위협
- elusive *a* 쉽게 찾을 수 없는
- feat *n* 위업, 공적
- get to ~에게 영향을 미치다
- lumber *n* 목재
- spook *v* 겁먹게 하다
- spell *n* 한동안
- spring a trap 덫이 찰칵 닫히게 하다
- pen *n* 우리
- cross one's path ~와 마주치다
- coax *v* 구슬리다
- clearing *n* 공터
- sniff *v* 냄새 맡다
- plank *n* 판자
- corner post 모서리 기둥
- trapdoor *n* 뚜껑문, 함정문

독해 실전 모의고사 2회

본문 pp.198~211

305 ②	**306** ③	**307** ④	**308** ④	**309** ③
310 ⑤	**311** ③	**312** ⑤	**313** ④	**314** ④
315 ④	**316** ③	**317** ③	**318** ①	**319** ③
320 ⑤	**321** ④	**322** ④	**323** ③	**324** ④
325 ③	**326** ③	**327** ②	**328** ③	**329** ④
330 ②	**331** ①	**332** ③		

---

305 답 ②

📖 급여를 인상해 줄 것을 요청하는 편지

전문해석

Browning 씨께,

저의 현재 직위는 연봉이 28,500파운드이고, 이것은 작년 3월에 평가되었습니다. 회사에 근무한 지 5년 동안, 저는 양심적으로 업무를 수행해왔다고 생각하며 최근에 추가적인 책임을 얻었습니다. **저는 저의 자질과 제 일의 성격이 더 높은 급여를 정당화한다고 생각하고,** 이미 연봉 3만 파운드로 다른 회사의 비슷한 자리를 제의받았습니다. 저의 현재 업무는 흥미롭고 저는 저의 일을 대단히 즐기고 있습니다. 회사를 떠나고 싶지 않지만, 제 급여에 약간의 인상이 조정될 수 없다면 이 제안을 거절할 수 있습니다. **급여 인상이 가능했으면 좋겠고, 곧 연락이 오길 기다립니다.**

Roger Moore 드림

정답풀이

지난 5년간의 근무 수행태도로 보아 자신은 더 높은 급여를 받을 만하고 다른 회사로부터 이미 더 높은 연봉을 제안받았다고 하며 급여 인상을 요청하는 글이므로, 글의 목적으로는 ②가 가장 적절하다.

구문풀이

13행 Although I have no wish (**to leave** the company), / I cannot afford to turn down this offer [**unless** some improvement (in my salary) can be arranged].

: 양보의 부사절과 주절로 이루어진 문장으로, 주절에는 [ ]로 표시한 '만약 ~하지 않는다면'이라는 if ~ not의 의미인 unless가 이끄는 조건의 부사절이 포함되어 있다. 첫 번째 ( )는 형용사적 용법으로 쓰인 to부정사구로 앞의 wish를 수식하고, 두 번째 ( )는 전치사구로 조건절의 주어인 some improvement를 수식한다.

어휘풀이

- appointment *n* 직위
- carry out 수행하다
- additional *a* 추가적인
- qualification *n* 자격, 자질
- per annum 1년에
- turn down ~을 거절하다
- annual salary 연봉
- conscientiously *ad* 양심적으로
- responsibility *n* 책임, 의무
- justify *v* 정당화하다
- thoroughly *ad* 대단히
- arrange *v* 조정하다

---

306 답 ③

📖 할머니를 만나러 가는 도중에 낯선 사람이 자신을 응시하고 따라온 경험

전문해석

지난 토요일 나는 런던의 다른 맞은편에 사시는 할머니를 방문하고 싶었다. 나는 여러 해 동안 할머니를 본 적이 없었고, 할머니의 맛있는 케이크를 몹시 먹고 싶었다. 나는 기차에 타서 한 노인 옆의 빈자리를 발견했다. 나는 그곳에 앉아서 창밖을 내다보았다. 나는 할머니와의 유쾌한 재회를 상상했고, "할머니, 보고 싶어요!" 하고 혼잣말을 했다. 그때 나는 그 노인이 나를 쳐다보고 있는 것을 알았다. 나는 책을 꺼냈고, 그는 나를 계속해서 쳐다보고 있었다. 마침내, 기차가 Kings Cross 역에 도착했고, 나는 할머니의 집을 향해 걷기 시작했다. 잠시 후, 나는 어떤 사람이 나를 따라오고 있다는 이상한 느낌이 들었다. 나는 뒤돌아보았다. 노인이 나를 향해 달려 오고 있었다. 나는 달아나려 했지만, 한 발자국도 움직일 수 없었다.

정답풀이

필자는 할머니를 만난다는 기대로 행복했는데, 기차를 탄 후에 자신을 계속 쳐다보고 따라오는 사람에게 공포를 느낄 것이다. imagined the joyful reunion with Grandmother에서는 기대감이 드러나고, I tried to run, but couldn't even move a step.에서는 공포감을 느낄 수 있다. 따라서 'I'의 심경 변화로 가장 적절한 것은 ③ '기대하는 → 겁먹은'이다.

① 감사하는 → 걱정하는　　　　② 공포에 떠는 → 안도하는
④ 기쁜 → 슬픈　　　　　　　　⑤ 실망한 → 신나는

구문풀이

4행 I [got onto the train], and [found an empty seat {next to an elderly man}].

: 두 개의 [ ]는 문장의 주어 I에 연결되는 술부이다. { }는 앞의 명사구 an empty seat를 수식하는 형용사구이다.

어휘풀이

- look forward to ~을 고대하다
- pull into (열차가) 역에 들어오다
- reunion *n* 재회
- turn round 돌아보다

307 답 ④

전문해석

시간은 우리의 가장 소중한 물자이고, 그것은 확실히 유한한 자원이다. 따라서 우리는 분명 그 모든 것을 할 수는 없다. 너무 자주, 우리는 사소한 일로 우리의 일정을 채우고 너무 바빠서 우리의 목표를 달성할 수 없는 것처럼 보인다. 우리는 이 수법을 우리 자신에게 사용하는데, 그것은 Steven Pressfield가 〈The War of Art〉에서 '저항'이라고 부르는 것이다. 잠재의식적으로, 우리는 만약 우리가 바쁘고 과도하게 일정을 잡는다면, 우리가 하고 있어야 한다는 것을 아는 위대한 일을 직면할 필요가 없다는 것을 안다. 우리는 삶의 항아리에 큰 돌들(여러분의 우선 사항들)을 먼저 넣는 것으로 Stephen Covey가 설명한 것을 해야 한다. **덜 중요한 것들은 여러분의 시간을 채울 수 있으니, 분명 그것들이 여러분의 우선 사항에서 시간을 훔치게 허용하지 말아라.** 무언가에 '예'라고 말할 때마다, 다른 무언가에 '아니요'라고 말하고 있다는 것을 깨달아라. 중요한 것에는 '예'라고 말하고, 주요 목적을 달성하는 데 필요한 시간과 에너지를 줄이는 프로젝트와 활동에 대해서는 '아니요'라고 말하는 것을 배워라.

정답풀이

시간은 유한한 자원이므로 사소한 일로 일정을 채워 정작 우선적으로 해야 할 중요한 일을 할 시간을 낼 수 없는 지경에 빠지지 말라는 내용이다. 따라서 필자가 주장하는 바로 가장 적절한 것은 ④이다.

구문풀이

6행 Subconsciously, we know [{if we keep ourselves busy and over-scheduled}, we won't have to face the great work {we know that we should be doing}].

: [ ]는 문장의 동사 know의 목적어 역할을 하는 명사절이다. 그 안에서 첫 번째 { }는 조건 부사절이고, 두 번째 { }는 선행사 the great work를 수식하는 관계절로 목적격 관계대명사 that 또는 which가 생략되어 있다.

어휘풀이

- commodity *n* 물자, 상품
- trick *n* 수법, 술수
- subconsciously *ad* 잠재의식적으로
- priority *n* 우선 사항
- significant *a* 중요한
- fulfill *v* (의무·직무 등을) 다하다, 수행하다
- finite *a* 유한한
- resistance *n* 저항
- face *v* 직면하다
- jar *n* 항아리
- diminish *v* 줄이다

308 답 ④

전문해석

정치에서 예측 가능성과 한계에 관한 논쟁이 맹렬히 계속된다. 한편에는 (비록 절대 확실한 것은 아닐지라도) 믿을 만한 탁월함이 가능하다고 주장하는 사람들이 있다. Philip Tetlock의 '슈퍼 예측가들'은 전형적인 여우들로, 개방적이고, 호기심이 많으며, 자기 비판적인 조사 습관을 키움으로써 대단히 예측을 잘 하는 보통 사람들이다. Bruce Bueno de Mesquita의 '예측 공학자들'은 다른 경로로(그들의 경우, 90퍼센트 비율의 예측 정확성), '기대 효용'이라는 엄밀한 논리에서 만들어진 세련된 모형을 정치적 결과를 생산하는 결정에 적용함으로써 비슷한 성공을 주장한다. 다른 한편에는 원론적으로도 믿을 만한 정치적 예측의 가능성을 의심하는 회의론자들이 있다. 장애물은 충분한 자료나 계산 능력으로 극복될지도 모르는 기술적인 것뿐만 아니라 정치 시스템의 복잡한 본질에 내재하는데, 역동적이고 순차적이지 않으며 혼란스럽고, 초기 조건에서 작은 변화에 매우 민감하다. 일식은 수 세기 전에 미리 분 단위까지 계산될 수 있지만, 날씨는 불과 며칠 앞 이상 예측될 수 없고 그나마 완벽하지 않다. 지진은 전혀 예측될 수 없다. 회의론자들의 주장에 따르면, 정치는 천문학이라기보다는 기상학이다.

정답풀이

정치적 예측의 가능성을 옹호하는 견해와 그것에 대해 의심하는 견해를 소개하면서 의심하는 쪽에서는 일식이 일어나는 때를 미리 정확히 계산하는 천문학과 달리, 정치는 날씨와 지진처럼 예측하기 어려운 것을 다루는 기상학과 같다고 설명하고 있으므로, 밑줄 친 부분이 의미하는 바로 가장 적절한 것은 ④ '정치를 예측하는 것은 매우 복잡하고 불확실하며 어렵다.'이다.

① 정치적 결과에 영향을 미치는 요소들이 많다.
② 정치 전문가의 견해는 예측하기 어렵다.
③ 정치적 결과는 의도적인 활동에 의해 결정된다.
⑤ 다른 영역들과 달리, 예측의 정확성은 정치에서 높다.

구문풀이

7행 Bruce Bueno de Mesquita's "predictioneers" claim similar success by a different route (in their case, a 90 percent rate of prediction accuracy), by **applying** refined models [built from the rigorous logic of "expected utility"] **to** decisions [that produce political outcomes].

: claim이 문장의 동사이며, by a different 이하는 부사구이다. 첫 번째 [ ]는 applying의 목적어인 refined models를 수식하는 분사구이고, 두 번째 [ ]는 decisions를 수식하는 관계절이다. 「apply A to B」는 'A를 B에 적용하다'의 의미이다.

어휘풀이

- debate *n* 논쟁
- extraordinarily *ad* 대단히, 몹시
- accuracy *n* 정확성
- rigorous *a* 엄밀한
- skeptic *n* 회의론자
- obstacle *n* 장애물
- non-linear *a* 순차적이지 않은
- initial *a* 초기의
- in advance 미리
- rage *v* 맹렬히 계속되다
- enquiry *n* 조사
- refined *a* 세련된
- expected utility 기대 효용
- in principle 원론적으로
- inherent *a* 내재하는
- chaotic *a* 혼란스러운
- solar eclipse 일식

309 답 ③

전문해석

아이들의 생물학적 장점과 약점이 그들의 발달하는 자존감에 영향을 미치지만, 가족과 사회 환경과의 상호작용도 또한 영향을 미친다. 사람들이 자기 자신을 어떻게 바라보게 되는지는 다른 사람들이 그들을 어떻게 바라보고 대하는지에 의해서 크게 영향을 받는다는 점에서, 자존감은 사회적 과정이다. 비록 자존감이 자기 판단을 지칭하지만, 이 판단은 아이들이 다른 사람에 의해서 대접받는 방식과 그들이 다른 사람과 상호작용을 하는 동안 자신에 대한 긍정적인 경험을 하는지의 여부에 의해서 쉽게 영향을 받는다. **따라서 부모는 아이들이 긍정적인 자존감을 발달시키는 것을 돕는 데 있어서 중요한 역할을 하는데, 그 이유는 부모가 아이들이 가장 빈번하게 상호작용하는 '다른 사람들'이기 때문이다.** 어린 아이들에게 부모보다 세상에서 더 중요한 사람은 없다. 부모는 의사소통하고, 사랑과 관심을 표현하고, 아이들에게 도전하라고 격려하고, 독립심을 기르고, 사회화를 자극하는 방식에 관심을 기울임으로써 아이들의 자존감에 이런 영향을 미친다.

정답풀이

자존감은 다른 사람과의 상호작용을 통해서 영향을 받으므로 아이들과 가장 빈번하게 상호작용하는 '다른 사람'이 부모이기에 부모가 아이들의 긍정적인 자

존감 형성에 중요한 역할을 한다는 내용의 글이다. 따라서 글의 요지로 가장 적절한 것은 ③이다.

구문풀이

4행 Self-esteem is a social process [in that {how people come to see themselves} is heavily underline{influenced} by {how others see and treat them}].

: 「in that ~」은 '~라는 점에서'라는 의미의 부사절이며, 첫 번째 { } 부분이 부사절의 주어이고, is influenced가 동사이다. 두 번째 { }는 전치사 by의 목적어 역할을 하는 명사절(의문사절)이다.

어휘풀이
- biological *a* 생물학적인
- interaction *n* 상호작용
- vital *a* 중요한, 필수적인
- take on (일 등을) 떠맡다
- independence *n* 독립(심)
- self-esteem *n* 자존감
- judgment *n* 판단
- exert *v* 가하다, 미치다
- foster *v* 기르다
- socialization *n* 사회화

310 답 ⑤

📖 상대방이 처한 상황을 알게 되면서 생기는 타인에 대한 이해

전문해석
당신이 한 조각의 파이를 먹기 위해서 도로변의 식당에 들렀다고 가정해 보자. 종업원이 주문을 받기 위해 왔지만 당신은 어떤 파이를 원하는지를 결정하는 데 어려움을 갖는다. 당신이 망설이는 동안에 그녀는 참지 못하여 그녀의 메모장을 펜으로 두드리고, 천장 쪽으로 눈을 굴리고, 당신을 노려보고는 마침내, "이봐요, 아시다시피 나는 시간이 하루 종일 있지 않아요!"라고 쏘아붙인다. 대부분의 사람들처럼 당신은 아마도 그녀가 불쾌하거나 불친절한 사람이라고 생각할 것이다. 하지만 당신이 그녀에 대해서 매니저에게 불평을 할지를 결정하는 동안에 한 단골손님이 당신에게 당신의 '신경질적인' 종업원이 출근하는 길에 차가 고장 난 혼자 사는 엄마이고, 그녀는 그것을 수리할 돈을 어디에서 구할지를 모르고 즉석 요리 전문 요리사가 자신을 만족시킬 정도로 그녀가 충분히 빠르게 주문을 받지 않기 때문에 그녀에게 계속 소리를 지르고 있다는 것을 말한다고 가정해 보자. 그 모든 정보를 고려하여 당신은 그녀가 반드시 불쾌한 사람은 아니며 그저 심한 스트레스를 받고 사는 평범한 한 인간이라고 결론을 내릴 수 있다.

정답풀이
불친절하게 행동하는 종업원의 사례를 통해, 상대방이 보이는 태도 이면에 그가 처한 상황을 알게 되면 그 사람의 그러한 태도를 이해할 수 있을 것이라는 점을 설명하는 글이다. 따라서 글의 주제로 가장 적절한 것은 ⑤ '상황의 고려에서 생기는 이해'이다.
① 효과적으로 불평하는 법 배우기
② 공적인 삶과 사적인 삶 사이의 경계 그리기
③ 성격의 관점에서 타인의 행동을 설명하기
④ 사회적 관계 유지를 위해 공감 능력 발달시키기

구문풀이

9행 But suppose, [{**while** you are deciding (**whether to** complain about her to the manager)}, a regular customer tells you {that your "crabby" server is a single parent (whose car broke down on her way to work) and she has no idea (where she will find the money to have it repaired); ~}].

: 접속사 while 이하는 suppose의 목적어 역할을 하는 명사절이고 while은 '~ 동안에'의 의미로 첫 번째 { }로 표시한 시간 부사절을 이끈다. 첫 번째 ( )는 '~할지'라는 의미의 「whether+to부정사」 구문이 쓰인 명사구로 앞의 are deciding의 목적어 역할을 한다. 이어지는 절에는 a regular customer가 명사절의 주어, tells가 동사이며,

두 번째 { }가 tells의 직접목적어이다. 이 직접목적어절에서 첫 번째 ( )는 a single parent를 수식하는 소유격 관계대명사절이고, 두 번째 ( )는 has no idea에 이어지는 의문사절이다.

어휘풀이
- roadside *a* 길가의
- impatiently *ad* 참지 못하여
- scowl *v* 노려보다, 쏘아보다
- nasty *a* 고약한, 불쾌한
- short-order cook 즉석 요리 전문 요리사
- scream *v* 소리 지르다
- enormous *a* 거대한
- empathy *n* 공감, 감정이입
- hesitate *v* 망설이다
- tap *v* 두드리다
- snap *v* 쏘아붙이다, 매섭게 말하다
- complain *v* 불평하다
- conclude *v* 결론내리다
- personality *n* 성격
- consideration *n* 고려

311 답 ③

📖 유기체의 생존에 있어서 중요한 다양성

전문해석
어떤 유기체가 생존하기 위해서는, 그것을 구성하는 부분들이 여러 가지 매우 다양한 임무를 수행할 만큼 충분히 다양해야 한다. 다양성이 손실되는 곳에, 필수적으로 허약함이 생긴다. 예를 들어, 쌀과 같은 식물 종에 있어서 가장 억세고 강한 식물은 다른 종들의 이종교배로부터 나온 잡종이다. 불행히도, 많은 사람들은 이런 간단한 진리를 이해하지 못하고 있다. 예를 들어, 히틀러와 나치는 유전적으로 균일하고 순수한 인간들을 교배시킴으로써 최고의 인종을 만들 수 있다고 생각했다. 그들은 그러한 획일성이 최고의 종족에 이르기는커녕 실제로 동종교배와 인간의 유전자 풀에 있어서 다양성의 손실에 이르게 한다는 것을 거의 깨닫지 못했다. 그러한 잘못된 정보를 알고 있던 사람들이 다양성은 파괴되어야 하기보다는 배양되어야 한다는 사실을 알았더라면, 생각건대 그들은 인종적, 종교적, 그리고 이데올로기적 다양성을 짓밟아 없애기보다는 장려했을지도 모른다.

정답풀이
어떤 유기체가 생존하기 위해서는 그것들을 구성하는 부분들이 다양해야 한다고 하며, 그 예시로 가장 강한 식물은 이종교배로부터 나온 잡종이라는 것을 들고 있다. 이렇듯 사람도 인종적, 종교적, 이데올로기적 다양성을 추구해야 한다는 내용이므로, 제목으로는 ③ '다양성: 강인함의 원천'이 가장 적절하다.
① 순수성의 중요성
② 오직 적자만이 생존할 수 있다
④ 인종적 증오의 부정적 영향들
⑤ 이종교배의 잠재적 위험들

구문풀이

14행 **Had** such misinformed people **known** [that diversity should be cultivated rather than destroyed], / they **might have** conceivably **encouraged** racial, religious, and ideological diversity, instead of stamping it out.

: 과거의 사실에 반대되는 상황을 가정하는 가정법 과거완료 구문(「If＋주어＋had p.p. ~, 주어＋조동사의 과거형＋have p.p. ~」)이 사용되었는데, 이 문장에서는 If가 생략되어 주어와 동사가 도치되었다. [ ]는 had known의 목적절이다.

어휘풀이
- organism *n* 유기체
- hybrid *n* 잡종, 교배종
- engineer *v* 설계하다, 계획하다
- uniform *a* 균일한
- inbreeding *n* 동종교배
- stamp out 짓밟다, 밟아 뭉개다
- rugged *a* 억센, 견디는
- interbreeding *n* 이종교배
- genetically *ad* 유전적으로
- uniformity *n* 획일
- conceivably *ad* 생각건대, 상상컨대
- hatred *n* 증오, 혐오

312 답 ⑤

📖 아시아 3개국의 인도에 대한 선호도

전문해석

위의 그래프는 2006년에서 2012년까지의 기간 동안 아시아 3개국의 사람들이 인도에 대해 호의적인 시각을 가지고 있는 비율을 보여준다. 이 3개 아시아 국가 가운데서 일본은 주어진 기간 동안 인도에 대해 호의적 견해를 가진 사람들의 비율이 가장 높았다. 2011년보다 11% 포인트가 증가하여, 2012년에는 일본 사람들의 70%가 인도에 대해 호의적인 견해를 가졌다. 대조적으로, 2012년에 중국인들의 23%만이 인도를 호의적인 관점에서 바라보았는데, 2006년보다 10% 포인트 줄어든 수치였다. 그리고 2011년에 파키스탄 사람들의 14%만이 인도에 대해서 호의적인 경향을 드러냈다. 2012년에 파키스탄의 인도에 대한 평가는 전년에 비해 8% 포인트 증가했지만, 2006년의 비율보다는 2% 포인트(→ 11% 포인트) 감소했다.

정답풀이

파키스탄 사람들이 인도에 대해 호의적인 시각을 가지고 있는 비율은 2012년에 22%로 전년인 2011년(14%)에 비해 8% 포인트가 증가한 수치이지만, 33%가 우호적인 2006년보다는 11% 포인트가 감소한 수치이므로 2006년보다 2% 포인트 감소했다고 한 ⑤가 도표와 일치하지 않는다.

구문풀이

[1행] The graph above shows the percent of people in three Asian nations [having a favorable view of India in the time period between 2006 and 2012].

: [ ]는 people in three Asian nations를 수식하는 현재분사구이다.

어휘풀이

- favorable *a* 호의[우호]적인
- in contrast 대조적으로
- in a favorable light 호의적인 관점에서
- disposed toward ~에 대해 어떤 마음을 갖고 있는
- appraisal *n* 평가

313 답 ④

📖 berberis의 특징

전문해석

남극과 호주를 제외하고 지구상의 모든 나라, 모든 기후에서 500종이 넘는 berberis가 자라고 있다. 모든 품종의 berberis는 먹을 수 있다. 이탈리아인들은 이 관목을 신성한 가시라고 부르는데, 이것이 예수의 가시관을 만드는 데 사용된 식물이라고 믿기 때문이다. 일부 품종, 예를 들어, Berberis darwinii는 정말로 끔찍하게 가시가 많고, 당신이 그것을 가지치기해야 한다면 두꺼운 장갑을 필요로 한다. 가지치기하는 동안, 나무줄기의 내부는 밝은 오렌지색이라는 것을 알아챌 것이다. 비슷한 색깔의 염료를 그 식물로부터 만들 수 있다. Berberis 관목은 단단하고 서리에 강하며 모든 종류의 토양과 날씨 조건에서 잘 자란다. Berberis 꽃은 홀로 피거나 노랗거나 오렌지 꽃으로 총상(總狀) 꽃차례로 매달려 피고, 다 익은 열매는 빨간색에서 짙은 자주색까지 색깔이 다양하며 둥글거나 뚜렷하게 타원형 모양일 수 있다.

정답풀이

berberis는 모든 종류의 토양과 날씨 조건에서 잘 자란다고 했으므로, ④는 글의 내용과 일치하지 않는다.

구문풀이

[6행] Some varieties, (for example Berberis darwinii), are indeed hellishly prickly and require thick gauntlets [**should you** need to prune it].

: ( )는 삽입구이고, 주어 Some varieties에 두 개의 동사 are와 require가 병렬 연결된 구조이다. [ ]는 조건 부사절로 if you should need to prune it에서 if가 생략되고 주어와 조동사인 should가 도치되었다.

어휘풀이

- apart from ~을 제외하고
- Antarctica *n* 남극 대륙
- edible *a* 먹을 수 있는, 식용의
- shrub *n* 관목
- holy *a* 신성한
- thorn *n* 가시
- hellishly *ad* 끔찍하게
- prickly *a* 가시가 많은
- gauntlet *n* 장갑
- prune *v* 가지치기하다
- dye *n* 염료
- tough *a* 강한, 힘든
- frost-hardy *a* 서리에 강한
- dangle *v* 매달리다
- distinctly *ad* 뚜렷이
- oval *a* 타원형의

314 답 ④

📖 방과 후 무술 프로그램 안내

전문해석

방과 후 무술 프로그램

매일 하는 무술 수업은 아이에게 인격 수양 교육을 제공합니다.

우리 방과 후 무술 프로그램은 아이의 방과 후 필요에 대한 해답입니다:

- 지역 학교에서 무료 교통편이 제공됩니다.
- 저희는 대부분의 휴일에도 열려 있습니다.

프로그램은 다음을 포함합니다:

매일 무술 수업 / 간식 시간 / 숙제 시간

금요일 즐거운 날에는 축구, 농구, 장애물 코스와 게임, 암벽 등반과 수영 등의 활동이 포함됩니다.

2024년 2월 15일까지 저희의 1년간 운영되는 프로그램에 가입하시고 100달러를 절약하세요!

크리스마스 휴일: 저희는 열려 있고 필요로 하는 이들에게 크리스마스 캠프를 제공할 것입니다.

지금 저희에게 전화하세요! 410-555-1234

정답풀이

2024년 2월 15일까지 1년간 운영되는 프로그램에 가입하면 100달러를 절약할 수 있다고 했으므로, 100달러에 등록할 수 있다고 한 ④는 안내문의 내용과 일치하지 않는다.

구문풀이

[18행] We will be open and offer a Christmas camp for those [who need it].

: be와 offer 두 동사가 조동사 will에 연결되어 병렬구조를 이룬다. [ ]는 those를 수식하는 관계절이다.

어휘풀이

- martial arts (동양의) 무술, 무도
- character *n* 인격, 품성
- transportation *n* 교통 기관, 운송, 수송
- obstacle *n* 장애물
- sign up for ~에 가입[신청]하다

315 답 ④

📖 해양 기술 연구 프로그램 참가 안내

해양 기술 연구 프로그램

프로그램 입학 요건
• 해양 기술 응용에 관심이 있는 대학생

프로그램 비용
• 식비, 숙박비, 프로그램 일부로서의 현지 여행을 포함한 1,500달러

등록 마감일
• 2024년 5월 19일

취소/환불 정책
• 프로그램 운영 시 최소 10명 이상 필요
• <u>최소 등록 인원이 충족되지 않으면 지불한 프로그램 비용 전액 환불</u>
• 최소 등록 인원 수가 충족되지 않으면 2024년 5월 31일에 등록한 학생들에게 통지되며, 통지되기 전에는 항공권을 구매하지 않는 것이 좋습니다.

정답풀이

최소 등록 인원이 충족되지 않으면 지불한 프로그램 비용 전액이 환불된다고 했으므로, ④가 안내문의 내용과 일치한다.

오답풀이

① 해양 기술 응용에 관심 있는 대학생을 대상으로 한다.
② 프로그램 비용에는 현지 여행비가 포함되어 있다.
③ 프로그램 운영 최소 인원이 10명이다.
⑤ 최소 등록 인원 미충족 시 2024년 5월 31일에 등록한 학생에게 통지된다.

구문풀이

15행 Registered students will be notified on May 31, 2024 [if the minimum enrollment number has not been met], / so it is recommended [not to purchase airline tickets in advance of being notified].

: 두 개의 절이 접속사 so로 연결된 구조이며, 첫 번째 [ ]는 첫 번째 절에 포함된 부사절이다. so 이하의 절에서 it은 가주어이고 [ ]로 표시한 to부정사구가 진주어이다.

어휘풀이

• entrance *n* 입학
• application *n* 응용
• registration *n* 등록
• enrollment *n* 등록자, 등록
• requirement *n* 요건
• accommodation *n* 숙박
• refund *n* 환불

---

316 답 ③

📖 공정한 세상에 대한 환상과 그 영향

전문해석

지난 반세기 동안, 사회적 정의는 사회 심리학자들에 대한 활발한 연구 분야였다. 대부분의 사람들은 정의에 관해 관심이 있는가? 냉소적인 사람들은 아니라고 말하며 사람들의 상호 비인간적 행위를 증거로 지적한다. 하지만 Melvin Lerner는 모든 사람들이 자신이 공정한 세상에 살고 있다고 상상하기를 원한다고 말하며, '공정한 세상에 대한 믿음'이라고 하는 이론을 제시했다. 실험들은 공정함의 환상을 유지하려는 사람들의 욕구가 그들로 하여금 잔인한 행동을 하도록 한다는 것을 보여준다. 만약 누군가가 나쁜 결과를 얻는다면, 다른 사람들은 그 사람을 보고 그 사람이 나쁜 결과를 받아 마땅하다고 믿는다. 이러한 믿음은 관찰자들이 자신들 스스로가 나쁜 사람들이 아니라는 것을 알기 때문에 불공정한 결과에 취약하다고 느끼는 것을 막아주지만, 그 과정은 또한 피해자에게 책임 전가를 초래한다.

정답풀이

③ **문장의 구조 파악**: show 다음에 접속사 that이 생략된 문장으로, 뒤에 완전한 구조의 절이 이어져야 한다. that절의 동사는 leads로 이미 존재하므로 maintains를 앞의 desire를 수식하는 to부정사인 to maintain으로 바꿔야 한다.

오답풀이

① **전치사**: '~로서'의 의미인 전치사로 올바르게 사용되었다.
② **분사구문**: 문장의 주어인 Melvin Lerner를 의미상의 주어로 하는 분사구문(~하면서)으로 올바르게 사용되었다.
④ **접속사 that**: 동사 believe의 목적어 역할을 하는 명사절 접속사로 올바르게 사용되었다.
⑤ **형용사**: observers를 의미상의 주어로 하는 동명사 feeling에 이어지는 형용사 보어로 올바르게 사용되었다.

구문풀이

12행 This belief **shields** observers **from feeling** vulnerable to unjust outcomes [because they <u>know</u> {that they themselves are not bad people}], / but the process also results in victim blaming.

: 두 개의 절이 등위접속사 but으로 연결되어 있다. 첫 번째 절은 주절과 [ ]로 표시한 이유 부사절로 나뉘는데, 주절에는 「shield A from -ing(A가 ~하는 것을 막다)」 구문이 사용되었다. 이유 부사절 안의 { }는 앞의 동사 know의 목적어 역할을 하는 명사절이다.

어휘풀이

• justice *n* 정의
• inhumanity *n* 비인간적 행위
• state *v* 말하다, 진술하다
• illusion *n* 환상
• lead ~ to *do* ~가 …하게 하다
• deserve *v* ~을 받아 마땅하다
• observer *n* 관찰자
• unjust *a* 불공정한
• victim *n* 피해자, 희생자
• point out ~을 지적하다
• propose *v* 제안하다
• just *a* 공정한
• fairness *n* 공정함
• cruel *a* 잔인한
• shield *v* 막다
• vulnerable *a* 취약한
• result in ~을 초래하다

---

317 답 ③

📖 문제의 원인에 맞춘 비판적 사고를 통해 문제 해결하기

전문해석

모든 문제가 광범위한 비판적 사고를 필요로 하는 것은 아니다. 때때로 문제의 원인에 대한 추정은 쉽게 이루어지며, 조직의 모든 사람에게 명백하다. 예를 들어, 한 지역 기념품 가게의 주인들이 길 건너편에 있는 최근 문을 연 할인 기념품 가게의 주차장에 있는 고객들의 차를 본다면, 문제는 분명하다. 고객이 비용 때문에 경쟁사의 제품을 구입하고 있다는 가정에 이의를 제기할 의심의 여지는 거의 없다. 가격을 얼마나 낮출지 결정하기 위해 조사가 필요하다는 가정이 성립할 수 있을 것이다. 하지만, 자신들의 제품에 자부심을 느끼는 가게 주인들이 대신 방문객들이 기념품을 살 때 어떤 혜택을 원하는지에 대한 조사를 한다면, 그들은 방문객들이 지역에서 만들어지고 있는 제품에 또한 관심이 있다는 것을 발견할 수 있다. 이것은 나아가 주인들에게 자신의 가게에서 파는 현지에서 생산되는 제품들을 홍보함으로써 경쟁적 위협에 대응하기 위한 아이디어를 제공할 수 있다.

정답풀이

(A) 바로 다음 문장에서 고객이 가격 때문에 경쟁사의 제품을 구매한다는 가정에 이의를 제기할 여지가 거의 없다고 한 부분에서 문제가 무엇인지는 분명한 것이므로 clear(분명한)가 적절하다. (unclear: 불분명한)

(B) 최근에 문을 연 할인 기념품 가게의 주차장에 있는 고객들의 차를 보고 문제가 있다고 느낀 상황이므로 조사를 한다면 가격의 할인 폭을 알기 위한 조사일 것이므로 lower(낮추다)가 적절하다. (raise: 올리다)

(C) 가게를 방문하는 사람들이 지역에서 만들어지고 있는 제품에 관심이 있다는 것을 발견한 상황이다. 따라서 가게 주인들은 자신의 가게에 있는 현지 생산 제품들을 홍보할 것이므로 promoting(홍보할)이 적절하다. (concealing: 감추는)

구문풀이

2행 Sometimes assumptions {about the cause of a problem} [are easily made] and [are evident to everyone in the organization].

: { }는 주어인 assumptions를 수식하는 전치사구이다. 핵심 주어(assumptions)가 복수이므로 동사는 are가 왔으며, 술부는 두 개의 동사구 [ ]가 병렬 연결되어 있다.

10행 The assumption might be made [that research is needed to determine how much to lower prices].

: [ ] 부분은 주어인 The assumption과 동격 관계인데 너무 길어서 동사 뒤에 위치하고 있다.

어휘풀이

- extensive *a* 광범위한
- assumption *n* 가정
- challenge *v* 이의를 제기하다, 도전하다
- competitor *n* 경쟁사
- locally *ad* 지역에서, 현지에서
- competitive *a* 경쟁의
- critical *a* 비판적인
- souvenir *n* 기념품, 선물
- take pride in ~에 자부심을 느끼다
- counter *v* 대응하다
- conceal *v* 감추다, 숨기다

318 답 ①

📖 독자를 설득하는 주요한 요소로서의 역할을 하는 세부사항

전문해석

특정한, 명백한, 구체적인, 특별한 세부사항, 이것은 허구의 생명이다. **세부사항은 (모든 훌륭한 거짓말쟁이들이 알고 있듯이) 설득력의 본질이다.** Mary는 Ed가 지난 화요일에 가스 요금을 내려 가는 것을 잊어버렸다고 확신하지만, Ed는 말한다. "내가 갔다는 걸 난 알고 있지, 왜냐하면 니트 조끼를 입은 이 나이 든 아저씨가 내 앞줄에 있었고 자기 쌍둥이 손녀들에 대해 계속해서 얘기했거든." 그리고 비록 난로[보일러]가 작동하지 않는다 해도 니트 조끼와 쌍둥이는 반박하기 힘들다. 〈허구의 기술〉에서 John Gardner는, 세부사항을 '증거', 즉 기하학 정리나 법정 소송 사건의 증거를 함께 보여주는 단계와 다소 비슷한 진실성의 지표라고 말한다. 그의 말에 따르면, 소설가는 "우리에게 거리, 가게, 날씨, 정치, 클리블랜드(혹은 배경 장소면 어디든)의 관심사에 대한 너무나 대단한 세부사항과 그의 캐릭터들의 외모, 제스처, 경험에 관한 너무나 대단한 세부사항을 제시해서 그가 우리에게 들려주는 이야기가 사실임에 틀림없다고 믿지 않을 수 없다."

정답풀이

세부사항은 진실을 나타내어 증거로서 효과가 있기에, 반박하기 어렵고, 소설가는 자기 작품에 세부사항을 풍부하게 부여하여 이야기를 사실로 믿게 만든다는 내용의 글이다. 따라서 세부사항이 가지는 힘은 ① '설득력'이라고 말할 수 있다.

② 정확성
③ 전체
④ 동정
⑤ 생생함

구문풀이

12행 The novelist, [he says], "gives us [**such** detail about the streets, stores, weather, politics, and concerns of Cleveland (or wherever the setting is)] and [**such** detail about the looks, gestures,

and experiences of his characters] **that** we **cannot help believing** [that the story {he tells us} must be true]."

: The novelist가 주어, gives가 동사이며, he says는 삽입절이다. 「such+명사+that ~」은 '너무나 대단한 …라서 ~하다'라는 의미를 나타내고, such로 시작하는 두 개의 [ ]가 병렬구조를 이룬다. 「cannot help -ing」는 '~하지 않을 수 없다'라는 뜻이다. 네 번째 [ ]는 believing의 목적어로 쓰인 명사절이고, 그 안의 { }는 목적격 관계대명사 which[that]가 생략된 관계절로 선행사 the story를 수식한다.

어휘풀이

- definite *a* 명백한
- stuff *n* 소질, 본질, 특성
- refute *v* 반박하다, 부인하다
- indicator *n* 지표
- theorem *n* 정리, 원리
- concrete *a* 구체적인
- vest *n* 조끼
- furnace *n* 난로, 화덕
- geometric *a* 기하학의
- court case 법정 (소송) 사건

319 답 ③

📖 익숙함에 의한 윤리적 사안에 대한 관심의 감소

전문해석

첫 번째 동물, 양 Dolly가 복제되었을 때, 그것은 신문에 대서특필되었으며 열띤 윤리적 논쟁을 일으켰다. 오늘날에는 인간 복제와 줄기 세포에 크게 열광한다. 그 사이에, 동물 복제는 대부분 받아들여졌고, 그 밖의 다른 종의 복제는 더 이상 제1면 기사로서의 자격이 거의 없다. '시험관 아기'가 처음 등장했을 때, 그들은 자칭 인간 윤리 지도자가 벌이는 격앙된 윤리 논쟁의 대상이었다. 세계 최초의 시험관 아기인 Louise Brown은 영국에서 1978년 7월 25일에 태어났다. 이후 백만 명 이상의 시험관 아기가 있으며, 오늘날 그 절차는 대부분의 건강 보험으로 비용이 처리된다. 이 주제의 '도덕성'은 더이상 거의 논의되지 않는다. 여성복의 유행 양식과 거의 같은 속도로 대부분의 근본적인 윤리 사안이 사라진다는 사실은 그것의 심오한 중요성에 의문을 던진다.

정답풀이

이 글은 복제된 동물이나 시험관 아기가 처음 등장했을 때 이 문제에 대해서 열띤 윤리적 논쟁이 일어났지만, 시간이 지나면서 사람들이 이 문제에 대해서 익숙해지면서 더 이상 윤리적 논쟁이 지속되지 않는다는 내용이다. 빈칸은 이 글의 가장 마지막에 위치하고 있으며, 앞의 내용을 종합하여 이것이 가지는 의미에 대해 언급하는 성격이 되어야 하므로 ③ '대부분의 근본적인 윤리 사안이 사라진다'를 넣어, 이러한 사실이 그것의 심오한 중요성에 의문을 던진다는 내용으로 이어지는 것이 적절하다.

① 생명공학에 대한 논쟁이 열기를 띤다
② 생명공학의 문제점들이 해결된다
④ 시험관 아기 비용이 보험으로 처리된다
⑤ 과학 연구에서의 도덕적 타락이 증가했다

구문풀이

14행 [The fact {**that** most fundamental ethical issues fade away at much the same rate as fashions in women's clothing}] brings their deep significance into question.

: [ ]는 문장의 주어에 해당하며, { }는 핵심 주어인 The fact의 내용을 구체적으로 설명한다. 동격 접속사 that은 생략할 수 없으며, 접속사이므로 that 다음에는 완전한 문장이 이어져야 한다. 문장의 동사는 brings이며 bring[throw] ~ into question은 '~에 의문을 갖게 하다'라는 의미이다.

어휘풀이

- clone *v* 복제하다
- moralistic *a* 윤리의
- yet another 또 하나의
- test tube baby 시험관 아기
- heated *a* 열띤
- stem cell 줄기세포
- qualify *v* 자격이 있다
- intense *a* 격앙된

- self-appointed *a* 자칭의
- insurance *n* 보험
- fade away 사라지다, 꺼지다
- procedure *n* 절차
- biotechnology *n* 생명공학

320 답 ⑤

📖 과학적 모델의 활용과 폐기

전문해석

과학적 모델의 역할은 건설 중인 대형 건물 주변에 세워져 있는 비계와 크레인의 역할에 비유될 수 있다. 이런 비계와 크레인이 없으면 건물을 지을 방법이 없지만 일단 공사가 끝나면 철거가 필요하다. 그러므로 그의 고전적인 저서 〈물리법의 특성〉에서, Richard Feynman은 이론이 항상 그것이 만들어진 모델로부터 **스스로를 분리하려고 노력해야 한다**고 주장했다. 그는 "가장 위대한 발견은 모델을 도외시하고, 모델은 결코 어떤 이익도 되지 않는다. Maxwell의 전기역학 발견은 공간 속의 많은 가상의 바퀴들로 처음 만들어졌다. 하지만 공간 속의 모든 바퀴와 다른 것들이 제거되었을 때 일은 잘 된다."고 썼다. **모델은 우리가 개념에 대한 통달을 얻는 것을 도와주지만, 개념 자체와 혼동하지 말아야 한다.** 가장 위대한 철학자 장자가 말한 것처럼, "토끼 올가미의 목적은 토끼를 잡는 것이다."

정답풀이

위대한 이론의 발견은 모델에 의존하지만, 일단 이론이 발견되면 그것이 만들어진 모델로부터 분리해야 한다는 것이 글의 요지이다. 빈칸에는 이러한 글의 요지를 비유적으로 가장 잘 표현한 말이 들어가야 하므로 빈칸에 들어갈 말로는 ⑤ '토끼 올가미의 목적은 토끼를 잡는 것이다'가 가장 적절하다.

① 지름길이 언제나 더 빠른 것은 아니다
② 적절하게 지니고 있으면 모든 도구가 무기이다
③ 현재를 알려면 과거를 봐야 한다
④ 나무는 숲을 보는 것을 허락하지 않는다

구문풀이

6행 Thus, in his classic book *The Character of Physical Law*, / Richard Feynman <u>argued</u> [that theory should always try to separate itself from <u>the models</u> {upon which it was built}].

: 부사구와 절로 이루어진 문장이다. [ ]는 문장의 동사인 argued의 목적어 역할을 하는 명사절이고 그 안의 { }는 관계절로 앞의 the models를 수식한다.

어휘풀이

- compare to ~와 비교하다
- construct *v* 세우다
- separate *v* 분리하다
- imaginary *a* 가상의
- concept *n* 개념
- philosopher *n* 철학자
- crane *n* 기중기, 크레인
- physical *a* 물리의
- electro-dynamics *n* 전기역학
- mastery *n* 숙달
- be confused 혼동되다

321 답 ④

📖 산업화로 인해 직접 요리하는 일이 줄어든 인간

전문해석

우리가 이 행성에서 번영하는 한 요리는 항상 인류 문화의 일부분이었다. 생존과 쾌락의 두 측면을 모두 지니고 있기에, 음식과 요리는 항상 우리 인간이 끌리는 것이었다. 요리를 통해서 우리는 도구를 사용하는 방법을 배웠으며, 어떤 사람들은 우리를 나머지 다른 동물들과 구별해 주는 것이 바로 우리의 요리하는 능력이라고 주장하기도 한다. 몇 천 년이 지나, 우리는 음식과 요리에 대해 매우 다른 견해를 갖고 있다. 비록 그것이 여전히 계속해서 우리의 일상생활에서 필수적인 부분이기는 하지만, 산

업화 덕분에 오늘날 과거에 했던 것보다 훨씬 더 적은 수의 사람들이 요리를 한다. 우리의 고도로 조직적이고 복잡한 문화 안에서, 우리들 대부분의 사람들이 무슨 일이 일어나고 있는지 모르는 공장 안에서 많은 음식 준비가 이루어진다. 이곳에서, 모든 재료가 완벽하게 조절되고 측정되어, 매번 우리가 좋아하는 똑같은 맛을 우리에게 가져다준다. 싸고 맛있는, 하지만 반드시 건강에 좋은 것은 아닌 음식이 인류 문화의 필수적인 부분이 되어, <u>점점 더 많은 사람들을 주방에서 쫓아냈다.</u>

정답풀이

빈칸은 싸고 맛있는 음식이 우리에게 가져다 준 변화에 대한 내용이 들어가야 한다. 도입부에서 음식과 요리가 우리의 일부분이라고 한 후, A few thousand years later, we have a much different view ~에서 그동안과 관점이 달라졌다고 언급하고 있는데, 이어지는 문장을 통해 이는 산업화로 인해 예전보다 훨씬 더 적은 수의 사람들이 요리를 한다(much fewer people cook today)는 것임을 알 수 있다. 따라서 싸고 맛있는 음식이 필수적인 부분이 되며 일어난 변화는 요리하는 사람들의 수가 줄어들었다는 것이므로, 빈칸에는 이와 맥락을 같이 하는 ④ '점점 더 많은 사람들을 주방에서 쫓아냈다'가 들어가는 것이 가장 적절하다.

① 사람들이 더 많은 여가 시간을 즐길 수 있게 해주었다
② 그 과정에서 생태계 파괴를 초래했다
③ 사람들이 채소보다 고기를 더 좋아하도록 부추겼다
⑤ 점점 더 많은 사람들이 더 맛있는 음식을 찾게 만들었다

구문풀이

5행 (Through cooking) we <u>learned</u> [how to use tools], / and some even <u>argue</u> [that **it is** our ability to cook {**that** separated us from the rest of the animals}].

: 두 개의 절이 and로 대등하게 연결된 구조이다. ( )는 전치사구이며, 첫 번째 절의 동사 learned는 첫 번째 [ ]로 표시한 「의문사+to부정사」를 목적어로 취하고 있는데, 여기서는 의문사로 how가 쓰여 '~하는 방법'의 뜻을 나타낸다. 두 번째 절에서 접속사 that이 이끄는 [ ]는 동사 argue의 목적어이며, 이 절에는 「it is ~ that ...(…한 것은 바로 ~이다)」의 강조구문이 쓰여, our ability to cook이 강조되고 있다. { }에는 「separate A from B(A와 B를 구별하다)」 구문이 쓰였다.

어휘풀이

- flourish *v* 번영하다
- survival *n* 생존
- separate *v* 분리하다
- industrialization *n* 산업화
- preparation *n* 준비
- ecological *a* 생태계[학]의
- planet *n* 행성
- be attracted to ~에 끌리다
- essential *a* 필수적인
- sophisticated *a* 복잡한, 정교한
- ingredient *n* (요리의) 재료, 성분
- destruction *n* 파괴, 붕괴

322 답 ④

📖 꿀벌에만 의존하는 수분 방식의 위험과 식물 수분에 필요한 생물 다양성

전문해석

수분을 오로지 꿀벌에만 의존하는 것은 위험한데, 꿀벌만으로는 생물학적 다양성의 견지에서 효과적이지 않기 때문이다. 단지 하나가 아니라 많은 꽃가루 매개자가 필요한데, 그것이 수분에서 더 많은 대체자를 확보할 것이기 때문이다. 즉, 만에 하나 한 무리의 꽃가루 매개자가 사라지거나 기상 조건에 의해 악영향을 받게 되더라도, 다른 무리들이 그것들의 감소된 수분을 만회할 수 있을 것이다. 생물 다양성은 이제 지극히 중요한데, 꿀벌이 그것의 개체군을 위협하고 있는 무수한 문제들을 겪고 있기 때문이다. 아마도 많은 꿀벌이 한곳에 머물러 있는 대신에 주기적으로 운송되고 있기 때문에, 꿀벌 수에 부정적으로 영향을 미치는 다수의 질병과 해충에 노출된다. (상업화된 꿀벌은 작업하기 쉽고 수분 작업 뿐만 아니라 꿀과 밀랍이라는 주목할 만한 경제적 산물을 생산한다.) 설상가상으로 이제 꿀벌은 벌집 폐사 장애라고 이름 붙여진 것으로 인해 엄청난 수가 사라지고 있는데, 그것의 원인은 알려지지 않았다.

수분을 위한 꽃가루 매개자로 꿀벌에만 의존하는 것은 꿀벌이 겪고 있는 여러 가지 문제를 고려하면 매우 위험하다고 볼 수 있으므로, 꽃가루 매개자의 생물 다양성을 도모해야 한다는 내용의 글이다. 따라서 상업화된 꿀벌의 여러 이점을 언급한 ④는 글 전체의 흐름과 관계가 없다.

구문풀이

11행 Possibly because many honey bees are regularly transported instead of being kept stationary, / they are exposed to a number of diseases and pests [that negatively affect honey bee numbers].

: 이유 부사절과 주절로 이루어진 문장으로 [ ]는 a number of diseases and pests 를 수식하는 관계절이다.

어휘풀이

- pollination *n* (식물) 수분 (작용)
- biodiversity *n* 생물학적 다양성
- insure *v* 확실히 하다, 보증하다
- make up for 만회[벌충]하다
- a myriad of 무수한
- stationary *a* 한곳에 머물러 있는, 고정된
- commercialized *a* 상업화된
- beeswax *n* 밀랍
- collapse *n* 폐사, 붕괴
- in terms of ~의 견지에서
- pollinator *n* 꽃가루 매개자
- substitute *n* 대신하는 것[사람]
- be subjected to ~을 겪다
- measurable *a* 주목할 만한, 중요한
- colony *n* 벌집, 군집
- disorder *n* 장애, 질환

323 답 ③

📖 포식자가 없는 환경 때문에 인간과 카메라를 무서워하지 않는 갈라파고스의 동물

전문해석

고립에는 여러 가지 흥미로운 면이 있다. 한 가지 진실로 매혹적인 면은 주목할 만한 포식자인 인간을 포함한 포식자로부터의 고립이다. (R) 그래서 **갈라파고스의 동물들은 (포식자가) 다가갈 때 달아나거나 피하는 것을 배우거나, 그런 것에 적응되지 않았다.** 많은 갈라파고스의 동물들에게 팔 하나의 거리로 다가갈 수 있으며, 놀랍게도 그것들은 달려들거나 도망가지 않을 것이다. (C) 이 경험은 즐거움과 놀라움의 끊임없는 원천이며, 우리들 중 많은 이들이 익숙해지기 어려운 경험이다. 우리는 손에 카메라를 들고 거리를 줄이기 위해 매우 강력한 망원 렌즈를 사용하면서 동물에게 천천히 접근하는 데 매우 익숙하다. (A) 갈라파고스에서는 이렇게 할 필요가 없으며, 사진 촬영 기회는 엄청난데, 보통의 일일 할당량보다 두 배에서 세 배 더 많이 촬영하게 될 정도이다.

정답풀이

포식자로부터 고립되는 것에는 매혹적인 면이 있다는 내용의 주어진 글 다음에, 그래서 포식자가 없는 환경에서 살아온 갈라파고스의 동물들은 도망치는 것을 몰라서 그들에게 아주 가까이 다가가도 피하지 않는다는 내용의 (B)가 이어져야 한다. 그리고 그렇게 다가가는 경험을 This experience로 받아 그 것이 즐거움과 놀라움을 준다는 내용의 (C)가 온 후, 갈라파고스의 동물들을 촬영할 때는 (C)에 언급된 보통의 야생 동물 촬영 방식을 택할 필요가 없다는 내용의 (A)로 마무리되는 것이 자연스럽다.

구문풀이

14행 This experience is a constant source of pleasure and amazement, / and **it**'s one [that is very difficult {for many of us **to get used to**}].

: 두 개의 절이 and로 연결된 문장이다. it은 앞 절에 나온 This experience를 가리키고, one은 an experience를 대신한다. [ ]는 one을 수식하는 관계절이며, { }로 표시된 to부정사구는 부사적 용법으로 쓰인 to부정사구로 형용사인 difficult를 수식한다. get used to는 '~에 익숙해지다'의 의미이며, for many of us는 to부정사의 의미상 주어에 해당한다.

어휘풀이

- isolation *n* 고립
- predator *n* 포식자
- to the point that ~하는 정도로
- flee *v* 달아나다
- fly off 급히 떠나다
- telephoto lens 망원 렌즈
- fascinating *a* 매혹적인
- noteworthy *a* 주목할 만한
- quota *n* 할당량, (해야 할) 몫
- shy away 피하다
- accustomed to ~에 익숙한
- cut down 줄이다

324 답 ④

📖 삼림 소방대원의 활동

전문해석

삼림 소방대원들은 종종 지상 기반 소방대원들이 도달하기에는 너무 먼 화재 현장으로 낙하된다. 대부분의 시나리오에서 사람들이 여가활동으로 낙하산을 탈 때는 착륙하기에 안정한 장소를 찾는 데 어려움이 없도록 넓은 풀밭을 선택한다. (C) 그러나 삼림 소방대원들은 그들이 진화해야 하는 화재 현장에 접근하기 위해서 식물이 무성한 거친 지대에 종종 착륙해야 하는데, 이것이 그 업무를 훨씬 더 복잡하게 만든다. 그것을 성취하기 위해서 그들은 모든 팀에 현 상황을 평가하고 최적의 착륙점을 결정하는 데 능숙한 투하지점 지시자(spotter)가 있다. (A) (낙하산으로) 내려오는 동안에, 때때로 그들의 장비는 나무에 걸리기 때문에 삼림 소방대원들은 침착함을 유지하고 활동할 준비가 되어 있는 상태에서, 어떤 것으로부터도 자유롭기 위해서 나무를 오르고 내려오는 데 능숙해야만 한다. (B) 일단 지상에 내려오면, 삼림 소방대원들은 48시간에서 72시간 동안 자급자족하며, 일반적으로 단순하지만 매우 효율적인 손 장비의 사용만으로 불이 붙고 있는, 또는 이미 진행 중인 불을 진압한다.

정답풀이

지상의 소방대원들이 갈 수 없는 화재 현장으로 낙하하는 삼림 소방대원에 관한 글이다. 사람들이 여가 활동으로 낙하산을 탈 때는 넓은 풀밭에 내린다는 주어진 글 다음에는, 역접의 연결어 however로 주어진 글과 대조적인 상황을 설명하는, 삼림 소방대원들은 거친 지대에 착륙한다는 (C)가 와야 한다. 그리고 낙하산을 타고 내려오는 동안 일어날 수 있는 일을 설명하는 (A)가 오고, 지상에 내려온 이후 활동에 대해 설명하는 (B)가 마지막에 오는 것이 가장 적절한 순서이다.

구문풀이

16행 Smokejumpers, however, <u>must</u> often <u>come</u> down on <u>rough terrain</u> [that is thick with vegetation] [**in order to** access the fires {they need to fight}], / **making** the task much more complex.

: Smokejumpers가 주어, must come이 동사이다. 첫 번째 [ ]는 rough terrain을 수식하는 관계절이고, 두 번째 [ ]는 '~하기 위해'라는 의미의 부사구이다. 이 안에 { }는 the fires를 수식하는 관계절로 목적격 관계대명사가 생략되었다. making 이하는 분사구문으로 의미상 주어는 앞 절 전체이다.

어휘풀이

- drop *v* 낙하시키다
- meadow *n* 목초지
- tangle *v* 엉키다
- descend *v* 내려오다
- ignite *v* ~에 불을 붙이다
- vegetation *n* (한 지방의) 식물, 초목
- remote *a* 멀리 떨어진
- gear *n* 장비
- adept *a* 숙련된, 능숙한
- self-sufficient *a* 자급자족할 수 있는
- terrain *n* 지대, 지역

325 답 ③

📖 재해를 몰고 오기도 하는 방글라데시의 축복인 세 강

방글라데시가 그것의 축복을 헤아려 본다면, 세 가지를 꼽을 수 있을 것인데 그것은 Brahmaputra 강, Meghna 강, 그리고 위대한 Ganges 강이다. 이 거대한 강들은 사실상 방글라데시의 유일한 천연 자원이다. 농업과 담수어업이 경제의 주요소인 대부분이 시골인 나라에서, 강들은 국민들의 생명선이다. 그러나 **이러한 축복들도, 그 지역의 여름 우기와 결합하면 또한 저주가 된다.** 해마다 거의 2미터의 비가 방글라데시에 내리기는 하지만, 3분의 2 이상은 단지 4개월 동안에 내린다. 연중 대부분, 세 강에 의해 형성된 거대한 삼각주는 바싹 말라있지만, 여름의 많은 날 동안에는 강들의 둑이 터져서 거대한 홍수가 일어난다. 적절한 위생과 물 저장 시설이 부족하여, 방글라데시는 또한 수인성 전염병에 취약하다.

정답풀이

주어진 문장은 여름 우기와 결합하면 축복도 저주가 된다는 내용으로, 저주에 해당하는 여름 우기에 집중적으로 쏟아지는 강우량에 대한 내용이 시작되기 전에 위치해야 하므로 ③에 들어가야 한다. ③을 기준으로 앞에는 축복에 관한 내용이 오고, 뒤에는 저주에 관한 내용이 와서 글의 흐름이 달라진다.

구문풀이

14행 [Lacking proper sanitation and water storage facilities], Bangladesh is also prone to epidemics of water-borne disease.

: [ ]는 이유를 나타내는 분사구문으로, As it(= Bangladesh) lacks proper ~로 이해할 수 있다.

어휘풀이

- ally *v* 결합하다, 동맹하다
- mighty *a* 위대한, 강력한
- agriculture *n* 농업
- parch *v* 바싹 말리다
- sanitation *n* 위생
- epidemic *n* 전염병
- curse *n* 저주
- predominantly *ad* 현저하게
- lifeblood *n* 생기의 근원, 생명선
- massive *a* 거대한
- prone to ~의 경향이 있는
- water-borne *a* 수인성의

326 답 ③

📖 사회보장 프로그램과 보험이나 연금 프로그램의 차이점

전문해석

미국에서 사회보장 프로그램은 보험의 원리에 기반을 둔 것이 아니다. 개인 보험과 연금 프로그램은 고객의 현재의 납부금을 건물, 농장, 또는 여타 부동산에 투자한다. 그렇지 않으면 그들은 부동산의 개발에 자금을 대는 주식과 채권을 산다. 이런 부동산은 연금 기금(또는 보험회사)이 자신의 고객들에게 미래의 의무를 이행하게 하는 수입을 발생시킨다. **사회보장은 이런 저금과 투자의 모델을 따르지 않는다. 그 대신 그것은 현재의 근로자들에게 세금을 부과하고 현재의 은퇴자들에게 줄 수당의 자금을 대기 위해 그 수입을 이용한다.** 오늘날의 근로자들에게 약속된 미래의 수당에 자금을 대기 위해 연방정부가 사용할 수 있는 생산적인 자산의 비축은 없다. 현재의 근로자가 은퇴할 때 그들에게 약속된 사회보장 수당은 미래 세대에 부과된 세금에서 나오게 해야 할 것이다.

정답풀이

주어진 문장에서 사회보장이 이러한 저금과 투자 모델을 따르지 않는다고 했으므로, 주어진 문장은 이러한 모델에 대한 설명이 나온 뒤에 와야 한다. 따라서 주어진 문장은, 투자를 통해 자금을 형성하여 그 돈으로 약정된 돈을 지급하는 보험이나 연금 프로그램에 대한 설명에서, 그런 투자 없이 현재의 근로자에게 거둔 세금으로 이미 은퇴한 사람에게 수당을 주는 사회보장 프로그램에 대한 설명으로 내용이 전환되는 자리인 ③에 들어가는 것이 가장 적절하다.

구문풀이

13행 There is no buildup of productive assets [that the federal government can use {to fund the future benefits promised today's workers}].

: [ ]는 productive assets를 수식하는 관계절이고, { }로 표시된 to부정사구는 '자금을 대기 위해'라는 의미로 목적을 나타내는 부사적 용법으로 쓰였다.

어휘풀이

- social security 사회보장(제도)
- pension *n* 연금
- alternatively *ad* 그렇지 않으면
- bond *n* 채권
- fulfill *v* (의무·직무 등을) 이행하다
- tax *v* 세금을 부과하다
- benefit *n* 수당
- buildup *n* 비축, 축적
- insurance *n* 보험
- real asset 부동산
- stock *n* 주식
- finance *v* 자금을 대다
- obligation *n* 의무
- revenue *n* 소득, 수입
- retiree *n* 은퇴자
- levy *v* (세금 등을) 부과[징수]하다

327 답 ②

📖 파트너에게 성가신 행동을 하여 애정을 확인하는 꼬리말이원숭이

전문해석

여러 해 동안 Costa Rica에서 꼬리말이원숭이를 관찰한 UCLA의 영장류학자인 Susan Perry는, 이 영장류들이 자신의 가장 좋아하는 사회적 파트너에게 온갖 종류의 신체적으로 거슬리고 화가 나게 하는 행동을 가함으로써 주기적으로 그들의 인내심을 시험한다고 보고했다. 예를 들면, 어린 꼬리말이원숭이는 자신이 좋아하는 사회적 파트너에게 다가가 손가락 하나를 그의 코에 찔러 넣고 반응을 기다릴지도 모른다. **그들의 관계가 좋으면 아무 일도 일어나지 않지만, 그 파트너가 그 관계에 대한 처음의 열정의 어느 정도를 잃었다면 화가 나게 하는 행동을 한 원숭이는 세게 얻어맞을 것이다.** Perry는 강한 사회적 유대관계를 가진 두 꼬리말이원숭이가 때로는 동시에 자신의 손가락을 서로의 코에 끼워 넣고 자신들의 얼굴에 행복한 표정을 지은 채로 몇 분에 이르는 동안 이 자세로 앉아서, 때로는 몸을 흔든다는 것을 알아차렸다. 꼬리말이원숭이들은 또한 자신이 가장 좋아하는 연합 파트너의 얼굴에서 털을 당기거나 그들의 귀를 깨물거나 그들의 손가락이나 발가락을 빨아서 그들을 괴롭힌다.

→ 꼬리말이원숭이들 사이의 일부 애정 표현은 그들의 가까운 친구들을 (A)화나게 하지만, 친구들이 그 행동을 용인하는 것은 그들이 그들의 관계를 (B)기꺼이 지속하려고 한다는 믿을 만한 증거를 제공한다.

정답풀이

꼬리말이원숭이는 상대의 코에 손가락을 찔러 넣는 등의 성가신 행동을 해서 상대의 반응을 보고 그들의 관계를 기꺼이 지속하려는 상대의 마음을 확인해 본다는 내용이므로, (A)에는 irritating(화나게 하는)이, (B)에는 willingness(기꺼이 하려고 함)가 가장 적절하다.

① 화나게 하는 – 꺼려함
③ 보호하는 – 무능함
④ 보호하는 – 기꺼이 하려고 함
⑤ 지원하는 – 꺼려함

구문풀이

1행 [Susan Perry, {a primatologist at UCLA (**who** has observed capuchin monkeys in Costa Rica for many years)}], has reported [that these primates periodically test {the patience (of their favorite social partners)} {by **subjecting** them to all kinds of physically intrusive and annoying behaviors}].

: 첫 번째 [ ]는 문장의 주어이고, 두 번째 [ ]는 동사 has reported의 목적어이다. 첫 번째 [ ]에서 핵심 주어는 Susan Perry로, 이와 동격인 어구인 첫 번째 { }에서 부연 설명되고 있으며 이 안에 ( )로 표시된 관계절은 a primatologist at UCLA를 수식한다. [ ]로 표시된 that절(목적절)에서 동사는 test이고 두 개의 { }는 각각 목적어(명사구)와 전치사구이다. 전치사구에는 '~함으로써'의 의미인 「by -ing」 구문이 쓰였다.

- **primatologist** *n* 영장류학자
- **periodically** *ad* 주기적으로
- **intrusive** *a* 거슬리는, 침해하는
- **enthusiasm** *n* 열정
- **simultaneously** *ad* 동시에
- **sway** *v* (몸을) 흔들다
- **coalition partner** 연합[연맹] 파트너
- **suck** *v* 빨다

- **primate** *n* 영장류
- **subject** *v* ~을 당하게 하다
- **initial** *a* 처음의
- **social bond** 사회적 유대관계
- **insert** *v* 끼워 넣다, 삽입하다
- **torture** *v* 괴롭히다, 고문하다
- **bite** *v* 깨물다
- **irritating** *a* 화나게 하는

328~329 답 ③ / ④

📖 아이들의 활동을 제약하는 가난과 그것의 해결 방법

전문해석

아이들은 어떻게 가난과 배제의 경험을 중재하고 협상하는가? 친구들과 함께 시내로 들어가거나 활동에 참여할 충분한 돈이 없으면, 아이들은 자신이 자신의 상황에 옭히는 것을 알게 된다. 가난과 불이익은 아이들의 자율적 행동 능력과 그들의 사회적 딜레마를 협상하고 해결하는 능력에 상당한 제약을 가한다. 이전의 연구는 아이들이 자신들의 부모에 대해 매우 보호적이며 이것은 욕구의 자제와 요구의 절제를 포함한 많은 형태를 취할 수 있다는 것을 보여주었다. 일부 아이들에게 이것은 가정 내 압박을 완화하기 위해, 기회를 추구하지 않거나 그들에 의해 너무 비용이 많이 드는 것으로 인지되는 활동에 주의를 끌지 않음으로써 활동으로부터 스스로를 제외시키는 것을 의미할 수 있다. 이 아이들은 적극적인 사회적 행위자들이며 자신들의 상황을 조정하거나 완화시키기 위해 다양한 전략을 사용한다. 아이들이 자신들의 환경에 대한 어느 정도의 통제력을 얻을 수 있는 한 가지 방법은 아이들이 또래들과 보다 더 충분히 참여할 수 있도록 하기 위해 이용될 수 있는 경제적 자원에 접근할 수 있는 대안적인 방법을 금지하는(→ 만드는) 것이다. 시간제 취업이 하나의 예이며, 그것은 사유와 독립의 척도를 위한 기회를 제공한다. 유급 고용으로부터의 수입은 아이들을 가족 환경의 경제적 제약으로부터 어느 정도 해방시키고 그들을 남에게 의존하지 않고 경제적 행위자로 만들 수 있다.

328

정답풀이

아이들이 가난으로 인해 사회적 활동에 제약을 받고 있다고 말하며 그 해결책을 제시하고 있는 글이다. 따라서 ③ '가난: 아이들의 활동을 제약하는 것'이 글의 제목으로 가장 적절하다.
① 아동 노동의 비참한 현실
② 스스로 동기를 부여하는 삶의 방식의 중요성
④ 양육 시 과도한 방임의 위험성
⑤ 어린 시절: 우리의 삶 전체를 결정하는 토대

329

정답풀이

뒤에 이어지는 예에서 시간제 취업은 아이들로 하여금 가난으로 인해 생기는 활동의 제약 문제를 해결하고 경제적 자원에 접근할 수 있는 대안적인 방법을 금지하는 것이 아니라 '만드는' 것이므로 (d)의 ban을 generate 정도로 바꿔야 한다.

오답풀이

① 가난은 아이들에게 자율적 행동 능력과 사회적 딜레마를 해결하는 능력에 '제약(constraints)'을 가한다는 문맥이다.
② 가난한 아이들은 부모에게 문제 해결을 요구하기보다 부모를 '보호하여 (protective)' 스스로 욕구에 대해 자제와 절제의 태도를 취한다는 흐름이다.
③ 가난한 아이들은 기회를 추구하지 않거나 비용이 많이 드는 활동을 원하지 않음으로써 그런 활동에서 '스스로를 제외시킬(self-exclusion)' 것이다.

⑤ 유급 고용은 아이들을 경제적 행위자로 만들고 그들의 가족이 처한 환경의 제약으로부터 '해방시킬(release)' 것이다.

구문풀이

5행 Poverty and disadvantage place considerable constraints on [children's capacity for autonomous action] and [their ability {to negotiate and resolve their social dilemmas}].

: Poverty and disadvantage가 주어, place가 동사이며, 두 개의 [ ]는 and로 연결되어 전치사 on의 목적어 역할을 한다. { }는 their ability를 수식하는 형용사적 용법의 to부정사구인데, 여기서 their social dilemmas는 앞의 negotiate와 resolve의 공통 목적어로, resolve 앞에는 to가 생략되어 있다.

19행 One way [in which children can gain some measure of control over their circumstances] is [to generate alternative ways of gaining access to economic resources {that can be used to enable them to participate more fully with their peers}].

: 첫 번째 [ ]는 문장의 주어인 One way를 수식하는 관계절이며, to부정사구인 두 번째 [ ]는 문장의 보어이다. { }는 앞의 명사구 economic resources를 수식하는 관계절이며, 여기에는 「enable+목적어+to부정사」 구문이 쓰여 '~가 …할 수 있게 하다'의 의미를 나타낸다.

어휘풀이

- **mediate** *v* 중재하다
- **exclusion** *n* 배제
- **disadvantage** *n* 불이익
- **capacity** *n* 능력
- **resolve** *v* 해결하다
- **protective** *a* 보호하는
- **moderation** *n* 절제
- **perceive** *v* 인지하다
- **alleviate** *v* 완화하다, 누그러뜨리다
- **mitigate** *v* 완화하다
- **gain access to** ~에 접근하다
- **measure** *n* 조치, 방법
- **to some degree** 어느 정도
- **in one's own right** 남에게 의존하지 않고
- **miserable** *a* 비참한, 불행한

- **negotiate** *v* 협상하다
- **circumstance** *n* 상황, 처지
- **constraint** *n* 제약, 속박
- **autonomous** *a* 자율적인
- **dilemma** *n* 딜레마
- **denial** *n* 거부
- **pursue** *v* 추구하다
- **in a bid to** *do* ~하기 위하여
- **agent** *n* 행위자
- **alternative** *a* 대안의
- **peer** *n* 친구, 동료
- **independence** *n* 독립
- **render** *v* (어떤 상태가 되게) 만들다
- **neglect** *n* 방치, 소홀

330~332 답 ② / ① / ③

📖 좋은 친구의 조건

전문해석

(A) 내가 스물다섯 살에 가르치는 일을 시작했을 때, 나보다 나이가 여덟 살 많은 동료 Peter Miller가 '나를 그의 날개 밑에 품어 보호해 주었다.' (a)그는 시간을 내어 내가 잘못하고 있는 것을 지적해 주었으며 나의 일부 학생들이 나에 대해 어떤 점을 좋아하지 않는지에 대해 설명해 주었다. 나는 항상 그의 비판을 고마워했으며, 이러한 분야에서 더 나아지기 위해 열심히 노력했다. 이따금 나는 내가 되고 싶어 하는 교사 혹은 사람이 될 수 있을지에 대해 의문을 품었다. 하지만 최소한 나에게는 언제나 내가 어디가 잘못 되었는지 알려주는 사람이 있었다.

(B) 내가 직장생활의 여섯 번째 해를 시작했을 때, Tim Hansel이 우리 학교의 교직원이 되었는데, 그는 다른 학교에서 전근을 온 것이었다. 우리는 두 가지 동일한 과목을 가르쳤고 그 중 한 과목에서 우리는 팀을 이루는 교사가 되었으므로, 우리는 매일 접촉하게 되었다. Tim은 아주 효율적이었고, 그래서 사람들이 아주 좋아했다. (b)그는 다른 사람들이 지니고 있는 최고의 특성을 끄집어내는 특별한 재능을 지니고 있는 것 같았다. 학생들에 대해서도, 그들의 실수를 부각시키지 않는 대신에, 그들이 잘해낸 것이나 그들이 '할 수 있는' 것들을 강조했다.

(D) 하지만 그것은 거기서 끝나지 않았다. Tim은 또한 항상 나에게 해줄 좋은 말을 갖고 있었다. 그는 내가 잘하고 있는 모든 것들을 지적해 주었다. (d)그는 나의 헌신적인 면에 대해서 감탄하고 있으며 나의 힘겨운 노력이 효과를 나타내고 있는 게 분명하다고 말했다. 그는 종종 나의 학생들이 얼마나 나를 좋아하는지 그리고 그들이 나의 가르침 덕분에 얼마나 많은 것을 배우고 있는지에 대해서 나에게 일깨워 주었다. 우리가 학교 밖에서 함께 시간을 보내기 시작했을 때, 그는 나에게서 칭찬해 줄 다른 점들을 찾아냈다. 이 모든 것의 결과는 전에는 나의 관심을 전혀 끌지 못했던 어떤 것들, 즉 교사 그리고 개인 모두의 자격으로 내가 '잘' 하고 있는 것을 내가 볼 수 있게끔 (e)그가 도와주었다는 것이었다.

(C) 이 두 사람과의 우정은 어떻게 되었을까? 애석하게도, 첫 번째 우정은 여러 해가 지난 후에 끝나버렸다. 이 사람은 내가 많이 존경했던 사람이므로, 나는 '애석하게도'라는 말을 쓴다. 나에 대한 그의 비판은 대부분 타당한 것이었으며, 나는 그로부터 많은 것을 배웠다. 하지만 그 우정이 끝나게 된 주된 이유들 중 하나는 그 비판이 너무 지속적이었다는 것이다. 그것은 결코 어떤 형태의 칭찬과도 균형을 이루지 못했으며, 결국에는 나를 지치게 만들었다. 다른 하나의 우정은 30년이 지난 후에도 계속 번성하고 있다. (c)그는 아직도 이 세상의 좋은 점과 나의 좋은 점에 대해 나에게 일깨워 준다.

정답풀이

330

내가 교직을 시작했을 때, 동료 교사인 Peter가 내가 잘못하고 있는 것들을 지적해주었고, 나는 그의 비판에 고마워했다는 (A) 다음에, Tim이 다른 학교에서 전근을 왔는데, 그는 학생들의 좋은 점을 부각시켜주었다는 (B)가 이어진다. 그리고 Tim이 학생들뿐만 아니라 나의 좋은 점도 찾아 알려주었다는 (D)가 나온 후, 이 두 우정 중, 내가 잘못한 것만 지적했던 Peter와의 우정은 끝이 났지만, 좋은 점을 찾아내어 알려준 Tim과의 우정은 유지되고 있다고 말하는 (C)로 이어지는 흐름이 자연스럽다.

331

(a)는 Peter Miller를 가리키고, 나머지는 모두 Tim Hansel을 가리킨다.

332

(C)에서 Most of his criticism of me was valid, and I learned a great deal from him.이라고 했으므로, Peter의 비판은 대부분 타당한 것이었다는 것을 알 수 있다. 그러므로 ③은 글의 내용과 일치하지 않는다.

구문풀이

33행 He said [that he admired me for my dedication] and [that **it** was obvious {**that** my hard work was paying off}].

: 두 개의 [ ] 모두 문장의 동사 said의 목적절이며, 밑줄 친 that은 모두 접속사이다. 두 번째 목적절에는 「가주어 it – 진주어(that절)」 구문이 사용되었다.

어휘풀이

- career *n* 직업, 경력
- colleague *n* 동료, 동업자
- appreciate *v* 고맙게 여기다, 감사하다
- criticism *n* 비판, 비평
- faculty *n* 교원, 교직원
- subject *n* 과목
- emphasize *v* 강조하다
- admire *v* 칭찬하다, 감탄하다
- valid *a* 정당한, 근거가 확실한
- wear down 피로하게 하다, 마멸시키다
- flourish *v* 번영하다, 번성하다
- dedication *n* 헌신
- pay off 성과가 나타나다
- compliment *v* 칭찬하다

---

① 적중 예상 문제

01 시설 02 되돌아보면 03 투명성 04 노골적으로, 전면적으로 05 엄청나게 큰 06 ~을 통해서, 경유하여 07 편집[편찬]하다 08 진공 09 장기적인 10 최종의, 순 11 불완전한 12 trap 13 당면한, 수중의 14 고민하다 15 비난하다, 질책하다 16 구두점 17 품위 18 적당히, 충분히 19 extraordinary 20 ~을 좌우하다, ~에 영향을 끼치다

② 적중 예상 문제

01 (신조어를) 만들어 내다 02 pronunciation 03 공들인 04 슬픈 05 피난, 퇴거 06 만족 07 실험실, 연구실 08 녹이 슨 09 ~에 관한 10 송어 11 불리하게, 반대로 12 현상 13 실체, 독립체 14 바위투성이의, 험한 15 밀도 16 위험 17 침, 타액 18 폭발 19 바람직한 20 colony

③ 적중 예상 문제

01 성, 성별 02 ~에 뒤지지 않다 03 부동산 04 (권력·영향력을) 행사하다; 노력하다 05 stereotype 06 변동성 07 몰입 08 지정하다 09 회복력이 있는 10 재고(품) 11 유지하다, 보유하다 12 중단하다 13 차별 14 기질 15 conservative 16 소매상 17 규범 18 (뚜렷한) 차이 19 성향, 경향 20 색깔

④ 적중 예상 문제

01 조절[조정]하다 02 ~을 다 써버리다, ~이 없어지다 03 농약, 살충제 04 손뼉을 치다 05 monotonous 06 신중한 07 평온, 고요함 08 치명적인 09 응시하다 10 이해관계자 11 연금 12 부재, 없음 13 차지하다, 구성하다 14 명령, 요청 15 medieval 16 결과, 영향 17 ~을 얻으려고 노력하다 18 이끌어내다 19 명성 20 충동적인

⑤ 적중 예상 문제

01 ~을 존경하다 02 설득 03 예의 바른, 공손한 04 ~인 것으로 드러나다[밝혀지다] 05 놀리다, 장난하다 06 꾸준히 07 계획적인, 의도적인 08 동시에 09 magnify 10 두려워하다, 몹시 무서워하다 11 순차적인, 잇따라 일어나는 12 자산 13 번성하다 14 비율, 비 15 완전히, 깊게 16 납작한, 편평한 17 ~을 알지 못하다 18 문학의 19 cheap 20 식물학자

① 독해 실전 모의고사

01 승리 02 온전한 03 syntax 04 (냄새·열·빛 등을) 내다, 발하다 05 대화, 논쟁 06 목재 07 불명확한 08 뇌반구 09 간극, 틈 10 진술, 말 11 탁월한, 눈부신 12 agenda 13 ~을 알아내다 14 의심하다 15 별개의, 뚜렷한 16 ~와 관련이 있다 17 길들인 18 produce 19 위업, 공적 20 상관관계 21 예기치 않은 22 냄새 맡다 23 멋진, 대단한 24 모호한, 불명료한 25 노력보다 26 도살하다 27 해독하다 28 그럴듯한 29 아낌없는, 후한 30 위협 31 ~와는 반대로 32 (경기·회담 등의) 장소 33 바꾸다 34 색이 바래다 35 fair 36 frequency 37 은유(법) 38 직물 39 만연, 창궐 40 ~은 말할 것도 없이 41 감소하다 42 완고한 43 ~을 고수하다 44 제초제 45 성쇠 46 starvation 47 분명한 48 먹이를 찾는, 수렵 채집의 49 옹호하다 50 독단적인

② 독해 실전 모의고사

01 경쟁의 02 중재하다 03 accommodation 04 내려오다 05 양심적으로 06 꽃가루 매개자 07 victim 08 복잡한, 정교한 09 (몸을) 흔들다 10 수행하다 11 분리하다 12 제약, 속박 13 ~을 거절하다 14 절제 15 생각건대, 상상컨대 16 취약한 17 ~을 겪다 18 칭찬하다, 감탄하다 19 먹을 수 있는, 식용의 20 위대한, 강력한 21 가시 22 저주 23 물자, 상품 24 reunion 25 번영하다 26 ~에 가입[신청]하다 27 전염병 28 어느 정도 29 자격, 자질 30 위생 31 만회[벌충]하다 32 유한한 33 conceal 34 평가 35 방치, 소홀 36 (일 등을) 떠맡다 37 괴롭히다, 고문하

다 **38** ~에 불을 붙이다 **39** 맹렬히 계속되다 **40** 칭찬하다 **41** 대신하는 것[사람]
42 중요한, 필수적인 **43** meadow **44** 성과가 나타나다 **45** 고약한, 불쾌한 **46** 혼
란스러운 **47** 은퇴자 **48** 거슬리는, 침해하는 **49** 소득, 수입 **50** 완화하다, 누그러뜨
리다

메가스터디 고등학습 시리즈

메가스터디 N제

영어영역 독해

정답 및 해설

메가스터디BOOKS

내용 문의 02-6984-6908 | 구입 문의 02-6984-6868,9 | www.megastudybooks.com

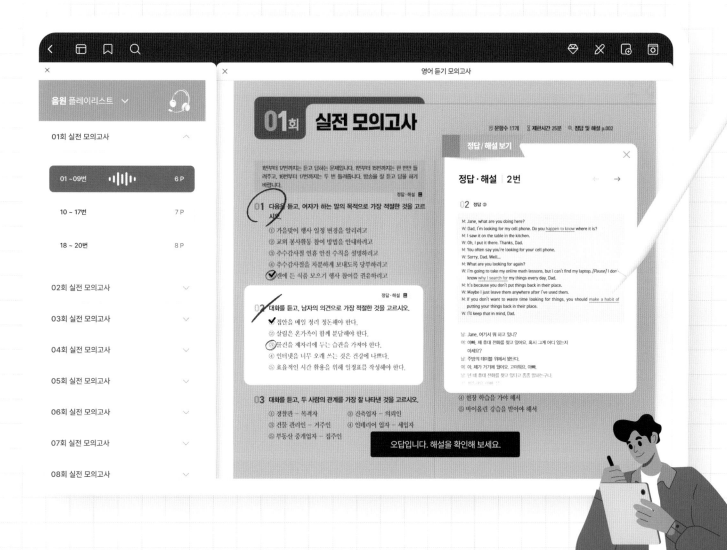

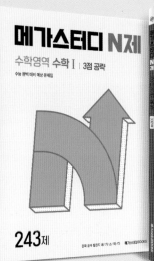